The Musician's Guide to Fundamentals

SECOND EDITION

Jane Piper Clendinning
Florida State University College of Music

Elizabeth West Marvin
Eastman School of Music

Joel Phillips
Westminster Choir College of Rider University

W. W. NORTON & COMPANY · NEW YORK · LONDON

W. W. Norton & Company has been independent since its founding in 1923, when William Warder Norton and Mary D. Herter Norton first published lectures delivered at the People's Institute, the adult education division of New York City's Cooper Union. The firm soon expanded its program beyond the Institute, publishing books by celebrated academics from America and abroad. By midcentury, the two major pillars of Norton's publishing program—trade books and college texts—were firmly established. In the 1950s, the Norton family transferred control of the company to its employees, and today—with a staff of four hundred and a comparable number of trade, college, and professional titles published each year—W. W. Norton & Company stands as the largest and oldest publishing house owned wholly by its employees.

Copyright © 2014, 2012 by W. W. Norton & Company, Inc.

All rights reserved
Printed in the United States of America
Second Edition

Editor: Maribeth Payne
Manuscript Editor: Justin Hoffman
Editorial Assistant: Michael Fauver
Emedia Editor: Steve Hoge
Emedia Editorial Assistant: Andrew Ralston
Proofreader: Debra Nichols
Associate Director of Production, College: Ben Reynolds
Art Director: Jillian Burr
Designer: Lisa Buckley
Photo Editor: Evan Luberger
Marketing Manager, Music: Christopher J. Freitag
Composition by Jouve North America
Music Engraving: David Reiffel
Manufacturing: RR Donnelley

Library of Congress Cataloging-in-Publication Data

Clendinning, Jane Piper, author.
  The musician's guide to fundamentals / Jane Piper Clendinning, Florida State University College of Music, Elizabeth West Marvin, Eastman School of Music, Joel Phillips, Westminster Choir College of Rider University.—Second edition.
     pages cm
  Includes indexes.
  Summary: "A hands-on approach to mastering the basics in class and online. The Musician's Guide to Fundamentals teaches the basics of music—listening, writing, and performing—using real music, from Bach to the Beatles, Broadway to the Black-Eyed Peas. A unique hands-on approach invites students to listen to music from day one as they learn to interpret musical notation and, eventually, to use it to compose songs of their own."
  ISBN 978-0-393-92388-9 (pbk.)
 1. Music theory.   I. Marvin, Elizabeth West, 1955- author.   II. Phillips, Joel, 1958- author.   III. Title.
 MT6.C5677 2014
 781—dc23
                                                                          2013046768

ISBN 978-0-393-92388-9

W. W. Norton & Company, Inc., 500 Fifth Avenue, New York, NY 10110
wwnorton.com

W. W. Norton & Company, Ltd., Castle House, 75/76 Wells Street, London W1T3QT

To our teachers, colleagues, and students—
with whom we have shared the joy of music, and from
whom we continue to learn—and, with thanks,
to our families for their patience and support

Brief Contents

CHAPTER 1 Pitch Notation and the Grand Staff   1
CHAPTER 2 Accidentals and Half and Whole Steps   27
CHAPTER 3 Simple Meters   47
CHAPTER 4 Beat Subdivisions and Syncopation   73
CHAPTER 5 Compound and Other Meters   97
CHAPTER 6 Major Scales and Keys   127
CHAPTER 7 Minor Scales and Keys   155
CHAPTER 8 Intervals   185
CHAPTER 9 Triads and the Dominant Seventh Chord   223
CHAPTER 10 Melody Harmonization and Cadences   255
CHAPTER 11 Form in Folk and Popular Songs   289
CHAPTER 12 Blues and Other Popular Styles   315
　　　　　　　Anthology   345

Appendix 1   Try It Answers   A-1
Appendix 2   Reading Review Answers   A-16
Appendix 3   Apply It Answers   A-18
Appendix 4   Glossary   A-29
Appendix 5   The Overtone Series   A-39
Appendix 6   The Diatonic Modes   A-40
Appendix 7   The C-Clefs   A-43
Appendix 8   Basic Guitar Chords   A-44
Appendix 9   Piano Fingerings for Selected Scales   A-48
Appendix 10 Connecting Chords   A-51

Contents

Preface xiii

CHAPTER 1 Pitch Notation and the Grand Staff 1

Musical Contour 1
Introduction to Pitch Notation: Letter Names 1
The Piano Keyboard: Naming White Keys 2
Staff Notation 3
Treble and Bass Clefs 3
Naming Pitches with Octave Numbers 6
Ledger Lines 6
The Grand Staff 9
Writing Music in a Score 11
Did You Know? 13 ■ Terms You Should Know 13 ■ Questions for Review 14 ■ Reading Review 14 ■ Apply It 15 ■ Workbook 19 ■ Aural Skills 25

CHAPTER 2 Accidentals and Half and Whole Steps 27

Sharps, Flats, and Naturals 27
Double Sharps and Flats 30
Writing Pitches with Accidentals 31
Half Steps and Whole Steps 32
Hearing Half and Whole Steps 34
Did You Know? 35 ■ Terms You Should Know 35 ■ Questions for Review 35 ■ Reading Review 36 ■ Apply It 37 ■ Workbook 39 ■ Aural Skills 45

CHAPTER 3 Simple Meters 47

Duple, Triple, and Quadruple Meters 47
Tempo Markings and Conducting Patterns 48
Rhythmic Notation 49
Meter Signatures 51
Counting Rhythms in Simple Meters 54
Rests 56
Did You Know? 58 ■ Terms You Should Know 58 ■ Questions for Review 58 ■ Reading Review 59 ■ Apply It 60 ■ Workbook 65 ■ Aural Skills 71

CHAPTER 4 Beat Subdivisions and Syncopation 73

Beat Subdivisions 73
Ties and Slurs 76
Syncopation 77
Triplets 79
Rhythmic Variations in Performance 80
Did You Know? 81 ■ Terms You Should Know 81 ■ Questions for Review 82 ■ Reading Review 82 ■ Apply It 83 ■ Workbook 89 ■ Aural Skills 95

CHAPTER 5 Compound and Other Meters 97

Compound Meters 97
Meter Signatures 98
Subdivisions 100
Other Compound Meters 102
Syncopation and Duplets 105
Asymmetrical Meters and Changing Meter 107
Did You Know? 110 ■ Terms You Should Know 110 ■ Questions for Review 110 ■ Reading Review 111 ■ Apply It 112 ■ Workbook 117 ■ Aural Skills 125

CHAPTER 6 Major Scales and Keys 127

Scales 127
Scale Types: Chromatic and Whole-Tone 128
Major Scales 129
Scale Degrees 130
Writing Major Scales 131
Major Key Signatures 133
The Circle of Fifths 137
Did You Know? 138 ■ Terms You Should Know 138 ■ Questions for Review 139 ■ Reading Review 139 ■ Apply It 140 ■ Workbook 145 ■ Aural Skills 151

CHAPTER 7 Minor Scales and Keys   155

Parallel Keys   155
Natural Minor   156
Harmonic Minor   157
Melodic Minor   160
Comparing Scale Types   161
Relative Keys   162
Minor Key Signatures and the Circle of Fifths   165
Identifying the Key from a Score   167
Did You Know?   168 ▪ Terms You Should Know   168 ▪ Questions for Review   169 ▪ Reading Review   169 ▪ Apply It   170 ▪ Workbook   175 ▪ Aural Skills   181

CHAPTER 8 Intervals   185

Intervals   185
Interval Quality   187
Inverting Intervals   190
Spelling Intervals   191
Augmented and Diminished Intervals   197
Compound Intervals   201
Consonance and Dissonance   202
Did You Know?   203 ▪ Terms You Should Know   203 ▪ Questions for Review   203 ▪ Reading Review   204 ▪ Apply It   205 ▪ Workbook   211 ▪ Aural Skills   219

CHAPTER 9 Triads and the Dominant Seventh Chord   223

Triads   223
Triad Qualities in Major Keys   224
Triad Qualities in Minor Keys   226
Spelling Triads   227
Triad Inversion   230
The Dominant Seventh Chord   233
Spelling the Dominant Seventh Chord   233
Seventh Chord Inversion   234
Did You Know?   236 ▪ Terms You Should Know   236 ▪ Questions for Review   236 ▪ Reading Review   237 ▪ Apply It   238 ▪ Workbook   243 ▪ Aural Skills   251

CHAPTER 10 Melody Harmonization and Cadences   255

Triads on $\hat{1}$, $\hat{4}$, and $\hat{5}$ and the seventh chord on $\hat{5}$ 255
Harmonizing Major Melodies with the Basic Phrase Model   259
Cadence Types   260
The Subdominant in the Basic Phrase   264
Melodic Embellishments and Melody Harmonization   265
Harmonizing Minor-Key Melodies   266
Did You Know?   269 ▪ Terms You Should Know   269 ▪ Questions for Review   269 ▪ Reading Review   270 ▪ Apply It   271 ▪ Workbook   277 ▪ Aural Skills   285

CHAPTER 11 Form in Folk and Popular Songs   289

Melody and Paired Phrases   289
Quaternary Song Form   290
Writing Melodies   293
Writing Keyboard Accompaniments   295
Form in Recent Popular Music   299
Did You Know?   301 ▪ Terms You Should Know   302 ▪ Questions for Review   302 ▪ Reading Review   302 ▪ Apply It   303 ▪ Workbook   307 ▪ Aural Skills   313

CHAPTER 12 Blues and Other Popular Styles   315

Pentatonic Scales   315
The Blues Scale and the 12-Bar Blues   318
Seventh Chords   321
Chord Extensions and Sus Chords   324
Did You Know?   326 ▪ Terms You Should Know   326 ▪ Questions for Review   326 ▪ Reading Review   327 ▪ Apply It   328 ▪ Workbook   335 ▪ Aural Skills   343

Anthology   345

"The Ash Grove"   346

Johann Sebastian Bach, Invention in D Minor   348

Bach, Prelude in C♯ Minor, from *The Well-Tempered Clavier*, Book I   350

Ludwig van Beethoven, Piano Sonata in C Minor, Op. 13 (*Pathétique*), second movement, excerpt   354

Frédéric Chopin, Prelude in C Minor, Op. 28, No. 20   356

"Come, Ye Thankful People Come" (St. George's Windsor)   357

Stephen Foster, "Jeanie with the Light Brown Hair"   358

Foster, "Oh! Susanna"   363

Patrick S. Gilmore, "When Johnny Comes Marching Home"   364

"Greensleeves"   365

"Home on the Range"   367

Elisabeth-Claude Jacquet de la Guerre, Gigue, from Suite No. 3 in A Minor   368

Scott Joplin, "Solace"   370

Jerome Kern, "Look for the Silver Lining"   374

Wolfgang Amadeus Mozart, String Quartet in D Minor, K. 421, third movement   379

Mozart, *Variations on "Ah, vous dirai-je Maman,"* excerpts   382

"My Country, 'Tis of Thee" (America)   385

John Newton, "Amazing Grace"   386

"O God Our Help in Ages Past" (St. Anne)   387

Joel Phillips, "Blues for Norton"   388

Franz Schubert, Waltz in B Minor, Op. 18, No. 6   392

"Simple Gifts"   394

Hart A. Wand and Lloyd Garrett, "Dallas Blues"   395

Appendix 1   Try It Answers   A-1
Appendix 2   Reading Review Answers   A-16
Appendix 3   Apply It Answers   A-18
Appendix 4   Glossary   A-29
Appendix 5   The Overtone Series   A-39
Appendix 6   The Diatonic Modes   A-40
Appendix 7   The C-Clefs   A-43
Appendix 8   Basic Guitar Chords   A-44
Appendix 9   Piano Fingerings for Selected Scales   A-48
Appendix 10   Connecting Chords   A-51

Music Credits   A-53

Photo Credits   A-54

Index of Musical Examples   A-55

Index of Terms and Concepts   A-58

Preface

We hope you have chosen this course because you have an interest in—even a love for—music. Perhaps you want to learn to read music, write your own songs, or just listen to music with more understanding. This book can help you do all three.

Have you ever tried to explain something, but didn't know the right words? Our study begins with the vocabulary that will help you communicate your musical ideas. You'll learn musical terms and symbols, and how to read and write pitches and rhythms, scales, intervals, and chords. We'll build on these basics and consider how music is put together, what musical elements are being used, and why it sounds the way it does.

When you finish this book, you'll have all the tools you need to compose a song, and we hope you'll perform it in class. What better way to demonstrate what you have learned than to write your own music!

In this course, you will study classical music, as well as rock, jazz and blues standards, and folk songs. We encourage you to explore music of other cultures and styles, too; much of what you'll learn is useful in thinking about any type of music. We hope that you will enjoy using this book, and that the concepts you learn will enrich the ways you think about music for many years to come.

With this new edition of our text, you will be able to learn more than ever online. New features described below—including an ebook, online notation from Noteflight, quizzes with listening, and more—offer resources for students and instructors in traditional and online classes.

Using this Text

This book offers a comprehensive set of materials for learning music fundamentals through repertoire, hands-on music-making, and creative music writing. The twelve chapters introduce everything you need to know to compose and notate a song of your own.

The *Musician's Guide to Fundamentals* is organized to make it as easy as possible for you to learn. It includes many useful features, described here, that will facilitate your study.

- **Listening icons** identify the nearly one thousand recordings accessible online at StudySpace (wwnorton.com/studyspace)—the student website for this text—and within the ebook.
- **Download icons** indicate excerpts from widely available recordings that you can purchase and download separately. Copyright restrictions make it impossible to supply recordings of these works, but you should find and listen to them whenever possible.
- **Key Concept** and **Summary** boxes highlight new ideas and gather essential information.

> **KEY CONCEPT** A **half step** (or **semitone**) is the interval between any pitch and the next closest pitch on the keyboard in either direction. The combination of two half steps forms a **whole step** (or **whole tone**). A whole step always has a note that could be inserted in the middle.

- **Try It** exercises are scattered throughout chapters to provide opportunities to practice new concepts. They give you immediate feedback on your understanding and prepare you for the assignments at the end of the chapter. When you see one of these exercises, try it, then check your answer in Appendix 1. Only then will you know that you understand the concept and can apply it in your music-making.

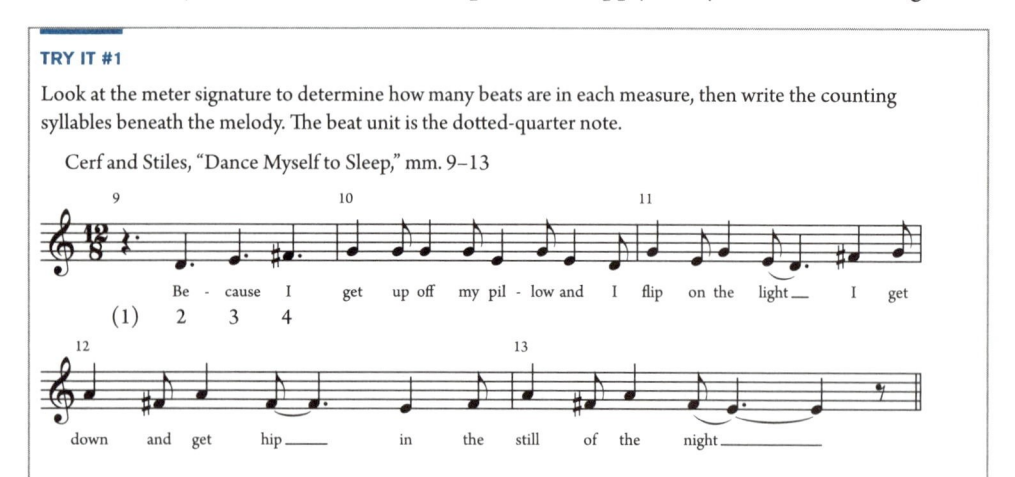

TRY IT #1

Look at the meter signature to determine how many beats are in each measure, then write the counting syllables beneath the melody. The beat unit is the dotted-quarter note.

Cerf and Stiles, "Dance Myself to Sleep," mm. 9–13

- Since many concepts can be learned in more than one way, **Another Way** boxes offer alternative explanations. Use the method that works best for you.

ANOTHER WAY A common mnemonic (memory) device to help you remember the first four flats is the word "bead." One handy sentence to remember for the order of both sharps and flats is "Father Charles Goes Down And Ends Battle." When you read it forward, the first letter of each word gives the order of sharps; when you read it backward ("Battle Ends And Down Goes Charles's Father"), you get the order of flats.

- Every chapter ends with a list of **Terms You Should Know**, **Questions for Review**, and a **Reading Review**. The **Questions for Review** are open-ended questions about chapter content; formulate answers to them in your own words. **Reading Reviews** are short matching quizzes; answers are provided in Appendix 2. These tools will help you test your mastery of the material covered before you move on to the next chapter.
- A **Did You Know?** box also appears at the end of each chapter to explain historical background for featured composers and pieces.

Did You Know?

Early rock and roll owes much to the blues. Not only did rock musicians borrow the 12-bar blues progression and the blues scale, in some cases they also reworked entire blues songs—either as covers (interpretations that acknowledged the original composers) or as "new" songs of their own. Rock-music scholars (and lawyers) have debated the question of when borrowed material becomes one's own and when it is protected by copyright law. For example, some of Led Zepplin's most famous songs have blues roots, raising both scholarly and legal controversies about their authorship. These songs include "Dazed and Confused" (compare with Jake Holmes's "I'm Confused"), "Whole Lotta Love" (compare with Willie Dixon's "You Need Love"), "Bring It on Home" (compare with a song with the same title by Willie Dixon), and the "Lemon Song" (compare with Howlin' Wolf/Chester Burnett's "The Killing Floor").

End-of-chapter activities and assignments invite you to practice what you've learned:

- **Apply It** activities emphasize the skills you need to understand and recall musical patterns. Activities include singing and rhythm reading, keyboard practice, short listening and writing activities, and more. So that you can assess your progress, answers to written Appy It exercises appear in the back of the book, and recordings of many melodies and rhythms are available online.
- Three or four double-sided, tear-out-and-turn-in **Workbook Assignments** give you the opportunity to master the concepts presented in each chapter. These assignments, which include abundant practice, reinforce concepts in the order that they appear in the chapter; headings indicate when you are ready to complete each assignment.
- One or two **Aural Skills Assignments** round out each chapter. These assignments often guide you through the process of listening to and notating recorded music.

In the back of the book, along with the answers to Try It, Reading Review, and Apply It exercises, you will find the **Glossary** and several **Appendixes** that provide additional information on topics such as guitar chords, the overtone series, the diatonic modes, and C-clefs.

Using the Anthology

As part of this text, we have included a short **Anthology** with musical scores for 23 pieces. Our spiral-learning approach revisits the anthology's core repertoire from chapter to chapter as you learn new concepts—a single piece might illustrate pitch, meter, scales, and triads. By the second or third time you "visit" a particular work, it will seem like an old friend. We hope that you will listen to the music until you know each work well enough to hear it in your head, the same way you can hear familiar songs from the radio, television, or movies just by thinking about them.

We have chosen music for study that we like and that our students have enjoyed. Some of the works should be familiar to you, and other pieces may be new. The anthology includes pieces for varied performing ensembles in contrasting musical styles—from American popular songs to classical sonatas, from a piano rag to a piano waltz, from a folk song to a choral hymn. Complete recordings of all the anthology pieces are available online.

Using Total Access

With Total Access—included free with every new copy of this text—you can access all the media you need for your music fundamentals course. Total Access includes:

- An **ebook**—with the same text as this book—that enables you to highlight, take notes, listen to musical examples, and access exercises
- **Noteflight**, a cloud-based notation program, that you can use to complete, listen to, and turn in most of the assignments in this text—as well as compose your own music—from any computer or mobile device with an Internet connection
- Expanded online **quizzes** that test your mastery of theoretical concepts—both aural and written—and offer immediate, detailed feedback
- Online **recordings** featuring performances by students and faculty at the Eastman School of Music
- A **Virtual Keyboard** and **Virtual Guitar** that you can use to practice finding notes, scales, and chords.

To begin Using Total Access, go to wwnorton.com/studyspace and register with the code on the card in the front of this book.

To the Instructor

The *Musician's Guide to Fundamentals* is a comprehensive teaching and learning package for undergraduate music fundamentals classes that integrates technological resources with a textbook and audio recordings. In addition, we have designed the package with numerous support mechanisms to help you efficiently prepare for class.

- The online **Answer Key** includes answers to all exercises in the same format and pagination as the text, plus instructions and resources for Apply It activities.
- The **Instructor's Manual** by Peter Martens (Texas Tech University) offers a wealth of materials, including chapter overviews, teaching strategies, class activities, supplemental repertoire, additional exercises, and test questions.
- **Coursepacks** enable your students to connect to Total Access through your campus learning-management system.
- You will no longer need to search online or in the library before class to find a recording of the work you will be studying; **recordings** of all the core repertoire and all dictation exercises are available online in high-quality performances. In addition, bonus tracks (Bach, Newton, and Joplin) demonstrate alternative performances.

To access these resources, visit wwnorton.com/instructors.

This new edition includes a number of additional resources that will prove especially useful to instructors of online and hybrid classes:

- With **Noteflight**, your students can complete and turn in—and you can grade—assignments electronically for a paperless class.
- Newly expanded **quizzes** report directly to your learning-management system gradebook and offer new ways of assessing proficiency in written and aural skills.
- New **Apply It** activities provide additional opportunities for self assessment with answers to written questions in the back of the text and online recordings of melodies and rhythms available for students to check their work.

We hope that all users of this textbook—student and teacher alike—will get to know the repertoire, find the class activities and aural assignments challenging and enjoyable, and emerge from this class with some new skills that will contribute to their lifelong engagement with music listening and performance.

Our Thanks to . . .

A work of this size and scope requires the help of many people. We are especially grateful for the support of our families. Our work together as coauthors has been incredibly rewarding, and we are thankful for that collaboration and friendship. While working on the project, we received encouragement and useful ideas from music fundamentals teachers across the country. We thank these teachers for their willingness to share their years of experience with us.

For subvention of the recordings that accompany the text, and for his support of strong music theory pedagogy, we thank Douglas Lowry (former Dean of the Eastman School of Music). For performance of many of the short examples in the text, we thank Richard Masters, whose sight-reading abilities, flexibility, and good grace are all appreciated. We also thank Don Gibson (former Dean and current Professor of Music Theory at Florida State University's College of Music) for his enthusiasm and unfailing support. For pedagogical discussions over the years, we are grateful to our colleagues at Florida State University, the Eastman School of Music, Westminster Choir College, and to the College Board's AP Music Theory Test Development Committee members and AP readers. Special thanks to Paul Murphy who stepped in on short notice to assist with aural skills materials. Thanks also to Peter Martens (Texas Tech University) for his work on the Instructor's Manual, to Elizabeth A. Clendinning (Emory University) for writing the online quizzes, and to Sarah Sarver (Oklahoma City University) for reviewing online materials.

We are indebted to the thorough and detailed work of our prepublication reviewers, whose careful reading of the manuscript inspired many improvements large and small. Reviewers of the second edition included Joel Galand (Florida International University), Courtenay Harter (Rhodes College), Barbara Murphy (University of Tennessee), Mark Richardson (East Carolina University), and Amelia Triest (University of California at Davis). First edition reviewers were Lyn Ellen Burkett (University of North Carolina at Asheville), Robert Carl (Hartt School, University of Hartford), Don Fader (University of Alabama), Taylor Greer (Pennsylvania State University), Judy Cervetto Hedberg (Portland Community College), Rebecca Jemian (University of Louisville), Joan F. Jensen (Tulane University), Laura L. Kelly (The University of Texas at San Antonio), Laila R. Kteily-O'Sullivan (University of North Texas), Linda Apple Monson (George Mason University), Kathy Murray (Missouri State University), Shaugn O'Donnell (The City College of New York), Malia Roberson (California Lutheran University), Peter J. Schoenbach (Curtis Institute of Music), Paul Sheehan (Nassau Community College), Jason Roland Smith (Ohio University School of Music), Jennifer Snodgrass (Appalachian State University), and Stephen Zolper (Towson University). We also acknowledge that the foundation of this book rests on writings of the great music theorists of the past and present, from the sixteenth to the twenty-first century, from whom we have learned the tools of the trade and whose pedagogical works have inspired ours.

For the production of the recordings, our thanks go to recording engineers Mike Farrington and John Ebert, who worked tirelessly with Elizabeth Marvin at Eastman on recording and editing sessions, as well as to Helen Smith, director of Eastman's Office of Technology and Media Production. We finally thank the faculty and students of the Eastman School who gave so generously of their time to make these recordings. The joy of their music-making contributed mightily to this project.

We are indebted to the W. W. Norton staff for their commitment to *The Musician's Guide to Fundamentals* and their painstaking care in producing this volume. Most notable among these are Justin Hoffman and Susan Gaustad, whose knowledge of music and detailed, thoughtful questions made them a pleasure to work with, and music editor Maribeth Payne, whose vision and great enthusiasm have helped launch this new edition. We are grateful for Norton's forward-thinking media editor Steve Hoge, who helped refine our ideas for the book's website and made them a reality. Lisa Buckley created the design, Debra Nichols provided expert proofreading, Chris Freitag developed marketing strategies, Amanda Sewell handled final editing of the recordings with a great eye and ear for detail, and Ben Reynolds oversaw the production of this text through to completion. Our gratitude to one and all.

Jane Piper Clendinning
Elizabeth West Marvin
Joel Phillips

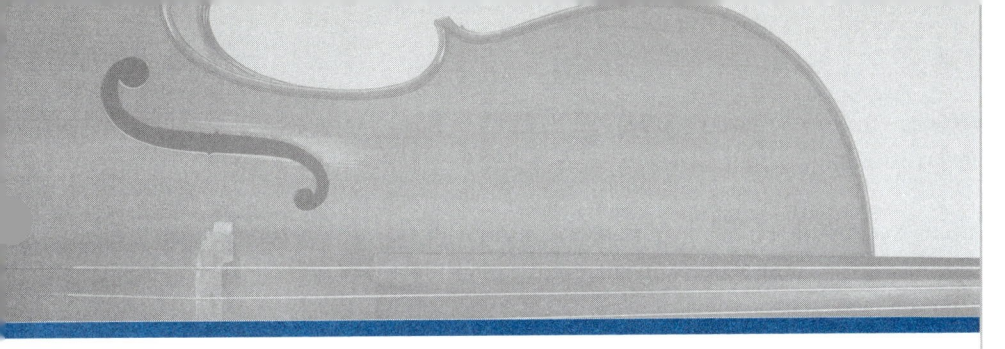

CHAPTER 1

Pitch Notation and the Grand Staff

TOPICS
- musical contour
- introduction to pitch notation: letter names
- the piano keyboard: naming white keys
- staff notation
- treble and bass clefs
- naming pitches with octave numbers
- ledger lines
- the grand staff
- writing music in a score

MUSIC
- Johann Sebastian Bach, Prelude from Cello Suite No. 2 in D Minor
- Elton John and Tim Rice, "Circle of Life," from *The Lion King*
- Scott Joplin, "Solace"
- John Lennon, "Imagine"
- John Newton, "Amazing Grace"
- Joel Phillips, "Blues for Norton"
- Lalo Schifrin, Theme from *Mission: Impossible*

Musical Contour

Listen to the hymn "Amazing Grace," shown in music notation in Example 1.1. Follow the shape of the musical line as you listen.

EXAMPLE 1.1   Newton, "Amazing Grace," mm. 1–8

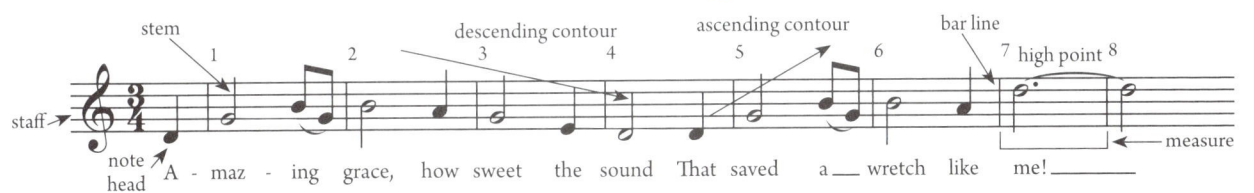

The musical notation above—the **score**—shows various symbols that represent musical sounds. The most basic symbol is the **note**. Each note, written as a small oval (either black or hollow) attached to a **stem** going either up or down, represents a single musical sound, or **pitch**. Notes are written higher or lower on the five horizontal lines of a musical **staff**; this shows graphically the "shape," or **contour**, of a melody. Notes 5 to 9 of "Amazing Grace" represent a **descending contour** and the notation on the staff likewise moves downward from left to right, each note lower than the previous one. The next three pitches move upward in an **ascending contour**. Most music—like this melody—moves both up and down, with melodic contours forming arches and waves, often with a single high point, as marked at the end of this phrase. The vertical lines on the staff, called **bar lines**, mark off equal amounts of time, called **measures**.

Introduction to Pitch Notation: Letter Names

Drawing a melody's contour may give a general idea of its shape, but you need more-precise information to play the tune correctly.

> **KEY CONCEPT** In a musical score, each note has a **letter name**—A, B, C, D, E, F, or G—which is determined by its position on the staff.

To count up beyond G, start over with A; to count down below A, start over again with G, as shown in Figure 1.1. You can also think of the seven letter names around a circle, like a clock. Think of the movement as upward when you count forward or clockwise, and downward when you count backward or counterclockwise. For example, five notes above E is B: E–F–G–A–B. Six notes below E is G: E–D–C–B–A–G. When counting, be sure to include the first and last letter names of the series: three above F is A (count F–G–A, not G–A–B).

FIGURE 1.1   Letter names

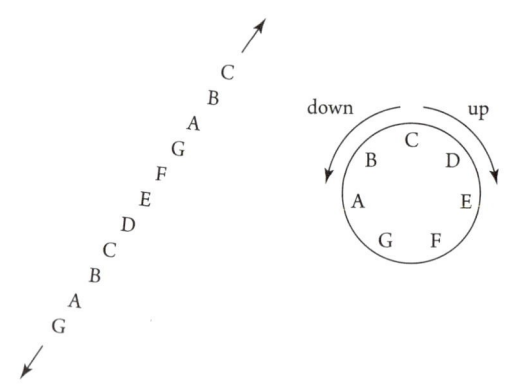

In this seven-name system, each letter name reappears every eighth position (eight above or below D is another D).

> **KEY CONCEPT** Pitches separated by eight letter names are an **octave** apart. The repetition of letter names reflects the way we hear: Pitches an octave apart sound similar. This principle is called **octave equivalence**.

TRY IT #1

Find the letter name requested.

(a) 7 above D: __C__
(b) 5 above A: ____
(c) 3 below B: ____
(d) 6 below C: ____
(e) 2 below E: ____
(f) 5 above F: ____
(g) 3 above C: ____
(h) 8 below D: ____
(i) 4 below E: ____
(j) 6 above G: ____
(k) 2 above G: ____
(l) 4 above B: ____
(m) 6 below D: ____
(n) 5 below F: ____
(o) 7 above E: ____

The Piano Keyboard: Naming White Keys

Look at the diagram in Figure 1.2 to identify pitch locations on the keyboard. (Or use the model keyboard in your text or the Virtual Keyboard on StudySpace.) The white key immediately to the left of any group of two black keys is a C, and the white key immediately to the left of any three black keys is an F; each is indicated by an arrow. Write in the remaining letter names for the white keys in the figure, using the black-key groupings to find your place.

> **KEY CONCEPT** Middle C is the C closest to the middle of the keyboard. No black key appears between E and F or between B and C.

FIGURE 1.2   Piano keyboard

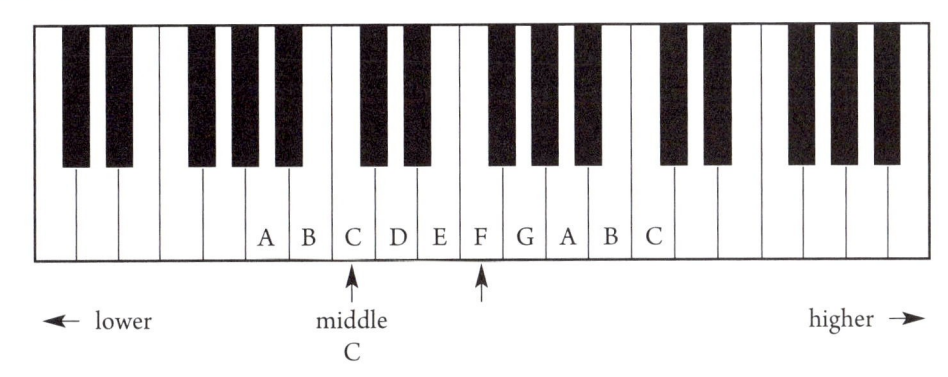

Staff Notation

As shown in Example 1.2, the staff (plural is staves) consists of five lines and four spaces, which are generally read from bottom to top, with the bottom line called the first and the top line the fifth. As a first step in writing pitches, ovals called notes or **note heads** are drawn on the lines or in the spaces of the staff (most notes will also require stems, as we'll see later). Filled note heads are played for a shorter duration than hollow ones. Higher pitches are notated toward the top of the staff, lower pitches toward the bottom, as marked.

EXAMPLE 1.2   Note heads on a staff

Treble and Bass Clefs

The letter names of the notes in Example 1.2 can't be identified without a **clef**, the symbol that appears on the far left of every staff. The clef shows which line or space represents which pitch (and in which octave). In Example 1.3, notes are written on the staff with a **treble clef**, sometimes called the G-clef. Its shape somewhat resembles a cursive capital G, and the end of its curving line (in the center) rests on the staff line for G. All the other pitches can be read from G by counting up or down in the **musical alphabet**. The note above the highest staff line (F) is G. The note below the lowest staff line (E) is D, and the note below that, with the little line through it, is middle C. The treble clef represents the higher notes on a keyboard.

As soon as possible, memorize the note names for each line and space. Learn the "line notes" together and the "space notes" together, as in Example 1.4.

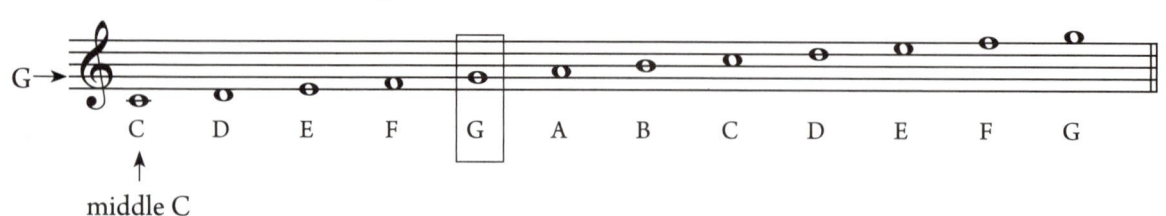

EXAMPLE 1.3   Treble clef (G-clef)

EXAMPLE 1.4   Treble-clef lines and spaces

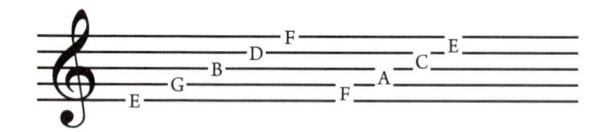

ANOTHER WAY To remember note names of the lines (E–G–B–D–F), you might make up a sentence whose words begin with these letters, like "Every Good Bird Does Fly." The spaces simply spell the word F–A–C–E.

TRY IT #2

(a) Write the letter name of each pitch in the blanks below.

(1) **B**   (2)___   (3)___   (4)___   (5)___   (6)___   (7)___   (8)___   (9)___   (10)___   (11)___   (12)___

(b) Write the letter names in the blanks, then circle the highest and lowest pitches.

Lennon, "Imagine," mm. 28–30

You____   You may say____   I'm a dream-er.   But I'm not the on - ly one.

(1) **E** (2)___   (3)___   (4)___ (5)___   (6)___   (7)___

CHAPTER ONE Pitch Notation and the Grand Staff

Now listen to Example 1.5, the beginning of Bach's Cello Suite No. 2, while looking at the music shown in the example. This lower-sounding melody is written in the **bass clef**.

EXAMPLE 1.5   Bach, Prelude, from Cello Suite No. 2 in D Minor, mm. 1–4

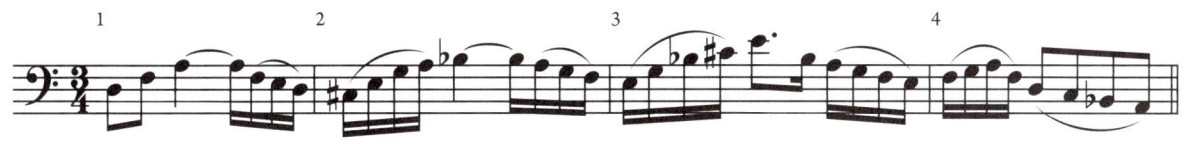

The bass clef, used for the lower notes on a keyboard, is also known as the F-clef: it somewhat resembles a cursive capital F, and its two dots surround the line that represents F. Other pitches may be counted from F, or memorized according to their positions on the staff, shown in Example 1.6. Example 1.7 shows the lines and spaces labeled with their letter names.

EXAMPLE 1.6   Bass clef (F-clef)

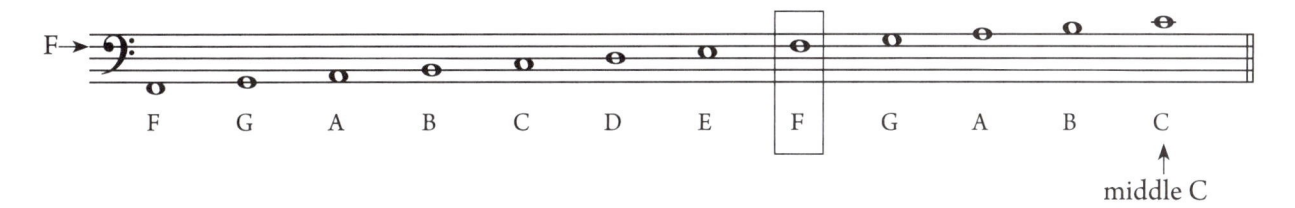

𝓕 = letter F → 𝄢

F G A B C D E F G A B C
                              ↑
                          middle C

EXAMPLE 1.7   Bass-clef lines and spaces

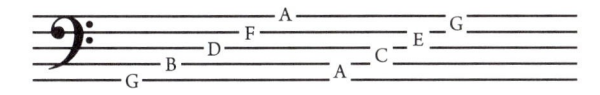

Lines (bottom to top): G–B–D–F–A
Spaces (bottom to top): A–C–E–G

> **ANOTHER WAY**   Two ways to remember the bass-clef spaces (A–C–E–G) are "All Cows Eat Grass" and "All Cars Eat Gas." The bass-clef lines (G–B–D–F–A) might be "Great Big Doves Fly Away."

TRY IT #3

(a) Identify the pitches on the bass staff below with letter names.

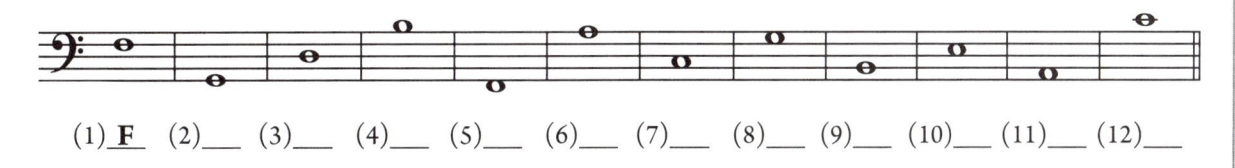

(1) **F** (2)___ (3)___ (4)___ (5)___ (6)___ (7)___ (8)___ (9)___ (10)___ (11)___ (12)___

TRY IT #3 (Continued)

(b) Listen to the beginning of "Blues for Norton." The lowest part is shown below. Then write the letter names for the pitches that have blanks beneath them. Circle the highest and lowest pitches.

Phillips, "Blues for Norton" (bass line), mm. 2–3

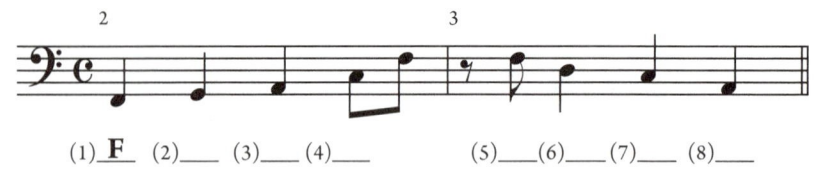

(1) **F** (2)___ (3)___ (4)___   (5)___(6)___(7)___ (8)___

ASSIGNMENT 1.1

Naming Pitches with Octave Numbers

As seen in the previous examples, letter names reappear in different octaves in the bass and treble clefs. To specify exactly in which octave a pitch appears, use octave numbers.

> **KEY CONCEPT** As Figure 1.3 shows, the lowest C on a standard piano keyboard is designated C1, and the highest is C8; middle C is C4. The number for a particular octave includes all the pitches from C up to the following B.

The B above C4, for example, is B4; the B below C4 is B3. The white notes below C1 on the piano are A0 and B0.

FIGURE 1.3 Piano keyboard with octave numbers

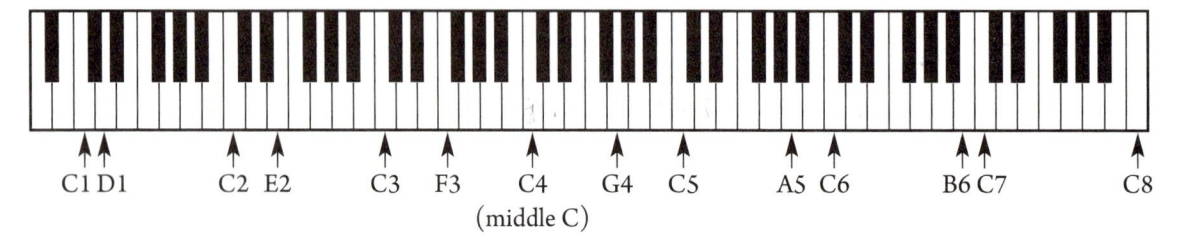

C1 D1   C2 E2   C3 F3   C4   G4 C5   A5 C6   B6 C7   C8
                          (middle C)

Ledger Lines

Some of the pitches on the piano keyboard, including middle C, cannot be notated on the five lines and four spaces of the treble or bass staff.

> **KEY CONCEPT** When music extends above or below the staff, extra lines—called **ledger lines**—are drawn to accommodate these notes (Example 1.8). Read ledger lines (and the spaces between them) just like other staff lines and spaces: by counting forward or backward in the musical alphabet.

6   CHAPTER ONE   Pitch Notation and the Grand Staff

EXAMPLE 1.8 Ledger lines above and below the staff

(a) Treble clef

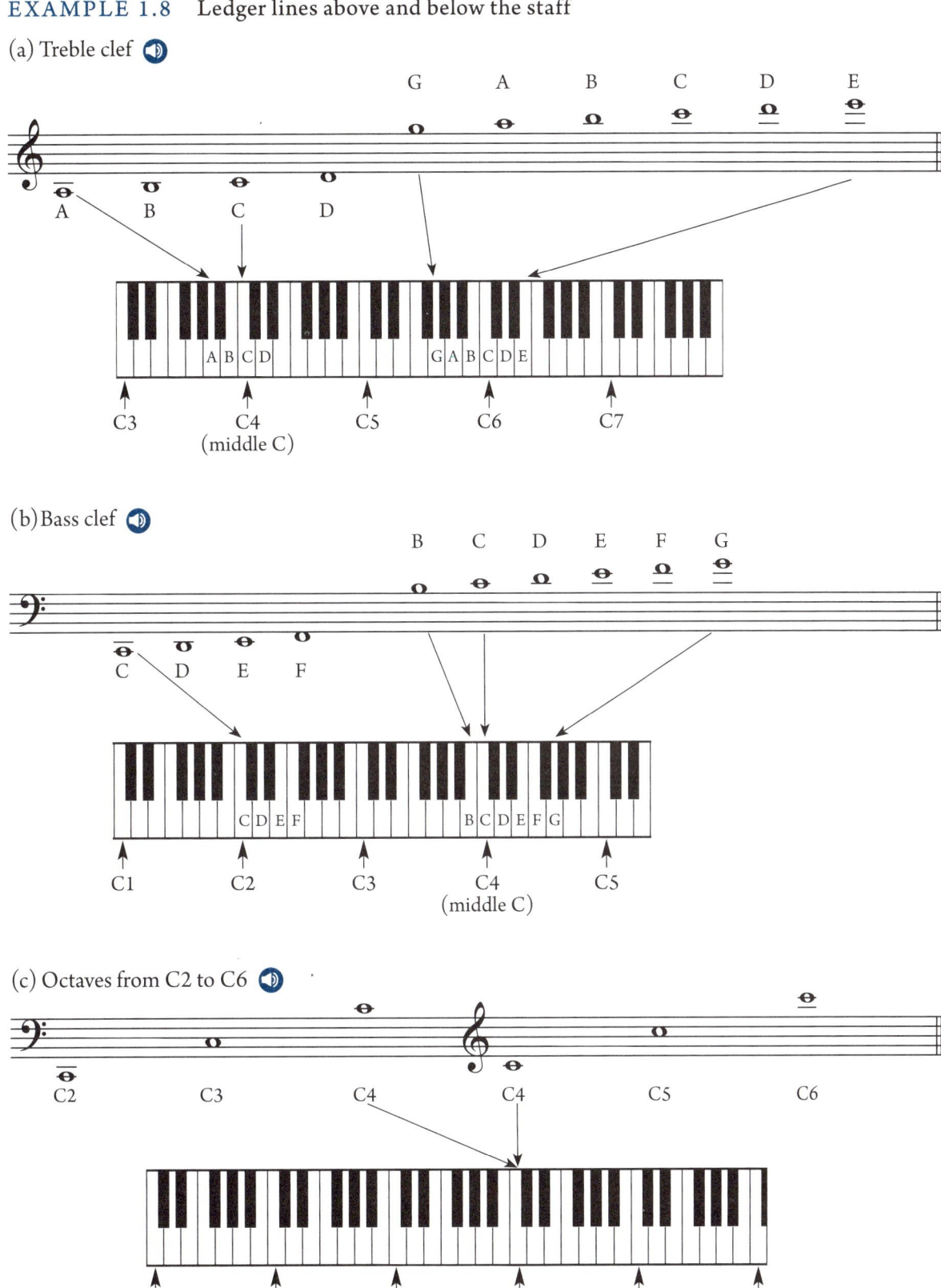

(b) Bass clef

(c) Octaves from C2 to C6

KEY CONCEPT The highness or lowness of a pitch (in other words, the octave in which it lies) is called its **register**.

Ledger Lines 7

Instruments and singing voices sound in different registers, which can be used to create certain moods and effects. In Example 1.9, from "Circle of Life," the low range of the melody is important to setting the mood. Some pitches are marked with their octave numbers; try identifying others.

EXAMPLE 1.9   John and Rice, "Circle of Life," from *The Lion King*, mm. 1–8

It takes a little practice to identify notes written with ledger lines. Example 1.10 provides a few landmarks for each clef.

> **KEY CONCEPT** The ledger-line notes below the treble staff are F–A–C; those above the staff are A–C–E. The ledger-line notes below the bass staff are A–C–E; those above the staff are C–E–G.

EXAMPLE 1.10   Ledger-line landmarks

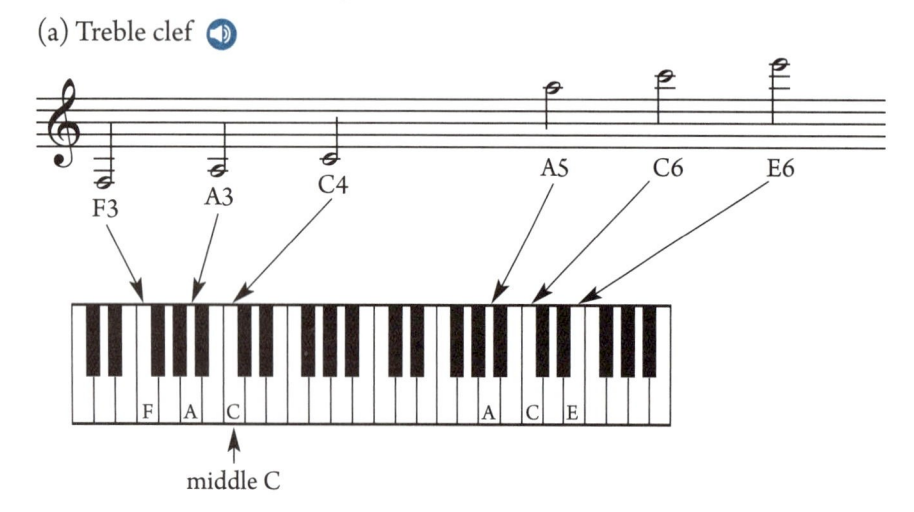

(a) Treble clef

8   CHAPTER ONE   Pitch Notation and the Grand Staff

(b) Bass clef

TRY IT #4

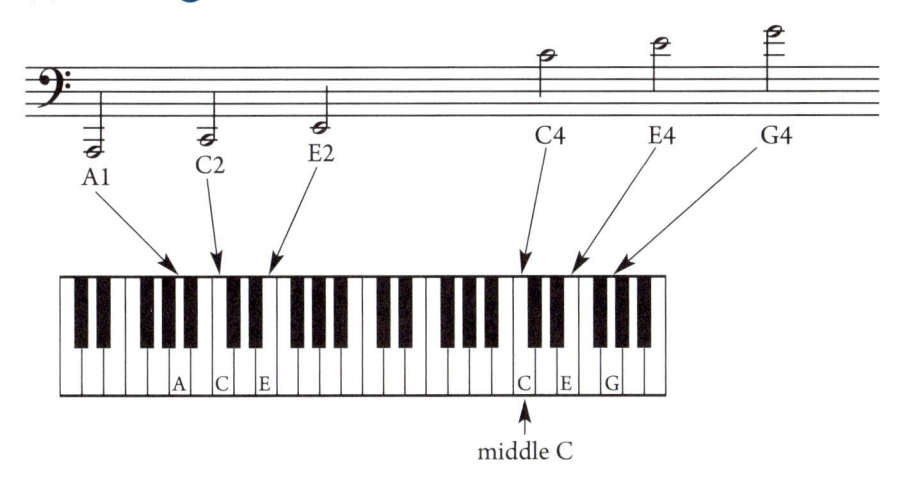

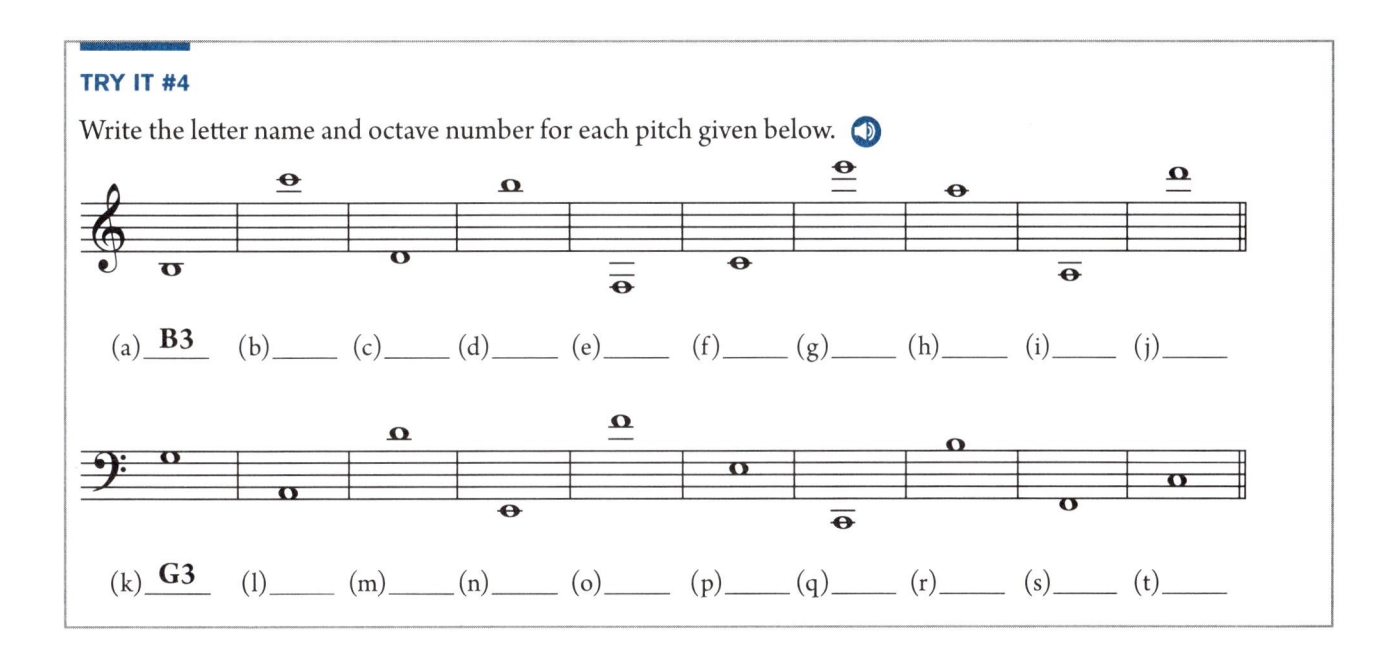

Write the letter name and octave number for each pitch given below.

(a) __B3__ (b) _____ (c) _____ (d) _____ (e) _____ (f) _____ (g) _____ (h) _____ (i) _____ (j) _____

(k) __G3__ (l) _____ (m) _____ (n) _____ (o) _____ (p) _____ (q) _____ (r) _____ (s) _____ (t) _____

ASSIGNMENT 1.2

The Grand Staff

Pitches for keyboards, and other instruments that play very high and low notes, are written on a grand staff like the one in Example 1.11.

> **KEY CONCEPT** A treble staff and a bass staff connected by a curly brace and a line make a **grand staff**.

Ledger lines may extend above and below the grand staff. Notes that fill in the middle, between the two staves, may be written in either clef. In the example, the notes in parentheses are alternate notations for those without parentheses.

EXAMPLE 1.11   The grand staff with pitches in its middle register

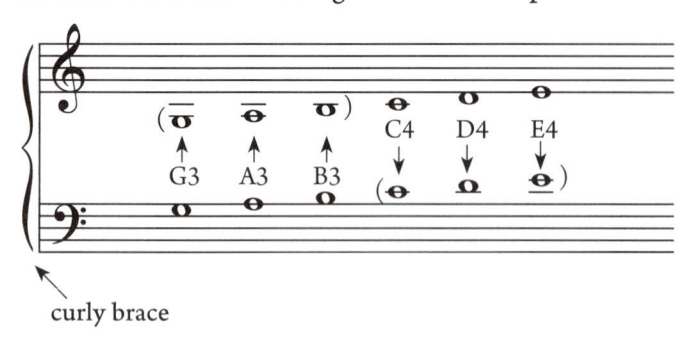

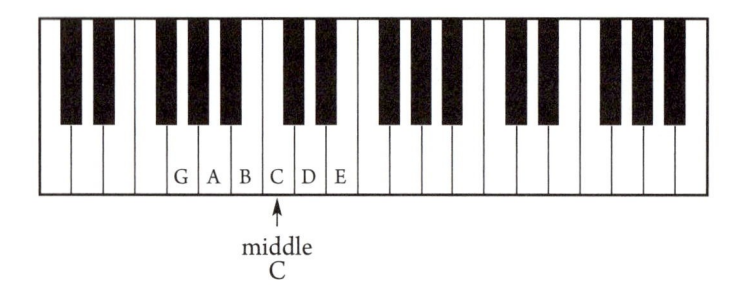

[musical example showing grand staff with notes G3, A3, B3, C4, D4, E4, and a keyboard diagram indicating middle C]

Listen to the opening of Joplin's "Solace" while following the score in Example 1.12. This passage shows ledger lines between the staves. In measure 5, the bass-clef F written with ledger lines is F4. This note could also have been written in the treble clef on the bottom space. In piano music with ledger lines written between the staves, the ranges of the two hands overlap; the clef shows which hand is supposed to play a particular note. Treble clef generally indicates the right hand, bass clef the left hand.

EXAMPLE 1.12   Joplin, "Solace," mm. 5–12

[musical score excerpt]

10   CHAPTER ONE   Pitch Notation and the Grand Staff

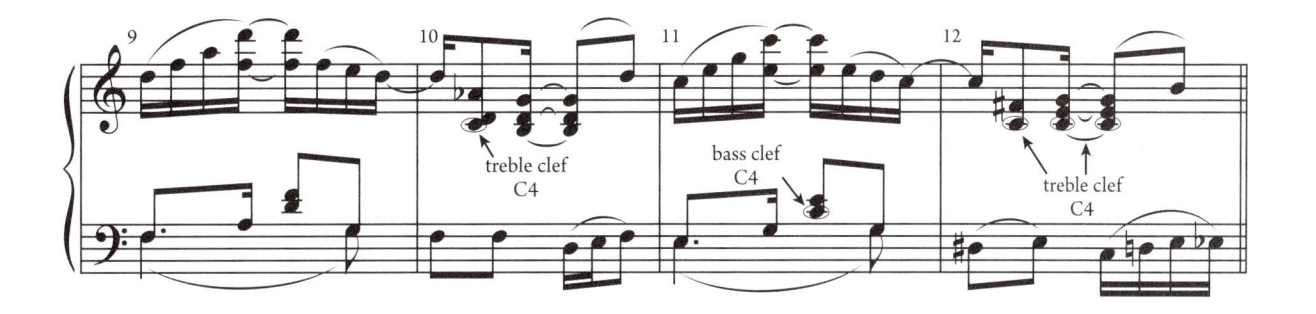

TRY IT #5

The example on the grand staff below includes many notes written with ledger lines. For each note with a blank beneath it, write the letter name and octave number. Then locate these pitches on a keyboard.

Schifrin, Theme from *Mission: Impossible*, mm. 1–2

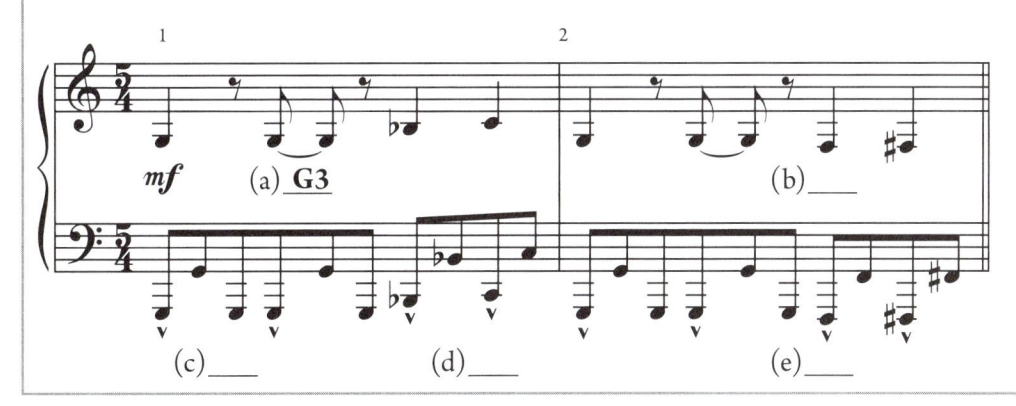

(a) **G3**   (b) ___   (c) ___   (d) ___   (e) ___

Writing Music in a Score

Writing music correctly (and neatly) helps those performing it to read fluently and without errors. You can draw a treble clef in a single continuous curved line, or in two strokes as shown in Example 1.13: (1) first draw a wavy line from top to bottom, like an elongated S, then (2) draw a second line that starts at the top and curves around it (ending on the G line). The bass clef is drawn in two steps as well: (1) draw an arc that looks a bit like a backward C, then (2) add two dots that surround the F line.

EXAMPLE 1.13 Drawing clefs

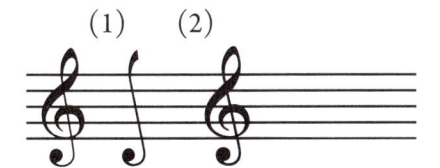

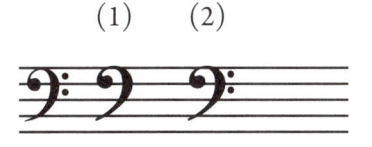

When you draw note heads on the staff, make them oval-shaped rather than round; they should not be so large that it's hard to tell whether they sit on a line or in a space (Example 1.14a).

> **KEY CONCEPT** Most notes have thin vertical lines, called stems, that extend above or below the note head. If a note lies below the middle line of the staff, its stem usually goes up, on the right side of the note head (♩); if a note lies on or above the middle line, its stem goes down, on the left side (♩).

The stem of a note on the middle line can, however, go up if the notes around it have stems up (both stem directions are shown in Example 1.14b). The length of the stem from bottom to top spans about an octave.

EXAMPLE 1.14 Notation guidelines
(a)

too round   too big   too small   perfect ovals

(b)

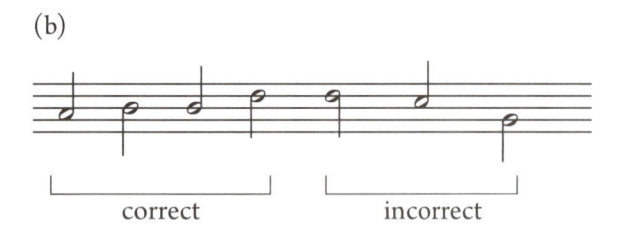

correct   incorrect

Example 1.15 shows ledger lines drawn correctly and incorrectly. When you write notes above the staff, draw ledger lines through the note heads or beneath them, but never above them. Note heads below the staff have ledger lines through them or above them, but never beneath. Draw ledger lines the same distance apart as staff lines.

EXAMPLE 1.15 Ledger-line pitches

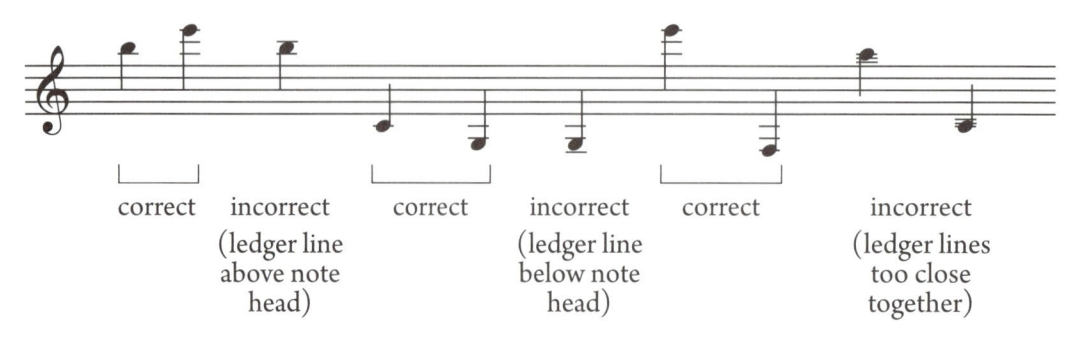

correct   incorrect   correct   incorrect   correct   incorrect
           (ledger line   (ledger line   (ledger lines
           above note   below note   too close
           head)   head)   together)

SUMMARY

When notating music, write neatly so that others can read your score easily and accurately.

- Draw a clef at the beginning of each staff.
- To indicate a grand staff, draw a long line and curly brace to connect the treble and bass staves on the left side.
- Draw both black and hollow note heads as neat ovals on or between staff lines.
- For ledger-line notes, draw ledger lines parallel to staff lines, the same distance apart, and between the note head and the top or bottom staff line.
- Draw straight, thin stems that span about an octave and follow the guidelines for stem direction.

You will learn more notational guidelines for rhythm and other topics in later chapters.

ASSIGNMENT 1.3, AURAL SKILLS 1.1

Did You Know?

Sir Elton John was born Reginald Kenneth Dwight in 1947. The child of a musician, he began studying piano at age four and won a scholarship to the Royal Academy of Music at age eleven. By the 1970s, John had become a pop superstar with a Top 40 single every year from 1970 to 1996. Among his most famous songs are "Your Song," "Goodbye Yellow Brick Road," songs from *The Lion King* (including "Circle of Life," Example 1.9), and "Candle in the Wind." This last song, originally a tribute to Marilyn Monroe, John rerecorded as a tribute to Princess Diana after her untimely death in 1997. "Candle in the Wind" became his biggest hit ever, selling over three million copies in the United States in its first week. John contributed royalties from this recording to Princess Diana's favorite charities.

Terms You Should Know

bar line	letter name	octave
clef	ledger line	octave equivalence
treble	measure	pitch
bass	middle C	register
contour	musical alphabet	score
ascending	note	staff
descending	note head	stem
grand staff		

Questions for Review

1. Which letters represent pitches?
2. Why are clefs necessary?
3. Why is a treble clef also called a G-clef? Why is a bass clef also called an F-clef?
4. What are the letter names for the lines on the treble staff? on the bass staff?
5. What are the letter names for the spaces on the treble staff? on the bass staff?
6. How many letter names apart are notes that span an octave?
7. What is the purpose of ledger lines?
8. When is a grand staff used? What does it consist of?
9. To which side of the note head do ascending stems connect? To which side do descending stems connect?
10. How do you decide whether stems should go up or down?

Reading Review

Match the term on the left with the best answer on the right.

_____ (1) E–G–B–D–F   (a) 𝄞
_____ (2) score   (b) five lines and four spaces on which music is notated
_____ (3) ledger lines   (c) notation of a piece of music
_____ (4) octave equivalence   (d) letter names for treble-clef spaces
_____ (5) clef   (e) attached to note heads above the middle line
_____ (6) contour   (f) similarity in sound of notes with the same letter name
_____ (7) F–A–C–E   (g) the shape of a musical line
_____ (8) treble-clef symbol   (h) letter names for treble-clef lines
_____ (9) G–B–D–F–A   (i) used to notate pitches above or below the staff lines
_____ (10) A–C–E–G   (j) ovals written on a staff to represent pitches
_____ (11) bass-clef symbol   (k) attached to note heads below the middle line
_____ (12) notes   (l) specifies the octave register of a pitch
_____ (13) octave number   (m) middle C
_____ (14) grand staff   (n) treble- and bass-clef staves joined with a curly brace
_____ (15) stems down   (o) letter names for bass-clef lines
_____ (16) C4   (p) letter names for bass-clef spaces
_____ (17) stems up   (q) symbol that gives notes on a staff their letter names
_____ (18) staff   (r) 𝄢

Additional review and practice available at wwnorton.com/studyspace

Apply It

Because singing and playing piano can help you understand and remember musical concepts, these performing activities will make up a significant part of your study. Most can be completed on your own or in class.

When singing:
- Don't be shy; sing out with enthusiasm!
- Don't worry about the quality of your voice. For our purposes, you only want to sing accurate pitches and rhythm.
- Sing every chance you get. Everything improves with practice.
- Sing a warm-up pattern first (like the one below) to orient your voice and ear to the music.

When playing on a keyboard:
- Keep your fingers curved.
- Don't depress any pedals for now.
- Typically, play different notes with different fingers. When it matters, specific fingering will be suggested.

If you don't have access to a piano:
- Practice on the Virtual Keyboard on StudySpace.
- Practice on the fold-out keyboard in the front of the book.
- Practice with a keyboard app.

A. Singing

For each warm-up pattern below, sing on the syllables given, in order to achieve an open and free sound. Also practice on the "lyrics" shown, *do-re-mi-fa-sol*, or numbers $\hat{1}$ to $\hat{5}$. You will learn more about these lyrics in Chapter 6. Listen first to the recording, then sing what you hear. You can check yourself at a keyboard.

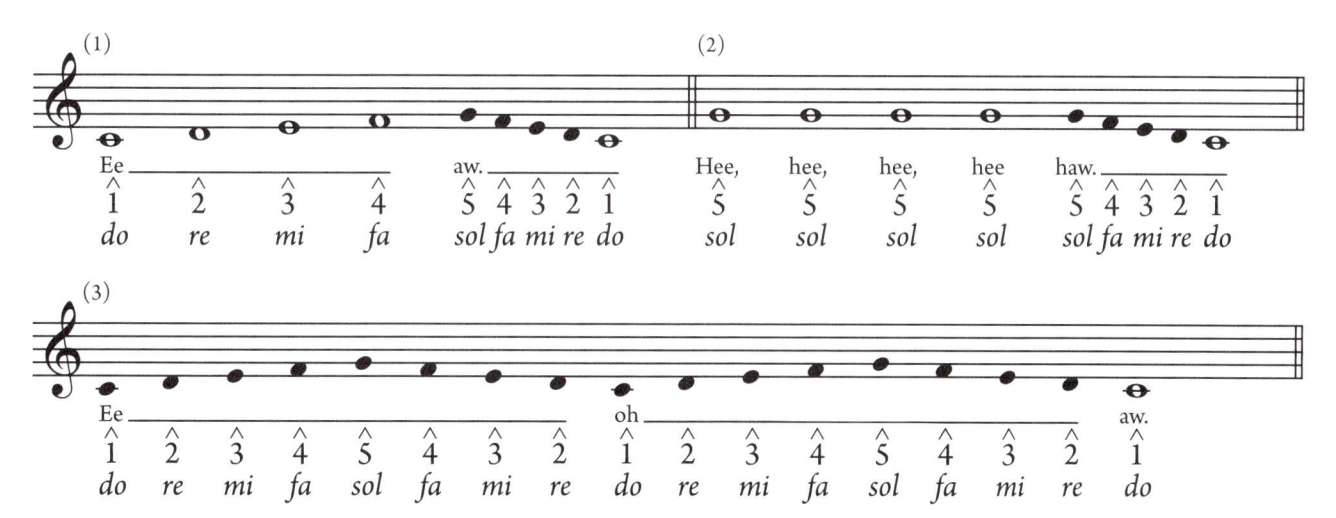

(1) Ee _____ aw. _____
$\hat{1}$ $\hat{2}$ $\hat{3}$ $\hat{4}$ $\hat{5}$ $\hat{4}$ $\hat{3}$ $\hat{2}$ $\hat{1}$
do re mi fa sol fa mi re do

(2) Hee, hee, hee, hee haw. _____
$\hat{5}$ $\hat{5}$ $\hat{5}$ $\hat{5}$ $\hat{5}$ $\hat{4}$ $\hat{3}$ $\hat{2}$ $\hat{1}$
sol sol sol sol sol fa mi re do

(3) Ee _____ oh _____ aw.
$\hat{1}$ $\hat{2}$ $\hat{3}$ $\hat{4}$ $\hat{5}$ $\hat{4}$ $\hat{3}$ $\hat{2}$ $\hat{1}$ $\hat{2}$ $\hat{3}$ $\hat{4}$ $\hat{5}$ $\hat{4}$ $\hat{3}$ $\hat{2}$ $\hat{1}$
do re mi fa sol fa mi re do re mi fa sol fa mi re do

Refer to this page when warming up each day. Sing these melodies often until your voice becomes stronger and your range wider. To begin, play a pitch on the keyboard that you can sing comfortably; sing a pattern starting on this pitch. Then play the next-higher note and sing the pattern again. Continue, each time one note higher, until the melody gets too high; then stop. You may also practice the pattern each time one note lower, until the melody gets too low. Choose a new pattern and repeat the process.

B. At the keyboard

1. Play the following notes on the keyboard in two or more different octaves. *Solo*: Play additional random white-key notes, then say their letter names. On the Virtual Keyboard, you can see the name of each note as you play it. *Duet*: One person plays a pitch and the other person names it, then switch roles. *Variation*: Sing each note as you play.

(a) C   (f) D   (k) G   (p) C
(b) A   (g) B   (l) F   (q) E
(c) E   (h) A   (m) D   (r) D
(d) G   (i) C   (n) A   (s) B
(e) F   (j) E   (o) B   (t) G

2. Play the following notes on the keyboard in the octave specified. The Virtual Keyboard extends from C2 to C6. Which of these notes are too high or too low to play on that keyboard?

(a) B5   (f) F5   (k) E5   (p) D6
(b) F3   (g) D4   (l) F4   (q) G4
(c) E2   (h) G6   (m) A3   (r) A5
(d) A4   (i) B3   (n) C1   (s) E3
(e) C6   (j) A2   (o) B4   (t) F6

C. Point and sing

After playing the home pitch, C, your teacher or a partner will create a melody by pointing to a series of notes—pitches on a staff, letter names, or piano keys—like those shown below.

1. When your partner points to a note, immediately sing it with its letter name.
2. Once the melody is complete, sing it until you have memorized it.
3. Write the melody with letter names or notate it on a staff.
4. For a solo activity, make your own point-and-sing exercises. Point to one or more notes, sing them, then check your singing by playing the notes at a keyboard. Begin with short patterns, and make your melodies longer as you practice.

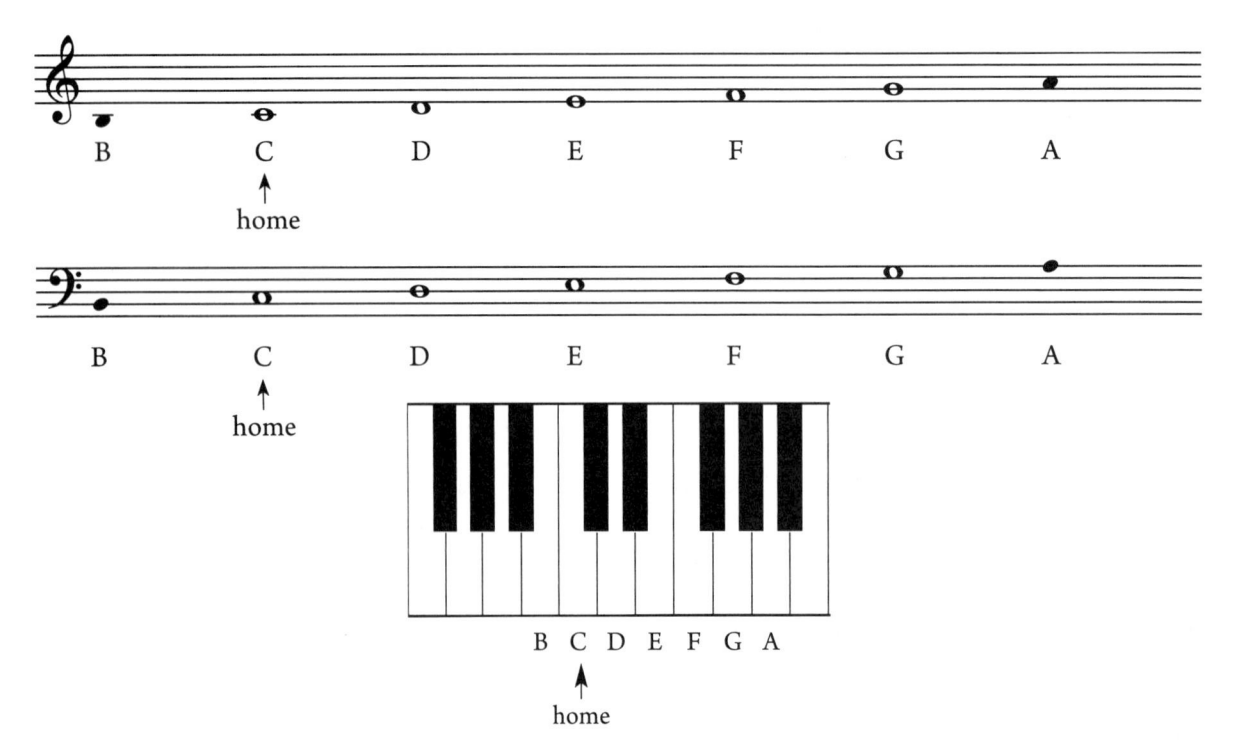

16   CHAPTER ONE   Pitch Notation and the Grand Staff

D. Listening and writing

Listen to each example, then write the letter names of its pitches. Finally, notate the melody with open note heads. 🔊

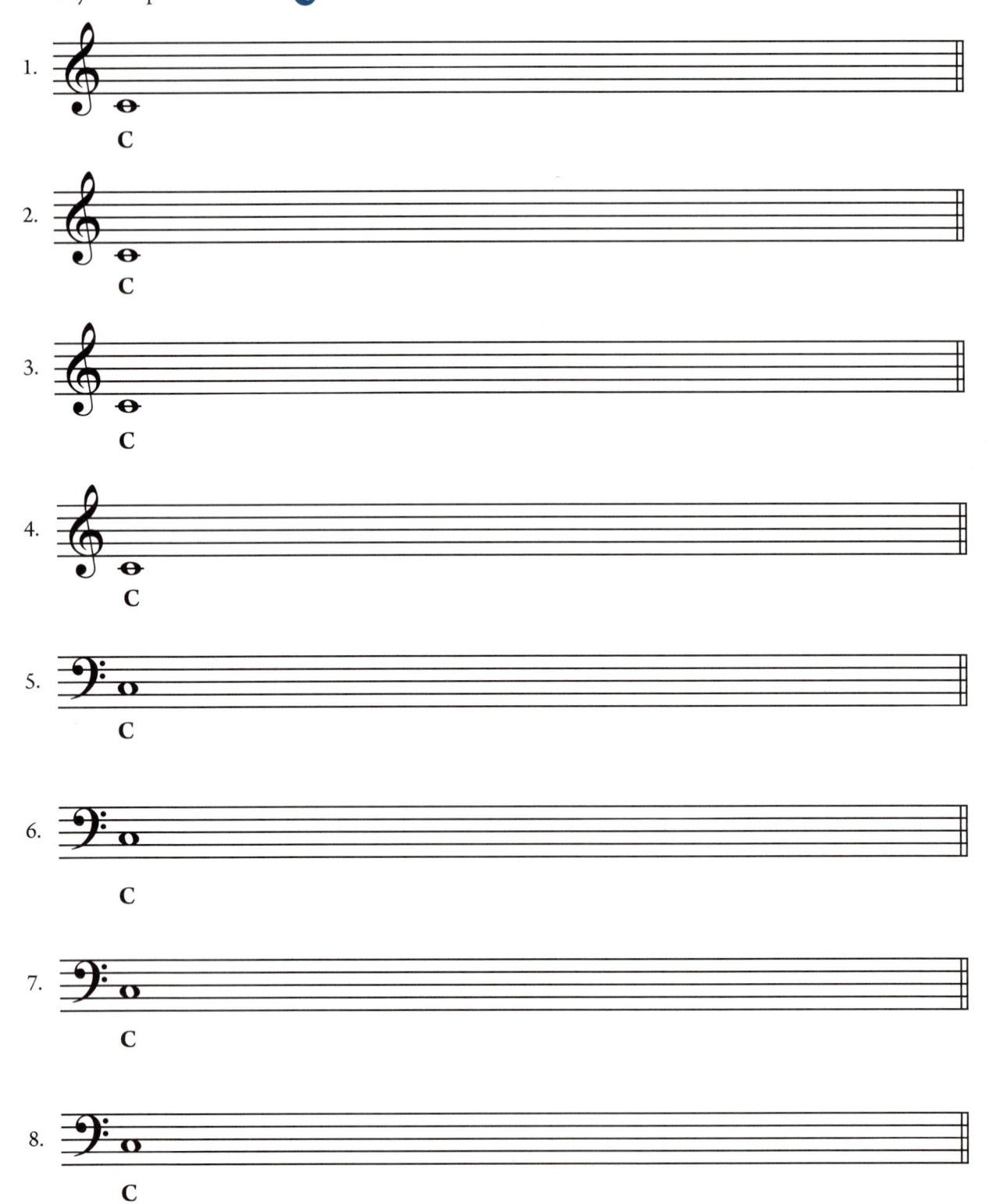

1. 𝄞 o
     C

2. 𝄞 o
     C

3. 𝄞 o
     C

4. 𝄞 o
     C

5. 𝄢 o
     C

6. 𝄢 o
     C

7. 𝄢 o
     C

8. 𝄢 o
     C

NAME _____

Workbook ASSIGNMENT 1.1

A. Letter names

Fill in the letter name requested. Remember to count the letter you begin with.

(1) 6 above C: __A__
(2) 3 above G: __B__
(3) 2 below F: __E__
(4) 7 below A: __B__

(5) 4 above D: __G__
(6) 2 above E: __F__
(7) 4 below D: __A__
(8) 5 below E: __A__

(9) 7 above C: __B__
(10) 5 below B: __E__
(11) 7 above G: __F__
(12) 3 below A: __F__

B. Identifying notes on the keyboard

On the keyboards below, write each letter name on its corresponding key.

(1) C, D, G, B

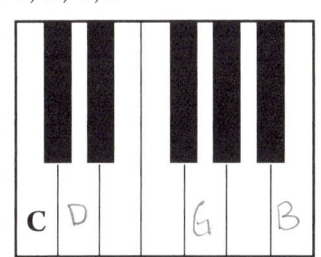

C D G B

(2) E, F, A, B

E F A B

On the keyboards below, write each letter name on *every* key with that name (in three octaves).

(3) C, E, A

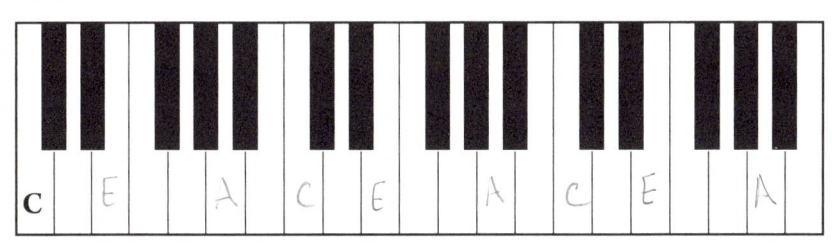

C E A C E A C E A

(4) G, B, D

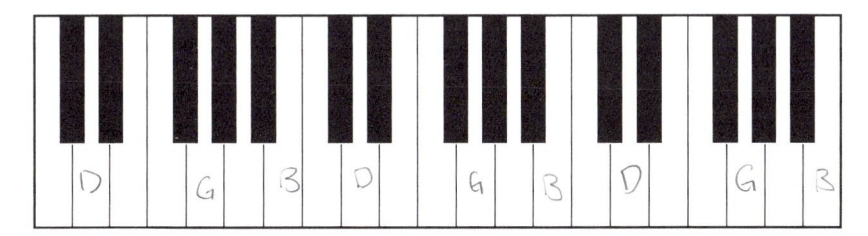

D G B D G B D G B

C. Drawing clefs

(1) Trace the treble clefs given in dotted lines, then draw additional clefs.

Assignment 1.1 **19**

(2) Trace the bass clefs given in dotted lines, then draw additional clefs.

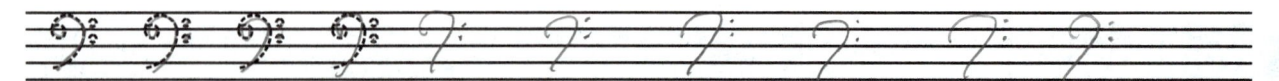

D. Reading notes in treble and bass clefs

Write the letter name of each pitch in the blank provided.

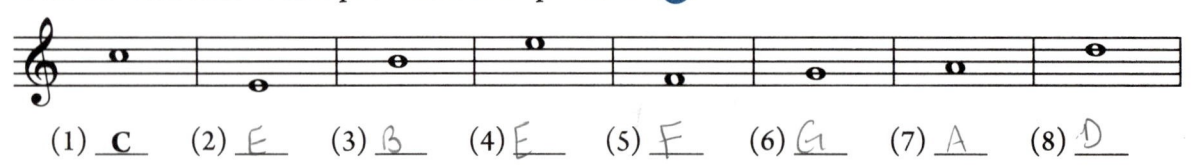

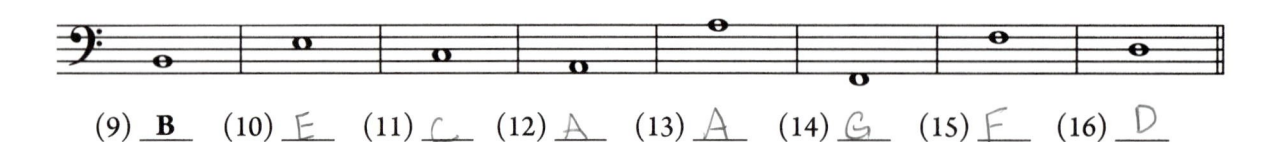

(1) __C__   (2) __E__   (3) __B__   (4) __E__   (5) __F__   (6) __G__   (7) __A__   (8) __D__

(9) __B__   (10) __E__   (11) __C__   (12) __A__   (13) __A__   (14) __G__   (15) __F__   (16) __D__

E. Reading notes in music

In each blank, write the letter name of the note above.

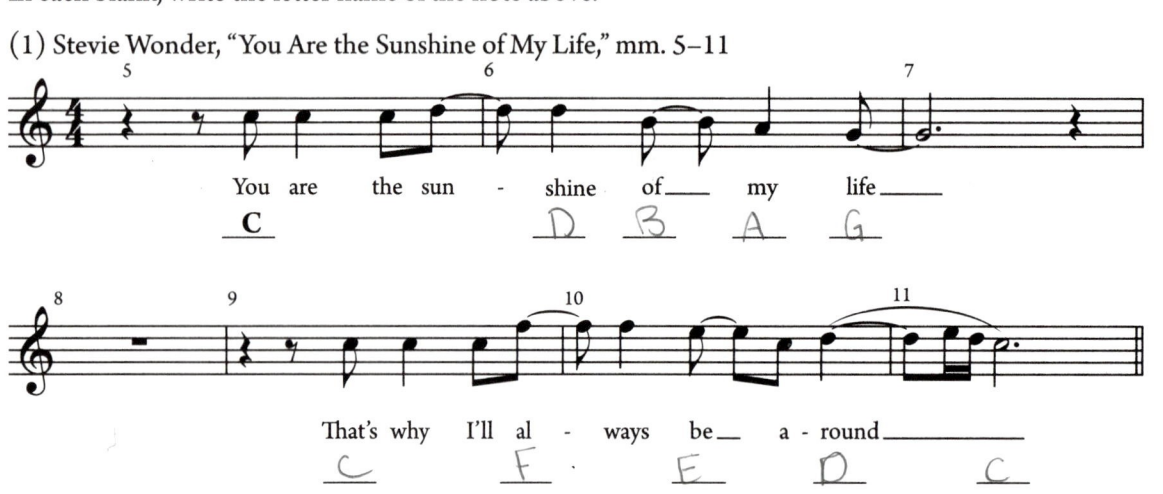

(1) Stevie Wonder, "You Are the Sunshine of My Life," mm. 5–11

You are the sun - shine of__ my life__
__C__   __D__ __B__ __A__ __G__

That's why I'll al - ways be__ a - round__
__C__   __F__   __E__   __D__   __C__

(2) Lennon and McCartney, "Hello, Goodbye," mm. 17–21

I say high__ You say low__ You say why__ and
__D__ __F__   __C__ __E__   __B__ __D__

I say I__ don't know__
__A__ __C__ __E__ __G__

20   CHAPTER ONE Pitch Notation and the Grand Staff

Workbook ASSIGNMENT 1.2

A. Identifying pitches with ledger lines

For each pitch notated on the staff, write its number on the correct key of the keyboard in the correct octave. Write the letter name on the blank beneath.

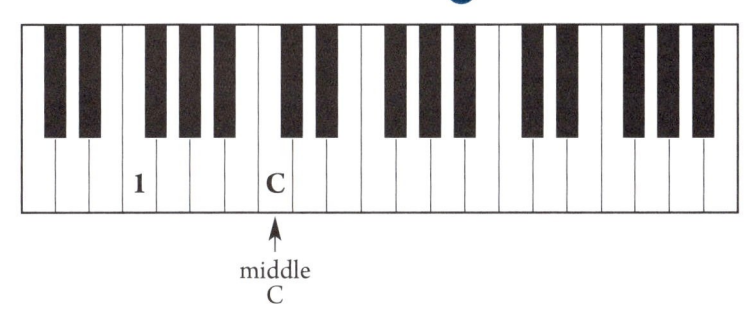

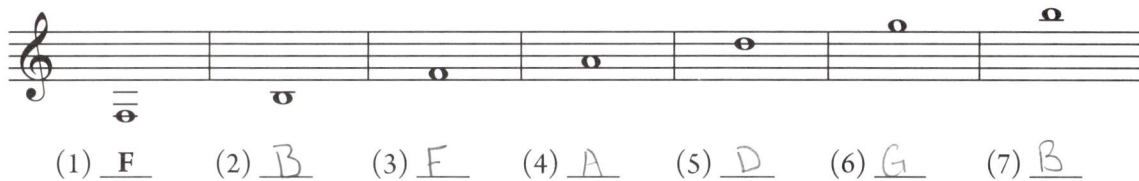

(1) **F**   (2) B   (3) F   (4) A   (5) D   (6) G   (7) B

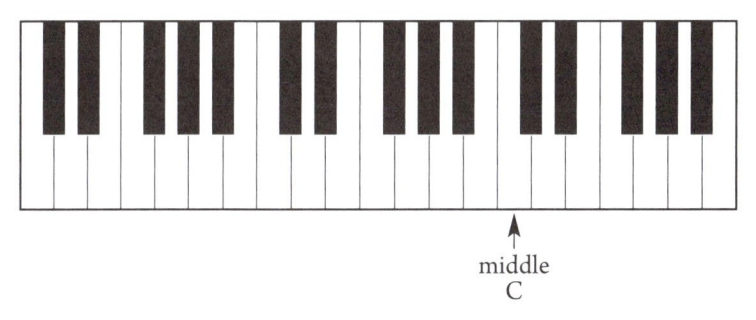

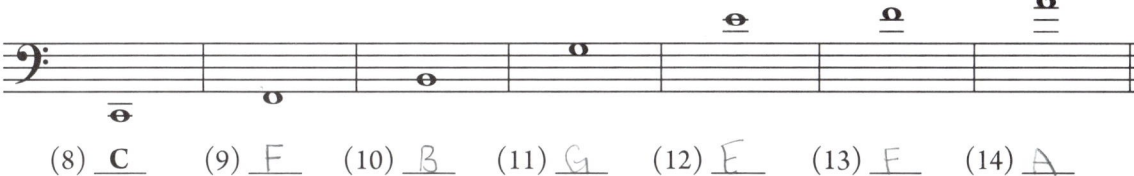

(8) **C**   (9) F   (10) B   (11) G   (12) E   (13) F   (14) A

Beneath each pitch, write its letter name and octave number.

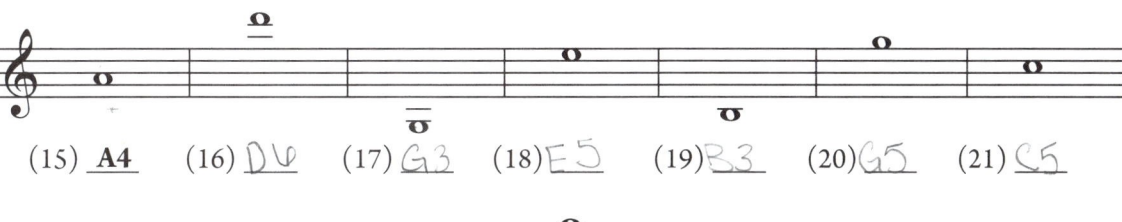

(15) **A4**   (16) D♭   (17) G3   (18) E5   (19) B3   (20) G5   (21) C5

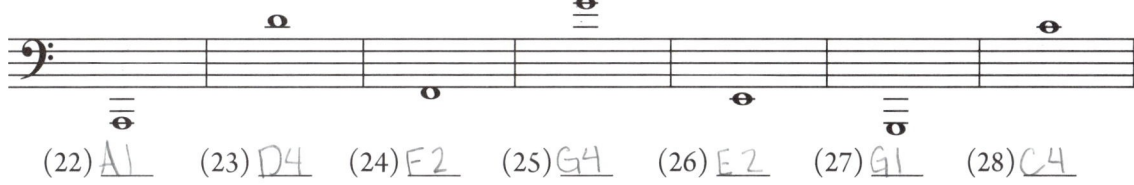

(22) A1   (23) D4   (24) E2   (25) G4   (26) E2   (27) G1   (28) C4

Assignment 1.2   21

B. Identifying pitches with ledger lines and octave numbers in music

In the passages below, write the letter name and octave number for any ledger-line note marked by an arrow.

(1) Mozart, *Variations on "Ah, vous dirai-je Maman,"* mm. 1–8

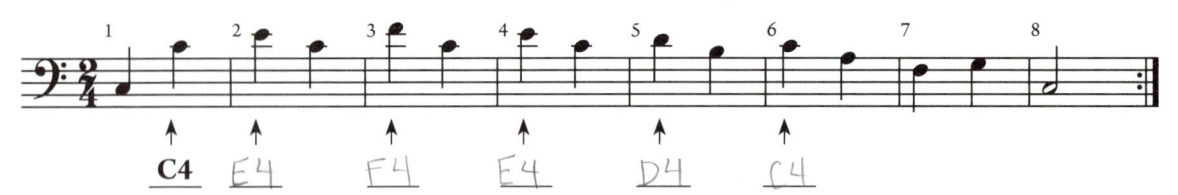

C4   E4   F4   E4   D4   C4

(2) Mozart, *Variations*, Var. VII, mm. 187–192

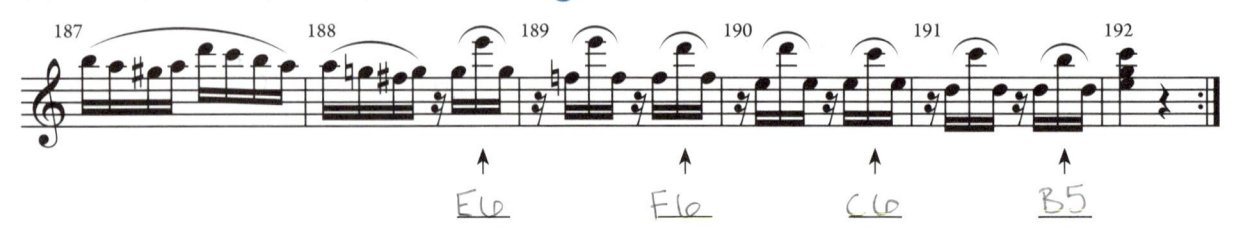

E6   F6   C6   B5

(3) Mozart, *Variations*, Var. XII, mm. 293–296

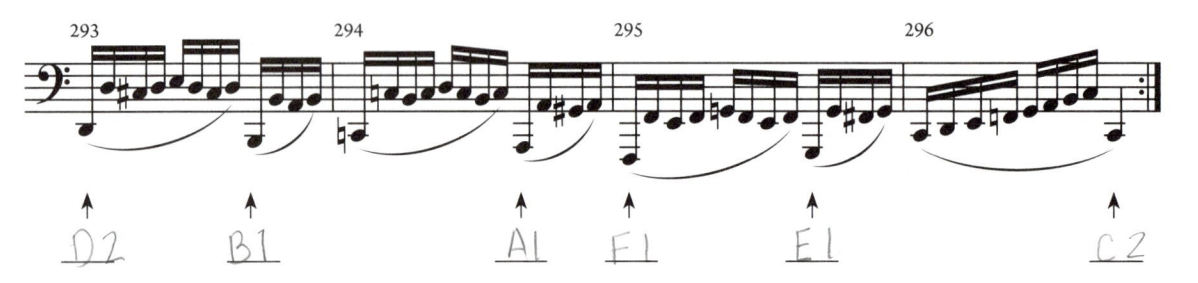

D2   B1   A1   F1   E1   C2

C. Writing pitches with ledger lines and octave numbers

For each number on the keyboard, write the corresponding note on the staff below it in the correct octave. Write the letter name and octave number in the blank provided.

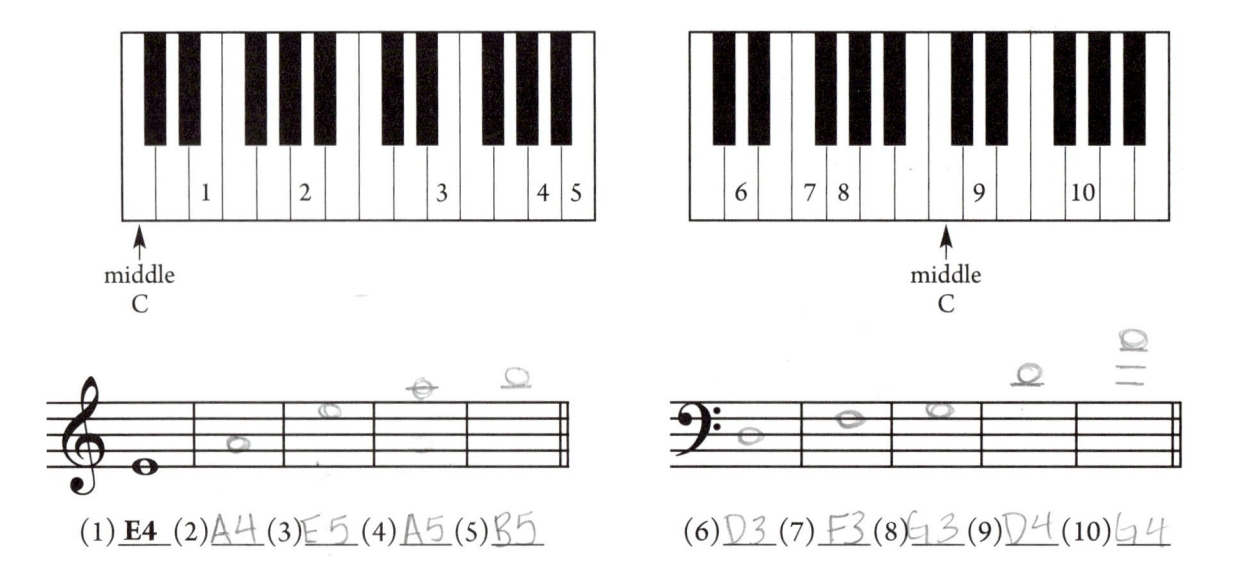

(1) **E4**   (2) A4   (3) E5   (4) A5   (5) B5   (6) D3   (7) F3   (8) G3   (9) D4   (10) G4

NAME _____

Workbook ASSIGNMENT 1.3

A. Writing pitches with ledger lines, stems, and octave numbers

For each note requested, neatly write a hollow note head on the correct line or space of the staff, then add a stem that extends in the correct direction.

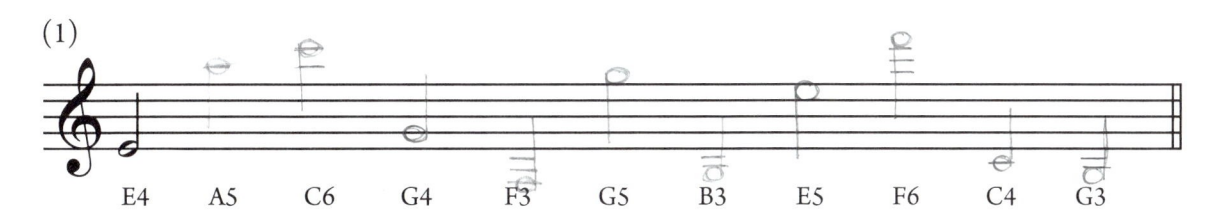

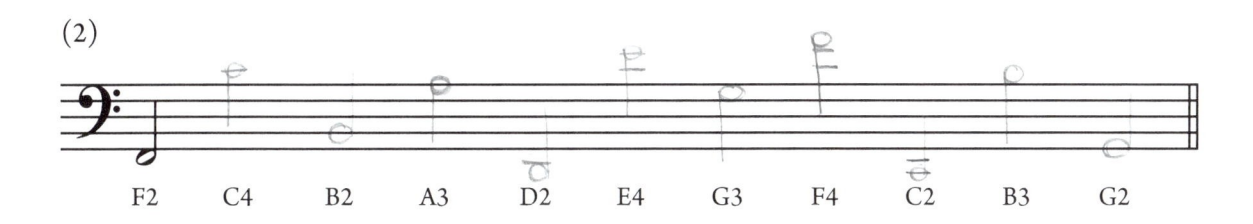

(1)

E4   A5   C6   G4   F3   G5   B3   E5   F6   C4   G3

(2)

F2   C4   B2   A3   D2   E4   G3   F4   C2   B3   G2

In the first row of blanks below the staff, label each pitch with letter name and octave number. Then, above or below the given note, rewrite the note in the new octave as specified. In the second row of blanks, write the letter name with its new octave number.

(3) Rewrite exactly two octaves lower.

Original: **A3**   F3   B3   C4   E4   D4   G3   G4   A3   A4
New letter name: **A1**   E1   B1   C2   F2   D2   G1   G2   A1   A2

(4) Rewrite exactly two octaves higher.

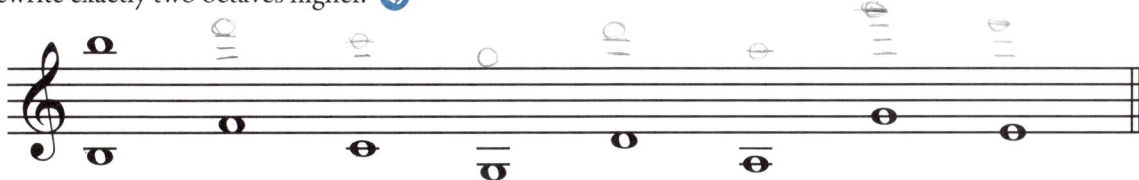

Original: **B3**   F4   C4   G3   D4   A3   G4   E4
New letter name: **B5**   F6   C6   G5   D6   A5   G6   E6

Assignment 1.3   23

B. Arranging: Changing clef and octave

Rewrite the pitches of each melody down one or two octaves as specified, on the staff provided. Copy the original notation (even the symbols that are unfamiliar to you) but change stem direction as needed. You do not need to copy the lyrics.

(1) Stephen Foster, "Jeanie with the Light Brown Hair," mm. 5–8. Write the music down one octave.

(2) Billy Joel, "Piano Man," mm. 72–78. Write the music down two octaves.

(3) Rewrite the beginning of "Amazing Grace" up one octave, as though scored for violin or flute. You'll need to use ledger lines.

24   CHAPTER ONE   Pitch Notation and the Grand Staff

NAME _____

Workbook AURAL SKILLS 1.1

Listen to an excerpt from a familiar melody. The excerpt consists of four segments. Segments 1 and 2 each include four pitches. Segments 3 and 4 each have three pitches. 🔊

(1) Focus on segment 1, the first four pitches. Which of the following best diagrams the segment's contour?

a. ╱   b. ╲   c. ╱╲   d. ╲╱

(2) Focus on the ending. Which of the following best diagrams segment 4's contour?

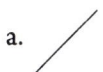

a. ╱   b. ╲   c. ╱╲   d. ╲╱

(3) Which of the following best describes how the segments are organized?

Segment 1	Segment 2	Segment 3	Segment 4
a. idea 1	idea 1 repeated	idea 2	idea 1 returns
b. idea 1	idea 1 repeated	idea 2	idea 2 repeated
c. idea 1	idea 2	idea 3	idea 4
d. idea 1	idea 2	idea 1 returns	idea 2 returns

(4) On the staff below, notate segment 1 with the pitches C, D, and E:

- Draw a treble-clef sign.
- Begin on middle C. First, draw its ledger line below the staff, then draw its oval note head on this ledger line. (Don't worry about stems or rhythm for now.)
- Notate the rest of segment 1's pitches. Make sure your note heads stay only on the appropriate line or in the appropriate space.

Aural Skills 1.1   25

(5) On the staff below, notate segment 4 with the pitches E, F, and G:

- Draw a treble clef.
- Begin on E4, the first (lowest) staff line. Draw its oval note head on this line. (Again, don't worry about stems or rhythm.)
- Notate segment 4's remaining pitches. Make sure your note heads stay only on the appropriate line or in the appropriate space. *Hint:* Think of the segment's contour (the answer to question 2).

(6) On the staff below, notate the pitches of the *entire* melody:

- Draw a treble clef.
- Begin with segment 1, your answer to question 4.
- To continue with segments 2 and 3, consult your answer to question 3.
- Conclude with segment 4, your answer to question 5.

Play your answer at the keyboard. Sing with the letter names C, D, E, F, and G. Use the keyboard to help you find the notes.

(7) On the staff below, notate the pitches of the entire melody in the bass clef, down one octave:

- Draw a bass clef.
- Consult your answer to question 6.

Again, play your answer at the keyboard.

(8) On the staff below, notate the entire melody in bass clef, beginning on middle C and using ledger lines. It should sound in the same octave as your answer for question 6.

26   CHAPTER ONE   Pitch Notation and the Grand Staff

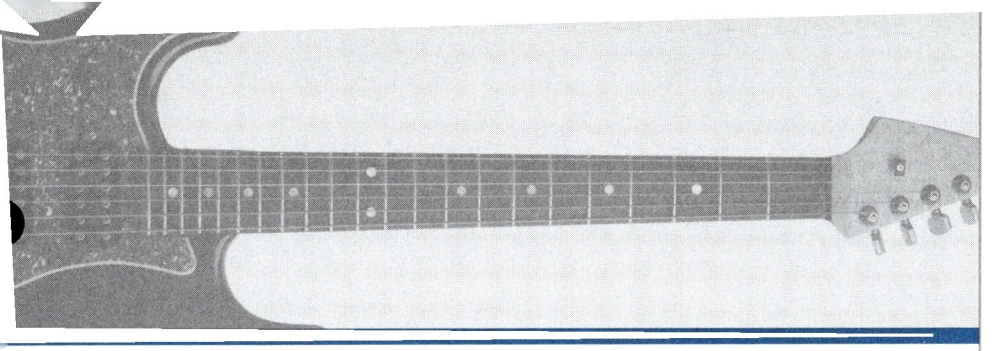

TOPICS

- sharps, flats, and naturals
- double sharps and flats
- writing pitches with accidentals
- half steps and whole steps
- hearing half and whole steps

MUSIC

- John Barry and Tim Rice, "All Time High"
- Scott Joplin, "Solace"
- Mel Leven, "Cruella de Vil," from *101 Dalmations*
- Willie Nelson, "On the Road Again"

CHAPTER 2

Accidentals and Half and Whole Steps

Sharps, Flats, and Naturals

Listen to the melody from Joplin's "Solace" while looking at Example 2.1. The first four notes in each line are marked on the keyboard below.

EXAMPLE 2.1   Joplin, "Solace," mm. 1–8 (right hand only)

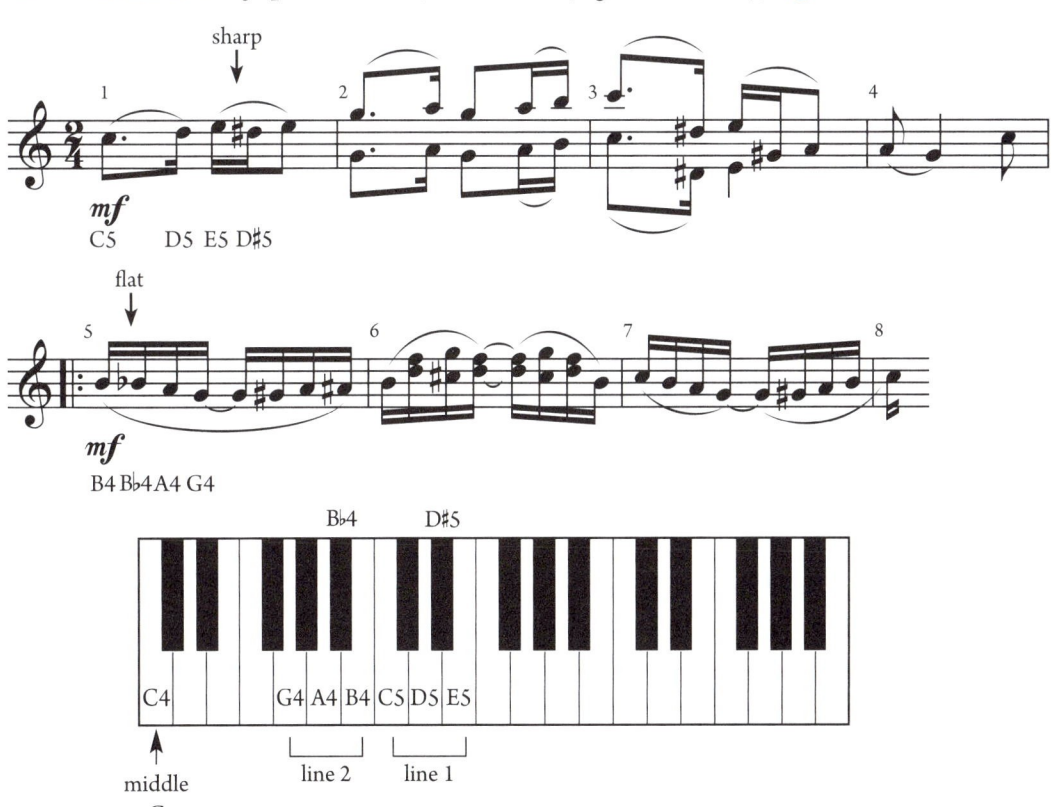

sharp

mf
C5 D5 E5 D♯5

flat

mf
B4 B♭4 A4 G4

B♭4   D♯5

C4   G4 A4 B4 C5 D5 E5
↑
middle C
    line 2   line 1

The fourth note of this melody is D♯5 (D-sharp 5), which is played on the black key between D5 and E5. On the second line, the second note is B♭4 (B-flat 4), played on the black key between B4 and A4.

The black keys are named in relation to the white keys next to them, as shown in Figure 2.1. The black key immediately *above* (to the right of) any white key takes the white key's name plus a **sharp** (♯). The two black keys grouped together are C♯ (C-sharp) and D♯, and the three black keys grouped together are F♯, G♯, and A♯.

FIGURE 2.1   Names for white and black keys

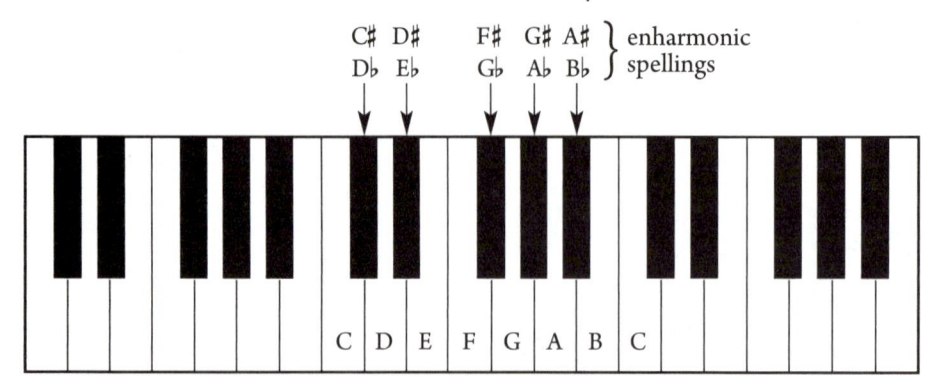

The black key immediately *below* (to the left of) any white key takes the white key's name plus a **flat** (♭). The group of two black keys may also be called D♭ (D-flat) and E♭, and the three black keys may also be called G♭, A♭, and B♭. Every black key has two possible names: one with a sharp and one with a flat. When pitches have different names but make the same sound and are played with the same key on the keyboard (D♭ = C♯), their spellings are called **enharmonic** (see Figure 2.1). Enharmonic notes sound the same but are spelled differently—like the words "too" and "two."

> **KEY CONCEPT**   A sharp sign (♯) raises any note to the next (often a black key, but sometimes a white key). A flat sign (♭) lowers any note to the next (often black, but sometimes white).

This span—from a note to its closest neighbor—is called a half step (see p. 32). Look again at Figure 2.1 to see C and C♯, or E and E♭: both pairs are half steps and include a white then a black key.

Sharp and flat symbols are called **accidentals**, though there is nothing "accidental" about their use or placement. A third common accidental, called a **natural** (♮), is shown in Example 2.2, from later in Joplin's piano rag. A natural returns a pitch to its "natural" state. In the left hand (bass clef) of Example 2.2, you would first play F♯ followed by F♮, and in the right hand (treble clef) D♯ followed by D♮—in both cases, a black key followed by a white one.

EXAMPLE 2.2   Joplin, "Solace," mm. 17–20

28   CHAPTER TWO   Accidentals and Half and Whole Steps

"Solace" has many accidentals. If a note with an accidental is repeated before the bar line, the accidental still applies. The bar line cancels an accidental.

There is no black key immediately to the right of E; the next note up is F. E♯ is therefore played on a white key and is enharmonic with F. B♯ is also a white key, and is enharmonic with C. On the flat side, C♭ is enharmonic with B, and F♭ is enharmonic with E. These enharmonic spellings for white keys are shown in Figure 2.2.

FIGURE 2.2 Enharmonic spellings for white keys

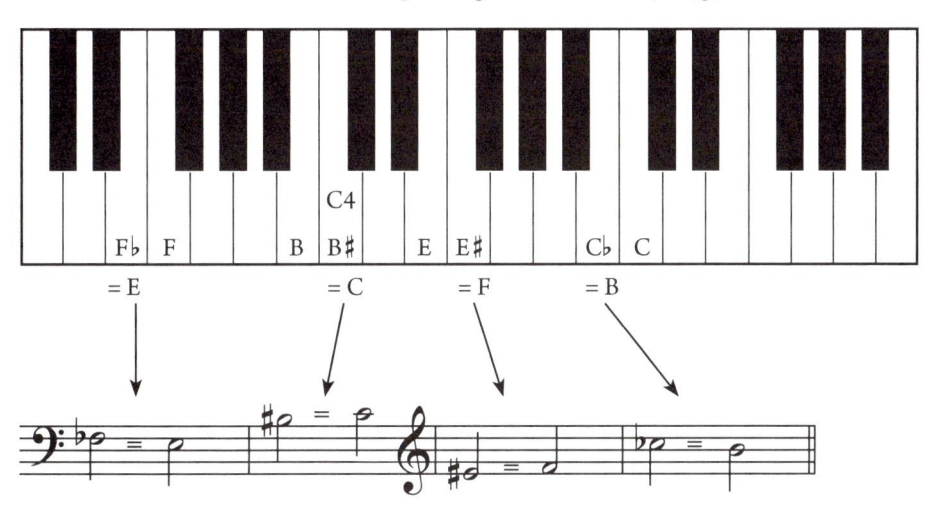

To see how composers use enharmonic notes in pieces of music, look back at the beginning of the second line of Example 2.1. Joplin has considered the musical context in which pitches appear, and written a B♭ as the musical line travels down, but an A♯ as the line moves up.

TRY IT #1

Name the enharmonic equivalent.

(a) G♭ is enharmonic with **F♯**

(b) B♯ is enharmonic with ____

(c) A♯ is enharmonic with ____

(d) E♯ is enharmonic with ____

(e) D♭ is enharmonic with ____

(f) B is enharmonic with ____

(g) A♭ is enharmonic with ____

(h) E♭ is enharmonic with ____

Double Sharps and Flats

Examples 2.3 and 2.4 show two other accidentals: the **double sharp** (𝄪) and **double flat** (𝄫). A double sharp (𝄪) raises a pitch two half steps (a whole step; see p. 32) above its letter name. A double flat (𝄫) lowers a pitch two half steps below its letter name. The double sharp (F𝄪4) appears on the first note of Willie Nelson's melody and in the second line. A double flat (B𝄫3) appears as marked in the bass-clef piano part of "All Time High."

EXAMPLE 2.3   Nelson, "On the Road Again," mm. 8–14

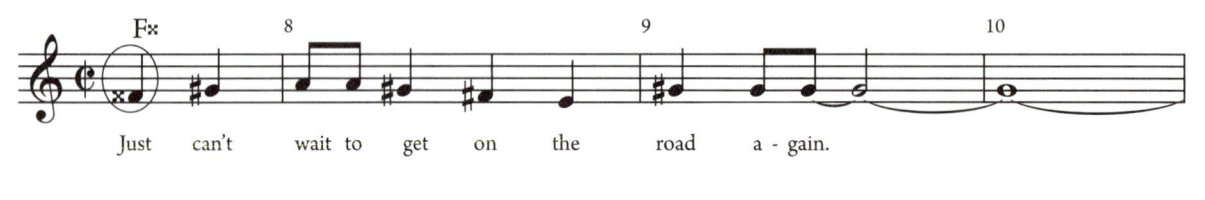

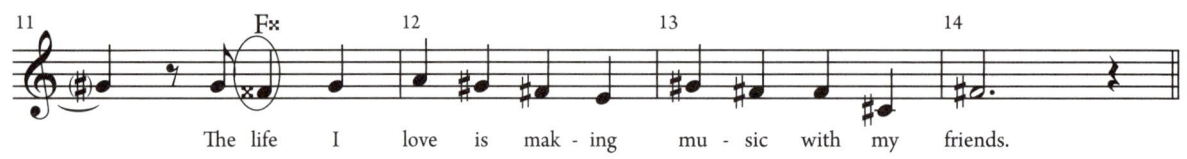

EXAMPLE 2.4   Barry and Rice, "All Time High," mm. 34–37

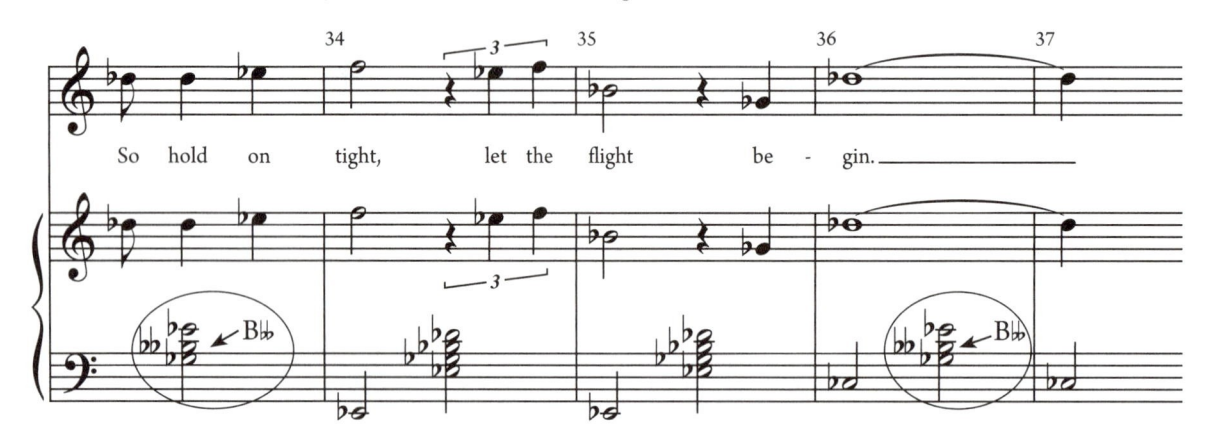

Double sharped or flatted notes are often played on the white keys of the piano. For example, the F𝄪4 in the Nelson song is enharmonic with G, and the B𝄫 in "All Time High" is enharmonic with A. Figure 2.3 shows other examples.

30   CHAPTER TWO Accidentals and Half and Whole Steps

FIGURE 2.3   Enharmonic pitches with double sharps and flats

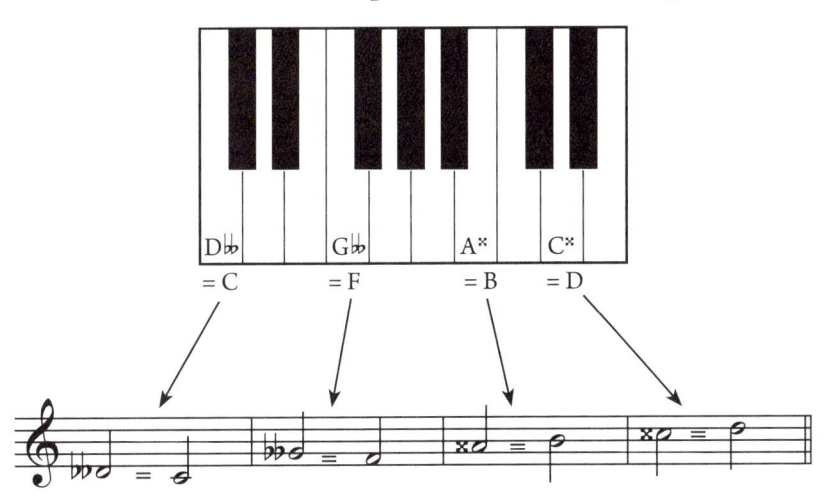

SUMMARY

Accidentals:
- ♯ (sharp)   raises the pitch a half step
- ♭ (flat)   lowers the pitch a half step
- 𝄪 (double sharp)   raises the pitch a whole step
- ♭♭ (double flat)   lowers the pitch a whole step
- ♮ (natural)   cancels a sharp, double sharp, flat, or double flat

Enharmonic notes: sound the same but are spelled differently

Writing Pitches with Accidentals

As you can see in Example 2.5, the beginning of "Cruella de Vil," an accidental is positioned before (to the left of) the note head in a musical score.

EXAMPLE 2.5   Leven, "Cruella de Vil," mm. 1–2

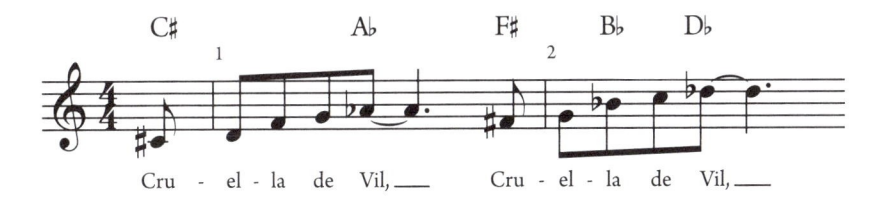

When you write or say note names, however, the accidental goes after (to the right of) the note name; for example, C♯ (C-sharp). For an accidental on a space (see the A♭ and F♯ above), the middle of the accidental is centered within the space, not on the line above or below. For an accidental on a line (see the B♭ and D♭), the line passes through its middle.

> **KEY CONCEPT** Always be careful to notate an accidental exactly on the line or space you intend, not floating above or below the note, and to place the accidental before the note.

TRY IT #2

Write the letter name in the space beneath each note below. Then write the enharmonically equivalent note in the blank measure to the right, and that note's name beneath.

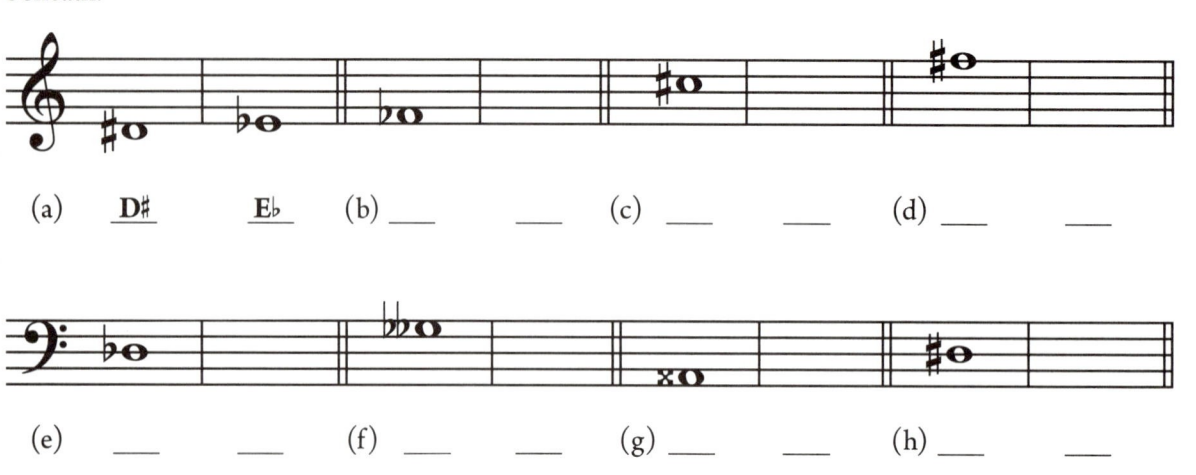

(a) __D♯__ __E♭__ (b) ___ ___ (c) ___ ___ (d) ___ ___

(e) ___ ___ (f) ___ ___ (g) ___ ___ (h) ___ ___

ASSIGNMENT 2.1

Half Steps and Whole Steps

The distance between any two notes is called an **interval**. The first two intervals in "Solace," shown in Example 2.6—B4 to B♭4 and B♭4 to A4—are half steps; the third, A4 to G4, is a whole step. Half and whole steps are basic building blocks in music.

EXAMPLE 2.6 Joplin, "Solace," mm. 5–8 (right hand only)

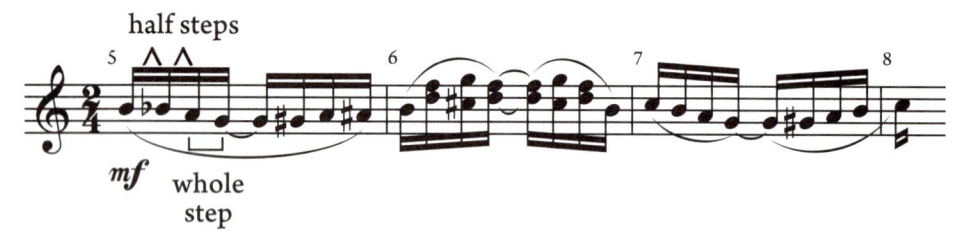

> **KEY CONCEPT** A **half step** (or **semitone**) is the interval between any pitch and the next closest pitch on the keyboard in either direction. The combination of two half steps forms a **whole step** (or **whole tone**). A whole step is always spelled with two adjacent letter names (F–G) and always has a note that could be inserted in the middle (F–F♯–G).

Example 2.7 shows half and whole steps on the keyboard. Usually a half step (Example 2.7a) spans a white key to a black key (like B to A♯) or black to white (like G♭ to G). The only exceptions are B to C and E to F, which naturally span a half step. Whole steps (Example 2.7b) usually span two keys of the same color: white to white (like C to D) or black to black (like B♭ to A♭). Again, those spelled with E, F, B, or C are exceptions.

32 CHAPTER TWO Accidentals and Half and Whole Steps

EXAMPLE 2.7 Half and Whole Steps

(a) Half steps

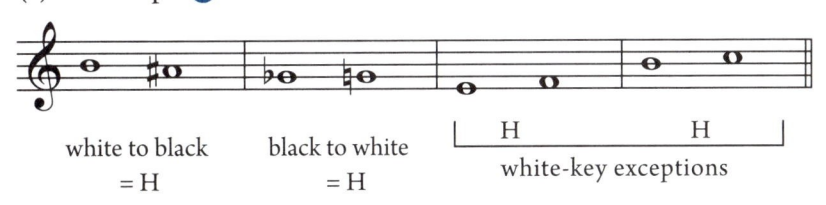

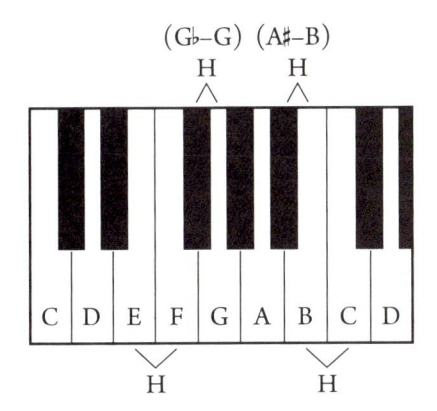

white to black = H   black to white = H   white-key exceptions (H, H)

(G♭–G) (A♯–B) — H, H
E–F, B–C — H

(b) Whole steps

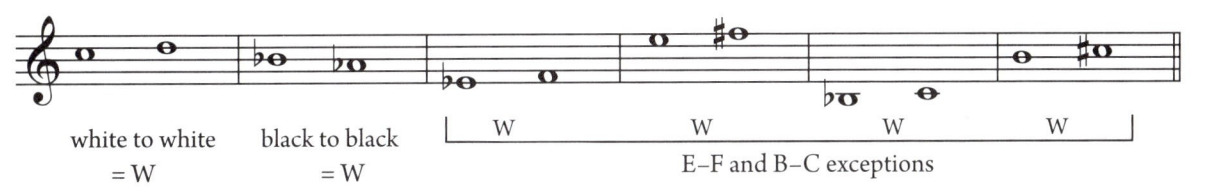

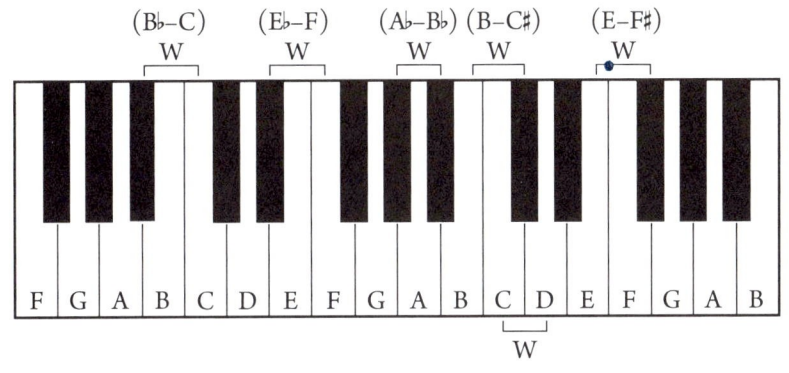

white to white = W   black to black = W   E–F and B–C exceptions (W, W, W, W)

(B♭–C) (E♭–F) (A♭–B♭) (B–C♯) (E–F♯)
W   W   W   W   W

C–D — W

Half steps that are spelled with two different letter names (G–A♭) are called **diatonic half steps**. Half steps that are spelled with the same letter name (G–G♯) are called **chromatic half steps**. Both spellings are correct; they are enharmonic equivalents. Both types of half steps are found in Example 2.7: B–A♯, E–F, and B–C are diatonic half steps; G♭–G♮ is a chromatic half step.

SUMMARY

- Half steps usually span keys of different colors: white to black or black to white. The exceptions are E–F and B–C, the white-key half steps (Example 2.7a).
- Whole steps usually span keys the same color: white to white or black to black. The exceptions are E♭–F, E–F♯, B♭–C, and B–C♯ (Example 2.7b).
- Double-check the spelling of any half or whole step that includes E, F, B, or C.

Half Steps and Whole Steps   33

TRY IT #3

(a) Name the pitch requested, then for the half steps, identify an enharmonically equivalent pitch. Do not use double sharps or double flats.

A half step: A whole step:

(1) above G: **G♯** or **A♭**   (6) above F♯: ___

(2) below C♯: ___ or ___   (7) below C: ___

(3) below B: ___   or ___   (8) above D: ___

(4) above E: ___   or ___   (9) above C♯: ___

(5) above D: ___   or ___   (10) below B♭: ___

(b) Identify whether each pair of pitches below spans a whole step (W), half step (H), or neither (N).

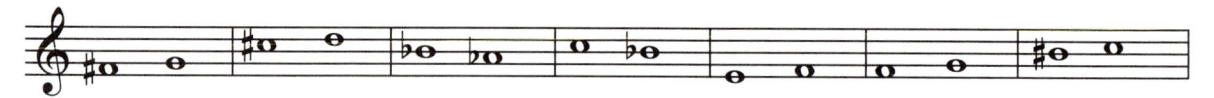

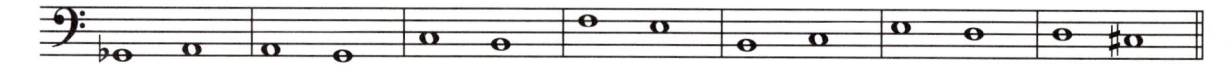

(1) **H**   (2) ___   (3) ___   (4) ___   (5) ___   (6) ___   (7) ___

(8) ___   (9) ___   (10) ___   (11) ___   (12) ___   (13) ___   (14) ___

(c) Identify each pair of bracketed pitches as a whole step (W), half step (H), or neither (N).

Leven, "Cruella de Vil," mm. 1–2

Cru - el - la de Vil, ___   Cru - el - la de Vil, ___

H   ___   ___   ___   ___

Hearing Half and Whole Steps

Listen to Example 2.8 to hear the difference in sound between half and whole steps. When you hear a whole step (C–D), you can imagine a note in the middle on the keyboard (C♯). When you hear a half step, you can't. Practice playing whole and half steps at the keyboard. For each whole step, insert the note between to hear how it divides the whole step in half.

EXAMPLE 2.8   Whole steps divided in half

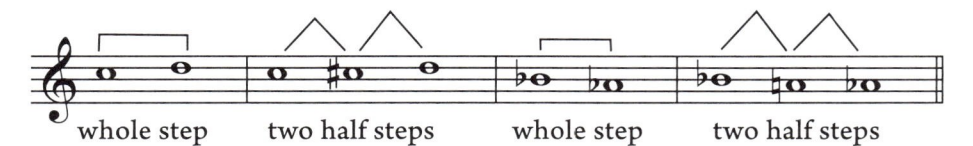

whole step   two half steps   whole step   two half steps

ASSIGNMENT 2.2, 2.3, AURAL SKILLS 2.1

Did You Know?

Scott Joplin's father was a former slave. One of Joplin's most famous compositions, "The Maple Leaf Rag" (published in 1899), earned him one penny for every sheet-music copy sold. His opera *Treemonisha* (composed in 1911) won an award for being the "most American opera" ever written, yet Joplin never saw it fully staged. Joplin's music was played in bars, dance halls, and other popular gathering places from the 1890s to the 1910s. It became popular once again in the 1970s after it was featured in the movie *The Sting* (1973), with Paul Newman and Robert Redford. Joplin's rags have remained among the best-known American music of the early twentieth century.

Terms You Should Know

accidentals
  flat (♭)
  sharp (♯)
  natural (♮)
  double flat (♭♭)
  double sharp (𝄪)

enharmonic
interval
  half step (semitone)
    chromatic half step
    diatonic half step
  whole step (whole tone)

Questions for Review

1. What is the effect of adding a sharp to a note? adding a flat? adding a natural?
2. What is an example of an enharmonic spelling?
3. What is the effect of adding a double sharp to a note? a double flat?
4. Does an accidental precede or follow a note's letter name when spoken or written? Does an accidental precede or follow the note head in a musical score?
5. Which pairs of white keys on the keyboard don't have a black key between them?
6. Which pairs of white keys span a half step? Which span a whole step?
7. Are there any half steps that span a black key to a black key?
8. How can you distinguish whole and half steps by ear?

Reading Review

Match the term on the left with the best answer on the right.

_____ (1) half step (a) symbol that raises a pitch a whole step
_____ (2) interval (b) the distance between two pitches
_____ (3) enharmonic spelling (c) symbol that raises a pitch a half step
_____ (4) ♯ (d) half step with a different letter name for each note
_____ (5) ♭ (e) interval between any key on the keyboard and the next closest key
_____ (6) whole step (f) symbol that lowers a pitch a whole step
_____ (7) ♭♭ (g) interval spanning two half steps
_____ (8) × (h) notes written with different letter names that sound the same
_____ (9) accidentals (i) half step with the same letter name for both notes
_____ (10) chromatic half step (j) symbols that indicate how much to raise or lower a pitch
_____ (11) natural (k) symbol that cancels a sharp or flat
_____ (12) diatonic half step (l) symbol that lowers a pitch a half step

Additional review and practice available at wwnorton.com/studyspace

Apply It

A. At the keyboard

1. Play the following pitches on a keyboard. Then name an enharmonic spelling. (Middle C is C4.)

   (a) C♯4   (f) D♯3   (k) G♭4   (p) C♭5
   (b) A♭3   (g) B♭5   (l) F♯2   (q) E♭2
   (c) E♭5   (h) A♭4   (m) D♭5   (r) D♯4
   (d) G♯2   (i) C♮2   (n) A♯2   (s) B♭4
   (e) F♯4   (j) E♯3   (o) B♯3   (t) G♭3

2. For each pitch shown in Exercise 1, play (and name):
   (a) The given pitch and a half step above.
   (b) The given pitch and a half step below.
   (c) The given pitch and a whole step above.
   (d) The given pitch and a whole step below.

3. Start with the given pitch, then move your finger on a keyboard, following the pattern of whole and half steps indicated. Write the name of the pitch at the end of the sequence.

   (a) Begin on C: down W, down H, down W, up H, up H = __**A**__
   (b) Begin on E: up W, up H, up W, down H, up W, up W = _____
   (c) Begin on F♯: down W, down W, up H, down W, down H, up W = _____
   (d) Begin on A♭: up W, up W, up W, down H, up W, up W = _____
   (e) Begin on C♯: down W, up H, up W, up W, up H, up H = _____
   (f) Begin on B: up H, up H, down W, down H, down W, down W = _____
   (g) Begin on D: up H, down W, down W, down H, down H, up W = _____
   (h) Begin on E♭: down W, down W, down H, down W, up H, up H = _____

B. Listening and writing

1. Hearing accidentals 🔊

Listen to the following pairs of notes (played in class or on your recording). First a pitch will be played, then raised or lowered one half step. Its original accidental is given. Circle the arrow that shows the pitch's change of direction, then circle its new accidental.

(a) sharp   ↑   (↓)   ♭   (♮)   ♯
(b) natural   ↑   ↓   ♭   ♮   ♯
(c) flat   ↑   ↓   ♭   ♮   ♯
(d) sharp   ↑   ↓   ♭   ♮   ♯
(e) natural   ↑   ↓   ♭   ♮   ♯
(f) natural   ↑   ↓   ♭   ♮   ♯

2. Hearing half and whole steps

Listen to the following pairs of notes (played in class or on the recording). The pitches make either a half step (H) or whole step (W). Write H or W in the blank, and ↑ for ascending or ↓ for descending.

(a) __W↑__   (f) _____   (k) _____   (p) _____
(b) _____   (g) _____   (l) _____   (q) _____
(c) _____   (h) _____   (m) _____   (r) _____
(d) _____   (i) _____   (n) _____   (s) _____
(e) _____   (j) _____   (o) _____   (t) _____

C. Singing and playing

Mark the half steps with brackets, as shown in Melody 1. Then perform the melodies below on a neutral syllable (like "la") or with letter names. Sing the hollow notes so that they last twice as long as the filled notes. Vary your performance in the following ways:

- Echo melodies after your teacher or the recording.
- Play the melodies at a keyboard.
- Play at a keyboard and sing along.
- Play on another instrument if you can.

Melody 1

Melody 2

Melody 3

Melody 4

Melody 5

Melody 6

Workbook ASSIGNMENT 2.1

A. Identifying pitches with accidentals

(1) On the keyboard below, write one letter name for each white key marked with an arrow; above, write two possible enharmonic names for each black key marked with an arrow.

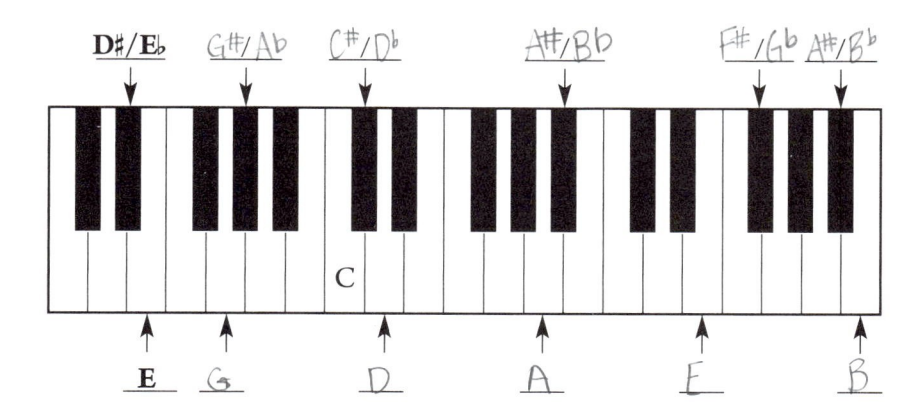

Above (black keys): D♯/E♭, G♯/A♭, C♯/D♭, A♯/B♭, F♯/G♭, A♯/B♭

Below (white keys): E, G, D, A, E, B

(2) Write the name of each pitch, together with its octave number, in the blank beneath the staff.

C♯3 _____ _____ _____ _____ _____ _____ _____ _____ _____

_____ _____ _____ _____ _____ _____ _____ _____ _____

B. Writing accidentals

Use the staves below to practice writing accidentals.

Write flat signs before each pitch.   Write natural signs.

Write sharp signs before each pitch.   Write natural signs.

C. Writing pitches with accidentals

Notate each numbered keyboard pitch with a hollow note head on the staff, above the corresponding number. Write the letter name and octave number in the blank. (Choose either enharmonic spelling for black keys.)

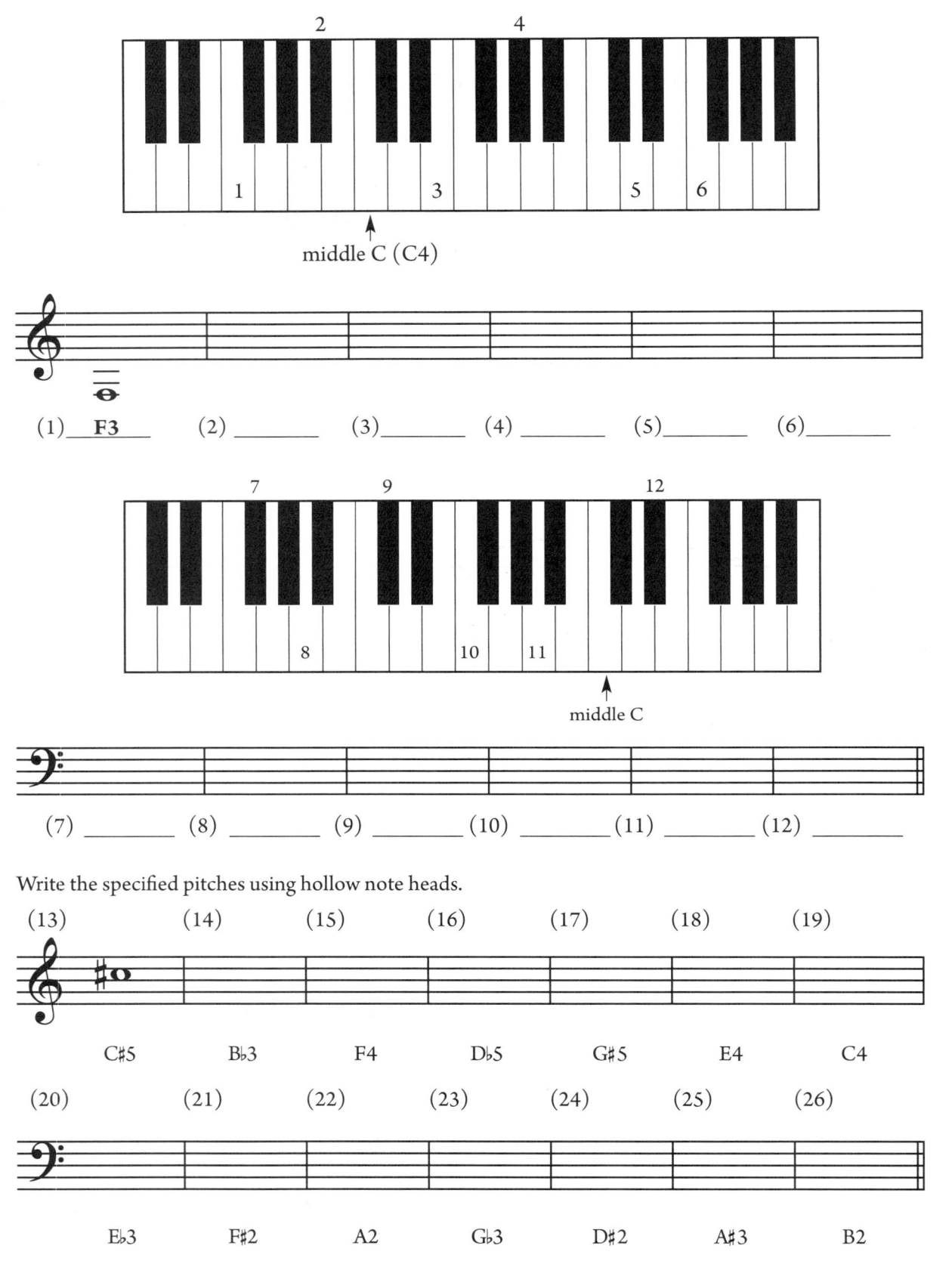

(1) __F3__ (2) _____ (3) _____ (4) _____ (5) _____ (6) _____

(7) _____ (8) _____ (9) _____ (10) _____ (11) _____ (12) _____

Write the specified pitches using hollow note heads.

(13) (14) (15) (16) (17) (18) (19)

C♯5   B♭3   F4   D♭5   G♯5   E4   C4

(20) (21) (22) (23) (24) (25) (26)

E♭3   F♯2   A2   G♭3   D♯2   A♯3   B2

40   CHAPTER TWO   Accidentals and Half and Whole Steps

NAME _____

Workbook ASSIGNMENT 2.2

A. Reading and writing enharmonic pitches

(1) In the first row of blanks below the staff, write the letter name for each pitch. In the second row, give the letter name of one possible enharmonic equivalent. 🔊

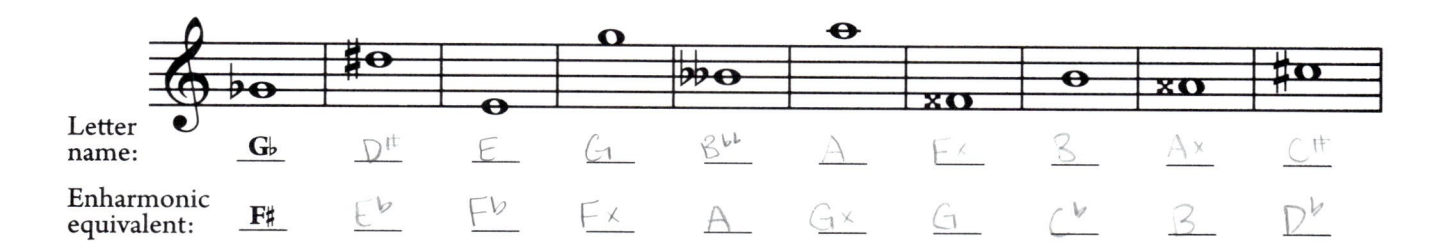

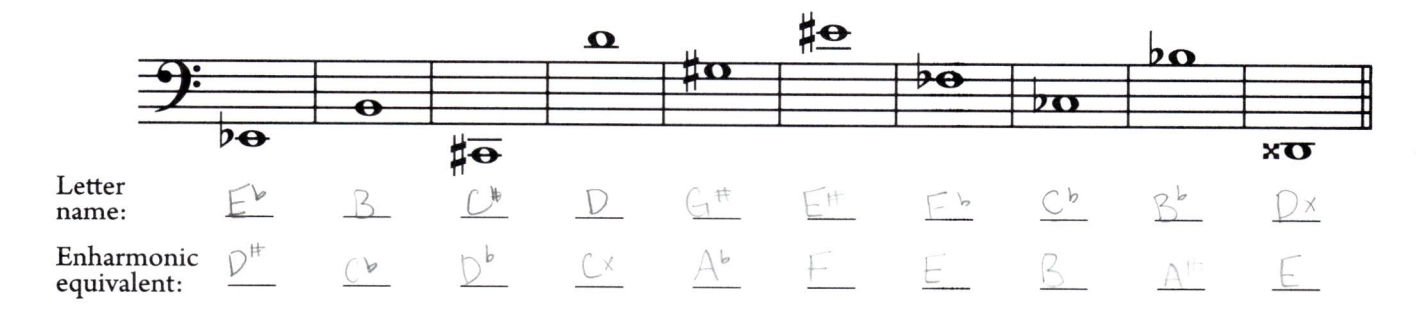

Letter name: **G♭**, D♯, E, G, B♭♭, A, E𝑥, B, A𝑥, C♯

Enharmonic equivalent: **F♯**, E♭, F♭, F𝑥, A, G𝑥, G, C♭, B, D♭

Letter name: E♭, B, C♯, D, G♯, E♯, E♭, C♭, B♭, D𝑥

Enharmonic equivalent: D♯, C♭, D♭, C𝑥, A♭, F, E, B, A♯, E

(2) Notate an enharmonic equivalent for each pitch below.

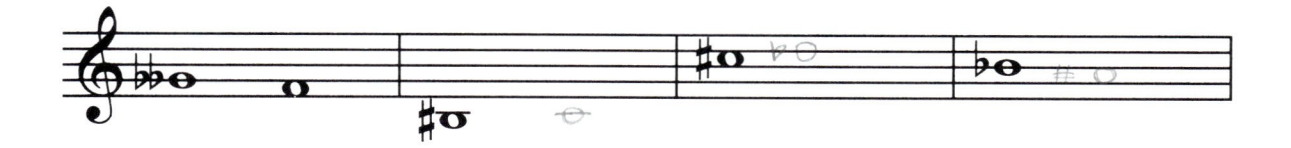

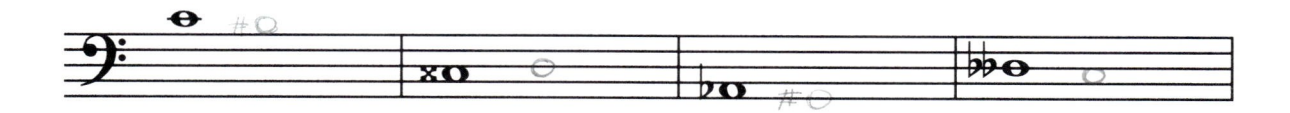

Assignment 2.2   41

B. Identifying and writing half and whole steps

For each pair of pitches, write W (whole step), H (half step), or N (neither) in the blank.

(1) G♯–A **H**
(2) E♭–F♯ N
(3) A♭–B♭ W
(4) B–C H
(5) F♯–G♯ W
(6) D♯–C♯ W
(7) A–G♯ H
(8) C–B♭ W
(9) E♯–F N

Write a whole step above the given note. Use adjacent letter names (not the same letter name). Write the note names and octave numbers in the blanks.

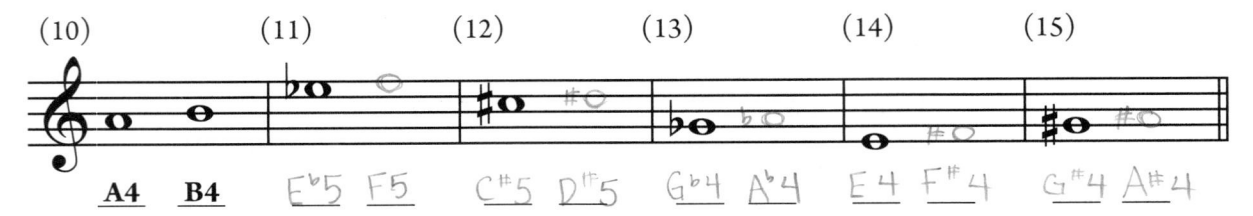

(10) **A4** B4
(11) E♭5 F5
(12) C♯5 D♯5
(13) G♭4 A♭4
(14) E4 F♯4
(15) G♯4 A♯4

Write a whole step below the given note. Use adjacent letter names. Write the note names and octave numbers in the blanks.

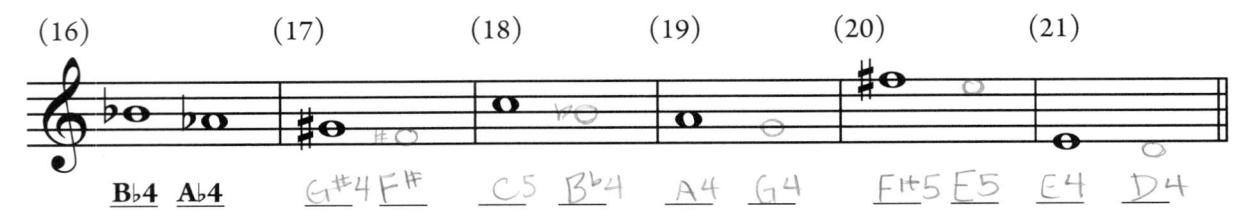

(16) **B♭4** A♭4
(17) G♯4 F♯
(18) C5 B♭4
(19) A4 G4
(20) F♯5 E5
(21) E4 D4

Write a half step above the given note. When you write black-key pitches, choose either enharmonic spelling; remember to write a natural sign, if needed, to cancel a sharp or flat. Write the note names and octave numbers in the blanks.

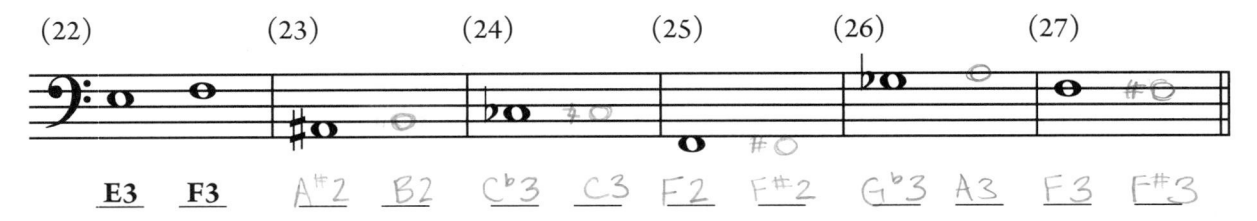

(22) **E3** F3
(23) A♯2 B2
(24) C♭3 C3
(25) F2 F♯2
(26) G♭3 A3
(27) F3 F♯3

Write a half step below the given note. For black-key pitches, use either enharmonic spelling. Write the note names and octave numbers in the blanks.

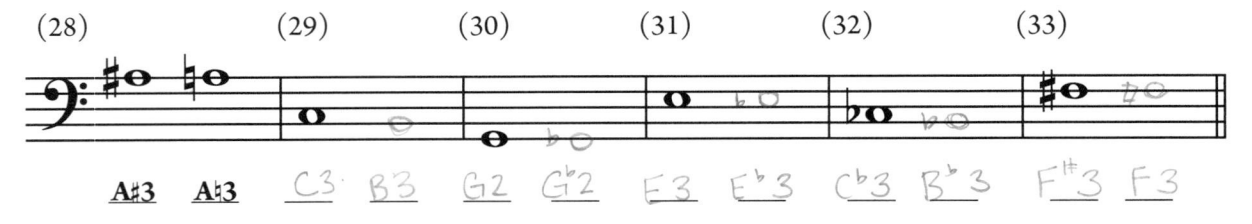

(28) **A♯3** A♮3
(29) C3 B3
(30) G2 G♭2
(31) F3 E3
(32) C♭3 B♭3
(33) F♯3 F3

Workbook ASSIGNMENT 2.3

A. Identifying and writing whole and half steps

Label each pair below as a whole step (W), half step (H), or neither (N).

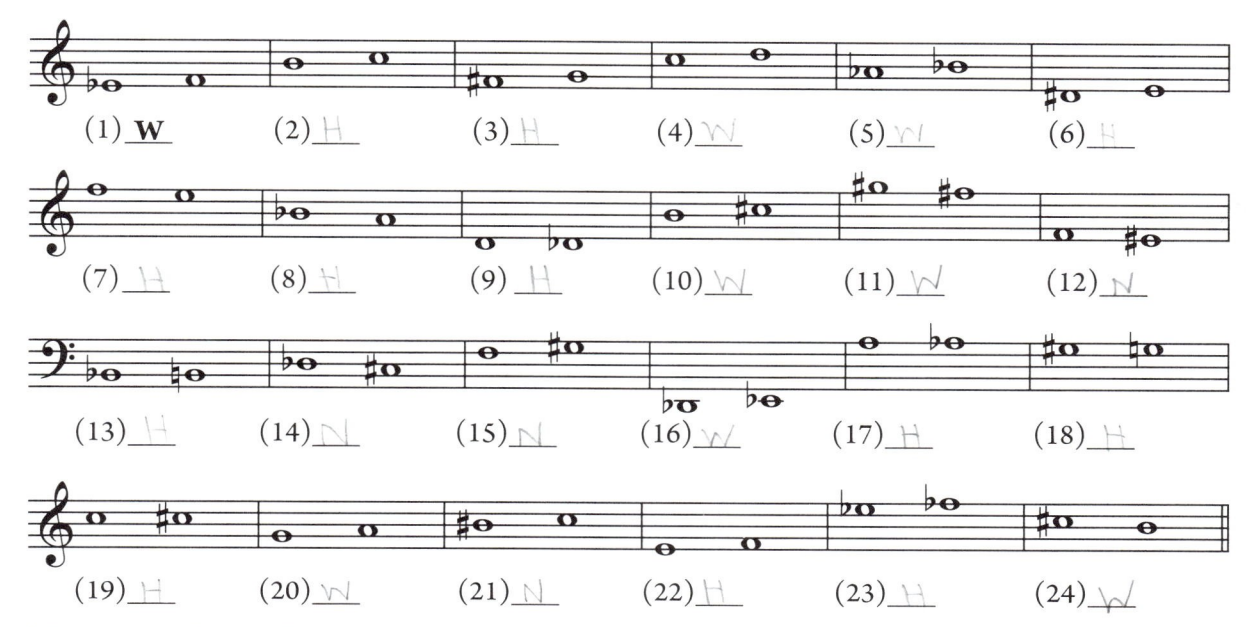

(1) **W**   (2) H   (3) H   (4) W   (5) W   (6) H

(7) H   (8) H   (9) H   (10) W   (11) W   (12) N

(13) H   (14) N   (15) N   (16) W   (17) H   (18) H

(19) H   (20) W   (21) N   (22) H   (23) H   (24) W

Write the specified whole or half step above the given note. For half steps, write the chromatic spelling (same letter names).

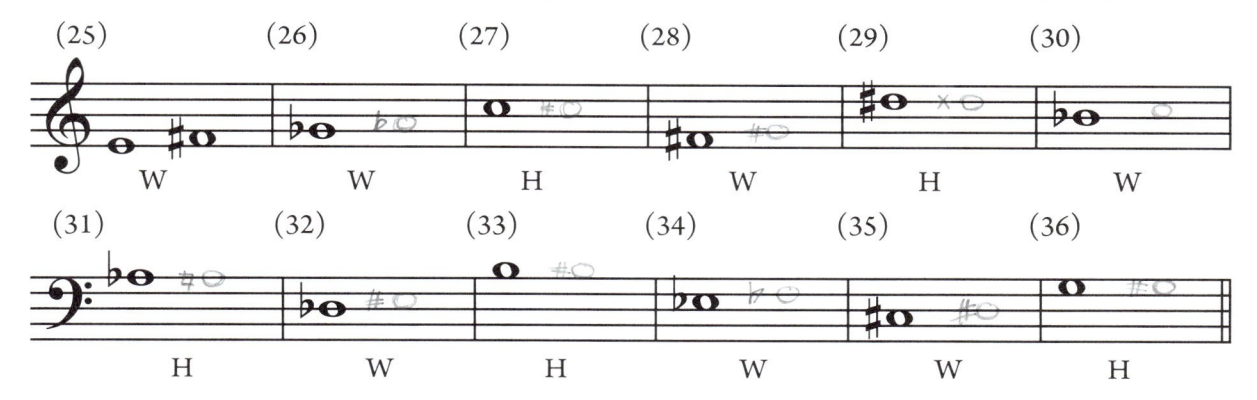

(25) W   (26) W   (27) H   (28) W   (29) H   (30) W

(31) H   (32) W   (33) H   (34) W   (35) W   (36) H

Write the specified whole or half step below the given note. For half steps, write the diatonic spelling (different letter names).

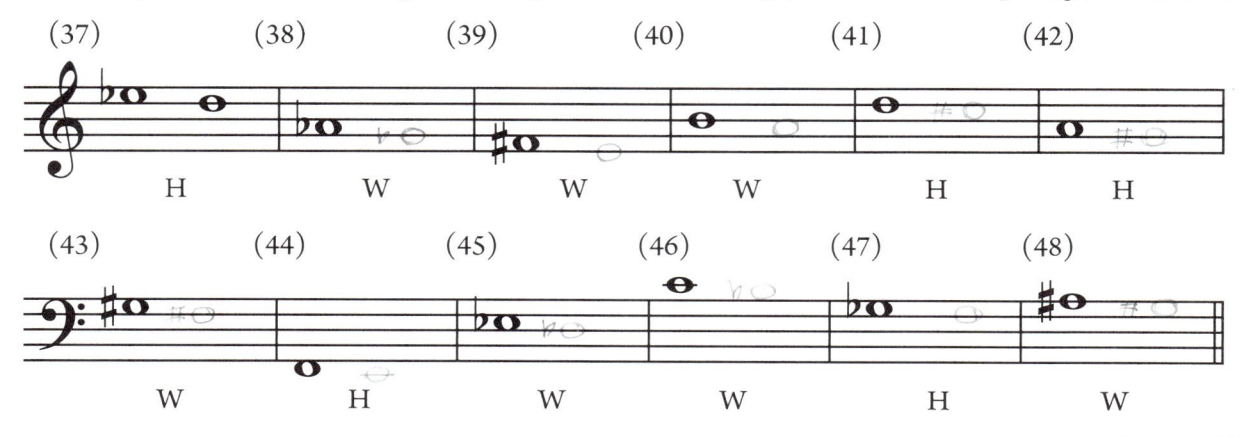

(37) H   (38) W   (39) W   (40) W   (41) H   (42) H

(43) W   (44) H   (45) W   (46) W   (47) H   (48) W

B. Identifying whole and half steps in music

Each melody below features whole and half steps. Beneath each bracketed interval, write W or H in the blank. Listen to the recorded examples to hear how the whole and half steps sound or play the pitches on a keyboard.

(1) Sousa, "The Stars and Stripes Forever," mm. 1–4

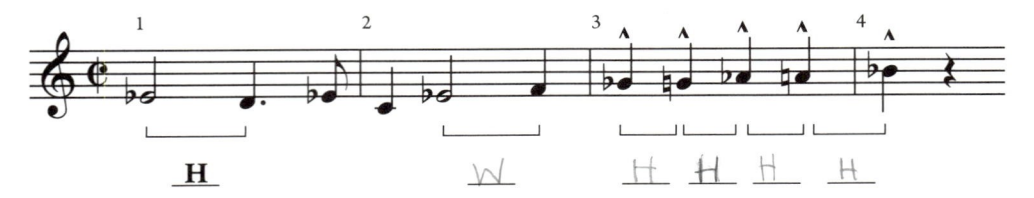

H   W   H   H   H   H

(2) Phillips, "Blues for Norton," mm. 20–24 (bass line)

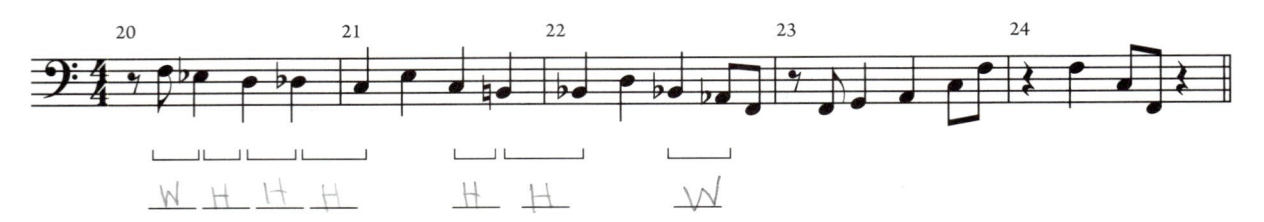

W H H H   H H   W

(3) Joplin, "Pine Apple Rag," mm. 1–4

W W H W W   H H W

(4) John Williams, "Imperial March," from *The Empire Strikes Back*, mm. 5–8

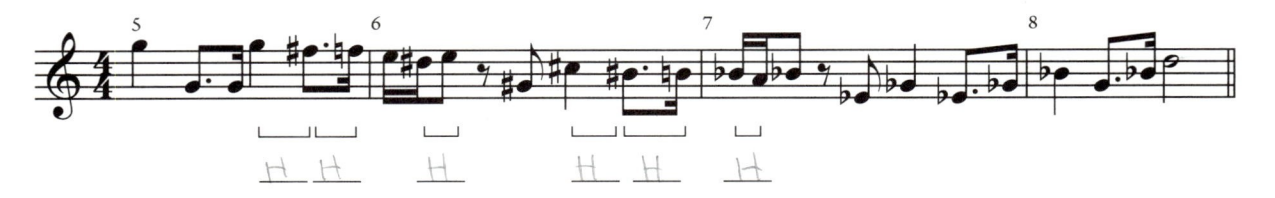

H H   H   H H   H

(5) Bruce Miller, Theme from *Frasier*, mm. 2–5

W H   H W H   H W

44   CHAPTER TWO   Accidentals and Half and Whole Steps

NAME _____

Workbook AURAL SKILLS 2.1

A. Playing and hearing half and whole steps

Play each of these half (H) and whole (W) steps at the keyboard in any octave. Name the second pitch you play with an adjacent (different) letter name and write it in the blank.

(1) H above A   **B♭**
(2) W below A♭   ___
(3) H above F♯   ___
(4) W below D♯   ___
(5) H above E   ___

(6) H below C   ___
(7) W above E♭   ___
(8) H below F♯   ___
(9) W above A♯   ___
(10) H below E♭   ___

(11) W above E   ___
(12) W below A   ___
(13) W above D♭   ___
(14) W below D♭   ___
(15) H above D♯   ___

Listen to the recording. Beginning with the given pitch, a two-pitch pattern will be played. In the blank beneath each exercise, write the interval between the two pitches, W or H. Notate the second pitch with an adjacent note name and with its accidental—♭, ♮, or ♯.

(16) W   (17) ___   (18) ___   (19) ___   (20) ___

(21) ___   (22) ___   (23) ___   (24) ___   (25) ___

(26) ___   (27) ___   (28) ___   (29) ___   (30) ___

(31) ___   (32) ___   (33) ___   (34) ___   (35) ___

B. Performing a melody at the keyboard

- Listen to the recording of either "Amazing Grace" or "Home on the Range" until you can sing it from memory.
- Sing each note of the melody, then find and play it on a keyboard. Do this until you can sing and play the entire melody.
- Draw a clef appropriate to your singing range—bass clef for men and treble clef for women—then draw an open note head for each pitch of the melody.

Aural Skills 2.1   45

- Locate the song in your anthology, and compare your notes with the printed music. Even if your clef is different, the notes should have the same letter names. If there are differences, listen again and make corrections.

C. Composing with whole and half steps

Compose two short melodies—one in the treble clef and one in the bass clef. Follow the steps below:
- Choose a different "home" pitch for each melody. Start and end each melody on this pitch.
- Include 10–12 pitches in each melody. Make a pleasing contour.
- Compose in a register you or a partner can sing comfortably. (Keep most pitches on the staff, with few ledger lines.)
- Use only adjacent letter names (e.g., B–C, F–G–A–G).
- Notate all accidentals, even naturals (on white keys).
- Write two or three times as many whole steps as half steps.
- Notate with note heads only. Mix hollow and filled note heads, playing or singing hollow ones twice as long as filled ones.

Prepare to perform your melodies in the following ways:

- Sing on a neutral syllable (such as "la") or with letter names.
- Play the melodies at the keyboard.
- Play at the keyboard and sing with a neutral syllable or letter names.
- Play melodies on another instrument.

Sample melody 1

C = home

Sample melody 2

B♭ = home

Your melodies

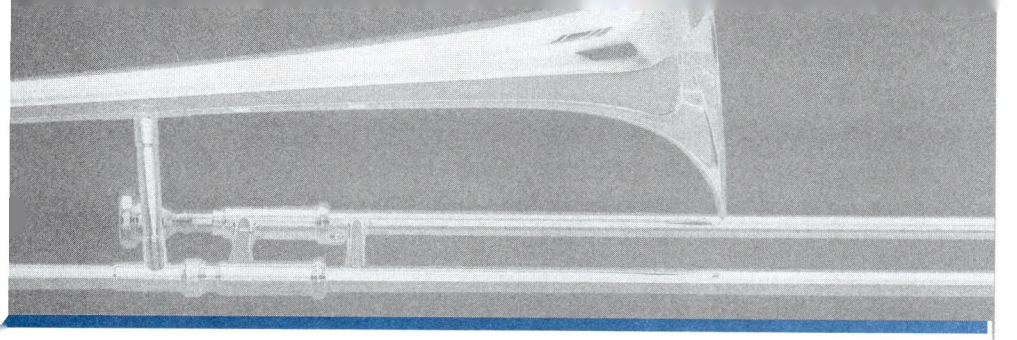

TOPICS

- duple, triple, and quadruple meters
- tempo markings and conducting patterns
- rhythmic notation
- meter signatures
- counting rhythms in simple meters
- rests

MUSIC

- Johann Sebastian Bach, Prelude in C Major, from *The Well-Tempered Clavier*, Book I
- "Come, Ye Thankful People Come"
- Stephen Foster, "Jeanie with the Light Brown Hair"
- Foster, "Oh! Susanna"
- John Lennon and Paul McCartney, "Hey Jude"
- Wolfgang Amadeus Mozart, Piano Sonata in C Major, K. 545
- Mozart, *Variations on "Ah, vous dirai-je Maman"*
- "My Country 'Tis of Thee"
- John Newton, "Amazing Grace"
- Joel Phillips, "Blues for Norton"
- John Philip Sousa, "The Stars and Stripes Forever"

CHAPTER 3
Simple Meters

Duple, Triple, and Quadruple Meters

Listen to an excerpt from "Oh! Susanna" by Stephen Foster and tap your foot in time to the music. This tap represents the work's primary pulse, or **beat**. Now listen for a secondary pulse moving faster than your foot tap. Tap the secondary pulse in one hand, while your foot continues with the beat. This secondary pulse is the **beat division**.

Beats typically divide into two or three parts. When you tap the beat division in your hand, you'll notice that there are two hand taps to one foot beat: the beat divides into two.

> **KEY CONCEPT** Pieces with beats that divide into two are in **simple meter**.

Listen again while tapping the primary beat and division as shown in Figure 3.1. Because the beat divides into twos, the song is in simple meter.

FIGURE 3.1   Meter in "Oh! Susanna"

Counts	1	2	1	2	1	2	1	2
Beats	tap	tap	tap	tap	tap	tap	tap	tap
Divisions	tap tap	tap tap	tap tap	tap tap	tap tap	tap tap	tap tap	tap tap
Lyrics	Oh!	Su-	san- na,		Oh!	don't you	cry for	me

Besides dividing, primary beats also group into twos, threes, or fours. As you listen to a piece, try saying "1-2-1-2" aloud (one number per primary beat); if the piece doesn't seem to fit that pattern, try "1-2-3-1-2-3." Listen now to "My Country, 'Tis of Thee," which groups into threes. Tap while following Figure 3.2.

FIGURE 3.2   Meter in "My Country, 'Tis of Thee"

Counts	1	2	3	1	2	3
Beats	tap	tap	tap	tap	tap	tap
Divisions	tap tap	tap tap	tap tap	tap tap	tap tap	tap tap
Lyrics	My	coun-	try,	'tis	of	thee

> **KEY CONCEPT** A work's **meter** tells (1) how its beats are divided, and (2) how they are grouped. When beats group into twos, the meter is called **duple**. When they group into threes, the meter is **triple**. When they group into fours, the meter is **quadruple**.

To determine the meter of a composition by ear:
1. listen for the beat and tap it with your foot,
2. listen for the beat division (simple meters will divide beats in two parts), and
3. listen for the groupings of the beat.

Try conducting (see the patterns in Figure 3.3) or counting to determine whether the meter is duple, triple, or quadruple.

Tempo Markings and Conducting Patterns

When only a few musicians are playing together, one may "count off" "1-2-1-2," "1-2-3," or "1-2-3-4" to help everyone start together at the same time and at the same speed, or **tempo** (plural is either "tempos" or "tempi"). Selecting the correct tempo for a performance is important to conveying the character or mood of a piece. The most common tempo indications (in Italian) are:

Slower tempos: *grave, largo, larghetto, adagio*
Medium tempos: *andantino, andante, moderato, allegretto*
Faster tempos: *allegro, vivace, presto, prestissimo*
Increasing in tempo (gradually faster): *accelerando* (abbreviated *accel.*)
Decreasing in tempo (gradually slower): *ritardando* (abbreviated *rit.*)

With larger groups, such as a band or choir, a conductor sets the tempo and helps keep the musicians playing to the same beat. Conductors outline specific patterns for each duple, triple, or quadruple meter, as shown in Figure 3.3. Conduct the duple pattern with the recording of "Oh! Susanna"; for "My Country," use the triple pattern. For a quadruple pattern, conduct "Come, Ye Thankful People Come."

FIGURE 3.3 Conducting patterns

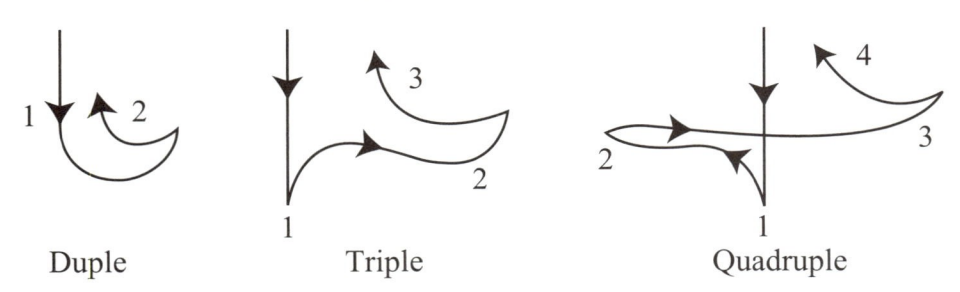

Duple Triple Quadruple

The following chart summarizes the meters of the pieces heard so far.

Piece	Meter type
"Oh! Susanna"	simple duple
"My Country, 'Tis of Thee"	simple triple
"Come, Ye Thankful People Come"	simple quadruple

As you practice **conducting patterns**, you may feel a physical weight on the **downbeat**—the downward motion of the hand on beat 1. You may also feel anticipation on the **upbeat**—the upward lift of the hand for the final beat of each pattern. The "weight" of the downbeat and the "lift" of the upbeat reflect the strong and weak beats of each measure.

> **KEY CONCEPT** In duple meters, the first beat is strong and the second is weak, making an alternating pattern of strong-weak. In triple meters, the pattern is strong-weaker-weakest, and in quadruple meters, strongest-weak-strong-weak. Strong beats in a meter are heard as **metrical accents**.

An **accent** adds weight, emphasis, or loudness to a musical element. Notated accents (>) instruct the performer to play with a sudden burst of loudness. Metrical accents are not necessarily louder; their emphasis comes from a strong beat.

In addition to showing the beat, a conductor's gestures and expressions may also convey the mood of the music, coordinate breaths, and indicate the volume, or **dynamic level**. As with tempo markings, dynamic markings are often in Italian, and are typically abbreviated.

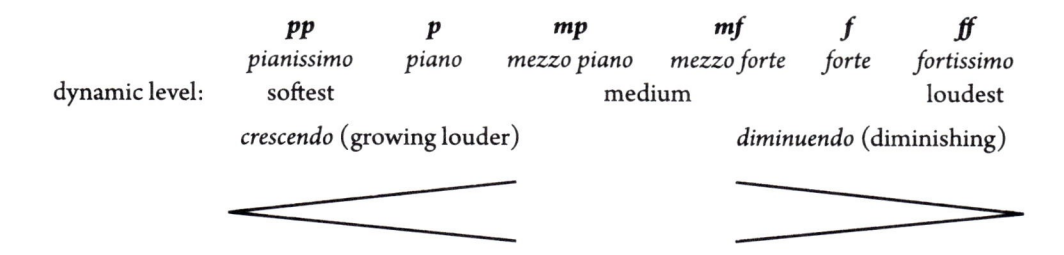

	pp	*p*	*mp*	*mf*	*f*	*ff*
	pianissimo	piano	mezzo piano	mezzo forte	forte	fortissimo
dynamic level:	softest		medium			loudest

crescendo (growing louder)   *diminuendo* (diminishing)

Rhythmic Notation

When you listened to the music at the beginning of the chapter, you probably noticed that some pitches lasted longer and others were shorter. The patterns of longer and shorter durations in music are called **rhythm**. Rhythm and meter are two different, but related, aspects of musical time. Meter defines beat groupings and divisions, while rhythm consists of durations of pitches and silences heard in relation to the underlying meter.

Look at Example 3.1, the beginning of "Amazing Grace." For now, focus on the labeled parts of the notation. The **bar lines** divide the staff into **measures**, or bars; numbers above the staff are measure numbers, to help you find your location in a piece.

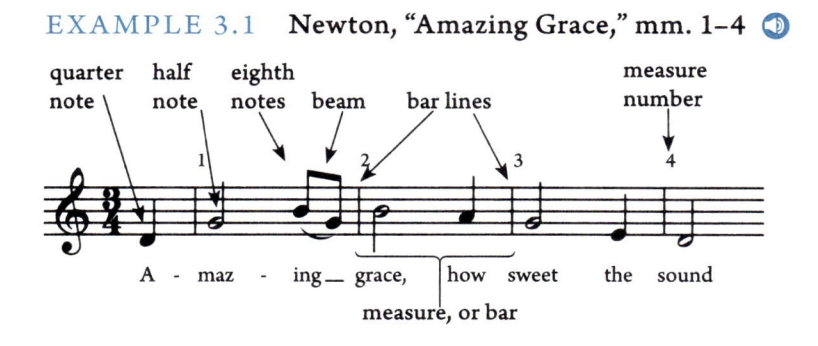

EXAMPLE 3.1 Newton, "Amazing Grace," mm. 1–4

The example features three of the most common note values in music: **quarter**, **half**, and **eighth notes**. A half note lasts twice as long as a quarter; a quarter note lasts twice as long as an eighth. Eighth notes can be written two ways: **beamed** together as in the example, or with a **flag** attached to the right of the stem, as in Figure 3.4. Write flags on the right side of the stem, whether the stem goes up or down. If eighth notes are beamed together, take the stem direction of the second note, as in the first measure of Example 3.1. For more than two beamed notes, choose the stem direction based on the majority of the pitches; don't change direction within the beamed group.

FIGURE 3.4 Parts of a note

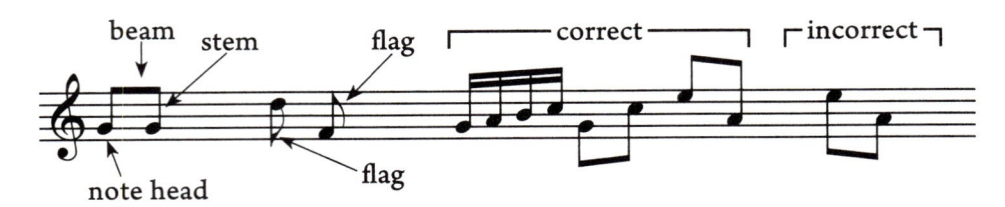

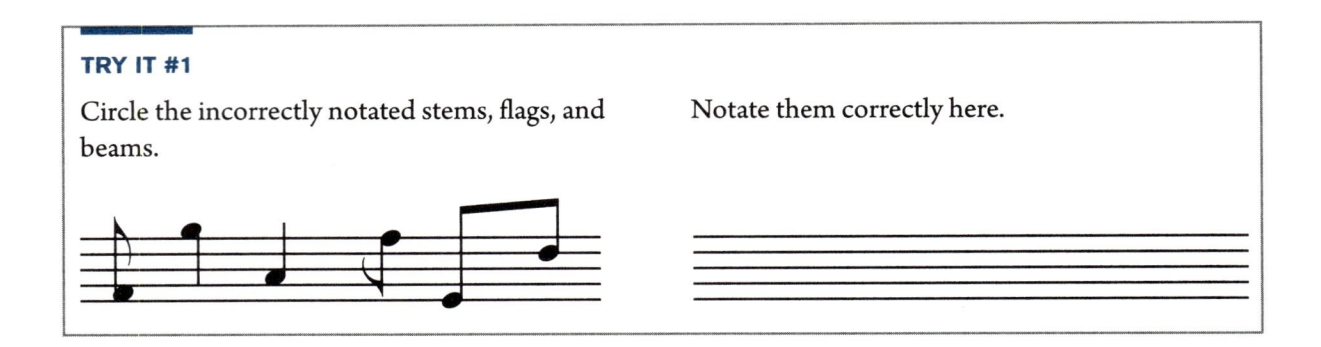

TRY IT #1

Circle the incorrectly notated stems, flags, and beams.

Notate them correctly here.

Now consider Example 3.2, the last few measures of a keyboard piece by J. S. Bach, to learn two additional note values.

EXAMPLE 3.2 Bach, Prelude in C Major, from *The Well-Tempered Clavier*, Book I, mm. 34–35

The notes with two beams are **sixteenth notes**. They may be written with either two beams or two flags, and they last half as long as eighth notes. The last measure contains **whole notes**—hollow note heads with no stem. A whole note lasts four times as long as a quarter note and twice as long as a half note.

The chart in Figure 3.5 sums up the basic note durations in simple meter and how these notes relate to each other: a whole note divides into two half notes, a half note divides into two quarters, and so on. You can create even smaller note values by adding beams or flags to the stem; a thirty-second note, for example, has three flags or beams and a sixty-fourth note has four.

FIGURE 3.5 Chart of rhythmic durations

Whole note   𝅝

Half notes   𝅗𝅥   𝅗𝅥

Quarter notes   ♩ ♩ ♩ ♩

Eighth notes   ♫ ♫ ♫ ♫

Sixteenth notes   ♬♬ ♬♬ ♬♬ ♬♬

SUMMARY

- A 𝅝 is equivalent to 𝅗𝅥 𝅗𝅥 or ♩ ♩ ♩ ♩
- A 𝅗𝅥 is equivalent to ♩ ♩ or ♫ ♫
- A ♩ is equivalent to ♫ or ♬♬

TRY IT #2

In each blank, write the value of the note above: W (whole note), H (half), Q (quarter), E (eighth), or S (sixteenth).

(a) Foster, "Jeanie with the Light Brown Hair" mm. 13–14 🔊

Ma - ny were the wild notes her mer - ry voice would pour,
E

(b) Lennon and McCartney, "Hey Jude," mm. 3–6

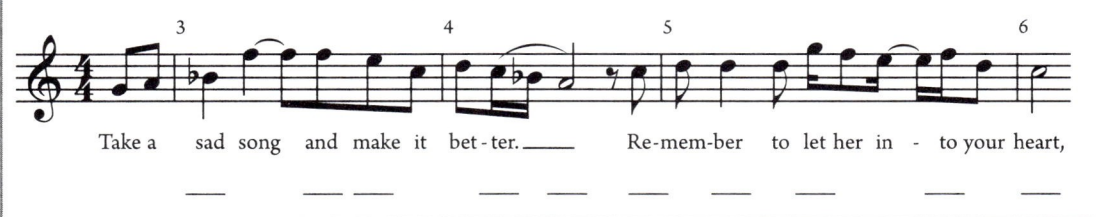

Take a sad song and make it bet - ter.___ Re - mem - ber to let her in - to your heart,

ASSIGNMENT 3.1

Meter Signatures

Listen again to the melody of "Amazing Grace," shown in Example 3.3, and tap or conduct along with the music. The meter is simple triple; this is indicated on the staff by the symbol $\frac{3}{4}$—called the **meter signature** (or time signature). The 3 means that there are three beats in a measure, and the 4 indicates that the quarter note gets one beat—it is the **beat unit**. The quarter note before the first bar line is an **anacrusis** (or upbeat or pickup)—a weak beat that precedes the first strong one.

EXAMPLE 3.3   Newton, "Amazing Grace," mm. 1–4

> **KEY CONCEPT** In simple meters: the top number of the meter signature—2, 3, or 4—shows the number of beats in a measure (duple, triple, or quadruple); the lower number represents the type of note that gets one beat (2 = half note, 4 = quarter note, 8 = eighth note, 16 = sixteenth note). In sum, the meter signature shows "how many" (top number) of "what" (bottom number) constitutes a measure.

Examples 3.4 and 3.5 show simple duple and simple quadruple meters. In Example 3.4, a familiar melody ("Twinkle, Twinkle, Little Star") used by Mozart, both hands play the beat unit—the quarter note. In Example 3.5, the rhythm moves primarily in quarter notes in a $\frac{4}{4}$ meter. On the grand staff or on multiple staves, the meter signature appears on each staff, as shown.

EXAMPLE 3.4   Mozart, *Variations on "Ah, vous dirai-je Maman,"* mm. 1–8

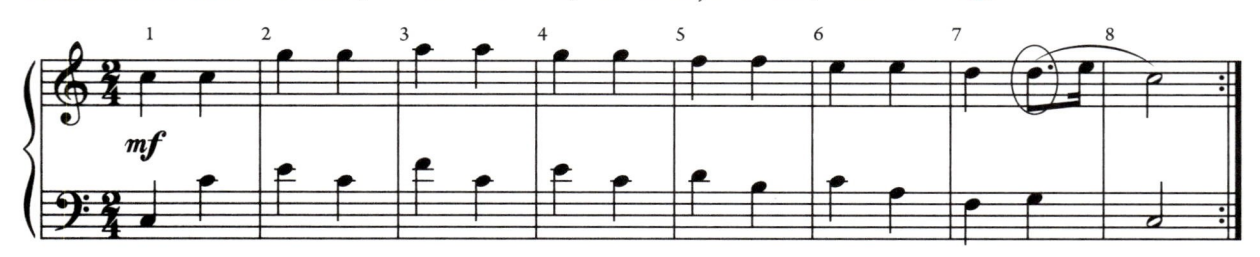

EXAMPLE 3.5   "Come, Ye Thankful People Come," mm. 1–4

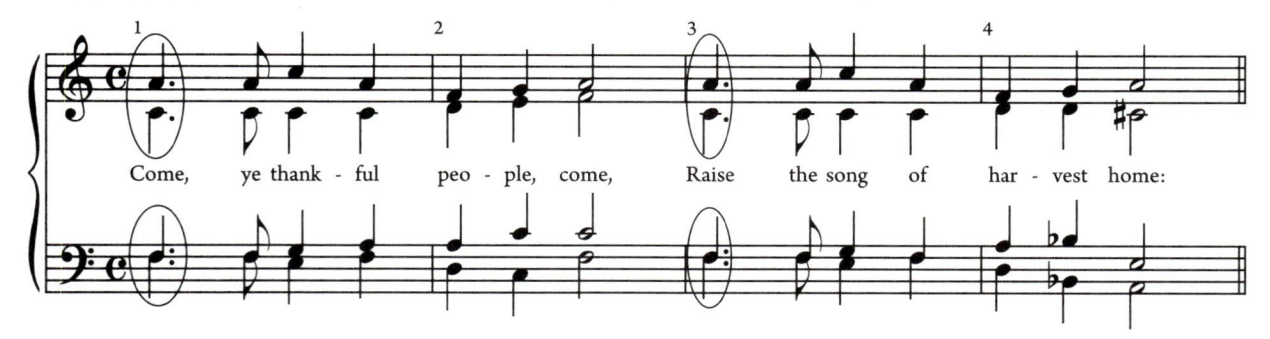

Both examples share another rhythmic device: a dot (circled).

> **KEY CONCEPT** A **dot** beside a note adds to that note half of its own value.

52   CHAPTER THREE Simple Meters

In Example 3.4, the dotted-eighth note in measure 7 lasts three-quarters of a beat. In Example 3.5, the dotted-quarters last a beat and a half.

You will often see meter signatures that consist of symbols other than numerals. For example, the symbol **C**, called "common time," is sometimes written instead of $\frac{4}{4}$, as in Example 3.6.

EXAMPLE 3.6   Mozart, Piano Sonata in C Major, K. 545, mm. 1–4

The quarter note is the most common beat unit, but it's not the only possibility. For example, "The Stars and Stripes Forever," shown in Example 3.7, is a march in a quick tempo with half notes felt as the beat unit and pairs of quarter notes as the beat division (see m. 3). The meter signature could be written as $\frac{2}{2}$—two beats to the measure, with a half note receiving the beat—but more often we find $\frac{2}{2}$ written as ¢, called *alla breve* or "cut time."

EXAMPLE 3.7   Sousa, "The Stars and Stripes Forever," mm. 1–4

There are various reasons why composers choose a particular beat unit. Sometimes it's to remind the performer of a particular compositional type—such as *alla breve* for marches. A piece may be notated with a longer beat unit for ease of reading, to avoid notating quick-moving rhythms with sixteenth or thirty-second notes. The meter may also suggest a tempo: an eighth-note beat unit might indicate a faster tempo and a lively motion.

SUMMARY

Meter signatures you are likely to see in simple meters include the following.

Simple duple	$\frac{2}{2}$	¢	$\frac{2}{4}$	
Simple triple	$\frac{3}{2}$	$\frac{3}{4}$	$\frac{3}{8}$	
Simple quadruple	$\frac{4}{2}$	$\frac{4}{4}$	**C**	$\frac{4}{8}$

Counting Rhythms in Simple Meters

To count rhythms in a simple-meter piece, you first need to look at the meter signature and identify the beat unit and beat division. For example, if the beat unit is a quarter note, the beat division is two eighths; if the beat unit is a half note, the beat division is two quarters. Figure 3.6 shows how to interpret various simple meter signatures; the first three are the most common.

FIGURE 3.6   Beat units and divisions in simple meters

Meter signature	Beats per measure	Beat unit	Beat division
2/4	2	♩	♫
3/4	3	♩	♫
4/4	4	♩	♫
3/2	3	𝅗𝅥	♩ ♩
3/8	3	♪	♬
4/8	4	♪	♬

TRY IT #3

For each meter signature given below, write its beat unit and division.

Meter signature	Beats per measure	Beat unit	Beat division
3/8	3	♪	♬
2/2	___	___	___
4/16	___	___	___
3/2	___	___	___
3/4	___	___	___

The next step in counting a rhythm is to locate the beats and divisions in the music.

KEY CONCEPT In 3/4, a measure of all quarter notes is counted 1-2-3; a measure of all eighth notes is counted 1 & 2 & 3 &.

In "Amazing Grace," shown in Example 3.8, the beat unit is the quarter note, but the melody mixes quarter notes with half notes and eighths. To count measure 1, write: 1 (2) 3 &, as shown in the example. The (2) indicates that the first half note extends through beat 2. The eighth-note division of beat 3 is written with an ampersand (3 &) and counted aloud as "three and."

EXAMPLE 3.8 Newton, "Amazing Grace," mm. 1–4

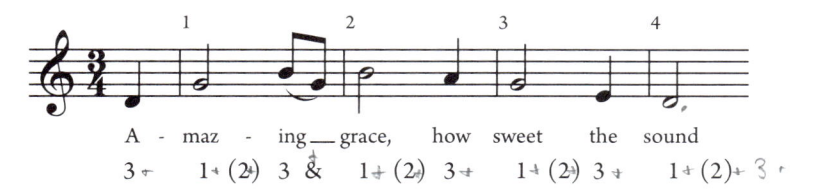

| A - maz - ing — grace, | how sweet | the sound |
| 3   1 + (2 +) 3 & | 1 + (2 +) 3 + | 1 + (2 +) 3 + | 1 + (2) + 3 |

The first quarter note of the melody, the anacrusis (or upbeat), counts as the final beat (3) of an incomplete measure. When an anacrusis begins a whole piece, as in this song, the measure numbering (above the staff) starts with the first *complete* measure. The last measure of the score is often incomplete, in order to "balance" the anacrusis.

Example 3.9 shows the counts for the same basic rhythm, notated in three different ways: with a quarter-note beat unit (a), half-note beat unit (b), and eighth-note beat unit (c). All three rhythms would be counted in exactly the same way, and all sound the same. While you may find the first easiest to read, you may also encounter the others in the music you play or sing. Practice reading rhythms with the less typical half-note or eighth-note beat units, as well as the more familiar quarter-note unit.

The rhythms in Example 3.9 are notated with a **rhythm clef**: two vertical lines preceding the meter signature. The rhythm clef is typically placed on a single line instead of a staff for percussion parts that play only rhythm, not specific pitches. The stems of notes on a rhythm clef typically point upward.

EXAMPLE 3.9 Equivalent rhythmic notation

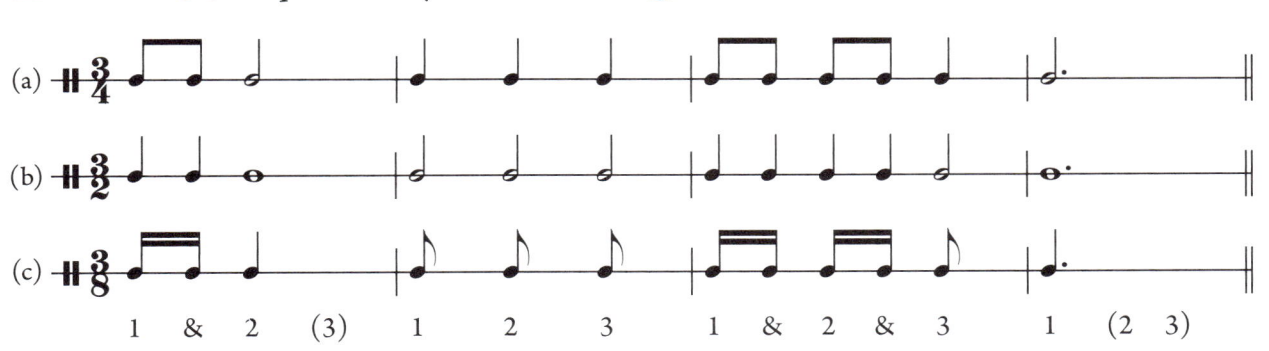

1 & 2 (3)   1 2 3   1 & 2 & 3   1 (2 3)

TRY IT #4

At each arrow, add one note value to complete the measure in the meter indicated. Write the counts beneath each rhythm.

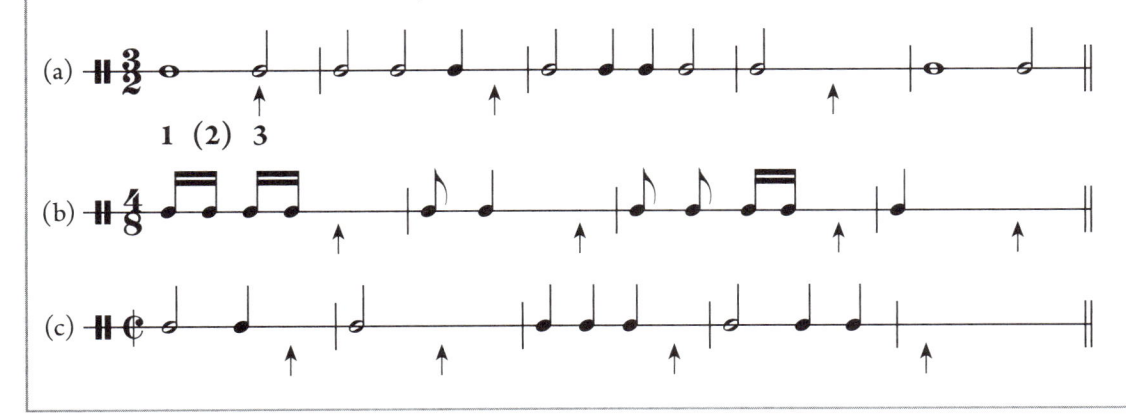

(a) 1 (2) 3

Counting Rhythms in Simple Meters   55

Rests

Listen to the beginning of *Blues for Norton*, shown in Example 3.10, to hear the effect of **rests**, or durations of silence. Here, the saxophone begins with a solo line while all the other instruments wait in silence for their first entrance. This silence is notated with rests.

EXAMPLE 3.10   Phillips, *Blues for Norton*, mm. 1–3

The **quarter rest** (𝄽) lasts as long as a quarter note, and the **eighth rest** (𝄾) lasts as long as an eighth note. These symbols in the example tell instrumentalists how long to count before beginning to play. Counts are shown below the temple-block part.

Figure 3.7 shows each type of rest with its corresponding note value in simple meter. A **whole rest** may represent four quarter-note beats or two half-note beats; it can also last a whole measure, regardless of how many beats are in that measure. Whole rests are usually centered between the bar lines, but smaller rests are positioned to reflect where the beats occur, as shown in Example 3.10. To write shorter rests, like the thirty-second (𝄿), just add additional flags to the sixteenth. Like other rhythmic values, rests may be dotted.

FIGURE 3.7   Note values and rests

whole (hangs below line 4)

half (sits on top of line 3)

quarter (centered on line 3)

eighth (centered on line 3)

sixteenth (sits on line 1)

ASSIGNMENT 3.2, 3.3

Counts for rests are written in parentheses to show that these durations don't actually sound. Listen to Example 3.11 and practice counting the rhythms along with the bass line. We will consider the rhythms of the upper lines in Chapter 4.

EXAMPLE 3.11   Phillips, "Blues for Norton," mm. 1–4

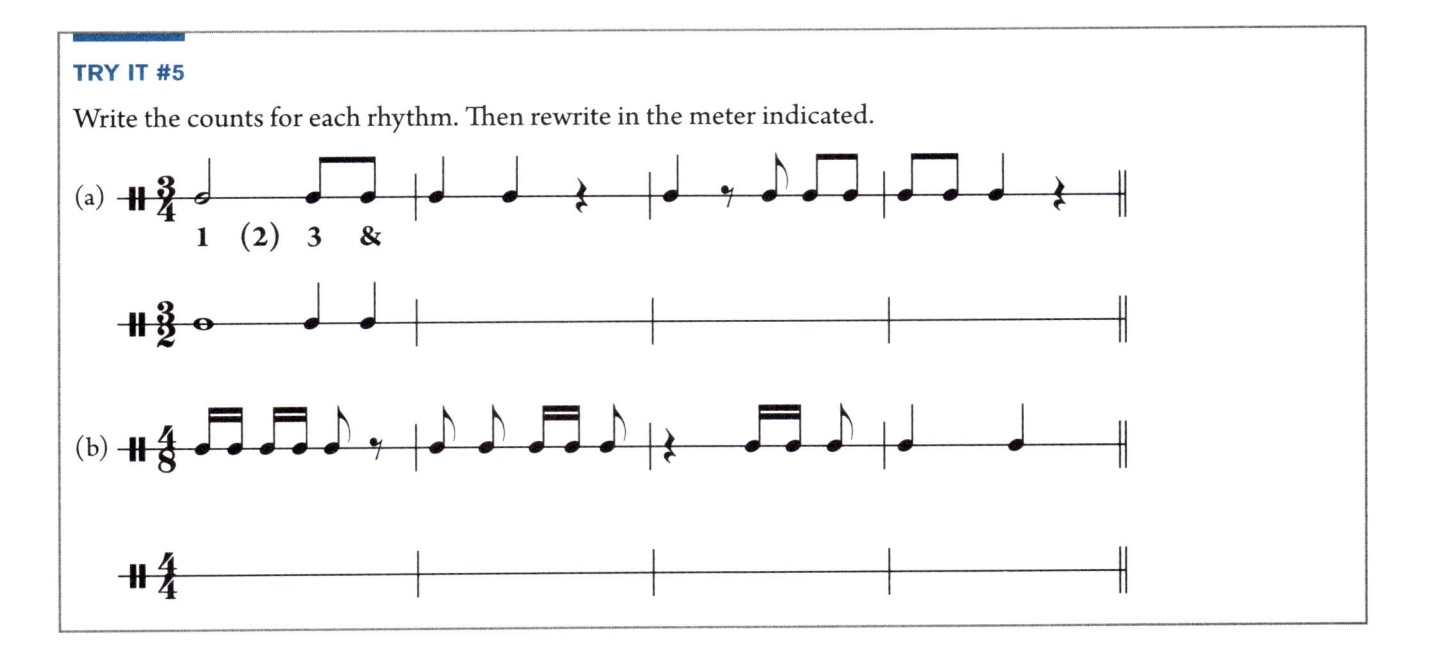

1   2   3   4 & (1) & 2   3   4   1   2   3   4 & (1) & 2   3   4

TRY IT #5

Write the counts for each rhythm. Then rewrite in the meter indicated.

(a)   1 (2) 3 &

(b)

AURAL SKILLS 3.1

Did You Know?

Much of the time when we think about music, we focus more on sounds and don't pay much attention to silences. Twentieth-century composer John Cage (1912–1992) forced us to do just the opposite when he composed his famous 4′33″ (1952)—a three-movement work where each movement has a duration selected by the performer, but is marked "Tacet" (a term usually used to tell certain instrumentalists not to play in one movement of a multimovement work). The title, 4′33″, refers to the duration of the whole piece. The performers indicate the start and end of each movement in some way—by lifting their instruments up and down or by opening and closing the piano keyboard cover—but make no sounds. The piece is not completely silent, however; normally people in the audience make some sound by moving, coughing, shuffling program pages, and so forth. Through this work and his writings, including *Silence* (1961), Cage inspired musicians and listeners to think about what happens between the sounds—in the silences.

Terms You Should Know

accent	measure	eighth
anacrusis	meter	sixteenth
bar line	simple	rest
beam	duple	whole
beat	triple	half
beat division	quadruple	quarter
beat unit	meter signature	eighth
conducting patterns	metrical accent	sixteenth
dot	note	rhythm
downbeat	whole	rhythm clef
dynamic level	half	tempo
flag	quarter	upbeat

Questions for Review

1. How do you decide if a piece is in duple, triple, or quadruple meter?
2. How do you decide which conducting pattern to use?
3. Where do the stronger metrical accents fall in simple triple meter? in simple duple meter? in simple quadruple meter?
4. Explain the difference between rhythm and meter.
5. Draw the parts of an eighth note. Draw one above the middle staff line and another below it.
6. On which side of a note are stems drawn? On which side of the stem are flags drawn?
7. What are the most common simple meter signatures?
8. What do the upper and lower parts of a meter signature represent in simple meters?
9. Which numbers may appear in the upper and lower positions of the meter signature in simple meters?
10. What is the beat unit in C? in ¢?

Reading Review

Match the term on the left with the best answer on the right.

_____ (1) quarter note (a) meter with beats that divide into two
_____ (2) beat unit (b) equal in duration to two quarter rests
_____ (3) rhythm (c) the type of note that gets one beat
_____ (4) whole note (d) ♪
_____ (5) C (e) the sequence of pitches and silences in music
_____ (6) simple meter (f) indicates how loud or soft the music should be
_____ (7) duple meter (g) 3/2, 3/4, and 3/8
_____ (8) dot (h) ♩
_____ (9) meter signature (i) counted the same as 4/4
_____ (10) triple meter (j) 2/2 and 2/4
_____ (11) 3/4 (k) the speed of the beats
_____ (12) sixteenth note (l) notation symbol that shows the beat unit and the number of beats in a bar
_____ (13) dynamic marking (m) has three quarter-note beats per measure
_____ (14) rhythm clef (n) *alla breve*, or cut time
_____ (15) anacrusis (o) upbeat
_____ (16) ¢ (p) adds half its value to a note or rest
_____ (17) half rest (q) used to notate unpitched percussion parts
_____ (18) tempo (r) duration equal to two half notes

Additional review and practice available at wwnorton.com/studyspace

Apply It

A. Listening for meter

Listen to the beginning of each of the following pieces. Focus on the grouping of the beats to decide whether the meter is simple duple, triple, or quadruple. Conduct along as you listen.

(1) Bach, Passacaglia in C Minor _____

(2) "Michael Finnigin" _____

(3) "Come, Ye Thankful People Come" _____

(4) Chopin, Prelude in C Minor, Op. 28, No. 20 _____

(5) Mozart, String Quartet in D Minor, K. 421, third movement _____

B. Reading rhythms

Perform the following rhythms as musically as possible, following dynamic markings. As you perform, tap or conduct the beats. Speak with rhythm syllables or counts (if instructed to do so) or a neutral syllable such as "ta," and give a slight emphasis to each downbeat.

Rhythm 1

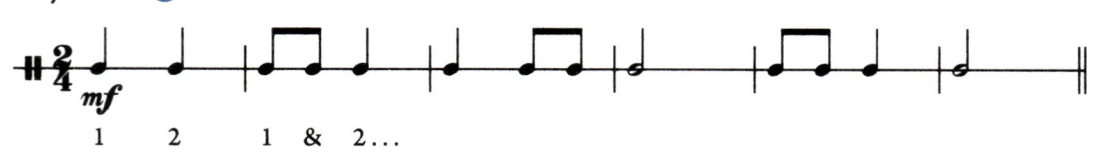

Rhythm 2

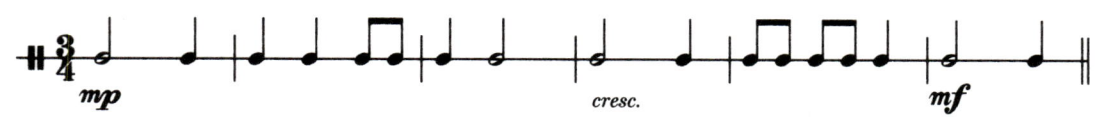

Rhythm 3

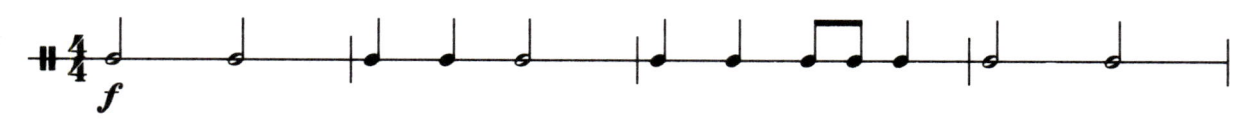

Rhythm 4

Rhythm 5 🔊

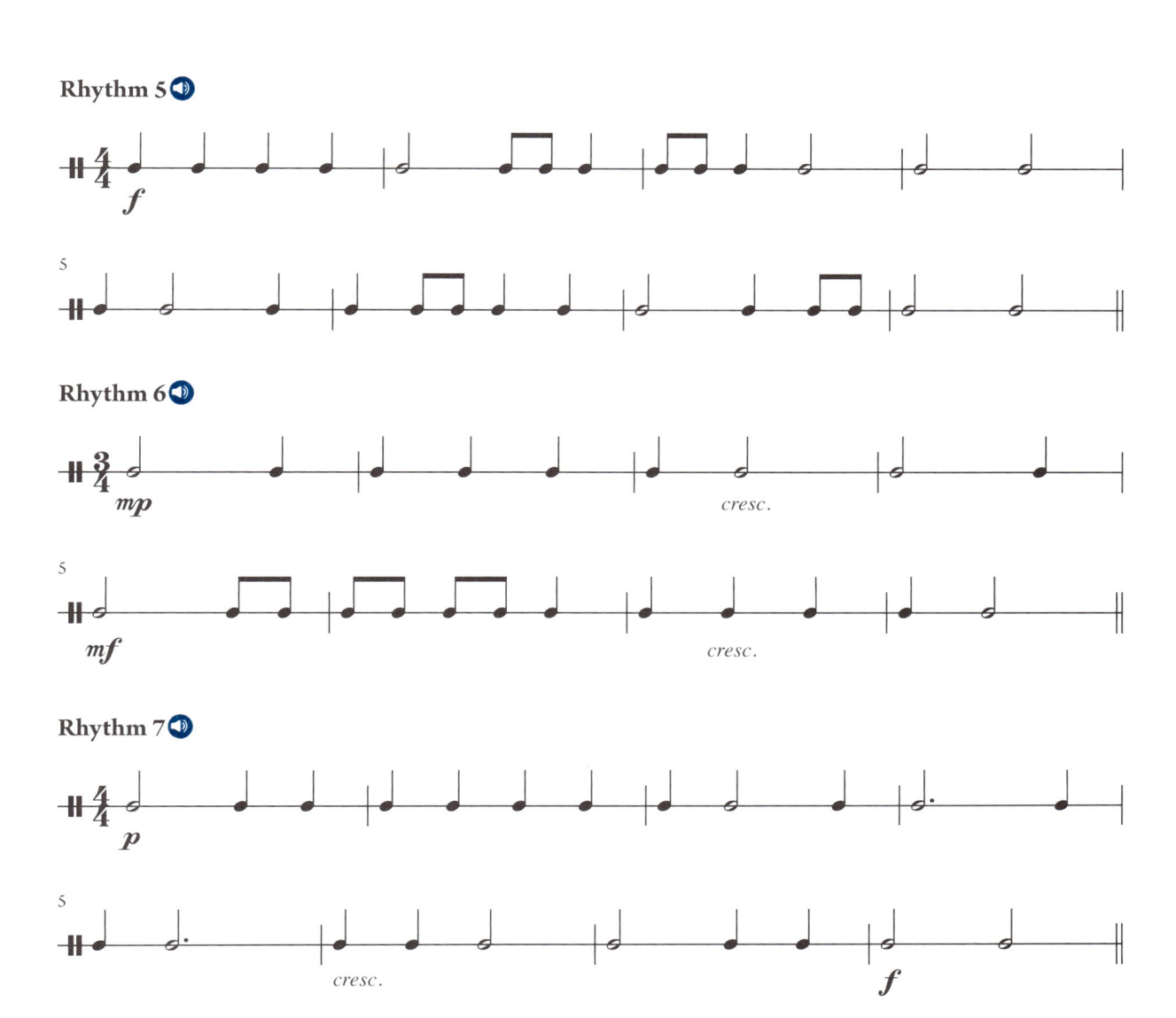

Rhythm 6 🔊

Rhythm 7 🔊

C. Composing a simple-meter rhythm

On your own, or with a team of three or four, compose an eight-measure rhythmic duet that features only the rhythmic patterns below. If you're working in a team, each person should notate one measure, then pass the marker to the next person. Repeat until the composition is complete. Add dynamic and tempo markings. Perform and critique in class.

Write in simple quadruple, simple triple, or simple duple meter. For simple triple, add one ♩ to every pattern.

Patterns

1   2   3   4   5

D. Singing at sight

- First review the vocal warm-ups in the Chapter 1 Apply It. Remember to warm up your voice each time you sing.
- Study the rhythm in each of the following melodies. Perform it on "ta," or on rhythm syllables, while tapping a steady beat (or conducting). Begin with a slow tempo; repeat at a faster tempo.
- Once you are confident with the rhythm, play the first note on a keyboard or another instrument, and begin learning the pitches, singing on the numbers or syllables marked. Practice without rhythm; play the pitches at

Apply It   61

a keyboard or sing together in class. Then sing the entire melody, checking the pitches at the keyboard *after* you sing. Finally put pitches and rhythm together at a slow tempo; repeat at a faster tempo.

Melody 1

Melody 2

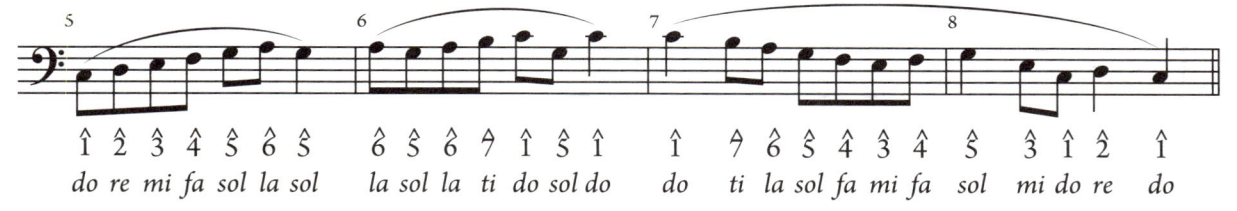

Melody 3 Mozart, *Variations on "Lison dormait,"* mm. 1–8 (adapted)

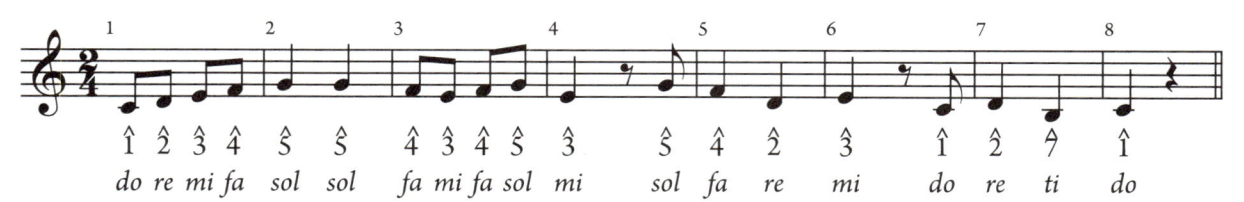

E. Listening and writing

Listen to rhythms made up of two patterns each from those below. Sing or tap what you hear, then write it on the staff provided.

Patterns

1. 　　2.

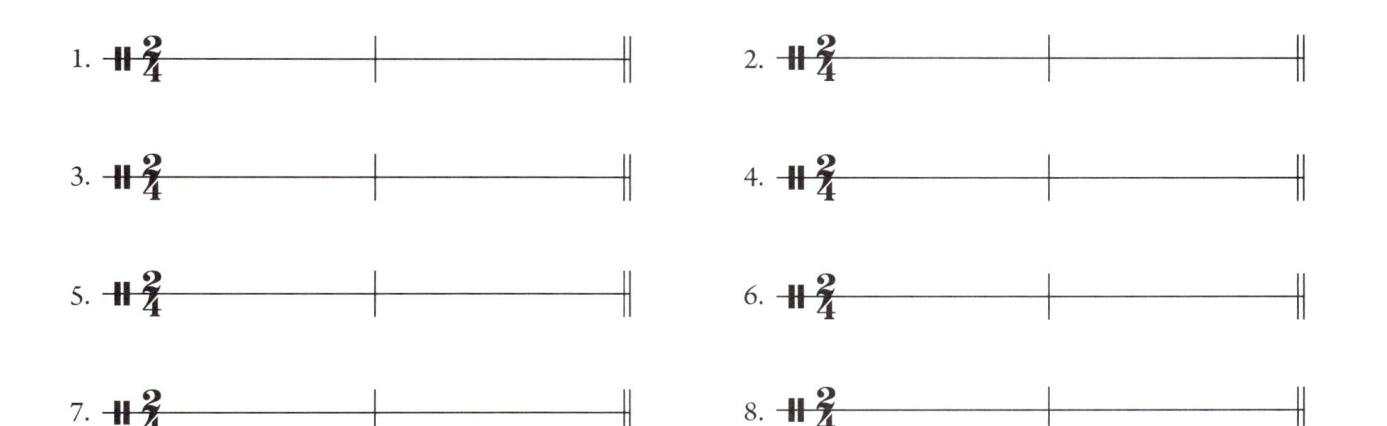

3. 　　4.

5. 　　6.

7. 　　8.

Listen to the rhythms combined with the pitches C–D–E–F–G. Sing what you hear, then write it on the staff provided.

9.

10.

11.

12.

13.

14.

15.

Apply It 63

16.

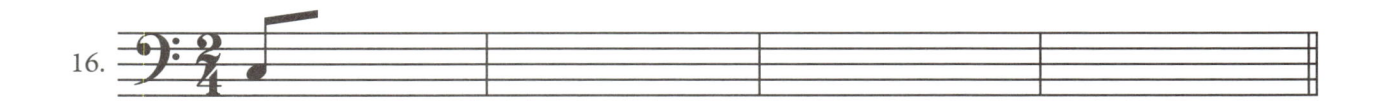

The next set of rhythms use the quadruple-meter patterns below combined with the pitches C–D–E–F–G. Each rhythm consists of four patterns. Sing what you hear, then write it on the staff provided.

Patterns

1   2   3   4   5

17.

18.

19.

20.

21.

22.

23.

24.

64   CHAPTER THREE   Simple Meters

NAME _____

Workbook ASSIGNMENT 3.1

A. Identifying note values

In the examples that follow, write W (whole), H (half), Q (quarter), E (eighth), or S (sixteenth) in each blank to indicate the value of the note above.

(1) James Horner, "My Heart Will Go On," mm. 25–28

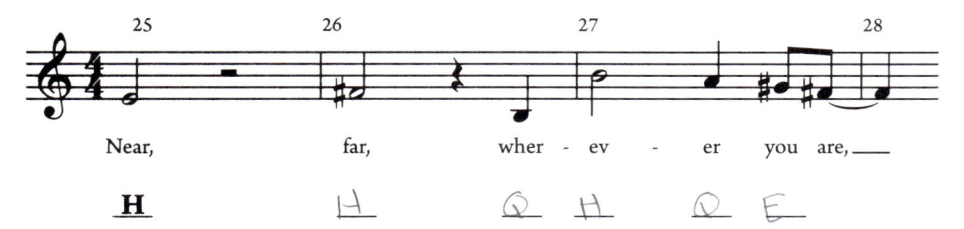

Near, far, wher - ev - er you are, ___

H   H   Q   H   Q   E

(2) Jonathan Larson, "Seasons of Love," from *Rent*, mm. 25–27

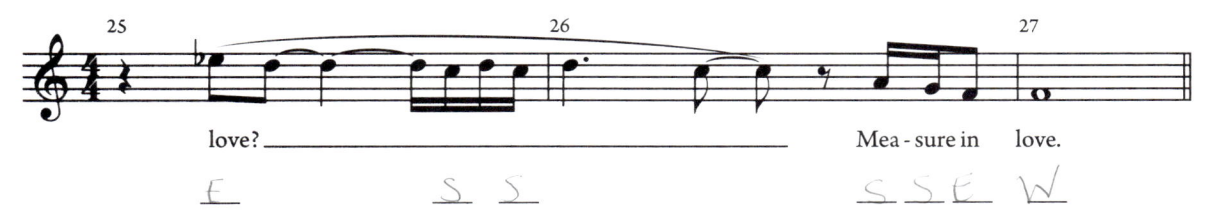

love? _____ Mea - sure in love.

E   S S   S S E   W

(3) Elton John and Bernie Taupin, "Your Song," mm. 9–10

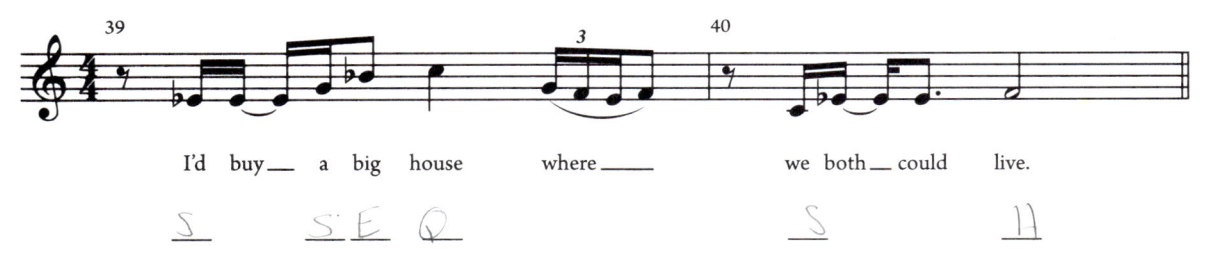

I'd buy ___ a big house where ___ we both ___ could live.

S   S E Q   S   H

B. Understanding duration

Fill in the blanks with a number to show the equivalent duration. Some numbers may be fractions (♪ = ½ ♩).

♩ = **4** ♬   o = 2 ♩   ♩ = 1/2 o

♩ = 4 ♬   o = 4 ♩   ♩ = 1/4 o

♩ = 2 ♬   ♪ = 1/2 ♪   ♪ = 1/4 ♩

o = 32 ♬   o = 8 ♪   ♩ = 1/2 ♩

♪ = 1/16 ♩   ♪ = 1/16 ♩   ♩ = 1/32 ♪

Assignment 3.1   **65**

C. Error detection in simple meters

In the rhythms below, the quarter note lasts one beat. Identify one measure in each example that has an incorrect number of beats for the meter specified. Circle the incorrect measure.

(1) simple triple

(2) simple duple

(3) simple quadruple

(4) simple triple

(5) simple quadruple

D. Notating quarter, half, and eighth notes with correct stem direction

Write the rhythms requested below, using notes on a variety of lines and spaces. Choose notes so that roughly half require stems up and half stems down. Be sure that your stem direction, flags, and beaming follow correct notation guidelines.

(1) In each measure, write two beamed eighth notes and a quarter note.

(2) In each measure, write a quarter note, then two eighth notes with flags.

(3) In each measure, write a half note, then two quarter notes.

(4) In each measure, write a quarter note, two beamed eighth notes, four beamed sixteenth notes, and a quarter note.

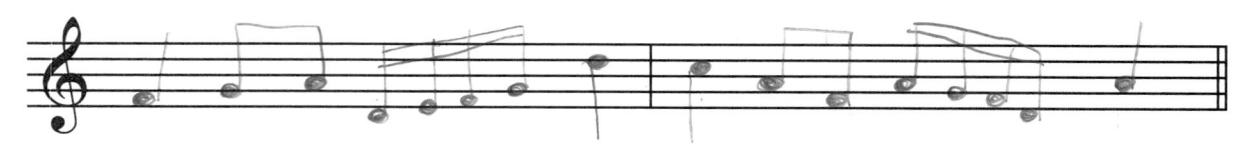

CHAPTER THREE Simple Meters

Workbook — Assignment 3.2

A. Reading meters with quarter-note beats

For each rhythm below, write the appropriate meter signature at the beginning of the line. Assume a quarter-note beat unit. Perform each rhythm.

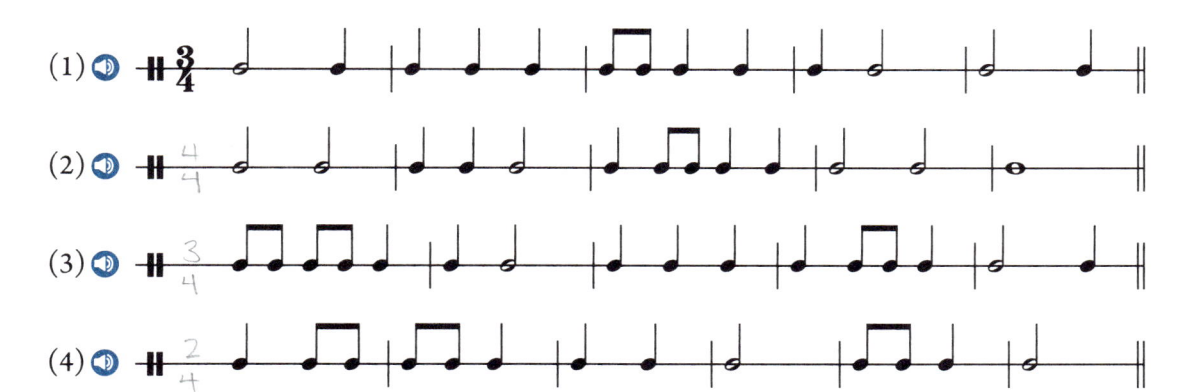

(1) $\frac{3}{4}$

(2) $\frac{4}{4}$

(3) $\frac{3}{4}$

(4) $\frac{2}{4}$

At each position marked by an arrow, add one note to complete the measure in the meter indicated.

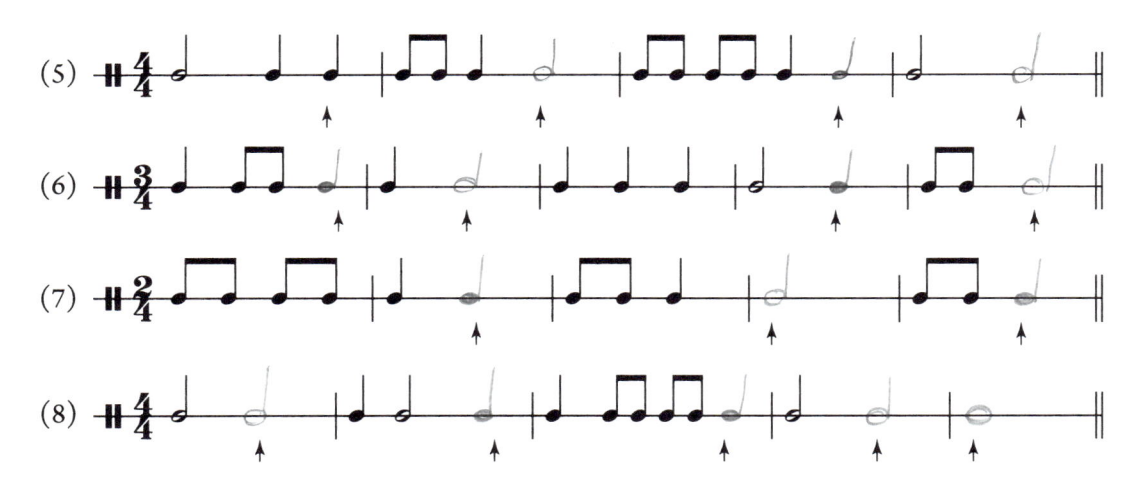

(5) $\frac{4}{4}$

(6) $\frac{3}{4}$

(7) $\frac{2}{4}$

(8) $\frac{4}{4}$

For each rhythm below, provide the missing bar lines that correspond with the meter signature given.

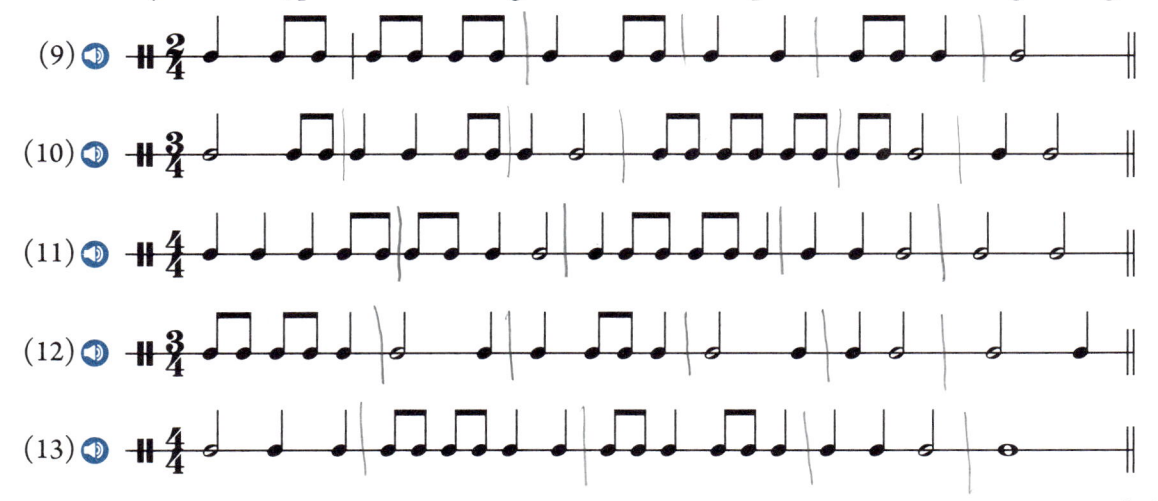

(9) $\frac{2}{4}$

(10) $\frac{3}{4}$

(11) $\frac{4}{4}$

(12) $\frac{3}{4}$

(13) $\frac{4}{4}$

B. Understanding dots

Finish the chart below to show the equivalent durations.

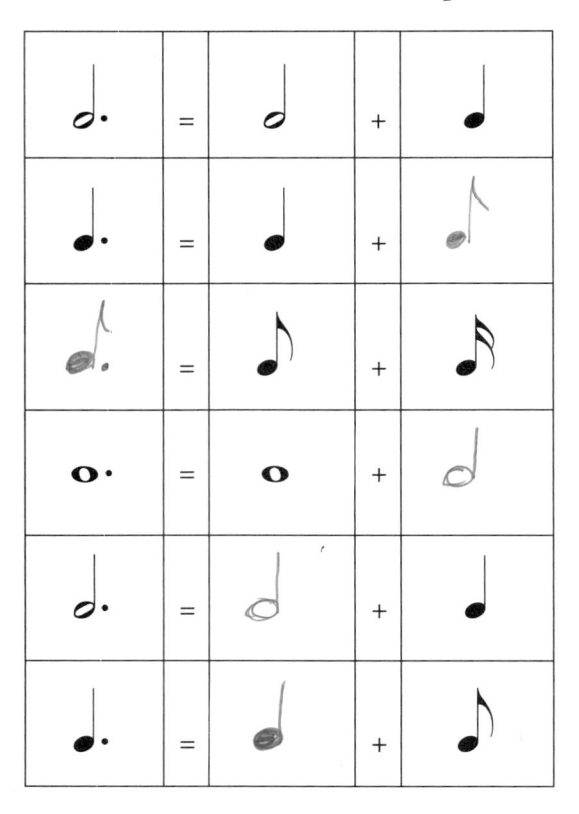

C. Writing rests

(1) On the staff below, write four whole rests, then four half rests.

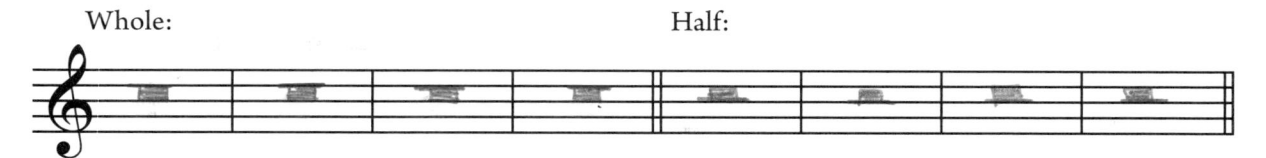

   Whole: Half:

(2) On the staff below, write four quarter rests, then four eighth rests.

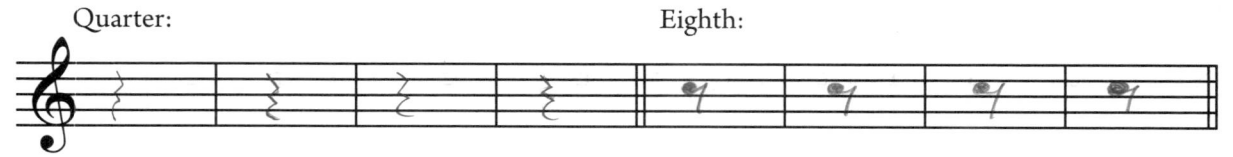

   Quarter: Eighth:

(3) Following each note, write a corresponding rest of the same duration.

Workbook ASSIGNMENT 3.3

A. Counting rhythms with quarter-note beats and rests

Write the counts (1 & 2 &) beneath each rhythm and melody below. Put the counts that occur during sustained notes or rests in parentheses.

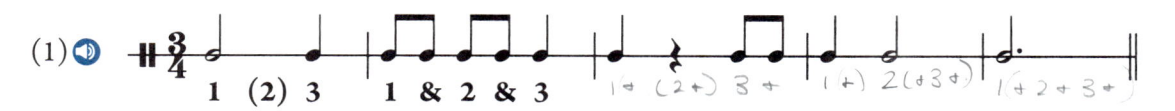

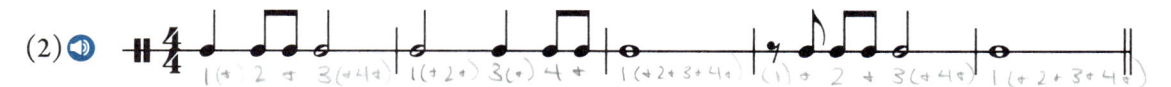

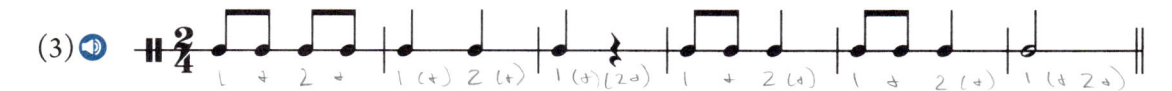

(1) [rhythm in 3/4]
1 (2) 3   1 & 2 & 3   1 + (2+) 3 +   1 (+) 2 (+ 3 +)   1 (+ 2 + 3 +)

(2) [rhythm in 4/4]
1 (+) 2 + 3 (+ 4 +)   1 (+ 2 +) 3 (+) 4 +   1 (+ 2 + 3 + 4 +)   (1) + 2 + 3 (+ 4 +)   1 (+ 2 + 3 + 4 +)

(3) [rhythm in 2/4]
1 + 2 +   1 (+) 2 (+)   1 (+) (2 +)   1 + 2 (+)   1 + 2 (+)   1 (+ 2 +)

(4) Lionel Richie, "Three Times a Lady," mm. 11–14

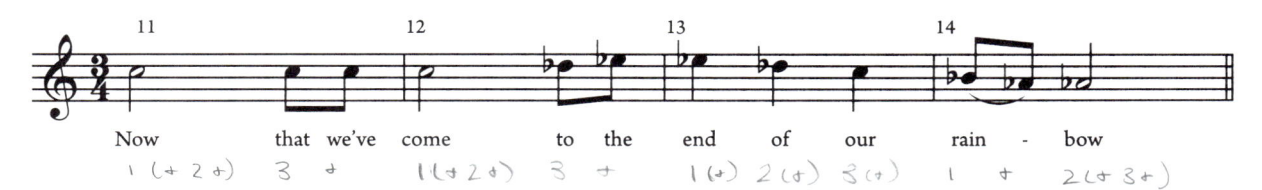

Now   that we've come   to the   end   of   our   rain - bow
1 (+ 2 +)   3   +   1 (+ 2 +)   3   +   1 (+) 2 (+) 3 (+)   1   +   2 (+ 3 +)

(5) Bono and U2, "Miracle Drug," mm. 29–32 (the last measure is incomplete)

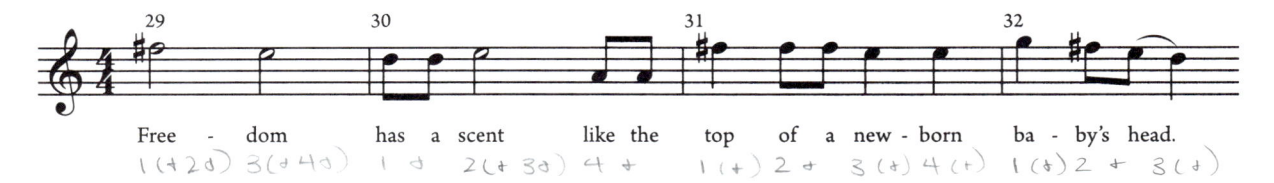

Free - dom   has a scent   like the   top   of a new - born   ba - by's head.
1 (+ 2 +) 3 (+ 4 +)   1   +   2 (+ 3 +)   4   +   1 (+) 2 + 3 (+) 4 (+)   1 (+) 2 + 3 (+)

(6) Richard Rogers and Oscar Hammerstein, "If I Loved You," from *Carousel*, mm. 5–11

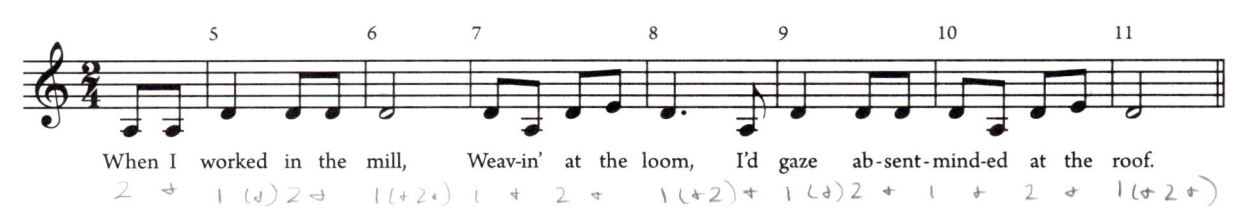

When I   worked in the mill,   Weav-in' at the loom,   I'd gaze   ab-sent-mind-ed at the roof.
2 +   1 (+) 2 +   1 (+ 2 +)   1 + 2 +   1 (+ 2) +   1 (+) 2 +   1 + 2 +   1 (+ 2 +)

B. Counting rhythms with half- and eighth-note beats

For each rhythm, provide the missing bar lines that correspond with the meter signature given. Then add the counts below.

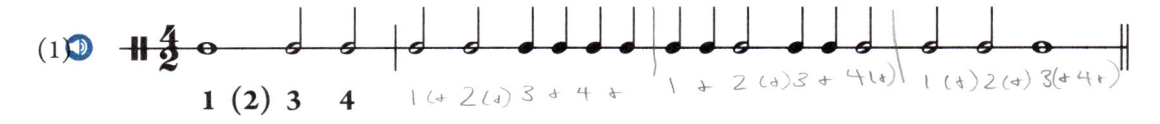

(1) [rhythm in 4/2]
1 (2) 3   4   1 + 2 (+) 3 + 4 +   1 + 2 (+) 3 + 4 (+)   1 (+) 2 (+) 3 (+ 4 +)

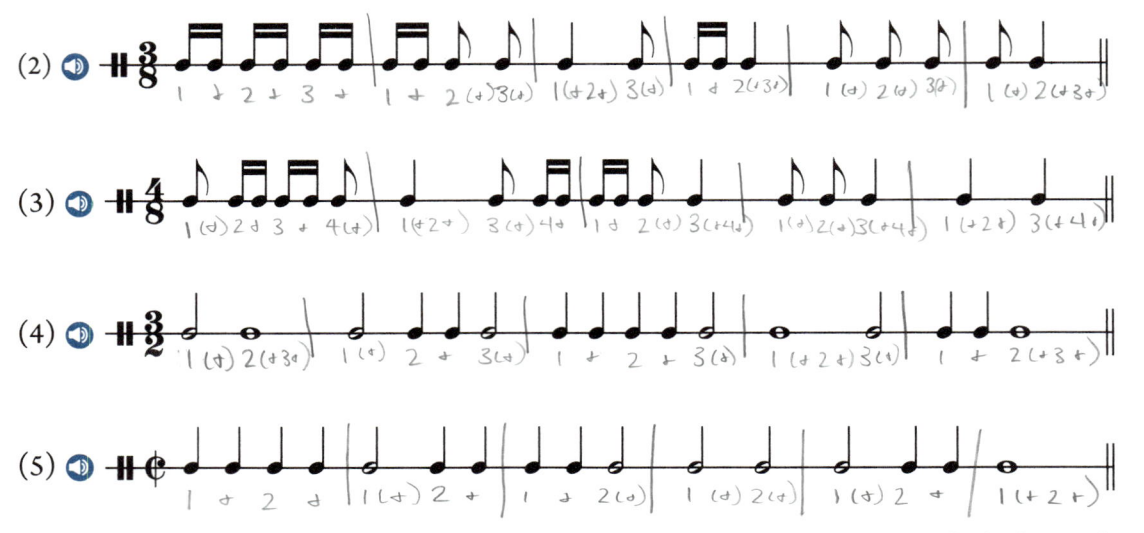

Rewrite each of the following rhythms on the line below it in the new meter specified. The resulting rhythm should sound the same as the original. Add the proper counts beneath the rhythm you have written.

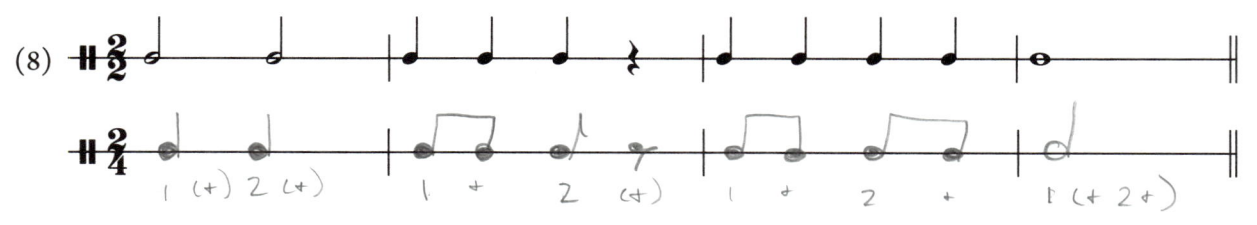

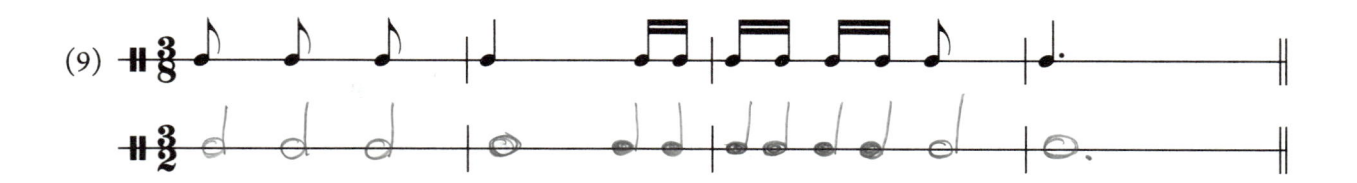

NAME _____

Workbook AURAL SKILLS 3.1

A. Hearing simple meters

Listen to the beginning of each of the following pieces. Focus on the grouping of the beats to decide whether the meter is simple duple, triple, or quadruple. Try conducting along as you listen. Write the meter type in the blank.

(1) Bach, "O Haupt voll Blut und Wunden" _____

(2) Joplin, "Solace" _____

(3) Schubert, Waltz in B Minor _____

(4) Beethoven, *Pathétique* Sonata, second movement _____

B. Listening to and writing a simple-meter rhythm

Listen to an English folk round, and complete the following exercises.

(1) Focus on the rhythm of this melody.

- Tap the beat with your foot. Then sing the melody from memory on "la." Keep a steady tempo, even if it is slower than the recording.
- Tap the beat with your foot and its divisions with your left hand. Then sing the melody from memory while tapping.
- Conduct the beats. When you are comfortable conducting, sing the melody from memory. As you sing, imagine the beat divisions to keep your rhythm precise.

(2) On the staff below, notate only the rhythm with the correct note values.

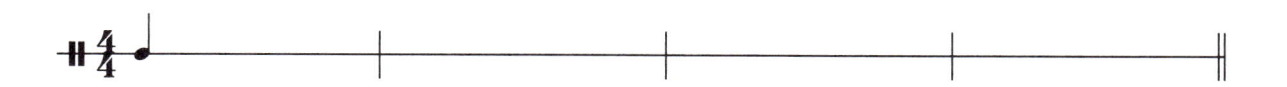

(3) On the staff below, notate the rhythm again, this time in $\frac{4}{8}$.

C. Writing a rhythmic composition

Write a four-measure rhythmic duet in which the top part speaks the word "yes" and the bottom part says "no," in a musical argument. Use the sample composition as a model. Write durations and rests so that the two words always begin on a different beat or part of the beat, never together. Be ready to perform with a partner, or have the entire class read your composition as a musical argument. In performance, slowly *crescendo* to the final measure.

Sample

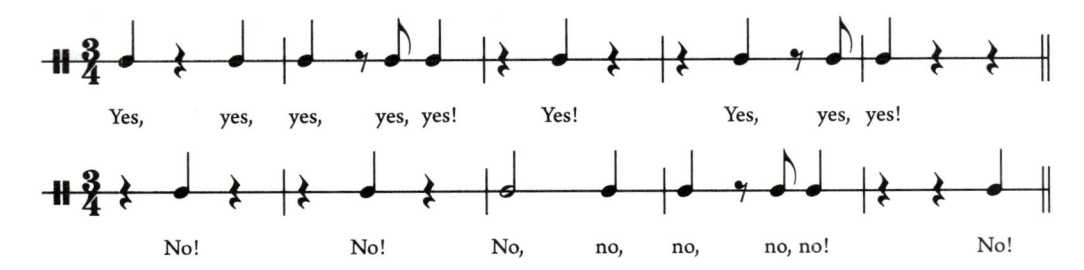

Yes, yes, yes, yes, yes! Yes! Yes, yes, yes!

No! No! No, no, no, no, no! No!

Space to work out your ideas

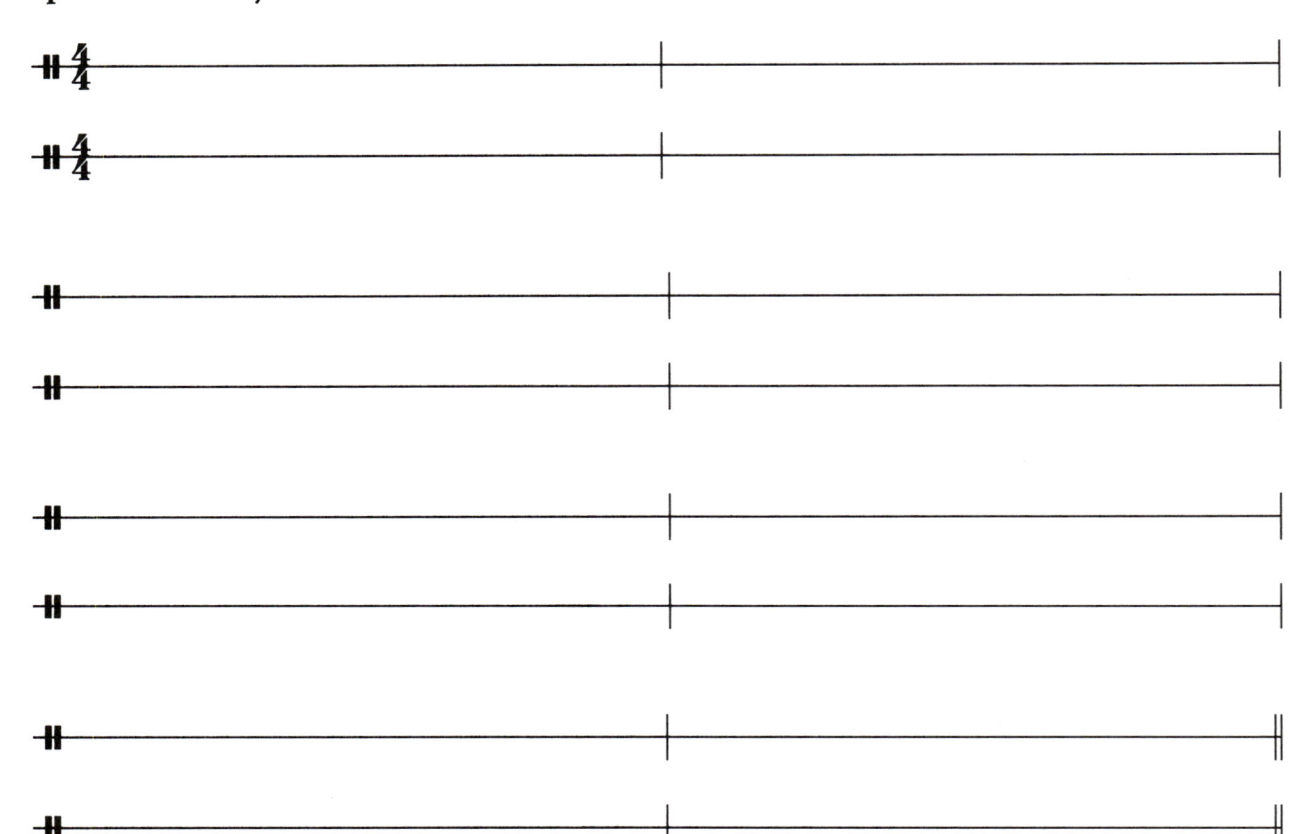

Final composition

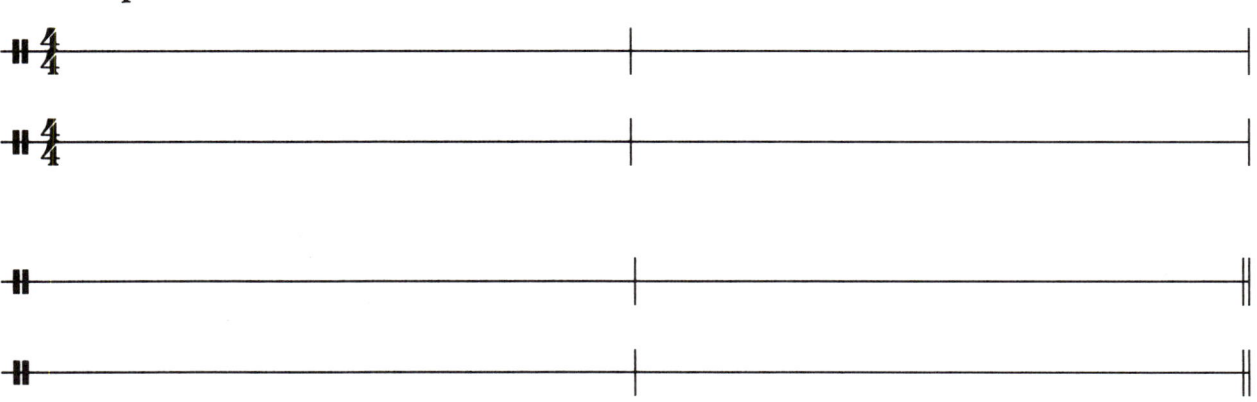

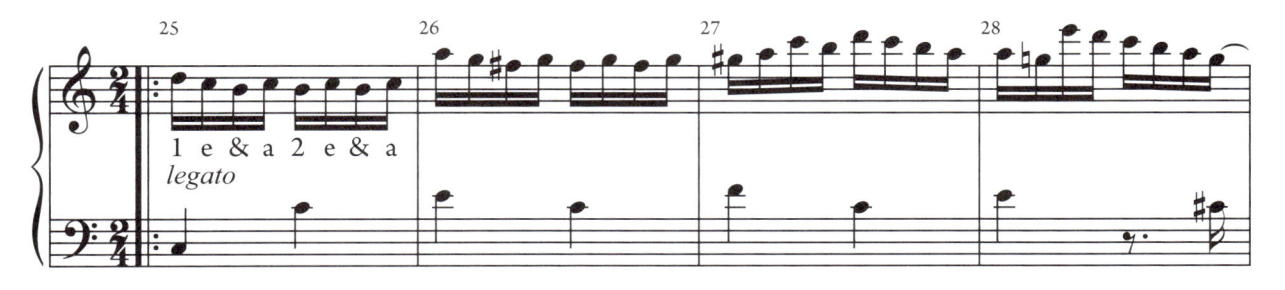

TOPICS

- beat subdivisions
- ties and slurs
- syncopation
- triplets
- rhythmic variations in performance

MUSIC

- Scott Joplin, "Pine Apple Rag"
- Joplin, "Solace"
- John Kander, Theme from *New York, New York*
- Jerome Kern, "Look for the Silver Lining"
- Don McLean, "American Pie"
- Wolfgang Amadeus Mozart, Variations on *"Ah, vous dirai-je, Maman"*
- John Newton, "Amazing Grace"
- Dolly Parton, "I Will Always Love You"
- Brian Wilson and Mike Love, "Girls on the Beach"

CHAPTER 4

Beat Subdivisions and Syncopation

Beat Subdivisions

Listen to an excerpt from Mozart's Variations on *"Ah, vous dirai-je, Maman,"* following the score in Example 4.1. The left-hand melody (in the bass clef) moves primarily in quarter notes with a few eighth notes at the end of the excerpt. These durations represent the beat and beat divisions of this simple duple meter. The sixteenth notes in the right hand represent the **beat subdivision**—counted 1 e & a, as labeled in the example.

EXAMPLE 4.1   Mozart, Variations on *"Ah, vous dirai-je, Maman,"* Var. I, mm. 25–32

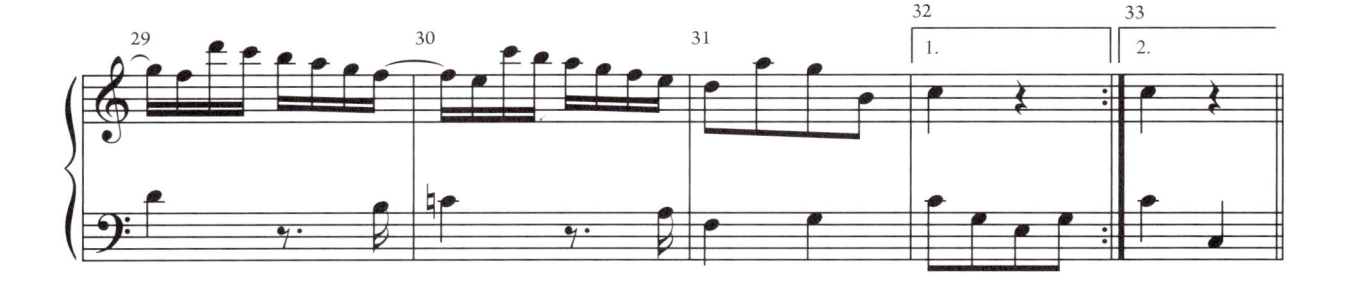

73

> **KEY CONCEPT** In simple meters, the beat divides into twos and subdivides into fours. A ♩ beat, for example, divides ♫ and subdivides into ♬♬ (or a combination, such as ♩♬).

There are only seven basic rhythmic patterns made from divisions and subdivisions of a quarter-note beat; all are shown in Figure 4.1 with counts written underneath. These patterns can be combined and recombined in many ways to create interesting and varied rhythms. Patterns 6 and 7 include dotted-eighth notes: since these last as long as three sixteenth notes, they are paired with a sixteenth note to complete the beat. A rest may be substituted for any duration in the following patterns; some examples are given in Figure 4.2.

FIGURE 4.1 Rhythmic patterns for one quarter-note beat

1
1 &

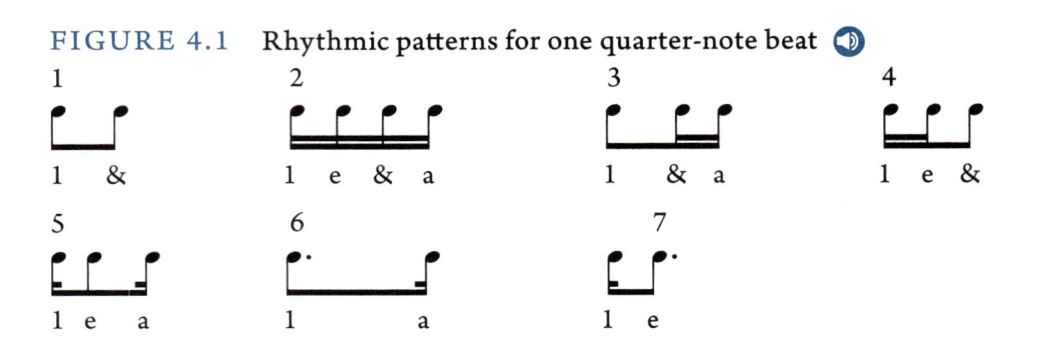

2
1 e & a

3
1 & a

4
1 e &

5
1 e a

6
1 a

7
1 e

FIGURE 4.2 Quarter-note beat patterns with rests

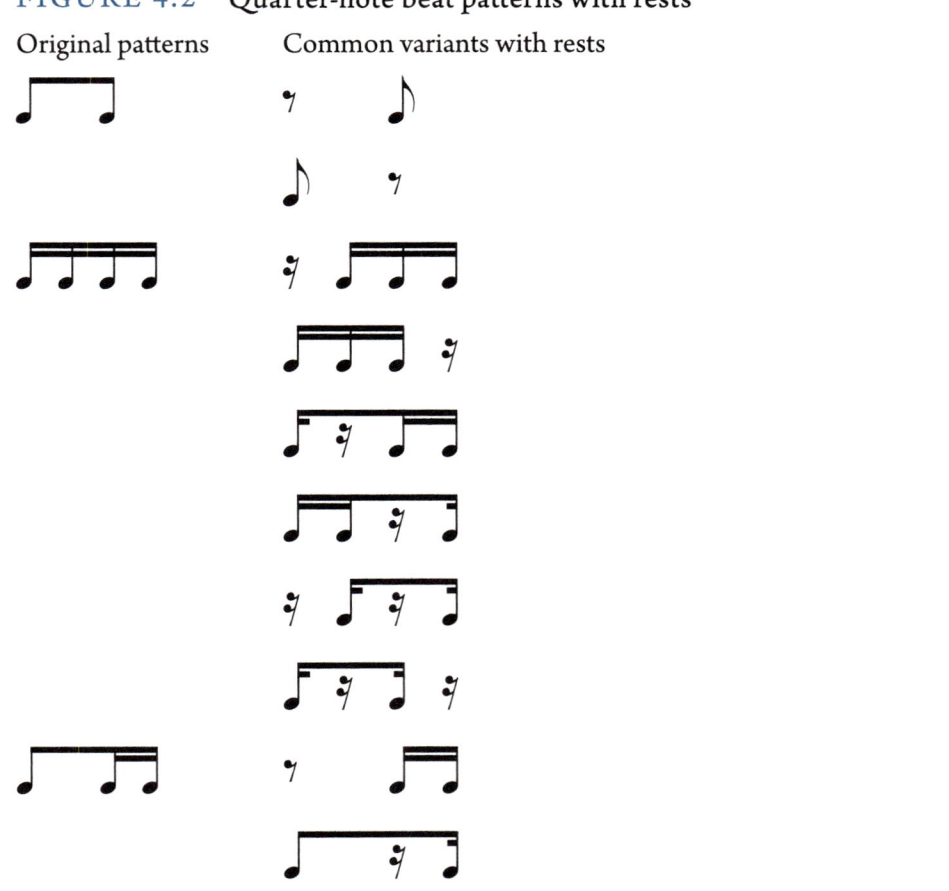

Original patterns   Common variants with rests

74   CHAPTER FOUR   Beat Subdivisions and Syncopation

Listen to the beginning of "Solace" while following the music in Example 4.2. Three of the seven patterns from Figure 4.1 appear in these measures. Locate the patterns, and write the counts underneath each one. In the last measure, which does not feature any of the seven patterns, the counts are written in for you.

EXAMPLE 4.2   Joplin, "Solace," mm. 1–4

KEY CONCEPT The beaming of rhythmic patterns should reflect the beat units, as in Example 4.2. Notes that sound within the same beat should be beamed together. Do not beam across the beat.

Example 4.3 shows incorrect beaming, and illustrates how correcting the notation clarifies the beat units.

EXAMPLE 4.3   Beaming to reflect the quarter-note and half-note beat unit
(a) Incorrect

Correct

1   2   3   &   4 e & a   1 e &   2   &   3 e & a   4

(b) Incorrect

Correct

1 (2) &   3   &   1 e & a 2   3   &   1   & a 2 e & a 3

Beat Subdivisions   75

Ties and Slurs

Another passage from "Solace," shown in Example 4.4, illustrates an element of rhythmic notation we have not yet considered: the tie.

> **KEY CONCEPT** **Ties** are small arcs connecting the note heads of two identical pitches, which may have the same or different durations. A tie makes the first note sound as long as the two notes' durations added together; the second note is not played separately. If an accidental is applied to the first note of a tie, it continues through the tie's duration.

In the right-hand part of measure 5, Joplin ties the final sixteenth note G4 of beat 1 to the first G4 of beat 2; similar ties are found in measures 6 and 7. When ties extend across a beat, as here, write the "silent" count in parentheses to remember where the beat comes, even if no new note sounds on it. Do the same for dots that extend across a beat.

EXAMPLE 4.4 Joplin, "Solace," mm. 5–8

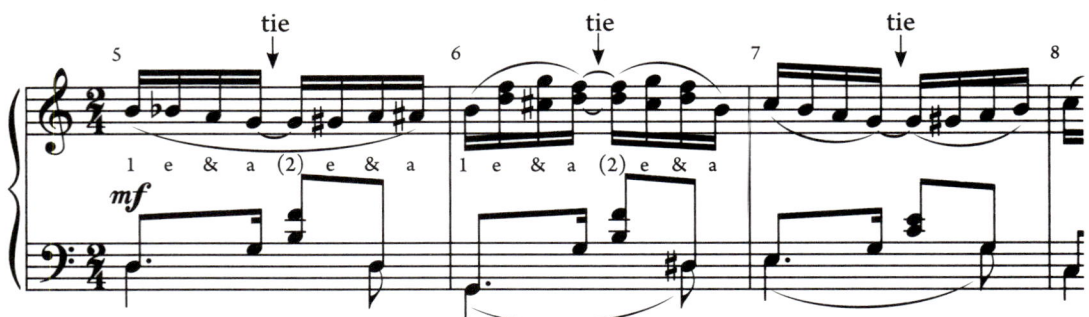

Every measure of Example 4.4 also includes arcs that connect two or more *different* pitches. These lines are called **slurs**. They affect **articulation** by showing how to bow a stringed instrument or tongue a wind or brass instrument, for example, but they don't change the duration of the pitches. In piano music, they tell the performer to play the slurred notes smoothly (or legato); in vocal music, the slurred notes are sung on one syllable or in one breath.

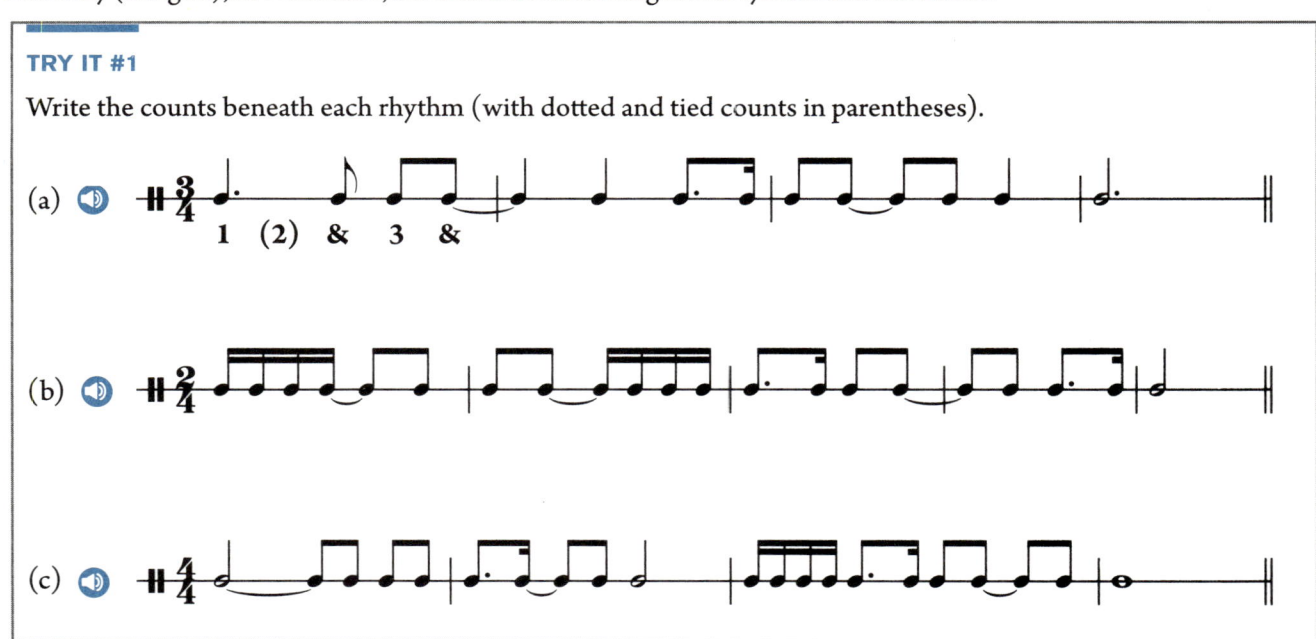

> **TRY IT #1**
>
> Write the counts beneath each rhythm (with dotted and tied counts in parentheses).
>
> (a) 1 (2) & 3 &
>
> (b)
>
> (c)

ASSIGNMENT 4.1

76 CHAPTER FOUR Beat Subdivisions and Syncopation

Syncopation

Look at Example 4.5, in cut time (¢), and tap the rhythm, using the counts underneath (think 1 e & a 2 e & a). This rhythm, one of the *clave* patterns from Afro-Cuban music, has been incorporated into many other popular styles. After the first note, all the notes are off the beat until the last one, which falls on beat 2.

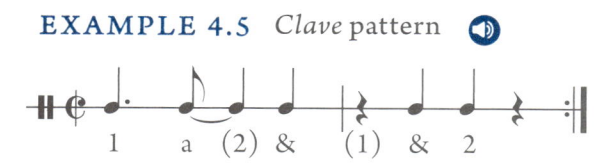

EXAMPLE 4.5 *Clave* pattern

> **KEY CONCEPT** **Syncopations** are created when an expected accent is displaced—moved to another beat or part of a beat by dots, ties, rests, dynamic markings, or accent marks.

We've already seen two syncopated rhythm patterns (5 and 7) in Figure 4.1 (both reproduced in Figure 4.3). In each, the longest duration of the rhythm is on the "e" of 1 e & a instead of the stronger (expected) 1 or &. Other types of syncopation are shown by the arrows in Example 4.6.

FIGURE 4.3 Syncopated patterns within a quarter-note beat

EXAMPLE 4.6 Types of syncopated rhythms

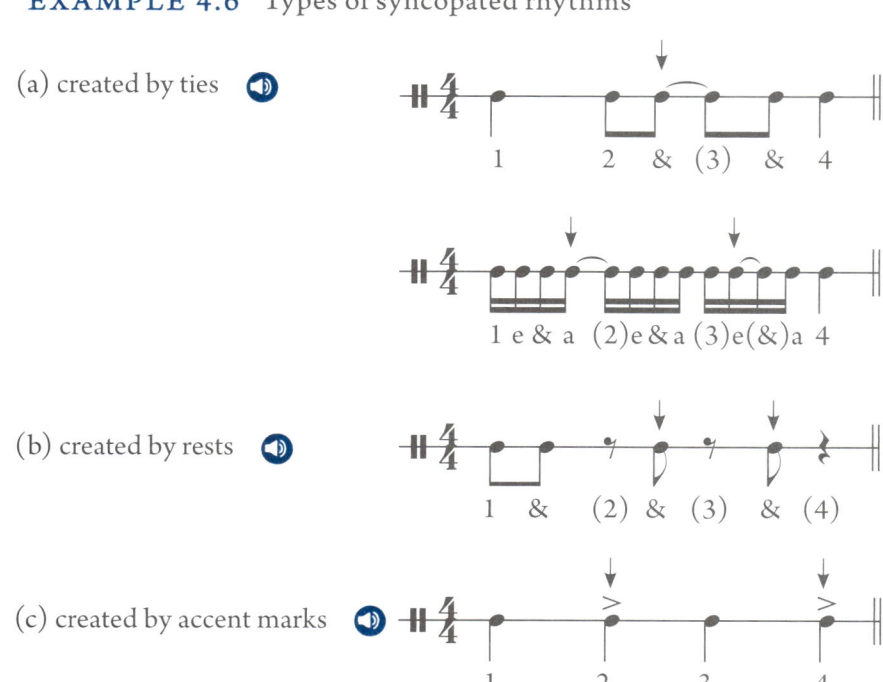

(a) created by ties

(b) created by rests

(c) created by accent marks

In Example 4.7, the arrows mark syncopations within the beat in measures 1 and 3 and across the beat in measures 2 and 4. Syncopations across the beat are usually notated with ties, like those in measures 2 and 4; here, the expected accent on beat 2 comes earlier, on the first of the tied notes.

EXAMPLE 4.7   Joplin, "Pine Apple Rag," mm. 1–4

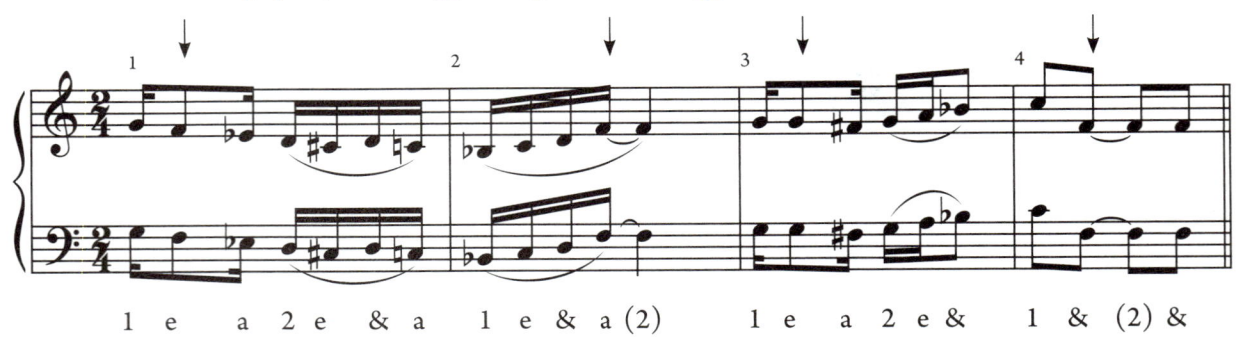

```
1 e   a 2 e  & a    1 e & a (2)     1 e   a 2 e &     1 &  (2) &
```

In Example 4.8, from "American Pie," the syncopations span two beats in 4/4 meter. The ♪ ♩ ♪ rhythm, counted "1 & (2) &" in measure 31, is a rhythmic **augmentation** of the ♫ ♫ pattern, counted "1 e a," in measure 1 of the Joplin rag. An augmentation lengthens the durations of a rhythm, often by doubling them, as here. The last syncopation in measure 31 is created by the entrance of the word "love" on the offbeat.

EXAMPLE 4.8   McLean, "American Pie," mm. 30–31

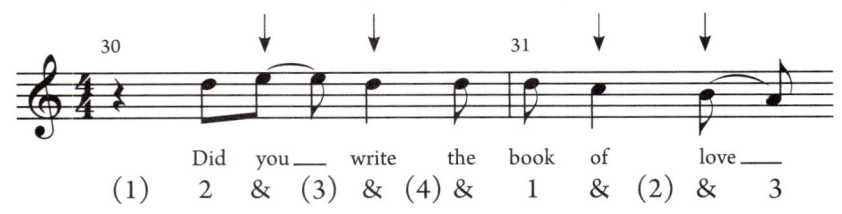

```
        Did  you    write   the   book   of        love
   (1)   2    &    (3)  &   (4)  &    1    &   (2)  &    3
```

Syncopations require a strong sense of the underlying beat for the displaced accents to play against. When you read music with syncopations, look first for the common patterns, and use the counting syllables to count any unfamiliar ones. When performing, tap the steady beat to feel the metrical displacement of the syncopation.

> **TRY IT #2**
>
> The rhythm below is drawn from measures 9–12 of Joplin's "Solace." Write the counts beneath, and mark each syncopation with an arrow. All arrows should line up with e or a of the 1 e & a pattern. Perform the rhythm aloud.
>
> 1 e & a

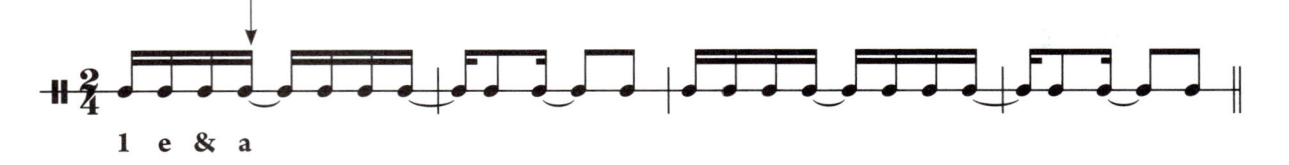

ASSIGNMENT 4.2

Triplets

In simple meters, it is possible to divide a beat into three parts instead of the usual two.

> **KEY CONCEPT** A **triplet** is a three-part division of the beat in a simple-meter piece.

Example 4.9 shows a passage from "Girls on the Beach." The piece is in $\frac{4}{4}$ meter, but in measures 11–12, three eighths are beamed together with a small 3 above the beam (♫). This indicates that three eighth notes make up the beat instead of two. We count the triplet "1 la li" to emphasize the even division into three parts, and to avoid confusing it with the counts for division in two or four parts.

EXAMPLE 4.9   Wilson and Love, "Girls on the Beach" mm. 11–14

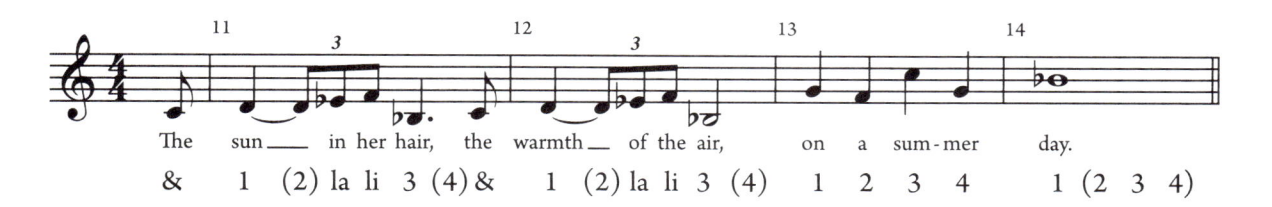

The	sun	in her hair,	the	warmth	of the air,	on	a	sum-mer	day.
&	1 (2) la li 3 (4)	&	1 (2) la li 3 (4)	1 2 3 4	1 (2 3 4)

You may also see triplets consisting of an eighth note and a quarter note (♪ ♩). The quarter substitutes for two eighths and is counted "1 la." The reverse (♩ ♪) is counted "1 li." Figure 4.4 summarizes the possibilities.

FIGURE 4.4   Notation of triplet divisions

Duration	Normal division	Triplet notation
♪	♫	♬♪ ♪♫ ♫♪
♩	♫	♬ ♩♪ ♪♩
𝅗𝅥	♩ ♩	♩♩♩ ♩𝅗𝅥 𝅗𝅥♩
𝅝	𝅗𝅥 𝅗𝅥	𝅗𝅥𝅗𝅥𝅗𝅥 𝅝 𝅗𝅥 𝅗𝅥 𝅝
1	1 &	1 la li 1 li 1 la

In popular songs notated in $\frac{4}{4}$, you may encounter triplet patterns notated with quarter notes, as in Example 4.10. Because this type of triplet pattern spans two beats of the notated meter, these are called **two-beat triplets**. To count these triplets, you might imagine the passage in cut time, with the half note as the beat unit. Measure 22 of Example 4.10 would be counted as 1 la li 2 &.

Triplets   79

EXAMPLE 4.10   Kander, Theme from *New York, New York*, mm. 20–23

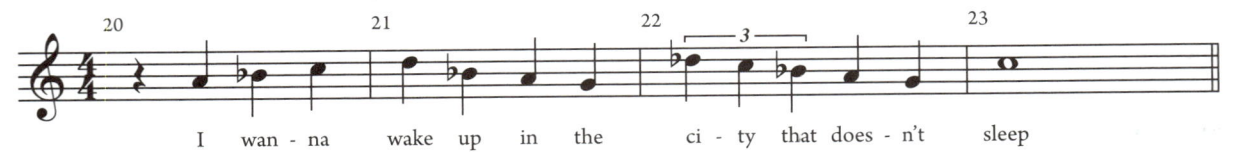

I wan - na wake up in the ci - ty that does - n't sleep

Rhythmic Variations in Performance

Blues, gospel, jazz, Broadway show tunes, and many other forms of popular music gain much of their character through their distinctive rhythm. A jazz improviser, for example, might take a simple but memorable melody and "jazz it up" by adding embellishments in rhythm and pitch. Gospel performance may also feature improvisation, and the pitches and rhythms you see on the score may differ substantially from what you hear. Listen to two versions of "Amazing Grace," while following the melody in your anthology (p. 386). In one performance, a verse sung by unaccompanied voice is followed by two verses with guitar. This arrangement is folklike in its simplicity, and the singer performs the melody as shown in the score. In contrast, the other performance, by a lower voice and piano, is highly embellished. The singer freely improvises on the tune with additional pitches, variations in the rhythm, and repeated text to create a performance that is uniquely her own, while the pianist improvises an accompaniment to match.

> **KEY CONCEPT** In another common rhythmic variation, known as **swung eighths**, the score shows pairs of eighth notes in simple meter, but the performer plays or sings them unevenly, holding on to the first eighth a little too long and bringing in the second one after the &—as if they were notated as triplets.

In jazz standards, such as "Look for the Silver Lining," shown in Example 4.11, rhythms notated in eighth notes may be performed swung, though performers may introduce other rhythmic variations as well. The exact lengths of swung eighth notes can vary; in a transcription (a score notated from a recorded performance), they may be notated as even eighth notes with the performance instruction "swung" or with triplet or dotted notation.

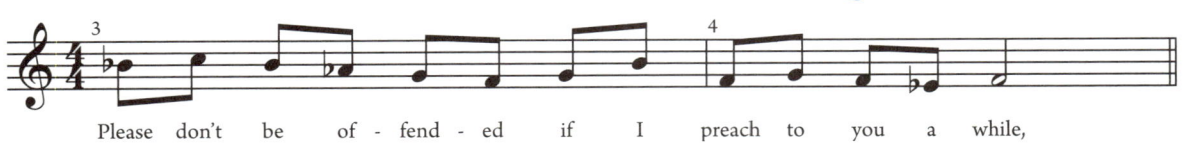

EXAMPLE 4.11   Kern, "Look for the Silver Lining," mm. 3–4

Please don't be of - fend - ed if I preach to you a while,

> **TRY IT #3**
>
> Listen again to Example 4.11 and notate the swung eighths using triplets.

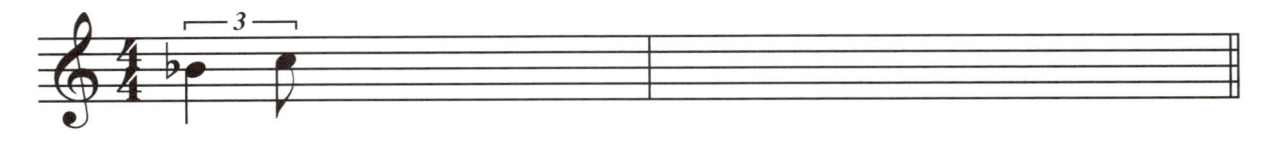

80   CHAPTER FOUR   Beat Subdivisions and Syncopation

When you compose songs of your own, you might first create a simple melodic line with a basic rhythm, and then vary it—for example, delay a pitch or pull it ahead of the beat to make syncopations, or use triplets. When you analyze rhythmically elaborate music, be alert for the underlying simpler framework, and consider how the composer took something basic and made it memorable.

ASSIGNMENT 4.3, AURAL SKILLS 4.1

Did You Know?

Popular music includes many more syncopations than classical music. Syncopated and embellished melodies may imply a simpler underlying tune. Compare two published versions of a passage from "I Will Always Love You," shown below. The first represents the melody as sung by Dolly Parton, who composed this song; the second is a simpler version of the melody. For example, in Dolly's performance (a), she sings the word "I'll" early in measure 6, making it syncopated (coming in on the & of beat 3); in the simpler version (b), the same word lands squarely on beat 4. Parton also adds many embellishments that alternate between two pitches, such as in measure 8, and other variants intensifying the emotional expression of her performance. If you like, listen to Dolly Parton's performance and to another performance by Whitney Houston to compare how each embellishes the underlying simpler melodic outline.

Dolly Parton, "I Will Always Love You," mm. 7–8

(a) Published version 1:

I'll think of you ev-'ry step of the way.

(b) Published version 2:

I'll think of you each step of the way.

Terms You Should Know

articulation	slur	tie
augmentation	swung eighths	triplet
beat subdivision	syncopation	two-beat triplet

Questions for Review

1. What is the difference between a beat division and a beat subdivision?
2. Write seven rhythmic patterns that fill one quarter-note beat unit in simple meter.
3. If the beat unit is a half note, what note values represent the beat division and subdivision?
4. In simple meter, what note value is generally paired with a dotted quarter to fill out the beat? What note value is generally paired with a dotted eighth?
5. What guidelines are used to determine which notes to beam together?
6. What types of rhythmic patterns make syncopations?
7. How is a tie different from a slur?
8. How do you represent a three-part division of a beat in simple meters?
9. What note values represent a triplet division of a quarter-note beat unit? of a half-note beat unit?

Reading Review

Match the term on the left with the best answer on the right.

_____ (1) ♫♫♫♫   (a) arc connecting the note heads of two identical pitches

_____ (2) tie   (b) arc connecting two or more different pitches

_____ (3) slur   (c) subdivision of a quarter-note beat

_____ (4) 1 e & a   (d) counting syllables for a common syncopation pattern

_____ (5) syncopation   (e) division of a quarter-note beat

_____ (6) ♫ ♩   (f) counting syllables for a subdivided beat

_____ (7) triplet   (g) counting syllables for a triplet

_____ (8) 1 e a   (h) rhythmic displacement of accents

_____ (9) 1 la li   (i) beat division into three parts in simple meter

Additional review and practice available at wwnorton.com/studyspace

Apply It

A. Reading rhythms

Perform the rhythms below on "ta" or counting syllables, as directed. Keep a steady beat by tapping the pulse or conducting, and follow the dynamic markings. Your teacher may ask you to write the counts below the rhythms.

Rhythm 1

Rhythm 2

Rhythm 3

Rhythm 4

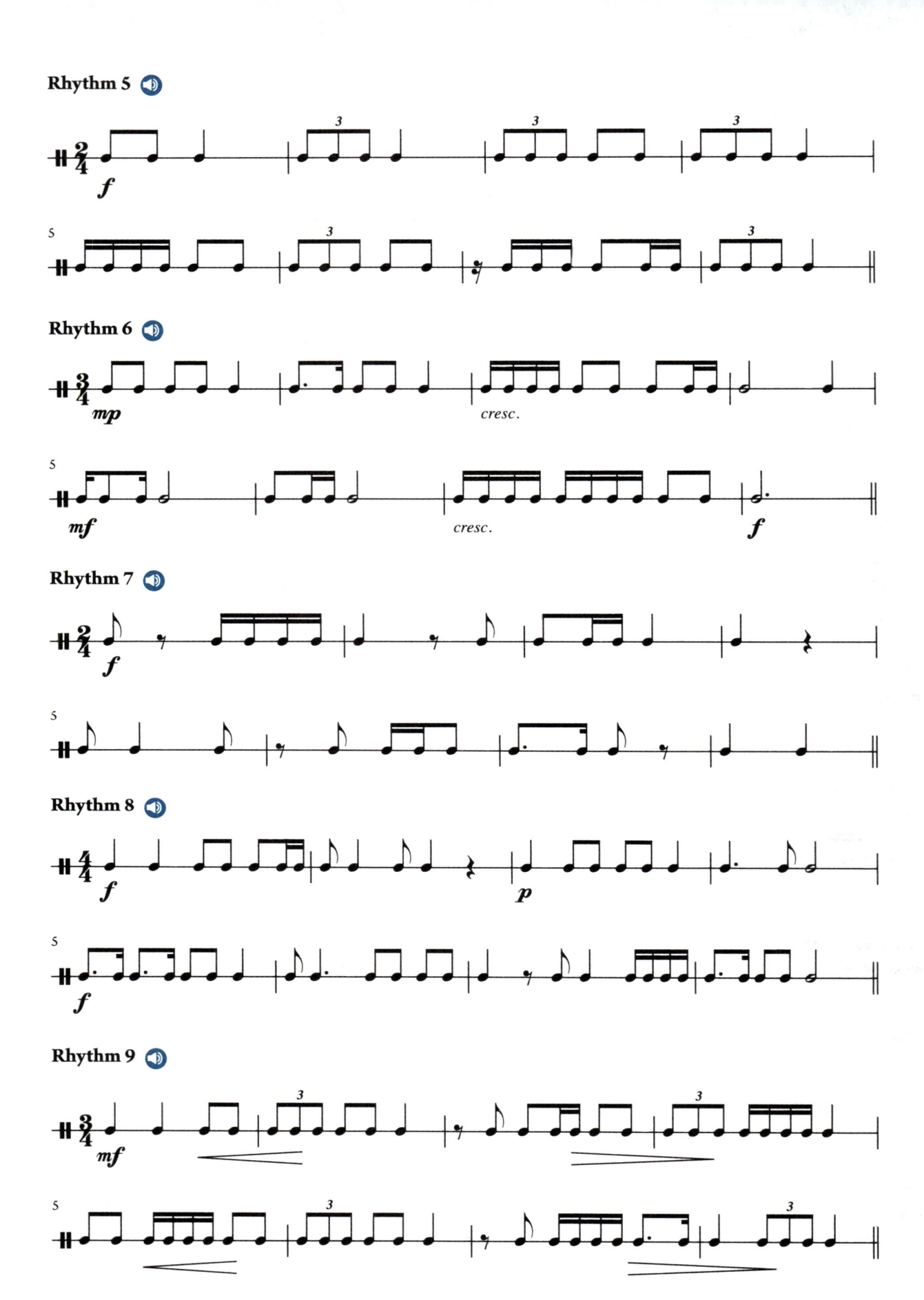

Rhythm 5

Rhythm 6

Rhythm 7

Rhythm 8

Rhythm 9

84 CHAPTER FOUR Beat Subdivisions and Syncopation

B. Rhythmic duets

Prepare each line of these duets. Perform them in class in groups with two different sounds (men vs. women, taps vs. claps, no vs. yes, etc.) so that the interplay between lines can be heard. Observe all dynamic markings. On your own, you can perform one part along with the recording of the other.

Duet 1

Duet 2

C. At the keyboard: Playing and singing melodies with triplets

For each melody:

- Practice the warm-up on the piano with your right hand. Begin with the thumb on the first note and use each finger. Play 1–2–3–4–5 ascending and descending, and sing along on "la." You can also warm up on the Virtual Keyboard.
- Practice just the rhythm of the melody on "ta" while tapping the beat (or conducting). Then practice just the pitches on the keyboard (don't worry about fingering for now).
- Sing the melody on the numbers given underneath at a slow tempo, then at a faster tempo. Play the melody at a keyboard at a slow tempo, then at a faster tempo.

Warm-up

Melody 1

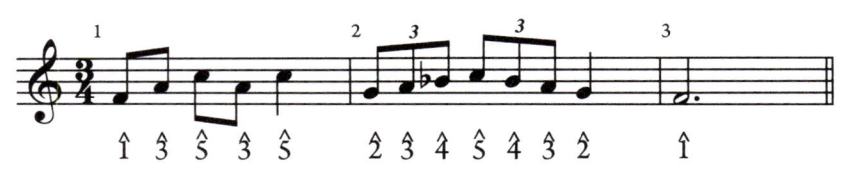

Warm-up

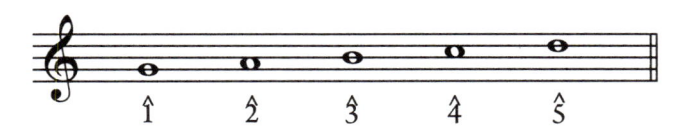

Melody 2

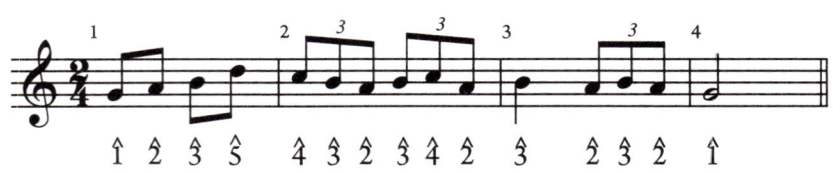

CHAPTER FOUR Beat Subdivisions and Syncopation

Warm-up 🔊

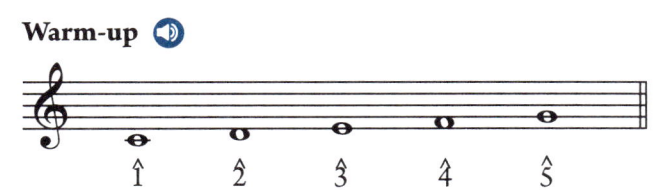

Melody 3 Alan Jay Lerner and Frederick Loewe, "Wand'rin' Star," from *Paint Your Wagon* (adapted), mm. 1–8

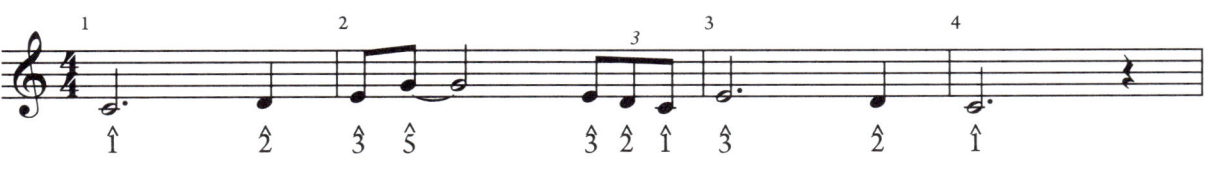

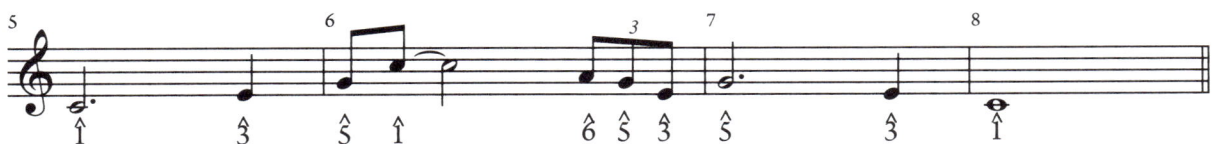

Warm-up 🔊

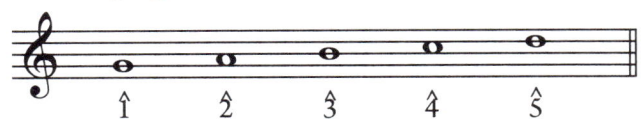

Melody 4 Clara Edwards, "Into the Night," mm. 3–6

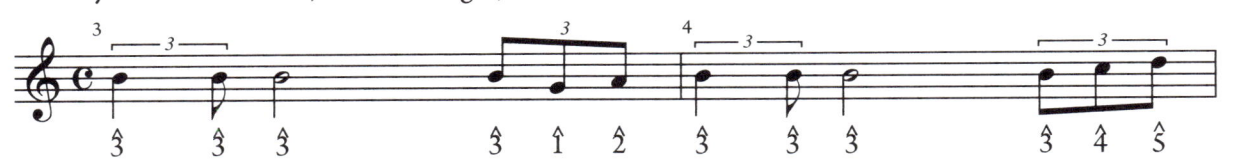

Warm-up 🔊

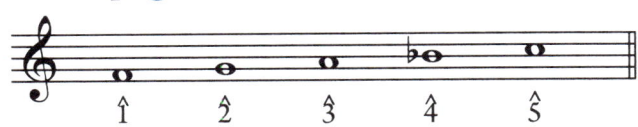

Melody 5 George David Weiss, Hugo Peretti, and Luigi Creatore, "Can't Help Falling in Love," from *Blue Hawaii*, mm. 5–12

D. Listening and writing

Listen to rhythms made of two patterns each from those numbered below. Sing or tap what you hear, then write it on the staff provided. 🔊

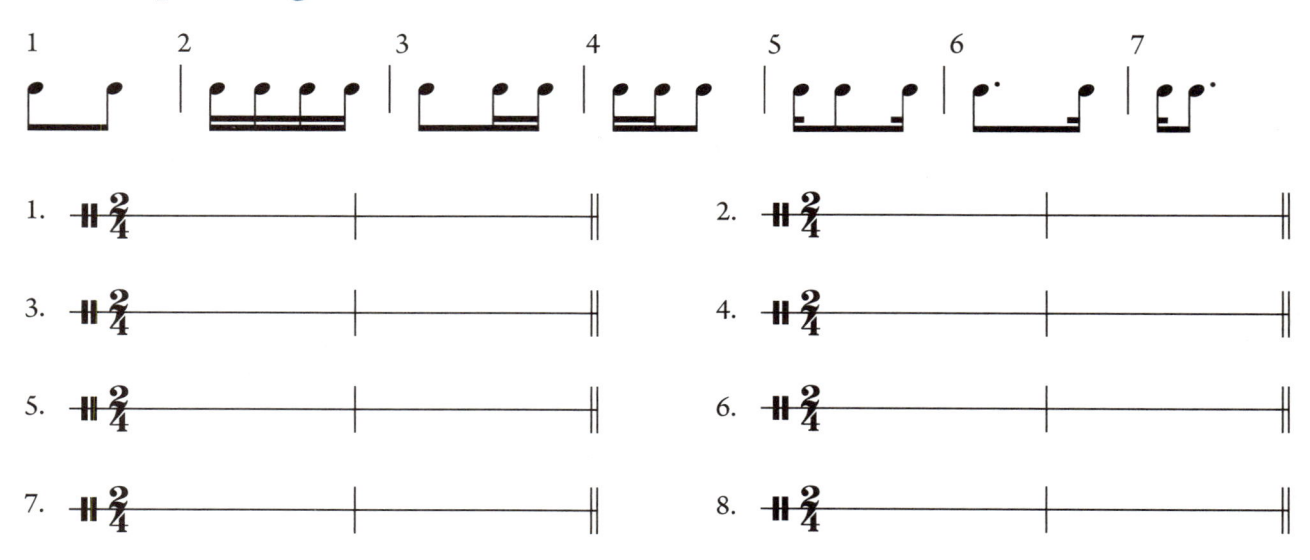

1. 2. 3. 4. 5. 6. 7.

1. 𝄽 2/4 ∣ ∥
2. 𝄽 2/4 ∣ ∥
3. 𝄽 2/4 ∣ ∥
4. 𝄽 2/4 ∣ ∥
5. 𝄽 2/4 ∣ ∥
6. 𝄽 2/4 ∣ ∥
7. 𝄽 2/4 ∣ ∥
8. 𝄽 2/4 ∣ ∥

Listen to the rhythms combined with pitches in the octave C to C. Sing what you hear, then write it on the staff provided. 🔊

9.
10.
11.
12.
13.
14.
15.

88 CHAPTER FOUR Beat Subdivisions and Syncopation

NAME _____

Workbook ASSIGNMENT 4.1

A. Dots and ties

For each rhythm below, provide the missing bar lines that correspond with the meter signature given.

(1) — (5) [rhythm exercises in 3/4, 4/4, 2/4, 4/4, 3/4]

Rewrite the following rhythms with dots in place of tied notes. Be careful to beam your answers correctly. Write the correct counts beneath the rewritten rhythm, then perform it.

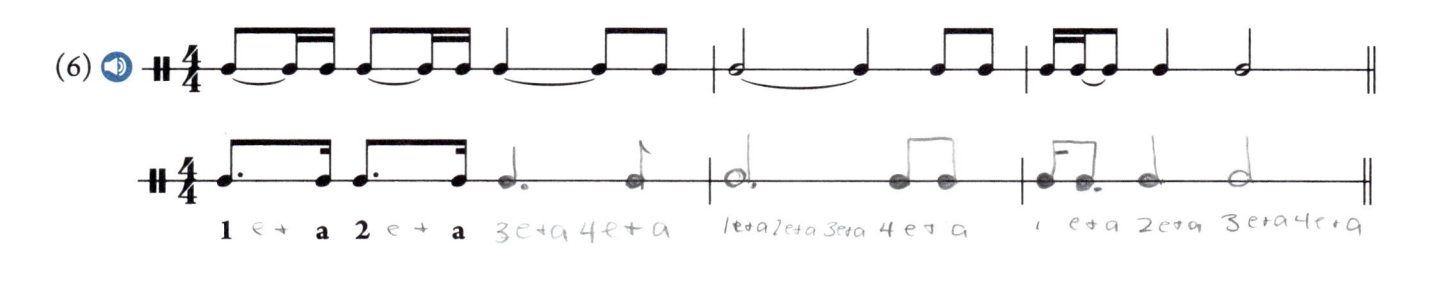

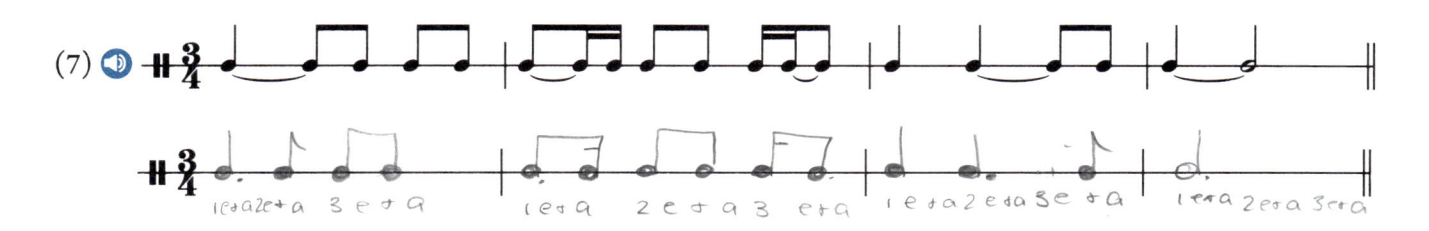

(6) [4/4 rhythm exercise]

Counts written: 1 e + a 2 e + a 3 e + a 4 e + a | 1 e + a 2 e + a 3 e + a 4 e + a | 1 e + a 2 e + a 3 e + a 4 e + a

(7) [3/4 rhythm exercise]

Counts written: 1 e + a 2 e + a 3 e + a | 1 e + a 2 e + a 3 e + a | 1 e + a 2 e + a 3 e + a | 1 e + a 2 e + a 3 e + a

Assignment 4.1   89

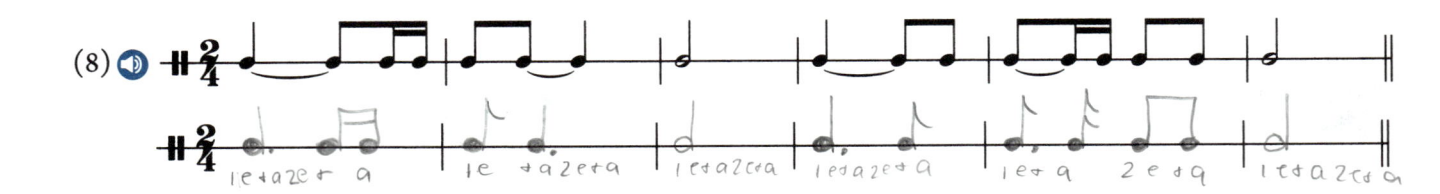

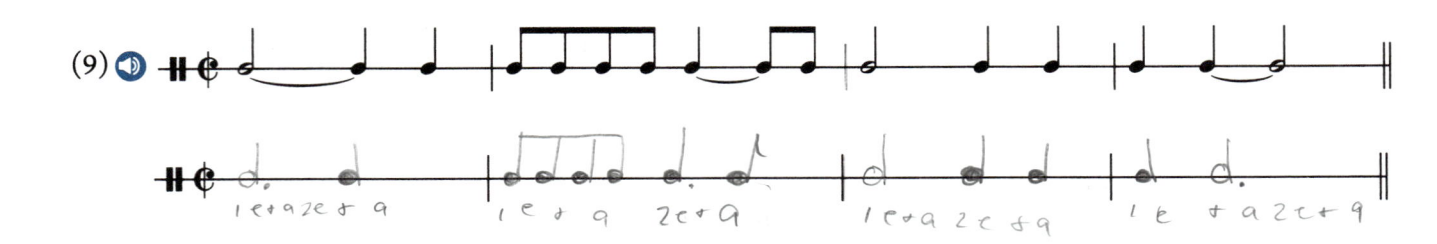

B. Beaming — Job of beaming is to break up notes into groups - belong to specific p...

Rewrite each of the following rhythms with correct beams to reflect the quarter-note beat unit. Add the proper counts beneath the rhythm and read the rhythm out loud on "ta" or with counting syllables.

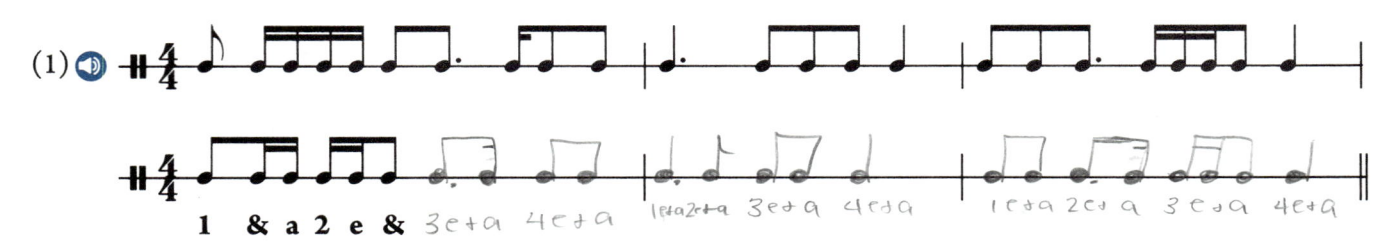

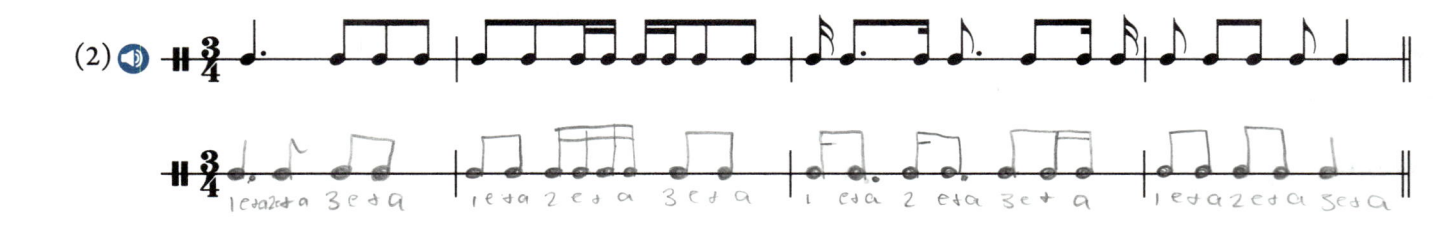

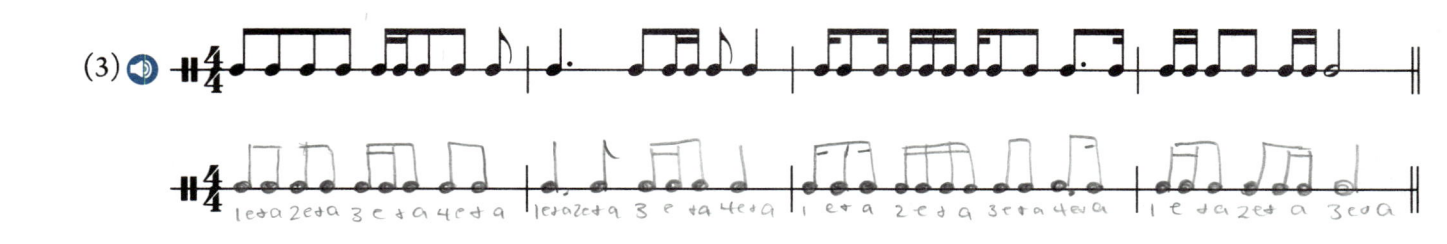

90 CHAPTER FOUR Beat Subdivisions and Syncopation

Workbook ASSIGNMENT 4.2

A. Rhythms with divisions, subdivisions, dots, and rests

For each rhythm below, provide the missing bar lines that correspond with the meter signature given.

At each arrow, add one note to complete the measure in the meter indicated. For now, don't worry about beaming guidelines.

B. Counting rhythms with dots, ties, and syncopations

In the melodies below, write the appropriate counts beneath the notes. (Note: The final measure of a melody may be incomplete.) Place an arrow above each syncopation.

(1) Joplin, "Solace," mm. 9–10

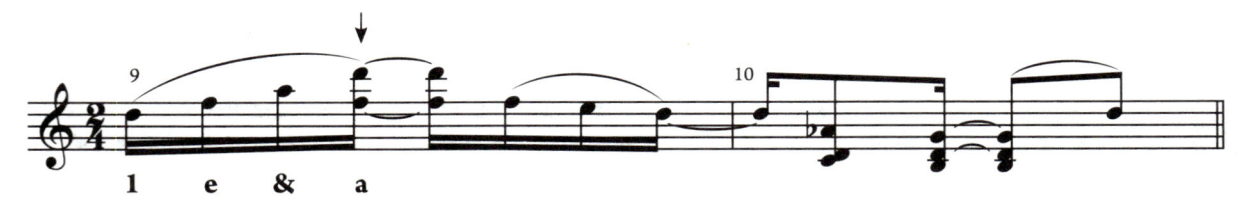

1   e   &   a

(2) Carole King, "You've Got a Friend," mm. 5–8

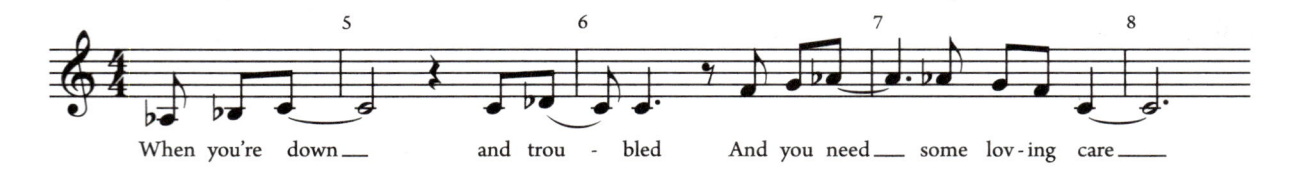

When you're down___ and trou-bled   And you need___ some lov-ing care___

(3) Antônio Carlos Jobim and Vinius de Moraes, "The Girl from Ipanema," mm. 13–19

When she walks, she's like___ a sam-ba that swings so cool and sways___ so gen-tle, that when

___ she pass-es, each one___ she pass-es goes "a-h-h!"

(4) Shania Twain, "You're Still the One," mm. 13–16

They said, "I bet___ they'll ne-ver make it." But just look at___ us hold-ing___ on.___

92   CHAPTER FOUR Beat Subdivisions and Syncopation

NAME _____

Workbook ASSIGNMENT 4.3

A. Syncopation and triplets

In each of the following examples, write an arrow above each syncopated rhythm. Then write in the appropriate counts below each rhythm.

(1) Frank Loesser, "Luck Be a Lady," from *Guys and Dolls,* mm. 3–6

They call you La - dy Luck but there is room for doubt At
    & 1 & 2 & 3 (4) &

times you have a ver - y un - la - dy like way of run - ning out.

(2) Jim Weatherly, "Midnight Train to Georgia" mm. 6–12

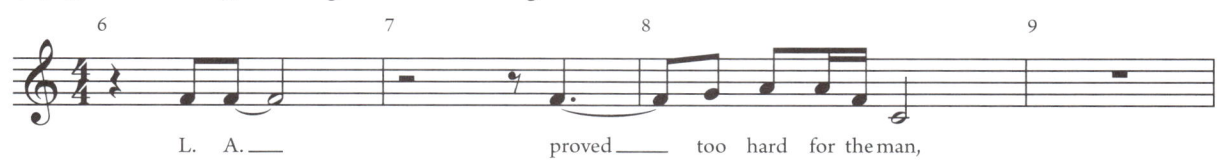

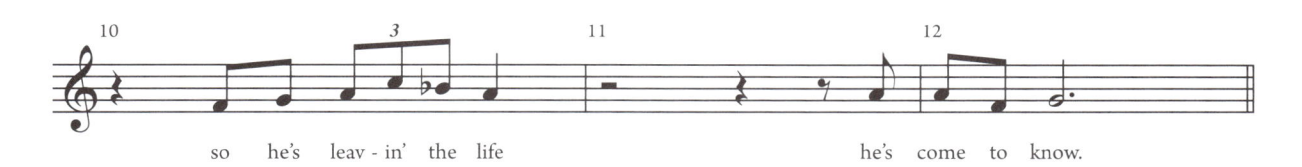

L. A. proved too hard for the man,

so he's leav - in' the life he's come to know.

B. Composition with dots, ties, and syncopations

Write a four-measure rhythm in $\frac{4}{4}$ that contains two syncopations (one using a tie), two dotted rhythms, and two rests.

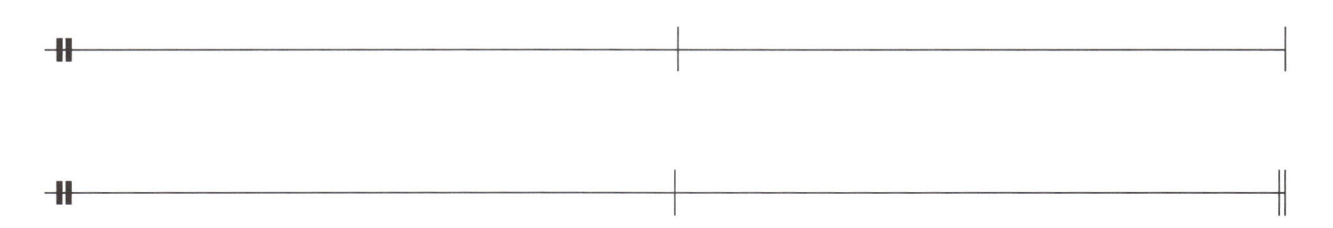

Assignment 4.3

C. Triplets

Supply the missing bar lines corresponding to the meter shown in each of the following rhythms.

At each arrow, add <u>one</u> note to complete any measure with too few beats. Write the counts beneath your answer, then perform the rhythm you have written.

Beneath (4): 1   (2) e & a 3   (4)   &

NAME _____

Workbook   AURAL SKILLS 4.1

A. Listening to and writing a melody with beat divisions

Listen to an excerpt from a piano sonata by Joseph Haydn and complete the exercises below. 🔊

(1) Focus on the rhythm of the higher part.
   - Tap the beat with your foot. Then sing the melody on a neutral syllable, such as "la." Keep a steady tempo, even if it is slower than the recorded performance.
   - Tap the beat with your foot and its divisions with your left hand. Sing the melody from memory on a neutral syllable as you tap.
   - Conduct the beats in duple meter. When comfortable conducting, sing the melody from memory. As you sing, imagine the beat divisions and subdivisions to keep your rhythm precise. Now conduct the beats in quadruple meter and sing as before.

(2) Notate the rhythm in quadruple meter.
   - On *each* staff below, draw a meter signature for common time.
   - On the treble staff, write a quarter-note anacrusis, then notate the rest of the melody's rhythm on any line or space. For divided or subdivided beats, beam notes to reflect the beat.
   - After the anacrusis, and then after every four beats, draw a bar line. On a grand staff, bar lines extend from the top line of the treble staff to the bottom line of the bass staff.

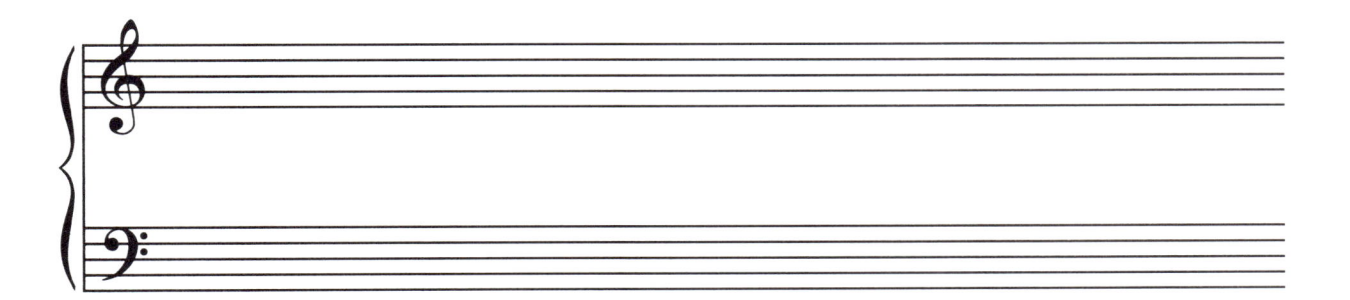

   - Now listen to the excerpt again, focusing on the rhythm of the lower part. On the bass staff, notate the rhythm of the lower part on any line or space. Vertically align notes in the bass and melody that sound at the same time. The bar lines will also help you to align the two parts.
   - Read your rhythmic notation. Tap the rhythm of the melody in one hand and the rhythm of the lower part in the other. Does your performance sound like the rhythm of the recording? Listen again to correct any errors.
   - If you had notated the rhythm in 2/4 instead of in common time (**C**), how would your answers be different?

B. Writing a rhythmic composition with beat subdivisions

Compose a rhythmic duet for two performers, using only the rhythmic patterns listed below.
- Write eight measures, in either $\frac{3}{4}$ or $\frac{4}{4}$ meter.
- Use no ties.
- Include eighth, quarter, and half rests only.
- Vary the complexity: both voices should sound together at times. At other times, when one voice is rhythmically active, the other voice may have rests or longer notes.
- Include dynamic markings to add musical interest.
- If you would like, write a text to be recited with your rhythm.

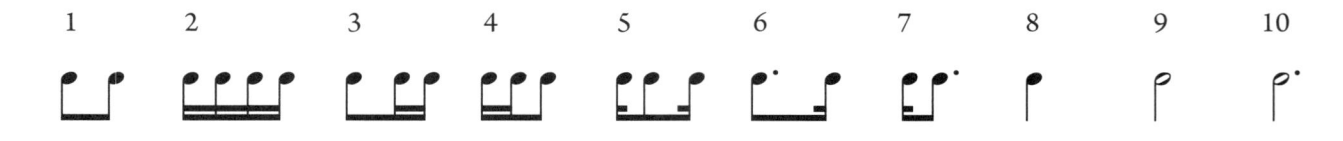

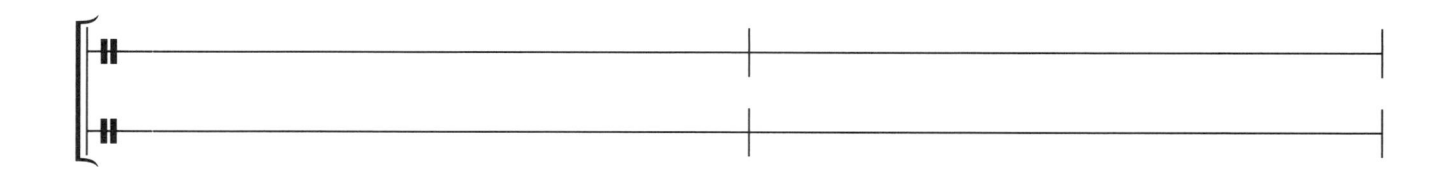

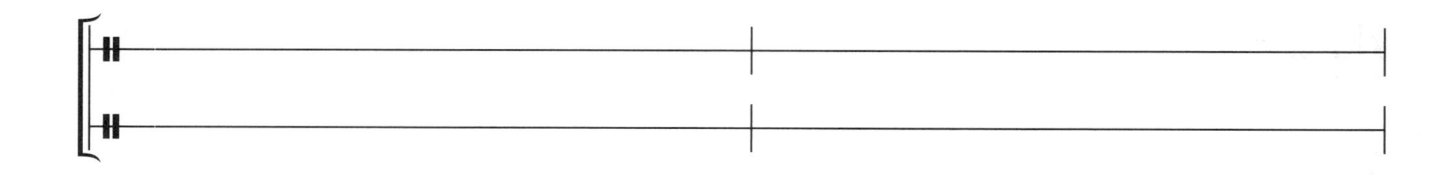

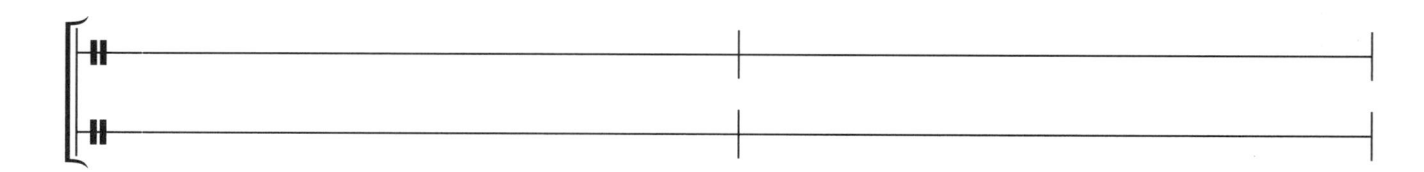

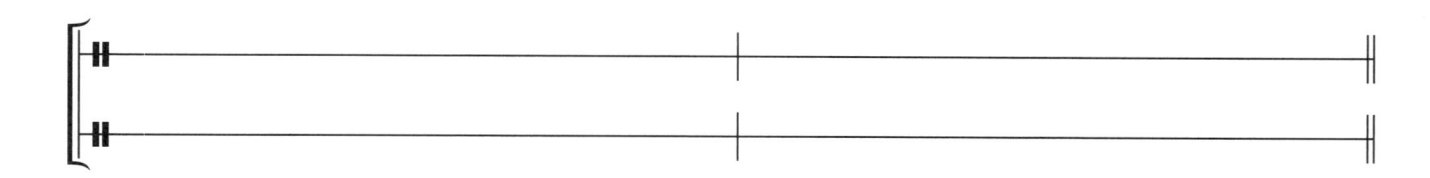

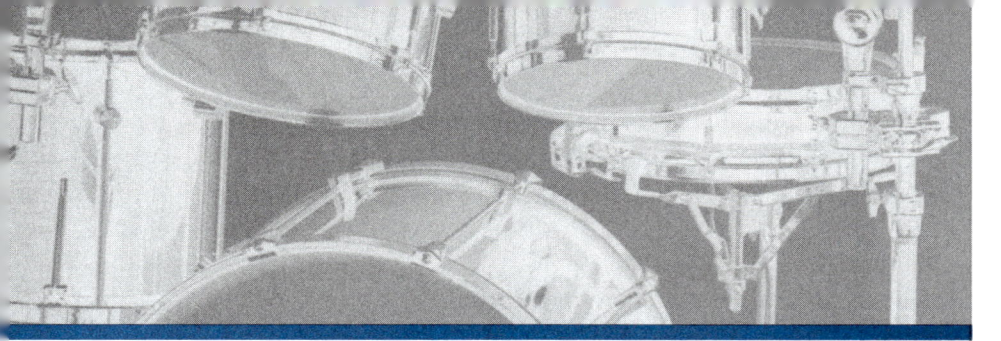

TOPICS

- compound meters
- meter signatures
- subdivisions
- other compound meters
- syncopation and duplets
- asymmetrical meters and changing meter

MUSIC

- Béla Bartók, "Bulgarian Rhythm," No. 115, from *Mikrokosmos*
- Bartók, "Syncopation," No. 99, from *Mikrokosmos*
- Dave Brubeck, "Blue Rondo à la Turk"
- Christopher Cerf and Norman Stiles, "Dance Myself to Sleep"
- Stephen Foster, "Beautiful Dreamer"
- Patrick S. Gilmore, "When Johnny Comes Marching Home"
- "Home on the Range"
- Elisabeth-Claude Jacquet de la Guerre, Gigue, from Suite No. 3 in A Minor
- Gustav Holst, Second Suite in F for Military Band, "Song of the Blacksmith"
- Elton John, Bernie Taupin, and Davey Johnstone, "I Guess That's Why They Call It the Blues"
- John Lennon and Paul McCartney, "Norwegian Wood"
- Smokey Robinson, "You've Really Got a Hold on Me"
- Lalo Schifrin, Theme from *Mission: Impossible*

CHAPTER 5
Compound and Other Meters

Compound Meters

Listen to "When Johnny Comes Marching Home." Tap the primary beat with your foot. The beat groups in twos; therefore the meter is duple. Now listen for the beat division and tap it with your hands; the beat divides into threes. Unlike triplets in simple meter—which occur only occasionally—the three-part division of the beat sounds all the way through the song. The meter is **compound duple**.

> **KEY CONCEPT** In **compound meters**, each beat divides into three parts. As in simple meters, the beats may group into twos (duple), threes (triple), or fours (quadruple); the conducting patterns for duple, triple, and quadruple compound meters are the same as for simple meters.

When counting beat divisions in compound meters, use the same syllables as for triplets: 1 la li 2 la li, and so on. Listen to the beginning of "When Johnny Comes Marching Home" again, this time following Example 5.1. Sing along using counting syllables. This passage features two of the most common rhythmic patterns in compound meter: ♫♪ (counted 1 la li) and ♩♪ (1 li). The tied notes in measure 3 work the same as in simple meters: the note sounds as long as the two durations connected by the tie, and the count for the tied beat is written in parentheses.

EXAMPLE 5.1 Gilmore, "When Johnny Comes Marching Home," mm. 1–4

Figure 5.1 shows how beats are divided and subdivided in compound meters with a dotted-quarter beat unit; each beat divides into three eighth notes. The dotted-quarter beat unit is typical in compound meters, analogous to the quarter-note beat unit in simple meters.

FIGURE 5.1 Note values and rests in compound meters with a dotted-quarter (♩.) beat unit

> **KEY CONCEPT** In compound meters with a dotted-quarter beat unit, the beat divides into three eighth notes and subdivides into six sixteenth notes.

The chart in Figure 5.2 gives typical rhythmic patterns in compound meters with a dotted-quarter beat unit. Patterns 1 to 3 only have divisions of the beat, while 4 and 5 include sixteenth-note subdivisions, and 6 is the dotted-quarter note, the beat unit itself. (Patterns 5 and 6 performed together may bring to mind the carol "Silent Night.")

FIGURE 5.2 Common patterns in compound meters with a dotted-quarter beat unit 🔊

1	2	3	4	5	6
1 la li	1 li	1 la	1 ta la ta li ta	1 ta li	1

Meter Signatures

In Example 5.1, "When Johnny Comes Marching Home," you may have noticed a meter signature we have not seen before: ⁶⁄₈. While simple-meter signatures are straightforward—the top number indicates the number of beats in the measure, and the bottom one is the beat unit—compound-meter signatures require extra steps to interpret. A signature like ⁶⁄₈ would seem to indicate six beats per measure, with an eighth note getting the beat, but we have already seen and heard that the dotted-quarter note is the beat unit. In $^6_8$, compound duple, there are only two beats per measure, counted 1 la li 2 la li. The numbers in compound-meter signatures represent the beat division.

> **KEY CONCEPT** In compound-meter signatures:
> - The top number is 6, 9, or 12, representing duple, triple, or quadruple meter, respectively. Divide this number by three to get the number of beats per measure (two, three, or four). For example, in $^6_8$ divide the number 6 by three to get two beats per measure.
> - The bottom number is usually 8, but may be 4 or 16. This number shows the note value of the beat *division*. Add together three of these note values to get the beat unit, which will always be a dotted note (♩., ♪., or ♬.). For example, in $^6_8$ add together three eighth notes to get a dotted-quarter beat unit.

Example 5.2 shows an excerpt of a piece in $^9_8$, Stephen Foster's "Beautiful Dreamer." To determine the number of beats per measure, divide the number 9 by three: there are three beats per measure. Therefore the meter is **compound triple**. To determine the beat unit, combine three eighth notes (bottom number) to get a dotted-quarter note.

EXAMPLE 5.2   Foster, "Beautiful Dreamer," mm. 5–8

Example 5.3, "Norwegian Wood," is in $^{12}_{8}$. This is **compound quadruple** meter, again with a dotted-quarter beat unit.

EXAMPLE 5.3   Lennon and McCartney, "Norwegian Wood," mm. 13–14

The beat divisions in compound meters are performed strong-weak-weak: the beats are stressed and the divisions are not. This pattern gives compound meters their characteristic lilting sound. At the measure level, the metrical accents are the same as for simple meters: duple meters receive a stronger accent on beat 1 and a weaker one on beat 2; triple is strong-weak-weaker, and quadruple is strongest-weak-strong-weak.

As in simple meters, a melody may begin with an anacrusis that precedes the first downbeat (see Example 5.1). In this case, the final measure will be incomplete to balance the anacrusis.

TRY IT #1

Look at the meter signature to determine how many beats are in each measure, then write the counting syllables beneath the melody. The beat unit is the dotted-quarter note.

Cerf and Stiles, "Dance Myself to Sleep," mm. 9–13

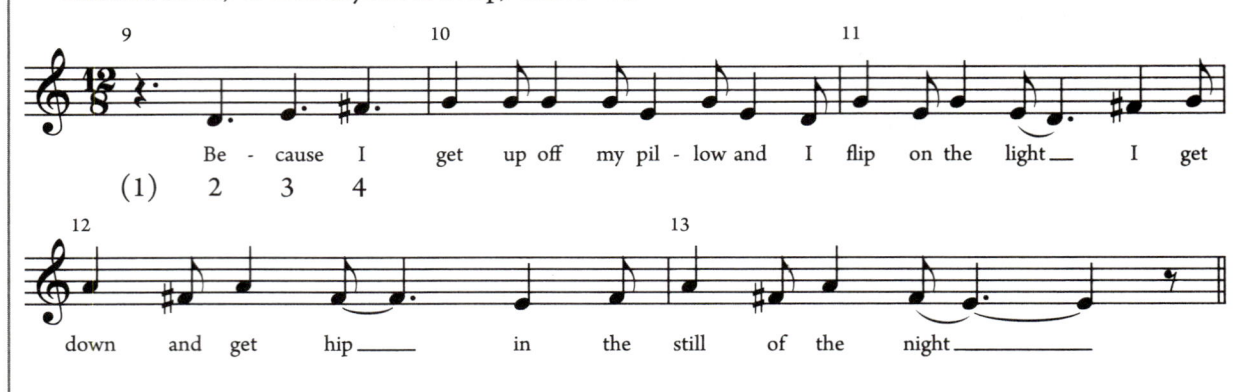

(musical score in 12/8, mm. 9–13, with lyrics: "Be - cause I get up off my pil - low and I flip on the light__ I get down and get hip__ in the still of the night__". Counting syllables shown under m. 9: (1) 2 3 4)

ASSIGNMENT 5.1

Subdivisions

In compound meters, the beat division further subdivides into two parts, just as in simple meters. Figure 5.3 lists common subdivision patterns for compound meters with a dotted-quarter note beat unit, along with their counting syllables.

FIGURE 5.3 Common beat subdivisions in 6/8 🔊

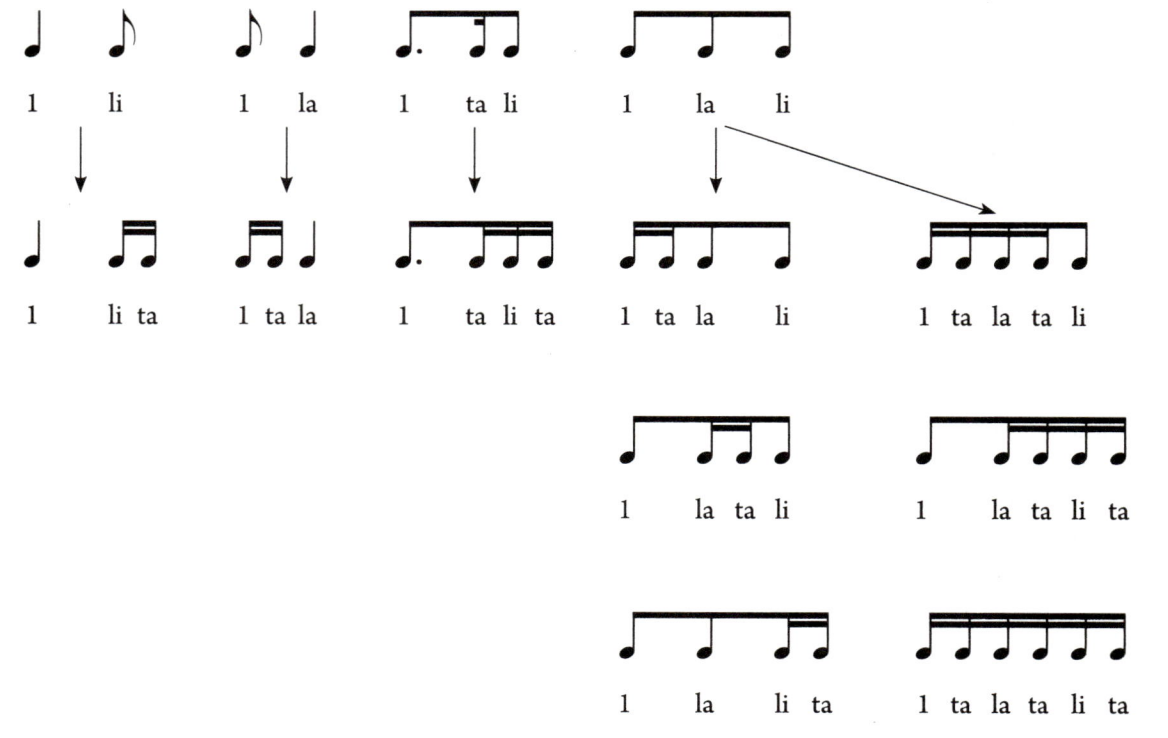

♩ ♪	1 li
♪ ♩	1 la
♩. ♫	1 ta li
♫ ♫ ♫ → ♩	1 la li
♩ ♬	1 li ta
♬ ♩	1 ta la
♩. ♬♬	1 ta li ta
♬ ♬ ♩	1 ta la li
♬ ♬ ♬ ♬	1 ta la ta li
♩ ♬ ♬	1 la ta li
♩ ♬ ♬♬	1 la ta li ta
♩ ♩ ♬	1 la li ta
♬♬ ♬♬ ♬♬	1 ta la ta li ta

100   CHAPTER FIVE   Compound and Other Meters

To read rhythms in compound meters easily, memorize these patterns with their syllables, and always beam them to reflect the beat, as shown in Figure 5.3. Other patterns can be made by replacing eighth notes with sixteenths, by adding ties or dots, or by substituting equivalent rests.

> **KEY CONCEPT** Always notate patterns with beaming that reflects beat groupings.

Example 5.4a shows the melody of "Home on the Range" written with correct beaming. Compare this with the notation in Example 5.4b, which makes the beat unit unclear and the rhythm more difficult to read.

EXAMPLE 5.4 "Home on the Range" with correct and incorrect beaming

(a) Correct beaming

Oh, give me a home, where the buf - fa - lo roam, Where the deer and the an - te - lope play
li 1 la li 2 li ta 1 ta li 2 li ta 1 li ta 2 ta li 1 (2)

(b) Incorrect beaming

Rests in compound meters should also be notated to reflect the beat and its division. Observe how the rests are written in the bracketed beats of Example 5.5: two eighth rests at the beginning of measure 7 reflect the beat division, and a dotted-quarter rest in measure 9 represents a full beat of silence. The rests in measure 11 are the most interesting; the two eighth rests finish out the second beat, while the quarter rest that follows makes clear that it belongs to beat 3. Although the notation of measures 7 and 11 differs, both are correct because the rests do not extend into the next beat.

EXAMPLE 5.5 Robinson, "You've Really Got a Hold on Me," mm. 6–11

I don't like you, but I love you;
1 2 li 3 4 li (1) li 2 li 3 4

Seems that I'm al - ways think - ing of you.
1 2 li 3 4 la (1) 2 li 3 4 la

Oh, oh, oh, you treat me bad - ly, I love you
1 2 3 li 4 li 1 la (2) (3) li 4 li

Subdivisions

TRY IT #2

Rewrite the following rhythms with correct beaming to reflect the beat. Practice the rhythms on "ta" or counting syllables and be prepared to perform them in class.

(a) 🔊

(b) 🔊

ASSIGNMENT 5.2

Other Compound Meters

The compound meters we have considered—$^6_8$, $^9_8$, and $^{12}_8$—are by far the most common, but others are also possible. Figure 5.4 lists the various possibilities and shows typical patterns for each beat unit. The dotted-half and dotted-eighth beat units were more prevalent in music written before the nineteenth century than they are today.

FIGURE 5.4   Compound-meter signatures and patterns

(a) Compound-meter signatures

        Meter signature (Beat unit)

compound duple: $^6_4$ (𝅗𝅥.) $^6_8$ (♩.) $^{6}_{16}$ (♪.)

compound triple: $^9_4$ (𝅗𝅥.) $^9_8$ (♩.) $^{9}_{16}$ (♪.)

compound quadruple: $^{12}_4$ (𝅗𝅥.) $^{12}_8$ (♩.) $^{12}_{16}$ (♪.)

102 CHAPTER FIVE Compound and Other Meters

(b) Typical patterns for each compound-meter beat unit

[rhythm patterns chart showing three columns for dotted-half, dotted-quarter, and dotted-eighth beat units]

1 la li   1 la li   1 la li

1   li   1   li   1   li

1 ta la ta li ta   1 ta la ta li ta   1 ta la ta li ta

1   ta li   1   ta li   1   ta li

Example 5.6 shows how "Home on the Range" would look if notated with three different beat units. The first version (a) is the familiar one, in $_8^6$; the other two versions (b and c) feature dotted-eighth and dotted-half beat units. All three are counted the same, and if performed at the same tempo they would sound the same, though they look quite different.

EXAMPLE 5.6 "Home on the Range" with dotted-quarter, dotted-eighth, and dotted-half beat units 🔊

(a) Original version, $_8^6$ (♩. beat unit)

Oh, give me a home, where the buf - fa - lo roam, Where the deer and the an - te - lope play;____

li 1 la li 2 li ta 1 ta li 2 li ta 1 li ta 2 ta li 1 (2)

(b) Written in $_{16}^6$ (♪. beat unit)

li 1 la li 2 li ta 1 ta li 2 li ta 1 li ta 2 ta li 1 (2)

(c) Written in $_4^6$ (𝅗𝅥. beat unit)

li 1 la li 2 li ta 1 ta li 2 li ta 1 li ta 2 ta li 1 (2)

Other Compound Meters

Example 5.7 shows the opening of a keyboard piece by Elisabeth-Claude Jacquet de la Guerre. This $_4^6$ movement has a dotted-half note beat unit and quarter-note beat division. Counts for the melody appear between the staves. (The symbols above and below some of the notes indicate ornaments, or embellishments, heard on the recording.)

EXAMPLE 5.7   Jacquet de la Guerre, Gigue, from Suite No. 3 in A Minor, mm. 1–6

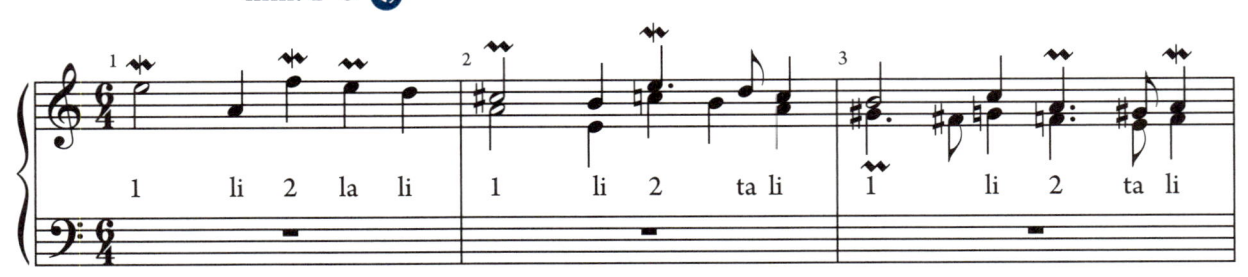

One challenge in counting compound meters with quarter-note beat divisions is that quarter notes ($_4^6$ ♩♩♩♩♩♩) are not beamed together like eighths ($_8^6$ ♫♫♫), removing a helpful visual cue for grouping. If you saw Example 5.8a without a meter signature, you might count the left hand of measure 17 as 1 & 2 & 3 & in $_2^3$ meter. But the dotted halves in measures 18–19 make it clear that this is compound meter, $_4^6$. Notating the rhythm in $_8^6$, as in Example 5.8b, introduces beams that show the compound groupings.

EXAMPLE 5.8   Jacquet de la Guerre, Gigue, mm. 17–20

(a) Original notation

(b) Rhythm of the melody notated in $_8^6$

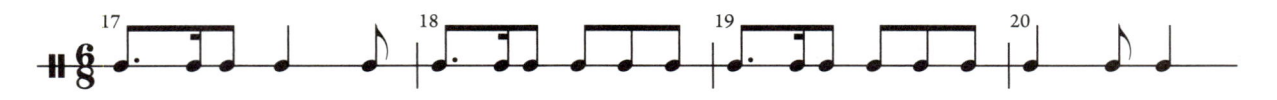

104   CHAPTER FIVE   Compound and Other Meters

TRY IT #3

For each rhythm below, provide the missing bar lines that correspond with the meter specified. Where possible, use beaming to help you decide.

(a) 6/4

(b) 9/16

(c) 12/4

(d) 6/16

AURAL SKILLS 5.1

Syncopation and Duplets

Just as in simple meters, ties and rests in compound meters can create offbeat accents, or syncopation. Three methods for writing syncopations in compound meters are shown in Figure 5.5.

FIGURE 5.5   Types of syncopation in compound meters

(a) Ties from a weak part of a beat across a stronger part

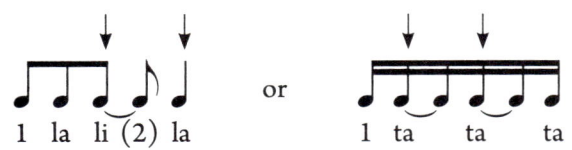

1 la li (2) la   or   1 ta ta ta

(b) An accent mark on a weak beat or the weak part of a beat

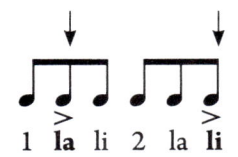

1 **la** li 2 la **li**

(c) A rest on the strong part of a beat that causes a weaker part to sound accented

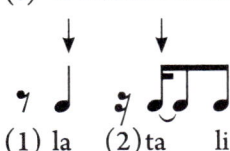

(1) la (2) ta li

Syncopation and Duplets   105

Example 5.9 shows syncopations in "I Guess That's Why They Call It the Blues." After the third beat of measures 22 and 23, a note that begins on the offbeat is tied over the fourth beat and is followed by another offbeat note. These syncopations sound like two-beat triplets, with three quarter notes dividing the two dotted-quarter beats evenly into three parts.

EXAMPLE 5.9   John, Taupin, and Johnstone, "I Guess That's Why They Call It the Blues," mm. 22–24

Typical syncopations within the beat are shown in Figure 5.6, where the dotted-quarter note is the beat unit. Ties are often renotated, as shown in the figure, so that an eighth note substitutes for two sixteenths tied together.

FIGURE 5.6   Typical syncopations within the beat in compound meters

While in simple meters you sometimes encounter triplets, which divide the beat into three parts instead of the usual two, the reverse is true in compound meters: you occasionally see a beat divide into two parts instead of the usual three. This two-part division is called a **duplet**. Look at Example 5.10, from "You've Really Got a Hold on Me." The melody is in 12/8, with an overall counting pattern of 1 la li 2 la li 3 la li 4 la li, but in measure 13, a duplet ("on me"), marked with a 2 above the beam appears on the second beat. This beat is counted 2 &, just as two eighths would be in simple meter with a quarter-note beat. Here, the second half of the duplet is tied over to make a syncopation.

EXAMPLE 5.10   Robinson, "You've Really Got a Hold on Me," mm. 12–13

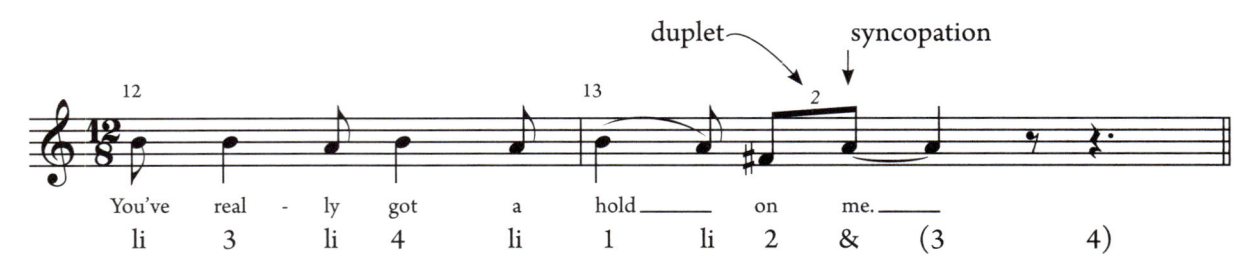

106   CHAPTER FIVE   Compound and Other Meters

Figure 5.7 shows how duplets are notated with each compound beat unit.

FIGURE 5.7   Notation of duplets

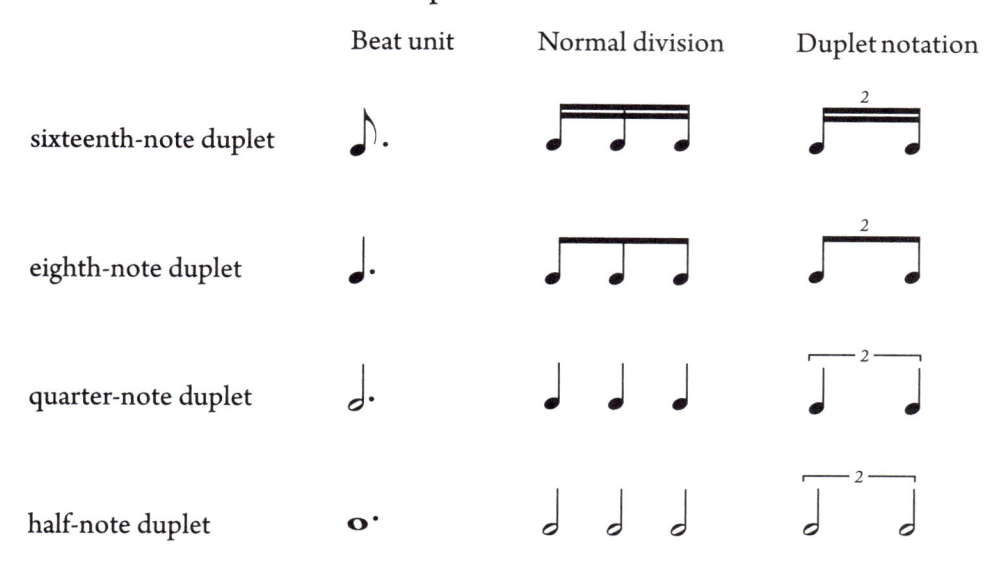

	Beat unit	Normal division	Duplet notation
sixteenth-note duplet	♪.	♬♬	♬²
eighth-note duplet	♩.	♫♫	♫²
quarter-note duplet	♩.	♩ ♩ ♩	♩ ♩²
half-note duplet	o·	𝅗𝅥 𝅗𝅥 𝅗𝅥	𝅗𝅥 𝅗𝅥²

ASSIGNMENT 5.3

Asymmetrical Meters and Changing Meter

All the simple and compound meters we have studied so far are considered **symmetrical**, with the primary beats in each measure equally spaced. Now listen to the beginning of Bartók's "Bulgarian Rhythm," shown in Example 5.11. The meter signature is 5/8—an **asymmetrical meter**—with primary beats of unequal duration (♩. ♩). Each measure lasts for five eighth notes and divides into two unequal "halves": three eighths in the first half, two in the second. You can see the unequal beat units in the left hand, which shifts between dotted-quarter and quarter notes. We count such rhythms by shifting between the syllables for compound and simple meters. For the right-hand rhythm, count 1 la li 2 &, making sure to keep the eighth-note duration consistent.

EXAMPLE 5.11   Bartók, "Bulgarian Rhythm," mm. 1–2

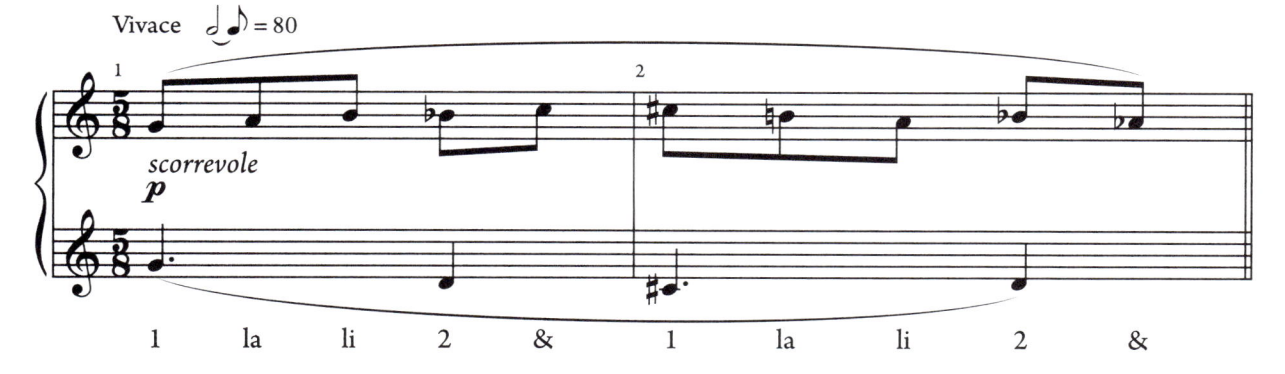

For another example of an asymmetrical meter, look at the *Mission: Impossible* theme shown in Example 5.12. The $\frac{5}{4}$ meter signature implies five quarter-note beats per measure, but the beaming and accent marks in the left hand's eighth notes indicate the grouping 3 + 3 + 2 + 2. Rather than counting this passage as five quarter-note beats, we hear four unequal beats (♩. ♩. ♩ ♩) in a driving, accented rhythm.

EXAMPLE 5.12   Schifrin, Theme from *Mission: Impossible*, mm. 1–2

Other asymmetrical meter signatures you might encounter are $\frac{5}{16}$, $\frac{7}{8}$, and $\frac{7}{16}$; meters with 5 as the top number are usually conducted in two uneven beats, those with 7 on top are generally conducted in three. Even symmetrical meters may be divided asymmetrically. For example, $\frac{9}{8}$ may be divided into 2 + 2 + 2 + 3 eighth notes, as in Example 5.13. This example has four beats per measure, with the fourth slightly longer than the others.

EXAMPLE 5.13   Brubeck, "Blue Rondo à la Turk," mm. 1–4

Finally, you might find more than one meter in a single piece. Look at Example 5.14, another composition by Bartók, where each measure has a different meter signature, as marked by arrows. This technique is called **changing meter**.

108   CHAPTER FIVE   Compound and Other Meters

EXAMPLE 5.14 Bartók, "Syncopation," mm. 1–3

EXAMPLE 5.15 Holst, Second Suite in F for Military Band, "Song of the Blacksmith," mm. 7–10

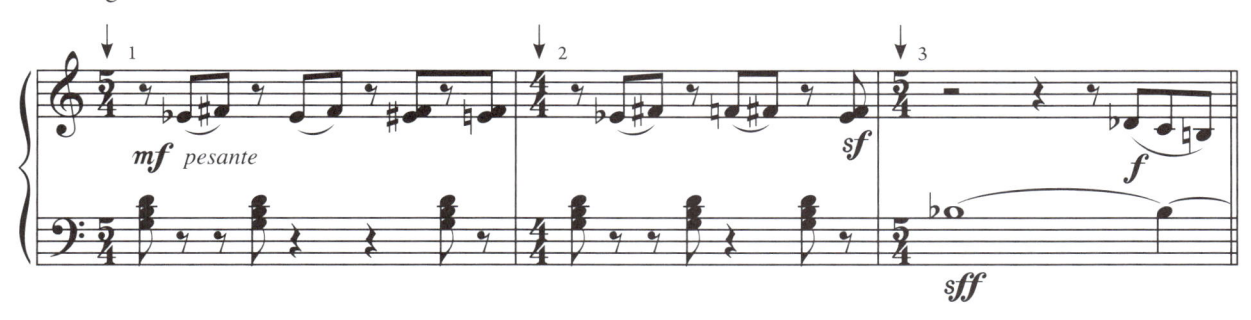

Changing meter is often found in twentieth-century and contemporary pieces, and may also appear in a popular or folk song, as in Example 5.15, an English folk melody set by Holst for band.

TRY IT #4

Write the correct meter signature for each rhythm below, then add the appropriate counts below the rhythm.

(a)

1 2 3 la li

(b)

ASSIGNMENT 5.4

Asymmetrical Meters and Changing Meter

Did You Know?

William "Smokey" Robinson was inducted into the Rock and Roll Hall of Fame in 1987, in honor of his extended career as singer-songwriter with the Miracles and his role as talent scout and record producer. During his long association with Detroit-based Motown Records—once the largest black-owned company in the United States—and its founder, Berry Gordy, Robinson worked as songwriter and producer with the Miracles, the Temptations, and Marvin Gaye. Gordy took Robinson under his wing when the young artist was still a teenager, and he released the Miracles' first single when Robinson was eighteen. The group became a hit during the 1960s and early 70s, with such songs as "You've Really Got a Hold on Me," "I Second That Emotion," and "The Tears of a Clown." With Ronnie White of the Miracles, Robinson wrote "My Girl," which became a #1 hit for the Temptations. After splitting from the Miracles in 1972, Robinson enjoyed a strong solo career. In 1999, he received a Grammy Lifetime Achievement Award.

Terms You Should Know

- asymmetrical meter
- changing meter
- compound meter
- compound duple
- compound triple
- compound quadruple
- duplet
- symmetrical meter

Questions for Review

1. Explain the difference between simple meter and compound meter.
2. How do you decide if a piece is in simple or compound meter?
3. How do you know whether a compound meter is duple, triple, or quadruple?
4. What do the upper and lower parts of a meter signature represent in compound meters?
5. Which numbers may appear in the upper and lower positions of compound-meter signatures?
6. What are the most common compound-meter signatures?
7. In 6/8 meter, how many beats does a dotted-half note last? a dotted-quarter?
8. If the beat unit is a dotted-quarter note, what note values represent the beat division and subdivision? if the beat unit is a dotted-half note?
9. What guidelines do you follow to decide which notes to beam together in compound meter?
10. Write four common rhythmic patterns that fill one dotted-quarter beat in compound meter.
11. How do you decide if a meter is symmetrical or asymmetrical?
12. How do asymmetrical meters sound different from symmetrical ones? Give an example of each.

Reading Review

Match the term on the left with the best answer on the right.

_____ (1) 1 ta li
_____ (2) changing meter
_____ (3) symmetrical meter
_____ (4) $\frac{9}{16}$
_____ (5) beat subdivision in $\frac{6}{8}$
_____ (6) duplet
_____ (7) asymmetrical meter
_____ (8) $\frac{6}{4}$
_____ (9) 2 + 2 + 3 grouping
_____ (10) 1 la li
_____ (11) compound meter
_____ (12) $\frac{12}{8}$
_____ (13) 3 + 2 grouping
_____ (14) 1 ta la ta li
_____ (15) beaming guideline
_____ (16) dotted note

(a) meter with equally spaced beats
(b) notation must reflect the beat unit
(c) type of note that gets one beat in compound meters
(d) type of meter where each beat divides into threes
(e) counting syllables for ♩ ♩ ♩ in $\frac{6}{8}$
(f) counting syllables for ♩. ♩ ♩ in $\frac{6}{8}$
(g) compound meter with four dotted-quarter beats per measure
(h) a grouping of eighths in $\frac{5}{8}$
(i) compound meter with three dotted-eighth beats per measure
(j) has adjacent measures with different meters
(k) division of the beat in two parts in compound meter
(l) ♫♫♫
(m) meter with unequally spaced beats
(n) compound meter with two dotted-half beats per measure
(o) counting syllables for ♫♫♩ in $\frac{6}{8}$
(p) a grouping of eighths in $\frac{7}{8}$

Additional review and practice available at wwnorton.com/studyspace

Apply It

A. Hearing simple and compound meters

Listen to the following examples to determine whether they are in simple or compound meter, then circle your choice. Tap the beats with your foot and the beat divisions with your hand. Remember that simple-meter beats divide into twos and fours, while compound-meter beats divide into threes.

1. simple   compound
2. simple   compound
3. simple   compound
4. simple   compound
5. simple   compound

B. Reading and writing rhythmic patterns in compound meters

1. Performing compound-meter beat patterns

Look at the example below, which features the most common compound-meter beat patterns. First tap all the beats with your foot and beat divisions with your hand; then chant the rhythm on a neutral syllable such as "ta" or with rhythm syllables. Memorize the look and sound of each pattern.

2. Composition

On your own or in teams of three to four people, compose a sixteen-measure rhythmic composition in 6/8 meter. Choose only from the beat patterns shown below. If you're working in a group, take turns composing one measure, then move on to the next team member. Keep taking turns until the composition is complete. Perform and critique your composition.

C. Reading rhythms

Perform the following rhythms on "ta" or rhythm syllables, as directed. Keep a steady beat by tapping the pulse or conducting, and follow the dynamic markings. (Optional: Write the counts below each rhythm.)

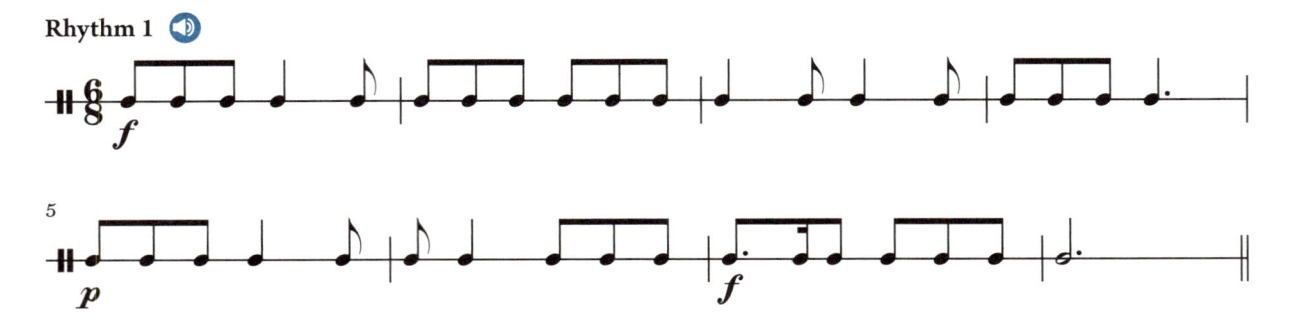

Rhythm 1

112   CHAPTER FIVE   Compound and Other Meters

Rhythm 2

Rhythm 3

Rhythm 4

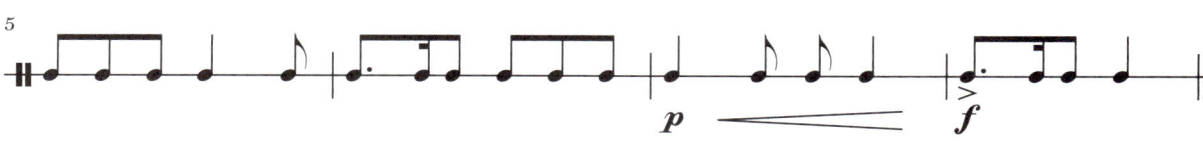

Rhythm 5

Perform as a duet. To help you practice, each voice is recorded individually.

Apply It

Rhythm 6

D. Playing and singing melodies in compound meter

The following melodies feature the $\hat{1}$–$\hat{2}$–$\hat{3}$–$\hat{4}$–$\hat{5}$ pattern from previous chapters, plus a few additional notes above and below. The $\hat{1}$–$\hat{2}$–$\hat{3}$–$\hat{4}$–$\hat{5}$ pattern appears as a warm-up for each, beginning on the same note as the melody.
- Practice the warm-up on a keyboard with your right hand. Begin with the thumb on the first note and use each finger. Play $\hat{1}$–$\hat{2}$–$\hat{3}$–$\hat{4}$–$\hat{5}$ ascending and descending, and sing along with it.
- Practice just the rhythm of the melody on "ta" or counting syllables while tapping the beat (or conducting). Then practice just the pitches on the keyboard (don't worry about fingering for now).
- Sing the melody on the numbers or syllables given, first at a slow tempo and then a faster tempo. Play the melody on a keyboard at a slow tempo, then a faster tempo.

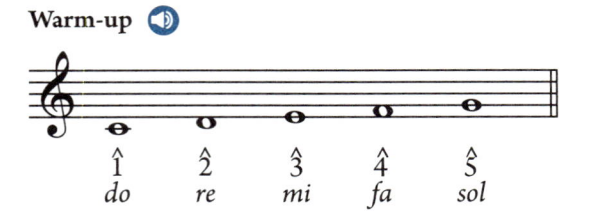

Warm-up

Melody 1   Harold Arlen and E. Y. Harburg, "We're Off to See the Wizard," from *The Wizard of Oz*, mm. 1–8

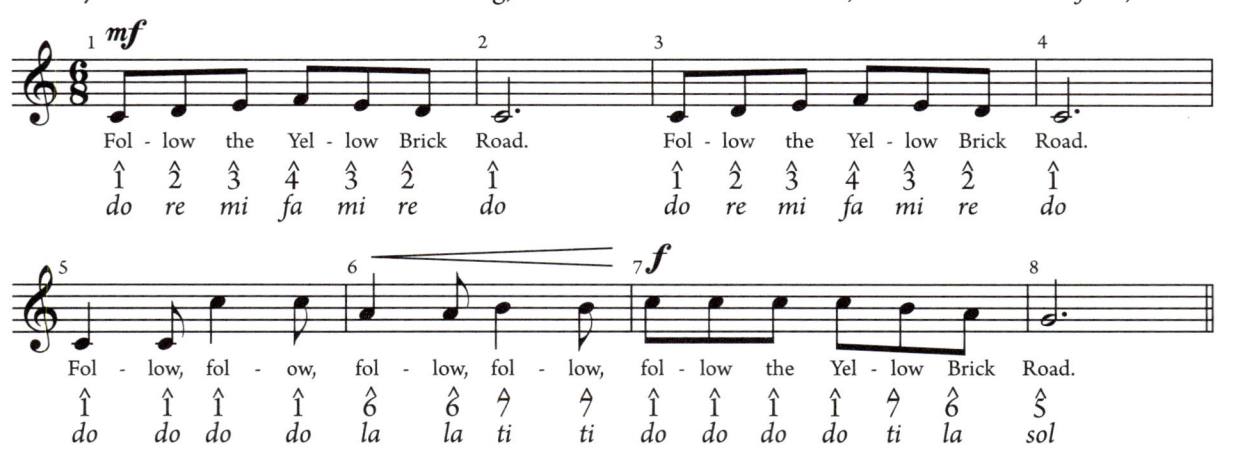

Melody 2   "Whoopee Ti-Yi-Yo" (abridged), mm. 1–8
Use the previous warm-up melody.

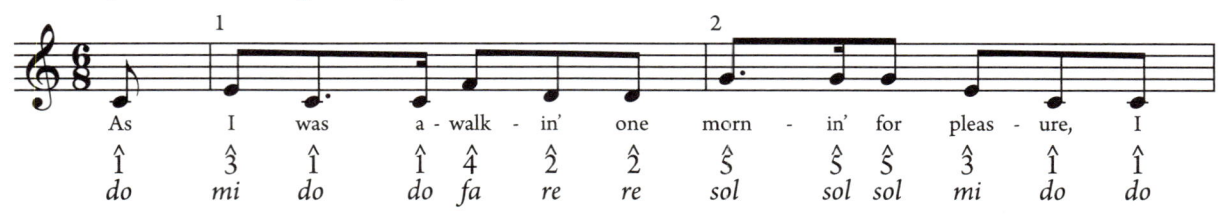

spied a cow-punch-er a-lop-in' a-long. Whoo-pee, ti- yi- yo, git a-
$\hat{4}$ $\hat{2}$ $\hat{2}$ $\hat{4}$ $\hat{2}$ $\hat{2}$ $\hat{5}$ $\hat{5}$ $\hat{5}$ $\hat{1}$ $\hat{1}$ $\hat{1}$ $\hat{1}$ $\hat{1}$ $\hat{3}$ $\hat{3}$ $\hat{3}$
fa re re fa re re sol sol sol do do do do do mi mi mi

long lit-tle do-gies, For you know that Wy- o- ming will be your new home.
$\hat{5}$ $\hat{5}$ $\hat{5}$ $\hat{3}$ $\hat{1}$ $\hat{1}$ $\hat{1}$ $\hat{4}$ $\hat{2}$ $\hat{2}$ $\hat{4}$ $\hat{2}$ $\hat{2}$ $\hat{5}$ $\hat{5}$ $\hat{5}$ $\hat{1}$
sol sol sol mi do do do fa re re fa re re sol sol sol do

Warm-up 🔊

$\hat{1}$ $\hat{2}$ $\hat{3}$ $\hat{4}$ $\hat{5}$
do re mi fa sol

Melody 3 Philip P. Bliss, "Wonderful Words of Life," mm. 1–8 🔊

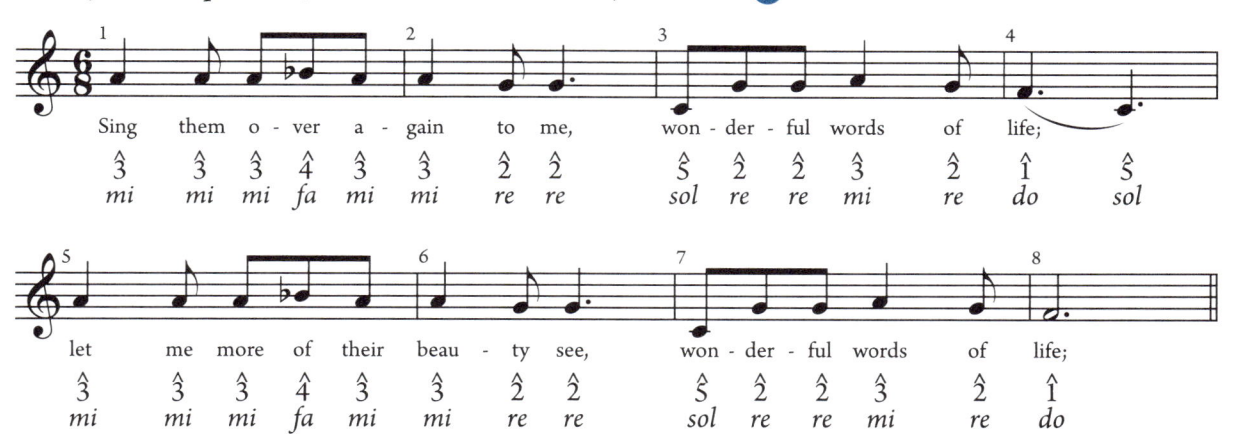

Sing them o- ver a- gain to me, won- der- ful words of life;
$\hat{3}$ $\hat{3}$ $\hat{3}$ $\hat{4}$ $\hat{3}$ $\hat{3}$ $\hat{2}$ $\hat{2}$ $\hat{5}$ $\hat{2}$ $\hat{2}$ $\hat{3}$ $\hat{2}$ $\hat{1}$ $\hat{5}$
mi mi mi fa mi mi re re sol re re mi re do sol

let me more of their beau- ty see, won- der- ful words of life;
$\hat{3}$ $\hat{3}$ $\hat{3}$ $\hat{4}$ $\hat{3}$ $\hat{3}$ $\hat{2}$ $\hat{2}$ $\hat{5}$ $\hat{2}$ $\hat{2}$ $\hat{3}$ $\hat{2}$ $\hat{1}$
mi mi mi fa mi mi re re sol re re mi re do

E. Listening and writing

Listen to rhythms made up of patterns from those numbered below. Sing or tap what you hear, then write it on the staff provided. 🔊

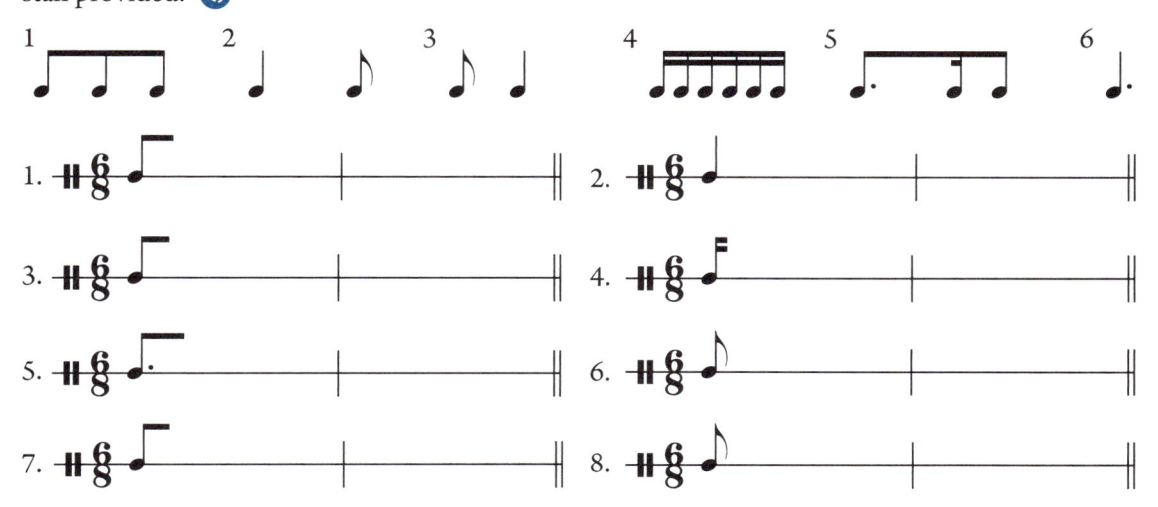

Apply It   115

Listen to melodies made from the rhythm patterns combined with pitches in the octave extending from C to C (C–D–E–F–G–A–B–C). Sing what you hear, then write it on the staff provided.

116   CHAPTER FIVE Compound and Other Meters

NAME _____

Workbook ASSIGNMENT 5.1

A. Simple and compound meters

For each meter in the chart below, provide the meter type (e.g., simple triple), the beat unit, and the number of beats per measure.

Meter	Meter type	Beat unit	Beats per measure
9/8	**compound triple**	♩.	3
¢	simple duple	♩	2
12/8	compound quad.	♩.	4
3/4	simple triple	♩	3
2/4	simple duple	♩	2
6/8	compound duple	♩.	2

B. Understanding beats and divisions

For each rhythm or melody below, write the rhythm counts below the staff.

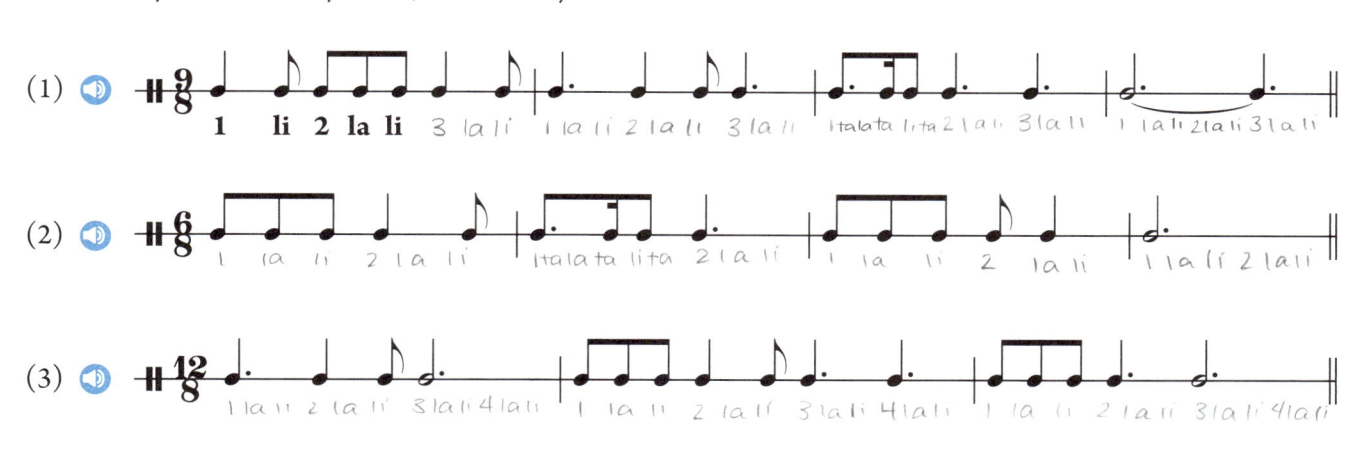

(1) 9/8 — **1 li 2 la li** 3 la li 1 la li 2 la li 3 la li 1 ta la ta li ta 2 la li 3 la li 1 la li 2 la li 3 la li

(2) 6/8 — 1 la li 2 la li 1 ta la ta li ta 2 la li 1 la li 2 la li 1 la li 2 la li

(3) 12/8 — 1 la li 2 la li 3 la li 4 la li 1 la li 2 la li 3 la li 4 la li 1 la li 2 la li 3 la li 4 la li

(4) Leigh Harline and Ned Washington, "Hi-Diddle-Dee-Dee," from *Pinocchio*, mm. 17–20

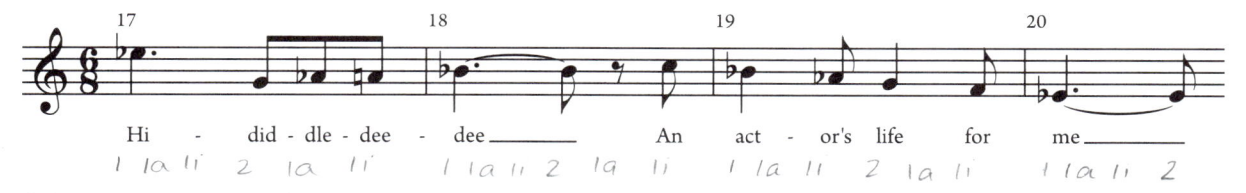

Hi - did - dle - dee - dee____ An act - or's life for me____
1 la li 2 la li 1 la li 2 la li 1 la li 2 la li 1 la li 2

(5) Jerry Herman, "Before the Parade Passes By," from *Hello, Dolly!* mm. 9–15

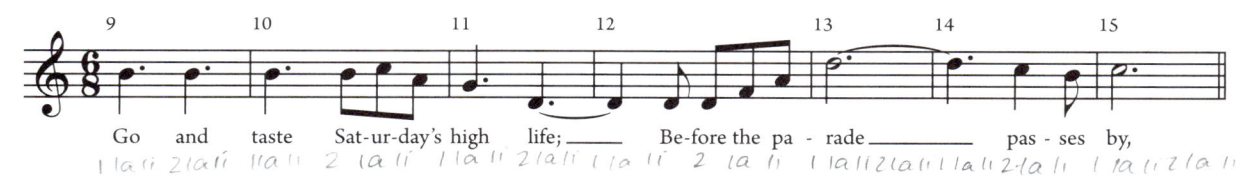

Go and taste Sat-ur-day's high life;____ Be-fore the pa - rade____ pas - ses by,
1 la li 2 la li 1 la li 2 la li 1 la li 2 la li 1 la li 2 la li 1 la li 2 la li 1 la li 2 la li 1 la li 2 la li

Assignment 5.1 117

At each position marked by an arrow, add one note value to complete the measure in the meter indicated.

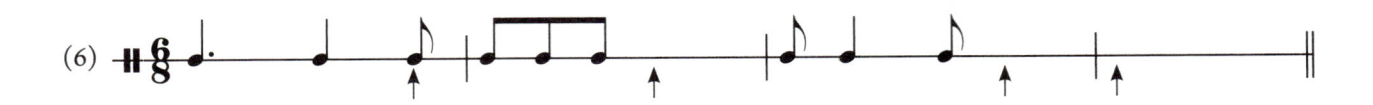

Notate the rhythm for each set of counts. Perform each rhythm after you've notated it.

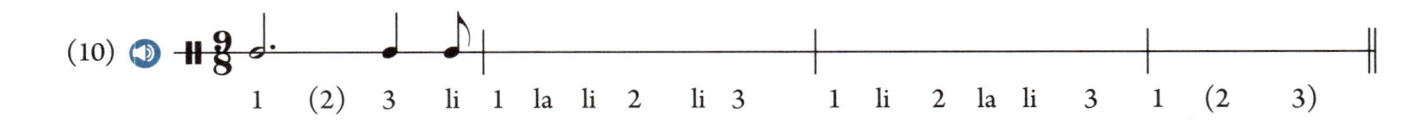

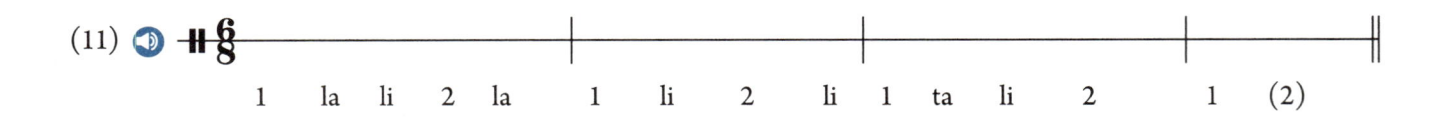

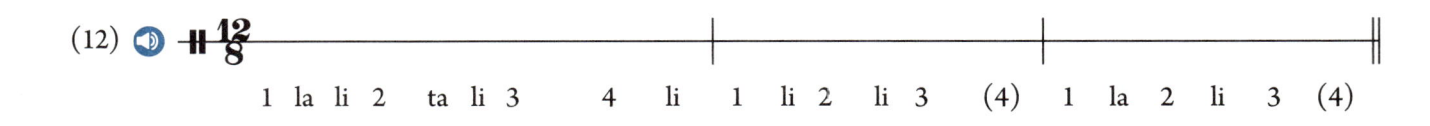

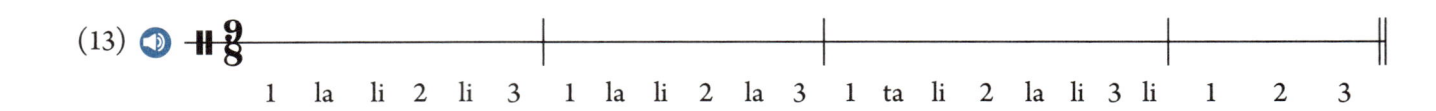

118 CHAPTER FIVE Compound and Other Meters

Workbook ASSIGNMENT 5.2

A. Divisions and subdivisions in compound meter

Write the counts beneath the staff, then perform each rhythm.

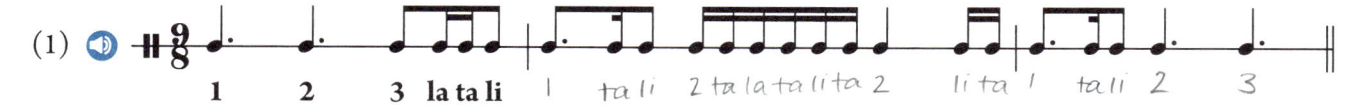

(1) $\frac{9}{8}$ — 1   2   3 la ta li | 1 ta li 2 ta la ta li ta 2 | li ta 1 ta li 2   3

(2) $\frac{6}{8}$ — 1 ta la li 2 la li | 1   li 2 | li ta 1 ta la ta li ta 2 la | 1 ta la 2

(3) $\frac{12}{8}$ — 1   li 2 li ta 3 | 1 la li ta 2 la li 3 ta li 4 | 1 ta la 2   3 la li 4

For each melody, provide the missing bar lines that correspond with the meter signature given.

(4) "The Butterfly"

(5) Fanny Mendelssohn Hensel, "Schwanenlied" (adapted)

(6) Ludwig van Beethoven, String Quartet in F Major, Op. 18, No. 1, second movement (cello part, adapted)

B. Understanding rests

Write the counts for the melodies below in the meter given. If the beginning of a beat coincides with a rest, write the count in parentheses.

(1) Wolfang Amadeus Mozart, "Sull aria," from *The Marriage of Figaro*, mm. 2–6

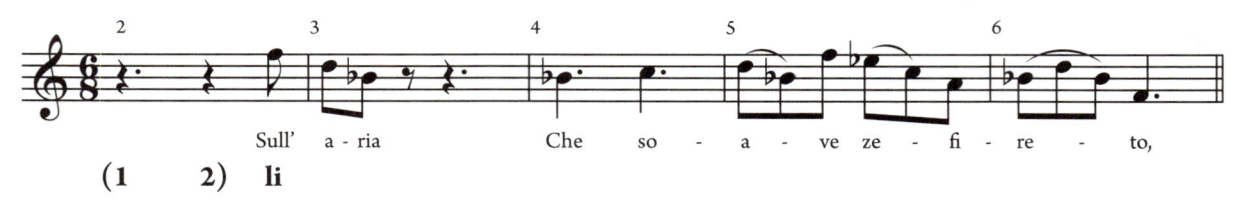

(1)   2) li

On the breeze, what a gentle zephyr [will whisper].

(2) Handel, "Rejoice Greatly," from *Messiah* (alternate version), mm. 9–14

At each position marked with an arrow, add one rest to complete the measure in the meter indicated. Then add counts beneath the rhythms, and practice counting aloud. If a beat begins with a rest, write the count in parentheses.

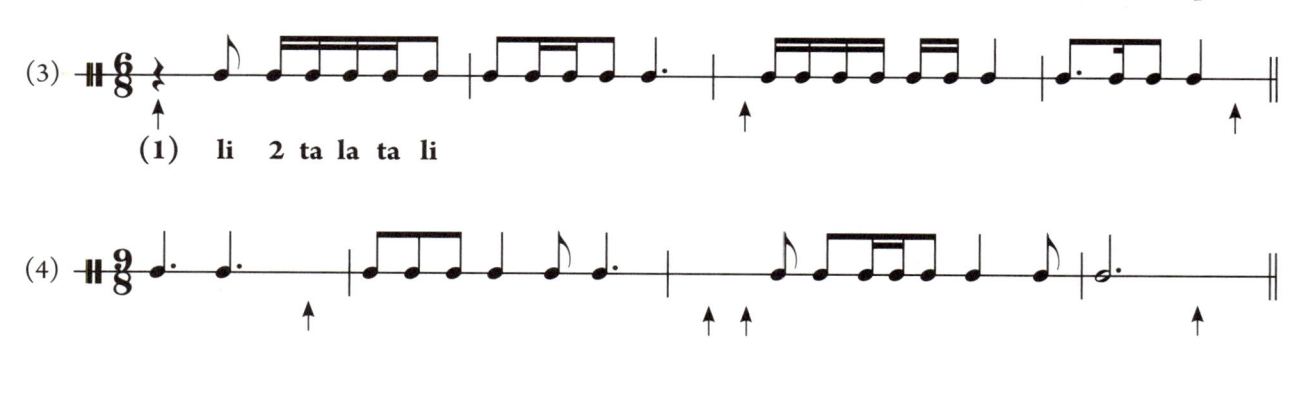

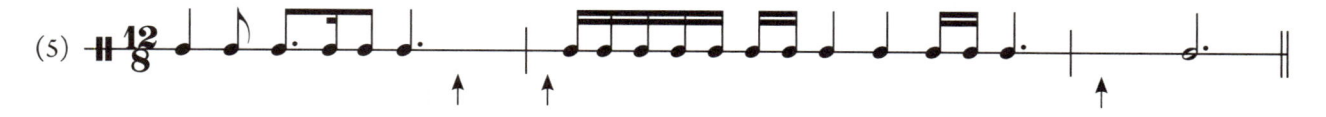

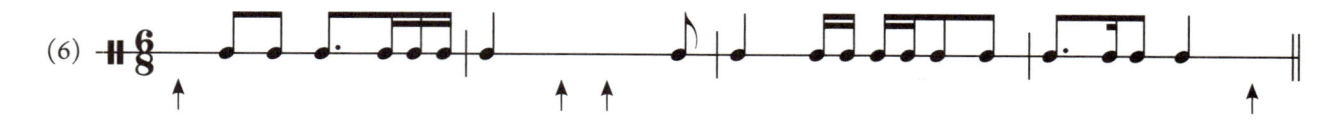

(3) **(1) li   2 ta la ta li**

(4)

(5)

(6)

120   CHAPTER FIVE   Compound and Other Meters

Workbook   ASSIGNMENT 5.3

A. Reading rhythms with 𝅗𝅥. and ♪. beat units

Each rhythm below has a 𝅗𝅥. beat unit. Rewrite the rhythm on the blank staff with a ♩. beat unit (for example, convert 6/4 to 6/8).

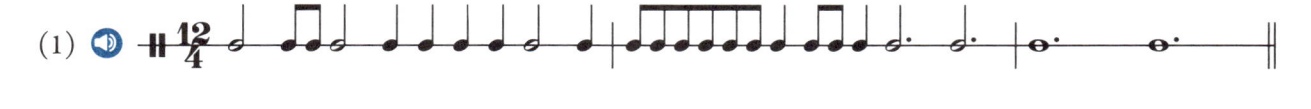

(1) 12/4 …

(2) 9/4 …

(3) 6/4 …

Jacquet de la Guerre, Gigue, from Suite No. 3 in A Minor, mm. 22–25

(4) 6/4 …

The rhythm below has a ♪. beat unit. Rewrite it with a ♩. beat unit.

(5) 6/16 …

Assignment 5.3

B. Beaming to reflect the meter

Rewrite the following rhythms with correct beaming to reflect the beat. Practice the rhythms on "ta" or counting syllables, and be prepared to perform them in class.

(1)

(2)

(3)

Vocal music, especially in older editions, is often written with beaming that corresponds to the syllables of the sung text. Rebeam the vocal line (using beams instead of flags) to reflect the meter and beat unit instead.

(4) George Frideric Handel, "How Beautiful Are the Feet of Them," from *Messiah* mm. 5–9

How beau-ti-ful are the feet ⎯ of them that preach the gos-pel of peace, How beau-ti-ful are the feet, how beau-ti-ful are the feet of them that preach the gos-pel of peace.

Workbook ASSIGNMENT 5.4

A. Syncopation in compound meters

Draw an arrow above each syncopated rhythm.

(1) Marc Shaiman and Scott Wittman, "It Takes Two," from *Hairspray*, mm, 6–7

They say it's a man's world. Well, that can - not ___ be de - nied. ___

(2) Andrew Lloyd Webber, "Memory," from *Cats*, mm. 17–20

Some - one mut - ters ___ and a street lamp gut - ters ___ and soon it will be morn - ing.

(3) Elton John, Bernie Taupin, and Davey Johnstone, "I Guess That's Why They Call It the Blues," mm. 12–15

And while I'm ___ a - way, ___ dust out ___ the de - mons in - side ___

B. Asymmetrical meters

Write the appropriate counts for each rhythm Use "1&" for a simple beat division and "1 la li" for compound.

(1) 7/8
1 & 2 & 3 la li

(2) 8/8

(3) 5/8

(4) 7/16

Assignment 5.4   123

The following excerpts are drawn from *Mikrokosmos*, a collection of piano pieces by Béla Bartók. Write the meter signature for each in the blank provided.

(5) "In the Style of a Folk Song," (No. 100), mm. 1–2

(6) "Fifth Chords," (No. 120), mm. 1–2

C. Changing meters

The following melodies, also from *Mikrokosmos*, feature changing meters. Write the correct signature in each position marked by an arrow. If the meter is unclear, consider the beaming as an additional clue.

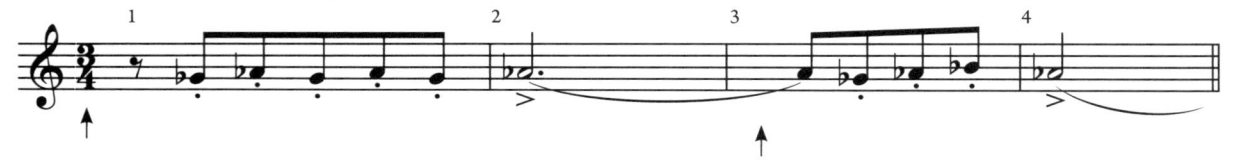

(1) "From the Diary of a Fly" (No. 142), mm. 1–4

(2) "Unison" (No. 137), mm. 1–5

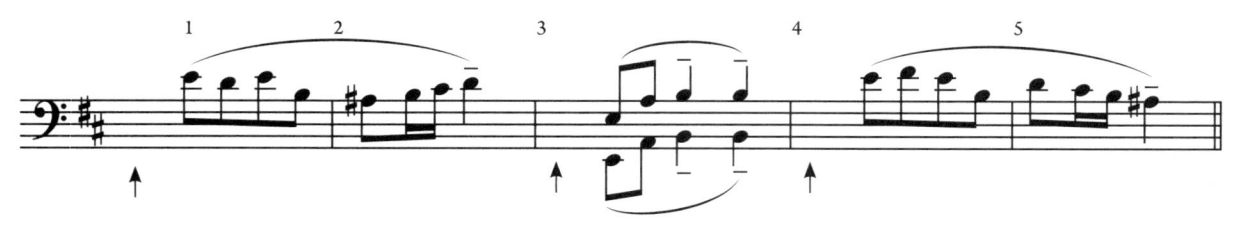

(3) "Change of Time" (No. 126), mm. 1–6

NAME _____

Workbook AURAL SKILLS 5.1

A. Listening to and writing rhythms in compound meter

Listen to two melodies in 6/8 meter. Each begins with an eighth-note anacrusis and consists of four two-measure segments. Notate only the rhythm, using the patterns on page 115.

(1) Hint: Segments 1–3 have the same rhythm; segment 4 has a different rhythm.

Segment 1

Segment 2

Segment 3

Segment 4

(2) Hint: Segments 1 and 3 have the same rhythm; segments 2 and 4 have different rhythms.

Segment 1

Segment 2

Segment 3

Segment 4

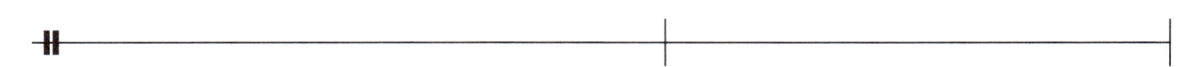

B. Writing a rhythmic composition with beat subdivisions in compound meter

Compose a rhythmic duet for two performers, using only the rhythmic patterns below.

- Write eight measures in 6/8 meter.
- Don't include ties. Use eighth, quarter, and dotted-quarter rests only.
- Vary the complexity: Both voices should sound together at times. At other times, when one voice is rhythmically active, the other voice may have rests or longer notes.
- Include dynamic markings to add musical interest.
- If you would like, write a text to be recited with your rhythm.
- Perform your composition with a partner.

TOPICS
- scales
- scale types: chromatic and whole-tone
- major scales
- scale degrees
- writing major scales
- major key signatures
- the circle of fifths

MUSIC
- "The Ash Grove"
- Stephen Foster, "Oh! Susanna"
- "Simple Gifts"
- John Philip Sousa, "The Stars and Stripes Forever"
- "Twinkle, Twinkle, Little Star"

CHAPTER 6

Major Scales and Keys

Scales

Listen to and compare the beginning of two melodies: Sousa's "The Stars and Stripes Forever" (Example 6.1) and "The Ash Grove" (Example 6.2). The melodies sound different because their pitches are drawn from different types of scales.

> **KEY CONCEPT** A **scale** is an ordered collection of pitches. When the primary pitches of a piece are written in ascending order without repetitions, they form a scale. Each note in a scale is separated from the next by a whole or half step. The first pitch is often repeated an octave higher at the end.

The collection of pitches in each melody, listed starting on E♭, appears below for comparison. (To make the two melodies easier to compare, the octaves of some pitches are changed.)

EXAMPLE 6.1   Sousa, "The Stars and Stripes Forever," mm. 1–4

(a) Melody

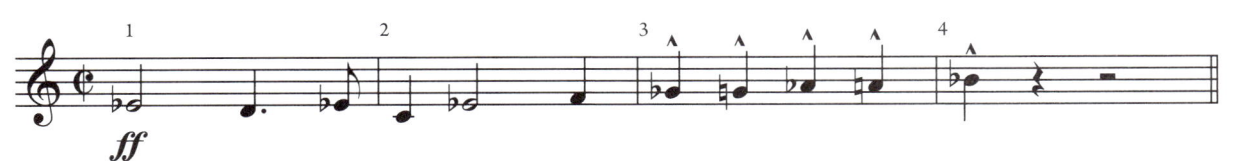

(b) Pitches of the melody

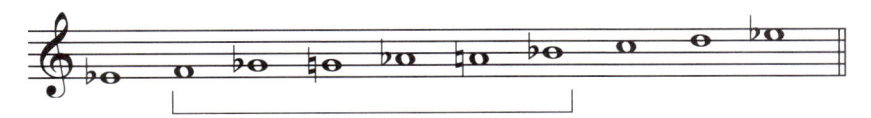

EXAMPLE 6.2   "The Ash Grove"

(a) Melody

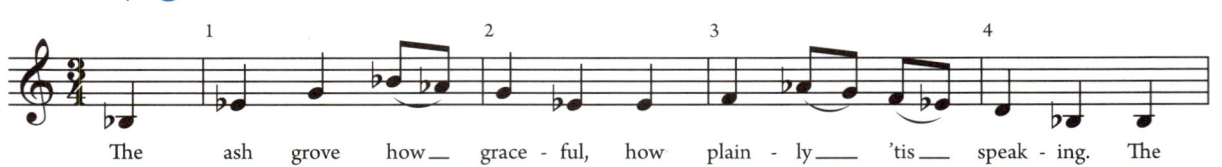

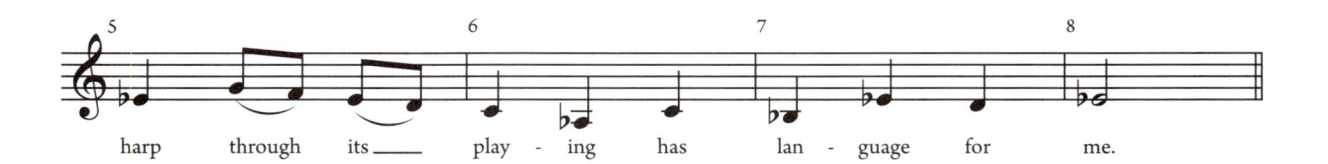

The ash grove how grace-ful, how plain-ly 'tis speak-ing. The harp through its play-ing has lan-guage for me.

(b) Pitches of the melody

Compare the pitches of Examples 6.1b and 6.2b. Except for the repeated E♭, the scale for "The Ash Grove" includes only one representative of each letter, but the scale for the Sousa march repeats some letter names with different accidentals, making chromatic half steps: G♭ and G♮, A♭ and A♮. In a portion of this scale, marked with a bracket, the pitches are all a half step apart: F G♭ G♮ A♭ A♮ and B♭.

Scale Types: Chromatic and Whole-Tone

Scales in which all pitches are equally spaced a half step apart are called **chromatic scales**. Example 6.3 shows a complete chromatic scale, beginning on E♭, with all twelve possible pitches within an octave. Portions of this scale are often found in showy or virtuosic music. Half steps written with the same letter name (like G♭–G♮) are called chromatic half steps because of their prevalence in the chromatic scale.

EXAMPLE 6.3   Chromatic scale, beginning on E♭

H   H   H   etc.

Unless the first pitch has a flat, it is customary to spell chromatic scales with sharps ascending and flats descending, as in Example 6.4. When the first note has a flat, it is typical to write flats and naturals ascending, as in Example 6.3, and flats descending.

EXAMPLE 6.4   Notation of the chromatic scale beginning on D

We can also construct a scale with all whole steps between the pitches as shown in Example 6.5. This scale, called a **whole-tone scale**, has only six different notes. Whole-tone scales are spelled with letter names in order but with one skipped, as in the example where D♭ is skipped; alternatively C♯ could be skipped and D♭ (in parentheses) used instead.

EXAMPLE 6.5   Whole-tone scale, beginning with E♭

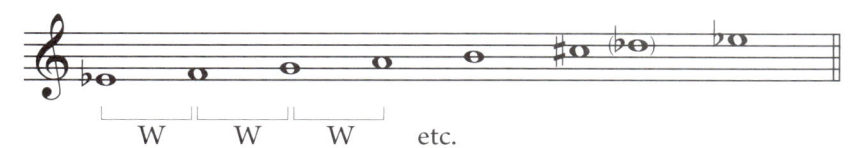

W   W   W   etc.

TRY IT #1

(a) Write a chromatic scale (ascending and descending) beginning with the pitches shown below. Use sharps ascending and flats descending. Do not add an accidental to the first note.

(1)   ascending   descending

(2)

(b) Write a whole-tone scale (ascending only) by adding accidentals to the pitches given below. Do not add an accidental to the first note.

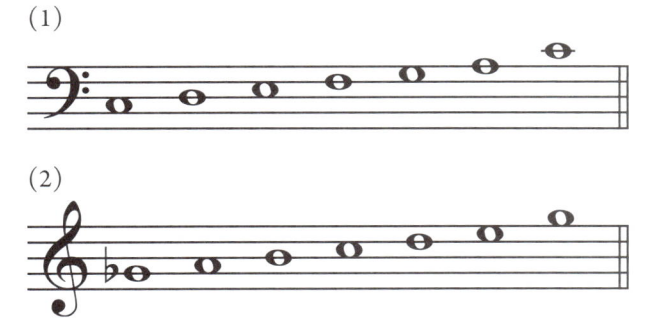

(1)

(2)

Major Scales

The ascending list of pitches in "The Ash Grove" (Example 6.2b) shows a different kind of scale E♭–F–G–A♭–B♭–C–D–E♭.

KEY CONCEPT The pattern of whole (W) and half (H) steps between these pitches is W–W–H–W–W–W–H, forming an ascending **major scale**. If you play the scale starting at the top and descend, the pattern is H–W–W–W–H–W–W.

Since the scale in Example 6.2 begins and ends on E♭, we call it an E♭ major scale (Example 6.6). Scales that are made up of half and whole steps, and include all seven letter names are **diatonic scales**. Half steps written with two different letter names are therefore diatonic half steps.

EXAMPLE 6.6   E♭ major scale

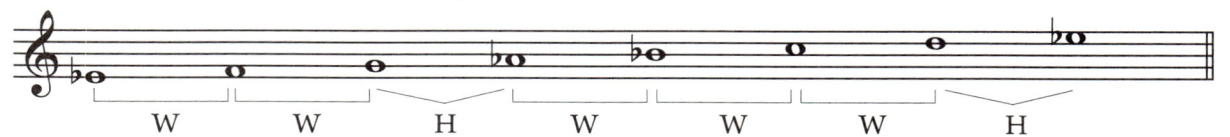

W W H W W W H

Scale Degrees

Each pitch of the major scale is a **scale degree**, or scale step. The beginning, or tonic, scale degree is important in scales and musical works based on them, as a home base to which other pitches gravitate. When a piece is based on a scale with a particular tonic, we say it is "in the key of" that scale. For example, "The Ash Grove" is in the key of E♭ major.

> **KEY CONCEPT** When music is in a **major key**, its pitches come primarily from a major scale and its melody gravitates to the tonic of that scale.

Musicians often refer to scale degrees using numbers from $\hat{1}$ to $\hat{7}$, written with a caret above. When singing music at sight, these scale-degree numbers can help you find your place in the scale. To keep track of tunes you hear or write, jot down the numbers as you sing or play, then translate the numbers into staff notation. Example 6.7 gives each scale step in C major, and Example 6.8 shows how to use them to write the beginning of "Twinkle, Twinkle, Little Star." To write this melody in another key (F, for example)—known as **transposing** the melody—use the same degrees in that scale: F (= $\hat{1}$)–F–C (= $\hat{5}$)–C–D (= $\hat{6}$)–D–C, and so on.

EXAMPLE 6.7   C major scale with scale-degree numbers and solfège syllables

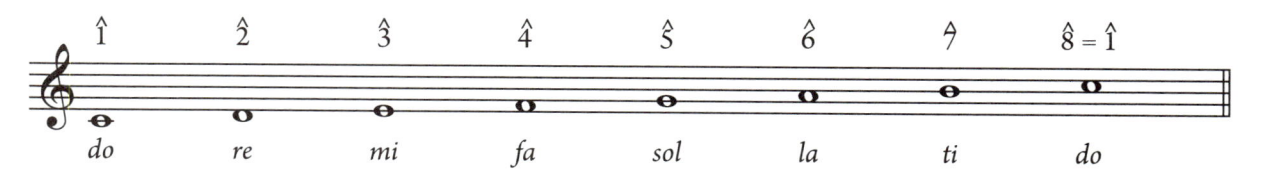

$\hat{1}$ $\hat{2}$ $\hat{3}$ $\hat{4}$ $\hat{5}$ $\hat{6}$ $\hat{7}$ $\hat{8} = \hat{1}$

do   re   mi   fa   sol   la   ti   do

EXAMPLE 6.8   "Twinkle, Twinkle, Little Star," mm. 1–4

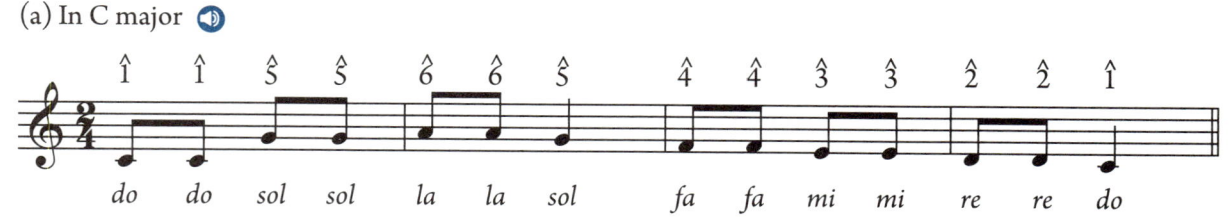

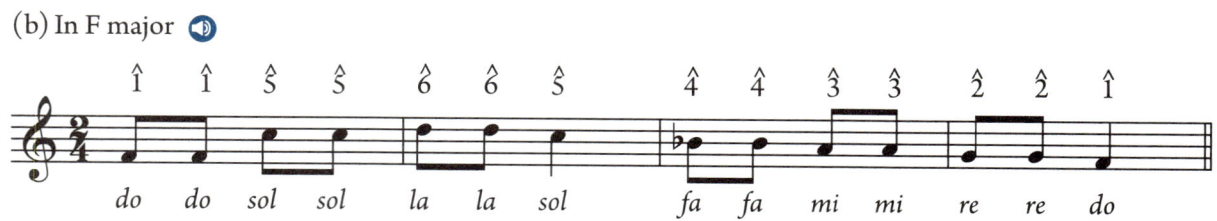

(a) In C major

$\hat{1}$ $\hat{1}$ $\hat{5}$ $\hat{5}$ $\hat{6}$ $\hat{6}$ $\hat{5}$ $\hat{4}$ $\hat{4}$ $\hat{3}$ $\hat{3}$ $\hat{2}$ $\hat{2}$ $\hat{1}$

do do sol sol la la sol   fa fa mi mi re re do

(b) In F major

$\hat{1}$ $\hat{1}$ $\hat{5}$ $\hat{5}$ $\hat{6}$ $\hat{6}$ $\hat{5}$ $\hat{4}$ $\hat{4}$ $\hat{3}$ $\hat{3}$ $\hat{2}$ $\hat{2}$ $\hat{1}$

do do sol sol la la sol   fa fa mi mi re re do

Another method for sight-singing, **movable-*do* solfège**, or **solfège** for short, assigns each scale degree a syllable—*do, re, mi, fa, sol, la, ti, do*—as shown beneath the scale in Example 6.7. In the movable-*do* system, $\hat{1}$ is always *do*, $\hat{2}$ is always *re*, $\hat{3}$ is always *mi*, and so on—no matter which scale is used, as Example 6.8 shows.

AURAL SKILLS 6.1

ANOTHER WAY A third method for sight-singing, called **fixed-*do* solfège**, always associates *do* with C, *re* with D, *mi* with E, *fa* with F, and so forth, regardless of the scale. Fixed-*do* solfège is analogous to singing letter names, while movable-*do* solfège is comparable to singing scale-degree numbers.

In addition to scale-degree numbers or solfège, musicians often refer to scale degrees by the names given in Example 6.9. Scale degree $\hat{1}$ is called the **tonic**—it is the "tone" on which the scale is built—while $\hat{5}$ is the **dominant**: its musical function "dominates" tonal music, as will be clear in future chapters. Scale degree $\hat{3}$ is the **mediant**, since it falls midway between $\hat{1}$ and $\hat{5}$. Scale degree $\hat{2}$ is called the **supertonic**—"super-" means "above" (as in "superhuman" or "superior")—to fix its position immediately above $\hat{1}$. As Example 6.9b shows, this relationship of $\hat{2}$ above $\hat{1}$ is mirrored by $\hat{7}$ below $\hat{1}$; $\hat{7}$, the **leading tone**, gets its name from its tendency to lead upward toward the tonic. (In fact, $\hat{7}$ is sometimes called a **tendency tone** because of this strong tendency to pull up to $\hat{1}$.) Scale degree $\hat{4}$ is the **subdominant**; "sub-" means "below" (as in "submarine" or "subordinate"). This label originates from the idea that $\hat{4}$ lies the same distance below the tonic as the dominant lies above. Similarly, the **submediant**, $\hat{6}$, lies three scale steps below the tonic (just as the mediant lies three scale steps above).

EXAMPLE 6.9 Scale-degree names
(a) Arranged $\hat{1}$ to $\hat{1}$

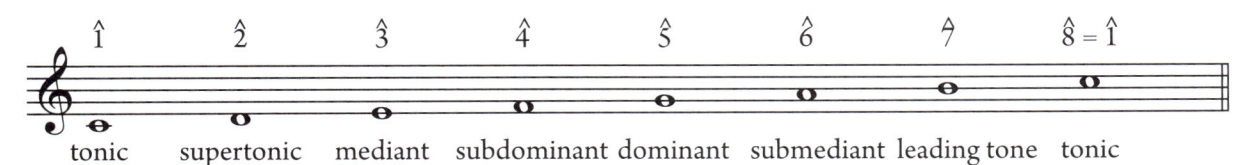

$\hat{1}$ — tonic
$\hat{2}$ — supertonic
$\hat{3}$ — mediant
$\hat{4}$ — subdominant
$\hat{5}$ — dominant
$\hat{6}$ — submediant
$\hat{7}$ — leading tone
$\hat{8} = \hat{1}$ — tonic

(b) Arranged with $\hat{1}$ in the middle

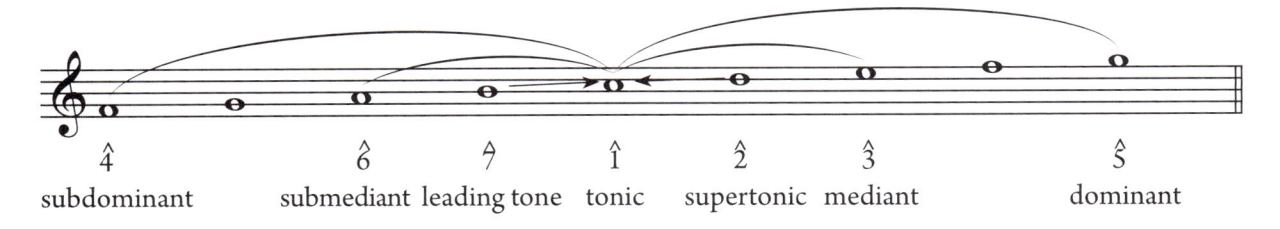

$\hat{4}$ — subdominant
$\hat{6}$ — submediant
$\hat{7}$ — leading tone
$\hat{1}$ — tonic
$\hat{2}$ — supertonic
$\hat{3}$ — mediant
$\hat{5}$ — dominant

Writing Major Scales

All major scales share the same pattern of whole and half steps between adjacent notes: W–W–H–W–W–W–H. An easy way to remember this pattern is to think of the position of half steps in a C major scale, which is made of the white keys from one C to the next.

Another easy way is to divide the scale into two four-note groups (or **tetrachords**) with a whole step between them, as shown in Example 6.10. These groups, each making the pattern W–W–H, are called **major tetrachords** because of their role in the major scale.

EXAMPLE 6.10   Major scale built from two major tetrachords

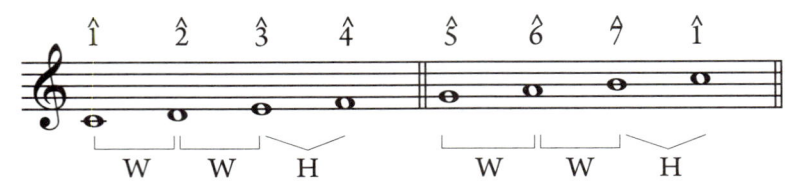

To write any major scale, follow the steps shown in Example 6.11, which builds the ascending D major scale.

a. Write $\hat{1}$ (which may or may not have an accidental).
b. Write the remaining seven notes (with no accidentals), one for each letter name, with $\hat{1}$ repeated at the top; these will fill one octave.
c. Write the interval pattern beneath the notes: W–W–H–W–W–W–H. (You could think of two major tetrachords, W–W–H, a whole step apart.)
d. Add accidentals if necessary to make the correct pattern of whole and half steps.

EXAMPLE 6.11   Steps to write an ascending major scale

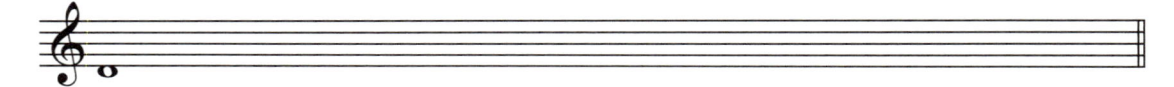

(a) Write $\hat{1}$.

(b) Add the remaining notes.

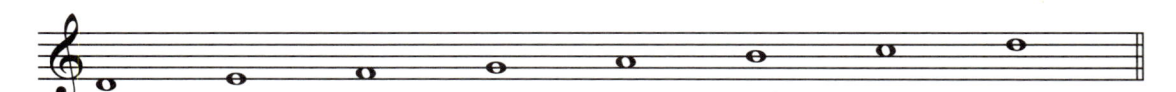

(c) Write the interval pattern.

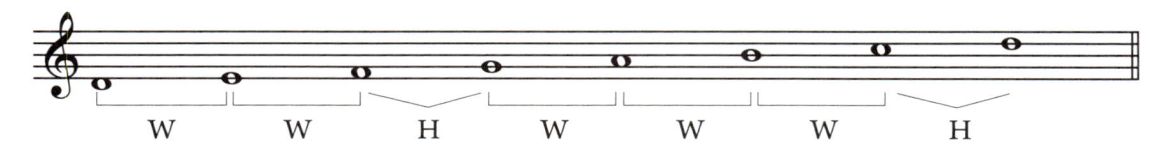

W W H W W W H

(d) Add accidentals, if needed.

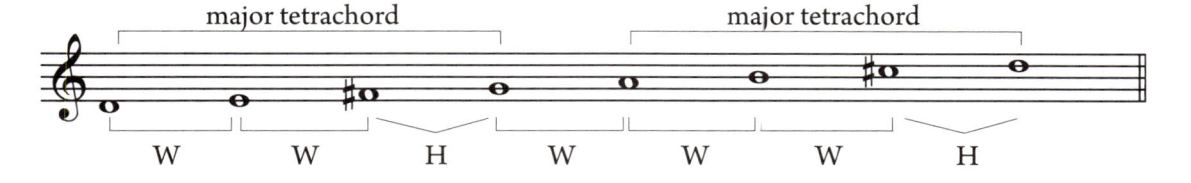

major tetrachord   major tetrachord

W W H W W W H

132   CHAPTER SIX   Major Scales and Keys

> **KEY CONCEPT** Any major scale you write should include eight pitches—all seven letters plus the tonic repeated at the end—and the accidentals should be either all sharps or all flats, not a mixture.

In the B♭ major scale, for example, it would be incorrect to write D♯ instead of E♭, as Example 6.12 demonstrates. This spelling would give both D and D♯ (a chromatic half step, instead of the diatonic D to E♭) and no E at all.

EXAMPLE 6.12   Notation of the B♭ major scale

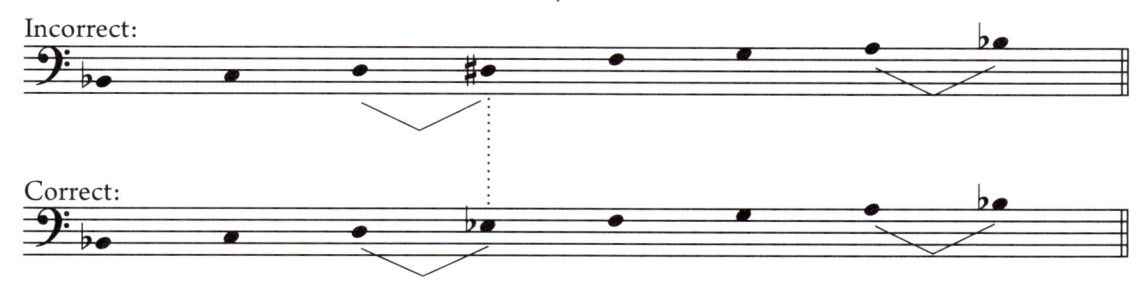

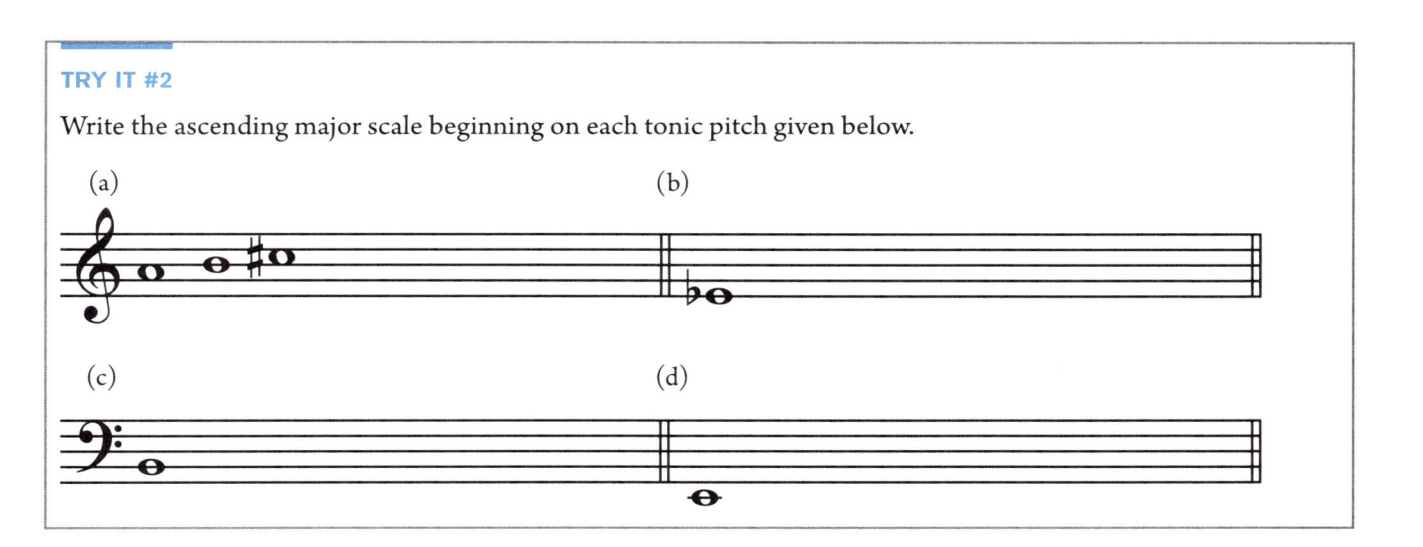

Incorrect:

Correct:

> **TRY IT #2**
> Write the ascending major scale beginning on each tonic pitch given below.
>
> (a)   (b)
>
> (c)   (d)

ASSIGNMENT 6.1

Major Key Signatures

Look at the melody of "Oh! Susanna," shown in Example 6.13, and examine the notation. This piece is in D major—whose scale includes two sharps—yet not a single accidental is notated next to any pitch. Instead, the **key signature** (circled) immediately following the clef sign instructs the performer to sharp every F and C throughout the song.

EXAMPLE 6.13   Foster, "Oh! Susanna," mm. 1–8

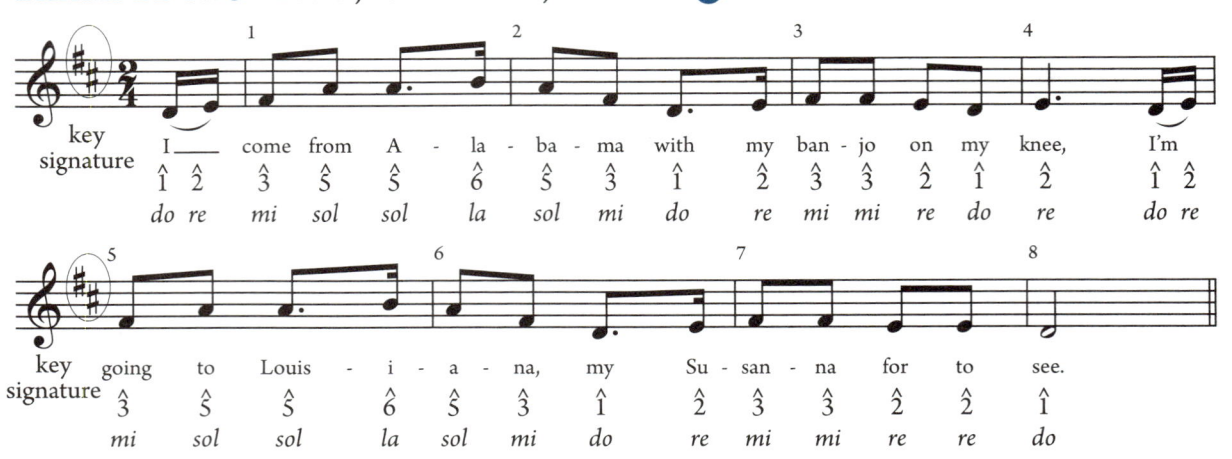

key signature | I — come from A - la - ba - ma with my ban - jo on my knee, I'm
1̂ 2̂ 3̂ 5̂ 5̂ 6̂ 5̂ 3̂ 1̂ 2̂ 3̂ 3̂ 2̂ 1̂ 2̂ 1̂ 2̂
do re mi sol sol la sol mi do re mi mi re do re do re

key signature | going to Louis - i - a - na, my Su - san - na for to see.
3̂ 5̂ 5̂ 6̂ 5̂ 3̂ 1̂ 2̂ 3̂ 3̂ 2̂ 2̂ 1̂
mi sol sol la sol mi do re mi mi re re do

A key signature represents the sharps or flats of the scale on which the work is based, and applies to pitches in all octaves. The key signature, together with the scale-degree relations between pitches, helps you determine the key of a piece. Occasionally, you may wish to alter a pitch by adding an accidental different from those in the key signature. Remember that such accidentals apply to all repetitions of the pitch (in that octave) for the rest of the measure; the next bar line cancels the accidental.

In Figure 6.1, all the major key signatures are notated in treble and bass clefs. You should memorize them, since many skills covered in future chapters build on this knowledge.

> **KEY CONCEPT**   In a key signature, the order of the sharps is F♯–C♯–G♯–D♯–A♯–E♯–B♯. The order of the flats is reversed: B♭–E♭–A♭–D♭–G♭–C♭–F♭. Sharps and flats must be written in this order and centered on the lines and spaces shown in Figure 6.1.

In a musical score, the key signature appears on every staff and is always written between the clef sign and meter signature (in alphabetical order: clef, key, meter). If the key is C major, there are no sharps or flats.

FIGURE 6.1   Major key signatures

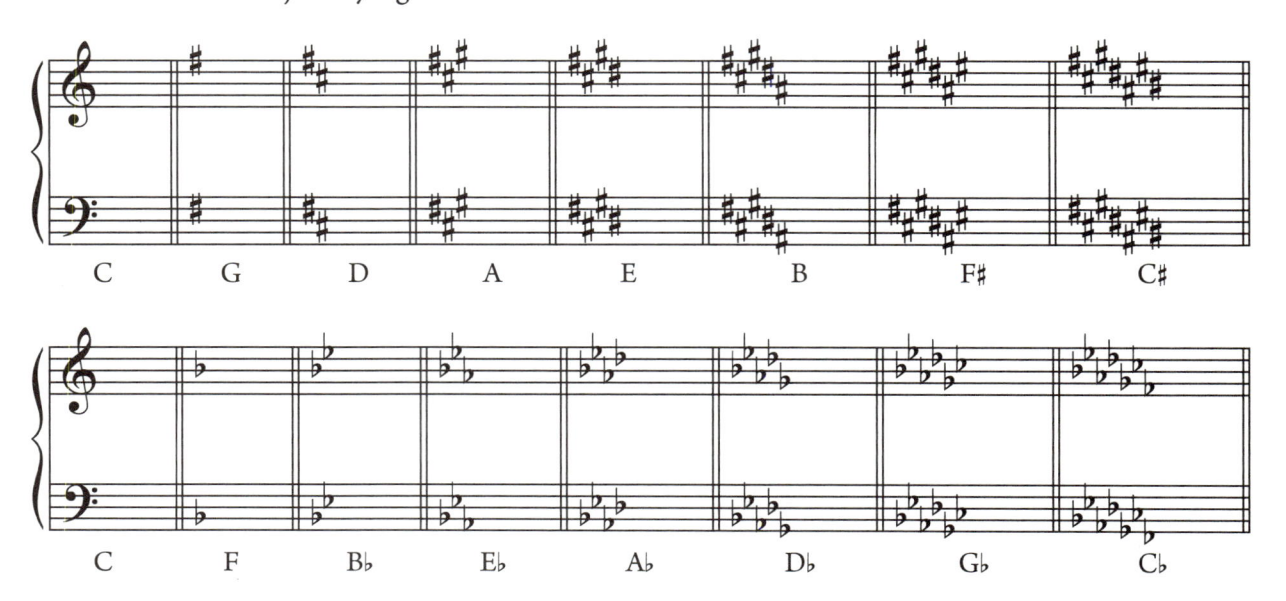

C   G   D   A   E   B   F♯   C♯

C   F   B♭   E♭   A♭   D♭   G♭   C♭

> **ANOTHER WAY** A common mnemonic (memory) device to help you remember the first four flats is the word "bead." One handy sentence to remember for the order of both sharps and flats is "Father Charles Goes Down And Ends Battle." When you read it forward, the first letter of each word gives the order of sharps; when you read it backward ("Battle Ends And Down Goes Charles's Father"), you get the order of flats.

TRY IT #3

Write the key signature for the major keys specified below, in both treble and bass clefs.

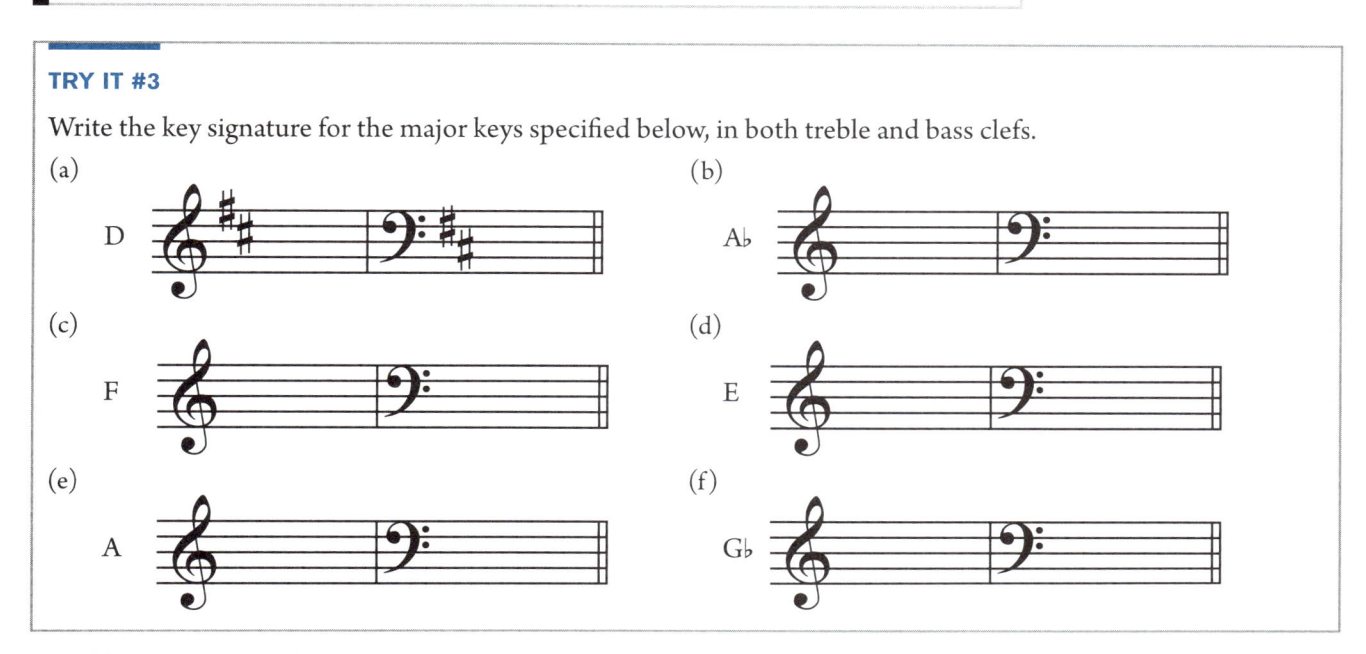

(a) D

(b) A♭

(c) F

(d) E

(e) A

(f) G♭

Although you should memorize which key signature goes with which key, you can also determine the key from the signature. For sharp keys, the last sharp of the signature is $\hat{7}$. To find the tonic, go up a diatonic half step. For example, in the key signature with four sharps (shown in Figure 6.2a), if D♯ is $\hat{7}$, then E is $\hat{1}$, and the key is E major. For flat keys, the last flat of the signature is $\hat{4}$ of the key. Beginning with that note, count down four scale steps (as in Figure 6.2b) to find the name of the key. As a shortcut (Figure 6.2c), take the next-to-last flat of the signature: that will be the name of the key (for example, for B♭–E♭–A♭, the key is E♭). For F major, however, since there is only one flat (B♭), you have to count down four steps (Figure 6.2d)—or better yet, memorize the signature.

FIGURE 6.2 Determining the major key from key signatures

(a) Sharp keys:
Count up a half step.
E major

(b) Flat keys:
Count down four scale steps.
E♭ major

(c) Flat-key shortcut:
Next-to-last flat.
E♭ major

(d) F major:
Count down four scale steps.
F major

Major Key Signatures

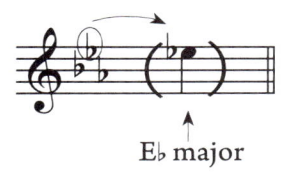

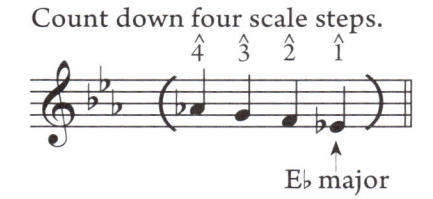

TRY IT #4

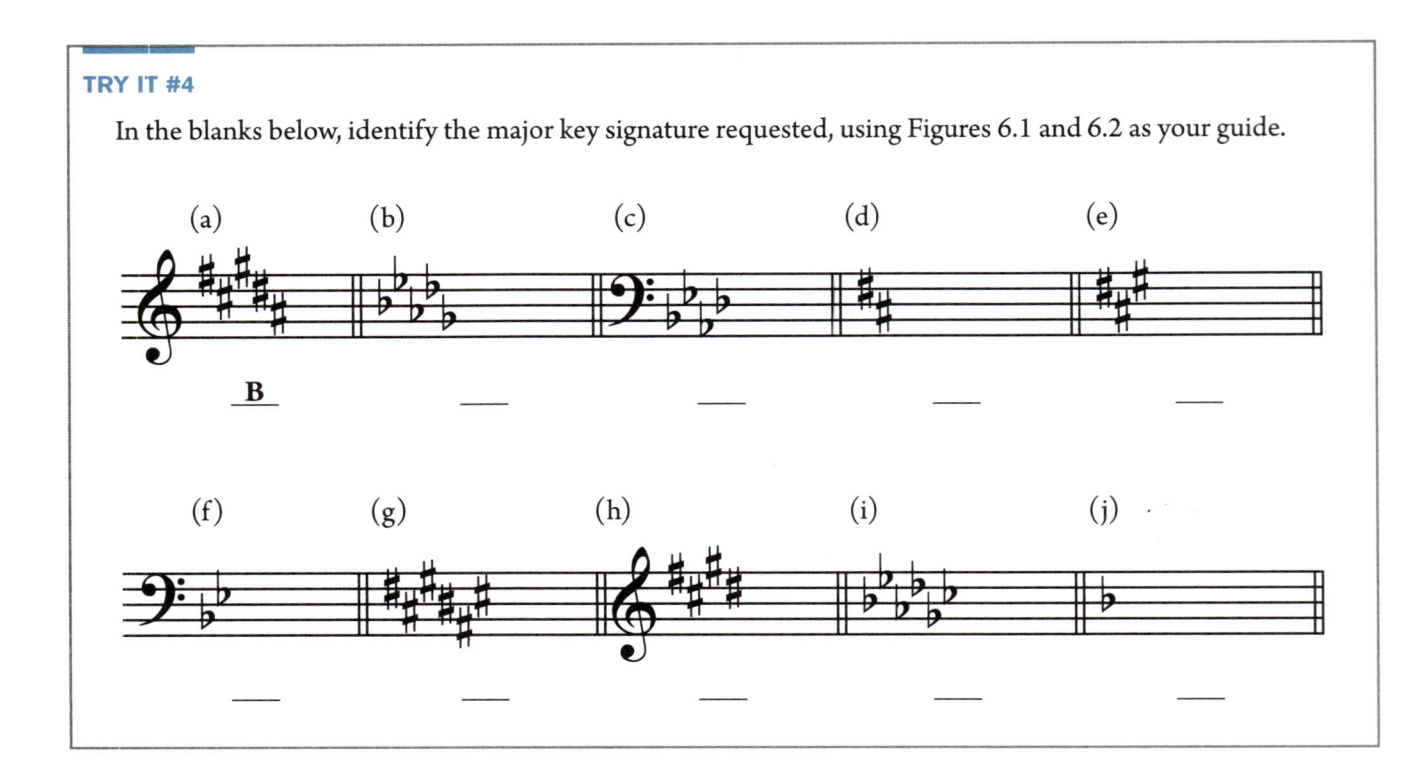

In the blanks below, identify the major key signature requested, using Figures 6.1 and 6.2 as your guide.

(a) B   (b) ___   (c) ___   (d) ___   (e) ___

(f) ___   (g) ___   (h) ___   (i) ___   (j) ___

ASSIGNMENT 6.2

If a piece has two sharps in its key signature, you might assume the piece is in D major, but the key signature alone is not enough to identify the key. (Two sharps can also indicate B minor, as we will see in Chapter 7.) To tell the key of a piece, always check the beginning and end of the melody or bass line for scale-degree patterns like $\hat{3}-\hat{2}-\hat{1}$ or $\hat{5}-\hat{1}$. Look back at Example 6.13, the beginning of "Oh! Susanna," and at Example 6.14, the end of the song. The melody in Example 6.13 starts with a D, $\hat{1}$ in D major, and the first two measures emphasize $\hat{1}-\hat{2}-\hat{3}$ and $\hat{5}-\hat{3}-\hat{1}$. The end of the melody (mm. 15–16 of Example 6.14) is $\hat{3}-\hat{2}-\hat{1}$. All are signs that the song is truly in D major.

EXAMPLE 6.14   Foster, "Oh! Susanna," mm. 13–16

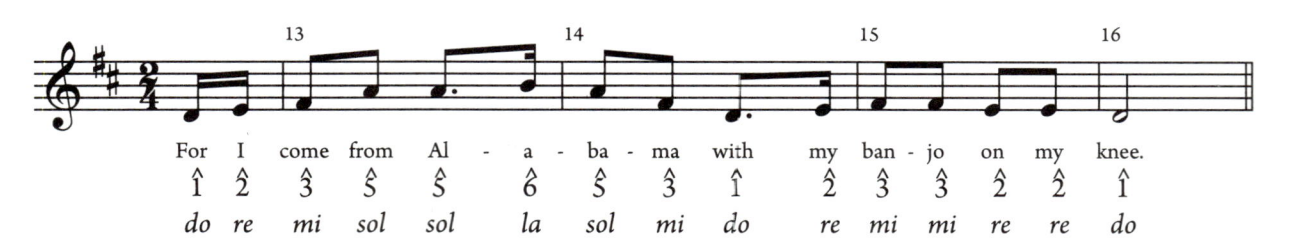

For I come from Al - a - ba - ma with my ban - jo on my knee.
$\hat{1}$ $\hat{2}$ $\hat{3}$ $\hat{5}$ $\hat{5}$ $\hat{6}$ $\hat{5}$ $\hat{3}$ $\hat{1}$ $\hat{2}$ $\hat{3}$ $\hat{3}$ $\hat{2}$ $\hat{2}$ $\hat{1}$
do re mi sol sol la sol mi do re mi mi re re do

TRY IT #5

In what key is "Simple Gifts"? How do you know?

- Key signature suggests what key? _____
- Last six scale degrees? _____
- First six scale degrees? _____
- Key of piece? _____

"Simple Gifts" 🔊

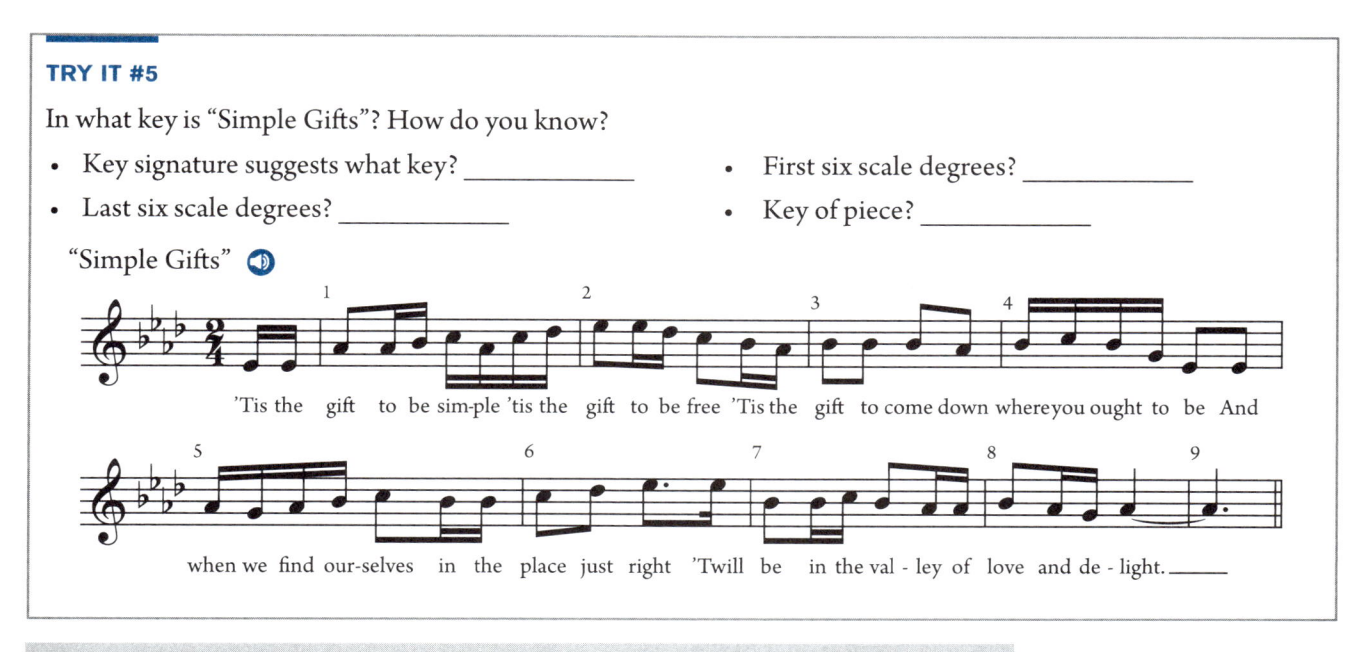

'Tis the gift to be sim-ple 'tis the gift to be free 'Tis the gift to come down where you ought to be And when we find our-selves in the place just right 'Twill be in the val - ley of love and de - light.

AURAL SKILLS 6.2

The Circle of Fifths

In Figure 6.1, each time a sharp is added, the new key is five steps higher than the last; and each time a flat is added, the key is five steps lower. C major has no sharps or flats, G major (five steps higher) one sharp, D major two sharps, and so on. This relationship between keys is represented by a circle, called the **circle of fifths** (Figure 6.3).

FIGURE 6.3 Circle of fifths

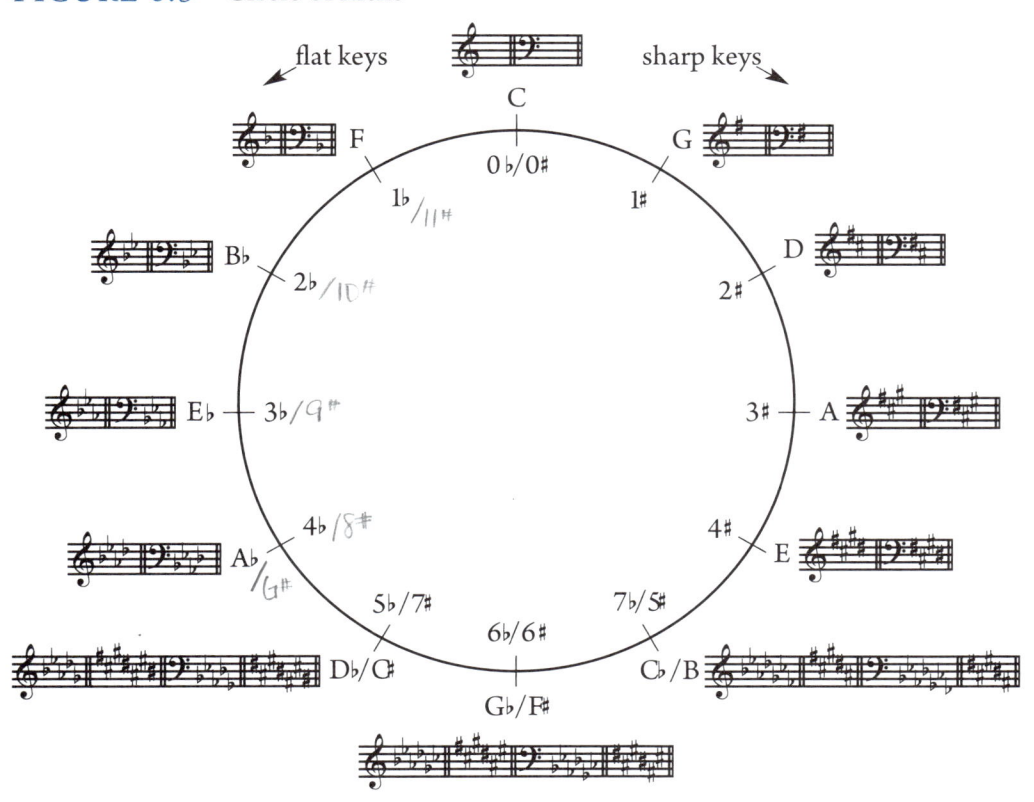

The Circle of Fifths 137

The keys that require sharps appear around the right side, with each key (proceeding clockwise from C) a fifth higher. The keys that require flats appear around the left side of the circle, with each key (going counterclockwise from C) a fifth lower. After F (one flat), each key on the left side of the circle has a flatted note as the tonic (B♭, E♭, A♭, etc.). You may find the circle of fifths a helpful aid as you memorize the key signatures.

ASSIGNMENT 6.3

Did You Know?

Who invented solfège? This innovation is usually attributed to Guido of Arezzo, an eleventh-century monk. Starting with a chant with phrases beginning on C, D, E, F, G, and A, he took the first syllable of each line of the Latin text to represent that note:

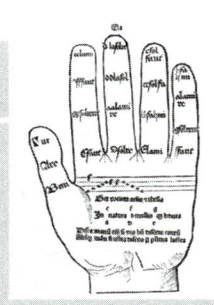

C: **Ut** queant laxis,
D: **Re**sonare fibris,
E: **Mi**ra gestorum,
F: **Fa**muli tuorum,
G: **Sol**ve polluti,
A: **La**brii reatum, Sancte Johannes

This six-syllable system worked well on the music of Guido's time, which could be sung using six-note segments called hexachords, starting on three different notes: C, F, and G. In fact, the three hexachords (called the natural, soft, and hard hexachords) are also the source of our modern notation for natural, flat, and sharp accidentals. Singers in Guido's day sang on syllables by moving between the three hexachords, and they used a mnemonic device based on the knuckles of the hand to remember the syllable changes. Today we call this a "Guidonian hand." Since Guido's time, the system has been altered, changing *ut* to *do*, and adding a seventh syllable, *ti*, for the leading tone in major and minor keys.

Terms You Should Know

circle of fifths	scale degree	solfège
key signature	tonic	movable *do*
major key	supertonic	fixed *do*
major tetrachord	mediant	tendency tone
scale	subdominant	transpose
chromatic	dominant	
diatonic	submediant	
major	leading tone	
whole-tone		

Questions for Review

1. How do you decide which accidentals to use in a chromatic scale?
2. How are chromatic and whole-tone scales similar? How do they differ from major scales?
3. What is the half- and whole-step pattern for an ascending major scale?
4. What systems can be used to label scale steps in a major scale? What are the characteristics of each?
5. What steps do you follow to write a major scale?
6. What is the difference between a chromatic half step and a diatonic half step?
7. Why do we use specific spellings of pitches to notate a major scale? For example, why would an E♭ major scale include an A♭ and not a G♯?
8. List the order of sharps in the key signature for F♯ major.
9. List the order of flats in the key signature for C♭ major.
10. What major key has three sharps? two flats? five flats?
11. What do you need to consider besides the key signature to identify the key of a piece?
12. How is the circle of fifths organized, and what does it show?

Reading Review

Match the term on the left with the best answer on the right.

_____ (1) key signature (a) has three flats in its key signature

_____ (2) circle of fifths (b) order of sharps in a key signature

_____ (3) D major (c) scale built of all half steps

_____ (4) F major (d) sharps or flats at the beginning of the staff (after the clef) that help determine the key

_____ (5) whole-tone scale (e) order of flats in a key signature

_____ (6) B–E–A–D–G–C–F (f) pattern of half and whole steps in a major scale

_____ (7) fixed *do* (g) arrangement of key signatures by number of sharps or flats

_____ (8) chromatic scale (h) has one flat in its key signature

_____ (9) W–W–H–W–W–W–H (i) has two sharps in its key signature

_____ (10) major tetrachord (j) order of symbols at the beginning of the staff

_____ (11) solfège syllables (k) system where $\hat{1}$ is *do*; like reading scale-degree numbers

_____ (12) E♭ major (l) scale built of all whole steps

_____ (13) clef, key, meter (m) *do–re–mi–fa–sol–la–ti*

_____ (14) F–C–G–D–A–E–B (n) pattern of W–W–H in a major scale

_____ (15) movable *do* (o) system where the note C is *do*; like reading letter names

Additional review and practice available at wwnorton.com/studyspace

Apply It

A. At the keyboard

1. Play the first five notes of a C major scale (with the W–W–H–W pattern), one note per finger, as shown in the diagram. Your thumbs are numbered 1, index fingers are 2, middle fingers are 3, and so on. In your left hand, begin with your fifth finger on $\hat{1}$ and end with your thumb on $\hat{5}$. In your right hand, begin with your thumb on $\hat{1}$ and end with your fifth finger on $\hat{5}$.

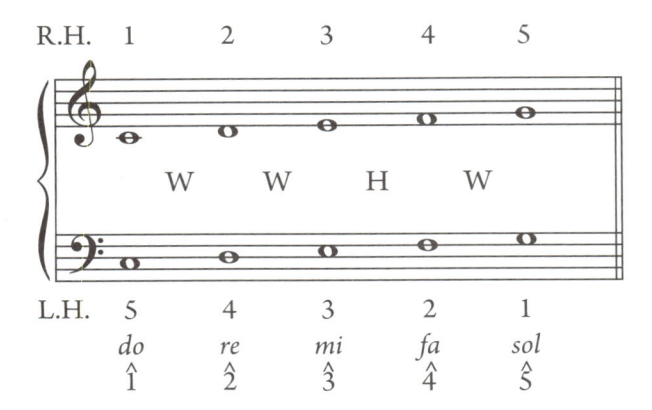

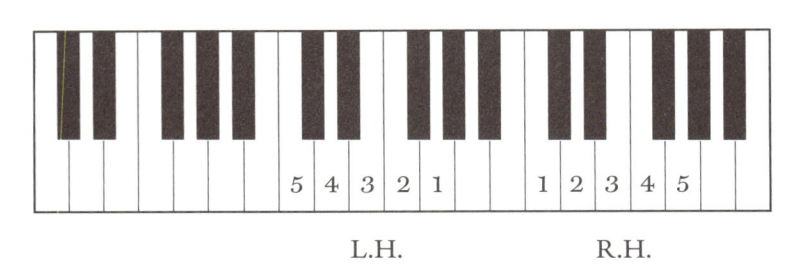

Beginning on each pitch below, play the five-finger pattern in both hands at the same time in separate octaves. While playing, sing with letter names, solfège syllables, or scale-degree numbers.

a. A (A–B–C♯–D–E)
b. F
c. G
d. E♭

e. B
f. F♯
g. E
h. C♯

i. A♭
j. B♭
k. D
l. G♭

2. Play a complete ascending major scale with the fingering shown. Each hand plays a major tetrachord (W–W–H), separated by a whole step.

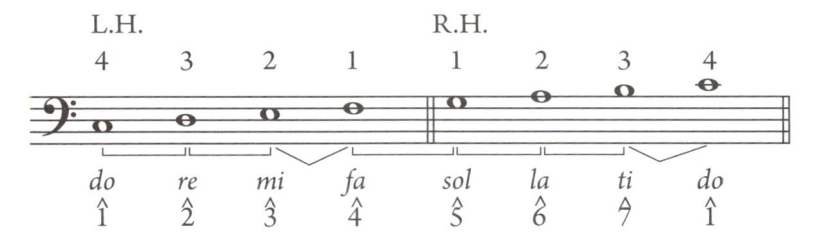

140   CHAPTER SIX   Major Scales and Keys

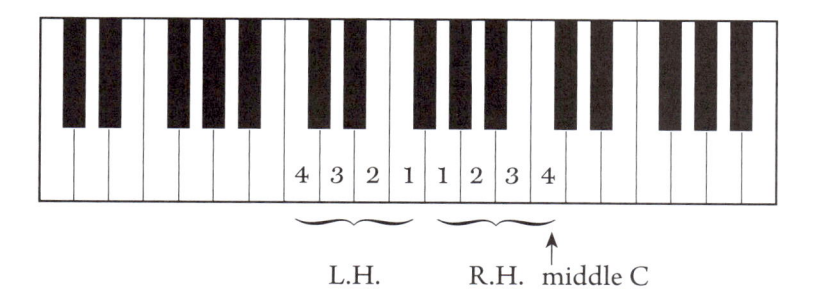

Playing all the following scales with this same fingering will help you remember the whole- and half-step "feel" of the pattern. (These fingerings are only for remembering the pattern; they don't replace traditional scale fingerings used by keyboard players.)

Beginning on each pitch below, play the major scale and sing each letter name. (Recall that each pitch must have a different letter name.) Play again and sing with solfège syllables or scale-degree numbers.

a. D
b. F
c. A♭
d. *B/C♭
e. E♭
f. *F♯/G♭
g. A
h. C
i. E
j. G
k. B♭
l. *D♭/C♯

*Consider each of these pitches as the tonic when you sing the letter names.

B. Review: Reading rhythms

Perform the following rhythms on "ta" or counting syllables, as directed. Keep a steady beat by tapping the pulse or conducting, and follow the dynamic markings.

Rhythm 1

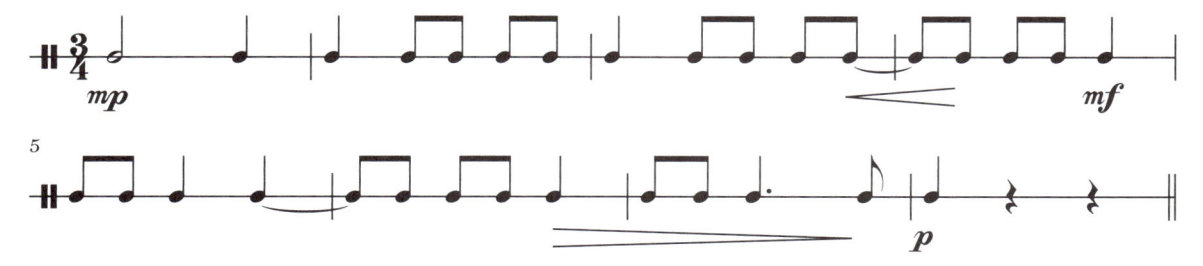

Rhythm 2

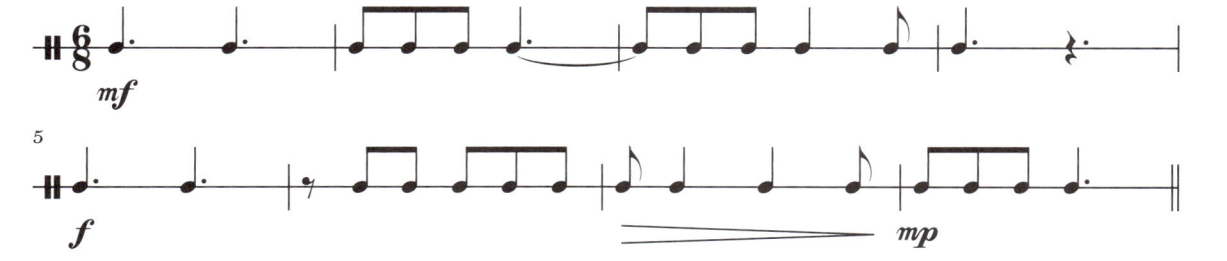

Rhythm 3

Rhythm 4

Rhythm 5

C. Singing at sight

1. The following melodies may be sung as a group activity in class or assigned as homework. First determine the key, and play the major scale at the keyboard (using the fingering you learned in Activity A2). Play the first pitch of the melody (if not $\hat{1}$), and sing down to the tonic pitch to orient yourself. Sing the scale on scale-degree numbers or solfège syllables as you play.
2. Then study the rhythm. Perform it on "ta" or on counting syllables, while tapping a steady beat (or conducting). Begin with a slow tempo; repeat at a faster one.
3. Once you are confident with the rhythm, begin learning the pitches. Sing in an octave that's comfortable for you. Sing on numbers, solfège, or la, as your teacher specifies. Practice without rhythm; play the pitches at a keyboard if it is helpful. Then sing the entire melody, checking the pitches at the keyboard *after* you sing. Finally put pitches and rhythm together at a slow tempo; repeat at a faster one.

Melody 1 "Lil' Liza Jane"

The repeat signs (:||) tell performers to repeat a section of the piece When you see a repeat sign, go back to the last repeat sign or the beginning of the piece and repeat the section once.

Melody 2 Bach, Musette, BWV Anh. 126, mm. 1–8 (adapted)
This melody begins on *sol* ($\hat{5}$).

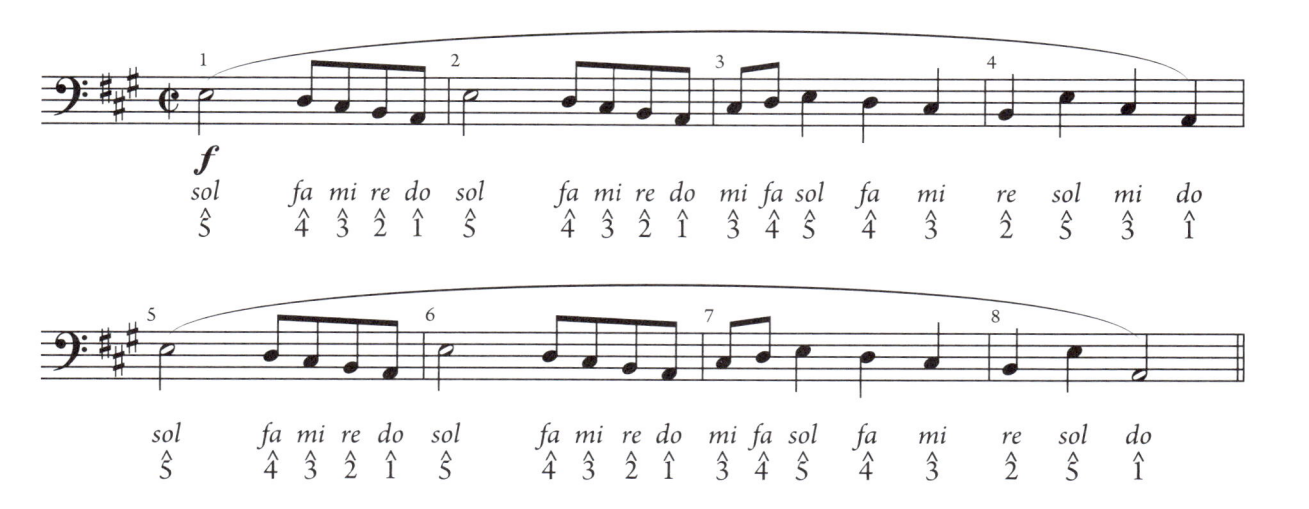

sol fa mi re do sol fa mi re do mi fa sol fa mi re sol mi do
$\hat{5}$ $\hat{4}$ $\hat{3}$ $\hat{2}$ $\hat{1}$ $\hat{5}$ $\hat{4}$ $\hat{3}$ $\hat{2}$ $\hat{1}$ $\hat{3}$ $\hat{4}$ $\hat{5}$ $\hat{4}$ $\hat{3}$ $\hat{2}$ $\hat{5}$ $\hat{3}$ $\hat{1}$

sol fa mi re do sol fa mi re do mi fa sol fa mi re sol do
$\hat{5}$ $\hat{4}$ $\hat{3}$ $\hat{2}$ $\hat{1}$ $\hat{5}$ $\hat{4}$ $\hat{3}$ $\hat{2}$ $\hat{1}$ $\hat{3}$ $\hat{4}$ $\hat{5}$ $\hat{4}$ $\hat{3}$ $\hat{2}$ $\hat{5}$ $\hat{1}$

Melody 3 Beethoven, Sonatina in G, Romanze (adapted), mm. 1–8
This melody begins on *mi* ($\hat{3}$). Write in solfège syllables or numbers as needed.

Melody 4 Harvey Worthington Loomis, "The Frog in the Bog"
The next two melodies are rounds. In a round, the circled numbers above the staff indicate when each part enters. To sing this round, divide into three groups. When the first group reaches ②, the second group sings from the beginning. When the first group reaches ③, the third group sings from the beginning. To practice the round on your own, play the recording, and begin singing at ②.

There once was a frog who lived in a bog and played a fid-dle in the mid-dle of a pud-dle. What a mud-dle! Bet-ter go round! Bet-ter go round!

Apply It 143

Melody 5 "Come, Follow Me"

This melody has a wide vocal range—start on a lower pitch if it is too high. Once you have learned the melody, sing it as a round.

Come, fol - low, fol - low, fol - low, fol - low, fol - low, fol - low me. Whith - er shall I fol - low, fol - low, fol - low, Whith - er shall I fol - low, fol - low thee? To the green - wood, to the green - wood, To the green - wood, green - wood tree.

D. Listening and writing

Listen to short melodies made from $\hat{1}$ to $\hat{5}$ of a major scale. Sing what you hear, then write it on the staff provided.

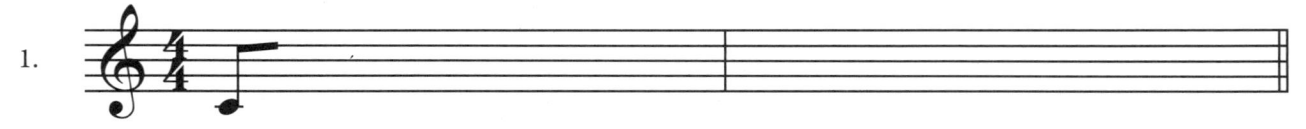

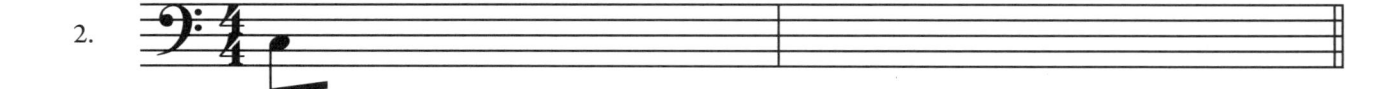

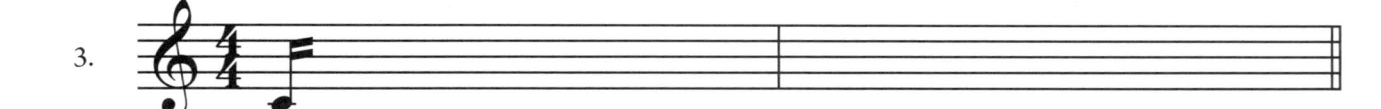

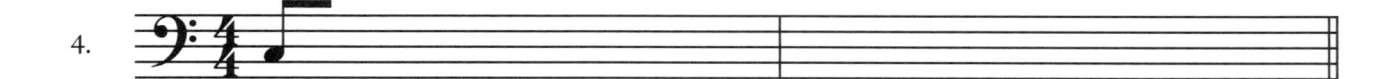

1.
2.
3.
4.
5.

144   CHAPTER SIX Major Scales and Keys

NAME _____

Workbook ASSIGNMENT 6.1

A. Writing chromatic scales

Write one-octave chromatic scales as requested below, both ascending (with sharps) and descending (with flats). For scales that begin with a flat, write flats and naturals ascending.

(1) C chromatic scale

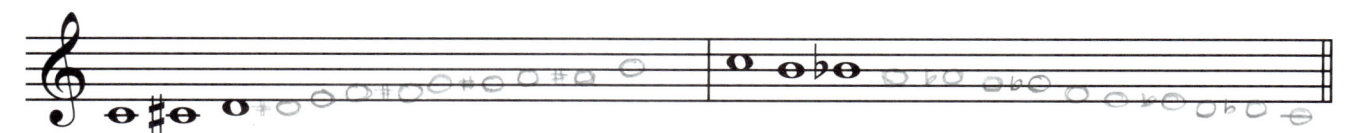

(2) A chromatic scale

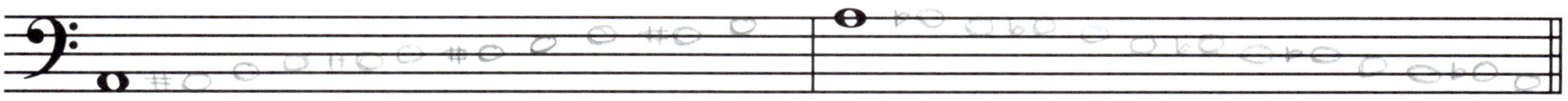

(3) F chromatic scale

(4) B♭ chromatic scale

B. Writing major scales

Beginning on the pitch given, build a major scale by adding flats or sharps to the left of the pitches as needed. Be sure to follow the correct pattern of whole and half steps: W–W–H–W–W–W–H. Label the whole and half steps.

(1) E♭ major   (2) D major

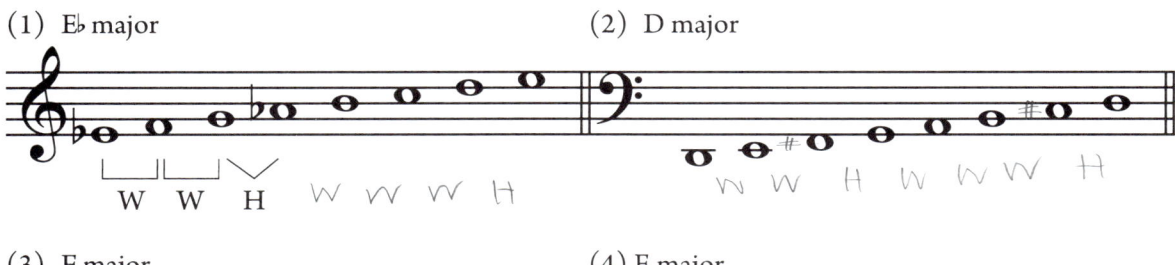

(3) F major   (4) E major

Assignment 6.1   145

C. Writing major scales with scale-degree numbers

Beginning on the pitch given, write an ascending and descending major scale, following the correct pattern of whole and half steps. Start by writing in the note heads, label whole and half steps, then add flats or sharps as needed. Write the scale-degree number above each note.

(1) F♯ major

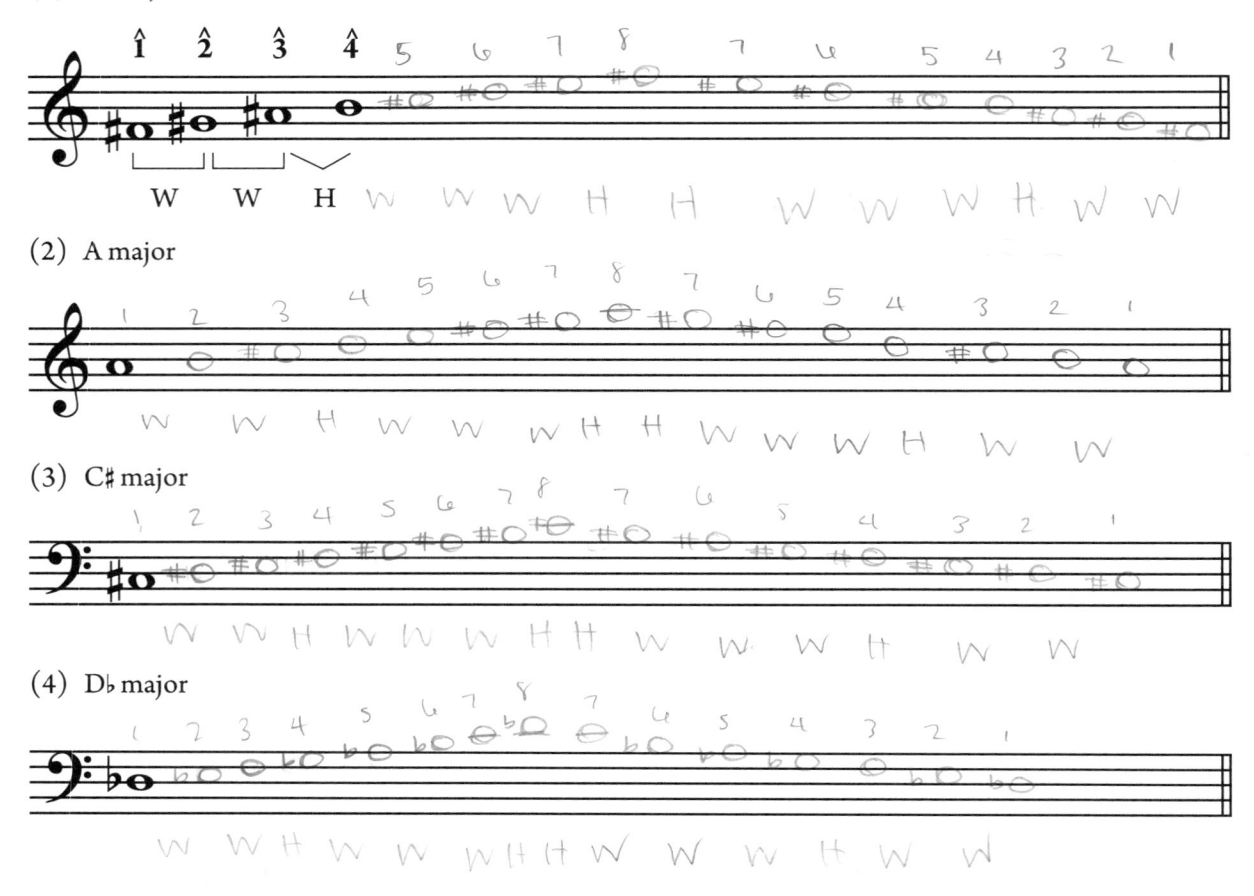

(2) A major

(3) C♯ major

(4) D♭ major

D. Writing whole-tone scales

For each set of pitches below, add accidentals to create a whole-tone scale. Label each whole step.

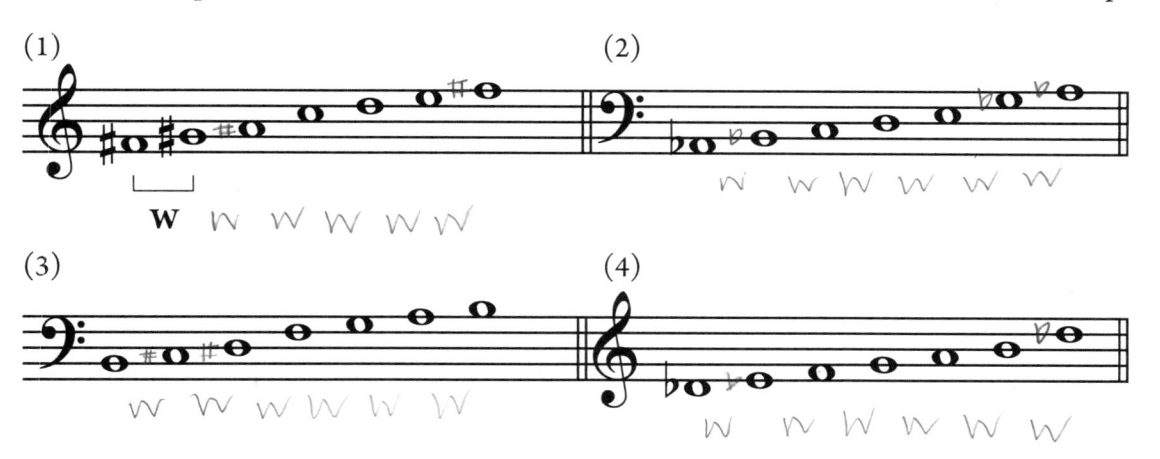

(1)   (2)

(3)   (4)

Workbook ASSIGNMENT 6.2

A. Key signature warm-up

On the staves below, copy the seven sharps and seven flats in order in each clef. As you write each sharp or flat, say the name of the major key that goes with the number of sharps or flats that you've written so far.

sharps   flats

sharps   flats

B. Writing key signatures

(1) Write the key signature for each sharp key below. Remember: Think one diatonic half step down from the name of the key; this note will be the last sharp.

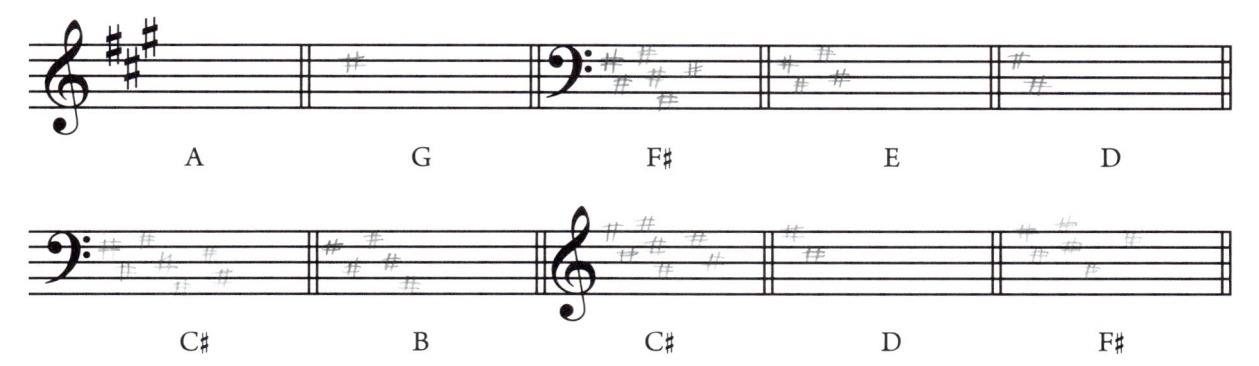

A   G   F♯   E   D

C♯   B   C♯   D   F♯

(2) Write the key signature for each flat key below. Remember: Write one flat beyond the name of the key.

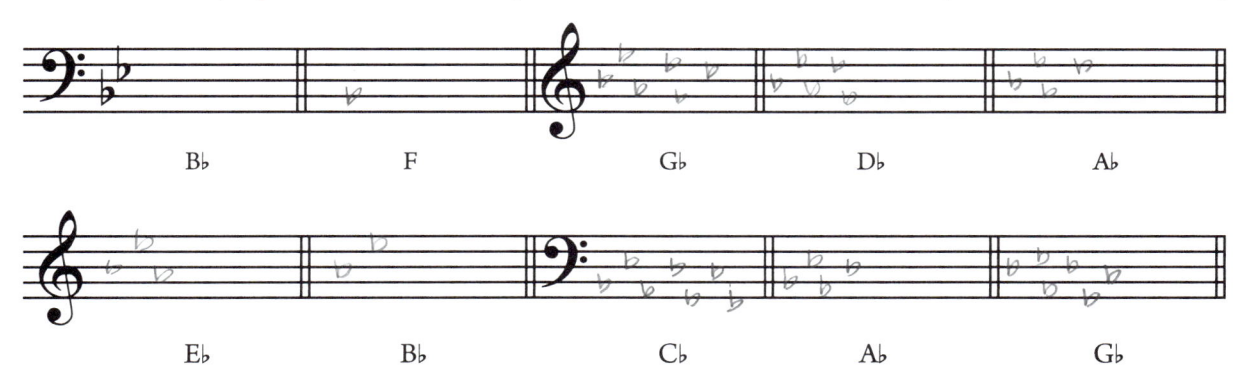

B♭   F   G♭   D♭   A♭

E♭   B♭   C♭   A♭   G♭

(3) Write the key signature for each major key indicated. Remember that the sharps and flats must appear in the correct order and octave.

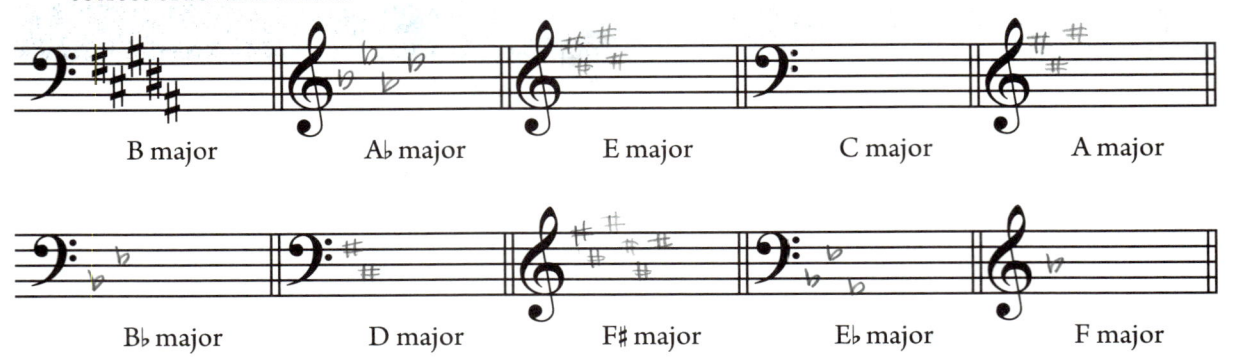

B major   A♭ major   E major   C major   A major

B♭ major   D major   F♯ major   E♭ major   F major

C. Identifying keys from key signatures

(1) Identify the name of each sharp key given below. Circle the last sharp (the leading tone of the key), then go up a half step to name the key.

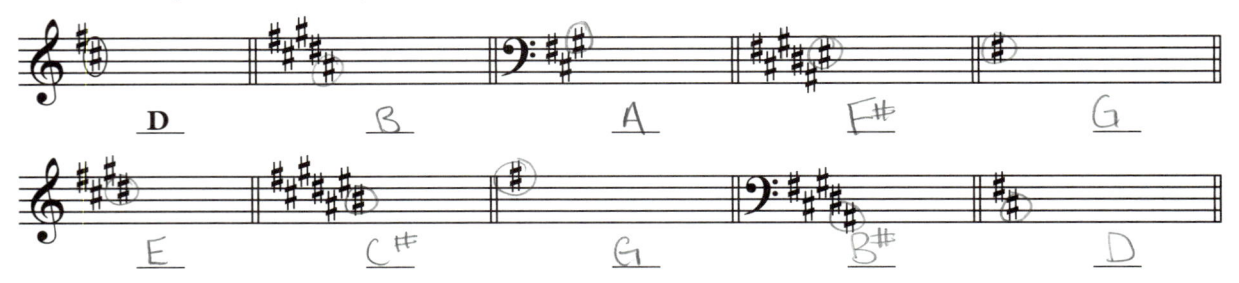

D   B   A   F♯   G

E   C♯   G   B♯   D

(2) Identify the name of each flat key below. Circle the next-to-last flat to get the name of the key (*or* go down four scale steps from the last flat).

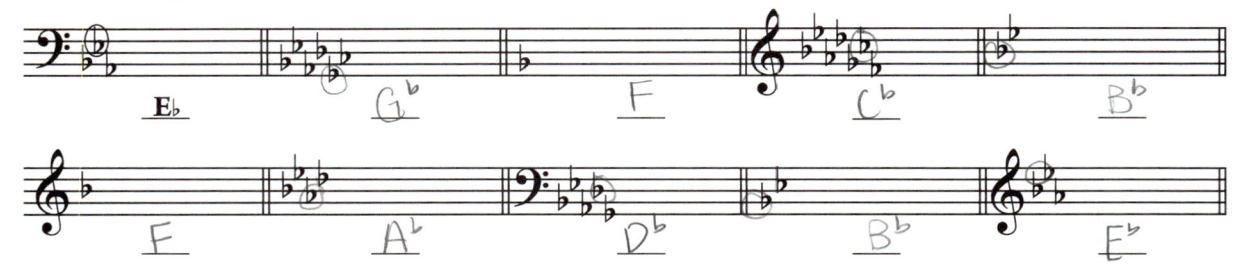

E♭   G♭   F   C♭   B♭

F   A♭   D♭   B♭   E♭

(3) Identify the name of the major key associated with each key signature below.

B♭   G   A♭   D   E♭   F♯   D♭   E

A   D   F   B   G♭   E♭   G   A♭

Workbook ASSIGNMENT 6.3

A. Writing major scales from scale degrees

Given the scale degree notated on the left, write the appropriate ascending major scale. Begin by writing whole notes on each line and space of the staff, then fill in the necessary accidentals. Write the scale-degree numbers to check your answer.

B. **Identifying the key from a melody**

Look at the key signature and melodic cues from the beginning and end of each song excerpt below to determine the key. Write the name of the major key or "not major" in the blank. If major, label the scale degrees of the notes to confirm that they fit well in the key you have chosen.

(1) "Drink to Me Only," mm. 1–4

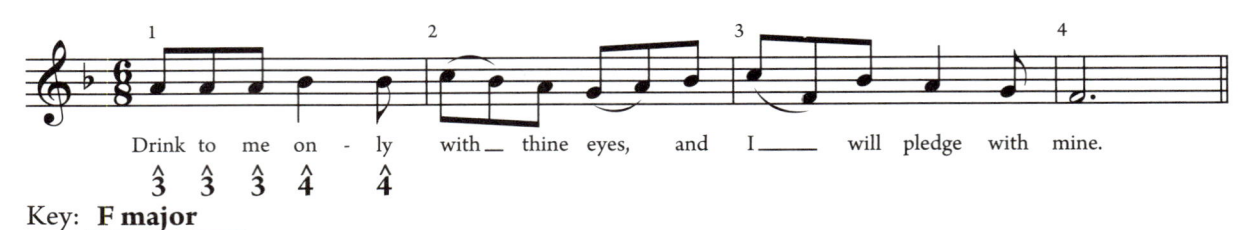

Drink to me on - ly with thine eyes, and I will pledge with mine.
$\hat{3}$ $\hat{3}$ $\hat{3}$ $\hat{4}$ $\hat{4}$

Key: **F major**

(2) Elvis Presley, "Love Me Tender," mm. 5–8

Love me ten - der, love me sweet, nev - er let me go.
5 1 7 1 2 6 2 1 7 6 7 1

Key: G major

(3) "Shalom, Chaverim," mm. 5–8

Le - hit ra - ot, le - hit ra - ot, Sha - lom, sha - lom.

Peace until we meet again

Key: not major

(4) Franz Schubert, "Der Lindenbaum," from *Winterreise*, mm. 9–12

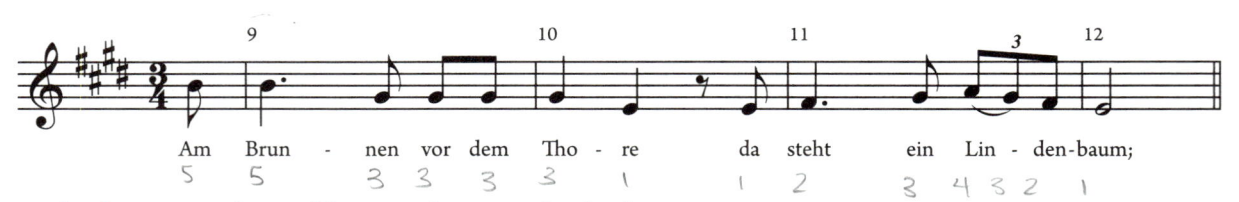

Am Brun - nen vor dem Tho - re da steht ein Lin - den-baum;
5 5 3 3 3 3 1 1 2 3 4 3 2 1

By the fountain in front of the gate, there stands a linden tree.

Key: E major

(5) "Masters in This Hall," mm. 5–8

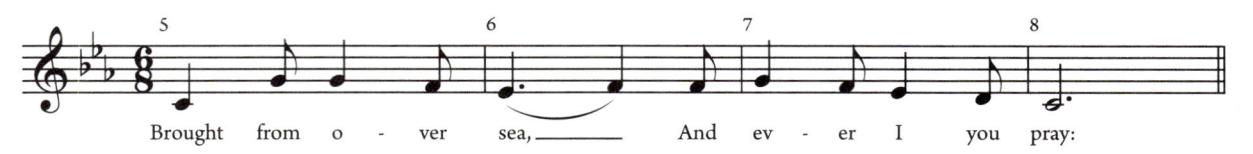

Brought from o - ver sea, And ev - er I you pray:

Key: not major

150   CHAPTER SIX Major Scales and Keys

Workbook AURAL SKILLS 6.1

A. Review: hearing half and whole steps

Listen to the recording. Beginning with the given pitch, a three-pitch melody will be played. In the blanks beneath each exercise, write W or H between pitches 1 and 2 and between pitches 2 and 3. Then notate pitches 2 and 3 with adjacent note names and the appropriate accidental.

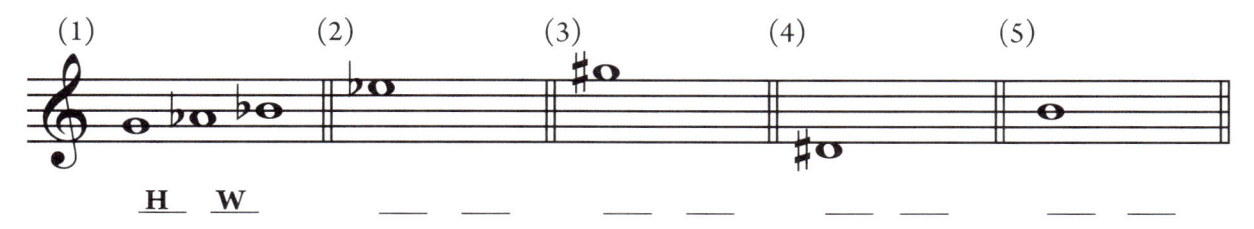

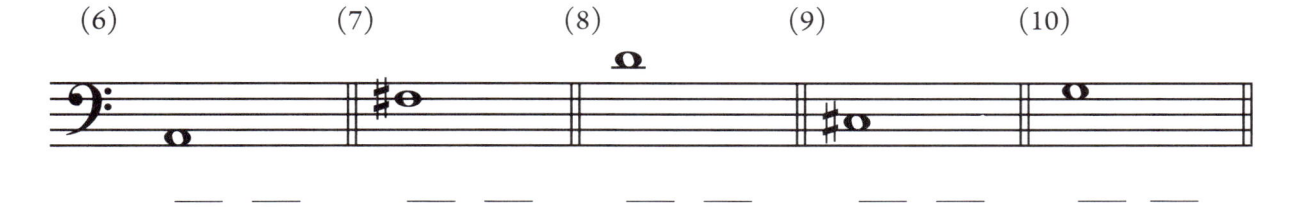

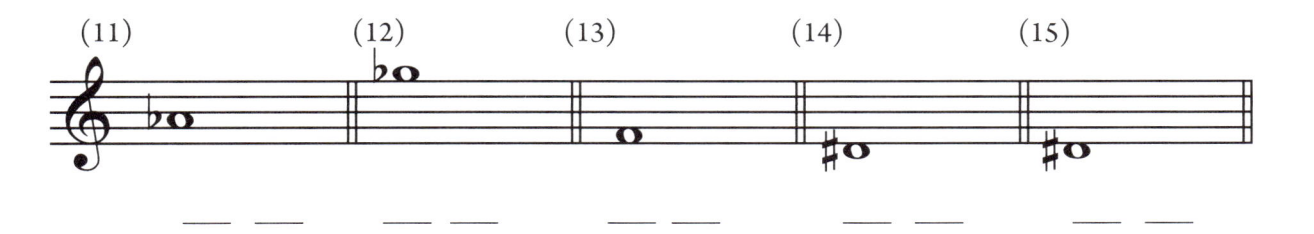

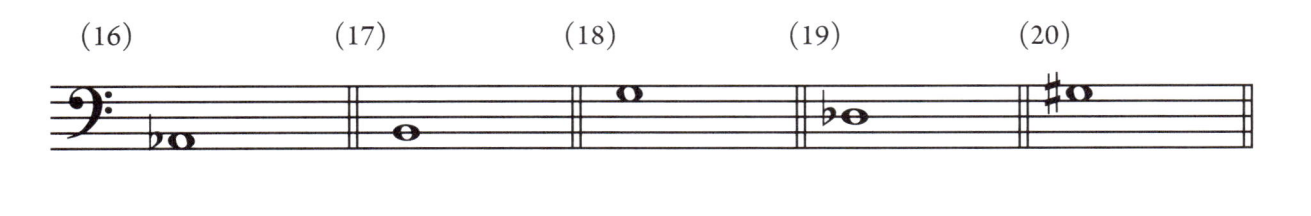

B. Identifying whole and half steps in a melody

Listen to an excerpt from a carol, then identify the melody's whole and half steps. Write W or H in the blanks beneath the staff. Then use this information to write the appropriate accidental before the other notes.

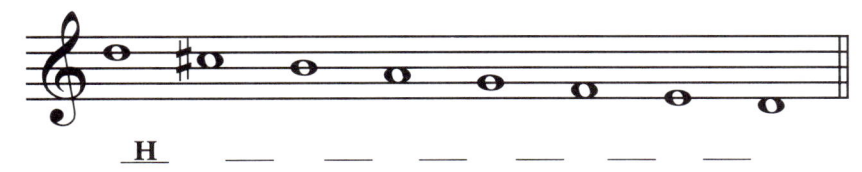

C. Listening to and writing a major-key melody

Listen to an excerpt from a familiar melody, and complete the following exercises. 🔊

(1) The excerpt consists of two five-note segments. Notate segment 1's five-pitch melody with scale-degree numbers or solfège syllables. The melody begins with $\hat{1}$ (*do*).

(2) On the staff below, notate segment 1's pitches with open note heads. Don't worry yet about rhythm. Write W under whole steps and H under half steps. Play your solution at a keyboard and compare with the recorded performance; correct any errors you hear.

(3) Now notate segment 2's five-pitch melody with scale-degree numbers or solfège syllables. The melody begins with $\hat{3}$ (*mi*).

(4) On the staff below, notate segment 2's pitches with open note heads. Between pitches, write W for whole step or H for half step. Check your solution at a keyboard and correct any errors.

(5) On the staff below, write the rhythm of the entire melody (segments 1 and 2). Use correct notation, beaming, and bar lines.

(6) Write pitches and rhythm of the entire melody on the staff below.

152   CHAPTER SIX   Major Scales and Keys

Workbook   AURAL SKILLS 6.2

A. Hearing half steps, whole steps, and skips

Listen to the recording. A three- or four-pitch major-key melody will be played starting on the given pitch. In the blanks beneath each exercise, write W (whole step), H (half step), or S (skip) between adjacent pitches. (Skips move from a line to the next line or a space to the next space.) Then, complete each melody with the correct notes and accidentals.

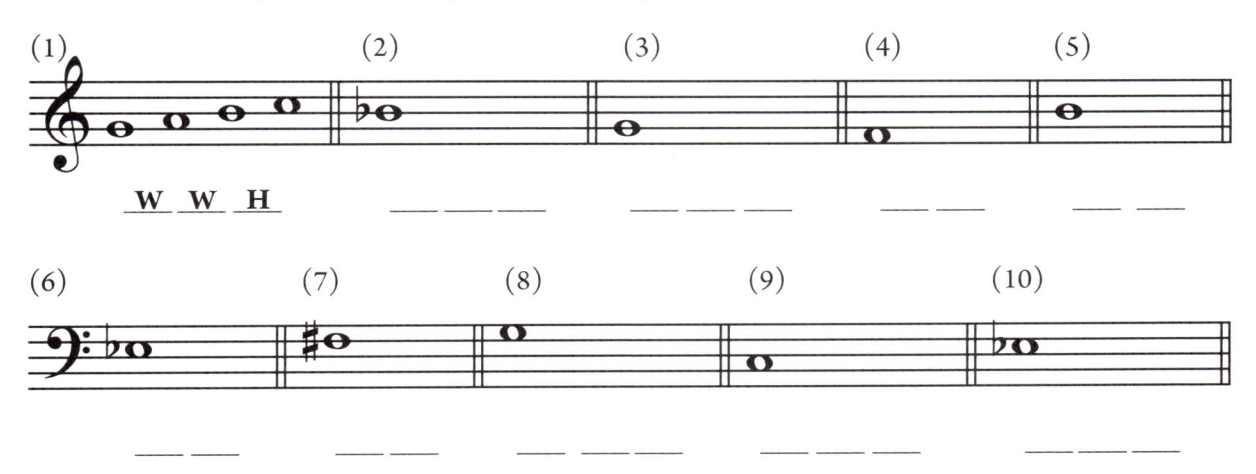

(1) W W H   (2)   (3)   (4)   (5)

(6)   (7)   (8)   (9)   (10)

B. Listening to and writing a major melody

Listen to an excerpt from a familiar melody, and complete the following exercises.

(1) The excerpt consists of three segments, the first two of which are the same. Notate segment 1's five-pitch melody in scale-degree numbers or solfège syllables. The melody begins on $\hat{1}$ (*do*).

(2) On the staff below, notate the pitches of segment 1 with open note heads. Don't worry yet about the rhythm. Between pitches 1–2 and 2–3 write W for whole step or H for half step.

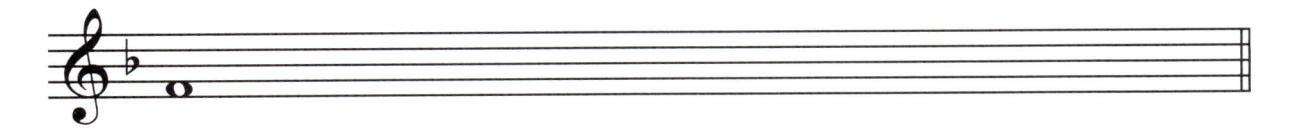

(3) Notate the melody of segment 3 in scale-degree numbers or solfège syllables. The melody begins on $\hat{1}$ (*do*).

Aural Skills 6.2   153

(4) Now notate the pitches of segment 3 with open note heads. Write W under each whole step and H under each half step.

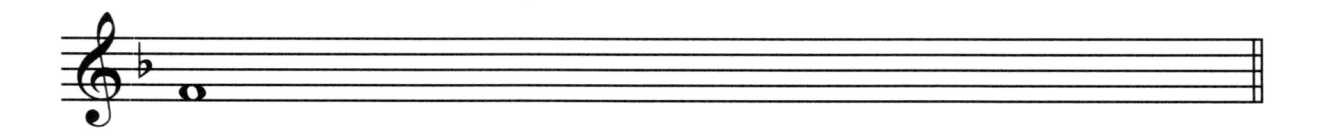

(5) On the staff below, write the rhythm of the entire melody (segments 1, 2, and 3). Use correct notation, beaming, and bar lines.

(6) Write pitches and rhythm of the entire melody on the staff below.

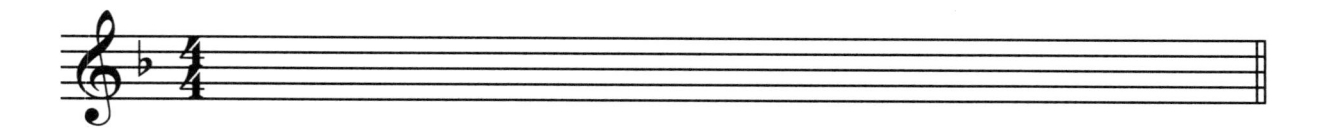

(7) Using your answer to question 5, convert the rhythm from $\frac{4}{4}$ to $\frac{4}{8}$ and notate it on the staff below.

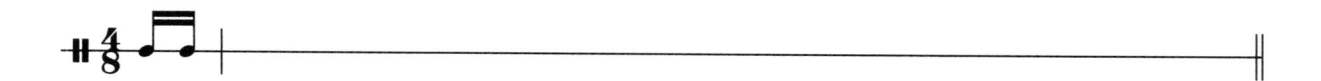

(8) Using your answer to question 6, notate the excerpt in the bass clef, starting on F3.

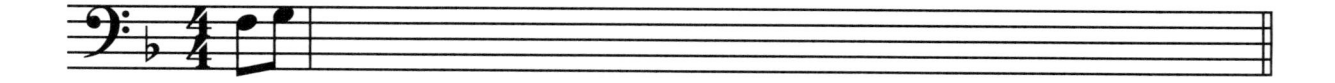

154   CHAPTER SIX   Major Scales and Keys

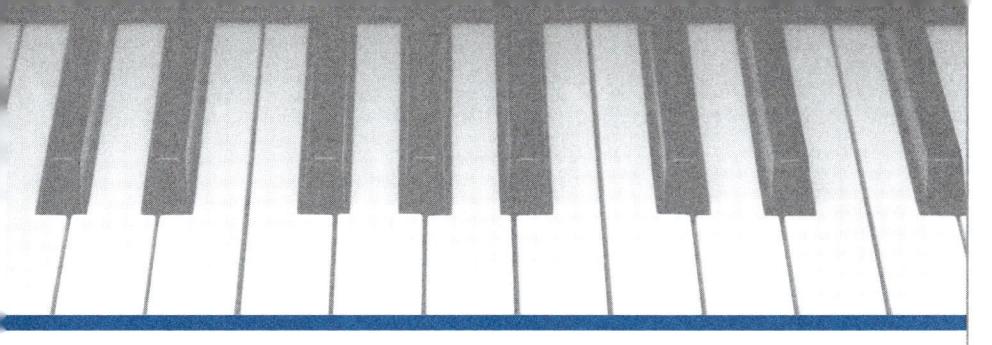

TOPICS
- parallel keys
- natural minor
- harmonic minor
- melodic minor
- comparing scale types
- relative keys
- minor key signatures and the circle of fifths
- identifying the key from a score

MUSIC
- Johann Sebastian Bach, Invention in D Minor
- Arcangelo Corelli, Allemanda, from Trio Sonata in A Minor, Op. 4, No. 5
- Jim Croce, "Time in a Bottle"
- Patrick S. Gilmore, "When Johnny Comes Marching Home"
- Wolfgang Amadeus Mozart, String Quartet, K. 421, third movement
- Mozart, *Variations on "Ah, vous dirai-je Maman"*
- Franz Schubert, Waltz in B minor, Op. 18, No. 6

CHAPTER 7

Minor Scales and Keys

Parallel Keys

Listen to the beginning of "Ah, vous dirai-je Maman" (otherwise known as "Twinkle, Twinkle, Little Star"), and a variation on the melody and compare the right-hand parts shown in Examples 7.1 and 7.2.

EXAMPLE 7.1 Mozart, *Variations on "Ah, vous dirai-je Maman,"* mm. 1–8

(a) Melody

(b) Pitches of the melody

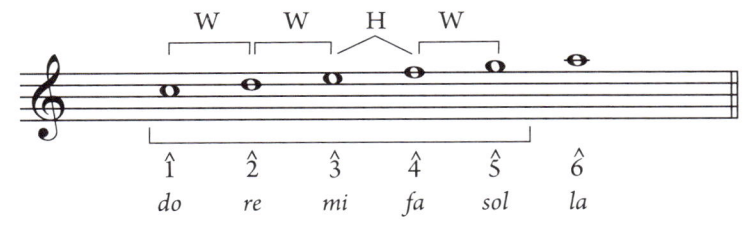

EXAMPLE 7.2 Mozart, *Variations*, Var. VIII, mm. 193–200

(a) Melody

(b) Pitches of the melody

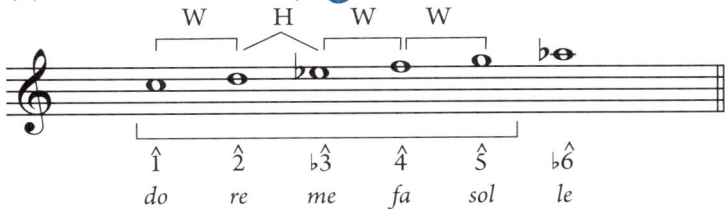

The beginning of Example 7.2 immediately signals the shift to the **minor mode** by its first three notes: C–D–E♭. The first five notes of the scale in each example—C–D–E–F–G in Example 7.1b and C–D–E♭–F–G in Example 7.2b—differ by only one note: $\hat{3}$ is lowered from E to E♭. (Write the third scale degree in minor as ♭$\hat{3}$ to show that it has been lowered when compared with major, even if the note itself does not have a flat.) These scale segments differ in their arrangement of whole and half steps: W–W–H–W in major becomes W–H–W–W in minor, as marked. Major and minor scales that share the same tonic always share their first five notes, except that $\hat{3}$ becomes ♭$\hat{3}$. In the Mozart example, $\hat{6}$ also becomes ♭$\hat{6}$. This is usually the case in minor keys, but it may vary between scales, as we will see shortly.

> **KEY CONCEPT** These melodies are written in **parallel keys**: C major and C minor. **Parallel major** and **minor** keys share the same tonic but have different key signatures and a different arrangement of whole and half steps.

The shared tonic between parallel keys is a powerful relationship. It is easy to move between them by changing the accidentals or key signature, as in the Mozart example. This shift is known as a **change of mode**.

Now look at the solfège syllables provided in Examples 7.1b and 7.2b. Sing $\hat{1}$, $\hat{2}$, $\hat{4}$, and $\hat{5}$ with the same syllables: *do, re, fa,* and *sol*; because the third scale degree differs, shift the syllable from *mi* in major to *me* in minor. (This system, called *do*-based minor, is only one of several for singing in minor keys. Your teacher may specify another.)

Natural Minor

One way to spell a **minor scale** is by taking the parallel major scale (Example 7.3a) and lowering $\hat{3}$, $\hat{6}$, and $\hat{7}$ one chromatic half step, to ♭$\hat{3}$, ♭$\hat{6}$, and ♭$\hat{7}$ (Example 7.3b). The result is known as the **natural minor** scale, with a W–H–W–W–H–W–W pattern. We refer to $\hat{3}$, $\hat{6}$, and $\hat{7}$ (with filled note heads in the example) as the **modal scale degrees** because they help distinguish between major and minor modes. Their solfège syllables reflect the change: *mi* becomes *me*, *la* becomes *le*, and *ti* becomes *te*.

EXAMPLE 7.3 Major scale and parallel natural minor

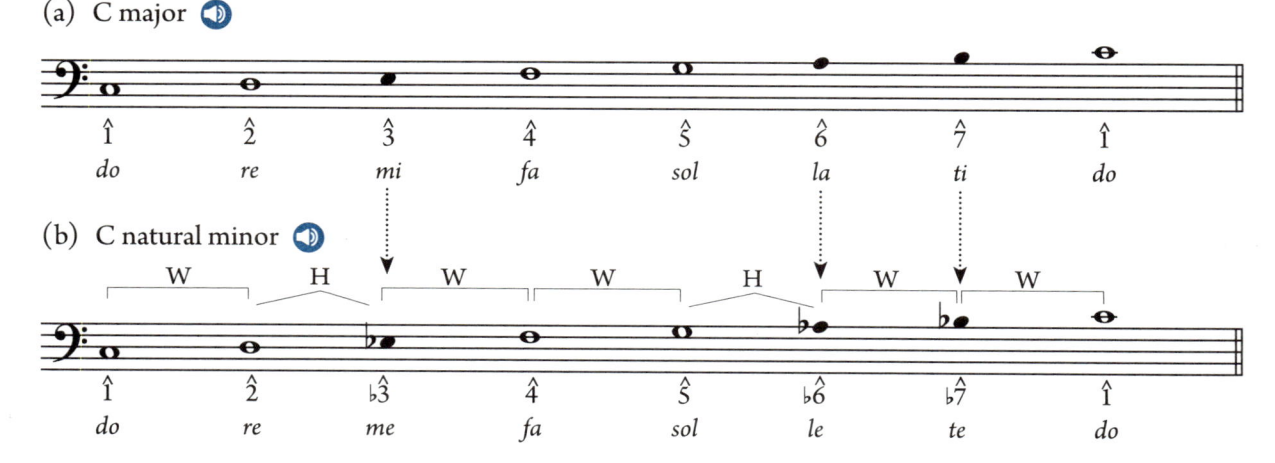

(a) C major

$\hat{1}$	$\hat{2}$	$\hat{3}$	$\hat{4}$	$\hat{5}$	$\hat{6}$	$\hat{7}$	$\hat{1}$
do	re	mi	fa	sol	la	ti	do

(b) C natural minor

$\hat{1}$	$\hat{2}$	♭$\hat{3}$	$\hat{4}$	$\hat{5}$	♭$\hat{6}$	♭$\hat{7}$	$\hat{1}$
do	re	me	fa	sol	le	te	do

In major keys, there is a special "pull" from $\hat{7}$ up to $\hat{1}$, from the half-step tension of the leading tone wanting to move up to the tonic (*ti* to *do*). In natural minor, there is no half-step pull between ♭$\hat{7}$ and $\hat{1}$ (*te* to *do*): these scale degrees are a whole step apart, a defining characteristic of the natural minor sound. Listen to Example 7.4a, in E minor, to hear the whole step D to E in measures 15–16. The E natural minor scale is written as in Example 7.4b. Here, ♭$\hat{7}$ (D) sounds relatively stable, and has none of the pull that a leading tone (D♯) would have to E.

EXAMPLE 7.4 Gilmore, "When Johnny Comes Marching Home"

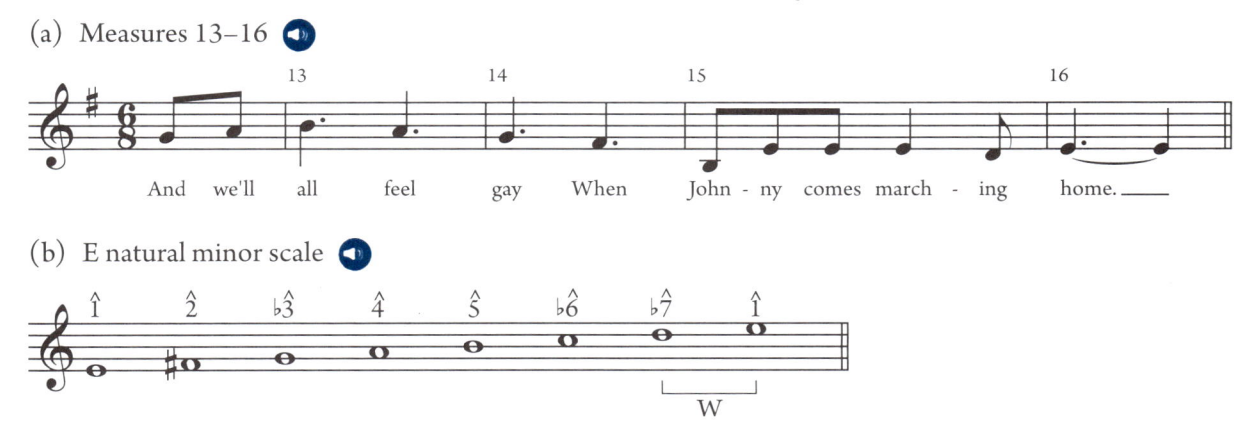

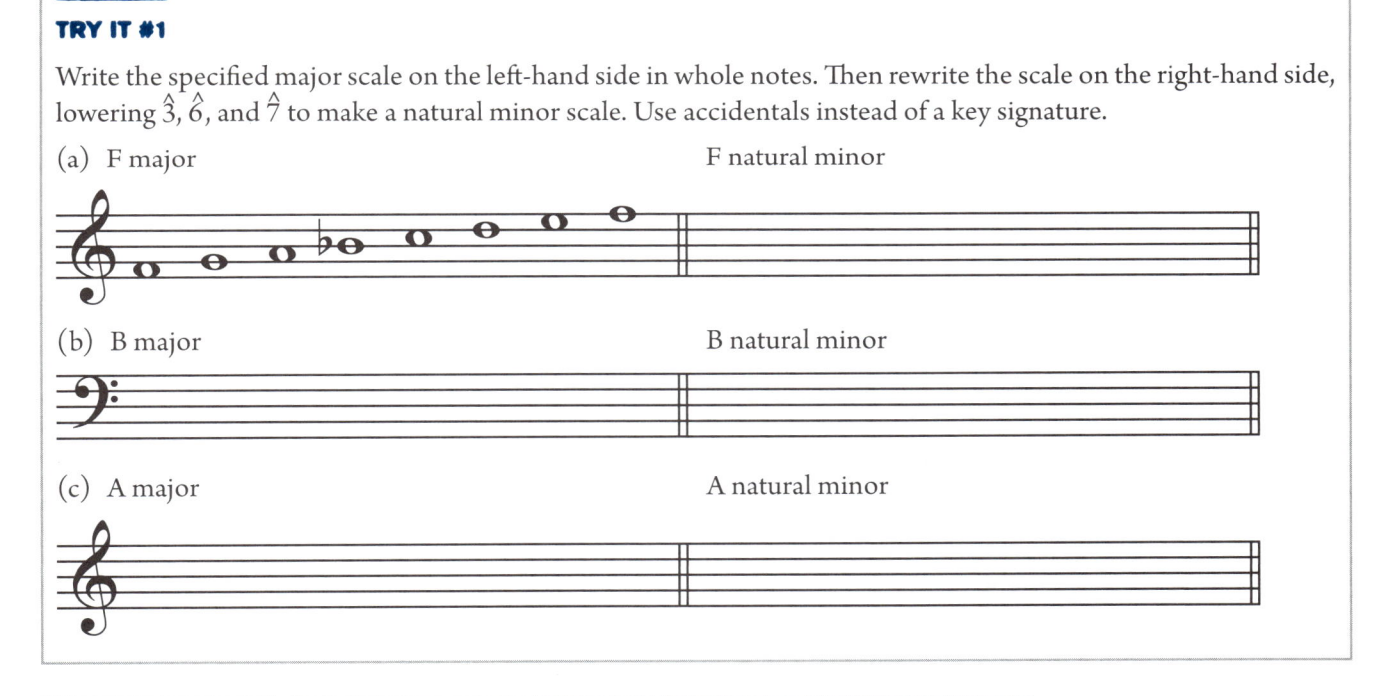

(a) Measures 13–16

(b) E natural minor scale

> **TRY IT #1**
>
> Write the specified major scale on the left-hand side in whole notes. Then rewrite the scale on the right-hand side, lowering $\hat{3}$, $\hat{6}$, and $\hat{7}$ to make a natural minor scale. Use accidentals instead of a key signature.
>
> (a) F major — F natural minor
>
> (b) B major — B natural minor
>
> (c) A major — A natural minor

ASSIGNMENT 7.1

Harmonic Minor

Now listen to the first eight measures of a minor-key waltz by Franz Schubert, shown in Example 7.5. In measure 1, the upper voice outlines $\hat{1}$, ♭$\hat{3}$, and $\hat{5}$ of the minor scale beginning on B. Every A in Schubert's waltz (left hand, mm. 2, 4, 6, and 7), however, has a sharp, which converts ♭$\hat{7}$ to $\hat{7}$, the leading tone to B. Here, there is the upward pull of leading tone to tonic, just as in major keys.

EXAMPLE 7.5   Schubert, Waltz in B Minor, mm. 1–8

Example 7.6 shows the scale that corresponds with the waltz. This scale, known as **harmonic minor**, features a half-step relation between $\hat{7}$ and $\hat{1}$ that was missing in natural minor. Because $\hat{7}$ now functions as a leading tone, we sing it on *ti* (not *te*), as in major.

EXAMPLE 7.6   B harmonic minor scale

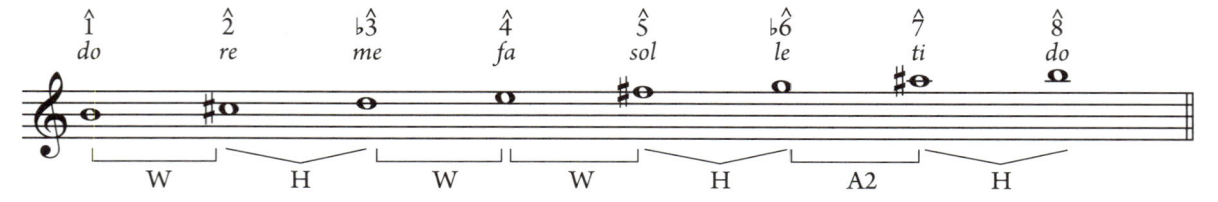

In this scale, the interval between $\flat\hat{6}$ and $\hat{7}$ (*le* and *ti*)—G to A♯ in Example 7.6—is larger than a whole step. It is an **augmented second (A2)**, equivalent to a step and a half. Because of the unusual sound of the A2, harmonic minor is not typically heard in pieces *as a scale*. Instead, the leading tone will generally appear as part of the harmony (the underlying chords, see Chapter 9), as in the Schubert waltz—hence the name, harmonic minor.

Listen to the opening of Bach's Invention in D minor (Example 7.7a), where $\flat\hat{6}$ and the leading tone appear melodically. Here Bach places $\hat{7}$ (C♯) below $\flat\hat{6}$ (B♭), in measures 1–2 and 5–6, to avoid the melodic A2. Example 7.7b shows how these scale degrees are typically handled: write $\hat{7}$ (*ti*) so that it moves up to $\hat{1}$ (*do*); write $\flat\hat{6}$ (*le*) so that it moves down to $\hat{5}$ (*sol*).

EXAMPLE 7.7   Bach, Invention in D Minor, mm. 1–7 (right hand)

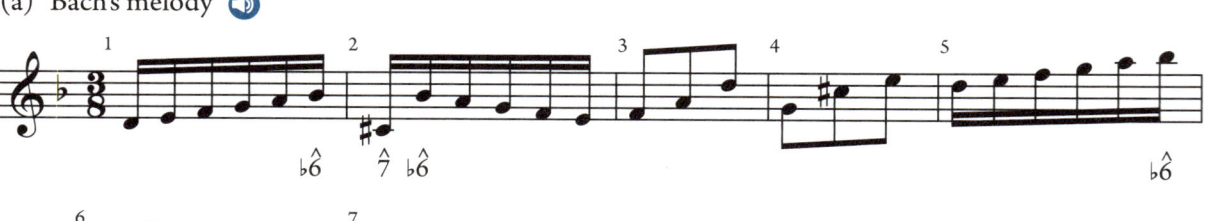

(a) Bach's melody

(b) Melodic separation of $\hat{7}$ from $\flat\hat{6}$ (*ti* from *le*)

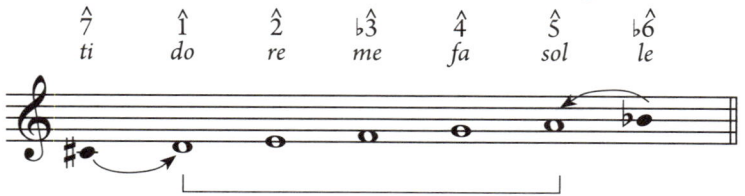

158   CHAPTER SEVEN   Minor Scales and Keys

KEY CONCEPT To write a harmonic minor scale, begin with natural minor and raise $\flat\hat{7}$ a chromatic half step to make the leading tone (*ti*). If you begin with a major scale, lower $\hat{3}$ to $\flat\hat{3}$ and $\hat{6}$ to $\flat\hat{6}$, but leave $\hat{7}$ unaltered.

These alterations sometimes result in odd-looking combinations of accidentals, as in Example 7.8. Example 7.8a shows a scale with flats and a sharp, the result of raising $\flat\hat{7}$ (F) to create a leading tone. The harmonic minor scale in Example 7.8b begins on a sharped note; such scales typically need a double sharp for the leading tone.

EXAMPLE 7.8 Spelling of harmonic minor scales

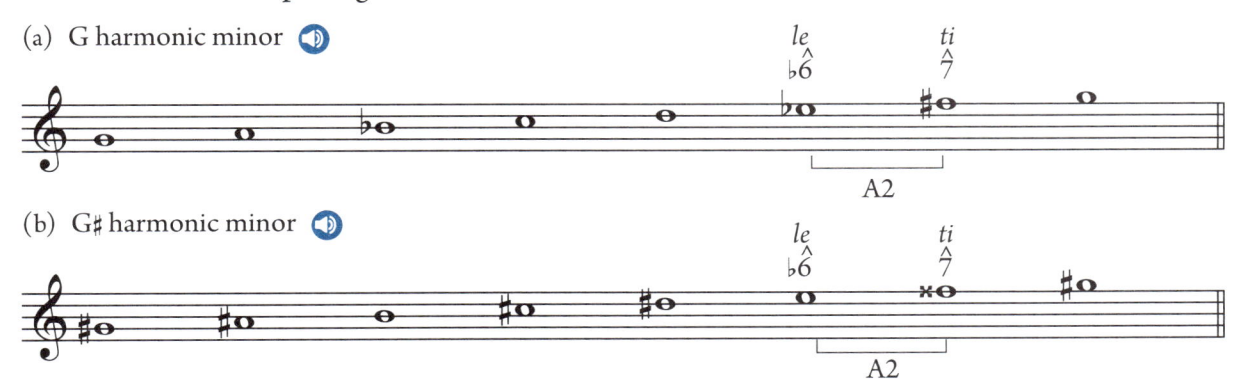

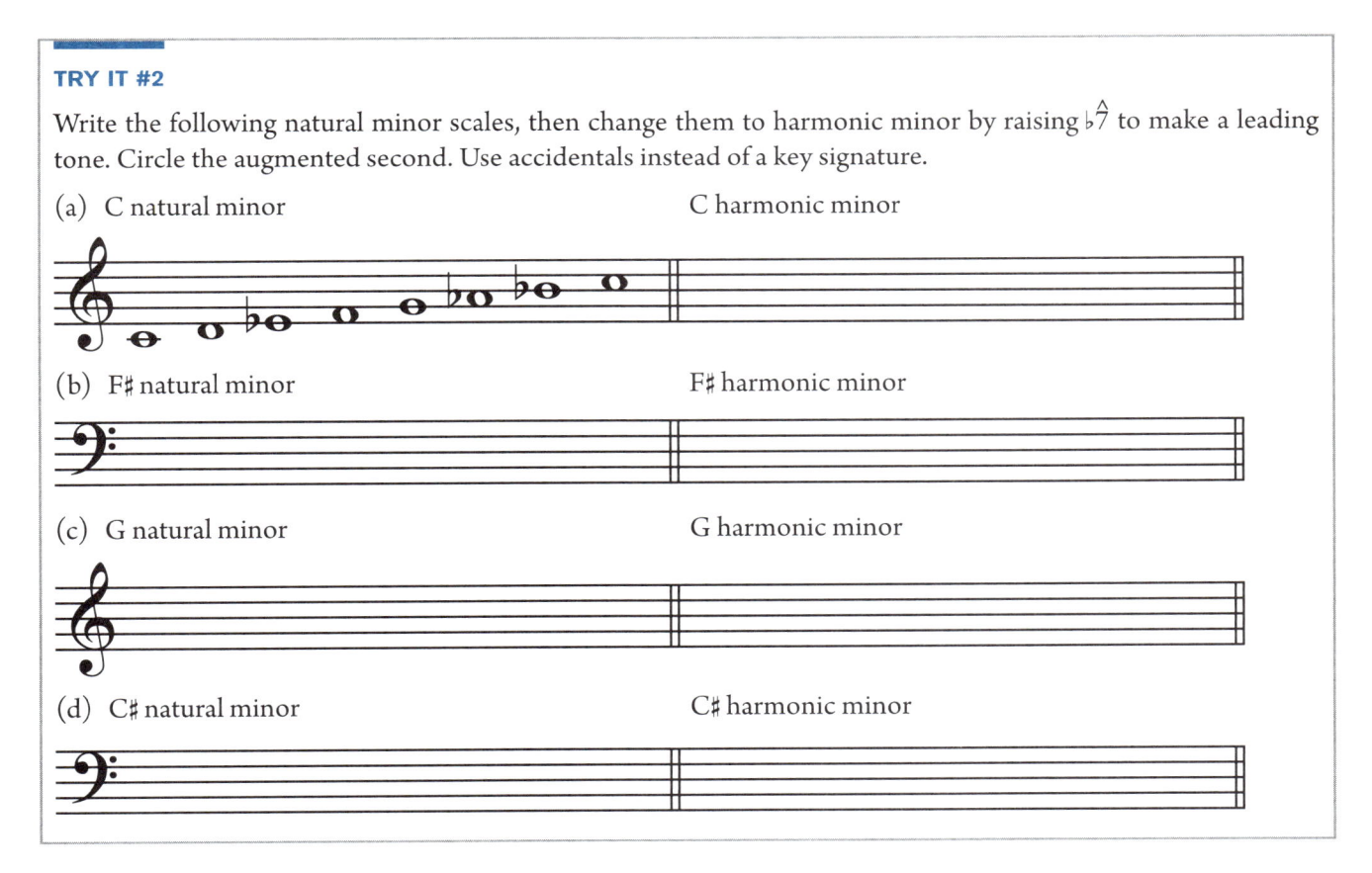

(a) G harmonic minor

(b) G♯ harmonic minor

TRY IT #2

Write the following natural minor scales, then change them to harmonic minor by raising $\flat\hat{7}$ to make a leading tone. Circle the augmented second. Use accidentals instead of a key signature.

(a) C natural minor   C harmonic minor

(b) F♯ natural minor   F♯ harmonic minor

(c) G natural minor   G harmonic minor

(d) C♯ natural minor   C♯ harmonic minor

AURAL SKILLS 7.1

Melodic Minor

Yet another variant of the minor scale is **melodic minor**, which differs in its ascending and descending forms.

> **KEY CONCEPT** Melodic minor is written with $\hat{6}$ and $\hat{7}$ when the scale ascends, reaching upward toward the tonic. In its descending form, it's written with $\flat\hat{7}$ and $\flat\hat{6}$ (like natural minor), pulling downward toward $\hat{5}$.

The left-hand part of the Mozart variation shown in Example 7.9, in C minor, illustrates how this scale is applied in music. In measure 197, Mozart raises $\flat\hat{7}$ to the leading tone (B♭ to B♮), but he also raises $\flat\hat{6}$ to $\hat{6}$ (A♭ to A♮) to avoid the potential augmented second (A♭ to B♮). In measure 198, $\flat\hat{6}$ (A♭) returns because the overall direction of the line here is downward.

EXAMPLE 7.9 Mozart, *Variations on "Ah, vous dirai-je Maman,"* **Var. VIII,** mm. 197–200

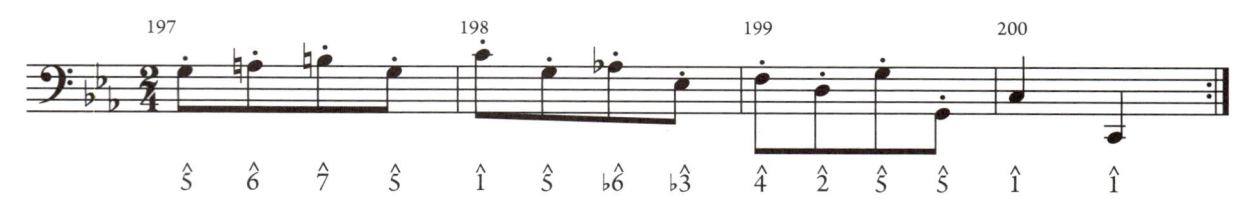

Example 7.10 shows the C melodic minor scale in its ascending and descending forms. Variability in the sixth and seventh scale degrees is typical in minor-key pieces. In C minor, the sixth may appear as A♭ or A♮, while the seventh may appear as B♭ or B♮ depending upon the context and the direction of the melodic line. Solfège syllables for the ascending form of melodic minor match those for major (*la–ti–do*), while syllables for the descending form match those for natural minor (*do–te–le*).

EXAMPLE 7.10 C melodic minor scale

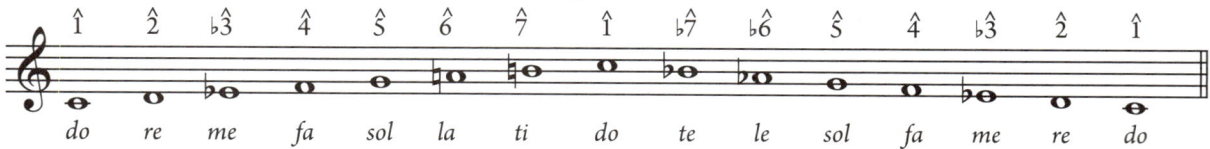

Follow the bass line of Example 7.11, a song in D minor, to see the variability of the sixth and seventh scale degrees in a different musical context. The bass descends chromatically from the tonic D in measure 9 to $\flat\hat{6}$ (B♭) in measure 13. The line then ascends back to D in measure 16, through the ascending melodic minor ($\hat{5}$–$\hat{6}$–$\hat{7}$, A–B♮–C♯) in measure 15.

EXAMPLE 7.11 Croce, "Time in a Bottle," mm. 9–16

chromatic scale segment

CHAPTER SEVEN Minor Scales and Keys

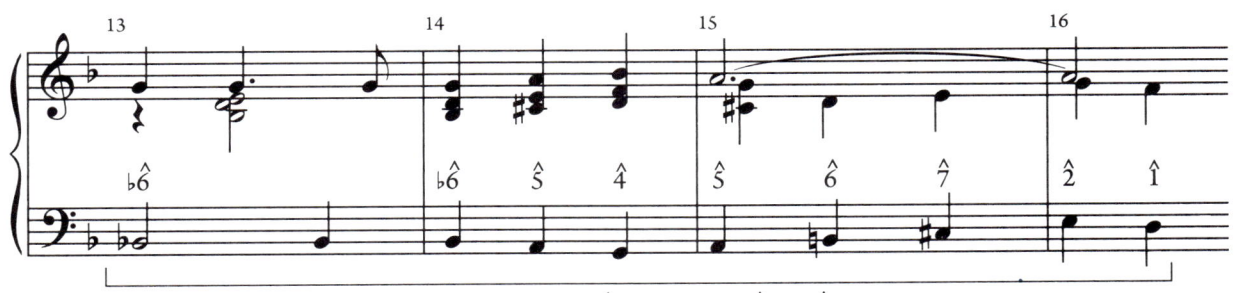

melodic minor segment ($\flat\hat{6}$ descending, $\hat{6}$ and $\hat{7}$ ascending)

Comparing Scale Types

In Example 7.12, C major is aligned with all three forms of the C minor scale. Play each scale. To tell them apart by ear, listen first for the quality of the third ($\hat{3}$ or $\flat\hat{3}$; *mi* or *me*). Then listen for the leading tone: there is no leading tone in natural minor (but $\flat\hat{7}$ instead). In harmonic minor, there *is* a leading tone, and you will hear it approached by the A2 ($\flat\hat{6}$–$\hat{7}$, or *le–ti*). Finally, you hear $\hat{6}$ (*la*) only in major or ascending melodic minor.

EXAMPLE 7.12 Four scales beginning on C

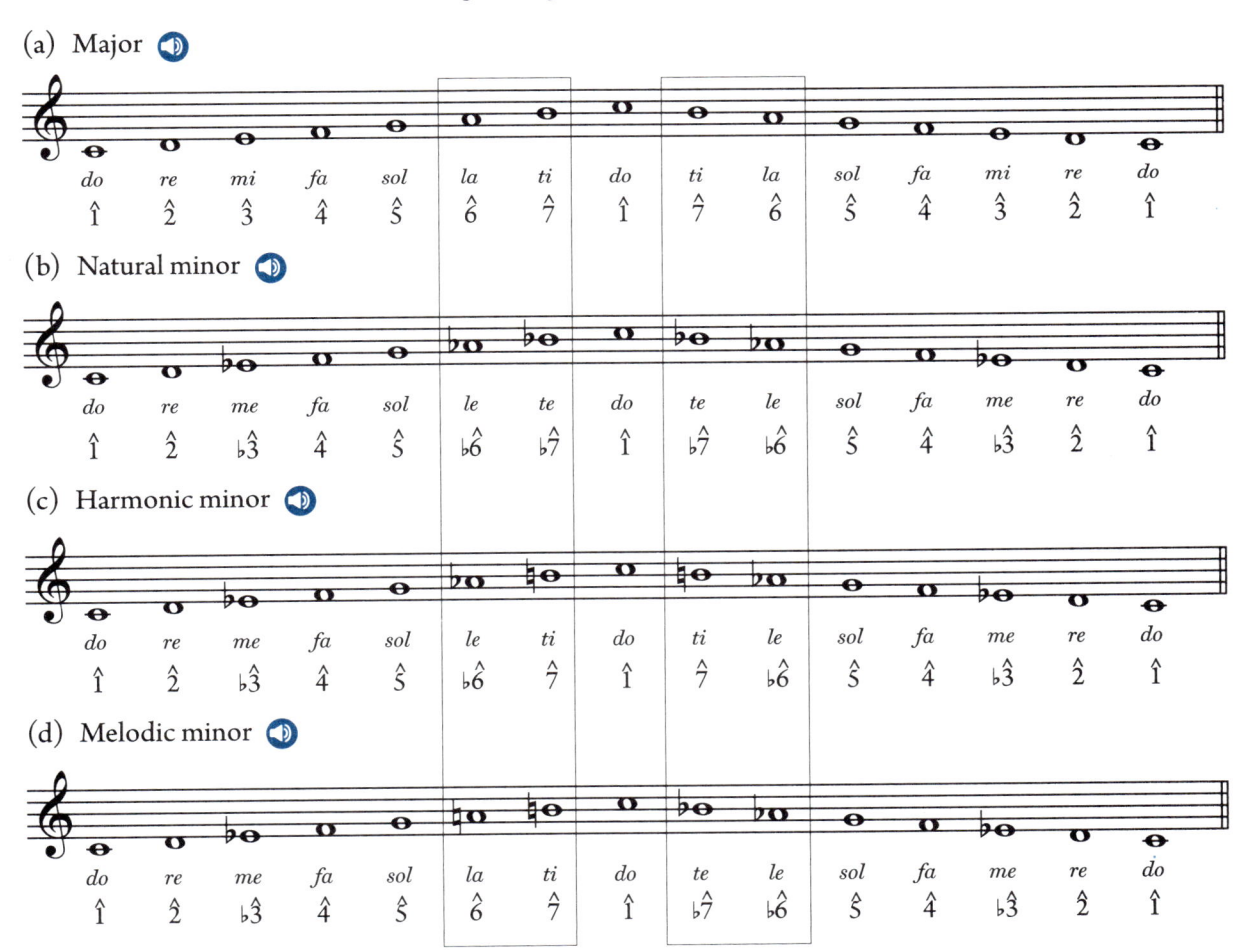

(a) Major

(b) Natural minor

(c) Harmonic minor

(d) Melodic minor

Scale-degree names in minor are identical to those in major (tonic, subdominant, etc.) with only a couple of exceptions. Scale-degree $\flat\hat{7}$ in natural minor is called the **subtonic** because of its placement a whole step below the tonic, and $\hat{6}$ in melodic minor is simply known as the **raised submediant**.

SUMMARY

- To write a natural minor scale, write a major scale, then add accidentals to lower $\hat{3}$, $\hat{6}$, and $\hat{7}$ a chromatic half step; or write whole and half steps above the tonic in the pattern W–H–W–W–H–W–W (use each letter name once).
- To write a harmonic minor scale, begin with a natural minor scale and then raise $\flat\hat{7}$ to $\hat{7}$, ascending and descending.
- To write a melodic minor scale, begin with a natural minor scale and then raise $\flat\hat{6}$ and $\flat\hat{7}$ to $\hat{6}$ and $\hat{7}$ ascending only. The ascending form is like major, with $\flat\hat{3}$. The descending form is identical to natural minor.

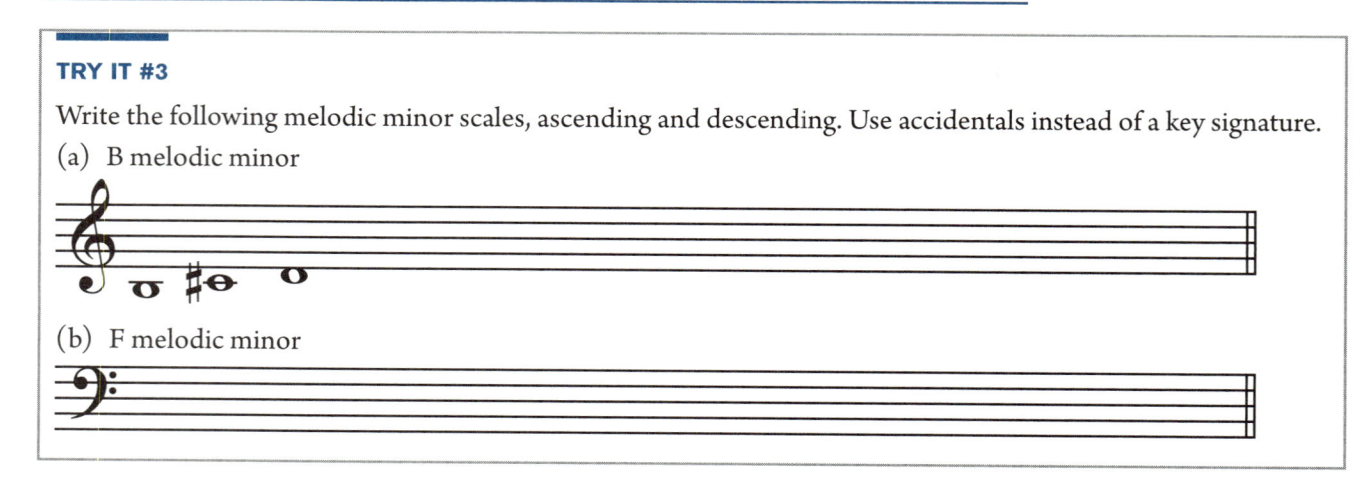

TRY IT #3

Write the following melodic minor scales, ascending and descending. Use accidentals instead of a key signature.

(a) B melodic minor

(b) F melodic minor

ASSIGNMENT 7.2

Relative Keys

Example 7.13 shows two phrases from a sonata by Corelli. Listen to the excerpts to determine the key of each passage. Decide by ear what the tonic pitch is; sing it, then listen for $\hat{3}$ or $\flat\hat{3}$ to decide whether the key is major or minor.

EXAMPLE 7.13 Corelli, Allemanda, from Trio Sonata, Op. 4, No. 5

(a) mm. 1–3

A minor: $\hat{1}$

(b) mm. 13–15

C major: $\hat{1}$

In Example 7.13a, you probably sang A, the first note of the violin part and the first and last notes of the accompaniment's bass line. This passage is in A minor: both violins begin with $\hat{1}$–$\hat{2}$–♭$\hat{3}$ and the bass line ends $\hat{5}$–$\hat{1}$ in A minor. Example 7.13b, in contrast, is in C major: the violin parts begin with $\hat{1}$–$\hat{2}$–$\hat{3}$ and the bass line ends $\hat{5}$–$\hat{1}$ in the new key. Though most of the music we have studied stays in one key throughout, many pieces (like this one) change keys; a process called modulation. In this piece, the change requires no new accidentals or key signature because A minor and C major share the same key signature: no flats or sharps.

> **KEY CONCEPT** Keys that share the same key signature (but different tonics) are called **relative keys**.

Example 7.14 aligns the scales of E♭ major and C natural minor to show how they are related: they share all the same notes but begin on different pitches.

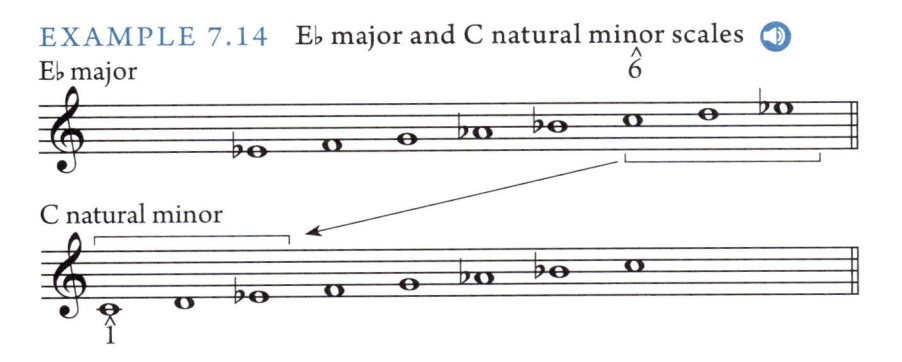

EXAMPLE 7.14 E♭ major and C natural minor scales

Every major scale has its **relative minor** scale, and every minor scale has its **relative major**. To find the relative minor of any major scale or key, identify $\hat{6}$ of the major scale: that pitch is the tonic of the relative minor. As Example 7.15 shows, the relative minor scale of G major is E minor.

Relative Keys

EXAMPLE 7.15 Finding the relative (natural) minor

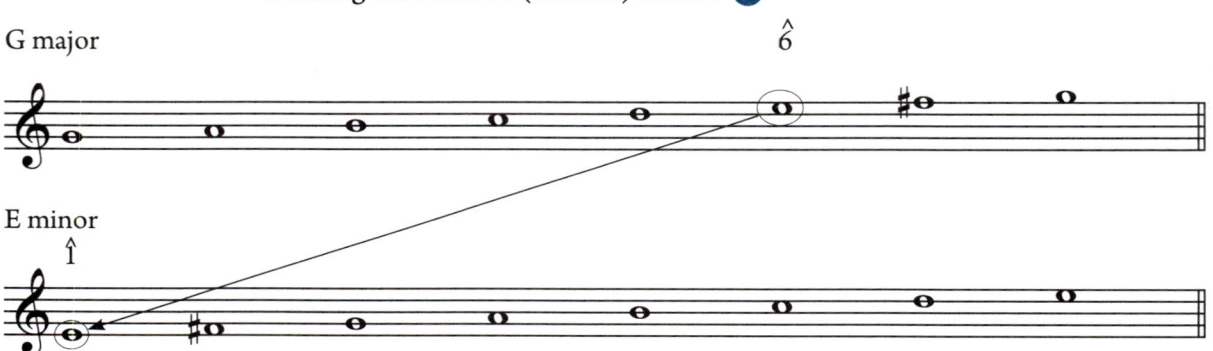

G major

E minor

ANOTHER WAY A shortcut for finding the relative minor key is to count *down* three half steps from the major-key tonic. Be sure to choose the correct spelling: it should conform to the key signature of the major key and span three different letter names. To find the relative minor of A major:

(1) Count down three letter names: A–G–F.
(2) Count down three half steps: A to A♭, A♭ to G, G to G♭.
(3) Change the spelling if it disagrees with step 1. We must respell G♭ as F♯, giving F♯ minor.

TRY IT #4

Given the major key or key signature below, supply the name of the relative minor.

Major key	Relative minor	Major key	Relative minor
(a) E major	**C♯ minor**	(g) B♭ major	_____
(b)	_____	(h) C major	_____
(c) D major	_____	(i)	_____
(d) E♭ major	_____	(j) F♯ major	_____
(e)	_____	(k)	_____
(f)	_____	(l)	_____

To find the relative major of any minor scale or key, identify ♭$\hat{3}$ of the minor scale: that note is the tonic of the relative major. As Example 7.16 shows, the relative major of G minor is B♭ major.

CHAPTER SEVEN Minor Scales and Keys

EXAMPLE 7.16 Finding the relative major

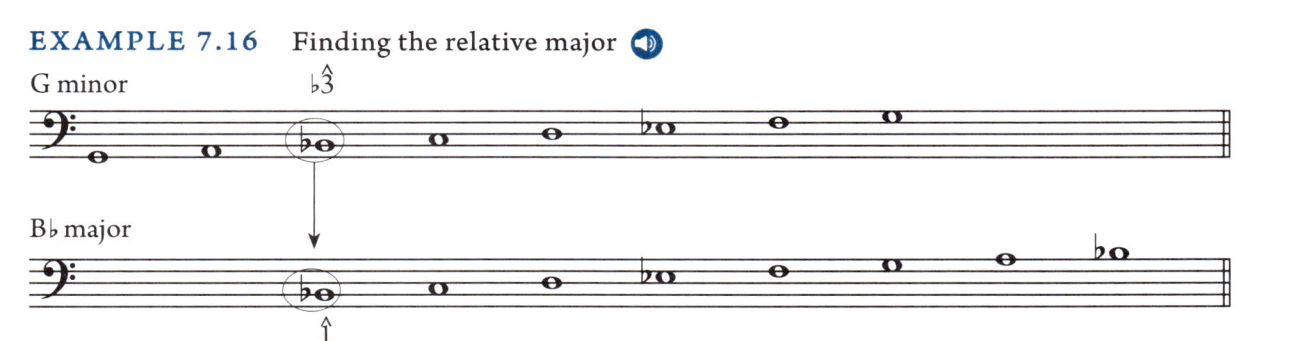

G minor

B♭ major

> **ANOTHER WAY** You can also find the relative major by counting *up* three half steps from the minor-key tonic. Again, choose a spelling three letter names away from the tonic. To find the relative major of F minor:
>
> (1) Count up three letter names: F–G–A.
> (2) Count up three half steps: F to F♯, F♯ to G, G to G♯.
> (3) Change the spelling if it disagrees with step 1. We must respell G♯ as A♭, giving A♭ major.

SUMMARY

- Parallel keys share the same tonic, but have different key signatures.
- Relative keys share the same pitches and key signature, but have different tonics.

Minor Key Signatures and the Circle of Fifths

Another way to write a natural minor scale is to think of the relative major and its key signature:

(1) Write the pitches from $\hat{1}$ to $\hat{1}$ of the minor scale without accidentals.
(2) Find its relative major.
(3) Write the relative major key signature next to the clef.

For harmonic or melodic minor, add the appropriate accidentals (e.g., a♯ or ♮ for the leading tone).

For speed and facility in sight-reading and analysis, memorize the minor key signatures just as you have the major ones. The circle of fifths in Figure 7.1 shows the key signatures shared by relative major and minor keys. It may help you memorize the minor key signatures. It may also help to remember that key signatures for parallel keys differ by three accidentals. For example, A major has 3 sharps, A minor has 0; B major has 5 sharps, B minor has 2; D major has 2 sharps, D minor has 1 flat.

FIGURE 7.1   Circle of fifths with major and minor keys and key signatures

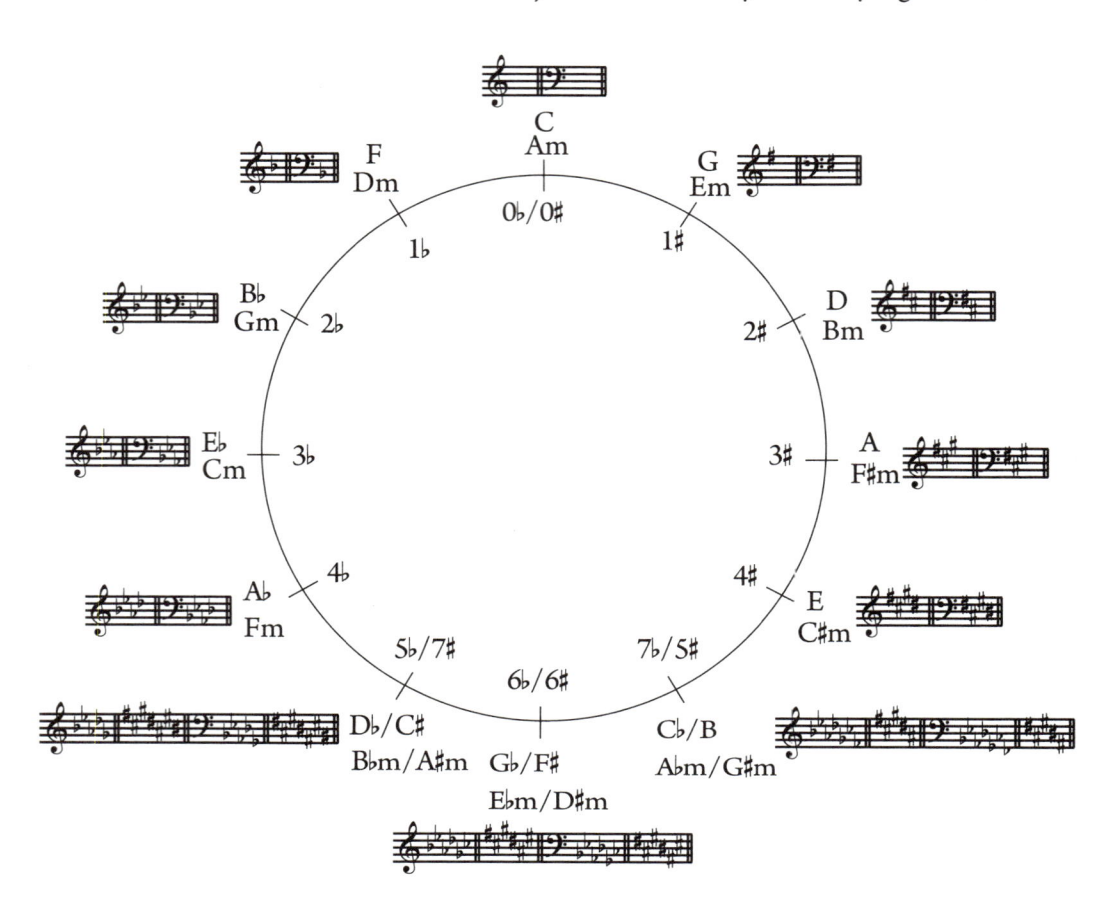

TRY IT #5

For each minor scale requested, first name the relative major key and write its key signature in the left-hand staff. Then, to the right, write the minor scale using that key signature plus accidentals to raise ♭$\hat{6}$ and ♭$\hat{7}$ as needed.

(a) F♯ harmonic minor

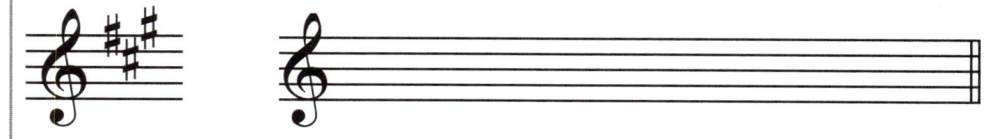

Relative major: __A__   F♯ harmonic minor scale

(b) E harmonic minor

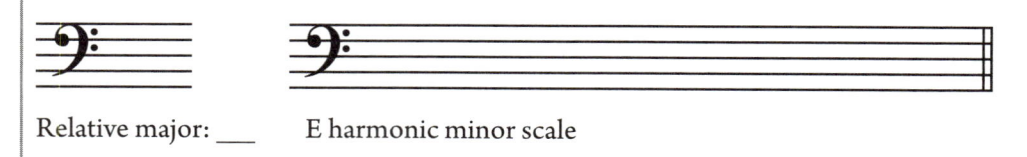

Relative major: ____   E harmonic minor scale

166   CHAPTER SEVEN   Minor Scales and Keys

(c) B melodic minor

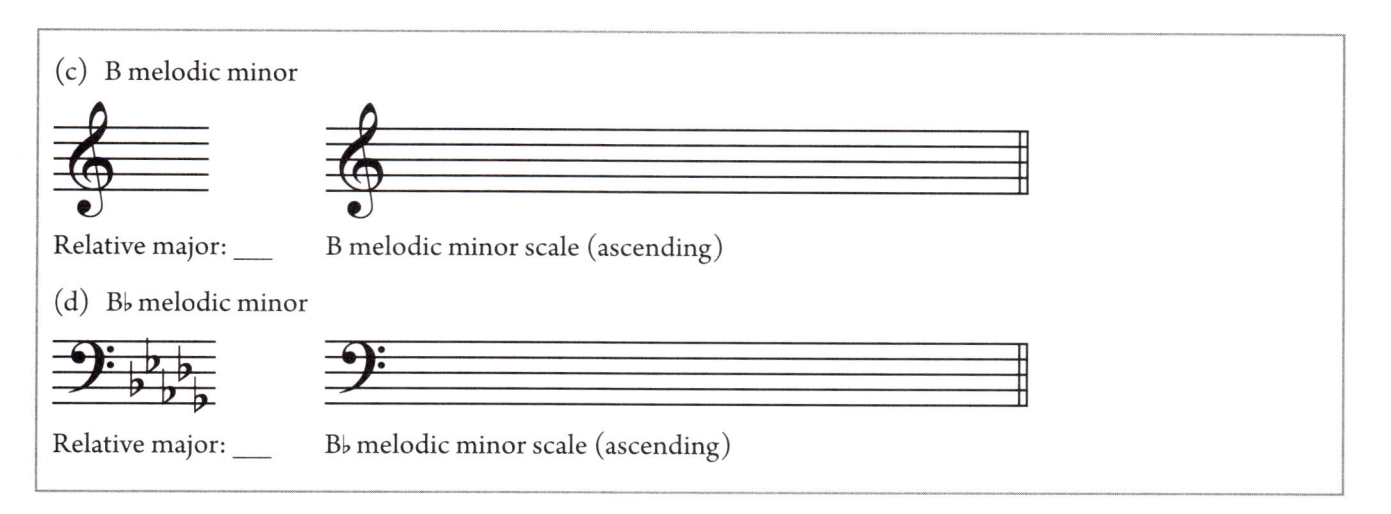

Relative major: ___   B melodic minor scale (ascending)

(d) B♭ melodic minor

Relative major: ___   B♭ melodic minor scale (ascending)

AURAL SKILLS 7.2

Identifying the Key from a Score

Finally, since a key signature can indicate either major or minor, how do you know which is the key of a piece? In Corelli's Allemanda (Example 7.13), we interpreted the scale degrees of the melody and the bass line to determine which phrase was in A minor and which was in C major.

> **KEY CONCEPT** Always imagine two possible tonics for a key signature: one for major and one for relative minor. Then look at the melody and bass lines for scale-degree patterns like $\hat{3}$–$\hat{2}$–$\hat{1}$ or $\hat{5}$–$\hat{1}$ at the beginning and end of the piece to signal which of the two possibilities is the tonic.

To practice, listen to the first ten measures of Mozart's String Quartet, K. 421, and follow the score in Example 7.17. There is one flat in the key signature, suggesting a key of either F major or D minor.

EXAMPLE 7.17   Mozart, String Quartet, K. 421, third movement, mm. 1–10

Listen first to the cello line, which begins with an extended D, held for three measures; it ends with A–D ($\hat{5}$–$\hat{1}$ in D minor). The melody (violin 1) likewise begins with a repeated D, and it ends with C♯–D ($\hat{7}$–$\hat{1}$ in D harmonic minor). This added accidental at the end of the phrase (to make $\hat{7}$–$\hat{1}$) is a strong signal of a minor key. These features together tell us that the piece is in D minor rather than F major.

SUMMARY

To determine the key of a piece:

1. Look at the key signature and identify both the major- and relative-minor-key tonics.
2. Look at the beginning and end of the melody and bass line for motion to or from one of these possible tonic pitches.
3. Look for an accidental that raises ♭$\hat{7}$ to $\hat{7}$ to create a leading tone. This signals a minor key.

ASSIGNMENT 7.3

Did You Know?

Wolfgang Amadeus Mozart's father, Leopold, a well-known violinist and teacher, took Wolfgang and his older sister "Nannerl" on performance tours through Europe before Wolfgang was even ten years old. Mozart also began improvising and composing music while still a child (he wrote his first opera when he was eleven). He went on to write a number of well-loved operas, including *The Marriage of Figaro* and *The Magic Flute*, symphonies, string quartets, and many piano works, including several sets of variations. In a time long before recordings were possible, variations on well-known tunes were popular. Composers and touring performers like Mozart sometimes would improvise variations as court entertainment. Listeners could then recognize the melody as it was embellished in different variations.

Terms You Should Know

augmented second (A2)	modal scale degree	scale-degree names in minor
change of mode	parallel keys	raised submediant
minor mode	parallel major	subtonic
minor scale	parallel minor	
natural minor	relative keys	
harmonic minor	relative major	
melodic minor	relative minor	

Questions for Review

1. Describe the relationship between parallel major and minor keys. Which scale degrees are different?
2. What are the differences between natural minor, melodic minor, and harmonic minor? Describe the steps you follow to change a major scale to each form of minor.
3. Why is the harmonic minor scale rarely found in a melody?
4. How do you know whether to use the raised form of $\hat{6}$ and $\hat{7}$ in melodic minor?
5. What changes in solfège syllables and scale-degree numbers do you make for each form of minor?
6. What do relative keys share? How can this relationship help you to spell minor scales quickly?
7. Given a major key, how do you determine its relative minor? Given a minor key, how do you determine its relative major?
8. When looking at a musical score, how can you tell whether the work is in a major or minor key?

Reading Review

Match the term on the left with the best answer on the right.

_____ (1) $\hat{3}$, $\hat{6}$, and $\hat{7}$
_____ (2) half step
_____ (3) natural minor scale
_____ (4) whole step
_____ (5) relative keys
_____ (6) raised submediant
_____ (7) harmonic minor scale
_____ (8) subtonic
_____ (9) parallel keys
_____ (10) descending melodic minor

(a) distance from $\hat{2}$ to $\flat\hat{3}$ in natural minor
(b) differs from major by three modal scale degrees
(c) D major and B minor
(d) D major and D minor
(e) $\flat\hat{7}$ in a natural minor scale
(f) differs from natural minor by the raised leading tone
(g) modal scale degrees
(h) $\hat{6}$ in an ascending melodic minor scale
(i) pitches are the same as in natural minor
(j) distance from $\flat\hat{7}$ to $\hat{1}$ in natural minor

Additional review and practice available at wwnorton.com/studyspace

Apply It

A. At the keyboard

Five-finger patterns

1. All three forms of the minor scale share $\hat{1}$ to $\hat{5}$. The parallel major scale shares these scale degrees as well, except that the third is $\hat{3}$ in major and $\flat\hat{3}$ in minor. Play each pattern below in both hands (separately, then together), one octave apart, fingerings 5–4–3–2–1 (left hand) and 1–2–3–4–5 (right hand). Sing on scale-degree numbers or solfège syllables as you play.

2. Follow the same model for each tonic note below. First play a major pattern ($\hat{1}$ to $\hat{5}$) with each hand in a separate octave (hands alone and then together). Then lower its third note by a half step and play a minor pattern. While playing, sing on letter names, scale-degree numbers, or solfège syllables. When you are satisfied with your performance, compare it to the recording.

   (a) A
   (b) F
   (c) G
   (d) E♭
   (e) B
   (f) F♯
   (g) E
   (h) C♯
   (i) A♭
   (j) B♭
   (k) G♯
   (l) D

Three types of minor scales

3. Play each of the following C minor scales while singing along on numbers or syllables, using the fingerings marked in the example. Listen for the changes in sound (always in the right hand) as you move from natural to harmonic and then to melodic minor.

(a) Natural minor

(b) Harmonic minor

170   CHAPTER SEVEN Minor Scales and Keys

(c) Melodic minor

L.H. 4   3   2   1   R.H. 1   2   3   4

do re me fa sol la ti do
1̂   2̂ ♭3̂ 4̂   5̂   6̂ 7̂   1̂

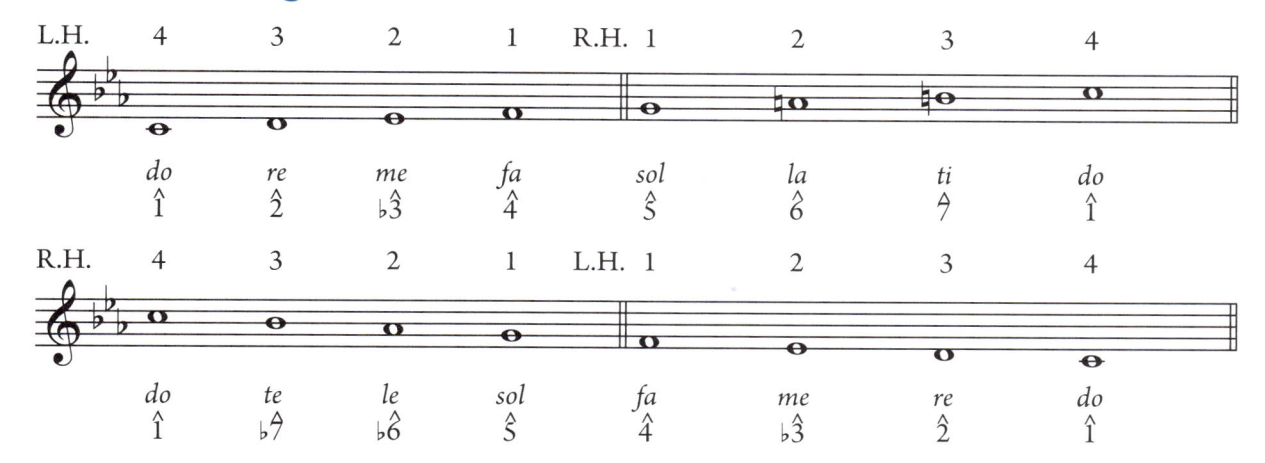

R.H. 4   3   2   1   L.H. 1   2   3   4

do te le sol fa me re do
1̂ ♭7̂ ♭6̂ 5̂   4̂ ♭3̂ 2̂   1̂

4. From each of the following tonic notes, perform the three types of minor scale—natural, harmonic, and ascending and descending melodic. As you play, sing each letter name, scale-degree number, or solfège syllable.

(a) D   (d) B   (g) A   (j) G
(b) F   (e) E♭   (h) C   (k) B♭
(c) G♯   (f) F♯   (i) E   (l) C♯

B. Review: reading rhythms

Perform the following rhythms on "ta" or counting syllables, as directed. Keep a steady beat by tapping the pulse or conducting.

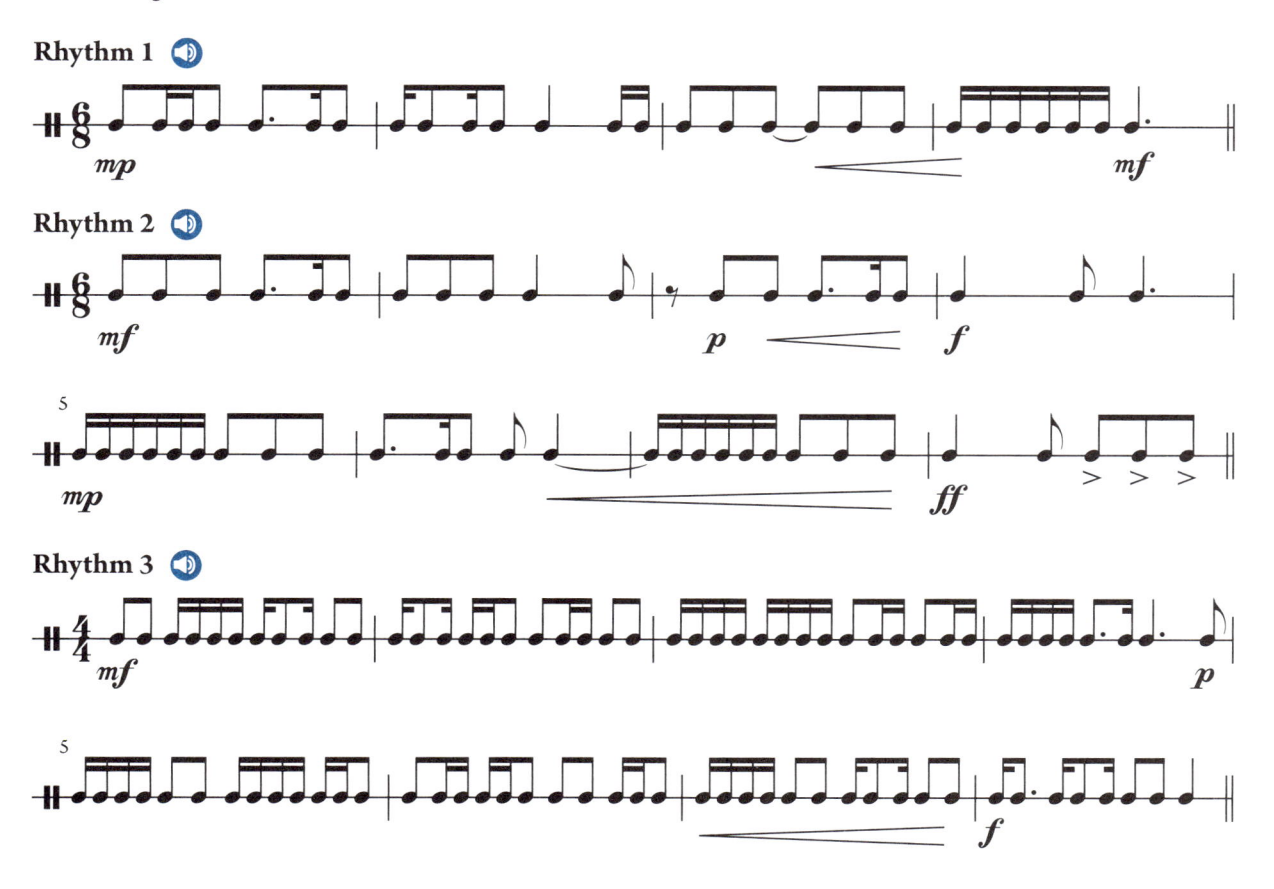

Rhythm 1

Rhythm 2

Rhythm 3

Apply It   171

Rhythm 4 (Duet: Perform with two people or groups.)

C. Listening for major and minor keys

Listen to the beginning of each excerpt to determine whether it is in a major or minor key, then circle your choice.

1. Franz Schubert, Allegretto, D. 915   major   minor
2. Fanny Mendelssohn Hensel, "Waldeinsam"   major   minor
3. Franz Schubert, *Wanderer* Fantasy, Op. 15, Adagio   major   minor
4. Ludwig van Beethoven, Sonata for Violin and Piano, Op. 30, No. 2, first movement   major   minor
5. Joseph Haydn, Piano Sonata No. 9, Scherzo   major   minor

D. Singing at sight

All of the following melodies are in minor keys. Before singing, determine each melody's key, and play that natural minor scale at the keyboard, using any fingering that is comfortable. Then identify scale segments, if present, that suggest harmonic or melodic minor (look for accidentals). When singing harmonic and melodic minor, concentrate especially on singing the whole and half steps in tune.

Work on the rhythm and pitches separately, using scale-degree numbers or solfège syllables to help you, before putting them together.

Melody 1 🔊

$\hat{1}$ $\hat{2}$ $\flat\hat{3}$ $\hat{4}$ $\hat{5}$ $\hat{4}$ $\flat\hat{3}$ $\hat{2}$ $\hat{1}$ $\hat{2}$ $\flat\hat{3}$ $\hat{4}$ $\hat{5}$ $\hat{4}$ $\flat\hat{3}$ $\hat{2}$ $\hat{1}$ $\flat\hat{3}$ $\hat{5}$
do re me fa sol fa me re do re me fa sol fa me re do me sol

$\hat{5}$ $\hat{6}$ $\hat{7}$ $\hat{1}$ $\flat\hat{7}$ $\flat\hat{6}$ $\hat{5}$ $\hat{5}$ $\hat{6}$ $\hat{7}$ $\hat{1}$ $\hat{5}$ $\hat{1}$ $\flat\hat{7}$ $\flat\hat{6}$ $\hat{5}$ $\hat{1}$ $\hat{5}$ $\hat{4}$ $\flat\hat{3}$ $\hat{2}$ $\hat{1}$
sol la ti do le te sol sol la ti do sol do te le sol do sol fa me re do

Melody 2 🔊

$\hat{1}$ $\hat{2}$ $\flat\hat{3}$ $\hat{4}$ $\hat{5}$ $\flat\hat{6}$ $\hat{5}$ $\hat{5}$ $\hat{4}$ $\flat\hat{3}$ $\hat{2}$ $\hat{1}$ $\hat{7}$ $\hat{1}$ $\hat{1}$ $\flat\hat{3}$ $\hat{5}$ $\hat{4}$ $\hat{2}$ $\hat{7}$ $\hat{1}$ $\flat\hat{3}$ $\hat{5}$ $\hat{4}$ $\flat\hat{3}$ $\hat{2}$
do re me fa sol le sol sol fa me re do ti do do me sol fa re ti do me sol fa me re

$\hat{1}$ $\hat{2}$ $\flat\hat{3}$ $\hat{4}$ $\hat{5}$ $\flat\hat{6}$ $\hat{5}$ $\hat{6}$ $\hat{5}$ $\hat{6}$ $\hat{7}$ $\hat{1}$ $\hat{5}$ $\hat{1}$ $\hat{1}$ $\flat\hat{7}$ $\flat\hat{6}$ $\hat{5}$ $\hat{4}$ $\flat\hat{3}$ $\hat{4}$ $\hat{5}$ $\flat\hat{3}$ $\hat{1}$ $\hat{2}$ $\hat{1}$
do re me fa sol le sol la sol la ti do sol do do te le sol fa me fa sol me do re do

Melody 3 "Once More My Soul" 🔊

This melody begins with an anacrusis on *sol* ($\hat{5}$)

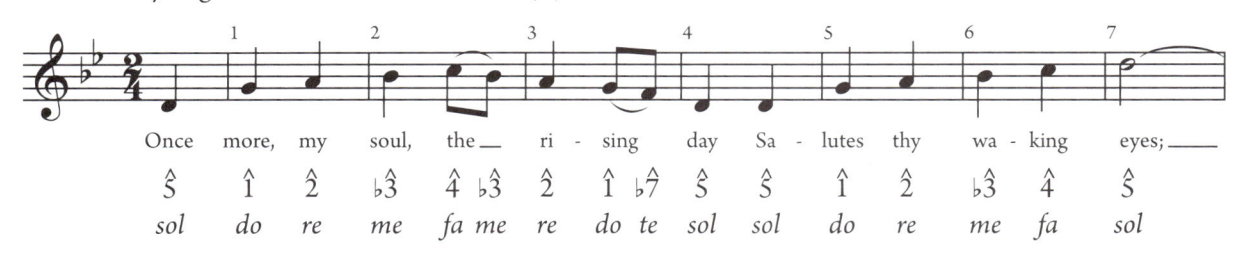

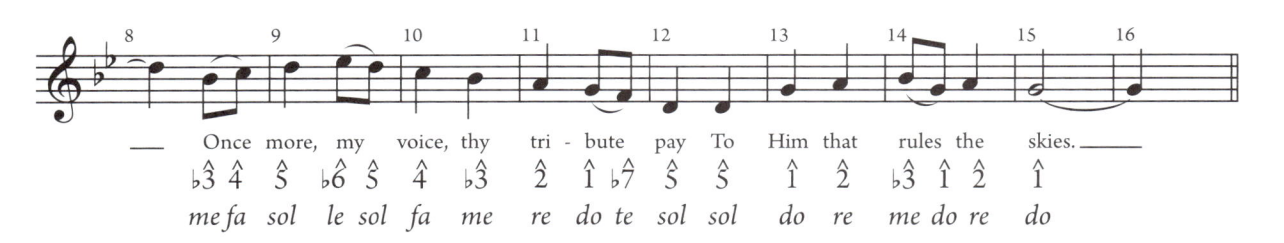

Once more, my soul, the ri - sing day Sa - lutes thy wa - king eyes;
$\hat{5}$ $\hat{1}$ $\hat{2}$ $\flat\hat{3}$ $\hat{4}$ $\flat\hat{3}$ $\hat{2}$ $\hat{1}$ $\flat\hat{7}$ $\hat{5}$ $\hat{5}$ $\hat{1}$ $\hat{2}$ $\flat\hat{3}$ $\hat{4}$ $\hat{5}$
sol do re me fa me re do te sol sol do re me fa sol

Once more, my voice, thy tri - bute pay To Him that rules the skies.
$\flat\hat{3}$ $\hat{4}$ $\hat{5}$ $\flat\hat{6}$ $\hat{5}$ $\hat{4}$ $\flat\hat{3}$ $\hat{2}$ $\hat{1}$ $\flat\hat{7}$ $\hat{5}$ $\hat{5}$ $\hat{1}$ $\hat{2}$ $\flat\hat{3}$ $\hat{1}$ $\hat{2}$ $\hat{1}$
me fa sol le sol fa me re do te sol sol do re me do re do

Apply It 173

Melody 4

1̂ ♭3̂ 5̂ ♭3̂ 4̂ ♭3̂ 2̂ 1̂ 5̂ 2̂ ♭3̂ 4̂ ♭3̂ 2̂ ♭3̂ 4̂ 5̂ 1̂ 2̂ ♭3̂ 4̂ ♭3̂ 2̂ 1̂ 5̂ 1̂
do me sol me fa me re do sol re me fa me re me fa sol do re me fa me re do sol do

E. Listening and writing

Listen to short patterns made from minor scales. Sing what you hear, then write it on the staff provided.

174   CHAPTER SEVEN   Minor Scales and Keys

NAME _____

Workbook ASSIGNMENT 7.1

A. Parallel major and natural minor

minor: W H W W
major: W W H W

The first five notes of a major or minor scale are given below. In the blank provided, identify the scale as "major" or "minor."

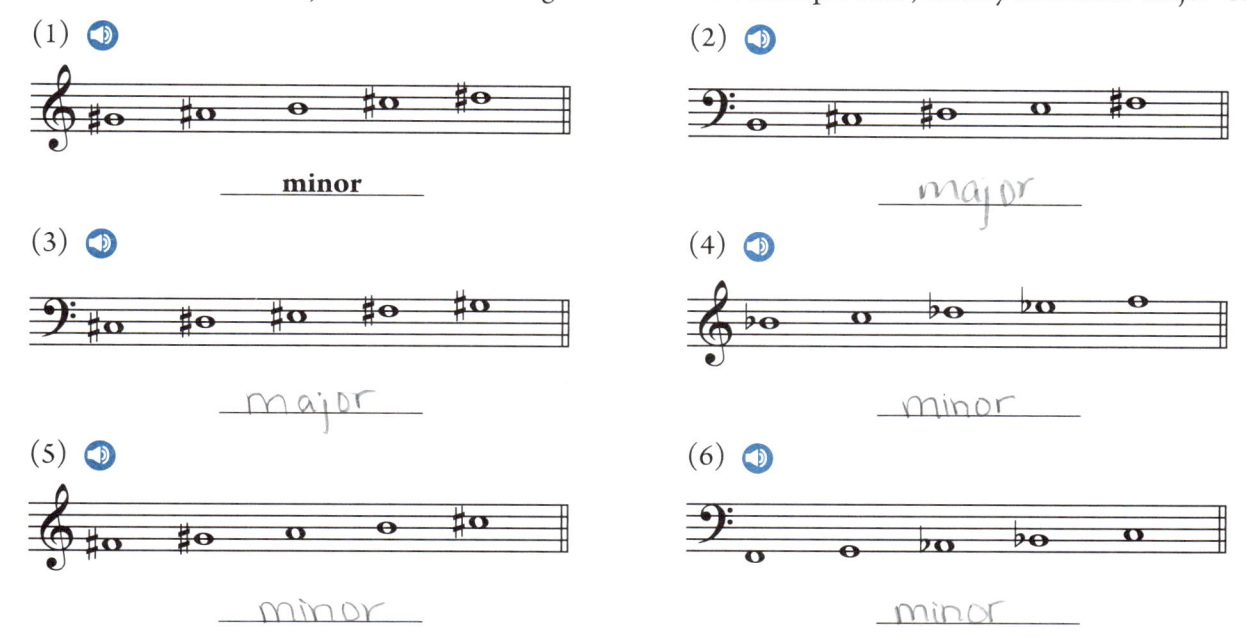

(1) _____minor_____

(2) _____major_____

(3) _____major_____

(4) _____minor_____

(5) _____minor_____

(6) _____minor_____

Write each specified major scale, using accidentals rather than a key signature. Next to each major scale, write its parallel natural minor scale (change $\hat{3}$, $\hat{6}$, and $\hat{7}$ to $\flat\hat{3}$, $\flat\hat{6}$, and $\flat\hat{7}$). Write either scale-degree numbers or solfège syllables beneath the minor scale.

(7) D major / D natural minor

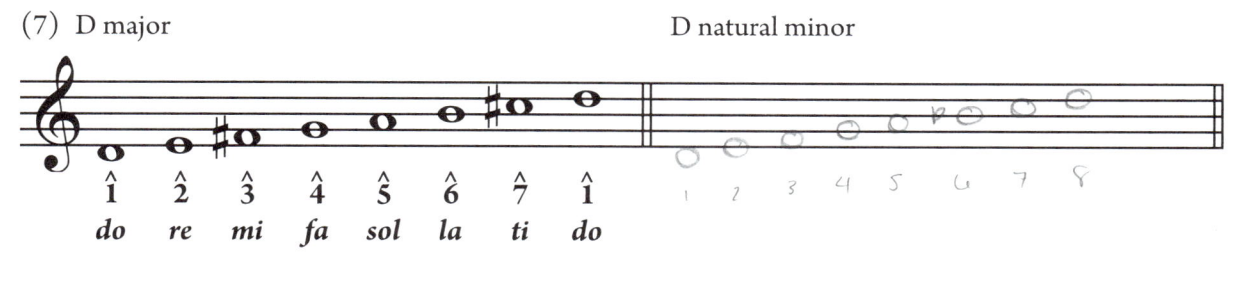

$\hat{1}$ $\hat{2}$ $\hat{3}$ $\hat{4}$ $\hat{5}$ $\hat{6}$ $\hat{7}$ $\hat{1}$
do re mi fa sol la ti do

(8) C♯ major / C♯ natural minor

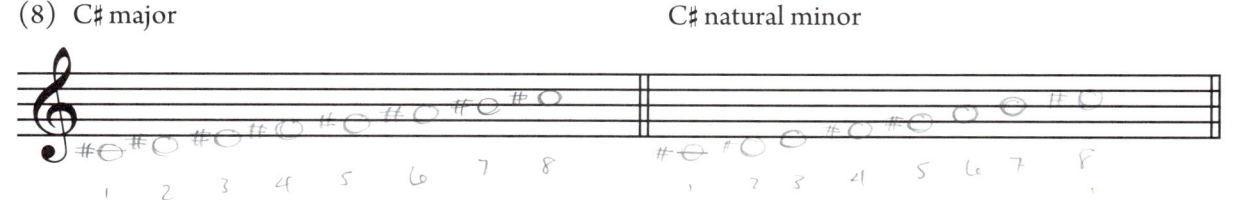

(9) E major / E natural minor

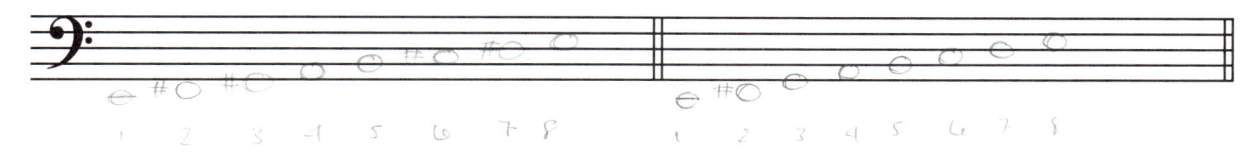

Assignment 7.1   175

(10) F♯ major   F♯ natural minor

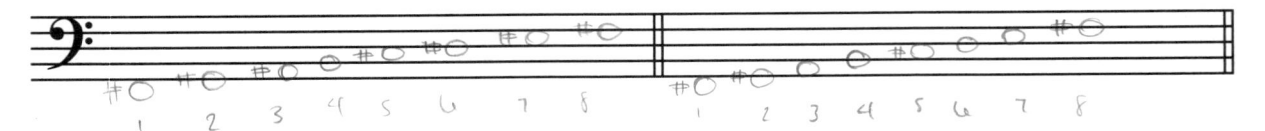

(11) B♭ major   B♭ natural minor

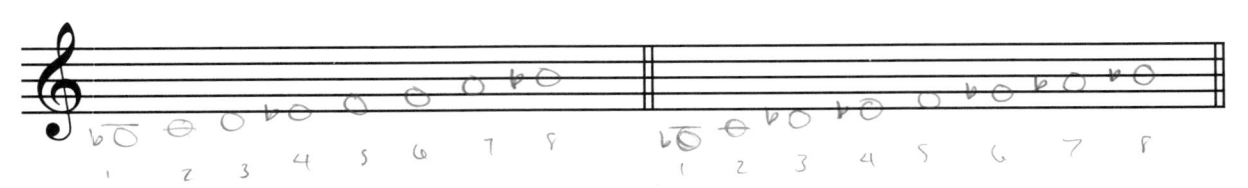

B. Writing natural minor scales

- Write the specified tonic pitch (which may have an accidental).
- Write the basic scale pitches above it (without accidentals).
- Either
   (1) Label the spaces between pitches with W–H–W–W–H–W–W.
   (2) Add the necessary accidentals to conform with the whole- and half-step pattern.

or
   (1) Imagine the parallel major key signature.
   (2) Use accidentals to lower scale degrees $\hat{3}$, $\hat{6}$, and $\hat{7}$.

(1) C natural minor

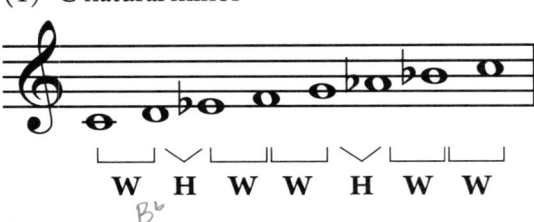

W H W W H W W

(2) B natural minor

(3) G natural minor

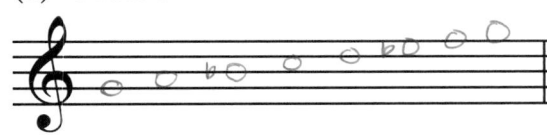

(4) D natural minor

(5) C♯ natural minor

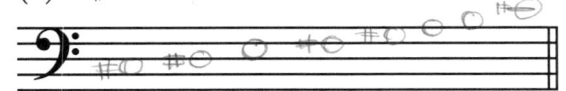

(6) F natural minor

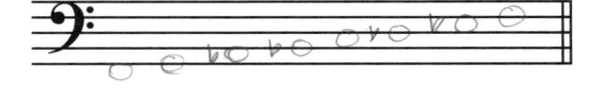

(7) E♭ natural minor

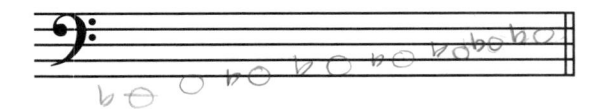

(8) F♯ natural minor

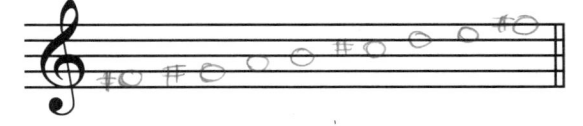

NAME _____

Workbook ASSIGNMENT 7.2

A. Writing harmonic minor

Write the natural minor scales specified below, using accidentals instead of key signatures. To the right, write a harmonic minor scale beginning on the same note. Circle the augmented second.

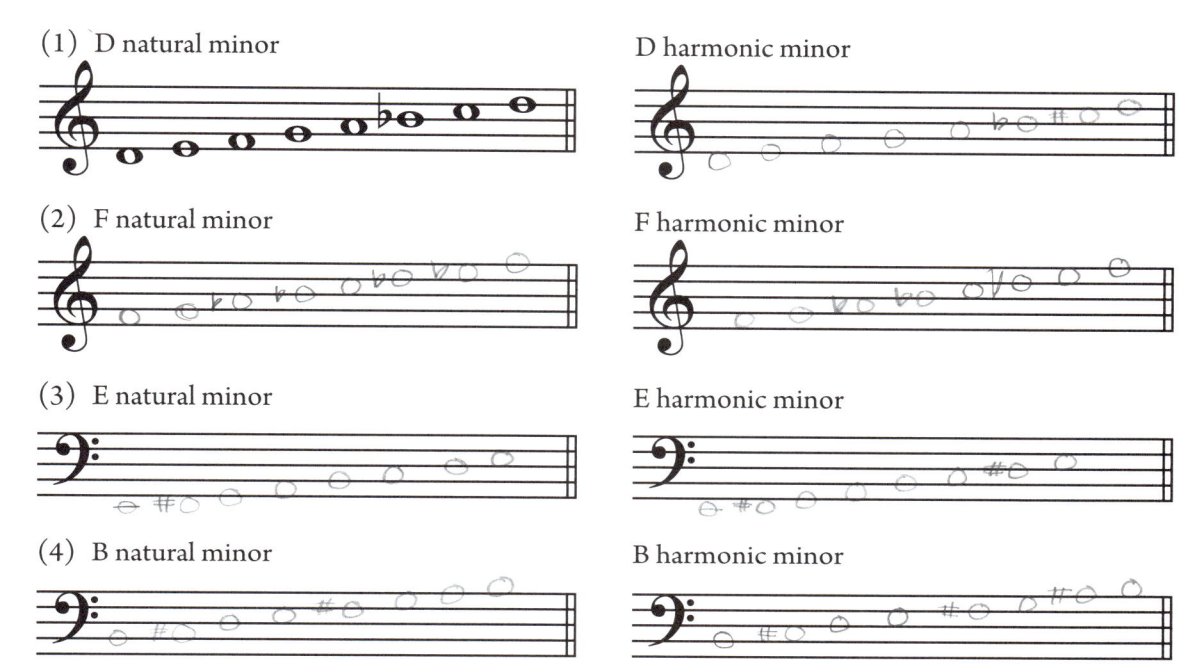

(1) D natural minor   D harmonic minor

(2) F natural minor   F harmonic minor

(3) E natural minor   E harmonic minor

(4) B natural minor   B harmonic minor

B. Notating melodies from scale degrees and solfège syllables

Notate the melodies given below in scale-degree numbers and solfège syllables (no rhythm required). If you know the name of the tune, write it in the blank. (Arrows indicate ascending or descending contour.)

(1) Write this melody in B minor.

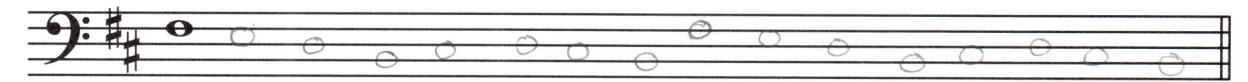

5̂ 4̂ ♭3̂ 1̂ 2̂ ♭3̂ 2̂ 1̂ 5̂ 4̂ ♭3̂ 1̂ 2̂ ♭3̂ 2̂ 1̂
sol ↓fa ↓me ↓do ↑re ↑me ↓re ↓do ↑sol ↓fa ↓me ↓do ↑re ↑me ↓re ↓do

Name of melody: We 3 Kings

(2) Write this melody in D minor.

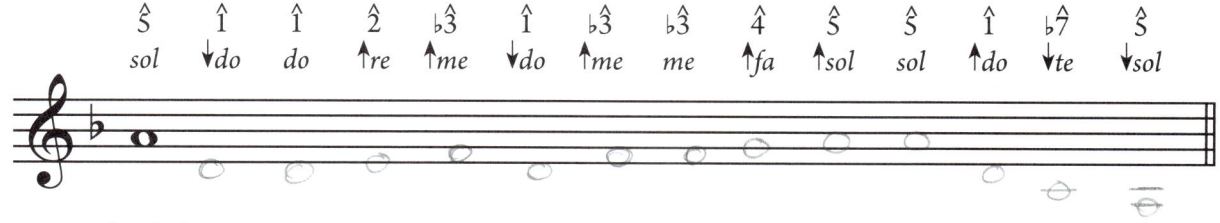

5̂ 1̂ 1̂ 2̂ ♭3̂ 1̂ ♭3̂ ♭3̂ 4̂ 5̂ 5̂ 1̂ ♭7̂ 5̂
sol ↓do do ↑re ↑me ↓do ↑me me ↑fa ↑sol sol ↑do ↓te ↓sol

Name of melody: _____

Assignment 7.2   177

C. Writing melodic minor

Write each natural minor scale specified using accidentals instead of a key signature. Then below it, rewrite as an ascending and descending melodic minor scale, adding accidentals as necessary. Finally, label each pitch of the melodic minor scale with the appropriate scale-degree number or solfège syllable.

(1) A natural minor

A melodic minor

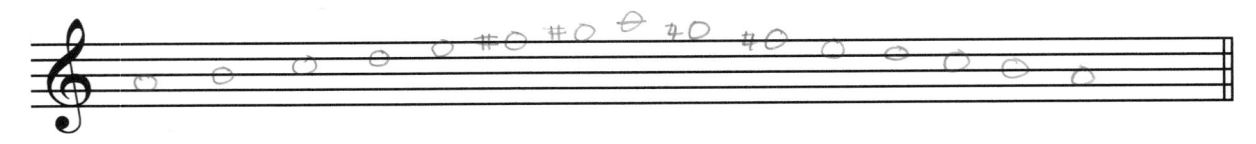

(2) F♯ natural minor

F♯ melodic minor

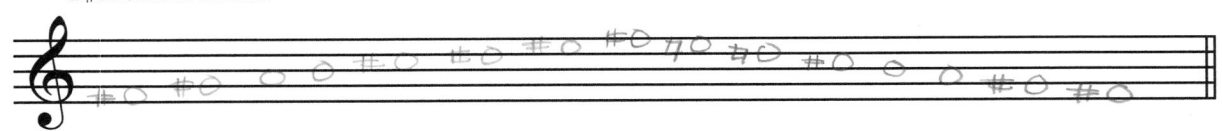

(3) G natural minor

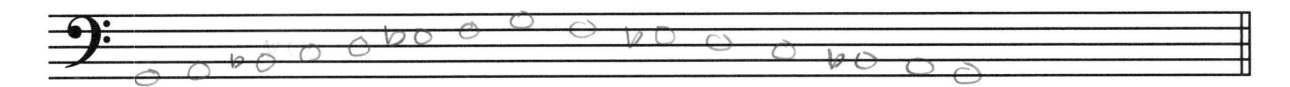

G melodic minor

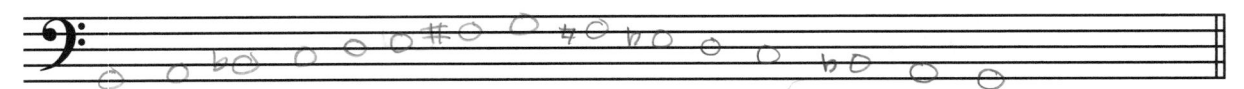

178   CHAPTER SEVEN   Minor Scales and Keys

Workbook — Assignment 7.3

A. Writing relative major and minor scales

- In each exercise below, first write the specified major scale using accidentals rather than a key signature. Circle $\hat{6}$ and write the letter name beneath.
- On the second staff, write the relative natural minor beginning with the circled $\hat{6}$.
- Copy the natural minor scales on the next two staves, altering as necessary to write the harmonic and melodic minor scale ascending.

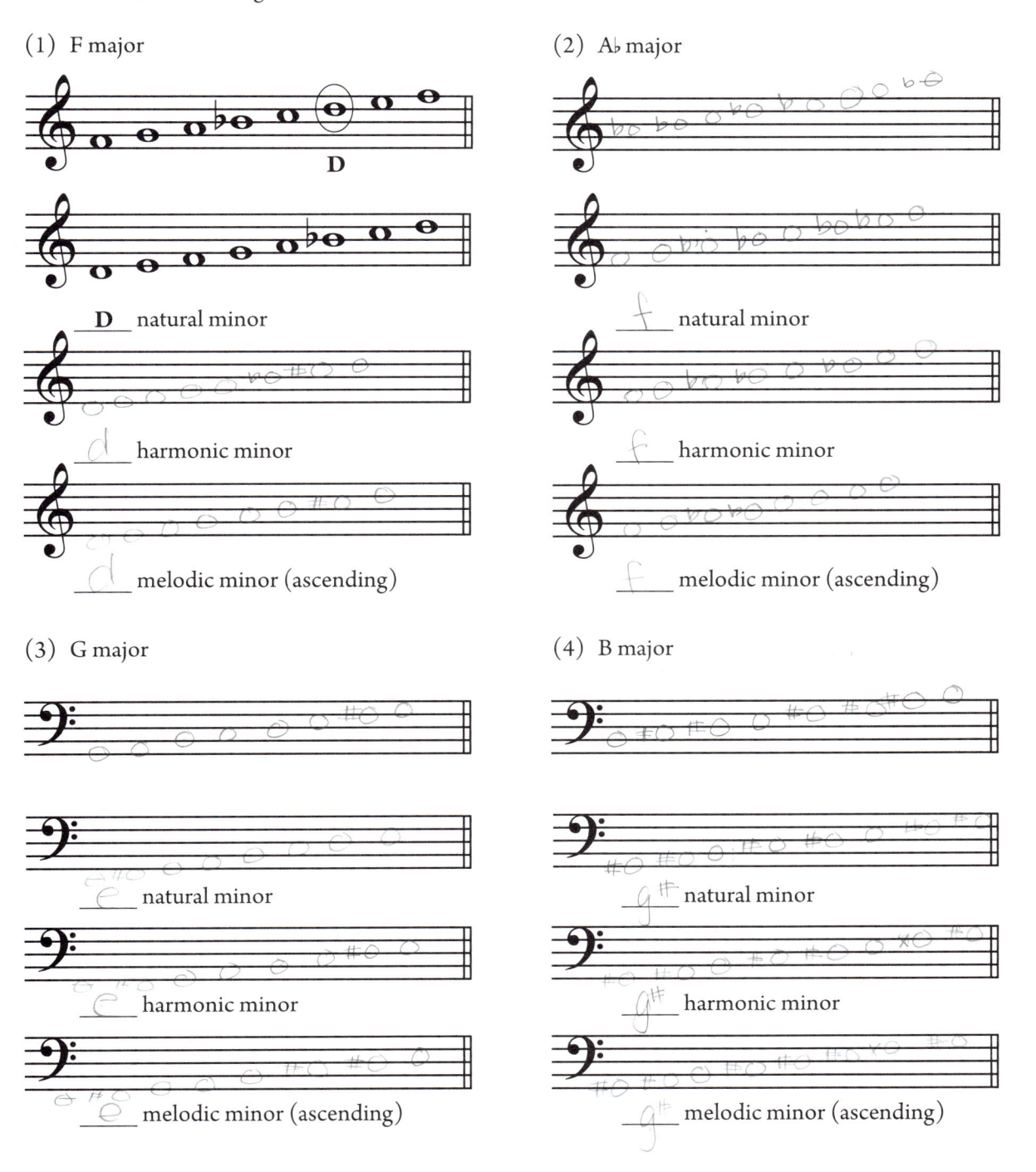

(1) F major

(2) A♭ major

(3) G major

(4) B major

B. Reading and writing minor key signatures

Write the name of the key represented by each signature. Write the major key (uppercase letter) in the top row, and minor key (lowercase letter) in the bottom row.

major: **B♭**, G, A♭, D, E♭, F♯, D♭, B
minor: **g**, e, f, b, c, d♯, b♭, g♯

major: A, D, F, E, G♭, E♭, G, D♭
minor: f♯, b, d, c♯, e♭, c, e, b♭

C. Analyzing keys from melodies

Determine the key of each melody from the key signature and scale degrees. Write the name of the key in the blank. Then circle the correct relationship between each pair of melodies below.

(1) Clarke, *Trumpet Voluntary*, mm. 5–8

Key: D major

(2) Tomás Luis de Victoria, "O magnum mysterium," mm. 5–9

et ad - mi - ra - bi - le sa - cra - men - - - - tum,

Key: d minor

Translation: [O great mystery] and wondrous sacrament

(3) Bach, Chorale Prelude on "Wachet auf," mm. 1–4

Key: E♭ major

(4) Henry Purcell, "Ah, Belinda, I am prest," from *Dido and Aeneas*, mm. 68–72

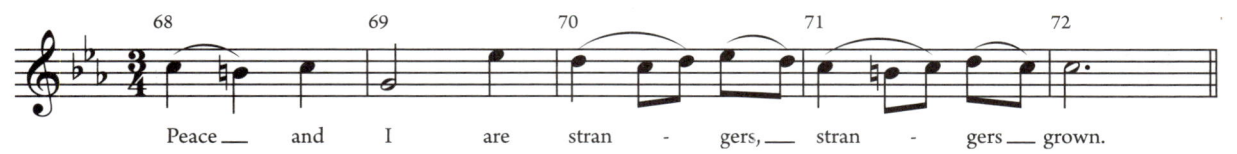

Peace — and I are stran - gers, — stran - gers — grown.

Key: C minor

(5) Clarke and Victoria are in   (parallel keys)   relative keys

(6) Bach and Purcell are in   parallel keys   (relative keys)

Workbook AURAL SKILLS 7.1

Listen to part of a traditional work song, and complete the following exercises.

Questions 1–4 focus on the singer's melody.

(1) Beginning with a quarter-note anacrusis, notate the rhythm on the staff provided. Beam notes to show the correct beat unit.

(2) Beginning on $\hat{5}$ (*sol*), write the melody with solfège syllables or scale-degree numbers.

(3) On the staves below, notate the pitches of the melody with hollow note heads in the key of G minor.

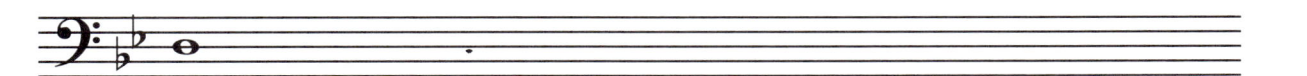

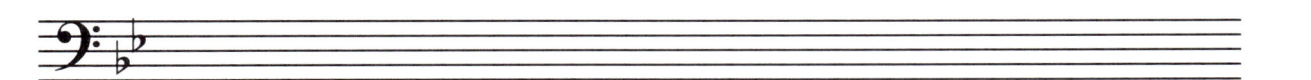

(4) Now notate both pitches and rhythm of the melody on the staves below. Remember to write a clef, key signature, and meter signature. For help, consult your answers to questions 1–3.

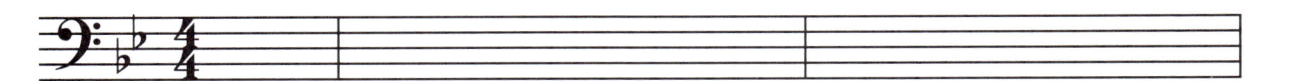

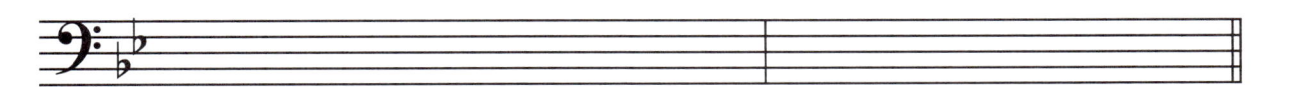

Questions 5–7 focus on the bass line, the lowest part in the piano.

(5) Beginning on $\hat{1}$ (*do*), write the first four pitches of the bass line with solfège syllables or scale-degree numbers.

(6) On the staff below, notate the first four pitches of the bass line in the key of G minor.

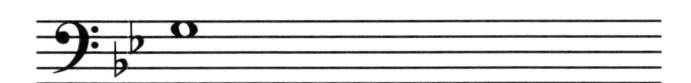

(7) The bass line's first four pitches belong to which minor scale form? Circle the correct answer.

a. natural (descending melodic)   ($\hat{1}$–♭$\hat{7}$–♭$\hat{6}$–$\hat{5}$; do–te–le–sol)

b. harmonic   ($\hat{1}$–$\hat{7}$–♭$\hat{6}$–$\hat{5}$; do–ti–le–sol)

c. ascending melodic   ($\hat{1}$–$\hat{7}$–$\hat{6}$–$\hat{5}$; do–ti–la–sol)

(8) Transpose the melody (the answer to question 4) to the key of E minor. Notate your response in the treble clef, beginning on B3. For help, recall the syllables or numbers in question 2.

182   CHAPTER SEVEN Minor Scales and Keys

Workbook AURAL SKILLS 7.2

(1) Follow the instructions below to compose two minor-key melodies.
- Write one melody in the treble clef and one in the bass clef, each should be eight measures long.
- For one melody, choose a simple meter signature; for the other, a compound meter signature. Include beat patterns from those below.

simple-meter beat patterns

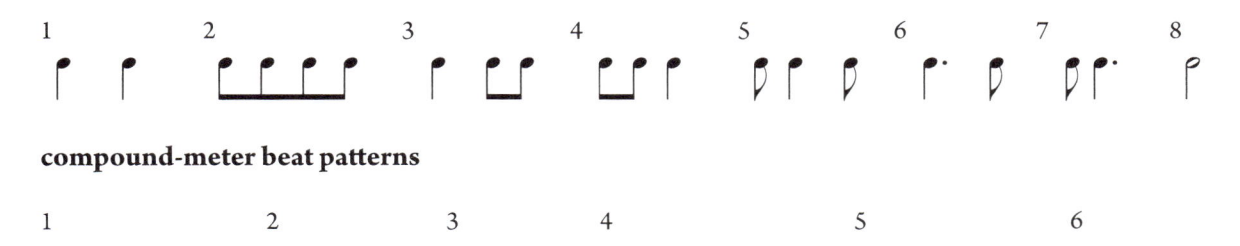

compound-meter beat patterns

- Choose a different tonic pitch in a key that you can sing comfortably for each melody. Begin and end each melody on the tonic pitch.
- Write the minor key signature that goes with the tonic pitch.
- Create an interesting contour.
- End measure 4 on $\hat{2}$, $\hat{5}$, or $\hat{7}$; end measure 8 conclusively on $\hat{1}$ or $\hat{3}$.
- When ascending from $\hat{5}$, choose pitches from the ascending melodic minor scale.
- When descending from $\hat{1}$, choose pitches from the natural (descending melodic) minor scale.

(2) Prepare to perform your melodies in the following ways.
- Sing with solfège syllables, scale-degree numbers, or letter names.
- Play them at the keyboard.
- Play at the keyboard and sing with syllables, numbers, or letter names.
- Play them on another instrument.

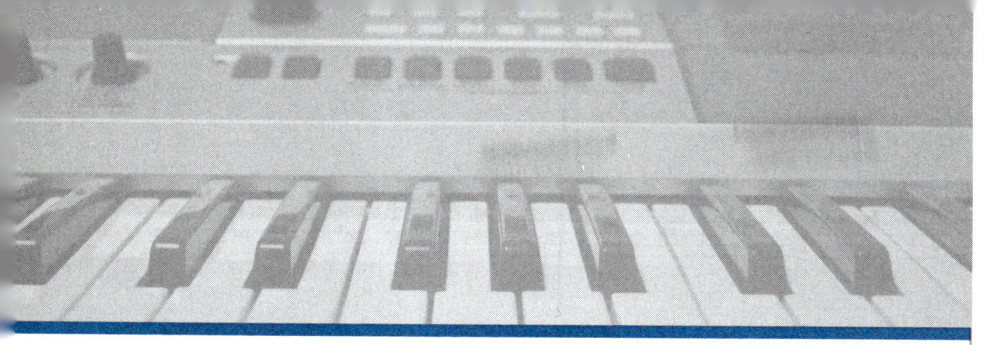

TOPICS
- intervals
- interval quality
- inverting intervals
- spelling intervals
- augmented and diminished intervals
- compound intervals
- consonance and dissonance

MUSIC
- "The Ash Grove"
- J. S. Bach, Invention in D Minor
- "Greensleeves"
- "Simple Gifts"

CHAPTER 8
Intervals

Intervals

Listen to the first two measures of "Simple Gifts" shown in Example 8.1. This melody, drawn from the A♭ major scale, is mostly made of whole and half steps, two of the most familiar musical intervals.

EXAMPLE 8.1 "Simple Gifts," mm. 1–2

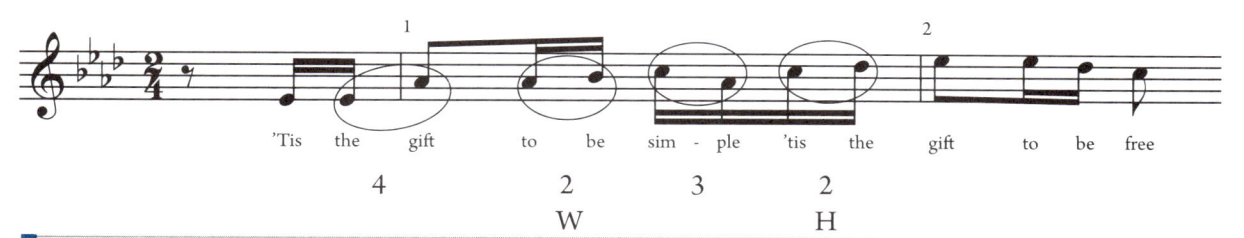

KEY CONCEPT An **interval** measures the distance between two pitches. Intervals are identified by their size (typically a number between 1 and 8) and quality (such as major or minor).

Four intervals are circled and labeled in the example. The first step in naming an interval is to identify its size, either by counting the letter names from one note to the next or by counting the number of staff lines and spaces spanned. Both half and whole steps are seconds, since both may span two adjacent letter names (or a line and a space). Only two intervals in the melody above are not seconds—the E♭4 to A♭4 in the anacrusis, and the C5 to A♭4 and back on the words "simple 'tis." The first interval, spanning four letter names (E♭–F–G–A♭), or four lines and spaces, is a fourth. The second interval is a third, spanning three letter names (C–B♭–A♭). When identifying an interval, always count the first and last notes.

Now listen to the first four measures of "Greensleeves," shown in Example 8.2. The first interval of the melody, A4 to C5, is a third (A–B–C). The melody in measure 1 features only seconds. These intervals and those in "Simple Gifts," measured between successive pitches, are called **melodic intervals**.

185

EXAMPLE 8.2   "Greensleeves," mm. 1–4

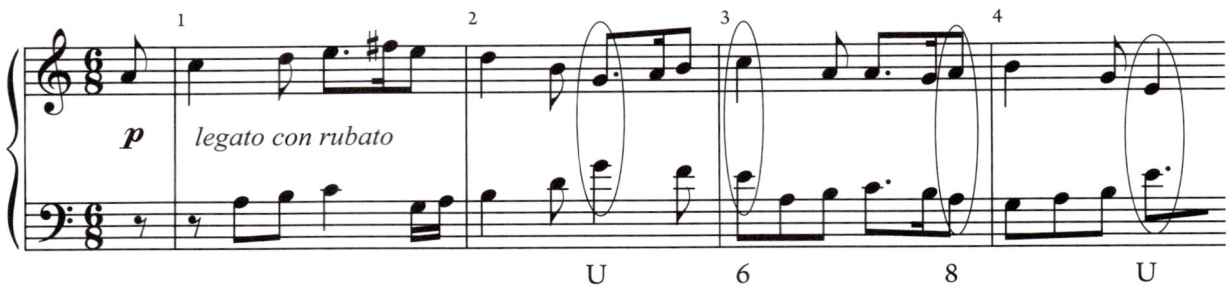

Listen again, paying attention to the intervals formed between the bass-clef pitches and the melody. Intervals between pitches heard at the same time are **harmonic intervals**. Name them the same way as melodic intervals—by counting the letter names or lines and spaces encompassed by the interval. In Example 8.2, the harmonic interval circled in the beginning of measure 3, between E4 and C5, is a sixth (E–F♯–G–A–B–C); the interval circled at the end of measure 3 is an **octave**. Octaves are abbreviated "8ve." You may also encounter the abbreviation "8va" from the Italian "ottava," appearing above or below a group of notes. This means to play the notes transposed up or down an octave.

If two parts play the exact same pitch, this "interval," which spans no actual space, is called a **unison** and abbreviated U. When all women or all men sing a melody together, they sing "in unison." (When women and men sing the same melody, they typically sing in octaves.) "Greensleeves" has unisons circled in measures 2 and 4. Example 8.3 illustrates harmonic and melodic interval sizes up to an octave.

EXAMPLE 8.3   Interval sizes

(a) Melodic intervals

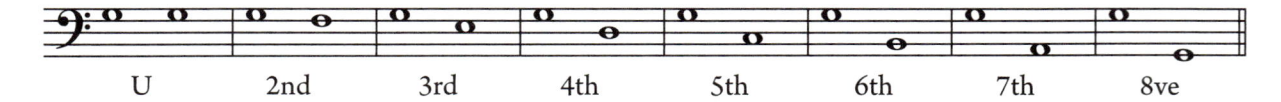

(b) Harmonic intervals

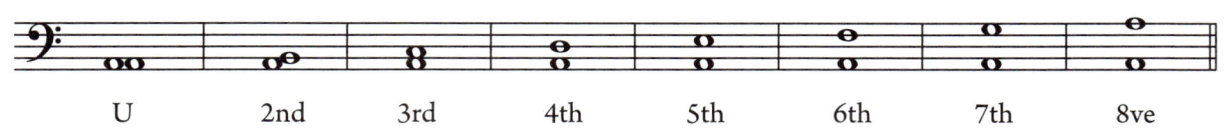

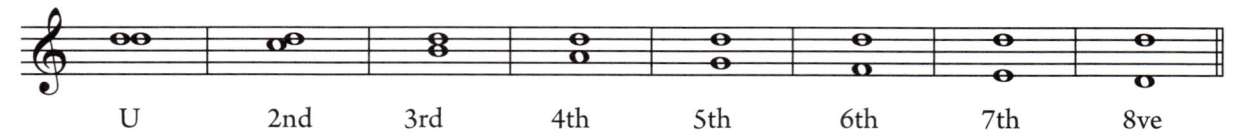

(c) Notation of unisons and seconds with stems

The two note heads in harmonic intervals should be aligned one above the other, except for unisons and seconds, whose note heads are side by side (Example 8.3b and c). A unison may be written as a single note head with two stems, one up and one down (Example 8.3c). The lower note of a second is written to the left, unless each note gets a separate stem.

> **KEY CONCEPT** Learn these landmarks on the staff to identify interval size quickly:
>
> - Thirds, fifths, and sevenths are always written with both pitches on lines or both on spaces.
>   - For thirds, the lines or spaces are adjacent.
>   - For fifths, skip one line or space.
>   - For sevenths, skip two lines or spaces.
> - Seconds, fourths, sixths, and octaves always have one pitch on a line and one on a space.

> **TRY IT #1**
>
> As quickly as possible, write the correct interval size beneath each example below. Identify intervals 3, 5, 7 by their line–line or space–space placement, and intervals 2, 4, 6, 8 by their line–space or space–line placement.
>
> (a) __3__   (b) ____   (c) ____   (d) ____   (e) ____   (f) ____

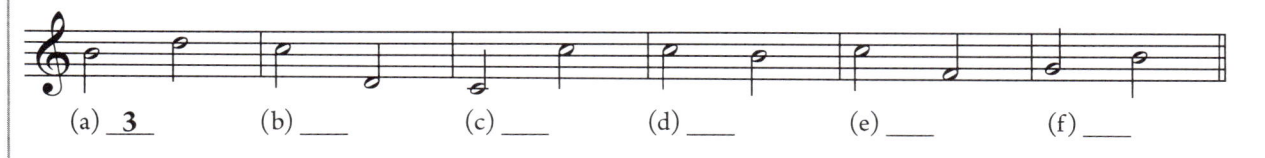

Interval Quality

Listen to "The Ash Grove" while following the melody line in Example 8.4. Five thirds are circled. If you play these thirds on a keyboard and count the half steps they span (remember to check the key signature!), you'll find that some span four half steps (the thirds from E♭ to G, and from D to B♭), and others span three half steps (from G to B♭ and F to A♭).

EXAMPLE 8.4   "The Ash Grove"

(a) mm. 1–4

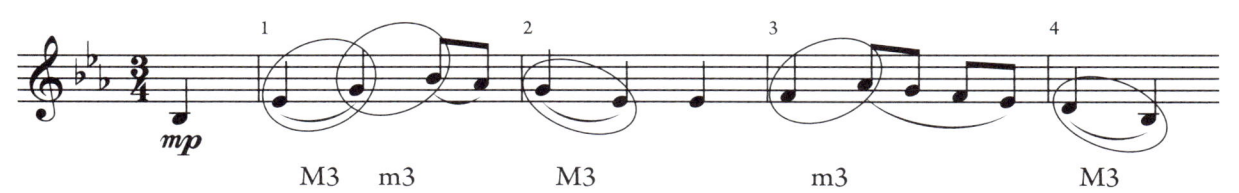

M3   m3   M3   m3   M3

(b) Thirds from mm. 1–4

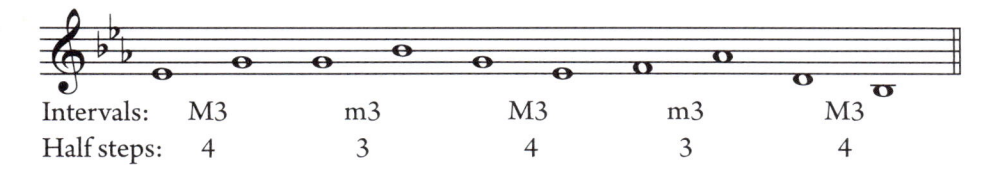

Intervals:	M3	m3	M3	m3	M3
Half steps:	4	3	4	3	4

The intervals that span three half steps are called minor thirds (abbreviated m3); those that span four half steps are called major thirds (M3). Both intervals are thirds, but their quality (major versus minor) differs. Similarly, a half step is a minor second (m2), and a whole step is a major second (M2); both intervals are shown in Example 8.5.

EXAMPLE 8.5   Interval qualities of seconds and thirds

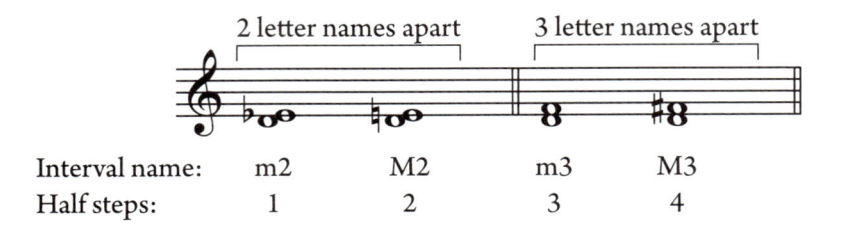

Interval name:	m2	M2	m3	M3
Half steps:	1	2	3	4

> **KEY CONCEPT** When two intervals of the same size (e.g., a third) span a different number of half steps, the difference in their sound is called the **interval quality**. Intervals are named by their size (number of letter names spanned) plus quality (such as **major**, **minor**, or **perfect**).

One good way to spell most intervals is by relating them to scales, where the interval's lower note is the tonic ($\hat{1}$). Compare $\hat{1}$, $\hat{4}$, $\hat{5}$, and $\hat{8}$ between the major and minor scales shown in Example 8.6: the pitches are exactly the same. In either kind of scale, the intervals from the tonic to the fourth, fifth, and octave above it are called perfect (abbreviated P). From the time of the earliest writings about music, around the fifth century B.C.E., these intervals were considered the purest acoustically, hence the name "perfect."

EXAMPLE 8.6   Perfect intervals in major and minor scales

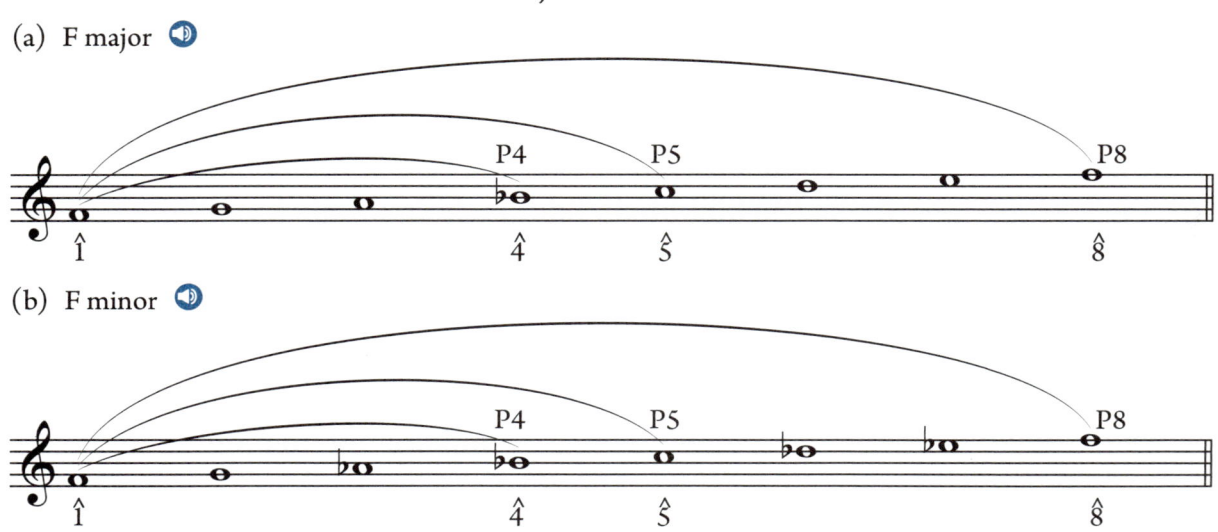

(a) F major

(b) F minor

188   CHAPTER EIGHT   Intervals

Now look at Example 8.7 and compare the intervals between the tonic and the third, sixth, and seventh scale degrees. In the major scale (a), these intervals form a M3, M6, and M7, respectively. In the minor scale (b), they span a m3, m6, and m7.

> **KEY CONCEPT** Major thirds, sixths, and sevenths are a half step larger than minor thirds, sixths, and sevenths.

EXAMPLE 8.7 Major and minor intervals in parallel keys

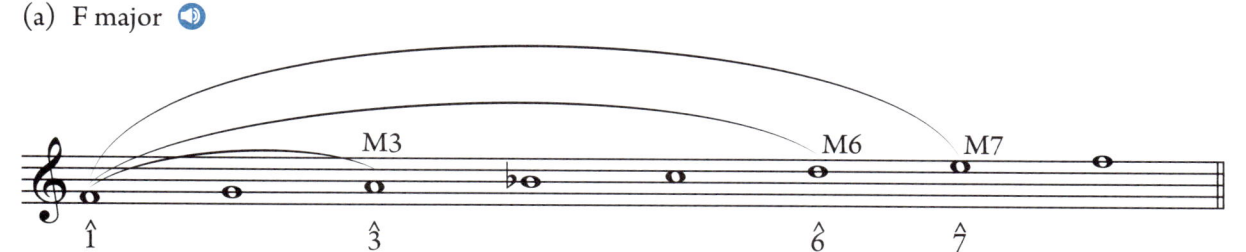

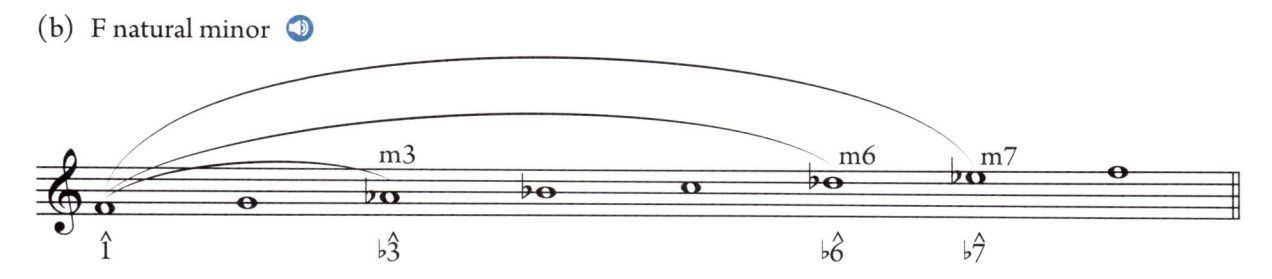

(a) F major

(b) F natural minor

In the descending major scale, the intervals beneath the tonic are all minor or perfect (Example 8.8a). In the descending minor scale, intervals are major or perfect, except from $\hat{1}$ down to $\hat{2}$, which is a m7 (Example 8.8b).

EXAMPLE 8.8 Major, minor, and perfect intervals in descending scales

(a) F major

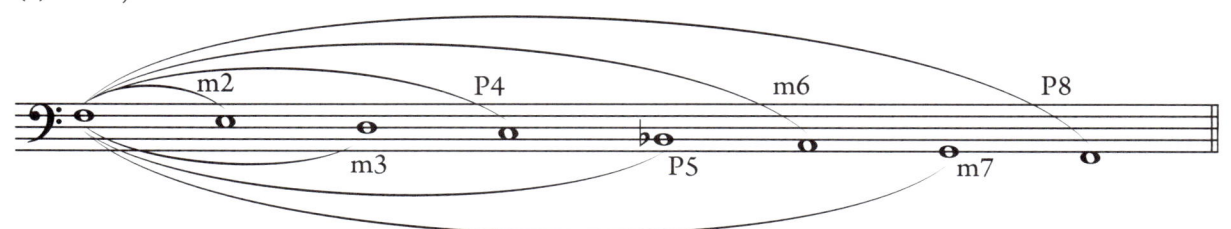

(b) F minor

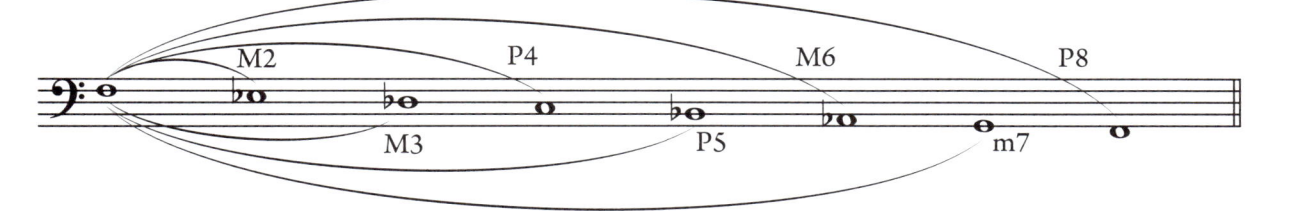

Interval Quality

SUMMARY

Interval size	Quality
2, 3, 6, 7	major or minor (not perfect)
U, 4, 5, 8	perfect (not major or minor)

Inverting Intervals

Example 8.9a shows a perfect fourth, F4 up to B♭4, followed by the same B♭4 up to F5. The second interval is a perfect fifth. Examples 8.9b and c show a major third and a minor sixth, as well as a major second and a minor seventh. Each interval pair in the example is inversionally related.

EXAMPLE 8.9 Inversionally related intervals

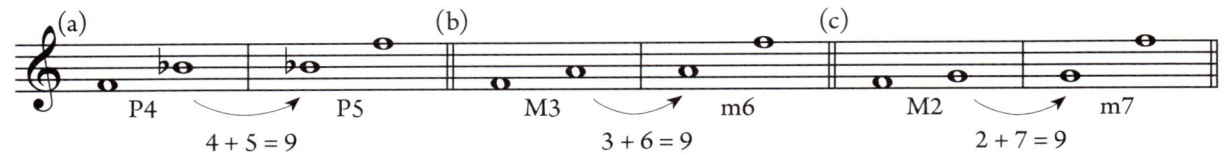

(a) P4 → P5   4 + 5 = 9
(b) M3 → m6   3 + 6 = 9
(c) M2 → m7   2 + 7 = 9

> **KEY CONCEPT** Intervals related by **inversion** share the same notes in reversed order (one of the two pitches is displaced by an octave). Intervals related by inversion are the unison and octave, second and seventh, third and sixth, and fourth and fifth; in each case, the sum of the two intervals is 9.

As Example 8.9 shows, a perfect interval inverts to another perfect interval. A major interval inverts to a minor interval (and vice versa): for example, a M3 inverts to a m6 (Example 8.9b) and a M2 inverts to a m7 (Example 8.9c).

SUMMARY

When inverting an interval:
1. Keep one pitch stable and move the other one up or down an octave.
   - Perfect intervals remain perfect.
   - Major intervals invert to minor.
   - Minor intervals invert to major.
2. The two interval sizes always sum to 9.
   - 1 inverts to 8.
   - 2 inverts to 7.
   - 3 inverts to 6.
   - 4 inverts to 5.
   - 8 inverts to 1.
   - 7 inverts to 2.
   - 6 inverts to 3.
   - 5 inverts to 4.

Spelling Intervals

In this chapter, you will learn three ways to identify and spell intervals: (1) by key signatures and scales, (2) by interval patterns in the C major scale, and (3) by inversion. Find the method that allows you to spell intervals most quickly and accurately, then use a second one to check your work.

Method 1 In this method, which works well for ascending intervals (with the bottom note given), you imagine the bottom note of an interval as the tonic of a major or minor key. The upper note lies somewhere in the scale and is spelled with accidentals belonging to that key. See Example 8.10 to follow these steps (shown in order vertically).
(1) Write the note heads of the interval on the lines or spaces.
(2) Think of the key signature of the bottom note. For major or perfect intervals, think of the major key signature; for minor intervals, think of the minor key signature.
(3) Add accidentals if necessary.
  - If perfect (U, 4, 5, 8) or major (2, 3, 6, 7), add an accidental to the upper note if needed to match the major key signature of the bottom note (Example 8.10a and c).
  - If minor (3, 6, 7), add an accidental to the upper note if needed to match the minor key signature of the bottom note (Example 8.10b and d).
  - If you want a m2, follow step 1, then add an accidental to the upper note to make a diatonic half step.

EXAMPLE 8.10   Spelling intervals from major and minor scales

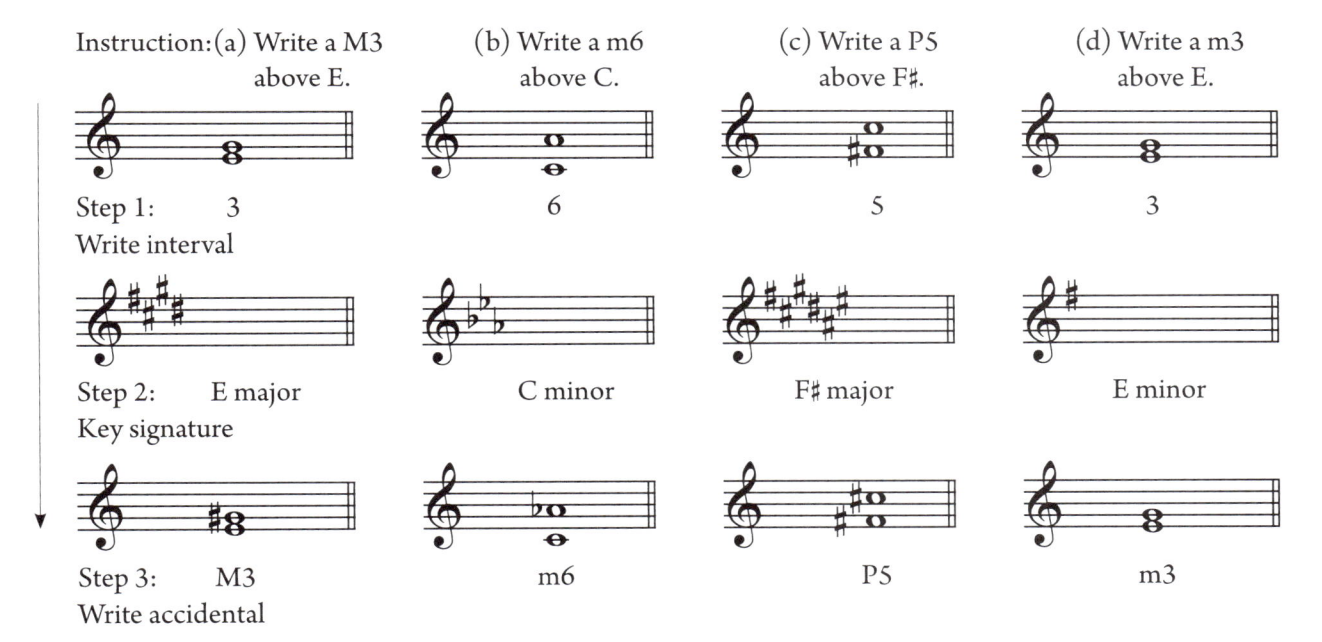

Instruction: (a) Write a M3 above E.   (b) Write a m6 above C.   (c) Write a P5 above F♯.   (d) Write a m3 above E.

Step 1: Write interval   3   6   5   3

Step 2: Key signature   E major   C minor   F♯ major   E minor

Step 3: Write accidental   M3   m6   P5   m3

Since a minor interval is a half step smaller than a major interval, you can also use a major key signature (if you know it better) to spell a minor interval, as shown in Example 8.11:
(1) Imagine the major key signature for the bottom note of the interval.
(2) Write the corresponding major interval based on the key signature.
(3) Lower the top note by a chromatic half step (don't change the letter name).

EXAMPLE 8.11   Spelling minor intervals from major key signatures

To spell a m7 above D:

(1) Write the major key signature.   (2) Spell a M7.   (3) Lower the top note.

To spell a m3 above G:

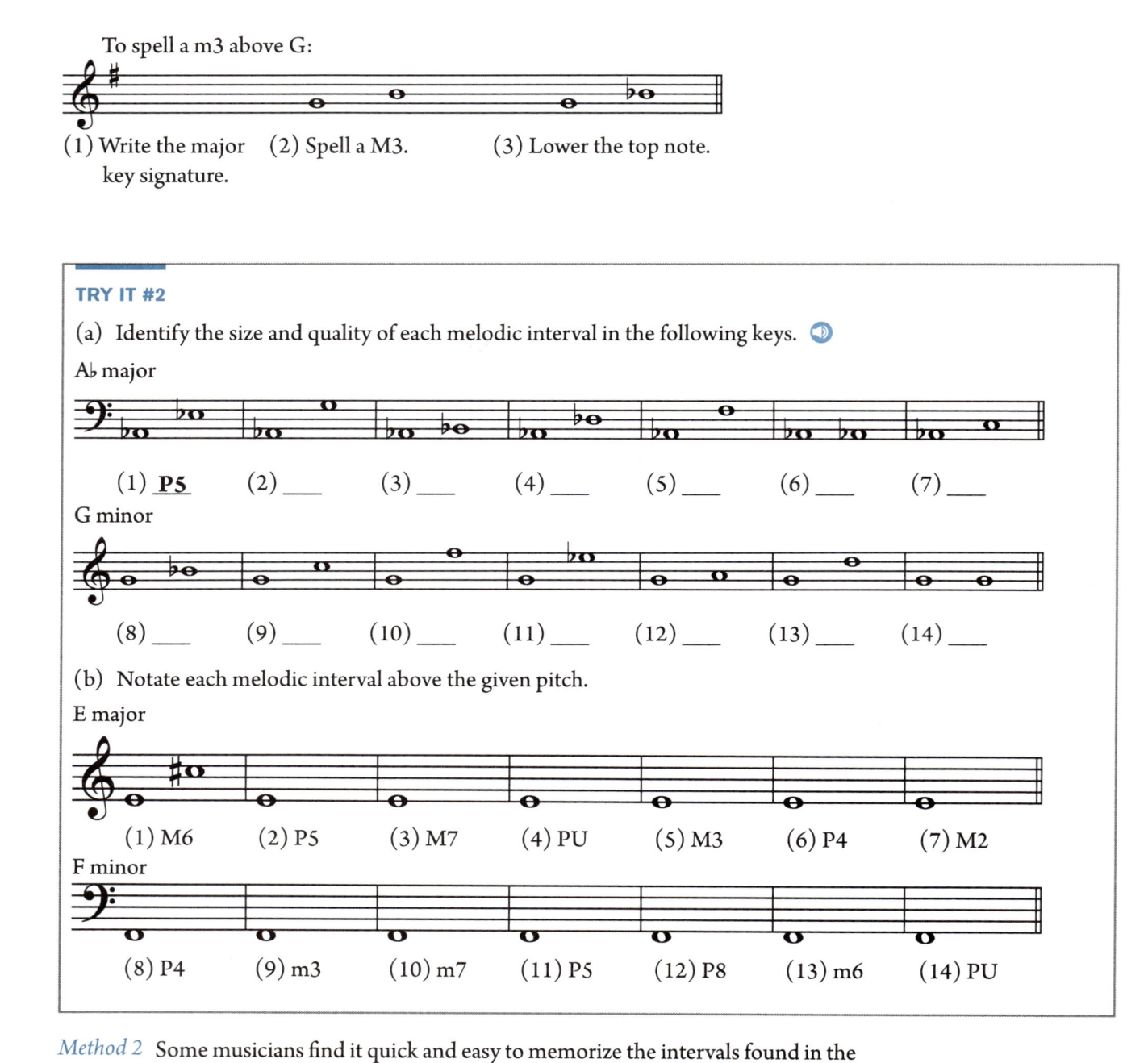

(1) Write the major key signature.   (2) Spell a M3.   (3) Lower the top note.

TRY IT #2

(a) Identify the size and quality of each melodic interval in the following keys.

A♭ major

(1) **P5**   (2) ___   (3) ___   (4) ___   (5) ___   (6) ___   (7) ___

G minor

(8) ___   (9) ___   (10) ___   (11) ___   (12) ___   (13) ___   (14) ___

(b) Notate each melodic interval above the given pitch.

E major

(1) M6   (2) P5   (3) M7   (4) PU   (5) M3   (6) P4   (7) M2

F minor

(8) P4   (9) m3   (10) m7   (11) P5   (12) P8   (13) m6   (14) PU

Method 2 Some musicians find it quick and easy to memorize the intervals found in the C major scale by visualizing them on the keyboard (the white-key notes), on another instrument, or on the lines and spaces of a staff with no accidentals. This method works well for both ascending and descending intervals, but be sure not to change the given note. Example 8.12 shows seconds, marked on the keyboard from C4 to C5 (a) and arranged on the staff (b). All seconds within the C major scale are M2, except for E–F and B–C, which are m2. As Example 8.12c shows, the interval quality is unchanged if you add the same accidental to both notes.

EXAMPLE 8.12 Seconds within the C major scale

(a) On the keyboard

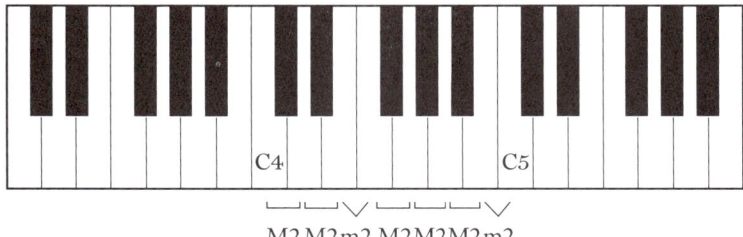

M2 M2 m2 M2 M2 M2 m2

(b) On the staff

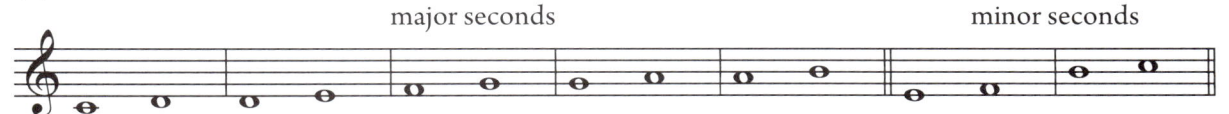

major seconds   minor seconds

(c) On the staff with matching accidentals added

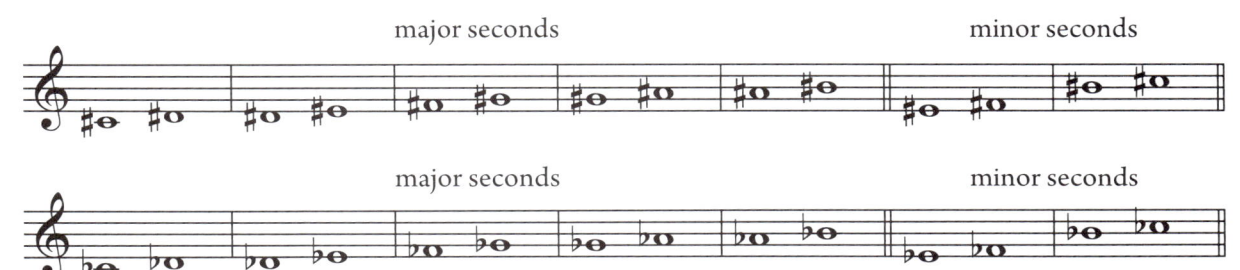

major seconds   minor seconds

major seconds   minor seconds

Memorize the qualities of the white-key thirds and fourths (Examples 8.13 and 8.14) as well, and play them at the keyboard. As with seconds, if a third or fourth has matching accidentals, it retains the size and quality of the white-key interval. For instance, all white-key fourths are perfect except F–B, and they remain perfect if matching accidentals are added to both pitches.

EXAMPLE 8.13 Thirds within the C major scale

(a) On the keyboard

m3 M3 m3

M3 m3 M3 m3

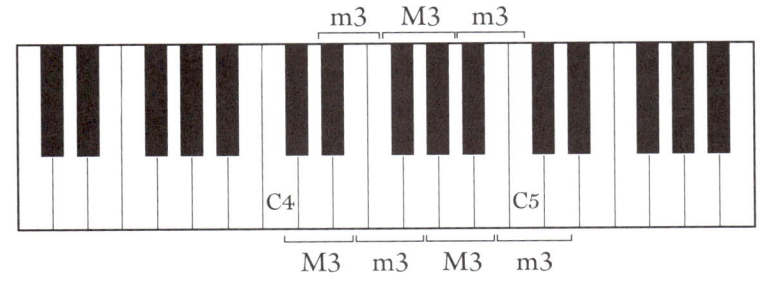

(b) On the staff

major thirds   also M3   minor thirds   also m3

Spelling Intervals   193

EXAMPLE 8.14 Fourths

(a) Within the C major scale

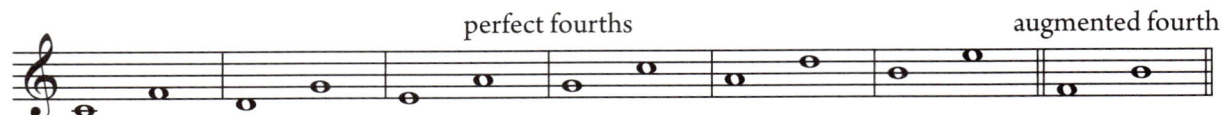

perfect fourths   augmented fourth

(b) With accidentals

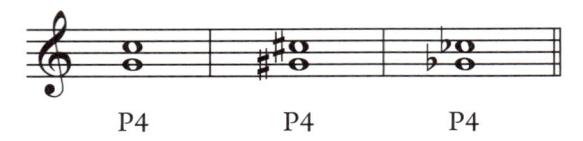

P4   P4   P4

TRY IT #3

Identify each second, third, and fourth below. Intervals with matching accidentals on both notes will have the same quality as their white-key counterparts.

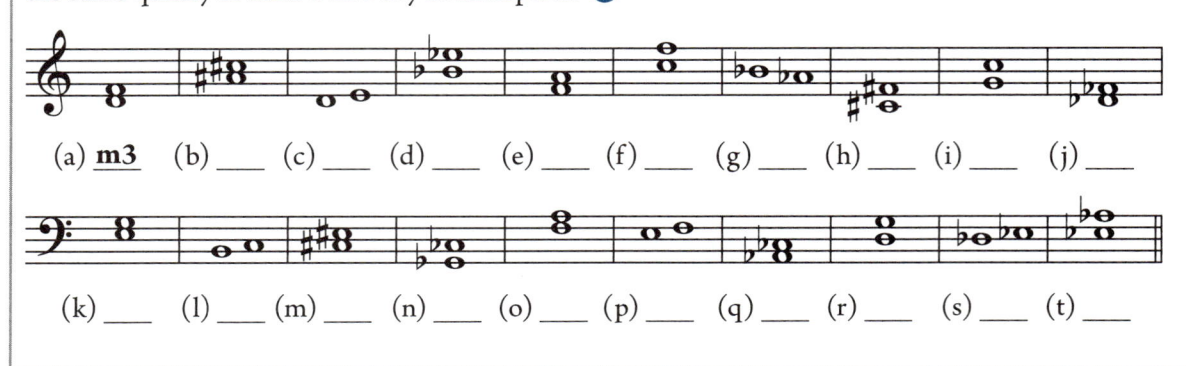

(a) **m3**   (b) ___   (c) ___   (d) ___   (e) ___   (f) ___   (g) ___   (h) ___   (i) ___   (j) ___

(k) ___   (l) ___   (m) ___   (n) ___   (o) ___   (p) ___   (q) ___   (r) ___   (s) ___   (t) ___

To spell intervals with the white-key (C major) method, remember:

- The quality of an interval remains unchanged when the same accidental is added to *both* notes. For example, F–G is a M2 as are F♭–G♭ and F♯–G♯.
- Minor intervals are a chromatic half step smaller than major. You can make a major interval into a minor one by lowering the top note (F–G becomes F–G♭) or raising the bottom note (F–G becomes F♯–G), in which case the accidentals no longer match.

To write any interval by the white-key method:

- If the given note is a white key, write the white-key interval first, and identify its quality (based on the pattern in C major). Then adjust its size by adding a flat or sharp to the other note (Example 8.15a).
    - To make a major interval minor, lower the top note or raise the bottom note.
    - To make a minor interval major, raise the top note or lower the bottom note.

- If the given note has an accidental, write the proper note head for the interval size and add a matching accidental, then follow the same procedure (Example 8.15b).
- If you are asked to write an interval up or down from a given note, do not change the given note; make any adjustments for quality to the other note.

EXAMPLE 8.15   Spelling intervals by C major patterns

(a) Start with a white-key interval and alter the second note.

1. Spell a m3 above C: 2. Spell a M3 above D: 3. Spell a M3 below D: 4. Spell a m3 below B:

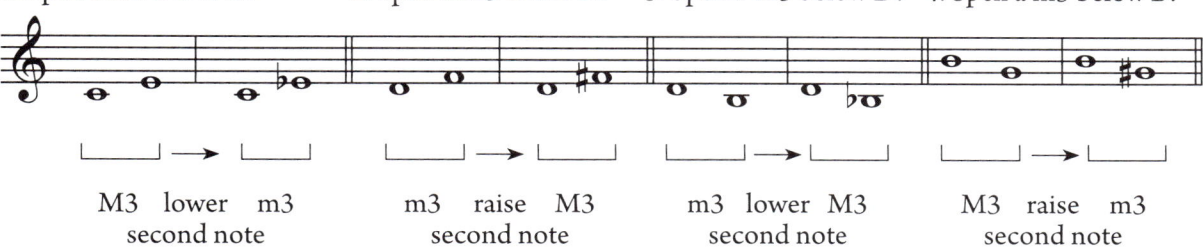

M3 lower m3   m3 raise M3   m3 lower M3   M3 raise m3
     second note   second note   second note   second note

(b) Start with matching accidentals and alter the second note.

1. Spell a m3 above C♯:   2. Spell a M3 above D♭:   3. Spell a M3 below D♭:   4. Spell a m3 below E♯:

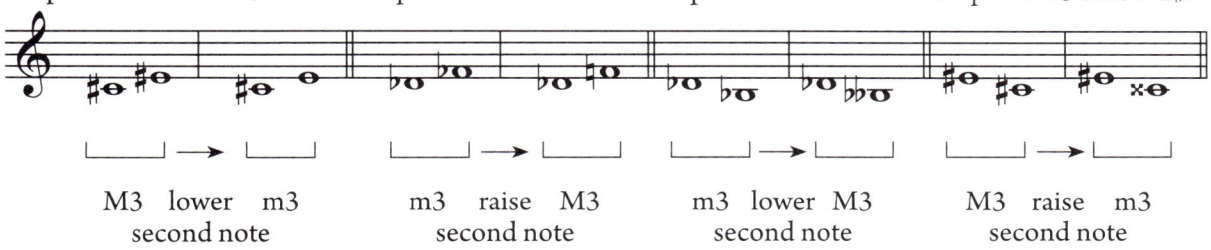

M3 lower m3   m3 raise M3   m3 lower M3   M3 raise m3
     second note   second note   second note   second note

ASSIGNMENT 8.1

Method 3 Inversions provide a quick shortcut for spelling wide intervals, such as fifths, sixths, and sevenths. As Example 8.16a shows, you can spell the minor seventh above D by thinking of its inversion, the major second. If you are asked to spell a large interval, think of its inversion: a major second below D is C, therefore a minor seventh above D is C. This process works with or without accidentals: since D♯ up to E is a minor second, D♯ down to E is a major seventh. Example 8.16b and c show how to spell fifths and sixths using inversions.

EXAMPLE 8.16 Spelling largest intervals from their inversions

(a) Spelling sevenths using seconds

1. Spell a m7 above D

2. Spell a M7 below D♯

M2 ⟶ m7   m2 ⟶ M7

(b) Spelling fifths using fourths

1. Spell a P5 above A

2. Spell a P5 below A♭

P4 ⟶ P5   P4 ⟶ P5

(c) Spelling sixths using thirds

1. Spell a M6 above A

2. Spell a m6 below D♭

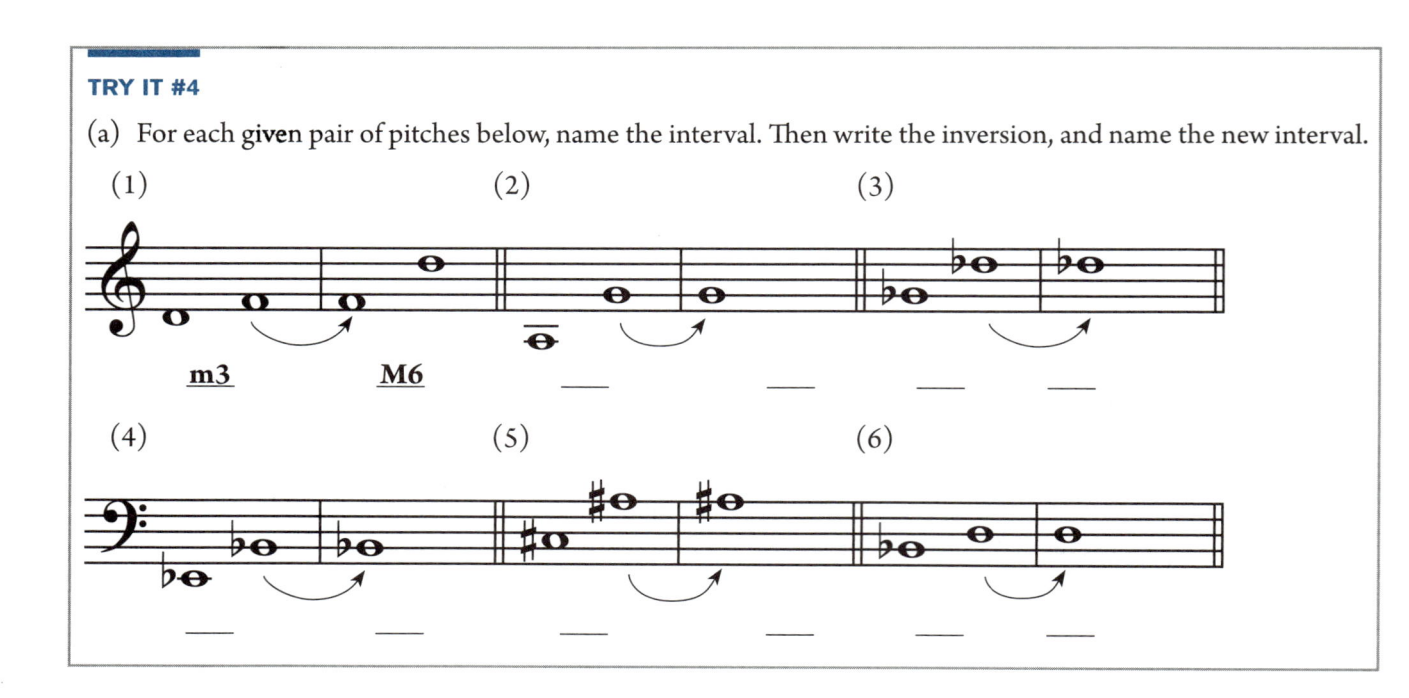

m3 ⟶ M6   M3 ⟶ m6

TRY IT #4

(a) For each **given** pair of pitches below, name the interval. Then write the inversion, and name the new interval.

(1) m3 M6

(2) ___ ___

(3) ___ ___

(4) ___ ___

(5) ___ ___

(6) ___ ___

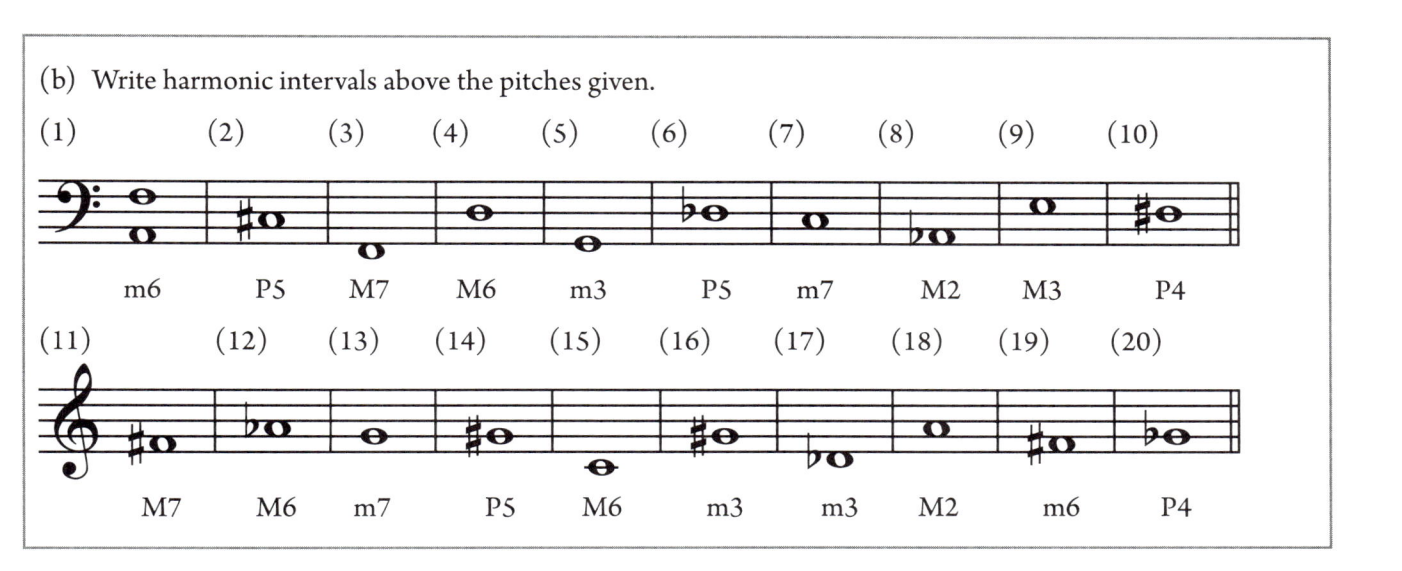

(b) Write harmonic intervals above the pitches given.

(1) m6 (2) P5 (3) M7 (4) M6 (5) m3 (6) P5 (7) m7 (8) M2 (9) M3 (10) P4

(11) M7 (12) M6 (13) m7 (14) P5 (15) M6 (16) m3 (17) m3 (18) M2 (19) m6 (20) P4

ASSIGNMENT 8.2

Finally, you can check the quality of any interval by counting its half steps. The table below summarizes the information you need to know. Be careful to write the note heads for the interval's size (spanning the correct number of letter names) first, before counting half steps. Otherwise, you may confuse enharmonic intervals like the A4 and d5 (tritones), which we consider next.

Interval name	Abbreviation	Interval type	Number of half steps
unison	U	1	0
minor second	m2	2	1
major second	M2	2	2
minor third	m3	3	3
major third	M3	3	4
perfect fourth	P4	4	5
tritone	A4 or d5	4 or 5	6
perfect fifth	P5	5	7
minor sixth	m6	6	8
major sixth	M6	6	9
minor seventh	m7	7	10
major seventh	M7	7	11
octave	P8	8	12

Augmented and Diminished Intervals

Bach's Invention in D minor (Example 8.17) provides examples of two additional interval types: **augmented** and **diminished**. Listen to the beginning, and focus on the bracketed intervals—the dramatic leap from B♭4 down to C♯4 and back up in measures 1–2, and the right-hand G4 to C♯5 in measure 4.

EXAMPLE 8.17 Bach, Invention in D Minor, mm. 1–5

mm. 1–2: m7   d7

m. 4: P4   A4

If the B♭ in measure 1 dropped down to a C4 instead of C♯4, as shown below the example, the interval would be a m7. The interval here is a half step smaller than a m7: a diminished seventh (d7). Now look at measure 4. If this interval were the white-key notes G4–C5, it would be a perfect fourth (P4); G4–C♯4 is a half step larger, making an augmented fourth (A4). These diminished and augmented intervals are produced by the variants of $\hat{6}$ and $\hat{7}$ that are available in harmonic and melodic minor scales.

> **KEY CONCEPT** When a major or perfect interval is made a chromatic half step larger, call it augmented (C up to A♯ is an A6). When a minor or perfect interval is made a chromatic half step smaller, call it diminished (C up to G♭ is a d5).

As previously mentioned, all the fifths and fourths made between pairs of white-key pitches are perfect except one: the interval between F and B (see Example 8.18). This interval may be spelled as a diminished fifth (d5) or an augmented fourth (A4), depending on where it is positioned within the major scale (Example 8.19). When $\hat{4}$ is lower than $\hat{7}$, it is an augmented fourth (F–B in C major); $\hat{7}$ lower than $\hat{4}$ makes a diminished fifth (B–F). Since the interval spans exactly three whole steps, it is called the **tritone** ("tri" means "three"). The A4 and d5 are the only inversionally related intervals that are exactly the same size: they each encompass six semitones.

EXAMPLE 8.18 Fourths made with white-key pitches

198   CHAPTER EIGHT   Intervals

EXAMPLE 8.19 The A4 and d5 in a C major scale

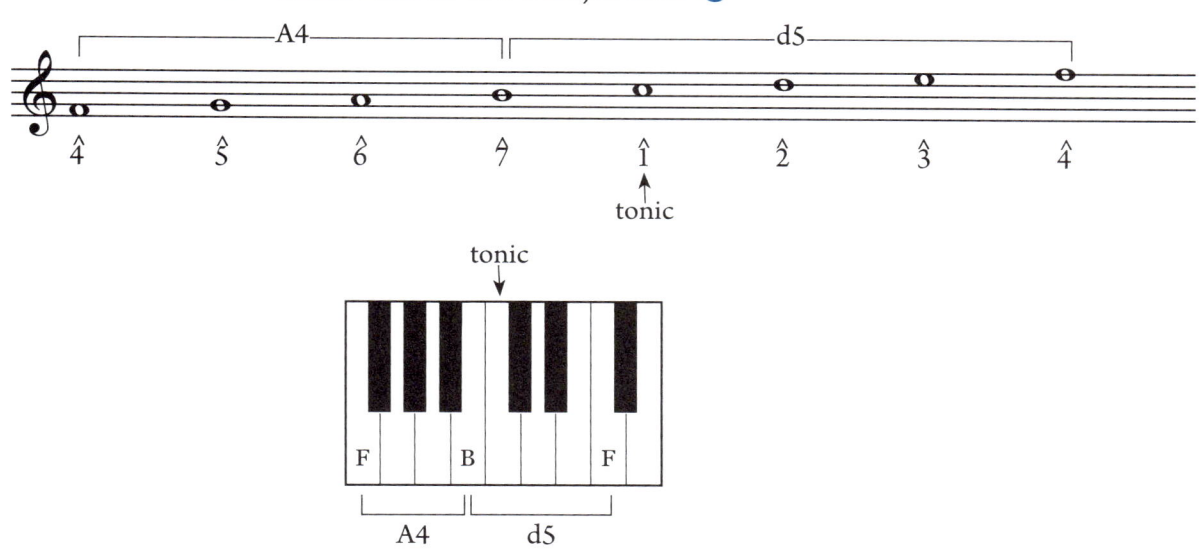

AURAL SKILLS 8.1

The A4 and d5 are the only diminished and augmented intervals that fall within the major and natural minor scales. Others can be made by raising or lowering diatonic scale degrees by a half step. Only a few—including the A2, A6, and d7—are often found in pieces of music. To spell an augmented or diminished interval, first spell a major, perfect, or minor interval, then use accidentals to adjust its size, as shown in Example 8.20. Don't change the letter name of either pitch.

EXAMPLE 8.20 Spelling augmented and diminished intervals

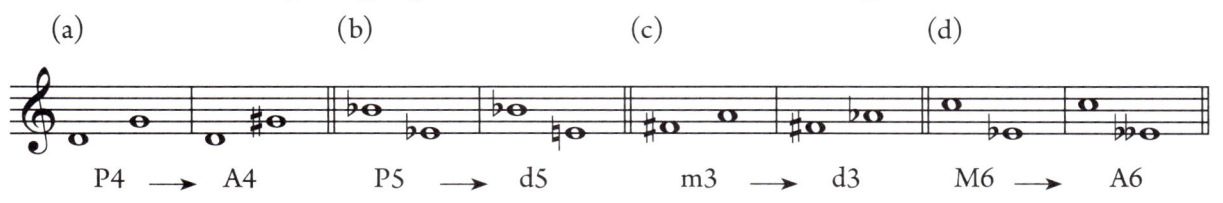

(a) P4 → A4   (b) P5 → d5   (c) m3 → d3   (d) M6 → A6

The charts below show the interval size produced when you make an interval one chromatic half step smaller (left arrow) or larger (right arrow):

d3 ← m3 → M3   d4 ← P4 → A4   d6 ← m6 → M6   d7 ← m7 → M7
m3 ← M3 → A3   d5 ← P5 → A5   m6 ← M6 → A6   m7 ← M7 → A7

For a	start with	add an accidental to move one pitch
diminished 3, 6, 7	minor 3, 6, 7	inward a half step
diminished 4, 5, 8	perfect 4, 5, 8	inward a half step
augmented 2, 3, 6	major 2, 3, 6	outward a half step
augmented 4, 5, 8	perfect 4, 5, 8	outward a half step

KEY CONCEPT Diminished and augmented intervals can usually be respelled as major or minor intervals. These spellings are **enharmonically equivalent:** for example, A2 and m3 (C–D♯ and C–E♭), d4 and M3 (C–F♭ and C–E), A5 and m6 (C–G♯ and C–A♭), and so on.

It is also possible to make doubly augmented or doubly diminished intervals, though they are rare. They are sometimes spelled with double sharps or double flats or with one note sharped and the other flatted (Example 8.21). To write them, follow the directions above (without changing any letter names), but move one pitch inward or outward a *whole* step, rather than a half.

EXAMPLE 8.21   Doubly augmented (dA) and diminished (dd) intervals

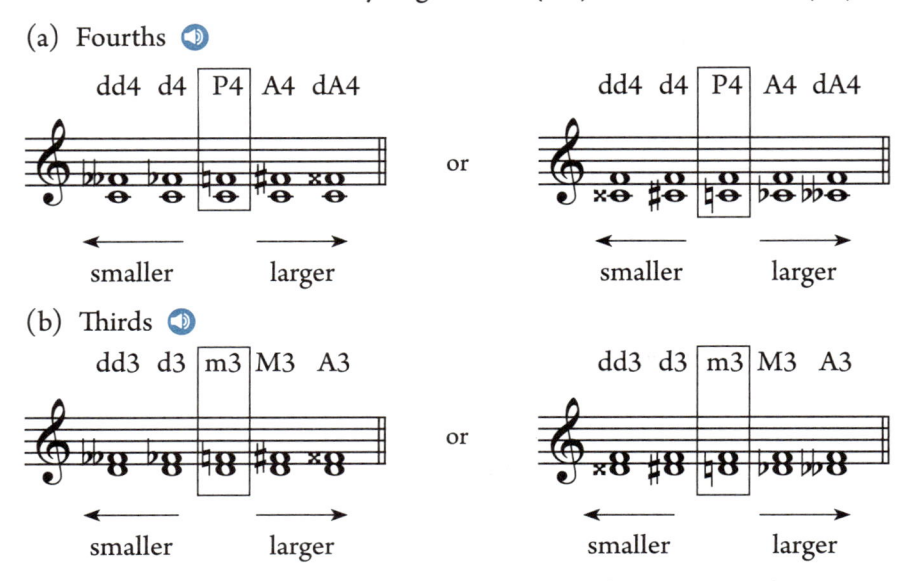

(a) Fourths

(b) Thirds

TRY IT #5

Spell the following augmented and diminished intervals above the given note. First spell a major, minor, or perfect interval as specified, then alter its quality. Don't change the given note by adding an accidental.

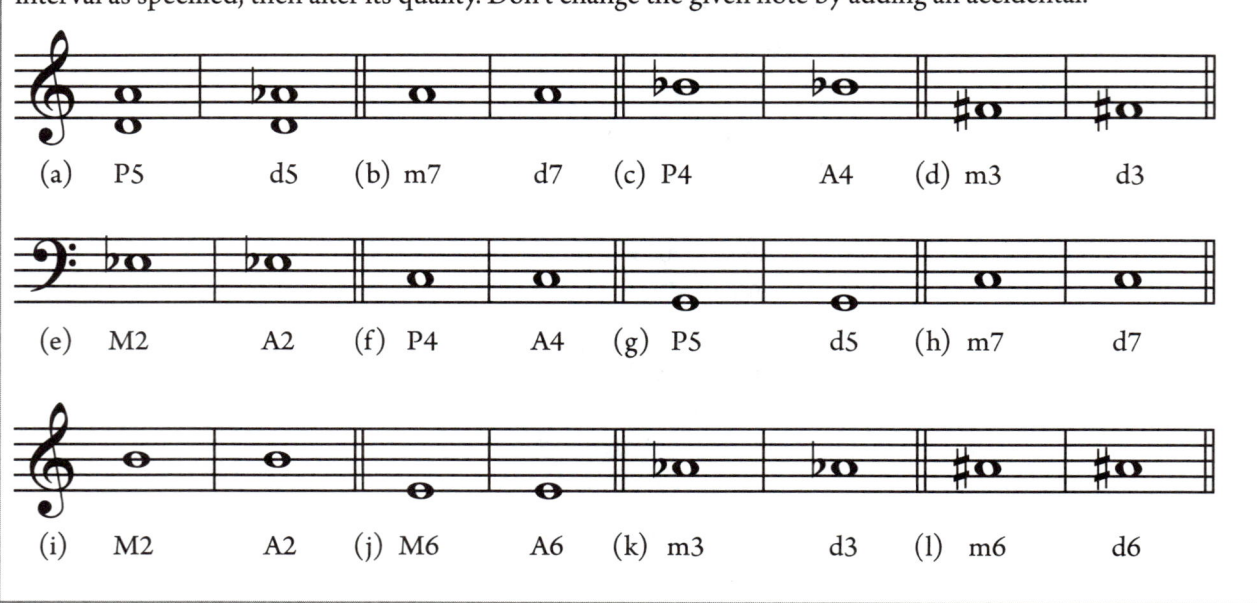

(a) P5   d5   (b) m7   d7   (c) P4   A4   (d) m3   d3

(e) M2   A2   (f) P4   A4   (g) P5   d5   (h) m7   d7

(i) M2   A2   (j) M6   A6   (k) m3   d3   (l) m6   d6

Compound Intervals

If you look back at the score of "Greensleeves" in Example 8.2 (reproduced in Try it #6), you will see that in measure 1 the first harmonic interval actually spans more than an octave: it is an octave plus a third, A3 to C5. This interval is sometimes called a tenth, since it spans ten letter names.

> **KEY CONCEPT** Intervals larger than an octave are **compound intervals**. **Simple intervals** are an octave or smaller in size.

The most common compound intervals are ninths, tenths, elevenths, and twelfths—which correspond to an octave plus a second, third, fourth, and fifth, as shown in Example 8.22. To name a compound interval, add 7 to the simple interval. (Add 7 rather than 8 because we began numbering the unison with 1 rather than 0.) For example, a second plus an octave equals a ninth, and a fourth plus an octave equals an eleventh.

EXAMPLE 8.22 Compound intervals

(a) Calculation

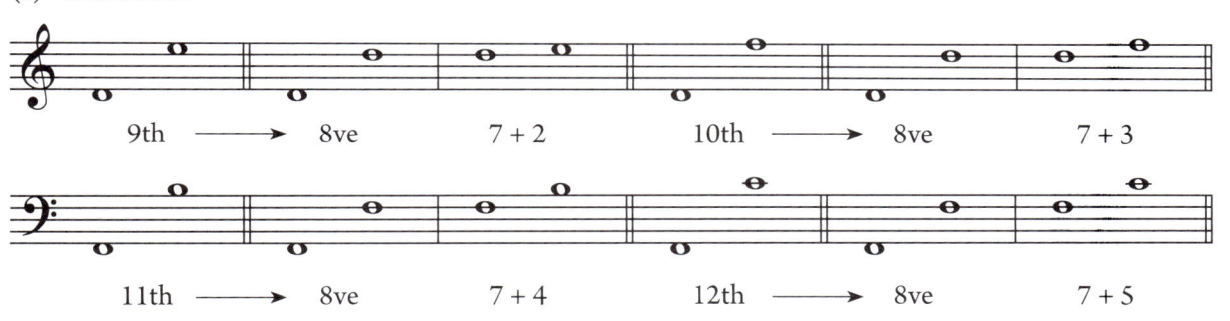

9th → 8ve   7 + 2   10th → 8ve   7 + 3

11th → 8ve   7 + 4   12th → 8ve   7 + 5

(b) Conversion chart

9th = 2nd   12th = 5th
10th = 3rd   13th = 6th
11th = 4th   14th = 7th

There are times when you need to label the span of an interval as a ninth, tenth, eleventh or twelfth because the exact musical space spanned by an interval is important to the way it sounds. However, you can usually label compound intervals as simple ones, without regard for the "extra" octaves between pitches, writing 4 instead of 11, or 5 instead of 12. Guidelines for determining the quality of compound intervals are the same as for simple ones.

TRY IT #6

Listen to "Greensleeves," and identify the harmonic intervals circled in measures 1–4. Identify the size and quality of each interval. For compound intervals, indicate the size and quality of the corresponding simple interval below.

"Greensleeves," mm. 1–5

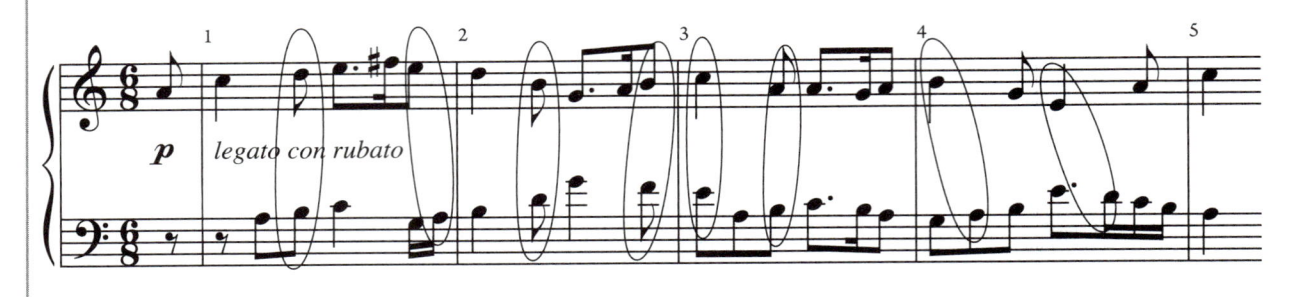

Interval: **m10** ____ ____ ____ ____ ____ ____

Simple equivalent: **m3** ____ ____ ____ ____ ____ ____

Consonance and Dissonance

Over the course of music history, intervals have been characterized as **consonant** if they sound pleasing to the ear or tonally stable, and **dissonant** if they sound jarring, clashing, or as if they need to move somewhere else to find a resting point. Consonance and dissonance are relative terms based on acoustics and compositional practice: what sounds consonant to us today may have sounded dissonant to musicians a century ago.

As a rule of thumb, consider perfect unisons, fifths, and octaves and major and minor thirds and sixths to be consonant. Consider seconds and sevenths to be dissonant, as well as any augmented or diminished intervals such as A4 and d5. The fourth as a melodic interval is consonant, but as a harmonic interval it may be treated as a dissonance.

Adding octaves doesn't change consonance or dissonance: tenths are consonances, as are thirds; ninths are dissonances, as are seconds. The concepts of consonance and dissonance will be useful when you write music of your own, since dissonant intervals tend to move toward consonant ones in pieces. This motion toward consonance is called **resolution**: dissonant intervals create the "need" to resolve, typically to the closest consonant interval, as illustrated in Example 8.23.

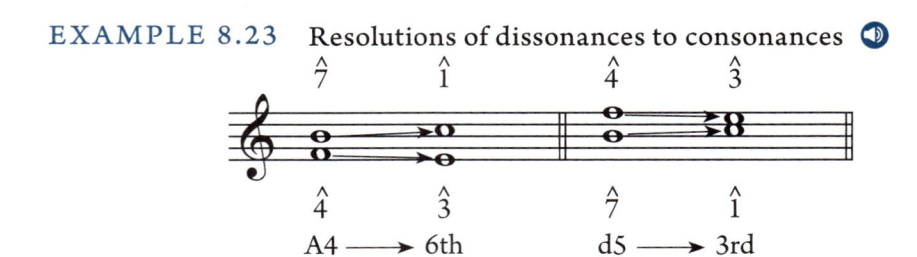

EXAMPLE 8.23   Resolutions of dissonances to consonances

A4 ⟶ 6th   d5 ⟶ 3rd

Common harmonic dissonances have standard resolutions: for example, the upper note of a minor seventh tends to resolve down. Resolutions of A4 and d5 are shown in the example above. As inversionally related intervals, they resolve in complementary ways: the A4 resolves out (to a sixth) and the d5 resolves in (to a third). For either, the underlying motion is the same, if viewed in relation to the scale: $\hat{7}$ resolves up to $\hat{1}$, while $\hat{4}$ resolves down to $\hat{3}$.

SUMMARY

- Consonant intervals: PU, P5, P8, m3, M3, m6, M6, melodic P4
- Dissonant intervals: m2, M2, m7, M7, any augmented or diminished interval, harmonic P4

ASSIGNMENT 8.3, 8.4, AURAL SKILLS 8.2

Did You Know?

"Simple Gifts" is a Shaker song composed in 1848 by Elder Joseph Brackett. The Shakers were a religious sect active in New England between the mid-eighteenth and early twentieth centuries, known today for music, furniture design, well-run farms, and a belief in equality of the sexes, which became a part of their teaching in the 1780s. "Simple Gifts," which was sung as a part of Shaker religious dance ceremonies, was little known until Aaron Copland set it 1944 in his ballet Appalachian Spring for Martha Graham's modern dance company.

Terms You Should Know

consonant	interval inversion	octave
dissonant	interval quality	resolution
interval	augmented	tritone
compound	diminished	unison
enharmonically equivalent	major	
harmonic	minor	
melodic	perfect	
simple		

Questions for Review

1. What is meant by interval size? by interval quality?
2. Which interval sizes may be major or minor? perfect? diminished or augmented?
3. How do you invert intervals?
4. Describe at least three methods for spelling intervals.
5. Describe how to label (or spell) larger intervals by inverting them.

6. How do you identify the name of compound intervals?
7. Which intervals are considered consonant? dissonant?
8. What should you alter to turn a P4 into a d5? a M6 into an A6? a m3 into an A3?
9. What interval is enharmonically equivalent to a d3? an A4? a m7?
10. Respell D–A♭ enharmonically, then provide the interval name for each spelling.

Reading Review

Match the term on the left with the best answer on the right.

_____ (1) interval quality   (a) the distance between pitches measured by counting letter names only
_____ (2) interval   (b) interval that spans two half steps
_____ (3) interval size   (c) interval that spans three half steps
_____ (4) melodic interval   (d) spans more than an octave
_____ (5) harmonic interval   (e) major, minor, perfect, augmented, or diminished
_____ (6) F–B   (f) distance to ♭$\hat{3}$, ♭$\hat{6}$, or ♭$\hat{7}$ above a minor-key tonic
_____ (7) minor interval   (g) U, 4, 5, 8
_____ (8) augmented interval   (h) the interval from $\hat{1}$ up to $\hat{5}$
_____ (9) P5   (i) the distance in pitch between any two notes
_____ (10) M3   (j) the distance in pitch between two successive notes in a melody
_____ (11) m3   (k) interval that spans four half steps
_____ (12) unison   (l) distance to $\hat{2}$, $\hat{3}$, $\hat{6}$, or $\hat{7}$ above a major-key tonic
_____ (13) P4   (m) "distance" between a note and itself
_____ (14) M2   (n) interval that spans one half step
_____ (15) enharmonic intervals   (o) the distance between two notes played simultaneously
_____ (16) perfect interval   (p) the distance between notes eight letter names apart
_____ (17) m6   (q) inversionally related intervals
_____ (18) E–F, B–C   (r) inversion of M3
_____ (19) major interval   (s) the only white-key seconds that are not major
_____ (20) diminished interval   (t) inversion of P5
_____ (21) octave   (u) the only white-key fourth that is not perfect
_____ (22) sum to 9   (v) half step larger than major or perfect interval
_____ (23) m2   (w) half step smaller than minor or perfect interval
_____ (24) compound interval   (x) sound the same but are spelled differently

Additional review and practice available at wwnorton.com/studyspace

Apply It

A. Singing and playing major-scale intervals at the keyboard

1. Perform the C major scale with the fingering shown. In a comfortable octave, sing up and down with scale-degree numbers, note names, or solfège syllables. 🔊

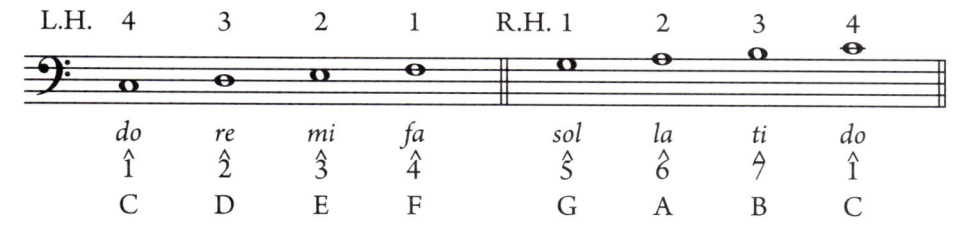

L.H. 4   3   2   1   R.H. 1   2   3   4

do	re	mi	fa	sol	la	ti	do
1̂	2̂	3̂	4̂	5̂	6̂	7̂	1̂
C	D	E	F	G	A	B	C

2. Use a and b below as models for playing and singing intervals above and below the tonic in a major scale. Try to associate particular intervals with particular fingerings and syllables. Begin as shown, and continue the pattern until you sing "perfect octave." In class, while one student or group plays the keyboard, the rest of the class should sing along. Refer to the interval summaries in c and d for help. When you have mastered C major, transpose these patterns to other keys.

(a) 🔊

L.H. 4 3   4 3   4 3   4 4 3 3   4 2   4 2   4 2   4 4 2

do re 1̂ 2̂   C D ma-jor sec-ond do mi 1̂ 3̂   C E ma-jor third (etc. . . .)

(b) 🔊

R.H. 4 3   4 3   4 3   4 4 3 3   4 2   4 2   4 2   4 4 2

do ti 1̂ 7̂   C B mi-nor sec-ond do la 1̂ 6̂   C A mi-nor third (etc. . . .)

(c) An ascending major scale produces all major and perfect intervals above its tonic pitch. 🔊

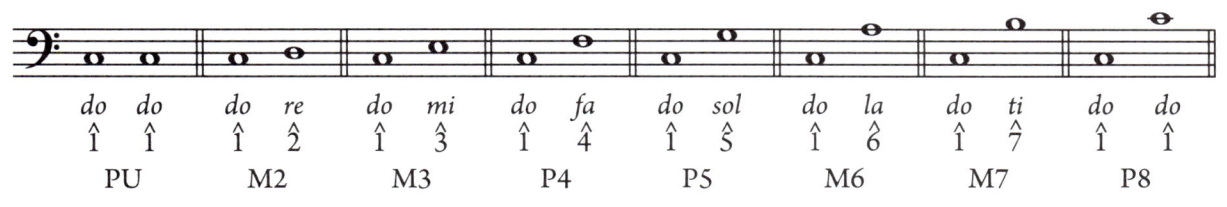

do do	do re	do mi	do fa	do sol	do la	do ti	do do
1̂ 1̂	1̂ 2̂	1̂ 3̂	1̂ 4̂	1̂ 5̂	1̂ 6̂	1̂ 7̂	1̂ 1̂
PU	M2	M3	P4	P5	M6	M7	P8

(d) A major scale produces all minor and perfect intervals below its tonic pitch. 🔊

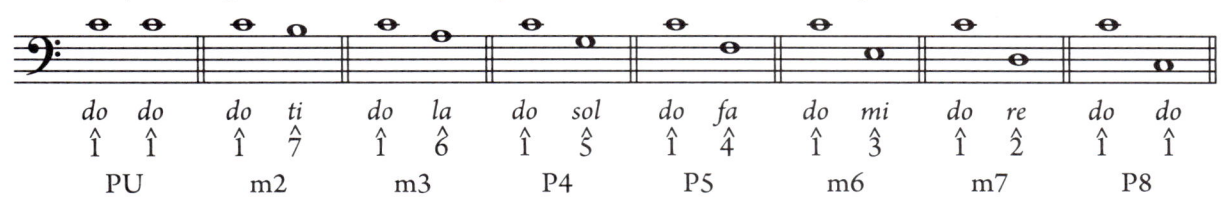

do do	do ti	do la	do sol	do fa	do mi	do re	do do
1̂ 1̂	1̂ 7̂	1̂ 6̂	1̂ 5̂	1̂ 4̂	1̂ 3̂	1̂ 2̂	1̂ 1̂
PU	m2	m3	P4	P5	m6	m7	P8

3. For each interval requested below, imagine the given pitch as the tonic of a major scale. Play and sing the pattern from activity A2 to find the interval.

Intervals above:

(a) M6 above D
(b) M2 above A♭
(c) M3 above F♯
(d) M7 above D♭
(e) P5 above B♭
(f) P4 above B
(g) M7 above E♭
(h) M6 above C♯
(i) M3 above G♭
(j) P8 above G
(k) M3 above A
(l) P5 above A♭
(m) M2 above D♭
(n) P4 above F
(o) M6 above E

Intervals below:

(a) m2 below A
(b) m6 below C♯
(c) P8 below A♯
(d) m7 below E♭
(e) m2 below D♭
(f) P4 below A♭
(g) m7 below B
(h) m3 below F♯
(i) m6 below E
(j) m3 below F
(k) m3 below A♭
(l) P5 below F
(m) m3 below C♯
(n) P4 below B♭
(o) P5 below A

B. Singing and playing minor-scale intervals at the keyboard

1. In order to practice singing and playing minor intervals, you can alter the natural minor scale by lowering $\hat{2}$ to ♭$\hat{2}$ so that all intervals above $\hat{1}$ are minor or perfect. Play the altered scale shown below, with a minor second between the first and second scale degrees, while singing scale-degree numbers, solfège syllables, or note names. For comparison, play the natural minor scale. 🔊

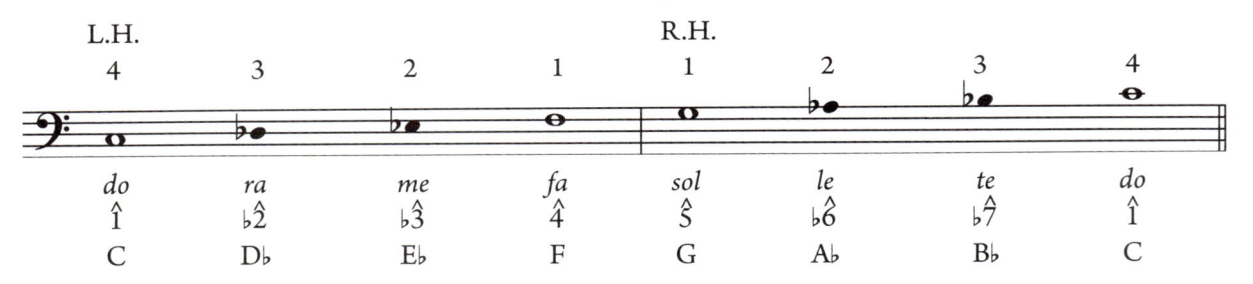

2. Use examples a and b below as models for playing and singing intervals above and below the tonic in a minor scale with ♭$\hat{2}$. Begin as shown, and continue the pattern until you sing "perfect octave." Refer to the interval summaries in c and d for help. When you have mastered C minor, transpose these patterns to other keys.

(a) 🔊

(b) 🔊

206   CHAPTER EIGHT   Intervals

(c) An ascending minor scale (altered with ♭2̂) produces all minor and perfect intervals above its tonic pitch.

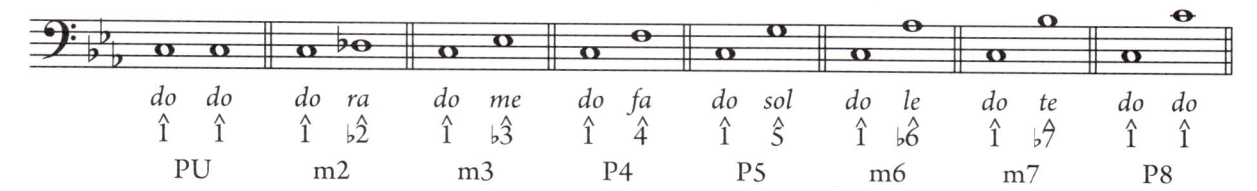

do do	do ra	do me	do fa	do sol	do le	do te	do do
1̂ 1̂	1̂ ♭2̂	1̂ ♭3̂	1̂ 4̂	1̂ 5̂	1̂ ♭6̂	1̂ ♭7̂	1̂ 1̂
PU	m2	m3	P4	P5	m6	m7	P8

(d) A descending minor scale (altered with ♭2̂) produces all major and perfect intervals below its tonic pitch.

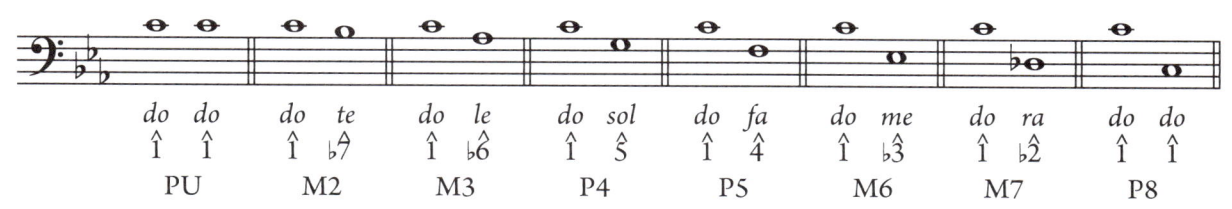

do do	do te	do le	do sol	do fa	do me	do ra	do do
1̂ 1̂	1̂ ♭7̂	1̂ ♭6̂	1̂ 5̂	1̂ 4̂	1̂ ♭3̂	1̂ ♭2̂	1̂ 1̂
PU	M2	M3	P4	P5	M6	M7	P8

3. For each interval requested below, imagine the given pitch as the tonic of an altered minor scale. Play and sing the pattern from activity B2 to find the interval.

Intervals above:

(a) m7 above G
(b) m6 above B
(c) m3 above E
(d) m7 above E♭
(e) P4 above G♭
(f) P5 above A
(g) m7 above D
(h) m3 above D
(i) m6 above E
(j) m3 above A
(k) P8 above F♯
(l) P5 above F
(m) m6 above C♯
(n) P4 above A♭
(o) m3 above F♯

Intervals below:

(a) M2 below D
(b) M6 below E♭
(c) M3 below B♭
(d) M2 below F♯
(e) M2 below D♭
(f) P4 below G
(g) M6 below B
(h) M7 below F♯
(i) M6 below E
(j) M3 below F
(k) M3 below A♭
(l) M7 below C
(m) M3 below C♯
(n) M6 below B♭
(o) M2 below A

C. Listening and writing: Interval identification

Each of the following exercises consists of a set of ten intervals that will be played for you. Each interval begins with the given pitch. In the blank beneath the staff, write the interval's quality and size (M3, m6, P5, etc.). Then write the second pitch in the staff, including any necessary accidental. Don't alter the given pitch.
You may wish to divide this activity into stages:

- On the first hearing, sing the interval back, then write the size only (6, 3, 2, 5, etc.). You may sing up or down the scale to count scale degrees.
- On the second hearing, sing back, and add the interval quality (M6, m3, m2, P5, etc.).
- On the third hearing, add notation on the staff and check your answer.

Ascending major and perfect intervals

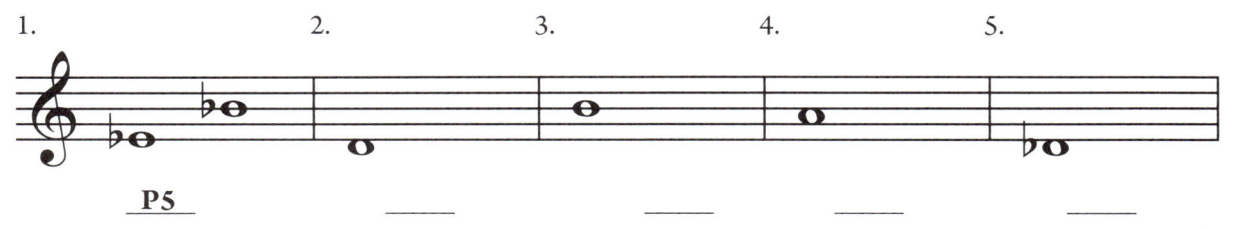

1. P5   2.   3.   4.   5.

Apply It

6. 7. 8. 9. 10.

Descending minor and perfect intervals

11. 12. 13. 14. 15.

m2

16. 17. 18. 19. 20.

Ascending minor and perfect intervals

21. 22. 23. 24. 25.

m3

26. 27. 28. 29. 30.

Descending major and perfect intervals

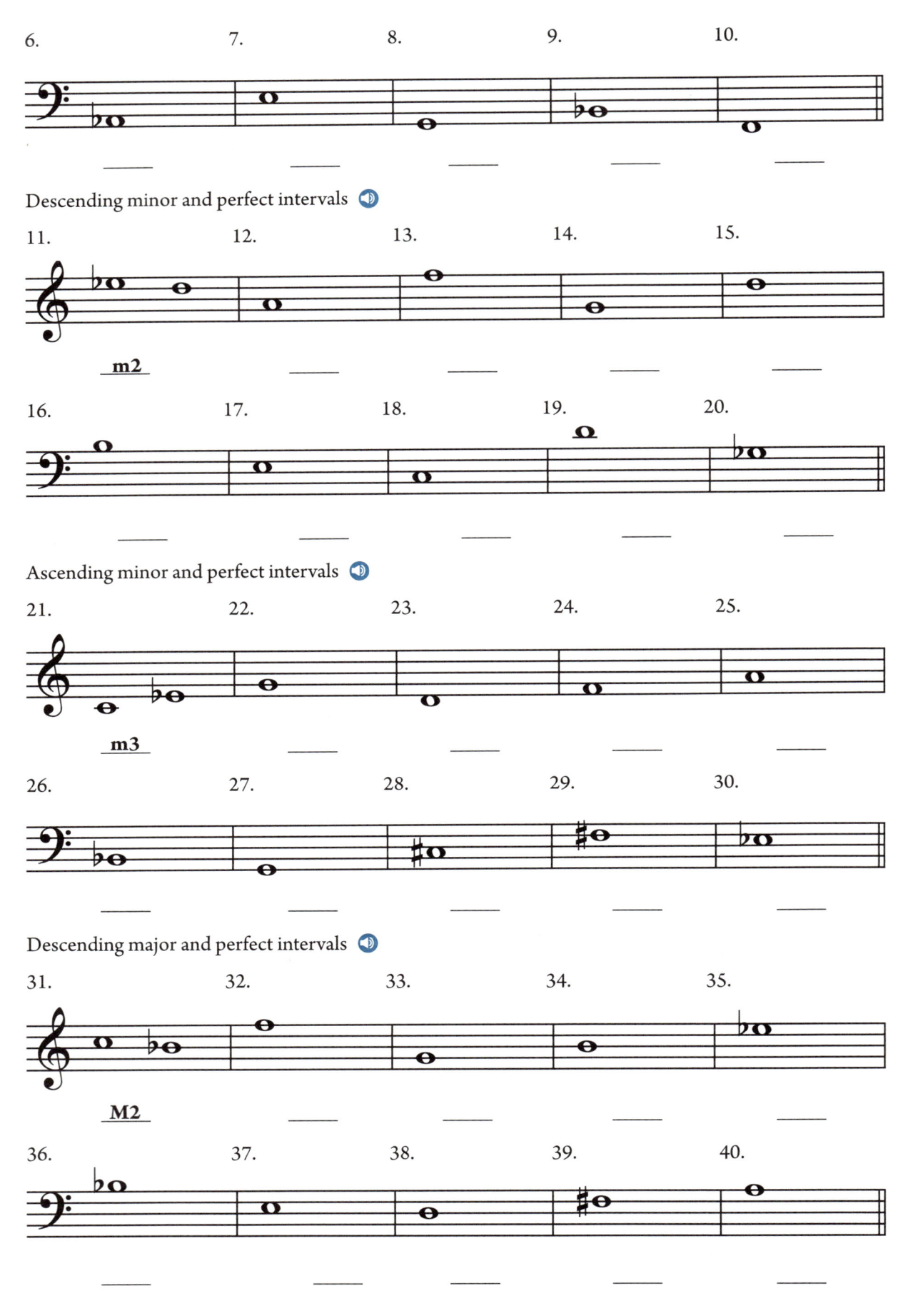

31. 32. 33. 34. 35.

M2

36. 37. 38. 39. 40.

D. Singing at sight

For each of the following melodies, first determine the key and play that major scale at the keyboard; sing along on scale-degree numbers or solfège syllables. Play the first pitch of the melody (if not $\hat{1}$) and sing up or down to the tonic pitch to orient yourself.

These melodies are ordered by type of interval featured. Before working on the melody, identify examples of the interval in the melody. Play and sing the interval; find its position in the scale you just played. Then practice rhythm and pitches separately before putting them together.

Melodies featuring seconds and thirds

Melody 1 "Banana Boat Song," mm. 1–10

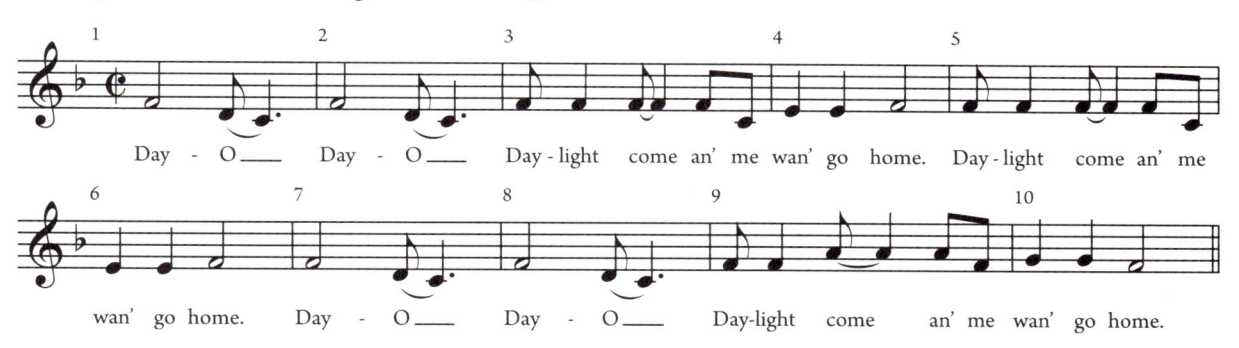

Melody 2 "Shenandoah"
Begins on *sol* ($\hat{5}$).

Melodies featuring fourths and fifths

Melody 3 Wolfgang Amadeus Mozart, "Alleluia," mm. 1–4
This melody may be sung as a round. You can practice singing the round with the recording; when it reaches ②, sing from the beginning.

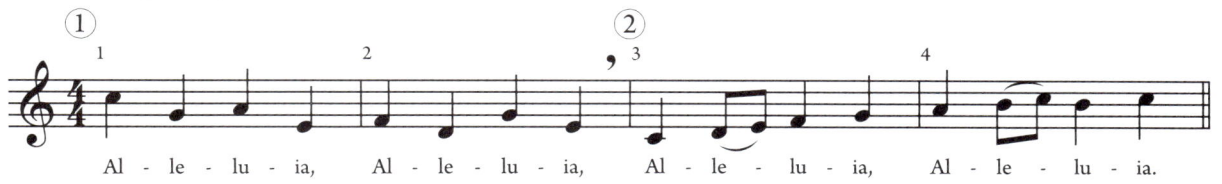

Apply It 209

Melody 4 Robert Lowry, "How Can I Keep from Singing," mm. 1–8
Begins on *sol* ($\hat{5}$).

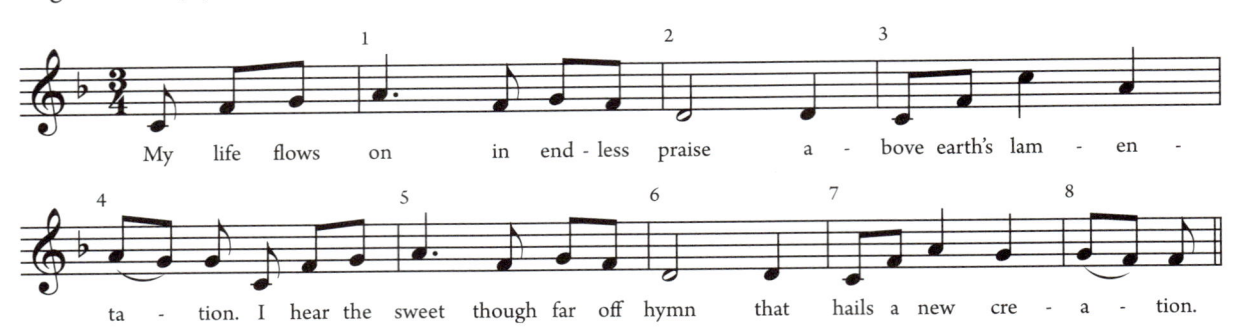

My life flows on in end-less praise a-bove earth's lam-en-ta-tion. I hear the sweet though far off hymn that hails a new cre-a-tion.

Melody 5 Schubert, "Am Flusse" (On the River), mm. 1–7
Begins on *sol* ($\hat{5}$).

Melodies featuring sixths and sevenths

Melody 6 George F. Root, "There's Music in the Air," mm. 1–8
Begins on *sol* ($\hat{5}$).

There's mu-sic in the air,_____ when the ear-ly morn is nigh, And faint its blush is seen_____ On the bright and laugh-ing sky.

Melody 7 "Music Alone Shall Live"
The melody begins on *mi* ($\hat{3}$) and may be performed as a round.

All things shall per-ish from un-der the sky. Mu-sic a-lone shall live, mu-sic a-lone shall live, mu-sic a-lone shall live, ne-ver to die.

NAME _____

Workbook ASSIGNMENT 8.1

A. Writing melodic intervals

Write a whole note on the correct line or space to make each interval specified below. Don't add sharps or flats. Check your answers by counting the letter names from the given note to the one you have written, remembering to include the given note.

Write the specified melodic interval above the given note.

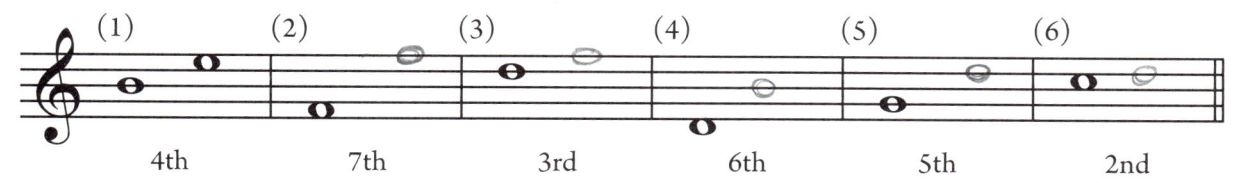

(1) 4th (2) 7th (3) 3rd (4) 6th (5) 5th (6) 2nd

Write the specified melodic interval below the given note.

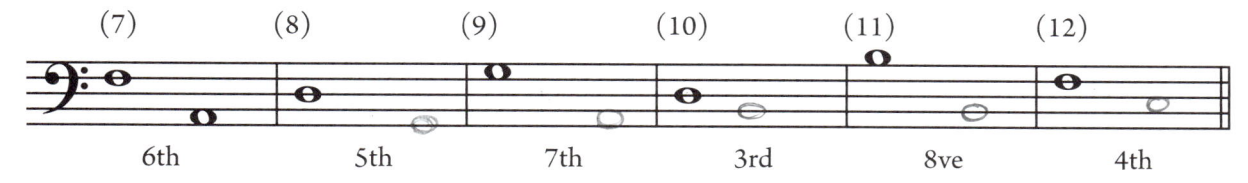

(7) 6th (8) 5th (9) 7th (10) 3rd (11) 8ve (12) 4th

B. Identifying interval size in context

For each circled interval, write the correct interval size in the blank provided.

(1) Mozart, Piano Sonata in C Major, K. 545, first movement, mm. 1–4

Top staff: 3, 6, 2, 2, 4, 2
Bottom staff: 5, 3, 4, 2, 6, 3, 6

(2) Bach, "Aus meines Herzens Grunde," mm. 1–4

Aus mei - nes Her - zens Grun - de

4, 3, 6, 8, 1, 3, 6, 8, 3

From my heart's foundation

C. Writing major and perfect intervals

First write a note head to make the correct interval size, then add a flat or sharp if necessary to make the correct quality. Don't change the given pitch.

Write the specified melodic interval above the given note.

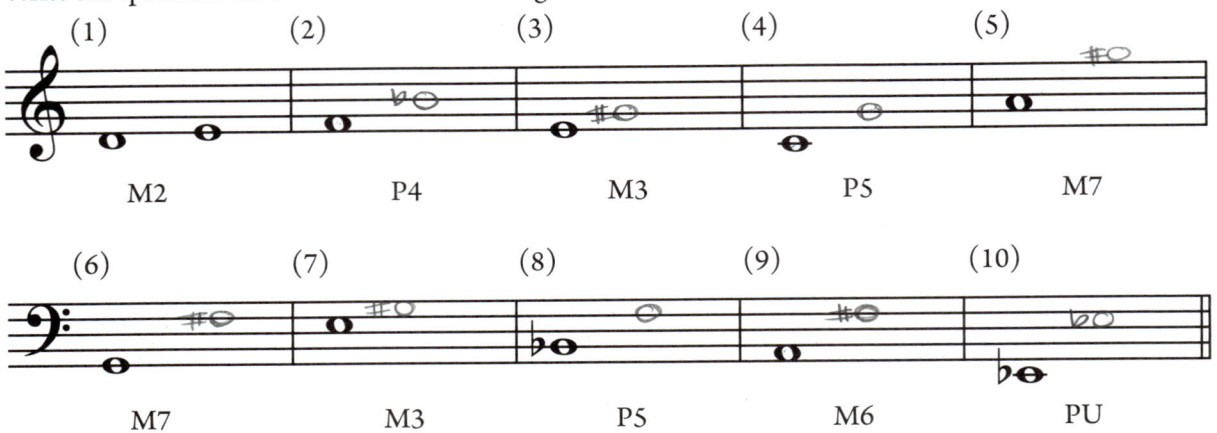

(1) M2 (2) P4 (3) M3 (4) P5 (5) M7

(6) M7 (7) M3 (8) P5 (9) M6 (10) PU

Write the specified harmonic interval above the given note.

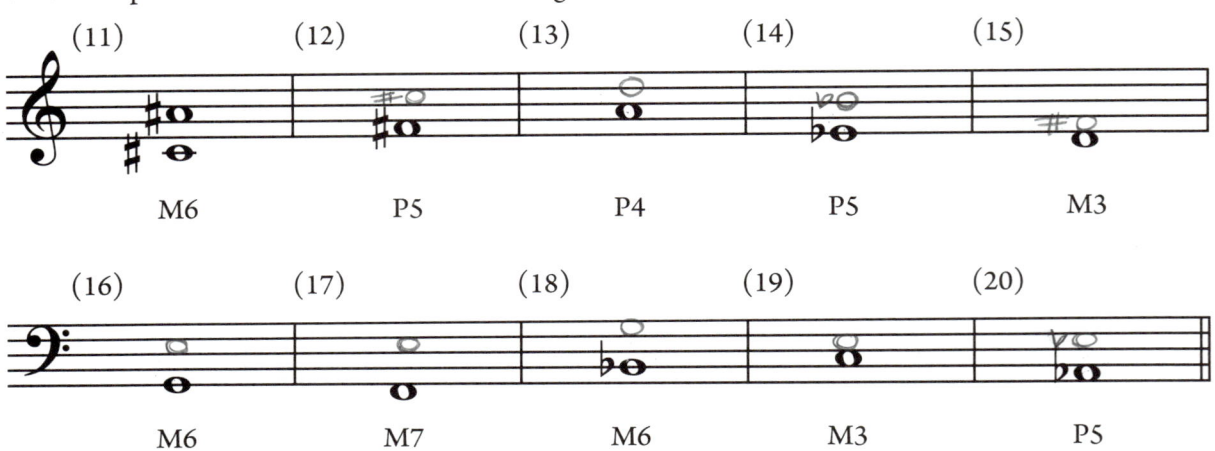

(11) M6 (12) P5 (13) P4 (14) P5 (15) M3

(16) M6 (17) M7 (18) M6 (19) M3 (20) P5

D. Identifying intervals

Label each interval with its quality and size (e.g., m6).

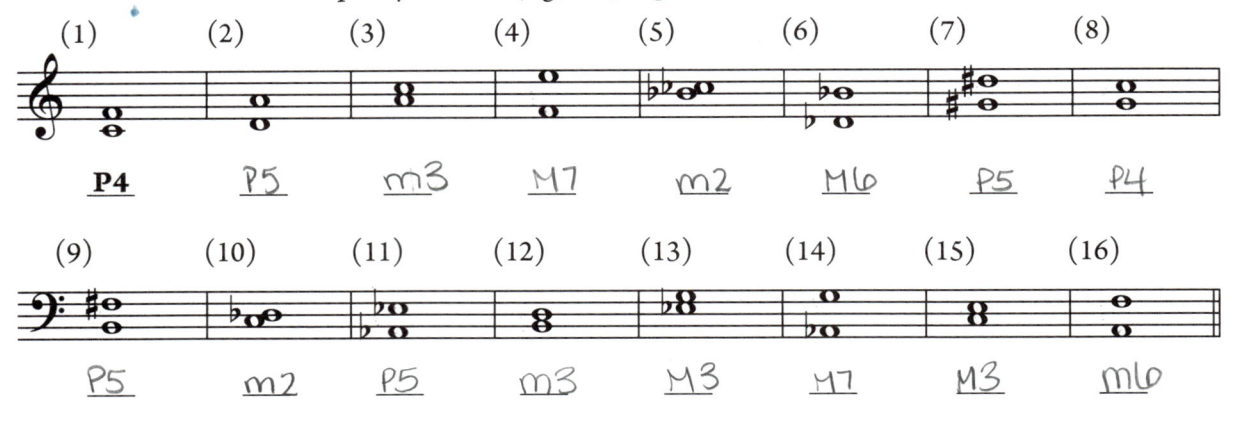

(1) **P4** (2) P5 (3) m3 (4) M7 (5) m2 (6) M6 (7) P5 (8) P4

(9) P5 (10) m2 (11) P5 (12) m3 (13) M3 (14) M7 (15) M3 (16) m6

Workbook ASSIGNMENT 8.2

A. Writing intervals

Write each specified harmonic interval above the given note. Don't change the given pitch.

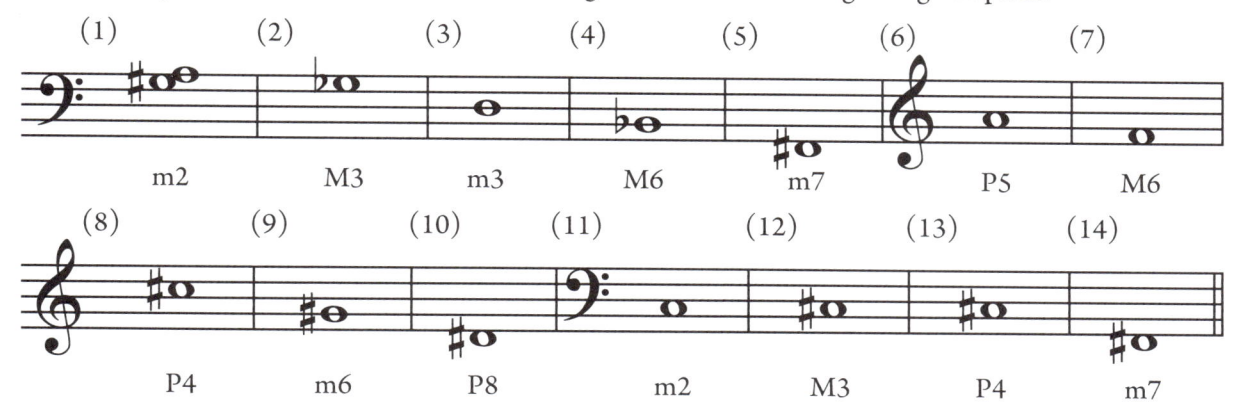

(1) m2 (2) M3 (3) m3 (4) M6 (5) m7 (6) P5 (7) M6
(8) P4 (9) m6 (10) P8 (11) m2 (12) M3 (13) P4 (14) m7

Write each specified harmonic interval below the given note.

(15) m7 (16) P4 (17) m3 (18) m2 (19) m3 (20) m7 (21) m6
(22) m6 (23) m7 (24) m6 (25) P5 (26) m3 (27) m3 (28) P4

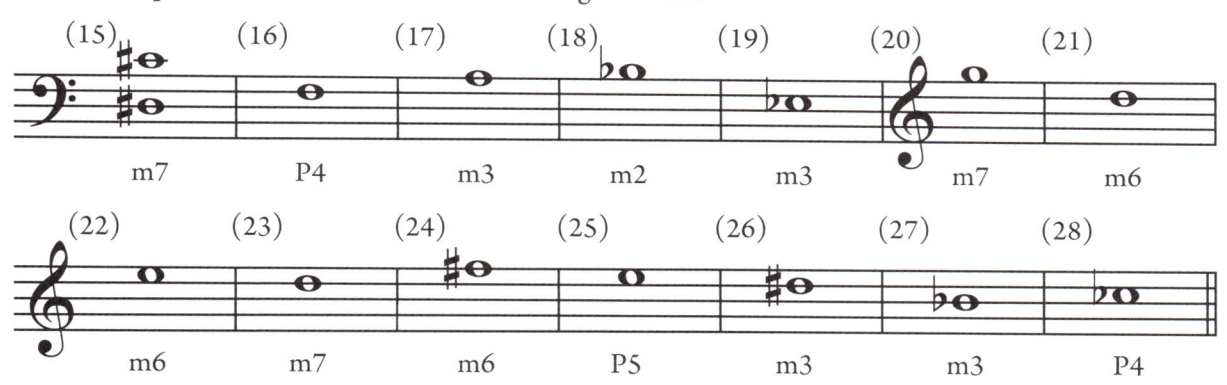

Write the specified melodic interval below the given note.

(29) M2 (30) P4 (31) M3 (32) P5 (33) M7
(34) M6 (35) M3 (36) P5 (37) P4 (38) P8
(39) P4 (40) M6 (41) M7 (42) M6 (43) P5

Assignment 8.2

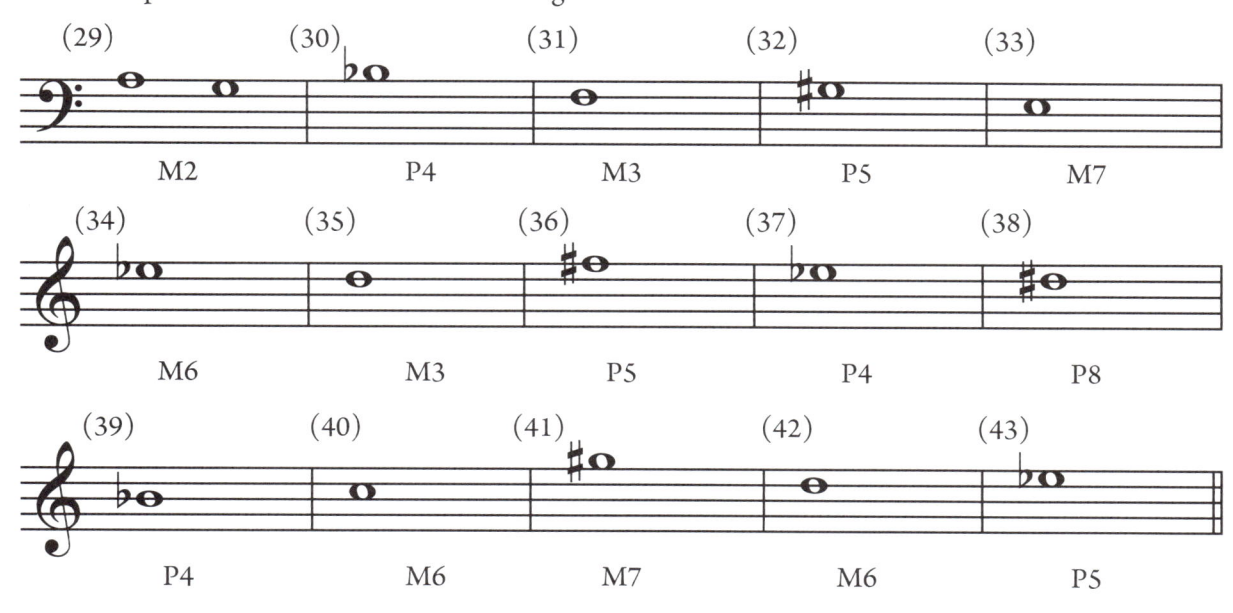

B. Inverting intervals

Identify each interval shown below, then invert the interval by rewriting the second note, followed by the first note transposed up an octave. Identify the new interval you have written.

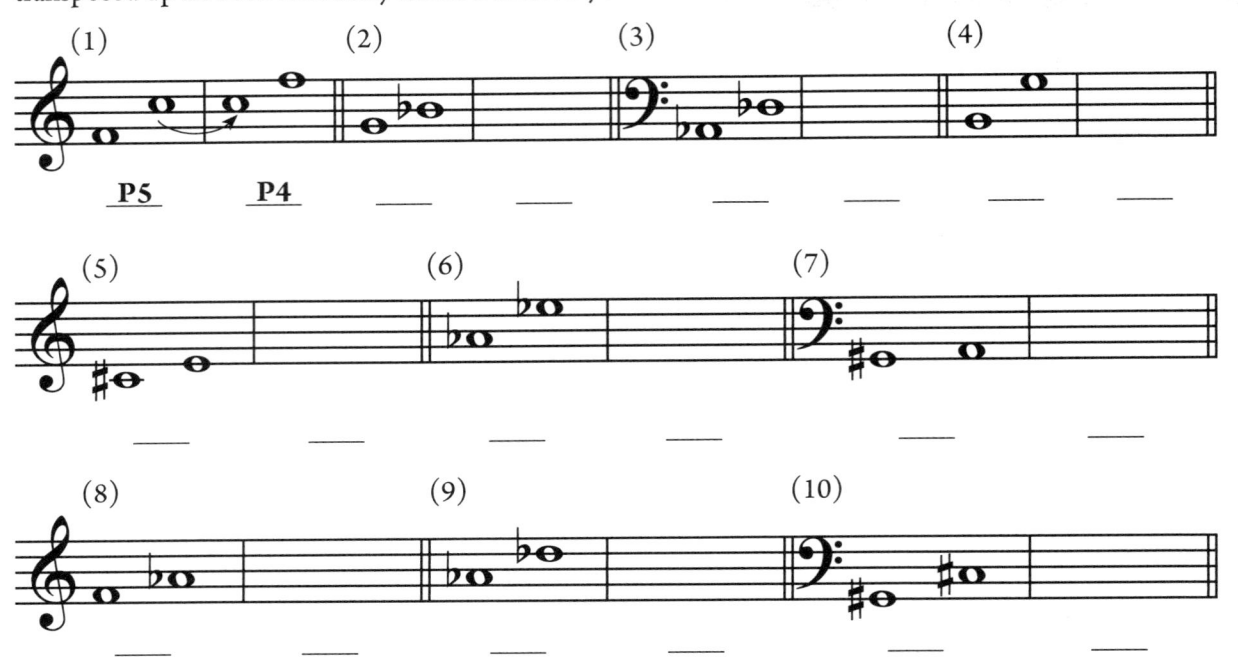

P5   **P4**   ___   ___

___   ___   ___

___   ___   ___

Identify each interval shown below, then invert the interval by rewriting the second note, followed by the first note transposed down an octave. Identify the new interval you have written.

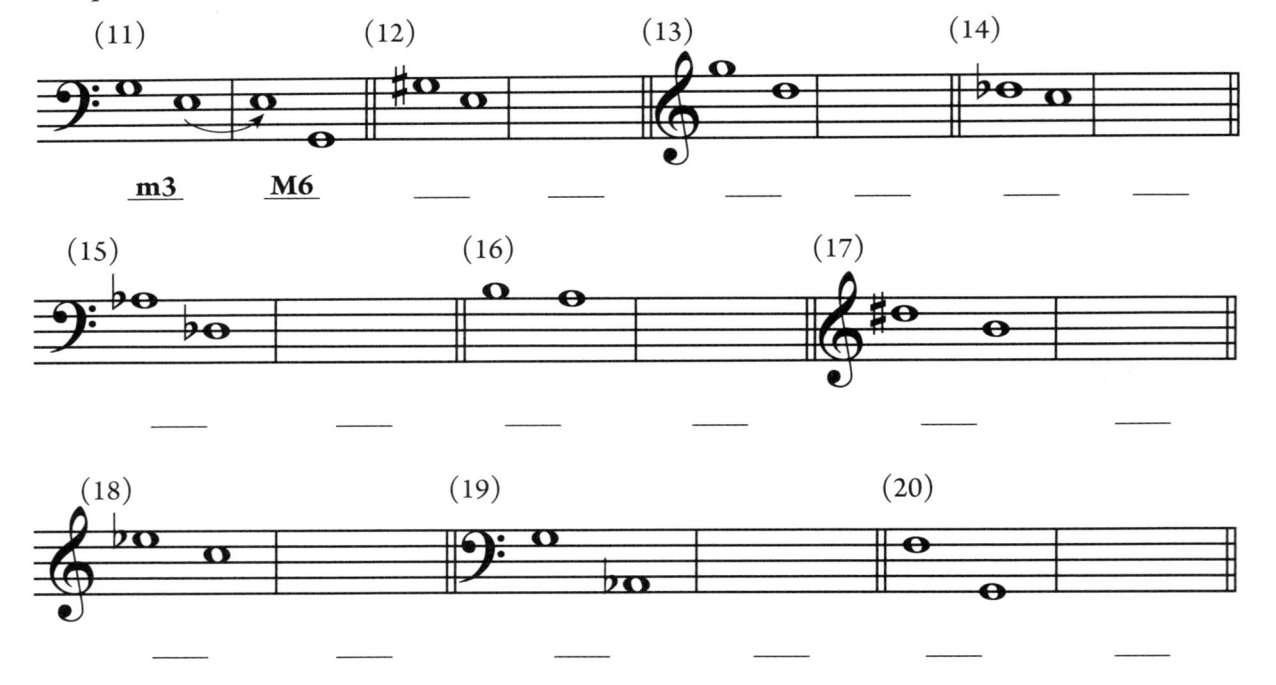

m3   **M6**   ___   ___

___   ___   ___

___   ___   ___

214   CHAPTER EIGHT   Intervals

NAME _____

Workbook   ASSIGNMENT 8.3

A. Identifying diminished and augmented intervals

Write the name (e.g., A4) under each interval.

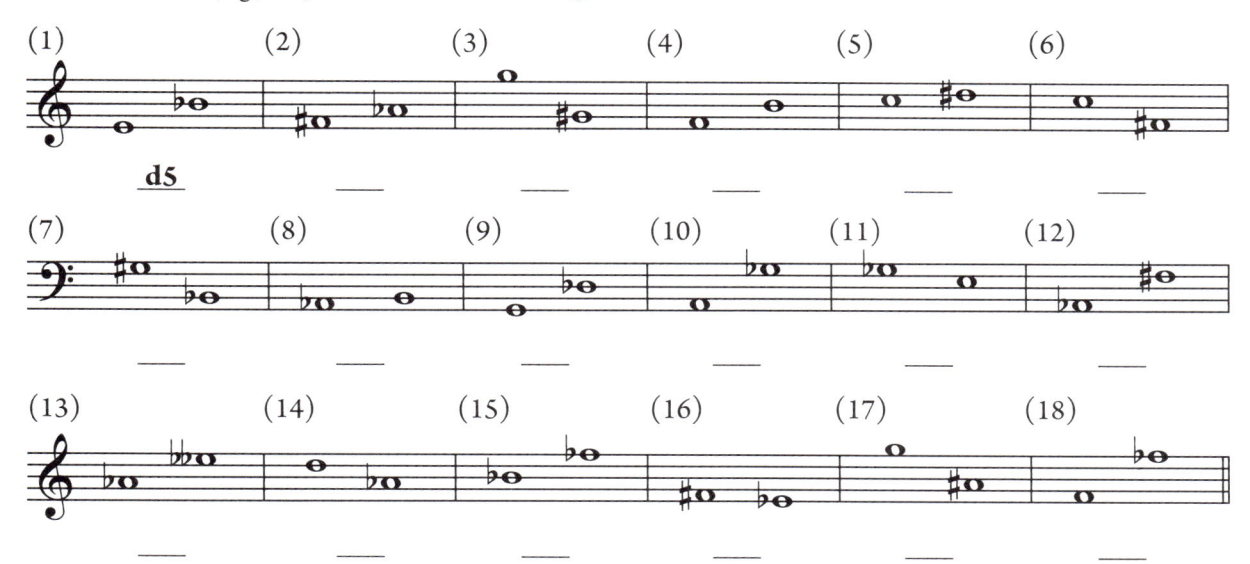

(1) **d5** (2) ___ (3) ___ (4) ___ (5) ___ (6) ___

(7) ___ (8) ___ (9) ___ (10) ___ (11) ___ (12) ___

(13) ___ (14) ___ (15) ___ (16) ___ (17) ___ (18) ___

B. Writing diminished and augmented intervals

Write each specified melodic interval below the given note.

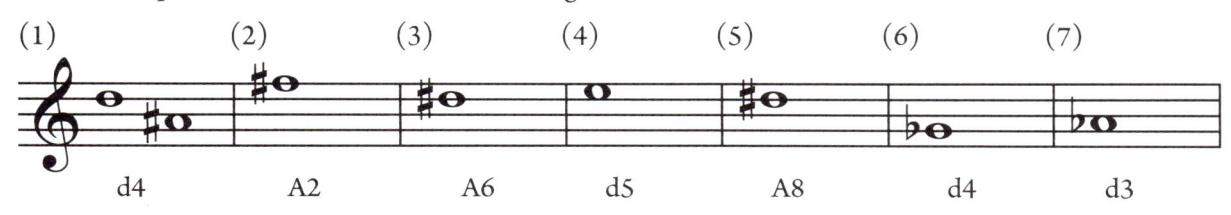

(1) d4   (2) A2   (3) A6   (4) d5   (5) A8   (6) d4   (7) d3

Write each specified melodic interval above the given note.

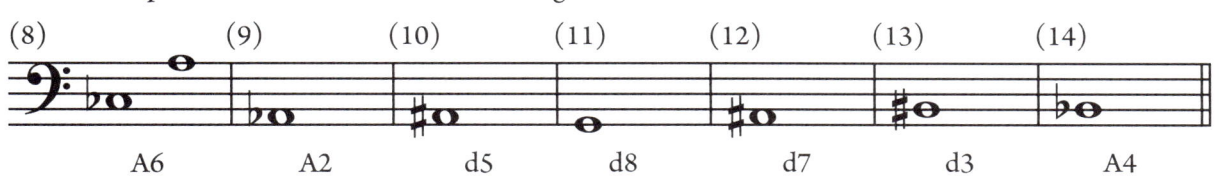

(8) A6   (9) A2   (10) d5   (11) d8   (12) d7   (13) d3   (14) A4

C. Writing melodic compound intervals

Write the specified melodic compound interval above or below the given note. (Hint: Subtract 7 to find the simple-interval equivalent.)

Write the compound interval above the given note.

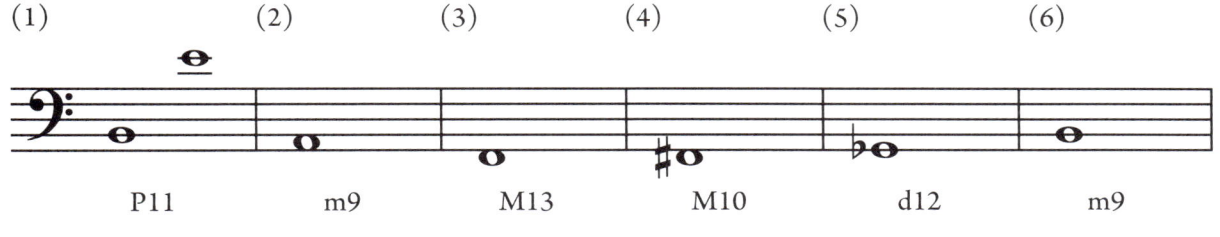

(1) P11   (2) m9   (3) M13   (4) M10   (5) d12   (6) m9

(7)	(8)	(9)	(10)	(11)	(12)
P12	m9	M10	M9	m13	m10

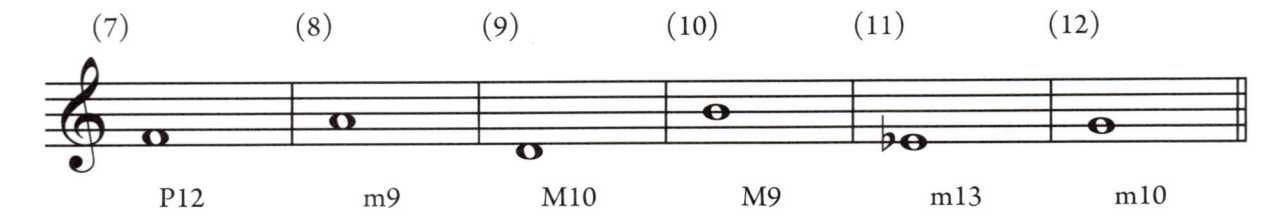

Write the compound interval below the given note.

(13)	(14)	(15)	(16)	(17)	(18)
M10	M9	M13	A11	M10	M9

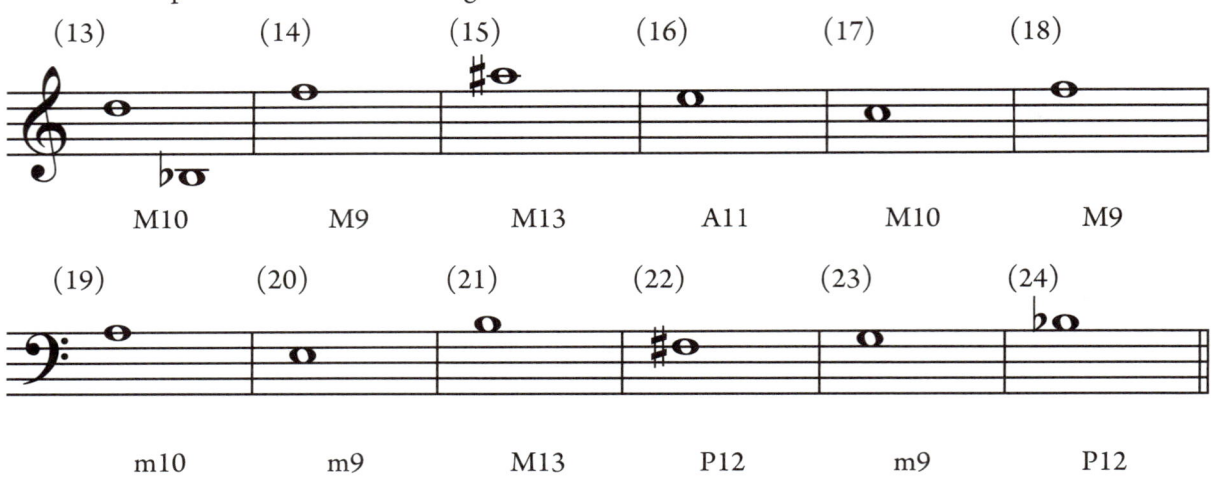

(19)	(20)	(21)	(22)	(23)	(24)
m10	m9	M13	P12	m9	P12

D. Intervals in context

Listen to the excerpt before analyzing it. Write the names of the circled pitches in the blank above the staff, incorporating accidentals from the key signature, then label the intervals with both quality and size (e.g., M7) in the blank below the staff.

Foster, "Jeanie with the Light Brown Hair," mm. 1–6

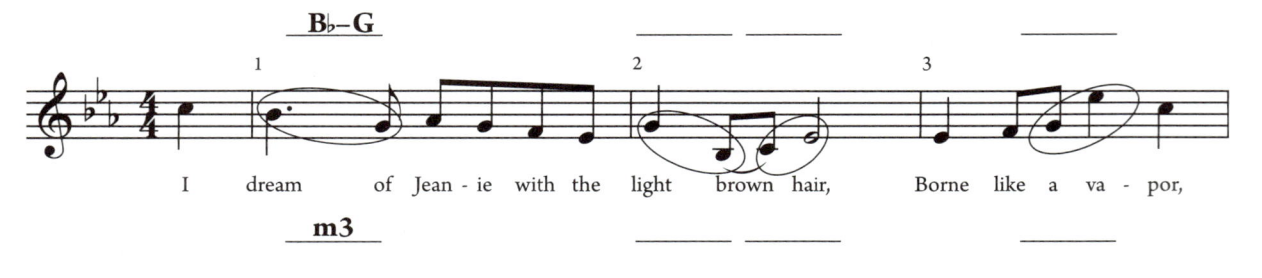

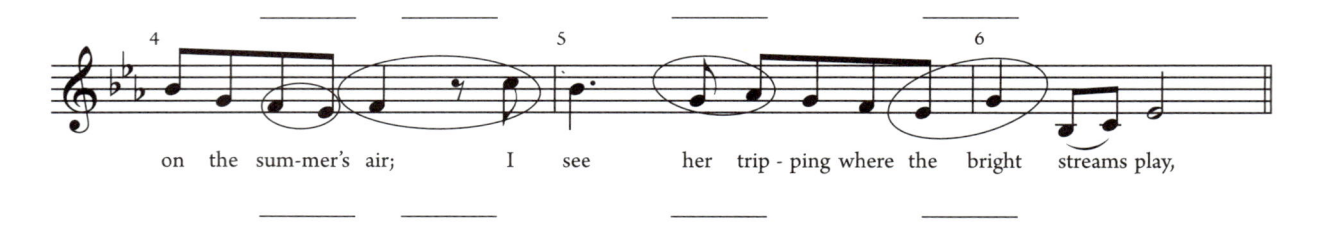

B♭–G

m3

I dream of Jean-ie with the light brown hair, Borne like a va-por,

on the sum-mer's air; I see her trip-ping where the bright streams play,

Workbook — Assignment 8.4

A. Identifying intervals

Label each interval with its quality and size (e.g., m6).

(1) **M2** (2) ___ (3) ___ (4) ___ (5) ___ (6) ___ (7) ___ (8) ___ (9) ___

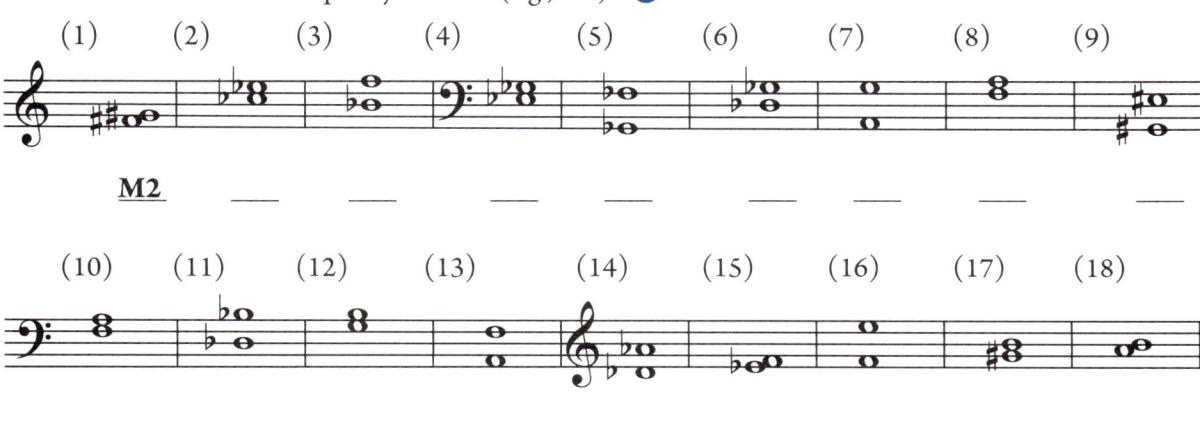

(10) ___ (11) ___ (12) ___ (13) ___ (14) ___ (15) ___ (16) ___ (17) ___ (18) ___

B. Writing melodic intervals

Write a whole note on the correct line or space to make each interval specified below. Don't add sharps or flats to the given note.

Write the specified melodic interval above the given note.

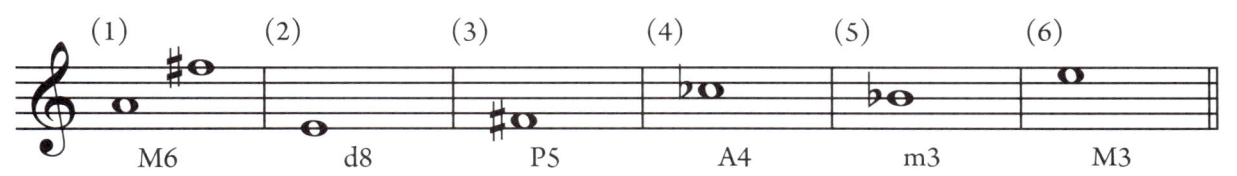

(1) M6   (2) d8   (3) P5   (4) A4   (5) m3   (6) M3

Write the specified melodic interval below the given note.

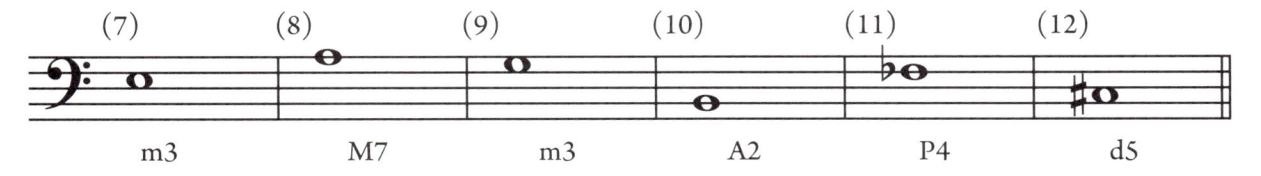

(7) m3   (8) M7   (9) m3   (10) A2   (11) P4   (12) d5

Write the specified interval above and below the given note.

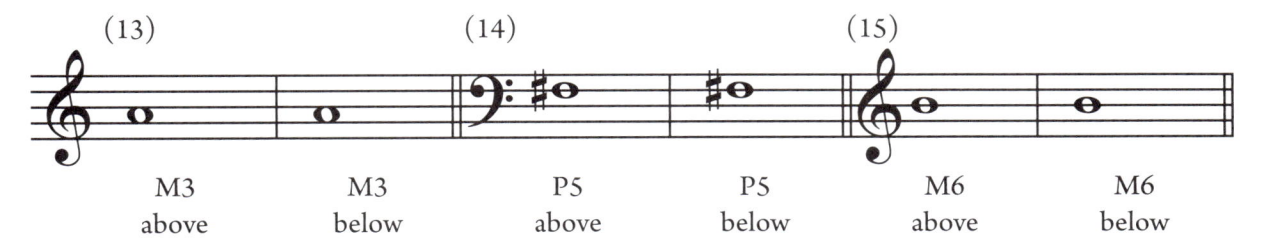

(13) M3 above   M3 below   (14) P5 above   P5 below   (15) M6 above   M6 below

C. Melodic intervals in context

Listen to the excerpts. Write the names of the circled pitches in the blank above the staff, incorporating accidentals from the key signature, then label the intervals with both quality and size (e.g., M7) in the blank below the staff.

(1) Phillips, "Blues for Norton," mm. 17–20

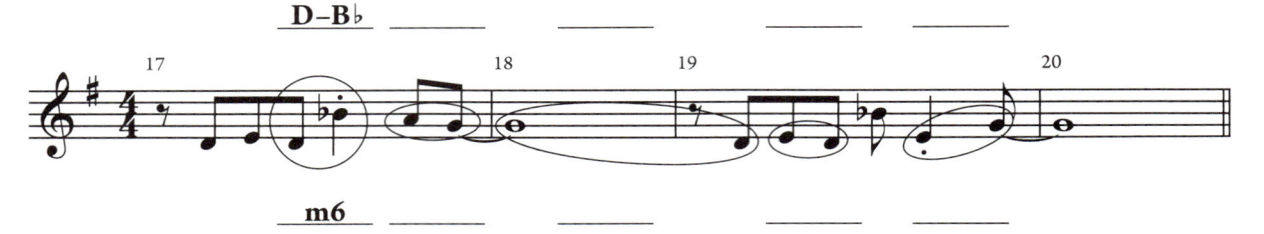

D–B♭ _____ _____ _____ _____

_____ m6 _____ _____ _____ _____

(2) Anonymous, Minuet in D Minor, from the Anna Magdalena Bach Notebook, mm. 9–16

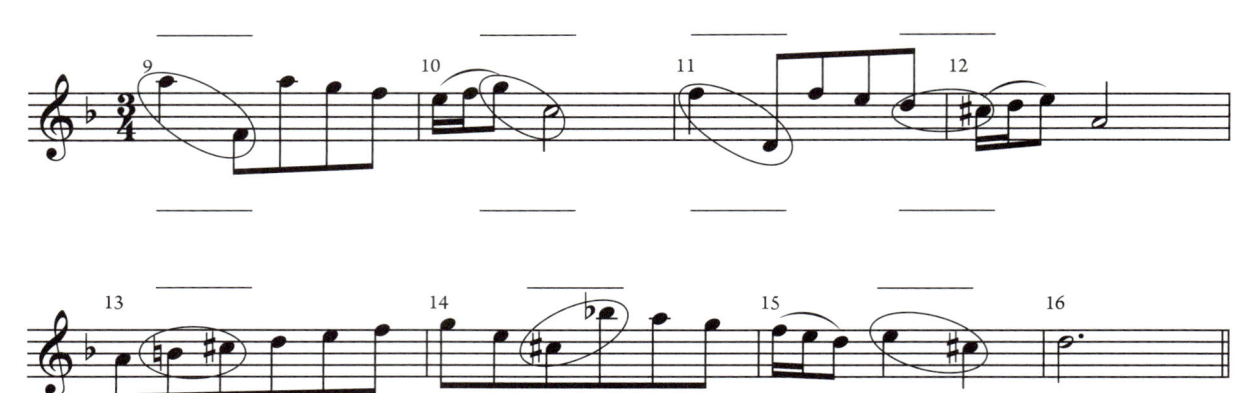

D. Harmonic intervals in context

Listen to measures 1–24 (the theme). Between the staves, write the number of the interval between the highest and lowest notes on each beat (ignore the small thirty-second notes in mm. 15 and 23, as well as the circled notes). Write the simple-interval number of any compound interval a twelfth or larger (e.g., 5 instead of 12).

Mozart, *Variations on "Ah, vous dirai-je Maman,"* mm. 1–24

Workbook   AURAL SKILLS 8.1

A. Interval identification

Each of the following exercises consists of a set of ten recorded intervals. Each interval begins with the given pitch. In the blank beneath the staff, write the interval's quality and size (M3, m6, P5, etc.), as well as an arrow up or down to show its direction. Then write the second pitch in the staff, including any necessary accidental. Don't alter the given pitch. 🔊

Perfect fourths, perfect fifths, and tritones (d5, A4)

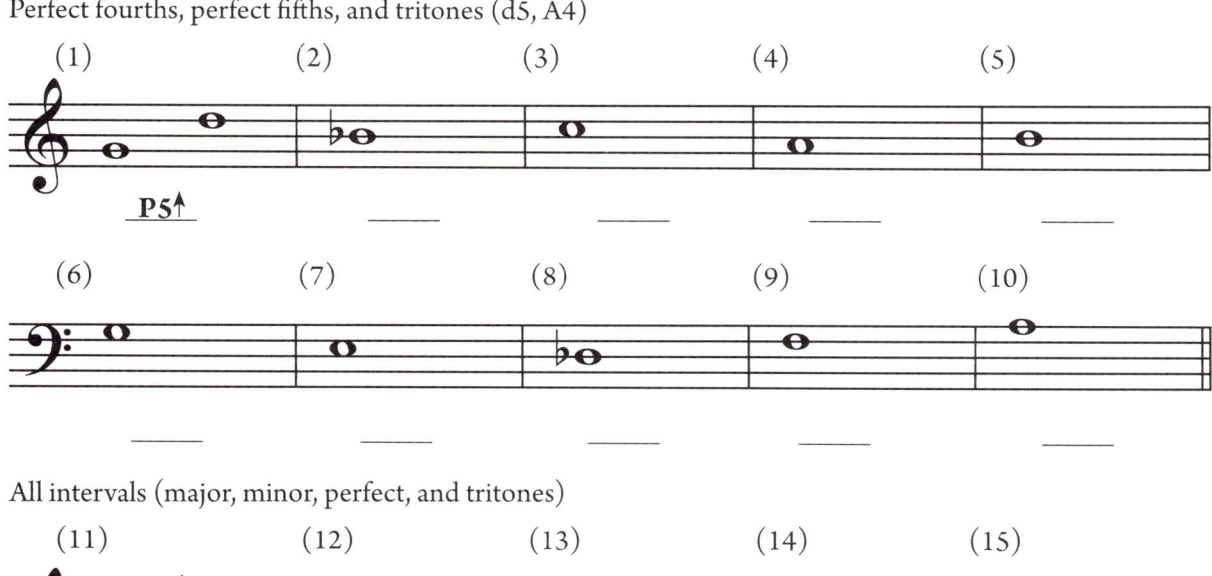

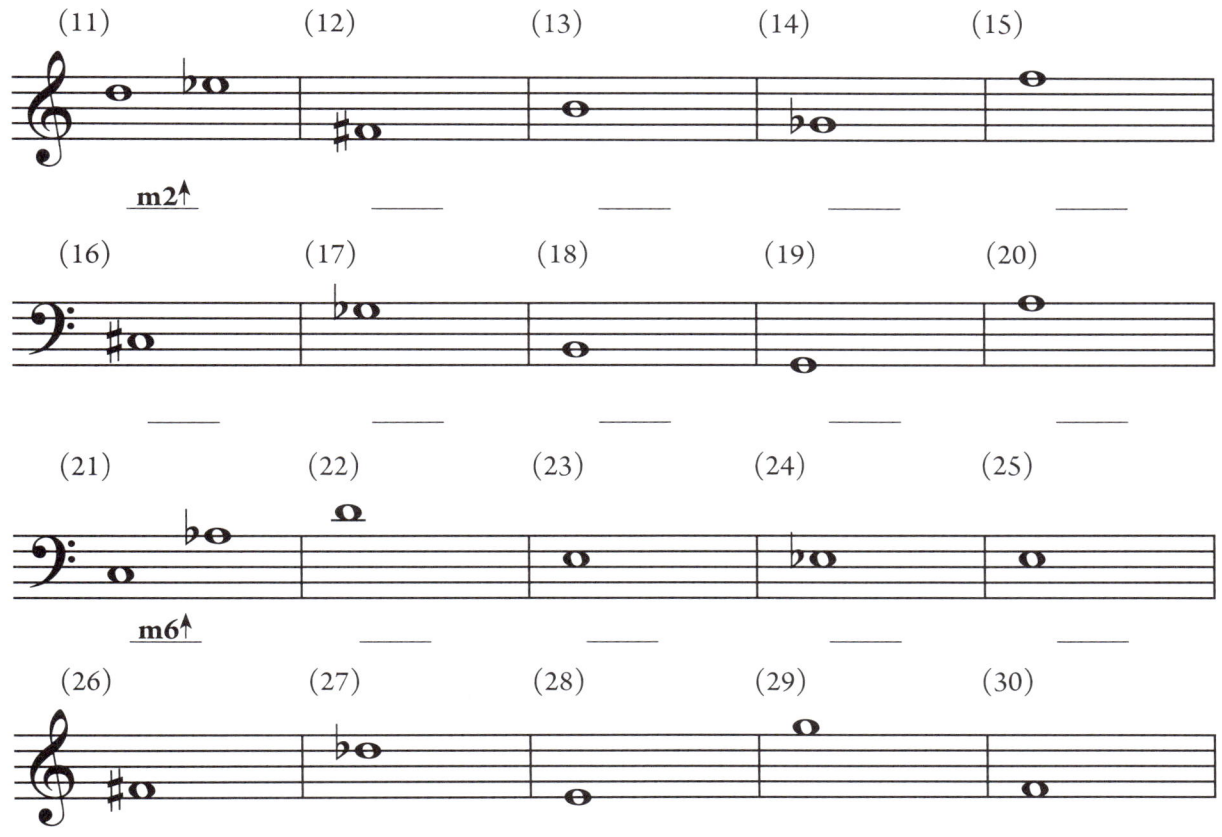

(1) P5↑ (2) ___ (3) ___ (4) ___ (5) ___

(6) ___ (7) ___ (8) ___ (9) ___ (10) ___

All intervals (major, minor, perfect, and tritones)

(11) m2↑ (12) ___ (13) ___ (14) ___ (15) ___

(16) ___ (17) ___ (18) ___ (19) ___ (20) ___

(21) m6↑ (22) ___ (23) ___ (24) ___ (25) ___

(26) ___ (27) ___ (28) ___ (29) ___ (30) ___

(31) (32) (33) (34) (35)

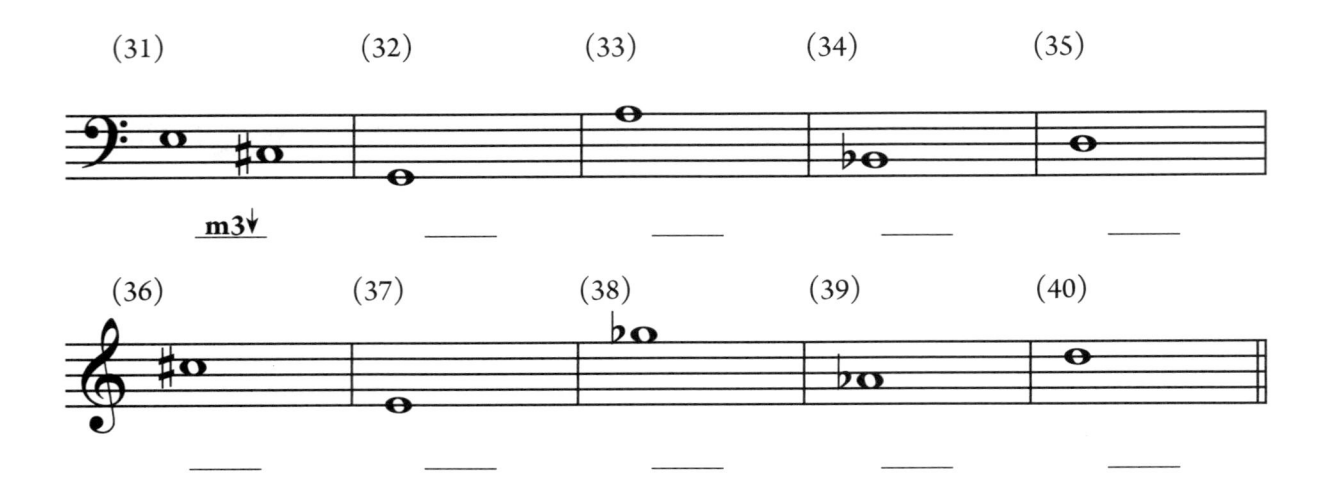

m3↓

(36) (37) (38) (39) (40)

B. Intervals from familiar music

Sometimes the easiest way to remember the sound of an interval is to associate it with a familiar melody. Play each interval below, then write the name of a piece that begins with or features the interval, either ascending or descending. Be prepared to sing your examples in class.

m2 _____

M2 _____

m3 _____

M3 _____

P4 _____

Tritone _____

P5 _____

m6 _____

M6 _____

m7 _____

M7 _____

P8 _____

NAME _____

Workbook AURAL SKILLS 8.2

Listen to a carol before completing the following exercises. 🔊

(1) Focus your attention on the right-hand melody. Which is the first harmonic interval in the right hand? (Hint: this harmonic interval is heard repeatedly.)

a. third b. fourth c. fifth d. sixth

(2) Notate the rhythm of the melody.

(3) Write the melody with scale-degree numbers or solfège syllables. Your answer should begin with $\hat{5}-\hat{6}-\hat{5}$ or sol–la–sol.

(4) Notate the pitches of the melody on the staves below.

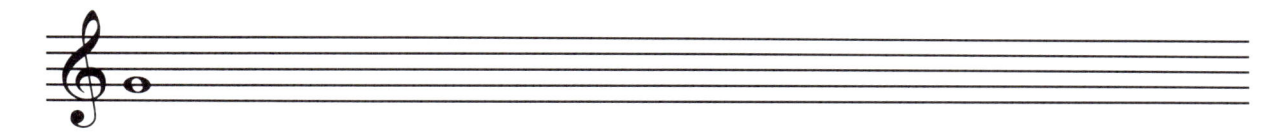

(5) Now focus your attention on the left-hand accompaniment. Which of the following repeated rhythms is heard in the accompaniment?

a.

b.

c.

d.

(6) The left-hand part begins with what harmonic interval?

a. m3 b. M3 c. P4 d. P5

(7) On the staff below, notate both pitches and rhythm of the melody in the key of C major.

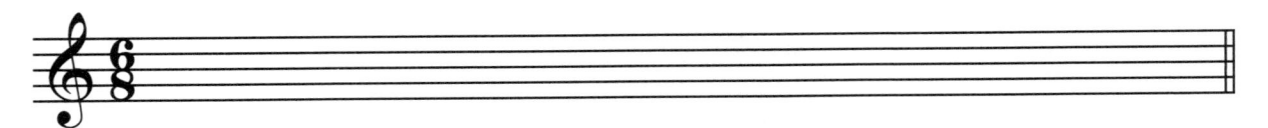

(8) Use the scale-degree numbers or solfège syllables to help you write the melody in B♭ major, beginning on F3. Write the correct key signature. Check your answer at a keyboard, and correct any errors.

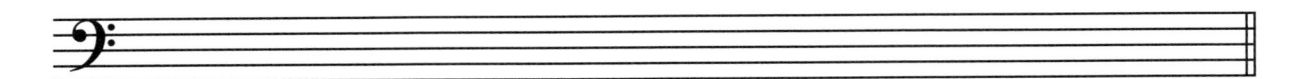

TOPICS
- triads
- triad qualities in major keys
- triad qualities in minor keys
- spelling triads
- triad inversion
- the dominant seventh chord
- spelling the dominant seventh chord
- seventh chord inversion

MUSIC
- "Come, Ye Thankful People Come"
- "My Country, 'Tis of Thee"

CHAPTER 9

Triads and the Dominant Seventh Chord

Triads

In most musical settings, melodic and harmonic intervals sound together; the horizontal and vertical components join to form a musical fabric, called a musical **texture**. For example, a hymn-style texture has four parts—two sung by women (labeled S for soprano and A for alto) and two sung by men (labeled T for tenor and B for bass). In hymn (or SATB) style, the top part—the soprano line—normally sings the melody, the lowest part—the bass line—provides a foundation, and the alto and tenor parts fill in between them. When all voices in a musical texture move together with nearly identical rhythm, as in hymn style, the texture is **homophonic**, and intervals made by the voices singing together form **chords**.

Listen to "My Country, 'Tis of Thee," shown in Example 9.1, to hear several different types of chords. As with scales, you can examine chord types by collecting the pitches used (leaving out repeated notes) and writing them in order within an octave. The pitches in each chord of the first measure of the example are shown below the staff; each of these chords is a triad, as shown in Example 9.1.

EXAMPLE 9.1 "My Country, 'Tis of Thee," mm. 1–6

KEY CONCEPT **Triads** are three-note chords; in their most basic position, they are built from stacking two thirds, one on top of the other, as shown in Example 9.2.

EXAMPLE 9.2   Intervals in major and minor triads

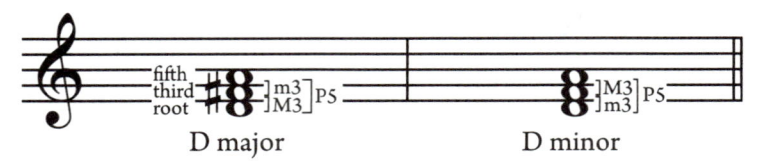

D major   D minor

The lowest note in this position is the **root** of the chord. The middle note (a third above the root) is the **third**, and the top note (a fifth above the root) is the **fifth**. The **major triad** has a M3 between its root and third and a m3 between its third and fifth; the **minor triad** has the opposite—a m3 between root and third and a M3 on the top. The difference between triad types is known as **quality**. Triads are named by the letter name of their root combined with their quality (e.g., G major or B minor). The first chord in "My Country" is an F major triad, the second is a D minor triad, and the third is a G minor triad, as shown. To make a four-note chord like those in Example 9.1, one of the members of the triad (usually the root) will be **doubled**—that is, the same chord member will appear in two places, one or more octaves apart.

Triad Qualities in Major Keys

Example 9.3 gives the quality for each triad built on scale degrees of the F major scale.

EXAMPLE 9.3   Triads built above the F major scale and their qualities

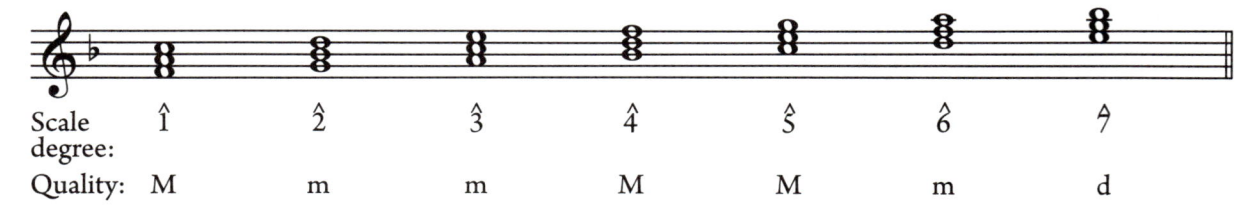

Scale degree:	$\hat{1}$	$\hat{2}$	$\hat{3}$	$\hat{4}$	$\hat{5}$	$\hat{6}$	$\hat{7}$
Quality:	M	m	m	M	M	m	d

In major keys, the triads built on $\hat{1}$, $\hat{4}$, and $\hat{5}$ are major, and the triads built on $\hat{2}$, $\hat{3}$, and $\hat{6}$ are minor. The triad built on $\hat{7}$, with a diminished fifth between its root and fifth and with both of its thirds minor, is called a **diminished triad**.

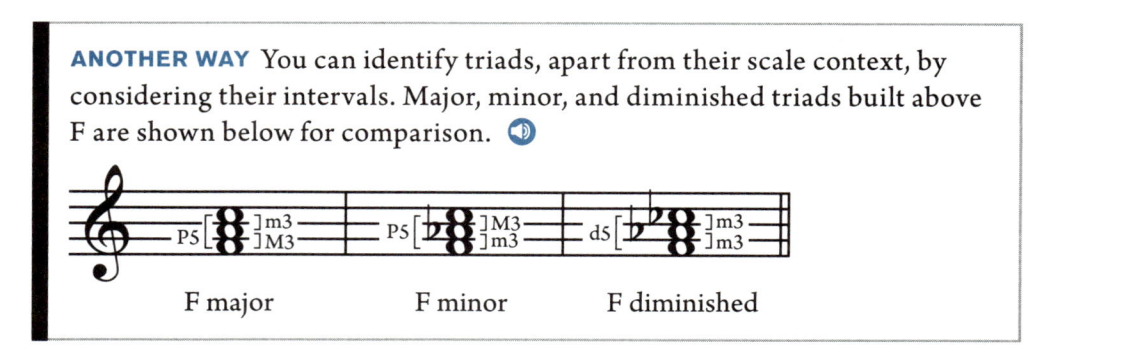

ANOTHER WAY You can identify triads, apart from their scale context, by considering their intervals. Major, minor, and diminished triads built above F are shown below for comparison.

F major   F minor   F diminished

CHAPTER NINE Triads and the Dominant Seventh Chord

There are several ways to label chords. You can refer to triads in a key by the scale degree on which they are built (for example, "a triad on $\hat{2}$") or by the scale-degree name. Tonic, subdominant, dominant, and so on refer both to the scale degrees and to the triads built on them. Musicians often label chords with Roman numerals, as shown in Example 9.4.

> **KEY CONCEPT** **Roman numerals** are a handy way of labeling both a chord's scale-degree position (I to vii°) and also its quality: a capital numeral indicates a major triad (I, IV, V), and a lowercase numeral a minor triad (ii, iii, vi). For diminished triads, add a small raised (superscript) circle to the lowercase numeral (vii°). When using Roman numerals, always indicate the key (as in Example 9.4).

EXAMPLE 9.4 Triad labels in F major

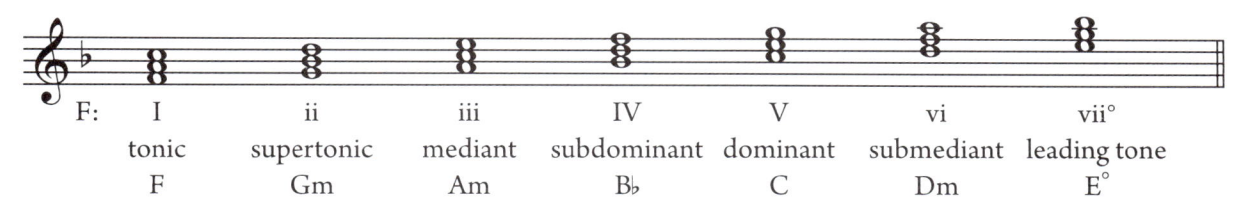

F:	I	ii	iii	IV	V	vi	vii°
	tonic	supertonic	mediant	subdominant	dominant	submediant	leading tone
	F	Gm	Am	B♭	C	Dm	E°

> **KEY CONCEPT** In popular music, chords are labeled by their root and quality, without a specific reference to their place in the key (without a Roman numeral). This book uses the following symbols for triads:
>
> | G major triad | G |
> |---|---|
> | G minor triad | Gm or Gmin |
> | G diminished triad | G° or Gdim |
> | G augmented triad | G⁺ (see p. 226) |

Your teacher may prefer another system, such as an uppercase letter for major and a lowercase letter for minor. There are many variants of these labels.

Example 9.5 illustrates how to label chords from "Come, Ye Thankful People Come." The key of the piece, F, is given to the left, before the Roman numerals.

EXAMPLE 9.5 "Come, Ye Thankful People Come," mm. 5–6

F: vi ii V I

Triad Qualities in Major Keys 225

Triad Qualities in Minor Keys

Example 9.6a shows the triads that can be built above the scale degrees of a natural minor scale. The triads on $\hat{1}$, $\hat{4}$, and $\hat{5}$ are minor; those on $\hat{3}$, $\hat{6}$, and $\hat{7}$ are major; and the triad on $\hat{2}$ is diminished.

EXAMPLE 9.6   Triads built above the G minor scale

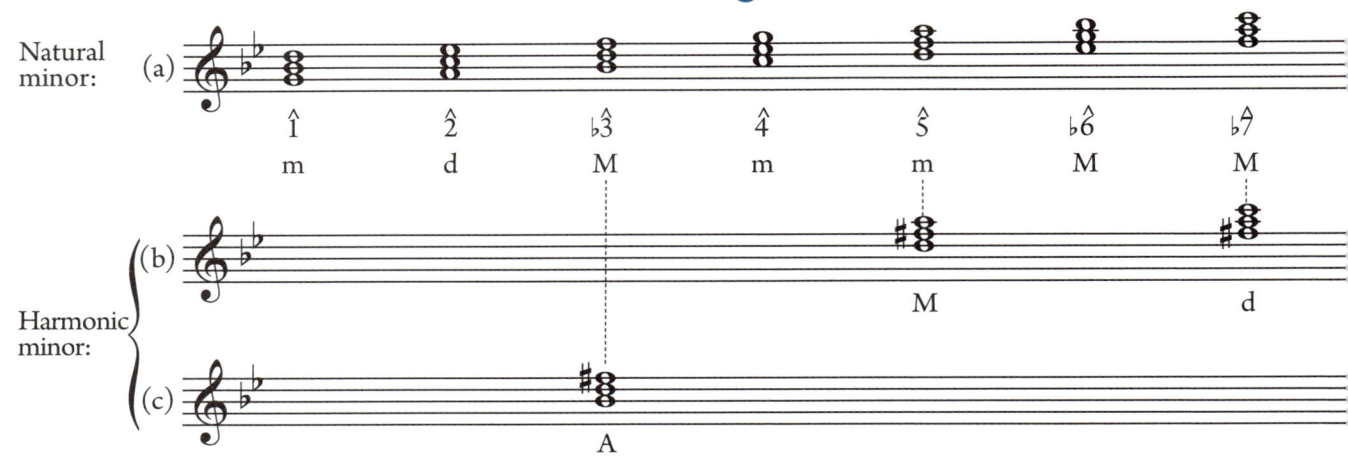

As we learned earlier, $\flat\hat{7}$ in minor is often raised to make a leading tone. In that case, the triads on $\hat{5}$ and $\hat{7}$ become major and diminished, respectively (Example 9.6b). Example 9.6c illustrates what happens to the triad on $\flat\hat{3}$ (B♭–D–F♯) with the raised leading tone: there are now major thirds between both root and third and third and fifth. Since the interval between the root and fifth is an augmented fifth, this type of chord is called an **augmented triad** (labeled A). Unlike the other triads in the example, this one is not usually found in minor-key pieces.

The Roman numerals for each triad in G minor are shown in Example 9.7, along with the scale-degree names and chord symbols.

EXAMPLE 9.7   Triad labels in G minor

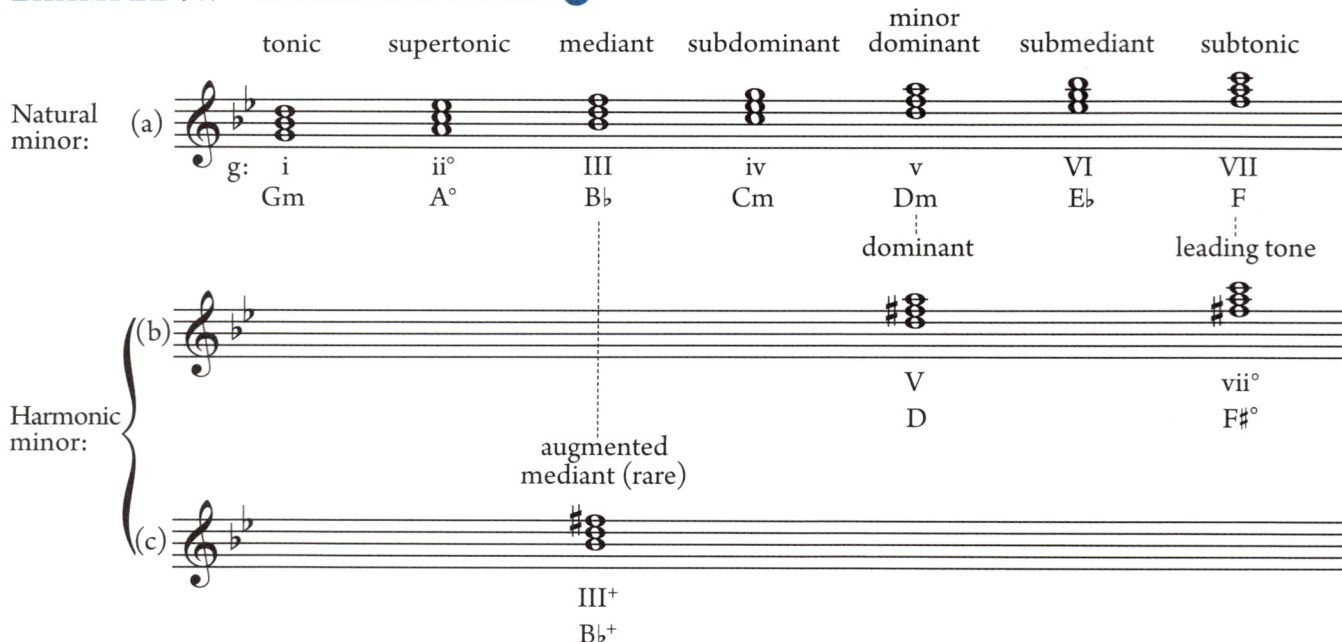

226   CHAPTER NINE   Triads and the Dominant Seventh Chord

To label an augmented chord (Example 9.7c), add a superscript plus sign to an uppercase Roman numeral (III⁺). When analyzing music with Roman numerals, always indicate the key at the beginning of your analysis (an uppercase letter for major keys, lowercase for minor keys, followed by a colon).

> **KEY CONCEPT** Triads that appear often in minor keys are i, ii°, iv, V, VI, and vii°. The major triad on $\hat{5}$ (V) and the diminished triad on the leading tone (vii°) are more typical than v and VII, because of their strong leading-tone-to-tonic motion. When you write V and vii° in minor keys, remember to raise $\flat\hat{7}$ to $\hat{7}$ to make the leading tone.

Spelling Triads

Triads are essential building blocks for music in many styles. Here are three ways to identify and spell triads: (1) by key signatures, (2) by triads in the C major scale, and (3) by intervals. Find the method that allows you to spell triads most quickly and accurately, then use a second one to check your work.

Method 1 This method draws on your knowledge of key signatures and scales. Always begin by writing the note heads stacked in thirds above the root, without accidentals: either line-line-line or space-space-space. Imagine a major triad in a major key, where the root is $\hat{1}$ and the upper notes are $\hat{3}$ and $\hat{5}$. Then think about which notes need accidentals, given the major key signature of the root. Example 9.8a illustrates the procedure for an A major triad. First write notes on three consecutive spaces starting from A, then think of the A major key signature: sharps on F, C, and G. C needs to be sharped: A–C♯–E. Example 9.8b follows the same procedure to spell an E♭ major triad.

EXAMPLE 9.8 Building a major triad from a major key signature

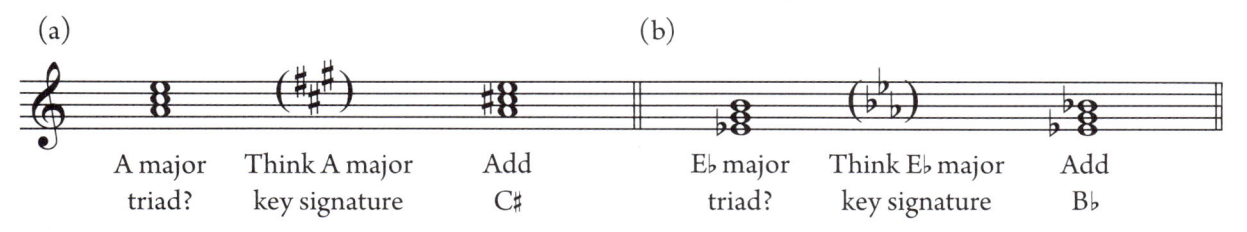

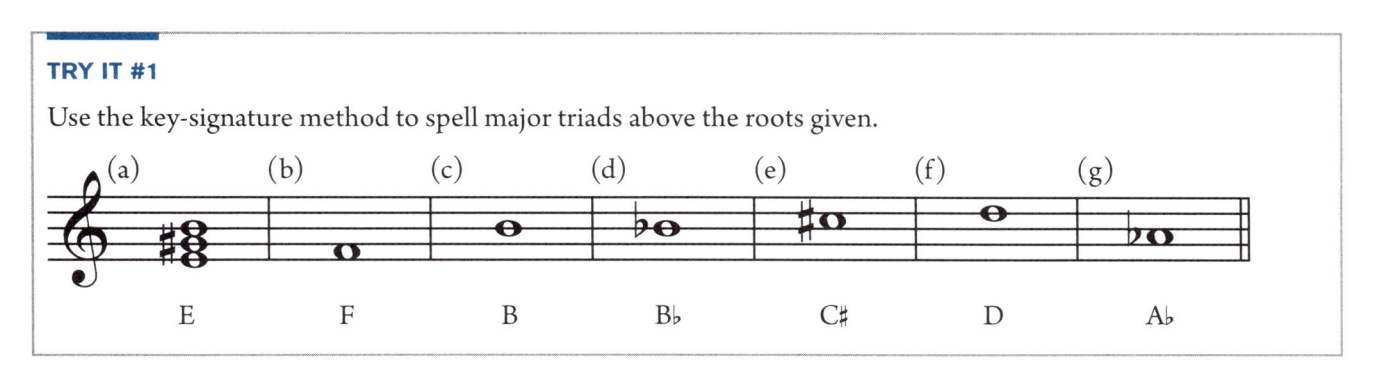

(a) A major triad? | Think A major key signature | Add C♯

(b) E♭ major triad? | Think E♭ major key signature | Add B♭

> **TRY IT #1**
> Use the key-signature method to spell major triads above the roots given.
> (a) E (b) F (c) B (d) B♭ (e) C♯ (f) D (g) A♭

For minor triads, you can use the same method but imagine the minor key signature, as shown in Example 9.9; or you can write a major triad and lower the third by a chromatic half step (without changing the letter name).

EXAMPLE 9.9 Building a minor triad from a minor key signature

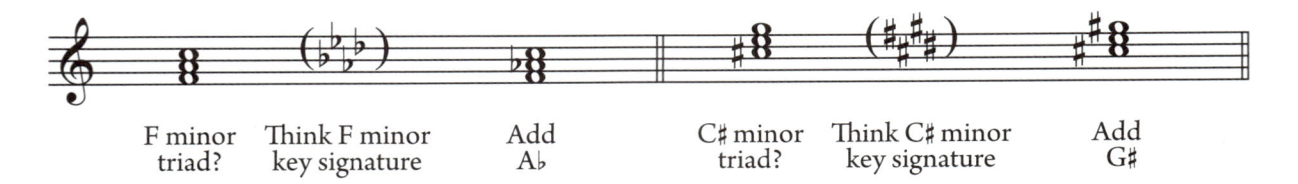

| F minor triad? | Think F minor key signature | Add A♭ | C♯ minor triad? | Think C♯ minor key signature | Add G♯ |

TRY IT #2

Use the minor key signature method to spell minor triads above the roots given.

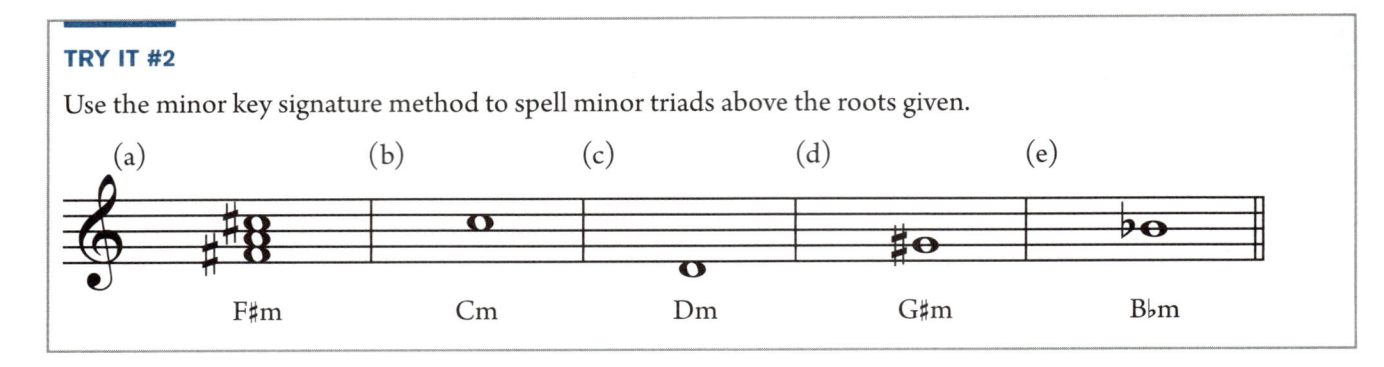

(a) F♯m (b) Cm (c) Dm (d) G♯m (e) B♭m

ASSIGNMENT 9.1, AURAL SKILLS 9.1, 9.2

Method 2 If you like to visualize triads on the keyboard or staff, first learn the qualities of each scale-degree triad in C major (Example 9.10a) from the piano white keys or note heads on the staff.

- Triads on C, F, and G remain major if all the accidentals match (Example 9.10b). To make a minor triad, lower the third a half step. To make an augmented triad, raise the fifth a half step.
- Triads on D, E, and A remain minor if all the accidentals match (Example 9.10c). To make a major triad, raise the third a half step. To make a diminished triad, lower the fifth a half step.
- Triads on B remain diminished if all the accidentals match (Example 9.10d). To make a minor triad, raise the fifth a half step. To make a major triad, raise both the third and fifth a half step.

EXAMPLE 9.10 Spelling triads from C major

(a) White-key triads

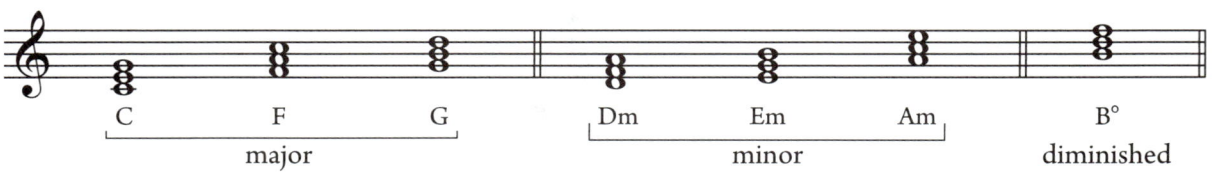

C F G — Dm Em Am — B°
major   minor   diminished

(b) For triads on C, F, and G

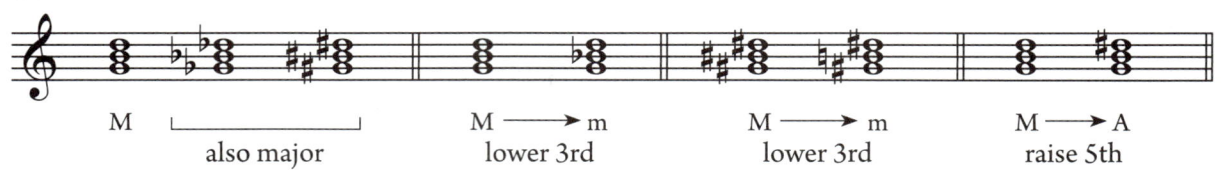

M — also major | M → m lower 3rd | M → m lower 3rd | M → A raise 5th

228   CHAPTER NINE Triads and the Dominant Seventh Chord

(c) For triads on D, E, and A

| m | also minor | m → M
raise 3rd | m → M
raise 3rd | m → d
lower 5th |

(d) For triads on B

| d | also diminished | d → m
raise 5th | d → M
raise 3rd and 5th |

TRY IT #3

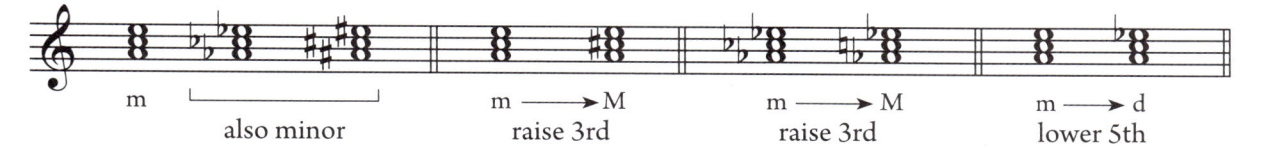

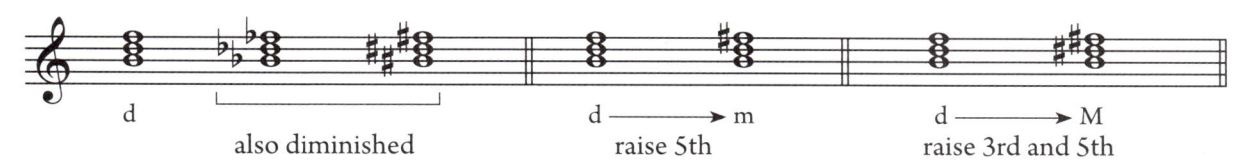

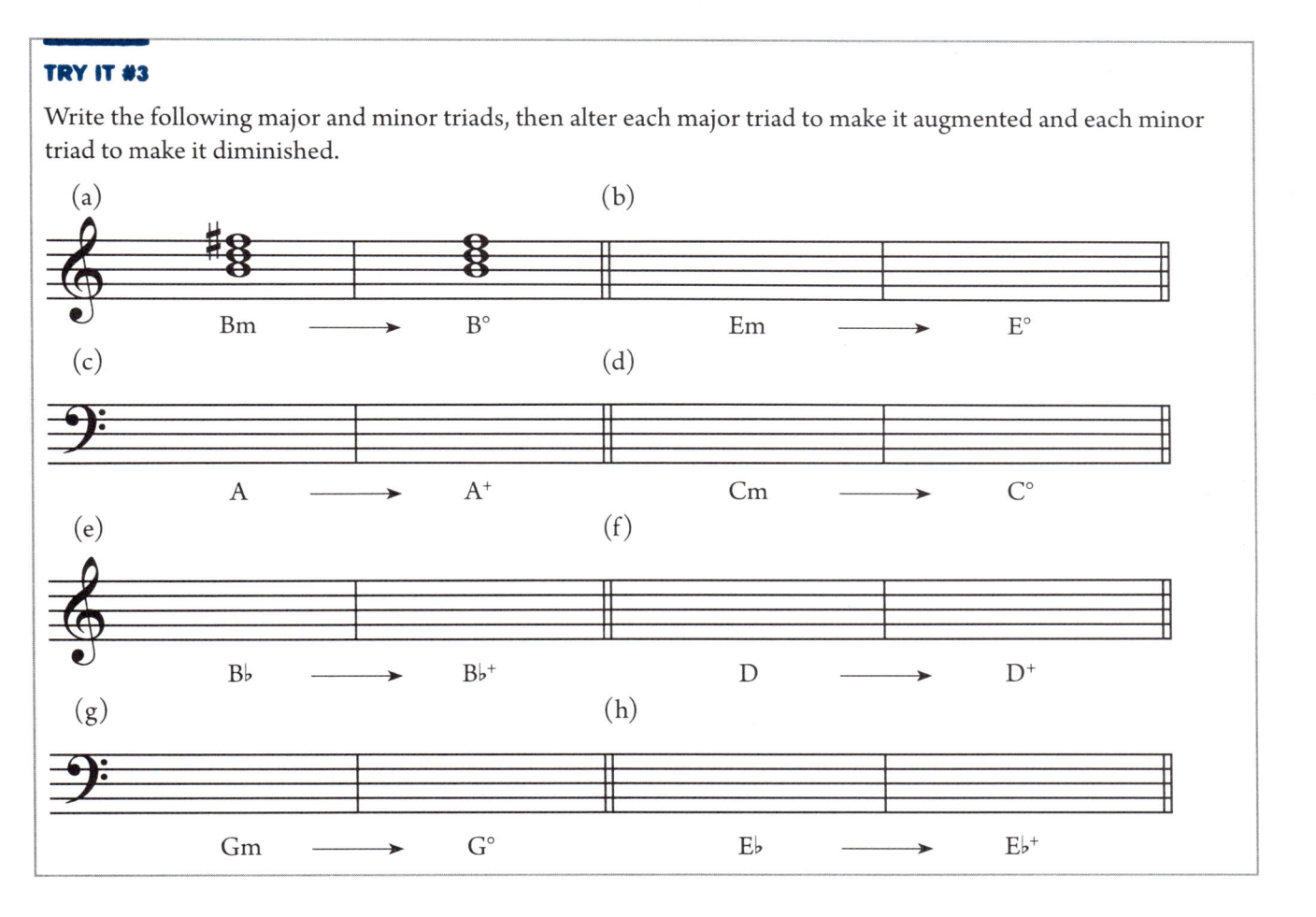

Write the following major and minor triads, then alter each major triad to make it augmented and each minor triad to make it diminished.

(a) Bm → B°   (b) Em → E°

(c) A → A⁺   (d) Cm → C°

(e) B♭ → B♭⁺   (f) D → D⁺

(g) Gm → G°   (h) E♭ → E♭⁺

Method 3 Finally, you can spell triads by dividing them into their component intervals, following the steps below (Example 9.11).

1. Write the root of the triad.
2. Add the fifth:
   (a) For a major or minor triad, write a P5 above the root.
   (b) For an augmented triad, make it an A5.
   (c) For a diminished triad, make it a d5.
3. Add the third:
   (a) For a major or augmented triad, add a M3 above the root.
   (b) For a minor or diminished triad, add a m3 above the root.

EXAMPLE 9.11   Spelling triads by intervals

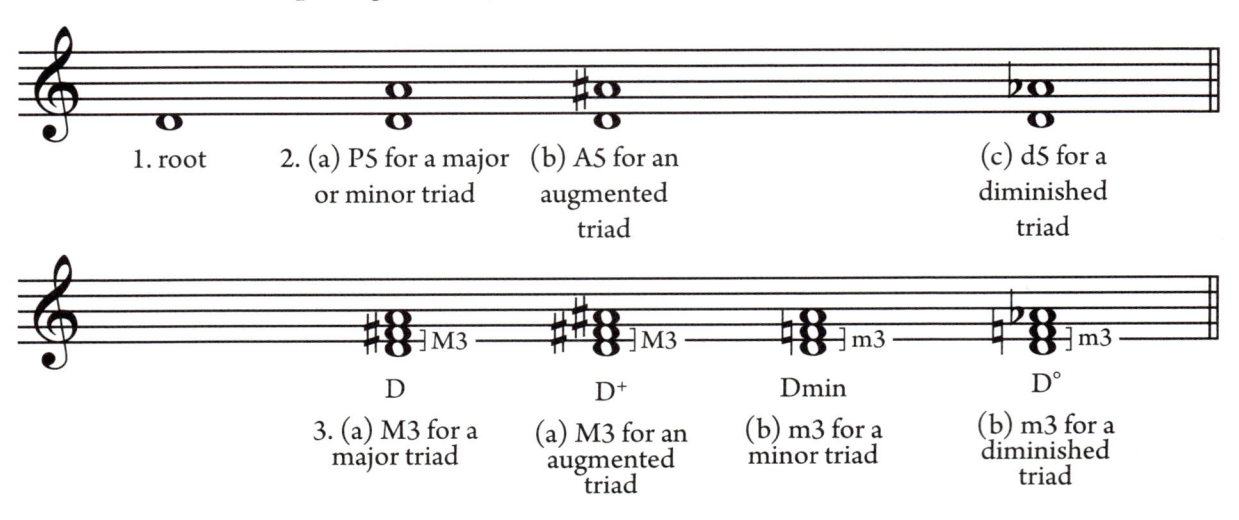

1. root
2. (a) P5 for a major or minor triad
   (b) A5 for an augmented triad
   (c) d5 for a diminished triad

D   D+   Dmin   D°

3. (a) M3 for a major triad
   (a) M3 for an augmented triad
   (b) m3 for a minor triad
   (b) m3 for a diminished triad

You can also spell root-position triads by stacking thirds (Example 9.12).

EXAMPLE 9.12   Spelling triads in stacked thirds

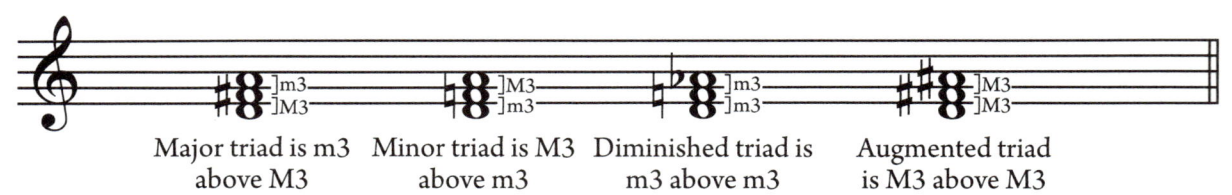

Major triad is m3 above M3   Minor triad is M3 above m3   Diminished triad is m3 above m3   Augmented triad is M3 above M3

Triad Inversion

Sometimes you will see triads arranged so that they are not stacked in thirds above their root. For an example, look at the third chord of "My Country" in Example 9.13. It is a G–B♭–D triad, but the third of the chord (B♭) is in the bass and also is doubled.

EXAMPLE 9.13   "My Country, 'Tis of Thee," m. 1

> **KEY CONCEPT** When the root of the chord is in the bass, the chord is in **root position**. If a chord member other than a root is in the bass, the chord is said to be **inverted**: when the third is in the bass, the chord is in **first inversion**; when the fifth is in the bass, the chord is in **second inversion**.

Inverted triads sound different from root-position triads because there are different intervals between the bass and upper parts. Inverted chords retain their basic harmonic identity, however, and are named by their root even when the root is not in the bass.

With root-position triads, you hear the intervals P5 and either M3 or m3 above the bass, but inversions bring out other intervals that can be made with the chord's tones, as shown in Example 9.14a: m6, M6, and P4. It is customary to label a triad and its inversions with numbers that represent their intervals, which are called **figures** from their use in an eighteenth-century compositional style called figured bass. Root-position triads have a fifth and third above the bass, for a figure of $^5_3$; this figure is often omitted because root position is assumed if there is no figure given. First inversion is labeled $^6_3$, or simply 6, and second inversion is labeled $^6_4$. Example 9.14b shows these chords voiced in four parts with typical doubling.

EXAMPLE 9.14   C major triad and its inversions

(a) Inversion labels

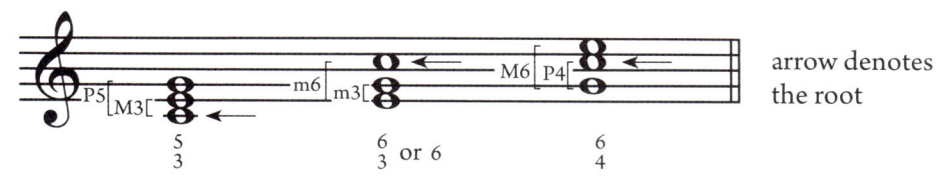

(b) Typical doubling

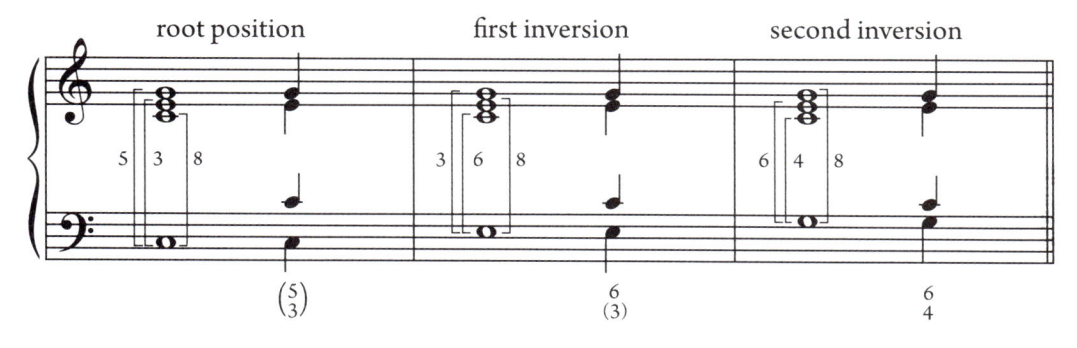

You can also show the inversion of a chord by adding its figure after its Roman numeral (V^6, ii^6) to show a chord's scale-degree, quality, and inversion in one space-saving label. In Example 9.15, the Roman numerals show how all three inversions of the F major chord sound in turn. Here, consider the F major chord to extend for all of measure 7, even though no F sounds on beats 2 and 3. If you were accompanying this with guitar, you would keep strumming the F major chord for both measures 7 and 8.

EXAMPLE 9.15 "My Country, 'Tis of Thee," mm. 7–10

Once you have spelled a triad, you can write it in one of the three triad positions by adding a fourth note in the bass. Example 9.16 shows each triad position in **keyboard style**, with three notes in the right hand and one in the left. In this style, the three notes in the right hand must fit within a single octave, so that they are easy to play on a keyboard. The note in the left hand—the bass note—determines whether the triad is in root position, first inversion, or second inversion.

EXAMPLE 9.16 Triad positions in keyboard style

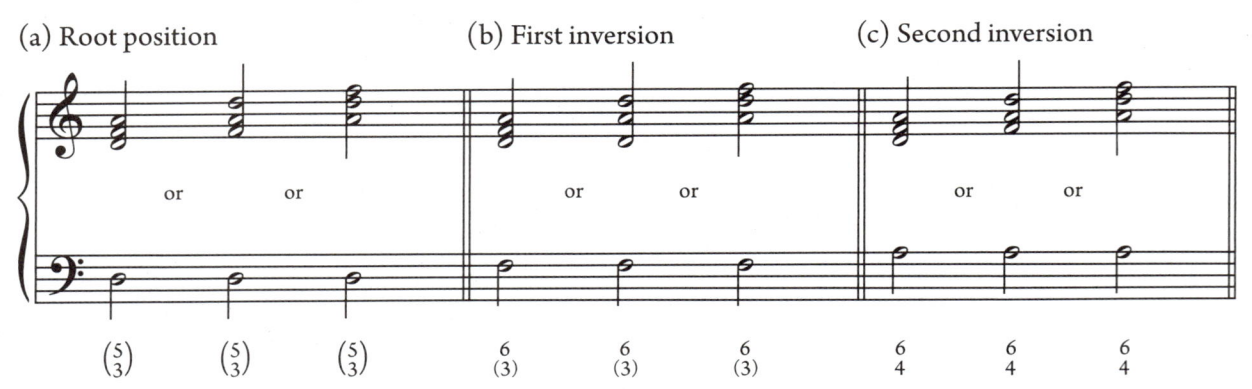

(a) Root position (b) First inversion (c) Second inversion

> **KEY CONCEPT** When you add a fourth voice, you must double one of the three notes of the triad. While there is some flexibility in choosing a doubling, it is customary to double:
>
> - the root of root-position triads,
> - any member of first-inversion major or minor triads except the leading tone,
> - the third of first-inversion diminished triads,
> - the fifth of second-inversion triads.

TRY IT #4

Write each triad in the inversion specified in keyboard style. Be sure that the arrangement of chord tones in the right hand fits within one octave and results in a correct doubling when the left hand is added.

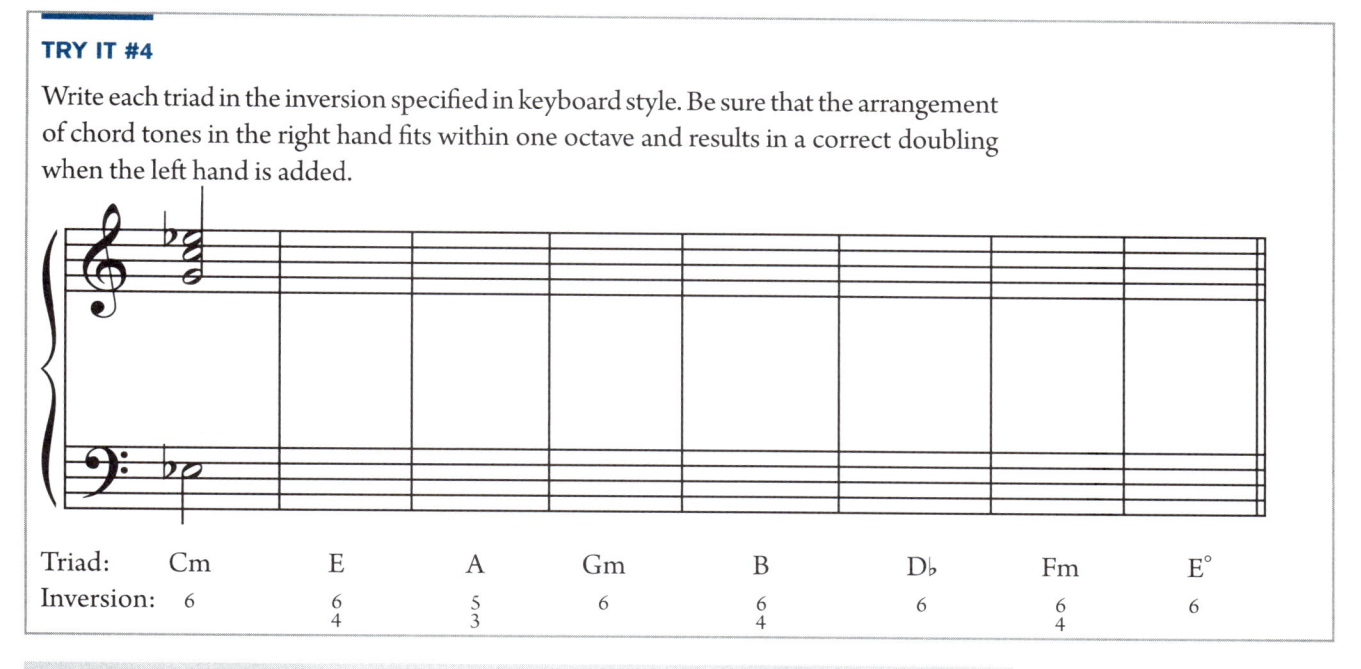

Triad:	Cm	E	A	Gm	B	D♭	Fm	E°
Inversion:	6	6/4	5/3	6	6/4	6	6/4	6

ASSIGNMENT 9.2, 9.3

The Dominant Seventh Chord

Some four-note chords have four *different* pitches (with no doubling), as shown in Example 9.17, the end of "My Country, 'Tis of Thee." The chord on the last beat of measure 13 has four notes stacked in thirds above $\hat{5}$ (C), as shown on the staff below: the C major triad (C–E–G) plus another third (B♭). This type of chord, with a **third**, **fifth**, and **seventh** above the **root**, is called a **seventh chord**. The most frequently encountered seventh chord, built on the fifth scale degree, is called the **dominant seventh chord**. The dominant seventh chord is normally written V⁷ ("five-seven") or indicated by the letter name of its root plus a 7 (for example, C7 for a dominant seventh chord built on the root C).

EXAMPLE 9.17 "My Country, 'Tis of Thee," mm. 13–14

Spelling the Dominant Seventh Chord

To spell a dominant seventh chord, use one of the methods below.

Spelling the Dominant Seventh Chord   233

Method 1 First write a major triad, then add a minor third above the triad's fifth, as shown in Example 9.18. Check that the interval between the root and seventh is a minor seventh.

EXAMPLE 9.18   Spelling a dominant seventh chord

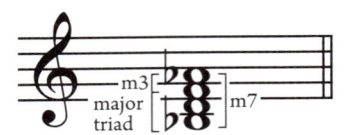

Method 2 Write the note head for the seventh chord's root, then stack three thirds above it (line-line-line-line or space-space-space-space). Ask yourself: In which key is this chord's root $\hat{5}$? Complete the spelling of the seventh chord using accidentals from that key signature. In Example 9.18, the B♭ root is $\hat{5}$ in the key of E♭ major. The key signature of three flats (B♭, E♭, A♭) requires that we spell the chord with A♭. Check the intervals above the bass using method 1 above.

TRY IT #5

Spell a dominant seventh chord above each of the roots provided.

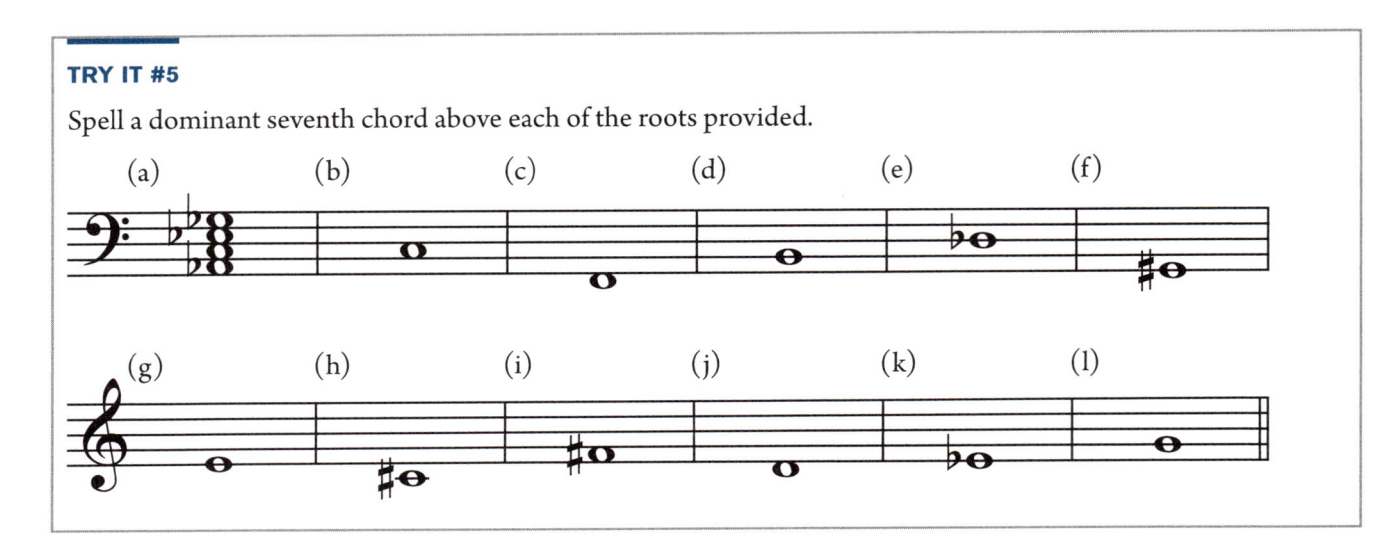

Seventh Chord Inversion

Seventh chords may also be inverted, as shown in measure 9 of Example 9.19. (The circled notes are not part of the chord.) The chord here is a dominant seventh (in the key of F), C–E–G–B♭, appearing successively with the root, third, and fifth in the bass.

EXAMPLE 9.19   "My Country, 'Tis of Thee," mm. 7–10

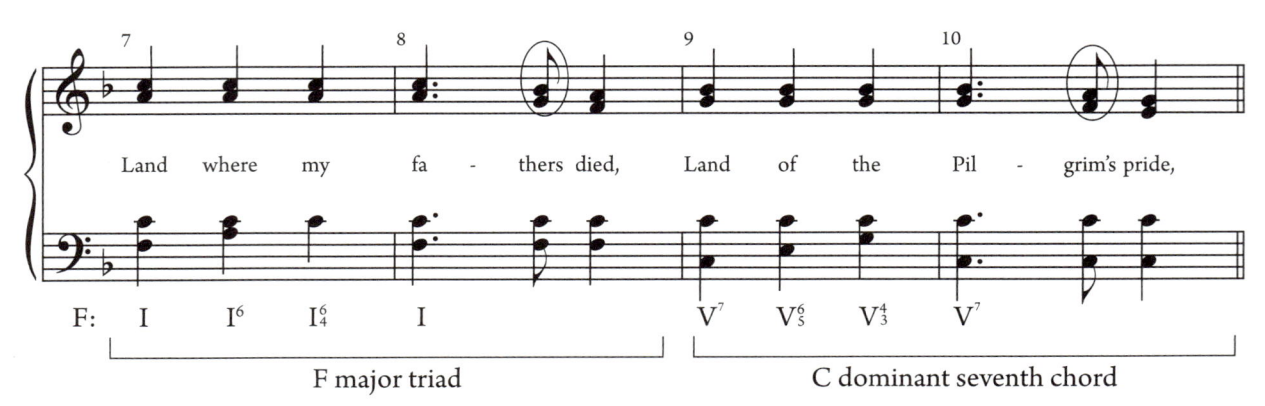

F: I   I⁶   I⁶₄   I   V⁷   V⁶₅   V⁴₃   V⁷

F major triad   C dominant seventh chord

234   CHAPTER NINE   Triads and the Dominant Seventh Chord

Since they include four chord members, seventh chords have three inversions in addition to root position. Example 9.20a shows a G dominant seventh chord (in the key of C) in root position, then first, second, and third inversion. The first set of numbers beneath each indicates all the intervals formed above the bottom note—for example, the root position has 7, 5, and 3 above the bass, while the first inversion has 6, 5, and 3. These figures are usually simplified: 7 for root position, $^6_5$ for first inversion, $^4_3$ for second inversion, and $^4_2$ or 2 for third inversion.

EXAMPLE 9.20 G dominant seventh chord and its inversions

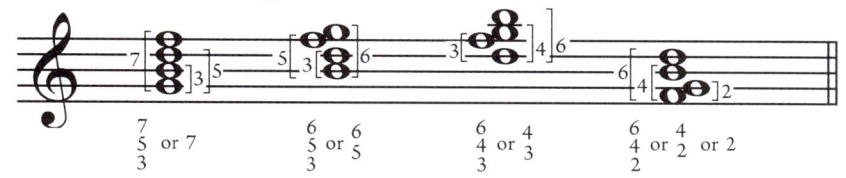

(a) On a treble staff

(b) In keyboard style and SATB style

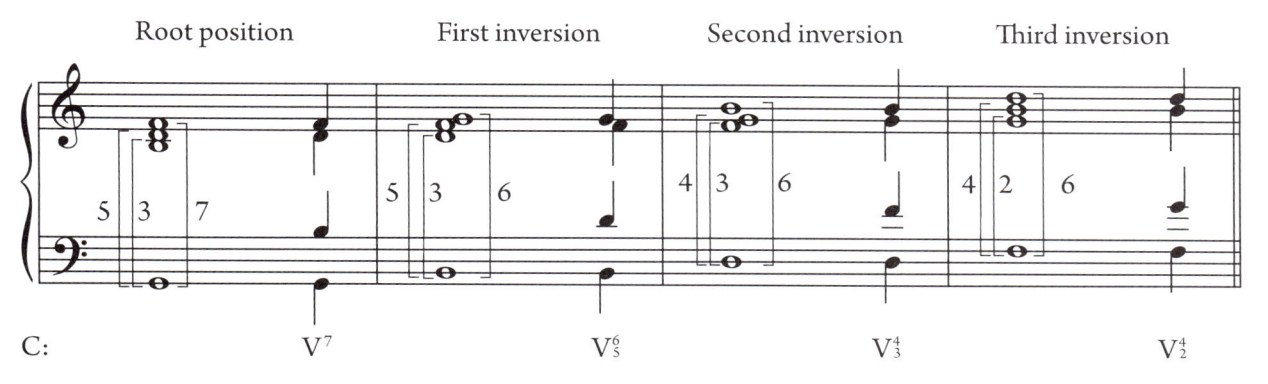

Example 9.20b shows the same chord in keyboard style (whole notes) and SATB style (quarter notes). Inverted seventh chords are usually complete in four parts—nothing is doubled—but you may encounter the root-position dominant seventh chord with two roots ($\hat{5}$), a third ($\hat{7}$), and a seventh ($\hat{4}$), but no fifth ($\hat{2}$).

SUMMARY

The inversion of a triad or seventh chord is determined by the bass, the lowest-sounding pitch.
- If the root is lowest (in the bass), it is **root position**.
- If the third is lowest, it is in **first inversion**.
- If the fifth is lowest, it is in **second inversion**.
- If the seventh of a seventh chord is lowest, it is in **third inversion**.

ASSIGNMENT 9.4

Did You Know?

The melody that we know as "My Country, 'Tis of Thee," or "America," is even more well-known in England as "God Save the King" (or "God Save the Queen," depending on the current monarch). The origin of the melody remains a mystery. It was first published in England in 1744, and became popular after a version with words by Thomas Arne was performed in London's Drury Lane and Covent Garden theaters in September 1745. Arne's lyrics rallied support for King George II and decried the Scots, led by "Bonnie Prince Charlie," his Stuart rival for the throne. Later, both Beethoven and Haydn incorporated this melody into their own compositions.

In the 1790s, the melody became the Danish national anthem, and, with the "God Save the King" text, it has also remained a national song for former British colonies besides the United States, including Canada and Australia. The text beginning "My country, 'tis of thee," written by Samuel Francis Smith, was first performed on July 4, 1831. Over a century later, on August 28, 1963, Martin Luther King quoted Smith's lyrics in his "I have a dream" speech from the steps of the Lincoln Memorial, as he called on the nation to "let freedom ring."

Terms You Should Know

chord
chord members
  root
  third
  fifth
  seventh
dominant seventh chord
doubling
figures
homophony
inverted chords
keyboard style

Roman numerals
seventh chord
texture
triad
triad names
  tonic
  supertonic
  mediant
  subdominant
  dominant
  submediant
  leading tone

triad qualities
  augmented
  diminished
  major
  minor
triad and seventh
chord positions
  root position
  first inversion
  second inversion
  third inversion

Questions for Review

1. What is the difference between a major and minor triad? a minor and diminished triad? a major and augmented triad?
2. What are the intervals in a major triad? in a minor triad?
3. What are several methods for spelling triads?
4. On which scale degrees are major triads found in major keys? in minor keys?
5. On which scale degrees are minor triads found in major keys? in minor keys?
6. On which scale degrees are diminished and augmented triads found in major keys? in minor keys?
7. What information does a Roman numeral provide?
8. Which Arabic numerals are used to show each triad position (root position, first inversion, second inversion)?
9. What are two methods for spelling a dominant seventh chord?

Reading Review

Match the term on the left with the best answer on the right.

_____ (1) Roman numerals
_____ (2) ^{6}
_____ (3) ^{7}
_____ (4) D–F–A
_____ (5) first inversion
_____ (6) third inversion
_____ (7) root
_____ (8) doubling
_____ (9) D–F♯–A♯
_____ (10) triad
_____ (11) root position
_____ (12) second inversion
_____ (13) $^5_3$
_____ (14) $^6_4$
_____ (15) D–F–A♭
_____ (16) $^6_5$
_____ (17) D–F♯–A
_____ (18) dominant seventh chord
_____ (19) $^4_3$
_____ (20) $^4_2$

(a) major triad
(b) chord position with the third in the bass
(c) minor triad
(d) diminished triad
(e) figure for a first-inversion triad
(f) chord position with the root in the bass
(g) figure for a root-position seventh chord
(h) the seventh chord built on $\hat{5}$
(i) augmented triad
(j) used to represent the scale degree of the root and the quality of triads and seventh chords
(k) figure for a first-inversion seventh chord
(l) figure for a second-inversion triad
(m) chord position with the seventh in the bass
(n) chord position with the fifth in the bass
(o) figure for a root-position triad
(p) the lowest note of a triad or seventh chord stacked in thirds
(q) figure for a second-inversion seventh chord
(r) placing one note of a triad in two voices to get four parts
(s) figure for a third-inversion seventh chord
(t) chord that may be represented as two stacked thirds

Additional review and practice available at wwnorton.com/studyspace

Apply It

A. At the keyboard

Major and minor triads

1. Play $\hat{1}$ to $\hat{5}$ of a major scale: think of the key signature or the pattern of whole and half steps (W–W–H–W). Now perform a major triad: $\hat{1}$, $\hat{3}$, and $\hat{5}$ of the scale segment you just played. Play with both hands an octave apart, and sing along with letter names, solfège syllables, or scale-degree numbers. (In class, one student may play while others sing.) 🔊

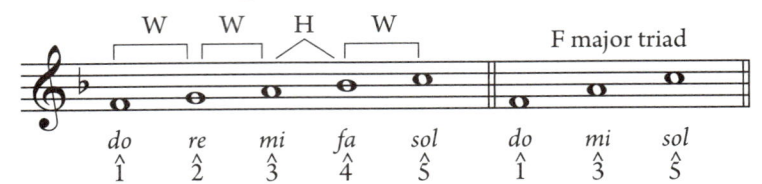

   W W H W — F major triad
   do re mi fa sol   do mi sol
   $\hat{1}$ $\hat{2}$ $\hat{3}$ $\hat{4}$ $\hat{5}$ $\hat{1}$ $\hat{3}$ $\hat{5}$

2. Play $\hat{1}$ to $\hat{5}$ of a minor scale: think of the key signature or the pattern of whole and half steps (W–H–W–W). Perform a minor triad: $\hat{1}$, $\flat\hat{3}$, and $\hat{5}$. Play with both hands an octave apart, and sing with letter names, solfège syllables, or scale-degree numbers. 🔊

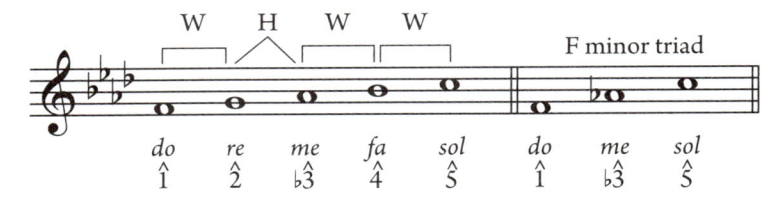

   W H W W — F minor triad
   do re me fa sol   do me sol
   $\hat{1}$ $\hat{2}$ $\flat\hat{3}$ $\hat{4}$ $\hat{5}$ $\hat{1}$ $\flat\hat{3}$ $\hat{5}$

3. For each pitch given below, follow instructions 1 and 2 above.
   When you have mastered the scale segment and triad at the keyboard, play *only* the tonic pitch and then sing the triad alone on syllables or numbers. Pay careful attention to the tuning of the third! When moving from major to minor, lower $\hat{3}$ to $\flat\hat{3}$. Compare your performance with the recording. You may also check your answers by playing triads on the Virtual Keyboard. 🔊

   (a) D   (f) B   (k) G♭
   (b) G   (g) E♭   (l) A♭
   (c) A   (h) C   (m) B♭
   (d) E   (i) C♯   (n) F♯
   (e) F   (j) D♭   (o) C♭

4. Augmented and diminished triads get both their name and their distinctive sound from the quality of their fifth. To make an augmented triad, perform a major triad, then raise its fifth a half step; the intervals from the root are a M3 and an A5. To make a diminished triad, perform a minor triad, then lower its fifth by a half step; the intervals are a m3 and a d5.

- Consider each given pitch to be the root of a chord. First perform a major triad, then raise the fifth a half step to create an augmented triad. While you play, sing the pitches with letter names. Each time you alter the fifth, keep the same letter, but change its accidental (for example, A becomes A♯, not B♭).
- From each of the given roots, perform a minor triad, then lower the fifth a half step to create a diminished triad. 🔊

   (a) C   (e) E   (i) F♯
   (b) A   (f) D   (j) B♭
   (c) G   (g) A♭   (k) C♯
   (d) F   (h) E♭   (l) G♯

B. Reading rhythms

These rhythms provide a review of duplets and triplets (Chapter 5). Perform using "ta" or counting syllables while tapping a steady beat or conducting. Remember to perform all dynamic indications and accents.

Rhythm 1

Rhythm 2

Rhythm 3

C. Singing at sight

First determine the key of the melody, and play that major or minor scale at the keyboard while singing along on scale-degree numbers or solfège syllables. Most of these melodies feature the tonic triad; sing a warm-up on $\hat{1}$–$\hat{3}$–$\hat{5}$–$\hat{3}$–$\hat{1}$–$\hat{7}$–$\hat{1}$ before beginning the melody. (You may write the syllables or numbers above or below the notes before singing.)

Practice singing the rhythm and pitches separately before putting them together. Check yourself at the keyboard or listen to the recording *after* you sing the melody.

Melody 1 "I Had a Little Nut Tree," mm. 1–4

Melody 2 Joseph Haydn, Seven German Dances, No. 6, mm. 1–8 (adapted)

Melody 3 Leopold Mozart, Burleske, mm. 1–8
How do measures 1–4 relate to 5–8?

Melody 4 "St. James Infirmary"
What is the quality of the triad outlined in this melody?

Melody 5 "Down in the Valley," mm. 1–8
This melody begins on *sol–do* ($\hat{5}$–$\hat{1}$).

Down in the val - ley, the val - ley so low, _____ Hang your head

o - ver, hear the wind blow. _____ Hear the wind blow, dear, hear the wind

blow, _____ Hang your head o - ver, hear the wind blow. _____

D. Listening and writing

Listen to melodies made from $\hat{1}$ to $\hat{5}$ of major and minor scales. Sing what you hear, then write it on the staff provided.

1.
2.
3.
4.
5.
6.
7.
8.
9.
10.
11.
12.

Apply It

E. Hearing triad qualities

Each exercise below consists of ten recorded root-position triads. These may be used in class or for individual practice. The root of each triad is notated on the staff; don't change the given pitch. In the blank, write the triad's quality (M, m, A, or d). Then notate the third and fifth, including any necessary accidentals. For example, if you hear a minor triad whose root is B♭, write "m" in the blank. Then notate the third and fifth.

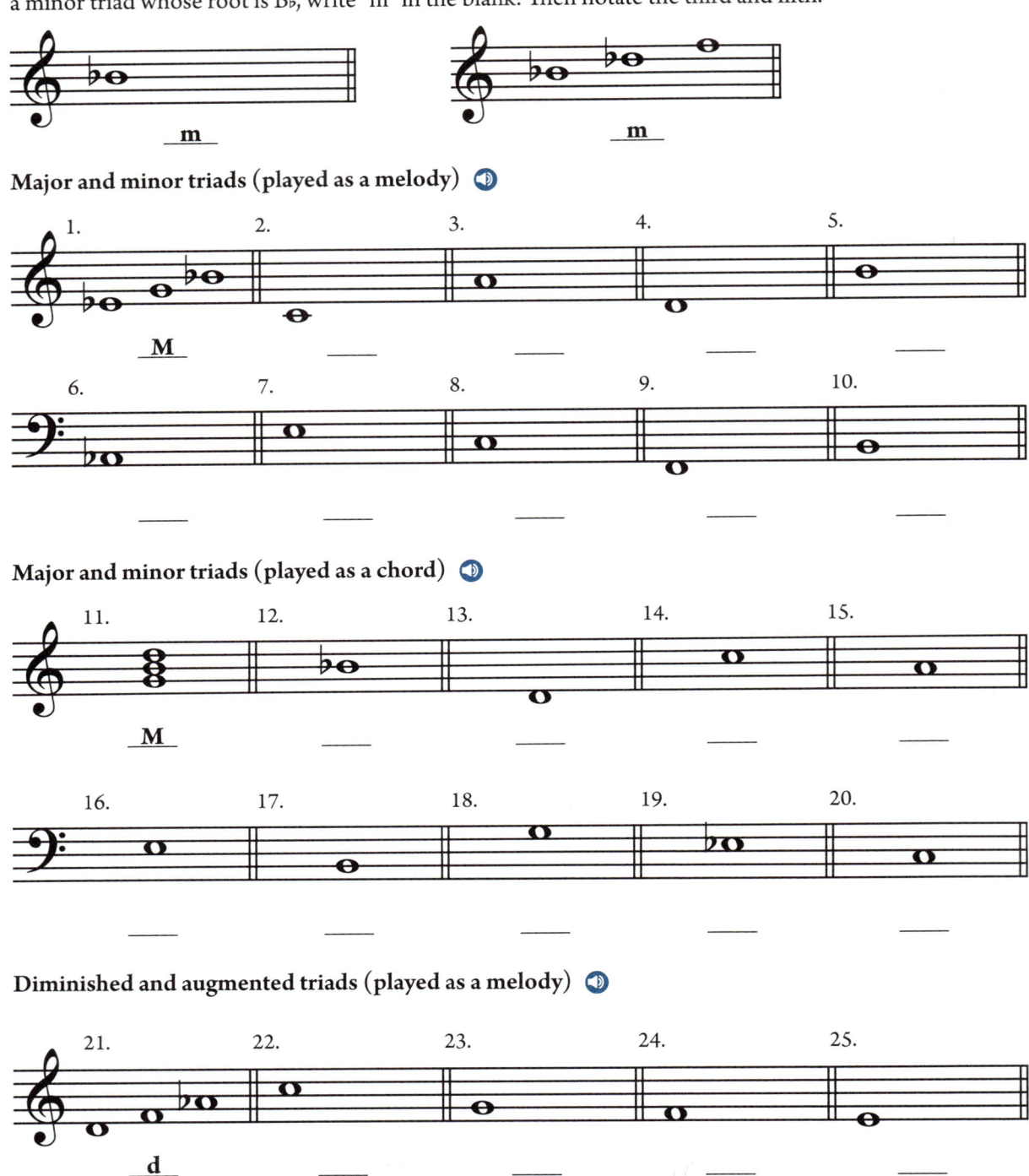

Major and minor triads (played as a melody)

1. M 2. ___ 3. ___ 4. ___ 5. ___

6. ___ 7. ___ 8. ___ 9. ___ 10. ___

Major and minor triads (played as a chord)

11. M 12. ___ 13. ___ 14. ___ 15. ___

16. ___ 17. ___ 18. ___ 19. ___ 20. ___

Diminished and augmented triads (played as a melody)

21. d 22. ___ 23. ___ 24. ___ 25. ___

26. ___ 27. ___ 28. ___ 29. ___ 30. ___

242   CHAPTER NINE   Triads and the Dominant Seventh Chord

NAME _____

Workbook ASSIGNMENT 9.1

A. Building triads above major scales

Write the requested ascending major scale in whole notes. Above each scale degree, write the third and fifth to make a triad, adding accidentals as needed for that key. Write M (major), m (minor), or d (diminished) under each triad to show the quality, then provide the Roman numeral.

(1)

Triad quality:	**M**	**m**	**m**	M	M	m	D°
Roman numeral:	F: **I**	**ii**	**iii**	IV	V	vi	vii°

(2)

Triad quality:	M	m	m	M	M	m	D°
Roman numeral:	A: I	ii	iii	IV	V	vi	vii°

(3)

Triad quality:	M	m	m	M	M	m	D°
Roman numeral:	E: I	ii	iii	IV	V	vi	vii°

(4)

Triad quality:	M	m	m	M	M	m	D°
Roman numeral:	D♭: I	ii	iii	IV	V	vi	vii°

Assignment 9.1

B. Writing triads

Write a triad of the specified quality above each root given.

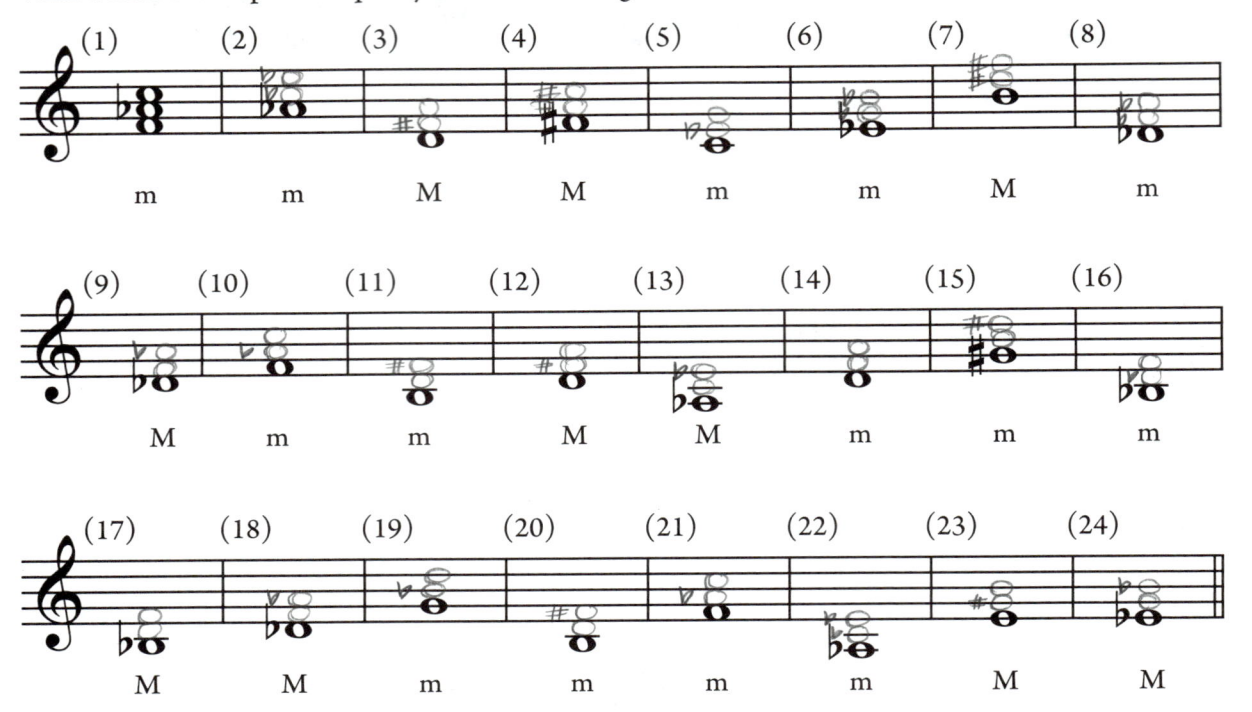

(1) m (2) m (3) M (4) M (5) m (6) m (7) M (8) m

(9) M (10) m (11) m (12) M (13) M (14) m (15) m (16) m

(17) M (18) M (19) m (20) m (21) m (22) m (23) M (24) M

C. Identifying major and minor triads in musical contexts

In the following excerpt, identify each chord by writing the triad (stacked in thirds) on the staff. Then in the blanks below, write M (for major) or m (minor) to indicate the chord quality. Remember to apply accidentals from the key signature. Finally, write a Roman numeral for each chord in the key specified.

"Old Hundredth," mm. 1–6

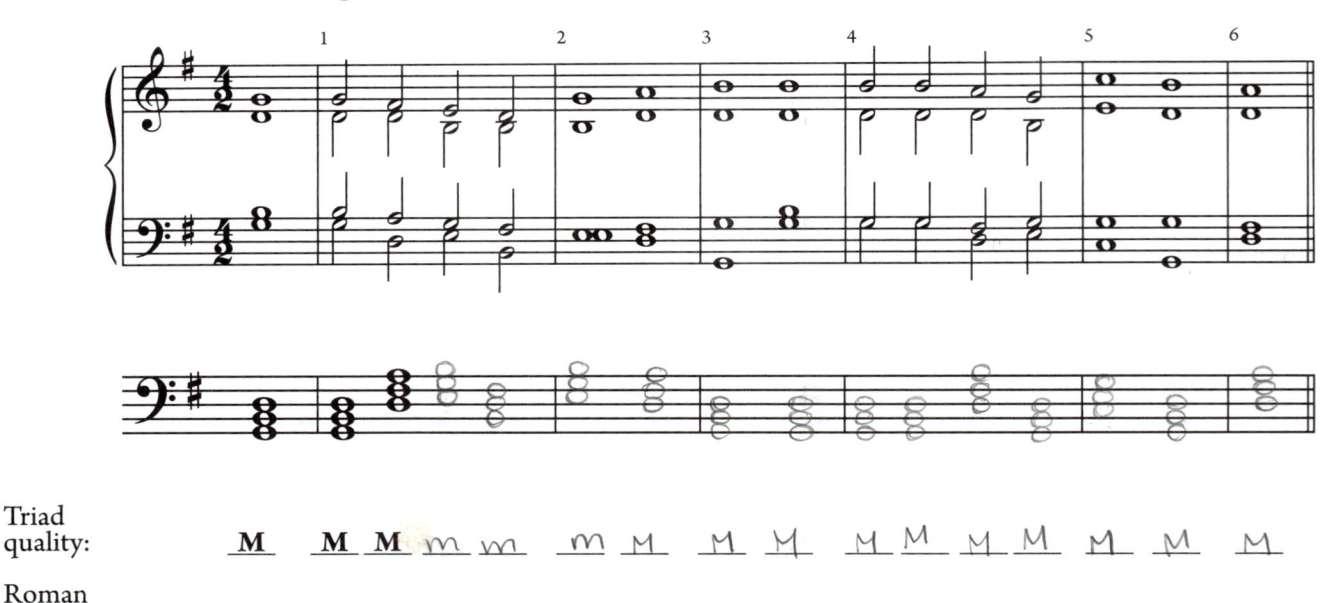

Triad quality: M M M m m m M M M M M M M M M M

Roman numeral: G: I I V vi iii vi V I I I I V I IV I V

Workbook — Assignment 9.2

A. Building triads above minor scales

Write the requested ascending harmonic minor scale in whole notes. Above each scale degree, write the third and fifth to make a triad, adding accidentals as needed for that key. Use the leading tone (raised) for triads built on $\hat{5}$ and $\hat{7}$. Write M (major), m (minor), or d (diminished) under each triad to show the quality, then provide the Roman numeral.

(1)

Triad quality:	m	d	M	m	m	M	M
Roman numeral: b:	i	ii°	III	iv	v	VI	VII

(2)

Triad quality:	m	d	M	m	m	M	M
Roman numeral: c:	i	ii°	III	iv	v	VI	VII

(3)

Triad quality:	m	d	M	m	m	M	M
Roman numeral: f#:	i	ii°	III	iv	v	VI	VII

(4)

Triad quality:	m	d	M	m	m	M	M
Roman numeral: d:	i	ii°	III	iv	v	VI	VII

B. Identifying major and minor triads

Identify the root and quality of each triad below (e.g., B♭m).

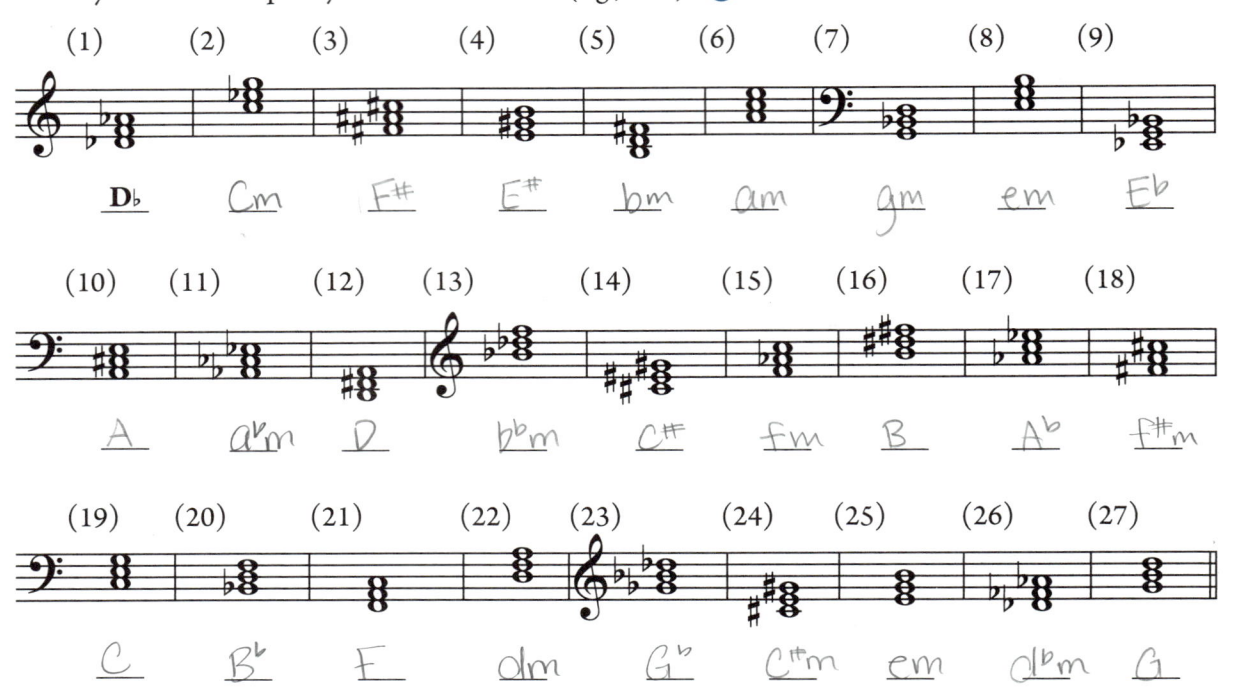

(1) D♭   (2) Cm   (3) F#   (4) E#   (5) bm   (6) am   (7) gm   (8) em   (9) E♭

(10) A   (11) a♭m   (12) D   (13) b♭m   (14) C#   (15) fm   (16) B   (17) A♭   (18) f#m

(19) C   (20) B♭   (21) E   (22) dm   (23) G♭   (24) c#m   (25) em   (26) d♭m   (27) G

C. Identifying major and minor triads in musical contexts

In the following excerpt, identify each chord by writing the triad (stacked in thirds) on the staff. Then in the blanks below, write M (for major) or m (minor) to indicate the chord quality. Remember to apply accidentals from the key signature. Finally, write a Roman numeral for each chord in the key specified. (For now, ignore circled notes.) Two chords are in first inversion: for these add the figure 6 to the Roman numeral.

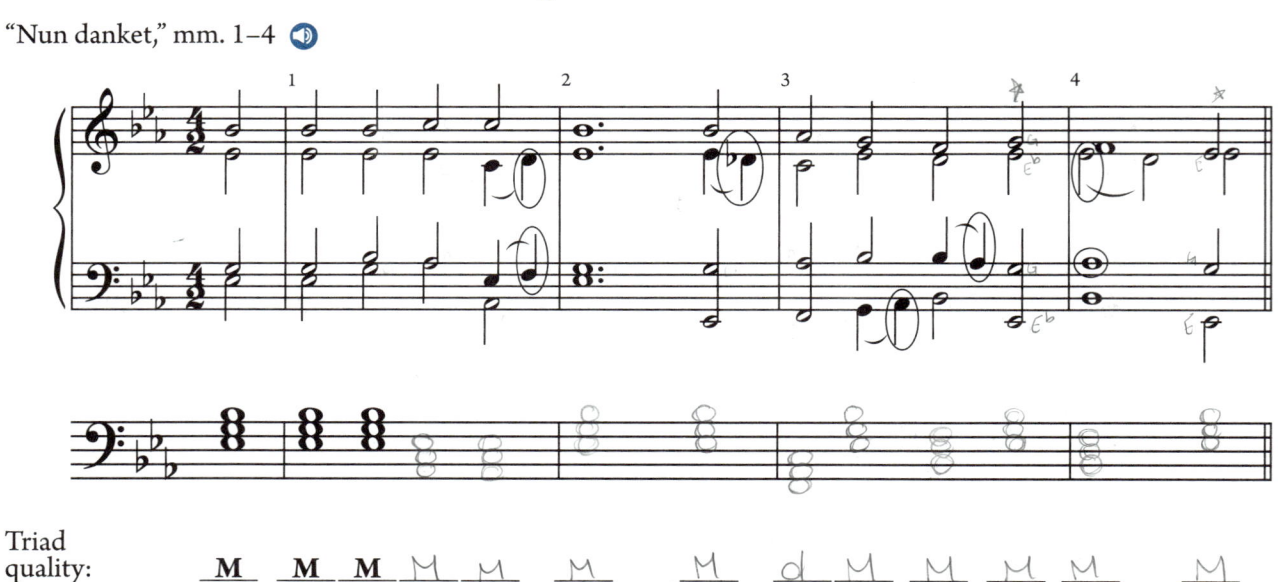

"Nun danket," mm. 1–4

Triad quality: M M M M M M M d M M M M M

Roman numeral: E♭: I I I⁶ IV IV I I ii° I⁶ III I III I

Workbook ASSIGNMENT 9.3

A. Writing major triads

Write the major key signature requested, then write the tonic triad (built from scale degrees $\hat{1}$, $\hat{3}$, and $\hat{5}$), using accidentals from the key signature.

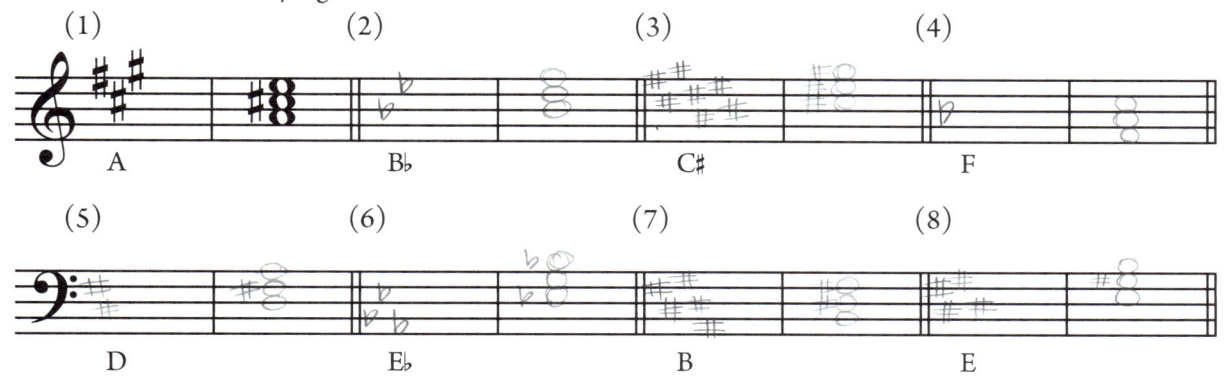

(1) A (2) B♭ (3) C♯ (4) F

(5) D (6) E♭ (7) B (8) E

Write major triads above each note below. First draw the note heads (line-line-line or space-space-space), then think of the major key signature of the bottom note to help you spell the chord.

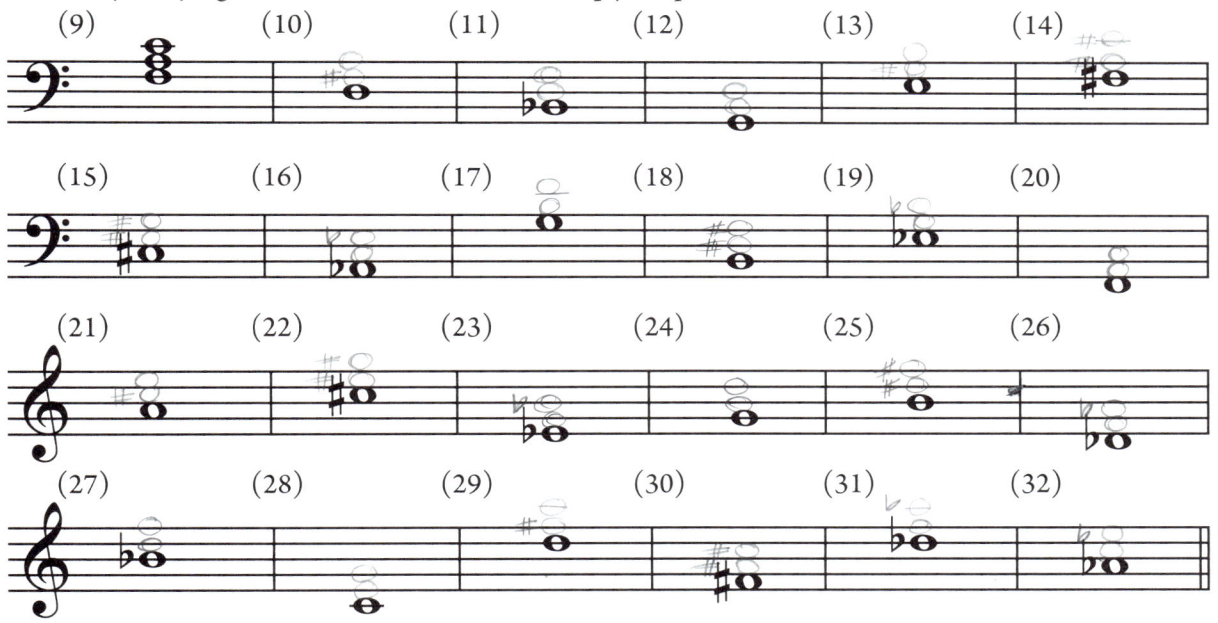

(9) (10) (11) (12) (13) (14)

(15) (16) (17) (18) (19) (20)

(21) (22) (23) (24) (25) (26)

(27) (28) (29) (30) (31) (32)

B. Writing minor triads

Rewrite each major triad below, lowering its third to make a minor triad.

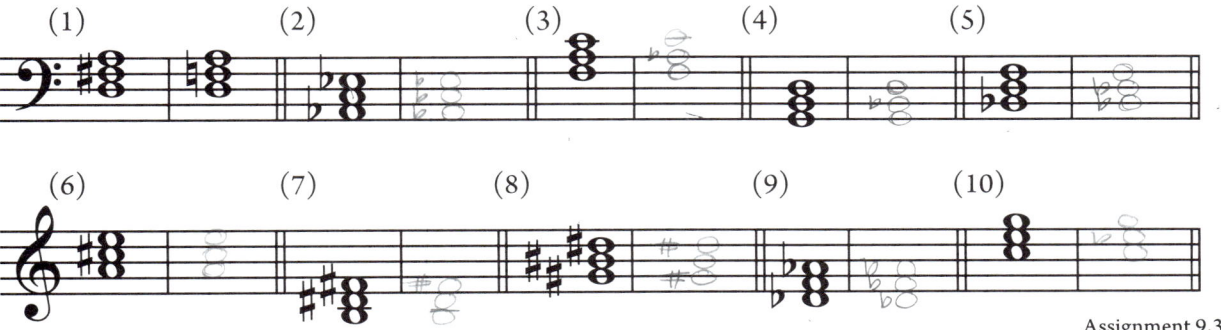

(1) (2) (3) (4) (5)

(6) (7) (8) (9) (10)

Assignment 9.3   247

Consider each pitch below as the root of a minor triad, then complete the triad.

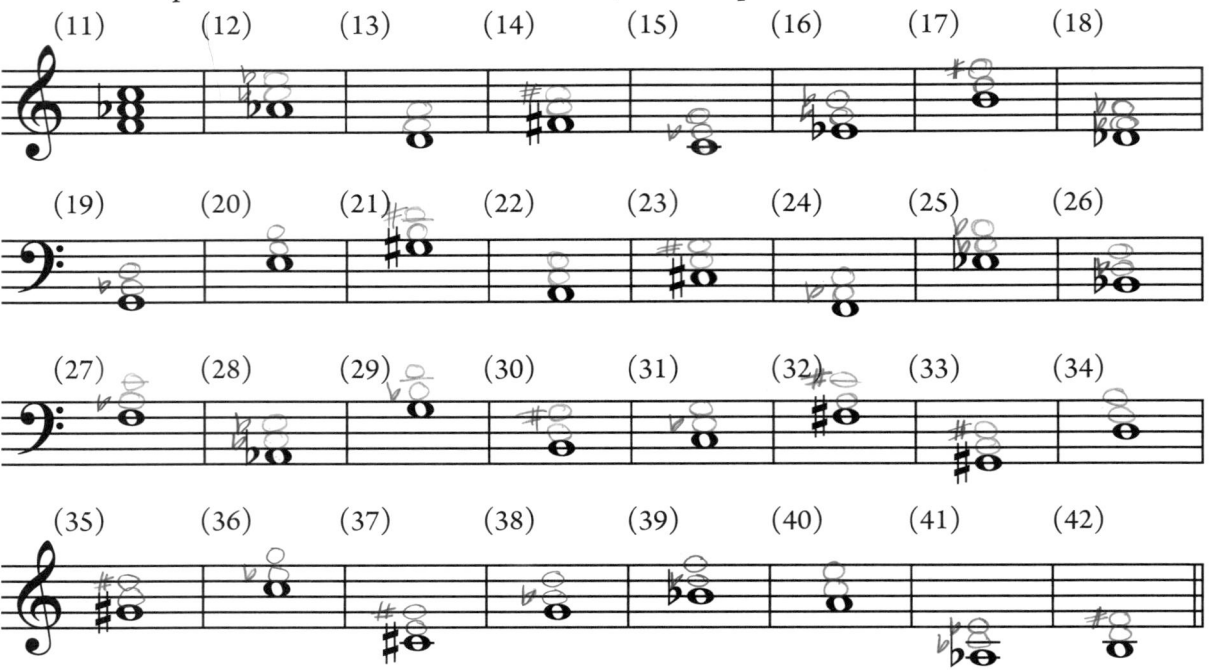

C. Writing triads in inversion

Write the specified triads in keyboard style (three notes in the right hand and one in the left).

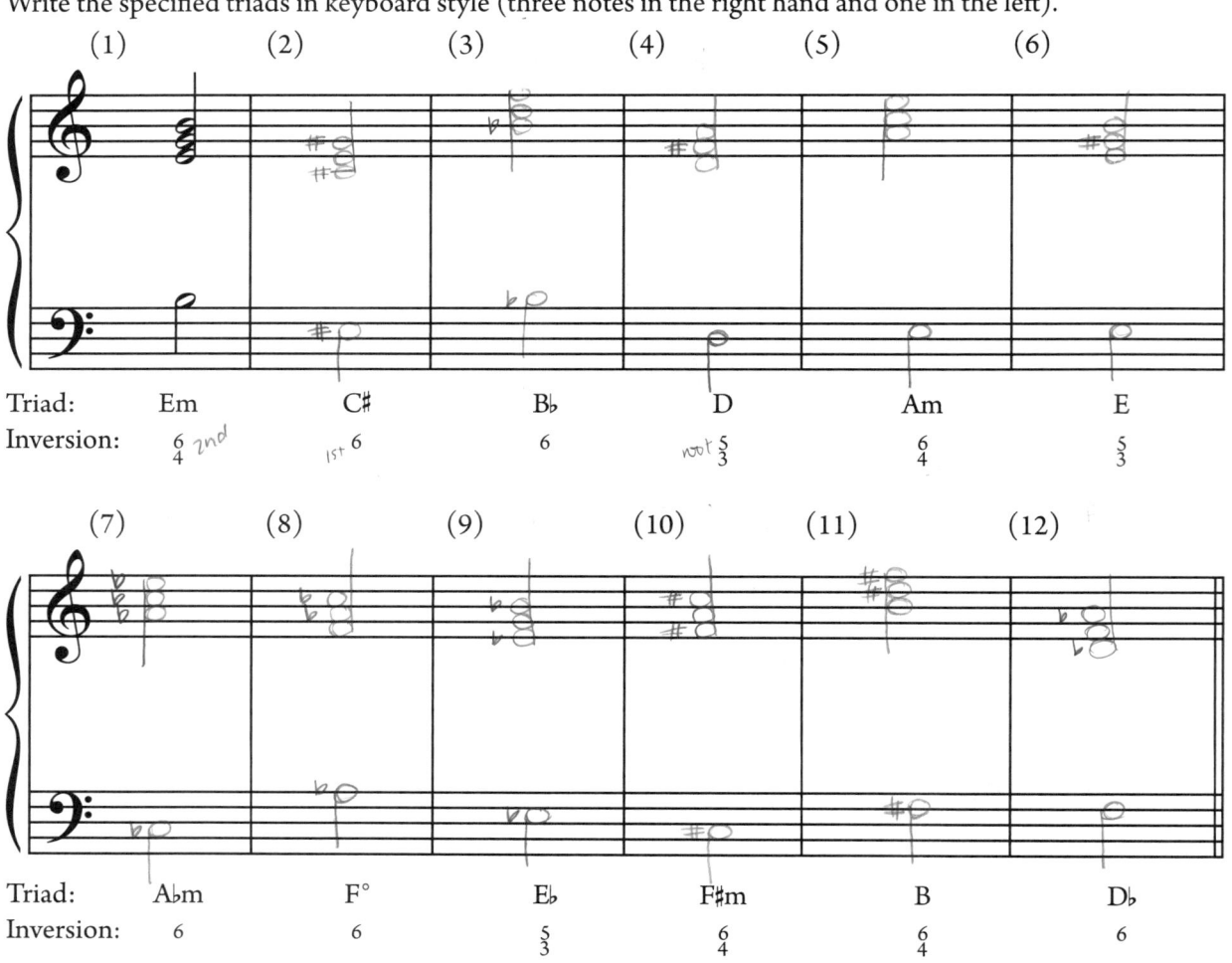

	(1)	(2)	(3)	(4)	(5)	(6)
Triad:	Em	C♯	B♭	D	Am	E
Inversion:	$^6_4$ 2nd	1st 6	6	root $^5_3$	$^6_4$	$^5_3$

	(7)	(8)	(9)	(10)	(11)	(12)
Triad:	A♭m	F°	E♭	F♯m	B	D♭
Inversion:	6	6	$^5_3$	$^6_4$	$^6_4$	6

248   CHAPTER NINE   Triads and the Dominant Seventh Chord

NAME _____

Workbook ASSIGNMENT 9.4

A. Writing major and minor triads

Write each triad specified below.

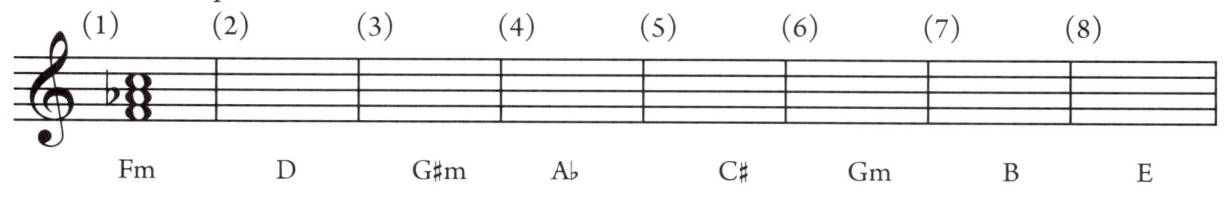

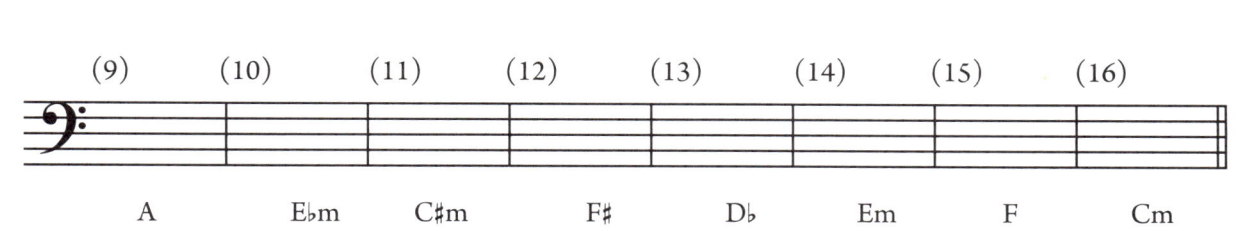

(1) Fm (2) D (3) G♯m (4) A♭ (5) C♯ (6) Gm (7) B (8) E

(9) A (10) E♭m (11) C♯m (12) F♯ (13) D♭ (14) Em (15) F (16) Cm

B. Writing dominant seventh chords

Write a dominant seventh chord above each given root, following one of the methods described in the chapter. Don't change the given pitch.

(1) (2) (3) (4) (5) (6) (7) (8)

(9) (10) (11) (12) (13) (14) (15) (16)

C. Writing triads

Write the requested triads below, following one of the methods described in the chapter. Don't change the given pitch. An example is shown for each set of triads, with the starting note indicated by an arrow.

Each pitch below is the root of a triad.

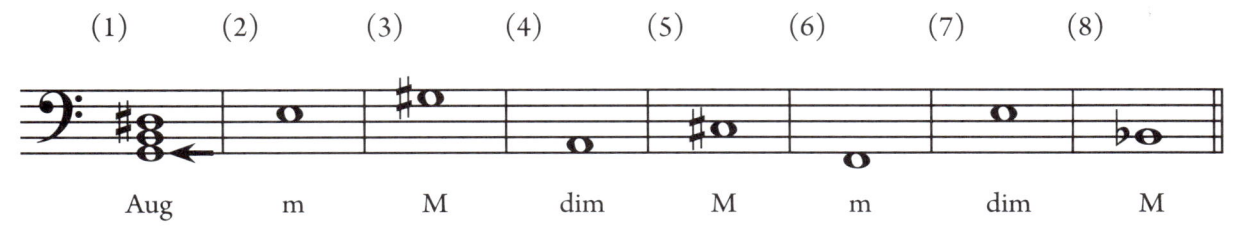

(1) Aug (2) m (3) M (4) dim (5) M (6) m (7) dim (8) M

Each pitch below is the third of a triad.

(9) (10) (11) (12) (13) (14) (15) (16)

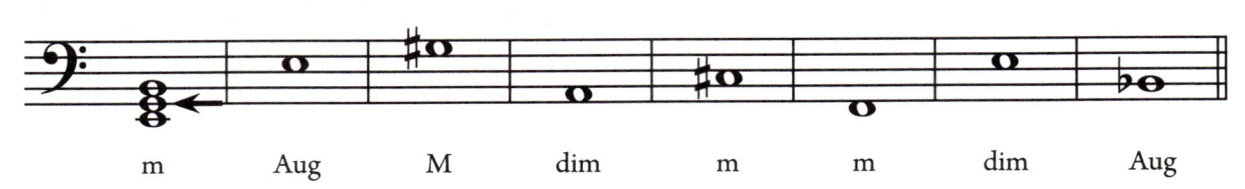

m   Aug   M   dim   m   m   dim   Aug

Each pitch below is the fifth of a triad.

(17) (18) (19) (20) (21) (22) (23) (24)

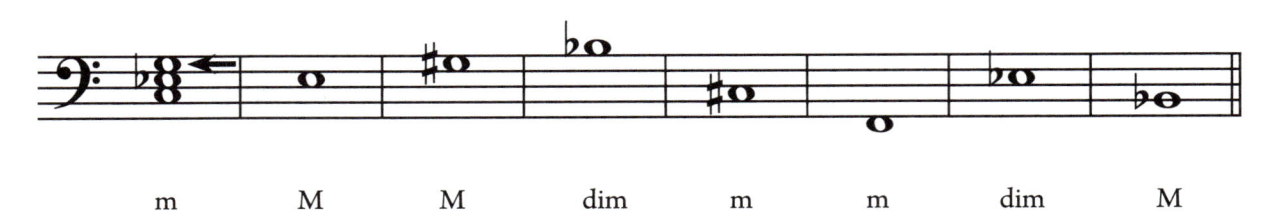

m   M   M   dim   m   m   dim   M

D. Identifying major and minor triads in musical contexts

In the following excerpt, identify each chord by writing the triad (stacked in thirds) on the staff. Then in the blanks below, write M (for major) or m (minor) to indicate the chord quality. Remember to apply accidentals from the key signature. Finally, write a Roman numeral for each chord in the key specified.

Johann Pachelbel, Canon in D Major, mm. 1–2

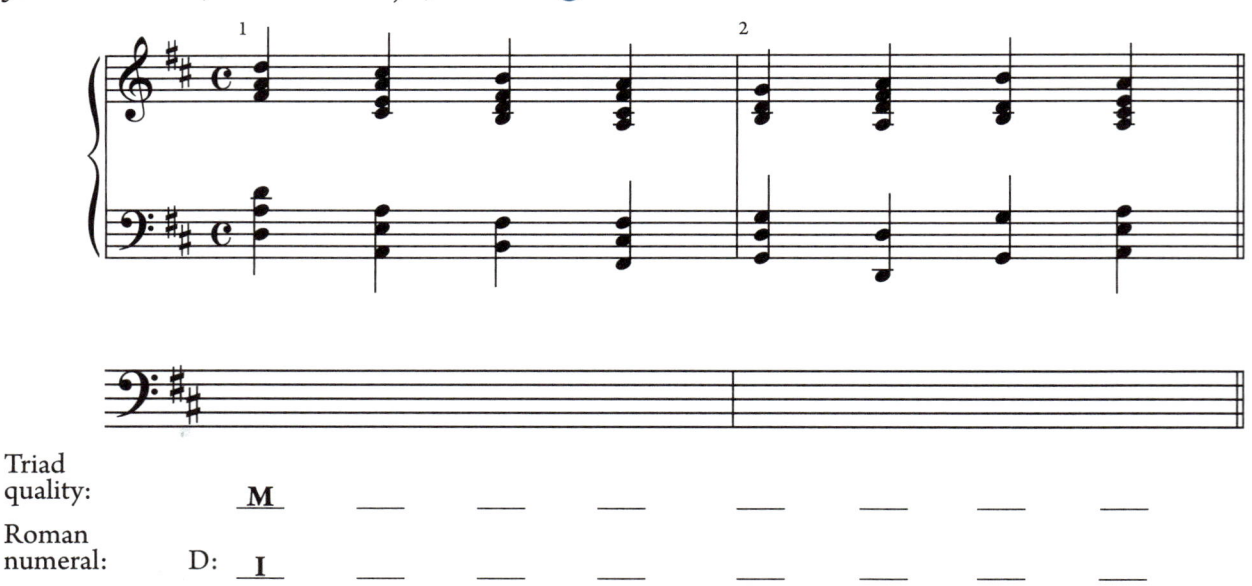

Triad quality: M ___ ___ ___ ___ ___ ___ ___

Roman numeral: D: I ___ ___ ___ ___ ___ ___ ___

Workbook   AURAL SKILLS 9.1

Listen to the beginning of a piano work by Franz Schubert, and complete the following exercises.

1. Throughout the excerpt, the melody is doubled at which interval?

(a) m3 (b) P5 (c) M6 (d) P8

2. Beginning with an eighth-note anacrusis, notate the rhythm of the excerpt in compound duple meter. Write bar lines and beam notes to show correct beat groups.

3. Beginning with $\hat{1}$–$\hat{1}$–♭$\hat{3}$–$\hat{5}$ (do–do–me–sol), write the melody with solfège syllables or scale-degree numbers.

4. Beginning with C4, notate the pitches of the melody on the staff below.

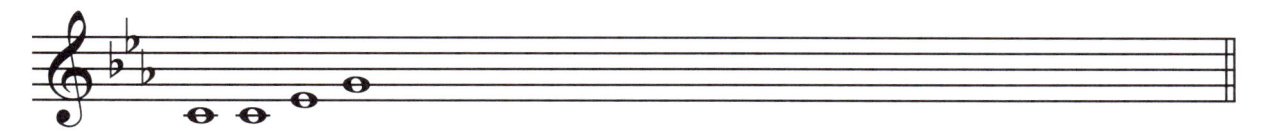

5. On which scale is this melody based?

(a) major   (c) harmonic minor
(b) natural minor

6. Referring to your answers to questions 2–4, notate both pitches and rhythm of the melody on the staff below.

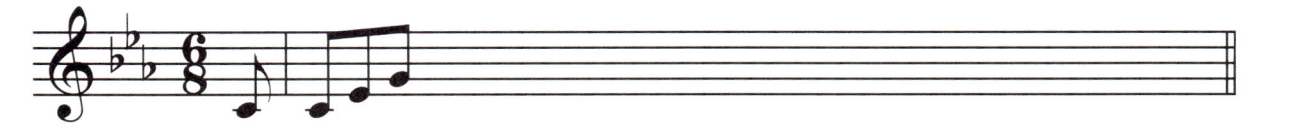

7. Rewrite the melody in the key of D minor. For help, recall the syllables or numbers in question 3.

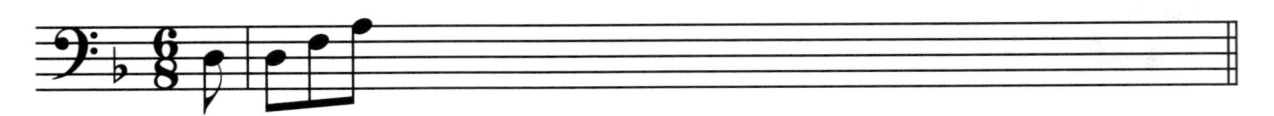

8. On the staff below, transcribe the answer to question 7 to its parallel major key. Write an appropriate key signature and then the time signature. (Remember: Parallel major has the same tonic pitch but a different key signature.)

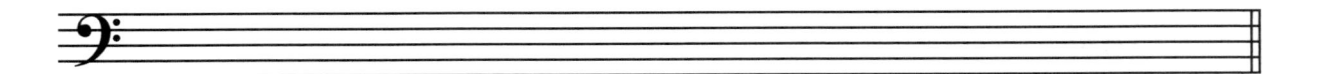

9. On the staff below, transcribe the answer to question 7 to its relative major key. Write key and time signatures.

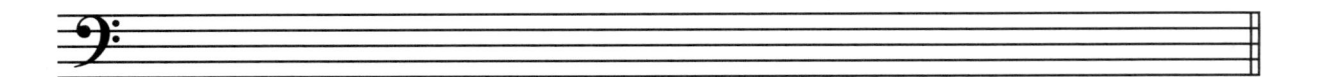

NAME _____

Workbook AURAL SKILLS 9.2

Composing and performing melodies

1. Compose two melodies that incorporate melodic thirds within the tonic triad.
   - Choose a different tonic pitch for each melody, one in a major key and one in a minor key. Write one in treble clef and one in bass clef.
   - Write the correct key signature. Choose a key that you can sing comfortably.
   - Include at least 10–12 pitches in each melody, starting on the tonic pitch. Create interesting rhythms and contours.
   - If you write $\hat{7}$, be sure that it moves up to $\hat{1}$. If you write $\flat\hat{7}$, it should move down to $\flat\hat{6}$.
   - Add tempo and dynamic markings, and make the score appear as musical as possible.

2. Prepare to perform your melodies in the following ways.
   - Sing on letter names, solfège syllables, or scale-degree numbers.
   - Play at the keyboard or other instrument.
   - Play on an instrument while you sing along.

Melody 1

Melody 2

TOPICS

- triads on $\hat{1}$, $\hat{4}$, and $\hat{5}$ and the seventh chord on $\hat{5}$
- harmonizing major melodies with the basic phrase model
- cadence types
- the subdominant in the basic phrase
- melodic embellishments and melody harmonization
- harmonizing minor-key melodies

MUSIC

- Johann Sebastian Bach, "Wachet auf"
- Chartres
- "Come, Ye Thankful People Come"
- "For He's a Jolly Good Fellow"
- Stephen Foster, "Oh! Susanna"
- "Go Down, Moses"
- "Home on the Range"
- "Michael Finnigin"
- "My Country, 'Tis of Thee"
- Joel Phillips, "Blues for Norton"
- Rosa Mystica
- Franz Schubert, Waltz in B Minor
- "Wayfaring Stranger"

CHAPTER 10
Melody Harmonization and Cadences

Triads on $\hat{1}$, $\hat{4}$, and $\hat{5}$ and the Seventh Chord on $\hat{5}$

Three triads often encountered in major- and minor-key pieces are those built on $\hat{1}$, $\hat{4}$, and $\hat{5}$—the tonic, subdominant, and dominant triads. They may appear as chords in an accompaniment or may form the framework for a melody. Listen to the opening of "Come, Ye Thankful People Come" in Example 10.1. The hymn begins with the pitches of the tonic triad in the key of F major: F–A–C ($\hat{1}$–$\hat{3}$–$\hat{5}$). The example ends with notes from the dominant triad in F major; C–E–G ($\hat{5}$–$\hat{7}$–$\hat{2}$), followed by a return of the tonic.

EXAMPLE 10.1 "Come, Ye Thankful People Come," mm. 1–2

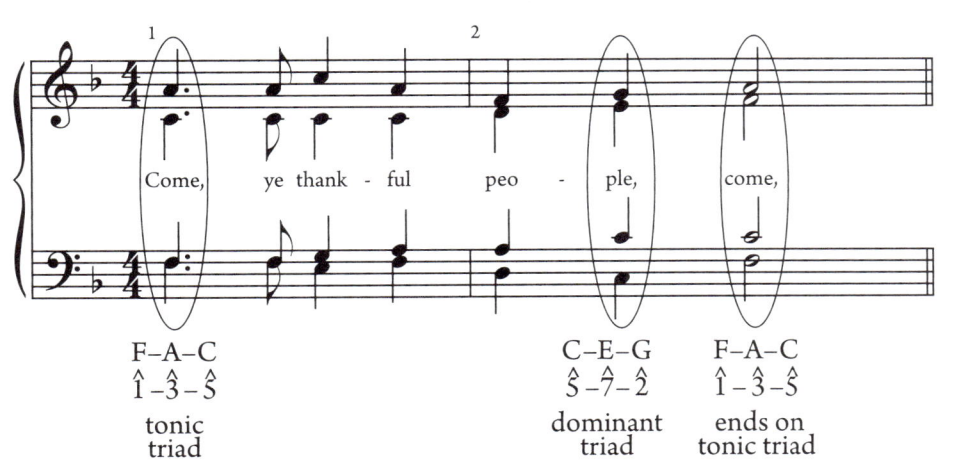

F–A–C
$\hat{1}$–$\hat{3}$–$\hat{5}$
tonic triad

C–E–G
$\hat{5}$–$\hat{7}$–$\hat{2}$
dominant triad

F–A–C
$\hat{1}$–$\hat{3}$–$\hat{5}$
ends on tonic triad

KEY CONCEPT The **tonic** triad—formed from $\hat{1}$, $\hat{3}$ (or $\flat\hat{3}$) and $\hat{5}$—is the most essential element in creating a sense of the key.

255

A good way to locate the tonic triad at the keyboard is to play the five-finger pattern from $\hat{1}$ to $\hat{5}$ in Example 10.2, then press your thumb, middle, and little fingers down to make the chord.

EXAMPLE 10.2   The tonic triad in major keys

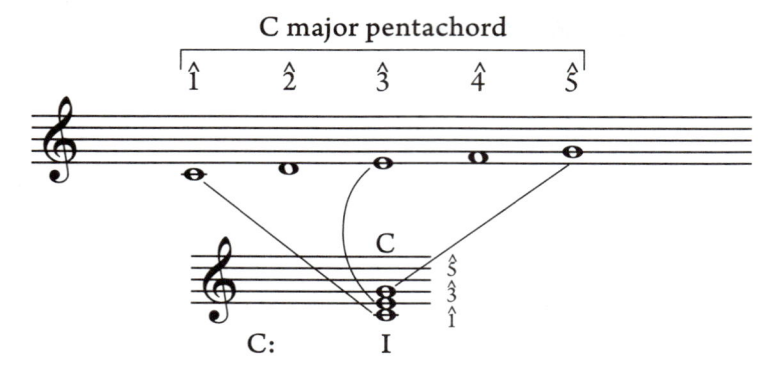

> **KEY CONCEPT** The next most essential chord for establishing a key is the **dominant** triad, $\hat{5}$–$\hat{7}$–$\hat{2}$ (Example 10.3).

Sometimes this triad is extended by another third to make $\hat{5}$–$\hat{7}$–$\hat{2}$–$\hat{4}$, the dominant seventh chord.

EXAMPLE 10.3   The dominant triad and dominant seventh chord in C major

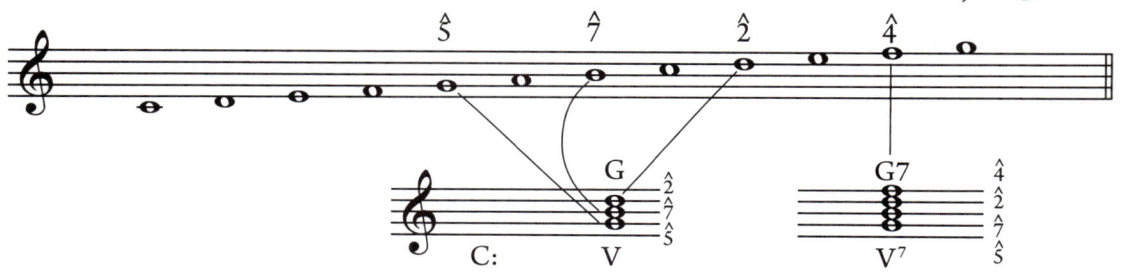

> **KEY CONCEPT** The chord built on $\hat{4}$, the **subdominant** triad, is $\hat{4}$–$\hat{6}$–$\hat{1}$ (Example 10.4).

Since the tonic, subdominant, and dominant triads in a major key are all major, they help give pieces a "major" sound.

EXAMPLE 10.4   The subdominant triad in C major

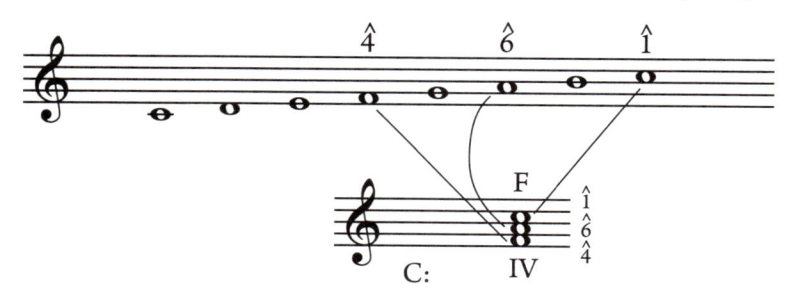

256   CHAPTER TEN   Melody Harmonization and Cadences

TRY IT #1

On the staves below, write the scale for each major key listed, using accidentals rather than key signatures. Label each pitch with a scale-degree number. Then write the tonic, subdominant, and dominant triads, as well as the dominant seventh chord, for each key, and label them with chord symbols above and Roman numerals below, as shown. The root of each chord is provided.

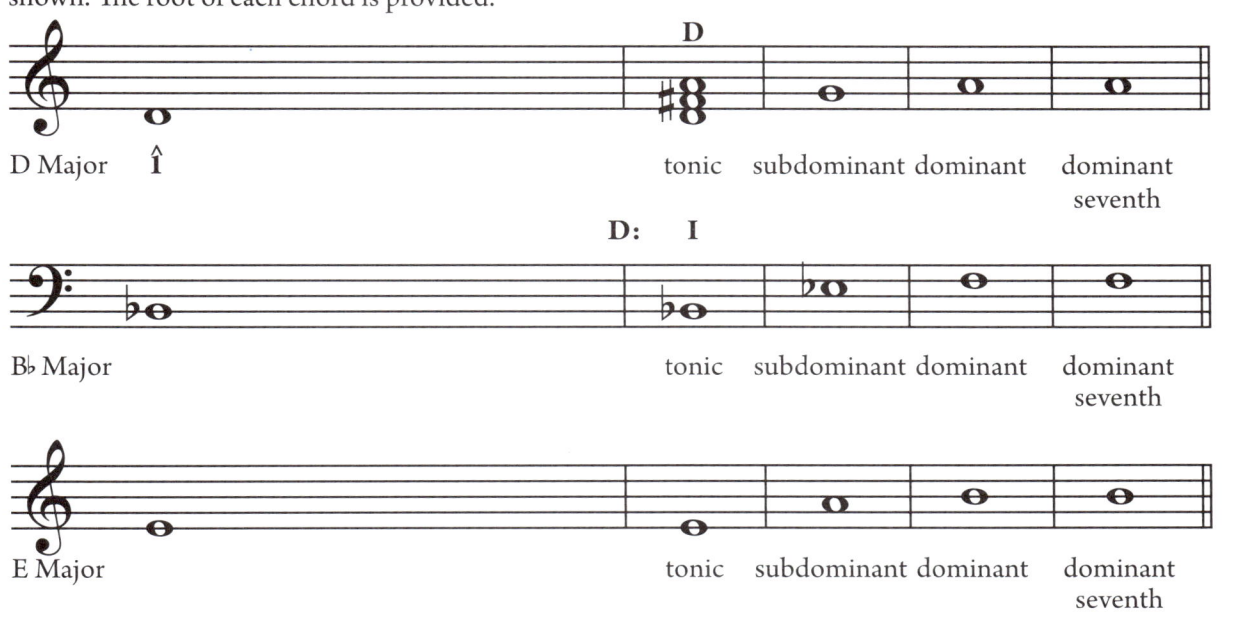

D Major $\hat{1}$ tonic   subdominant dominant   dominant seventh
          D: I

B♭ Major   tonic   subdominant dominant   dominant seventh

E Major   tonic   subdominant dominant   dominant seventh

The most common triads in minor-key pieces are also the tonic, subdominant, and dominant. If you spell these triads with the accidentals from a minor key signature, each has a minor quality. As we have seen, it is standard practice for composers to raise ♭$\hat{7}$ to make a leading tone, yielding the harmonic minor scale and a major dominant triad (Example 10.5).

EXAMPLE 10.5   Triads on $\hat{1}$, $\hat{4}$, and $\hat{5}$ (and V^7) in B harmonic minor

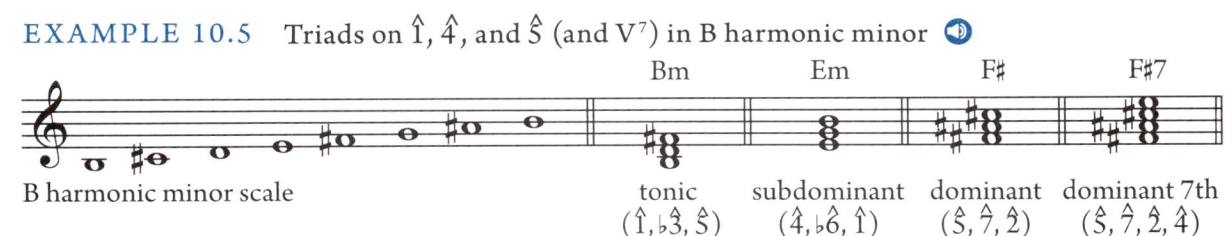

B harmonic minor scale

tonic ($\hat{1}$, ♭$\hat{3}$, $\hat{5}$)   subdominant ($\hat{4}$, ♭$\hat{6}$, $\hat{1}$)   dominant ($\hat{5}$, $\hat{7}$, $\hat{2}$)   dominant 7th ($\hat{5}$, $\hat{7}$, $\hat{2}$, $\hat{4}$)

b: i   iv   V   V^7

Listen to the opening measures of Schubert's Waltz in B Minor, consisting of a minor-key melody accompanied by the tonic triad and dominant seventh. Focus first on the melody in the right-hand part (treble clef), then write scale-degree numbers over the melody notes for measures 1–4.

EXAMPLE 10.6   Schubert, Waltz in B Minor, mm. 1–8

In measure 1, the scale degrees in both hands are exactly the same—$\hat{1}$, $\flat\hat{3}$, and $\hat{5}$ (*do–me–sol*), the tonic triad in B minor—but in different octaves and arrangements. The melody in this measure outlines the tonic triad, and is harmonized with that chord. In measure 2, the melody has $\hat{2}$, $\hat{4}$, and $\hat{5}$—pitches of the V^7 chord, which are accompanied by $\hat{5}$, $\hat{7}$, and $\hat{4}$. Both hands together make the complete V^7 (F♯–A♯–C♯–E).

> **KEY CONCEPT** When writing an accompaniment in a minor key, raise $\flat\hat{7}$ in the dominant harmony to make a leading tone (see Chapter 9), unless the melody features $\flat\hat{7}$ from the natural minor scale.

The arrangement of musical lines in Example 10.6—with melody in one hand and chords in the other—is called **melody and accompaniment**, one of the most common musical textures.

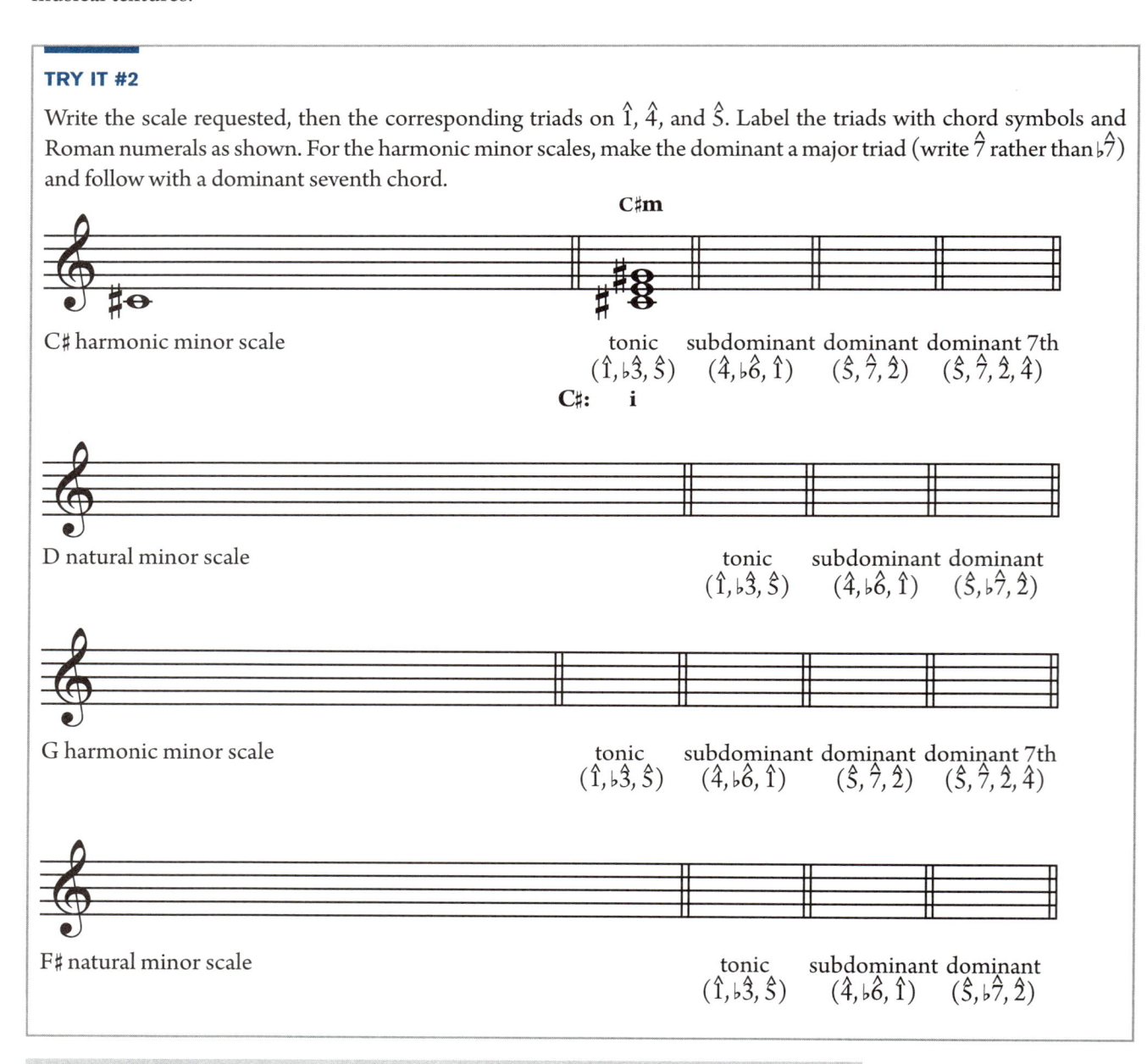

TRY IT #2

Write the scale requested, then the corresponding triads on $\hat{1}$, $\hat{4}$, and $\hat{5}$. Label the triads with chord symbols and Roman numerals as shown. For the harmonic minor scales, make the dominant a major triad (write $\hat{7}$ rather than $\flat\hat{7}$) and follow with a dominant seventh chord.

C♯ harmonic minor scale

             C♯m

tonic   subdominant dominant dominant 7th
($\hat{1}$,$\flat\hat{3}$,$\hat{5}$) ($\hat{4}$,$\flat\hat{6}$,$\hat{1}$) ($\hat{5}$,$\hat{7}$,$\hat{2}$) ($\hat{5}$,$\hat{7}$,$\hat{2}$,$\hat{4}$)

C♯: i

D natural minor scale

tonic   subdominant dominant
($\hat{1}$,$\flat\hat{3}$,$\hat{5}$) ($\hat{4}$,$\flat\hat{6}$,$\hat{1}$) ($\hat{5}$,$\flat\hat{7}$,$\hat{2}$)

G harmonic minor scale

tonic   subdominant dominant dominant 7th
($\hat{1}$,$\flat\hat{3}$,$\hat{5}$) ($\hat{4}$,$\flat\hat{6}$,$\hat{1}$) ($\hat{5}$,$\hat{7}$,$\hat{2}$) ($\hat{5}$,$\hat{7}$,$\hat{2}$,$\hat{4}$)

F♯ natural minor scale

tonic   subdominant dominant
($\hat{1}$,$\flat\hat{3}$,$\hat{5}$) ($\hat{4}$,$\flat\hat{6}$,$\hat{1}$) ($\hat{5}$,$\flat\hat{7}$,$\hat{2}$)

ASSIGNMENT 10.1

Look again at the opening of Schubert's waltz, shown in Example 10.7, focusing this time on the chords in the left-hand part. The Roman numerals below the staff indicate where Schubert uses tonic and dominant harmonies. The two harmonies alternate, one per measure, until measures 7–8. There, the pace of harmonic change speeds up, with two chords in measure 7 leading to a resting point in measure 8. This measure concludes a musical phrase.

> **KEY CONCEPT** A **phrase** is a basic unit of musical thought, similar to a sentence in language. The typical phrase—like most sentences—has a beginning, a middle, and an end. The end is marked by a **cadence**: the harmonic, melodic, and rhythmic features that make the phrase sound like a complete thought. Phrases are typically 4 or 8 measures in length.

EXAMPLE 10.7   Schubert, Waltz in B Minor, mm. 1–8

b: i V^7 i V^7 i V^7 i V^7 i
                                                          cadence

The rate at which chords change, called the **harmonic rhythm**, is one of the ways you can distinguish one style from another: a harmonic rhythm of one or two chords per measure is typical of waltzes; in hymns, every beat may have a new chord type; and in folk styles, the same chord may last for two or three measures. In all of these styles, the harmonic rhythm tends to speed up at the cadence to articulate the phrase ending.

Harmonizing Major Melodies with the Basic Phrase Model

We will now consider how to choose chords to accompany a melody. This process is called **harmonizing** a melody.

Listen to "Oh! Susanna" while following the score in your anthology (p. 363). At the second verse, where the guitar accompaniment begins, listen to how the chords change.

Example 10.8 shows the second verse harmonized with two chords: D (the tonic) and A7 (the dominant seventh). The melody helps the accompanist decide which chords to use. For example, measures 1–3 feature Ds, F♯s, and As, while measure 4 begins with an E that would clash with a D chord but works well with an A7. (The circled notes, labeled P and N, are not part of the chord; these will be discussed on p. 265.)

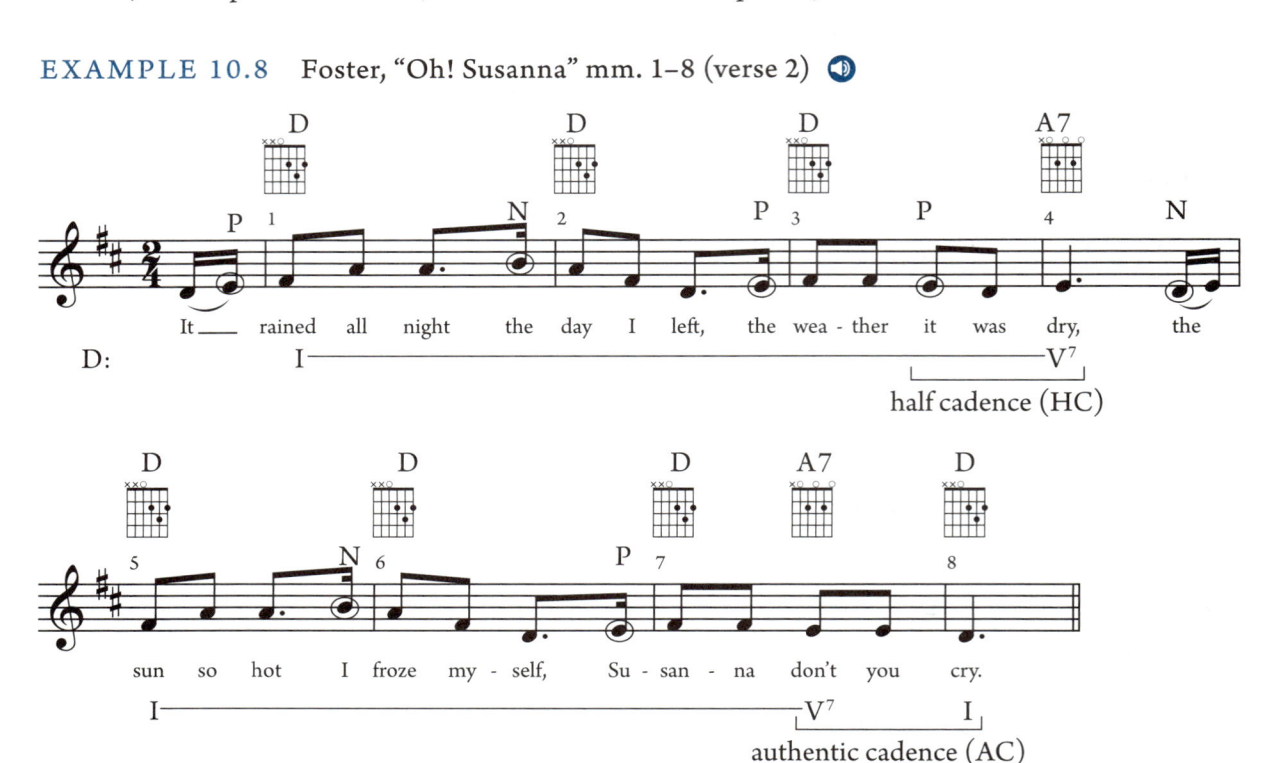

EXAMPLE 10.8   Foster, "Oh! Susanna" mm. 1–8 (verse 2)

[Musical notation: measures 1–4 with lyrics "It rained all night the day I left, the weather it was dry, the" — chords D, D, D, A7. Harmonic analysis in D: I——V⁷, marked half cadence (HC). Circled notes labeled P and N.]

[Musical notation: measures 5–8 with lyrics "sun so hot I froze myself, Susanna don't you cry." — chords D, D, D, A7, D. Harmonic analysis: I——V⁷—I, marked authentic cadence (AC).]

Also shown above the staff as part of the chord symbols are fretboard diagrams, illustrating guitar fingerings. The vertical lines represent guitar strings, the horizontal lines show the frets, and the black dots indicate where to place your fingers. (See Appendix 8 or explore the Virtual Guitar on StudySpace for more on guitar chords.)

Chords that harmonize a melody usually appear in a specific order, called a **chord progression**. A simple folk song may require only two chords: tonic and dominant. The tonic chord usually comes first to establish the key, followed by a dominant triad or seventh chord.

> **KEY CONCEPT** After the chords progress from tonic to dominant, they almost always return "home" to tonic in a progression known as the **basic phrase**: I–V–I. Use the basic phrase progression to guide you in melody harmonization; as we add more chords we will show their positions within the basic phrase.

Cadence Types

Every phrase ends with a cadence. Cadences are typically marked by a longer melody note (as in mm. 4 and 8 of Example 10.8) or by rests that break up the flow of the tune. Importantly, they are also marked by specific melodic–harmonic patterns known as the half, authentic, plagal, and deceptive cadence types. Of these, the half and authentic types are by far the most common.

Phrases may end on a dominant chord for an inconclusive sound. Listen again to Example 10.8, focusing on the end of the first phrase, at the words "it was dry" (m. 4). This type of ending is called a **half cadence** (abbreviated **HC**). The word "half" signals that the musical idea has not come to an end but must continue to another phrase before it can sound complete. Half cadences end on a dominant harmony accompanying a melody that ends on $\hat{2}$ (or less commonly on $\hat{5}$ or $\hat{7}$).

Often, as in "Oh! Susanna," a phrase ending on a half cadence is paired with another phrase that begins the same way but returns to tonic. This basic phrase progression sounds more complete, and the music can end here. Measures 5–8 of Example 10.8 follow this pattern. The cadence in measure 8, called an **authentic cadence** (**AC**), is formed when a dominant harmony moves to a tonic harmony to make a conclusive phrase ending. For the strongest type of ending, called a **perfect authentic cadence** (**PAC**), use the progression V or V^7 to I with both chords in root position (root of the chord in the bass) and the melody ending with $\hat{2}$–$\hat{1}$ or $\hat{7}$–$\hat{1}$. For a somewhat less conclusive authentic cadence—an **imperfect authentic cadence** (**IAC**)—end the melody on $\hat{3}$ or $\hat{5}$ or write the dominant harmony in an inversion.

You may encounter two additional types of inconclusive cadences in music: the deceptive cadence and the plagal cadence. To see a deceptive cadence, look at Example 10.9, a chorale by J. S. Bach. The melody in measures 19 and 20 descends $\hat{3}$–$\hat{2}$–$\hat{1}$ to the tonic (E♭), and the V^7 seems prepared to resolve to I, but instead it moves to vi—a chord that shares two of its three pitches with I (E♭ and G), but has a minor quality. This bait-and-switch strategy gives the cadence its name: a **deceptive cadence** (**DC**) moves from V or V^7 to vi, instead of I. In this chorale, Bach places the deceptive cadence here because he is setting two phrases with different text but the same melody—after the DC, the repetition of the phrase (mm. 21–24) ends with a PAC.

EXAMPLE 10.9   Bach, "Wachet auf," mm. 17–24

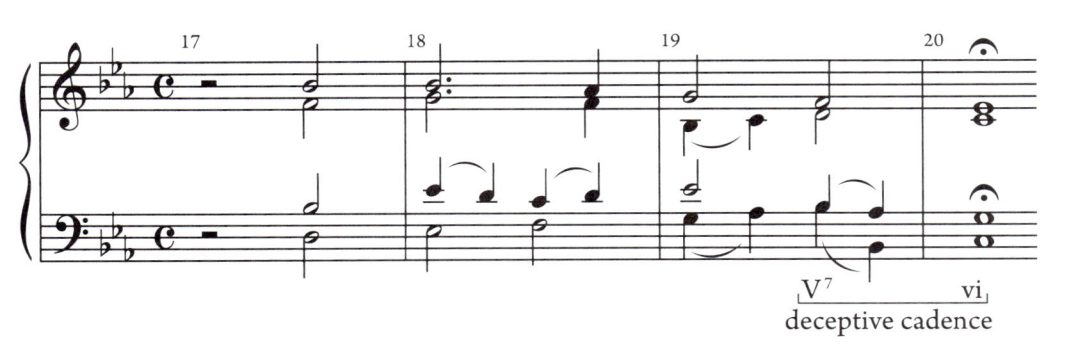

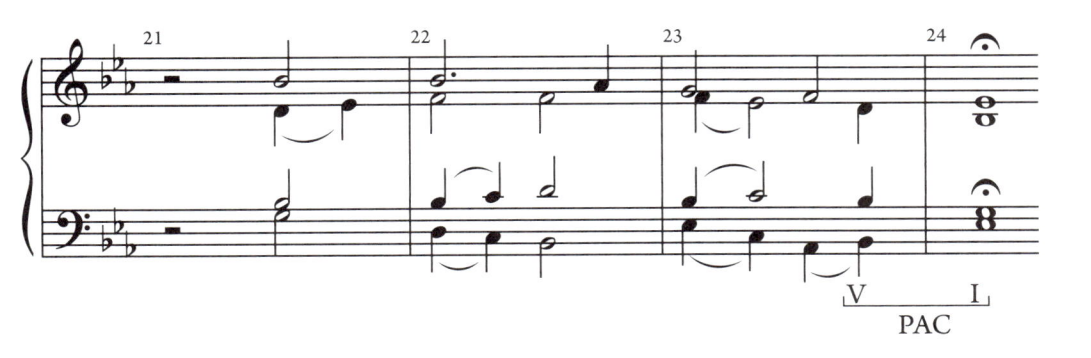

Not all V–vi motion creates a deceptive cadence; you may instead find a deceptive resolution of the dominant harmony in the middle of a phrase that cadences a few beats, or even a few measures, later. For an example, listen to the opening of "My Country, 'Tis of Thee," shown in Example 10.10.

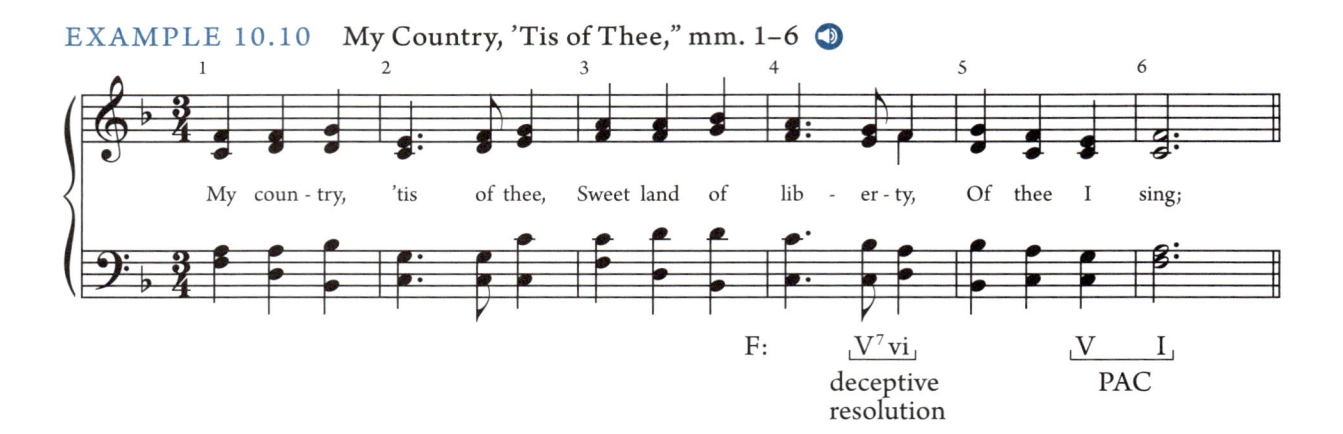

EXAMPLE 10.10 My Country, 'Tis of Thee," mm. 1–6

Although phrases are typically organized in four-bar units, this one consists of four bars plus two additional measures that end with a PAC. The first four bars end with a **deceptive resolution** of V^7 to vi; here, the deception is not really a cadence, since the music moves on immediately to the PAC. This type of V–vi deceptive resolution is more common than a phrase ending with a true DC.

Plagal cadences consist of the root-position chords IV–I. This cadence is sometimes called an "Amen" cadence, because the progression IV–I harmonizes the word "Amen" in many hymn books. Listen, for example, to the last words of "My Country, 'Tis of Thee" followed by the plagal "Amen" (Example 10.11). The PAC in measures 13–14 creates a stronger arrival on tonic than the plagal cadence, because of its leading-tone-to-tonic resolution. For this reason, plagal cadences directly following a PAC are often viewed as an extension of the tonic sound, rather than as a true cadence. Another typical context for a plagal cadence is in the blues (see Chapter 12), as shown in Example 10.12. In this style, either the IV or I chord may include a seventh.

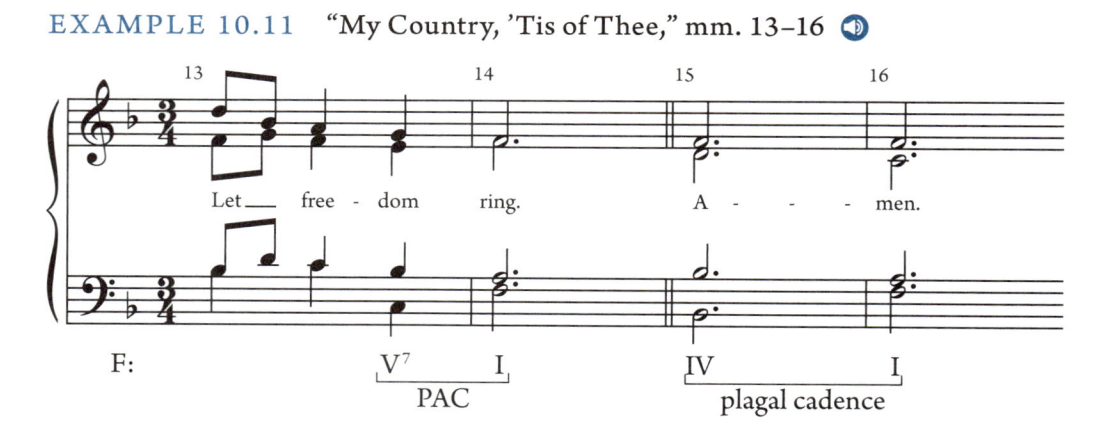

EXAMPLE 10.11 "My Country, 'Tis of Thee," mm. 13–16

EXAMPLE 10.12   Phillips, "Blues for Norton," mm. 20–24

[Musical score: Clarinet, Alto saxophone, Piano, and Bass parts. Piano and Bass show chord symbols C7, B♭7, F7. Roman numeral analysis in F: V⁷ — IV⁷ — I⁷, labeled "plagal cadence."]

SUMMARY

- Perfect authentic cadence (PAC), V or V⁷ to I or i in root position: ends with $\hat{1}$ in the soprano; the strongest conclusive cadence.
- Imperfect authentic cadence (IAC), V or V⁷ to I or i: ends with $\hat{3}$ or, less commonly, $\hat{5}$ in the soprano, or places the dominant harmony in inversion; a less conclusive cadence.
- Half cadence (HC), ends on V or V⁷; an inconclusive cadence.
- Deceptive cadence, V or V⁷ to vi or VI: avoids the expected tonic resolution; an inconclusive cadence.
- Plagal cadence, IV to I (or iv to i): may follow a stronger authentic cadence; more typical in popular styles such as the blues.

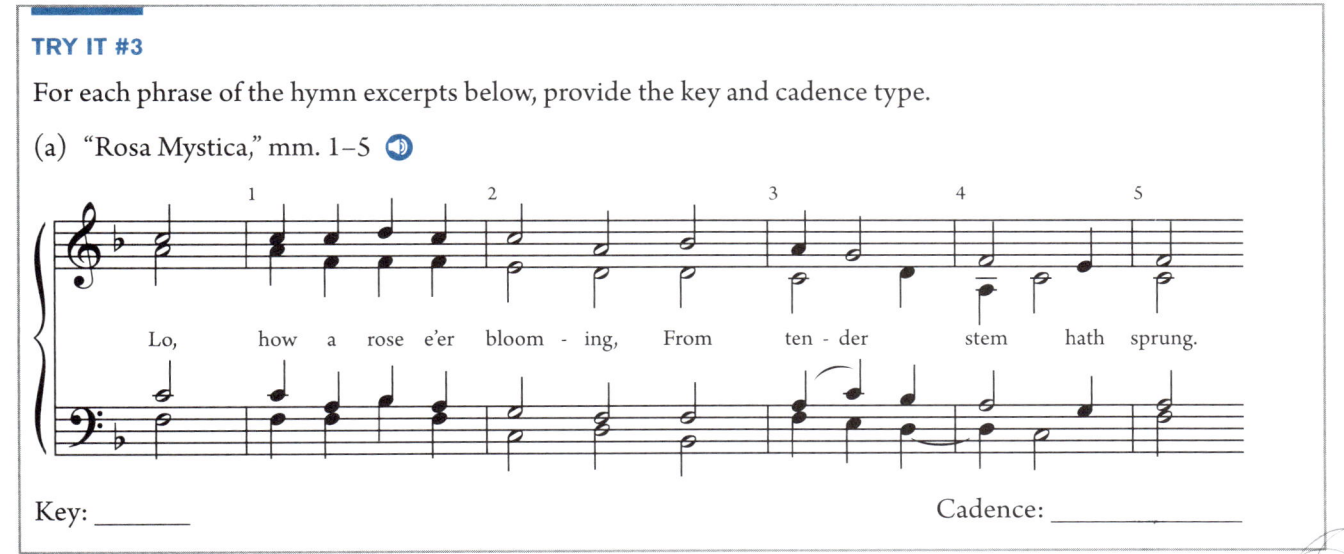

TRY IT #3

For each phrase of the hymn excerpts below, provide the key and cadence type.

(a) "Rosa Mystica," mm. 1–5

[Musical score: SATB hymn setting with text "Lo, how a rose e'er bloom-ing, From ten-der stem hath sprung."]

Key: _____   Cadence: _____

Cadence Types   **263**

TRY IT #3 (continued)

(b) Chartres, mm. 9–12

[Musical notation: Chartres, mm. 9–12, with lyrics "So of old the wise men watch-ing saw a lit-tle stran-ger star"]

Key: _____   Cadence: _____

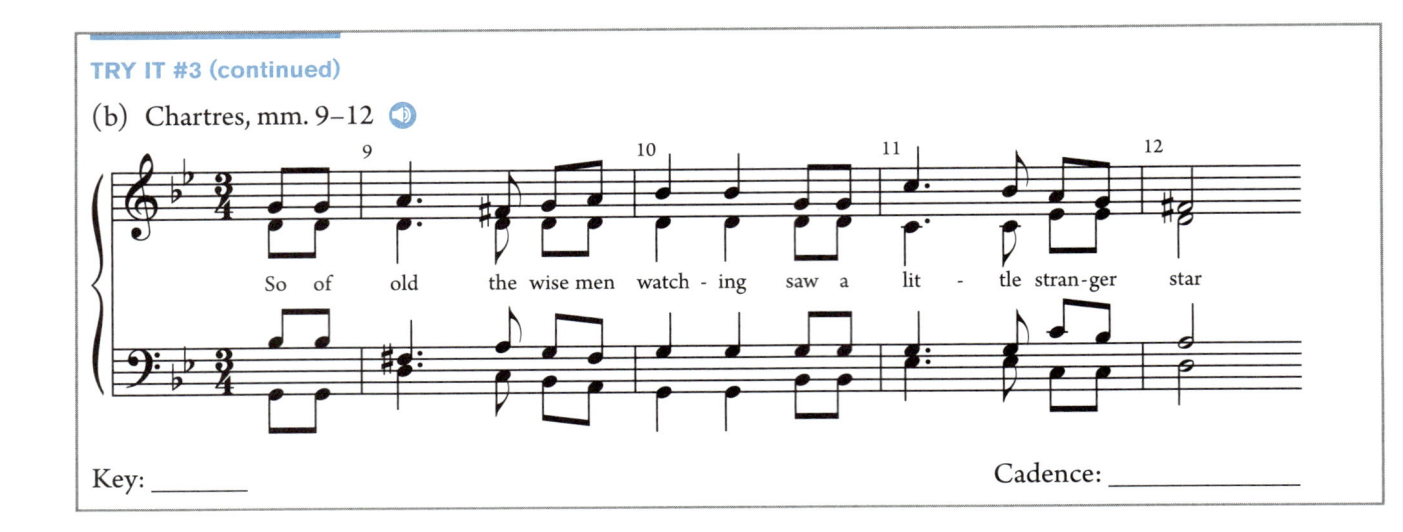

ASSIGNMENT 10.2, AURAL SKILLS 10.1, 10.2

The Subdominant in the Basic Phrase

To harmonize a slightly more elaborate phrase, you may need a subdominant chord. This triad usually appears in one of two places within the basic phrase. First, because it shares $\hat{1}$ with the tonic triad, it can appear between two tonic triads to extend the tonic sound. We hear this technique in "Home on the Range" (Example 10.13). Scale degrees $\hat{6}$ (E) and $\hat{4}$ (C) in measure 2 indicate that the IV chord would work well there. As in previous examples, circled notes are not part of the harmonies specified by the guitar chords.

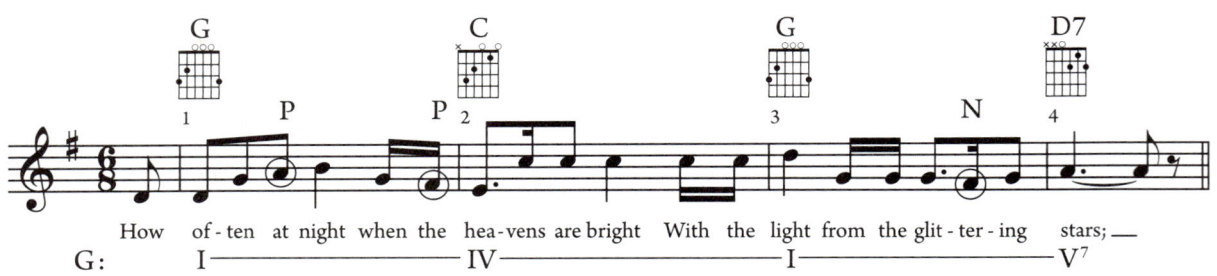

EXAMPLE 10.13   "Home on the Range," mm. 1–4 (verse 2)

[Musical notation with guitar chords G, C, G, D7; lyrics "How of-ten at night when the hea-vens are bright With the light from the glit-ter-ing stars;" harmonic analysis in G: I—IV—I—V⁷]

The second place you might see the subdominant triad is between the phrase's initial tonic and the dominant.

> **KEY CONCEPT** The subdominant harmony completes the basic phrase model: I–IV–V–I.

The subdominant provides additional harmonic interest in the phrase, leading away from tonic harmony and preparing for the arrival of the dominant. Example 10.14 illustrates both contexts for the subdominant triad in "For He's a Jolly Good Fellow." In the second half of the song, the F major triad in measure 5 leads to the subdominant (B♭) to prepare the V⁷–I perfect authentic cadence. In the first half, a IV chord appears in measure 2 between two tonic triads.

EXAMPLE 10.14   "For He's a Jolly Good Fellow," mm. 1–8

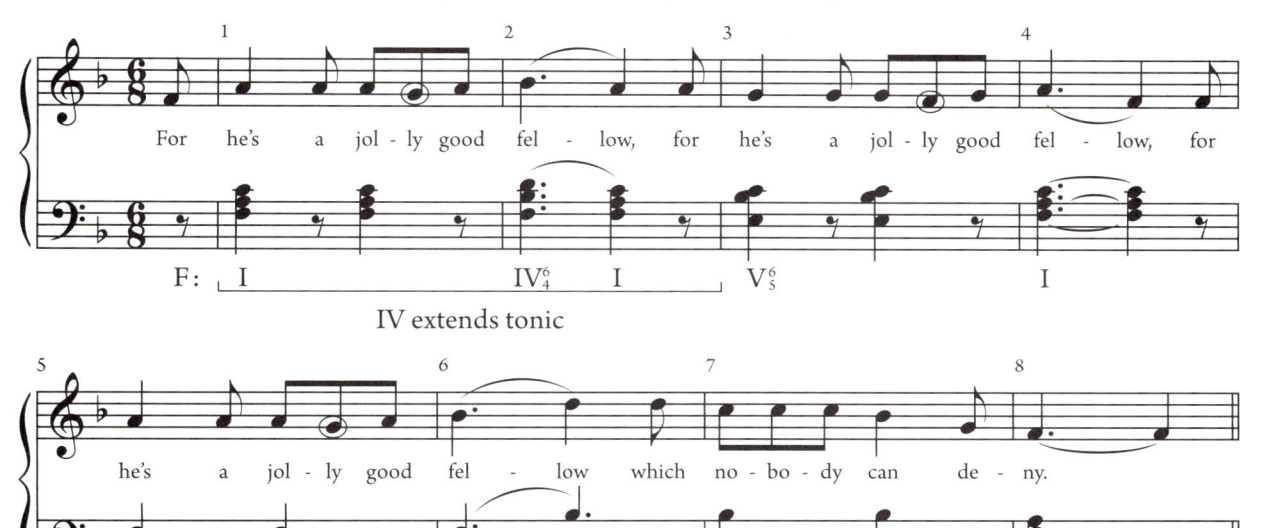

F: I   IV$^6_4$ I   V$^6_5$ I
        IV extends tonic

I   IV   V^7 I
     IV prepares dominant

SUMMARY

When harmonizing a melody, think of the melody as scale degrees.

- When $\hat{1}$, $\hat{3}$, and $\hat{5}$ appear near each other, harmonize them with a tonic triad.
- If $\hat{1}$ is repeated for a long time or if $\hat{4}$ and $\hat{6}$ appear, you might insert a subdominant triad, which can move back to the tonic or on to a dominant harmony.
- Though $\hat{5}$ can be harmonized with the tonic, when it appears in close proximity to $\hat{7}$ or $\hat{2}$, harmonize it with a V or V^7 chord.
- Keep this basic phrase progression in mind: I–IV–V–I.

Melodic Embellishments and Melody Harmonization

In the melodies we have looked at so far, there are some notes that don't fit into the accompanying chord. These notes are called **embellishing tones**: they embellish, or decorate, the melody by filling in between members of the chord. Look back at "Home on the Range" (Example 10.13). The circled A4 and F♯4 in measure 1 are called **passing tones**: the A4 passes by step between two chord tones (G4 and B4). The F♯4 passes between G4 (part of the I chord) and E4 (part of the IV chord). The circled F♯4 near the end of measure 3 is a **neighbor tone**—it moves by step away from the chord tone (G4) and comes right back. Passing tones and neighbor tones are the most common types of embellishing tones.

> **KEY CONCEPT** Neighbor tones reverse direction, stepping up (or down) from the chord tone to the neighbor, then stepping back down (or up) to the chord tone. Passing tones move in a single direction by step between two chord tones, filling in a third or fourth. Often embellishing tones appear on less emphasized beats or parts of the beat, or are shorter in duration than chord tones. When analyzing music, circle embellishing tones to show that they are not part of the chord.

In "Home on the Range," (Example 10.13) the chord tones appear on strong beats, and the embellishing tones are on weaker parts of the beat, which is typical for passing and neighbor tones. The embellishing tones are also relatively short in duration compared with the chord tones.

With your understanding of common embellishing tones, the basic phrase, and cadence types, you now should be able to harmonize a major-key melody on your own. Sing through or listen to "Michael Finnigin," given in Example 10.15, and write Roman numerals below the staff and chord symbols above to harmonize the tune. Find at least one place to write a IV chord. For each circled note, write P or N (for passing or neighbor tone), and label each cadence.

EXAMPLE 10.15   "Michael Finnigin"

[Musical notation: 8 measures in G major, 2/4 time, with lyrics:]

There was an old man named Mi-chael Fin-ni-gin, He had whis-kers on his chin-i-gin, The wind blew them off and they grew in-i-gin, Poor old Mi-chael Fin-ni-gin. Be-gin-i-gin!

G:

In the first two measures, most of the notes are $\hat{1}$, $\hat{3}$, and $\hat{5}$, members of the tonic triad in G major. These are harmonized with a tonic triad (G); you should have placed the chord symbol G above the staff and Roman numeral I below. Measures 3 and 4 feature mostly $\hat{5}$, $\hat{7}$, and $\hat{2}$, which belong to the dominant triad, D major. These four measures make a phrase with a tonic-to-dominant progression, ending with a HC in measure 4. Measures 5–6 are the same as measures 1–2 and may be harmonized the same. To create contrast between measure 5 and measure 1, you could insert a subdominant chord (C) between two tonic chords, I–IV–I, to harmonize the repeated Gs: "wind" (I), "blew them" (IV), "off" (I). Scale degrees $\hat{2}$ and $\hat{5}$ in measure 7 should be set with a V^7 (D7), leading to the final I chord (G) and making an AC in measure 8. Measures 5–8 make a complete basic phrase.

Harmonizing Minor-Key Melodies

You can harmonize minor melodies with triads on $\hat{1}$, $\hat{4}$, and $\hat{5}$ in much the same way as major-key melodies. The only difference is in the treatment of the seventh scale degree—whether to add an accidental to make a leading tone or to use the minor dominant (v). Compare the seventh scale degrees in two melodies, "Go Down, Moses" and "Wayfaring Stranger," shown in Examples 10.16 and 10.17, to consider how they should be harmonized.

EXAMPLE 10.16   "Go Down, Moses," mm. 1–8

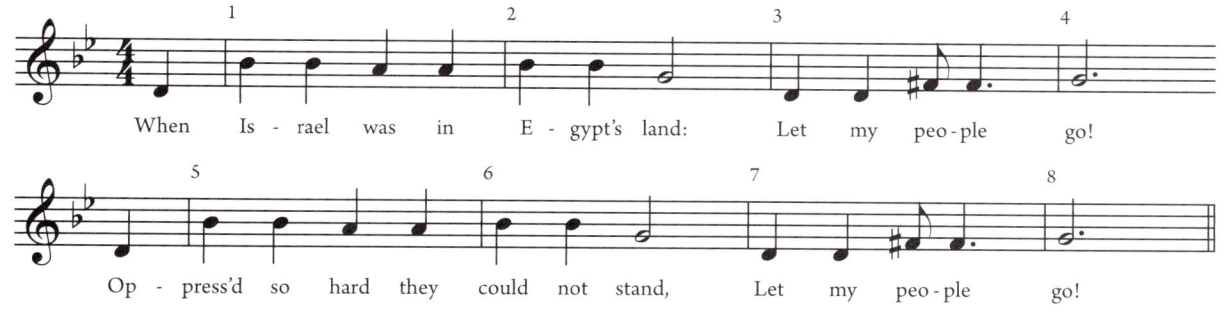

When Is - rael was in E - gypt's land: Let my peo - ple go!

Op - press'd so hard they could not stand, Let my peo - ple go!

EXAMPLE 10.17   "Wayfaring Stranger," mm. 1–8

I am a poor_____ way - far - ing stran - ger_____ a trav - 'ling

through_____ this world of woe;_____ yet there's no sick - - ness, toil or

dan - ger_____ in that bright world to which I go._____

KEY CONCEPT Before beginning any harmonization, sing through the melody on scale-degree numbers or solfège syllables or play it on an instrument to hear how it sounds. Then use the numbers or syllables to help choose appropriate chords.

"Go Down, Moses" is based on the G harmonic minor scale, with two flats in the key signature and an F♯ leading tone (making $\hat{7}-\hat{1}$). In contrast, "Wayfaring Stranger" shows no leading tone (C♯) and ends ♭$\hat{7}-\hat{1}$ (C♮–D); its pitches are drawn from the natural minor scale. Each melody ends with dominant-to-tonic motion, but "Go Down, Moses" calls for a major dominant triad in measure 7, and "Wayfaring Stranger" takes a minor dominant. To harmonize these melodies, use the chords in G harmonic minor and D natural minor, respectively.

In Example 10.18, the beginning of "Go Down, Moses," scale degrees appear beneath the staff and chord symbols above. Each chord choice corresponds with the melody, and the progression of chords follows the i–V–i basic phrase model. The dominant seventh at the cadence makes a harmonically strong ending.

EXAMPLE 10.18   "Go Down, Moses," mm. 1–4

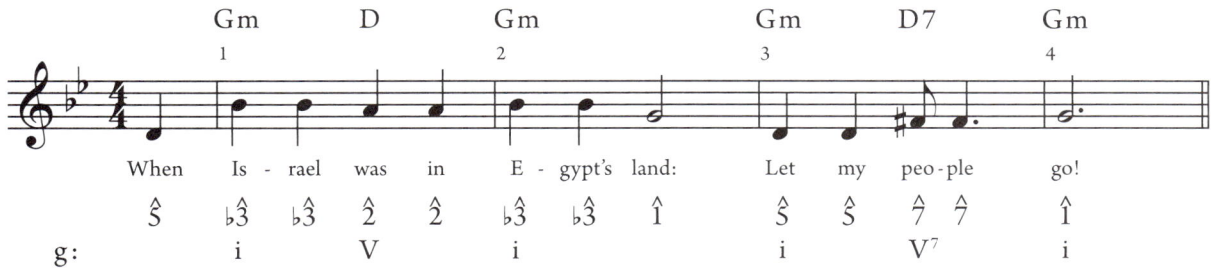

| Gm | D | Gm | Gm | D7 | Gm |

When Is - rael was in E - gypt's land: Let my peo - ple go!

$\hat{5}$ ♭$\hat{3}$ ♭$\hat{3}$ $\hat{2}$ $\hat{2}$ ♭$\hat{3}$ ♭$\hat{3}$ $\hat{1}$ $\hat{5}$ $\hat{5}$ $\hat{7}$ $\hat{7}$ $\hat{1}$

g: i   V   i   i   V⁷   i

Harmonizing Minor-Key Melodies   267

The second phrase of Example 10.16 is the same as the first and can be harmonized as shown in Example 10.18.

In Example 10.19, the end of "Wayfaring Stranger," the subdominant (Gm) in measure 7 harmonizes $\hat{4}$ (G) and extends the tonic sound. The circled G in measure 5 is a passing tone, moving between the chord tones F and A. Sing the melody while playing these chords on a guitar or keyboard.

EXAMPLE 10.19   "Wayfaring Stranger," mm. 5–8

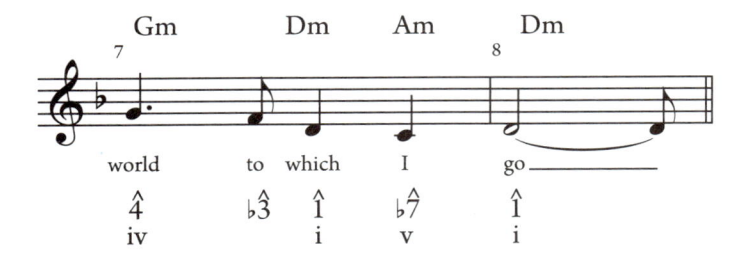

SUMMARY

To harmonize a melody with triads on $\hat{1}$, $\hat{4}$, and $\hat{5}$:
- First play or sing it with scale-degree numbers or solfège syllables.
- Let the scale-degree function of the melody notes (tonic, dominant, etc.) help you choose appropriate chords:

If the melody features	use
$\hat{1}$ or $\hat{3}$ (♭$\hat{3}$ in minor)	tonic harmony (I or i).
$\hat{2}$ or $\hat{7}$	dominant harmony (V or V^7).
$\hat{4}$ or $\hat{6}$ (♭$\hat{6}$ in minor)	subdominant harmony (IV or iv).
♭$\hat{7}$ in minor	minor dominant (v).
$\hat{5}$	either tonic or dominant harmony; let your ear be your guide.

- Plan phrase beginnings and endings first, then fill in the remaining chords.
- Listen for the end of each phrase. If the melody ends on $\hat{2}$, $\hat{5}$, or $\hat{7}$, use dominant harmony. If it ends on $\hat{1}$ or $\hat{3}$, use tonic harmony.
- If a portion of the melody includes several members of a triad, harmonize it with that triad.
- Where possible, follow the I–V–I or I–IV–V–I progression of the basic phrase; you may also use IV between two tonic triads.
- Aim for a fairly uniform harmonic rhythm. In folk or popular styles, the chord may change just once or twice per measure.

TRY IT #4

Harmonize measures 1–4 of the melody from Example 10.17 and write the Roman numerals beneath the staff.

"Wayfaring Stranger," mm. 1–4

I am a poor way-far-ing stran-ger a trav-'ling through this world of woe;

d:

ASSIGNMENT 10.3, 10.4

Did You Know?

Stephen Foster (1826–1864) is considered the first great American songwriter. His melodies, many written as parlor ballads or for minstrel shows, are so much a part of American culture that we often think of them as traditional folk songs rather than published, attributed compositions. "Oh! Susanna" was premiered in Andrews' Eagle Ice Cream Saloon in Pittsburgh on September 11, 1847. This song, with its nonsensical lyrics, became the unofficial theme song of the California gold rush, which began in January of the following year.

Terms You Should Know

basic phrase	chord progression	phrase
cadence	deceptive resolution	triad
authentic (AC)	embellishing tone	dominant
deceptive (DC)	neighbor tone	subdominant
imperfect authentic (IAC)	passing tone	tonic
perfect authentic (PAC)	harmonic rhythm	
plagal (PC)	harmonize	
half (HC)	melody and accompaniment	

Questions for Review

1. Which scale degrees make up the dominant seventh chord?
2. How do you know when a phrase ends?
3. What are the chords in a basic phrase progression?
4. For each cadence type, what harmonies end a phrase?
5. What are two typical ways for a IV chord to be used in a phrase?
6. How do you know whether a note in a melody is a chord member or an embellishing tone?

7. What are the steps in harmonizing a major-key melody?
8. What quality (major or minor) are the chords built on $\hat{1}$, $\hat{4}$, and $\hat{5}$ of a major scale? of a natural minor scale? of a harmonic minor scale?
9. Which scale degree is typically raised in minor? In which chords is it usually raised?
10. How is harmonizing a minor-key melody different from harmonizing a major-key melody?

Reading Review

Match the term on the left with the best answer on the right.

_____ (1) tonic triad
_____ (2) harmonic rhythm
_____ (3) perfect authentic cadence
_____ (4) dominant triad
_____ (5) chord progression
_____ (6) deceptive cadence
_____ (7) subdominant triad
_____ (8) cadence
_____ (9) phrase
_____ (10) plagal cadence
_____ (11) embellishing tones
_____ (12) passing tone
_____ (13) neighbor tone
_____ (14) half cadence

(a) an embellishing tone approached and left by step in the same direction
(b) phrase ending on the dominant (V or V^7)
(c) triad built on $\hat{5}$
(d) the rate at which chords change
(e) triad built on $\hat{1}$
(f) the harmonic, melodic, and rhythmic features that end a musical phrase
(g) phrase ending with IV–I
(h) an embellishing tone that moves by step away from a chord tone, then returns
(i) the order of chords harmonizing a melody
(j) a basic unit of musical thought, similar to a sentence in language
(k) dominant-to-tonic phrase ending, with $\hat{1}$ in the melody and $\hat{5}$–$\hat{1}$ in the bass.
(l) notes in a melody that are not a part of the harmony
(m) triad built on $\hat{4}$
(n) substitutes vi for I at the phrase ending

Additional review and practice available at wwnorton.com/studyspace

Apply It

A. At the keyboard

1. Play the following major scales (using any fingering) and sing along with letter names, solfège syllables, or scale-degree numbers. Then play major triads built on $\hat{1}$, $\hat{4}$, and $\hat{5}$ and the dominant seventh chord built on $\hat{5}$.

Example: D major

D: I   IV   V   V⁷

(a) D major   (d) B♭ major   (g) E major
(b) G major   (e) C major   (h) E♭ major
(c) F major   (f) A major   (i) A♭ major

2. Play the following natural minor scales (using any fingering) and sing along with letter names, solfège syllables, or scale-degree numbers. Then play minor triads built on $\hat{1}$, $\hat{4}$, and $\hat{5}$. Play the harmonic minor scale, then play the major triad and dominant seventh chord built on $\hat{5}$.

Example: D minor

d: i   iv   v

d: V   V⁷

(a) D minor   (d) B minor   (g) E minor
(b) G minor   (e) C minor   (h) F♯ minor
(c) F minor   (f) A minor   (i) C♯ minor

B. Ensemble singing at sight

Each of the following sight-singing examples draws on your study of triads. Play the first pitch on a keyboard or other instrument. Sing on scale-degree numbers or solfège syllables while tapping a steady pulse or conducting.

Melody 1 Stephen Foster, "Better Times Are Coming"

This melody is harmonized with I, IV, and V chords. Identify the chord in each measure, as well as any passing or neighboring tones. Sing in class along with the piano accompaniment or on your own with the recorded accompaniment.

Melody 2 Bach, "Jesu, Priceless Treasure" (adapted), mm. 1–2 🔊

This tune sets the triads in four parts. Practice singing each line in a comfortable register, then sing the four parts together as a class with piano accompaniment. Which part is the most challenging?

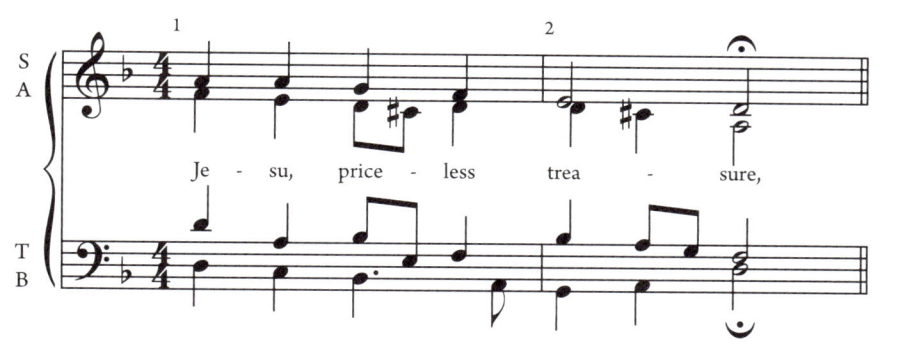

Melody 3 "Dona nobis pacem" 🔊

This melody begins with notes drawn from the tonic triad and dominant seventh chord. Practice on your own, then sing it as a round in class. A new group of voices begins when the previous group reaches ②. You can practice singing as a round with the recording; begin singing when the recording reaches ②.

Grant us peace

Melody 4 William Boyce, "Alleluia" 🔊

This melody begins with a descending major scale. At ②, the melody features notes drawn from the tonic and dominant triads. Practice it on your own, and sing it as a round in class. The melody ends on $\hat{3}$.

C. Group improvisation

Improvise a melody to go with the harmonic accompaniment given below. Make this a class project, with the teacher at the piano and members of the class improvising melodies with their voices or another instrument they play. If a member of the class plays guitar, add guitar accompaniment; read the guitar chords above the piano music. If any class members play a bass instrument (or have a bass voice), they can play the bass line to create a small ensemble. You may prepare an improvisation on your own by playing or singing along with the recorded piano part.

The music, in G major, is organized in four two-measure units, which may be repeated as many times as you like, with different class members supplying an improvised melody each time. Each unit consists of three major triads: I, IV, and V. The final measure, a tonic triad, is to be added at the conclusion of the performance. 🔊

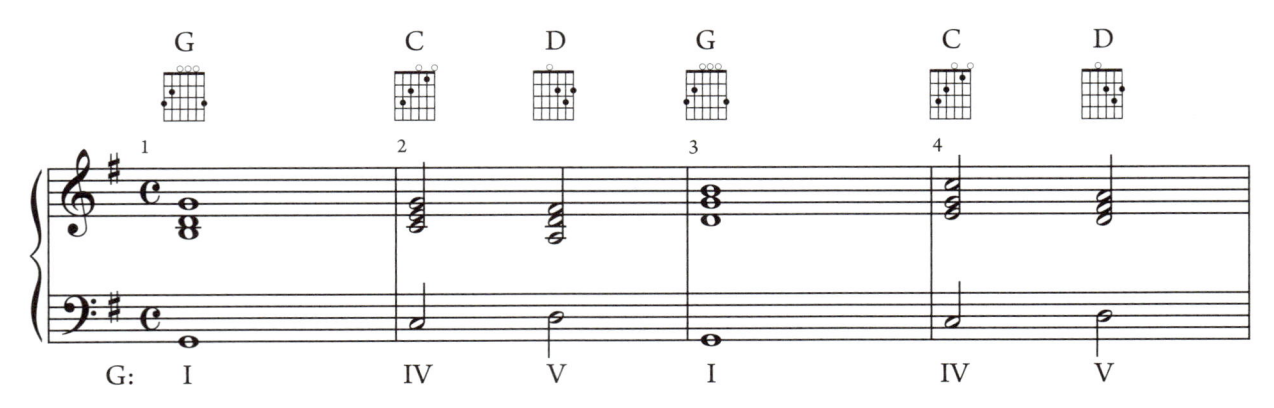

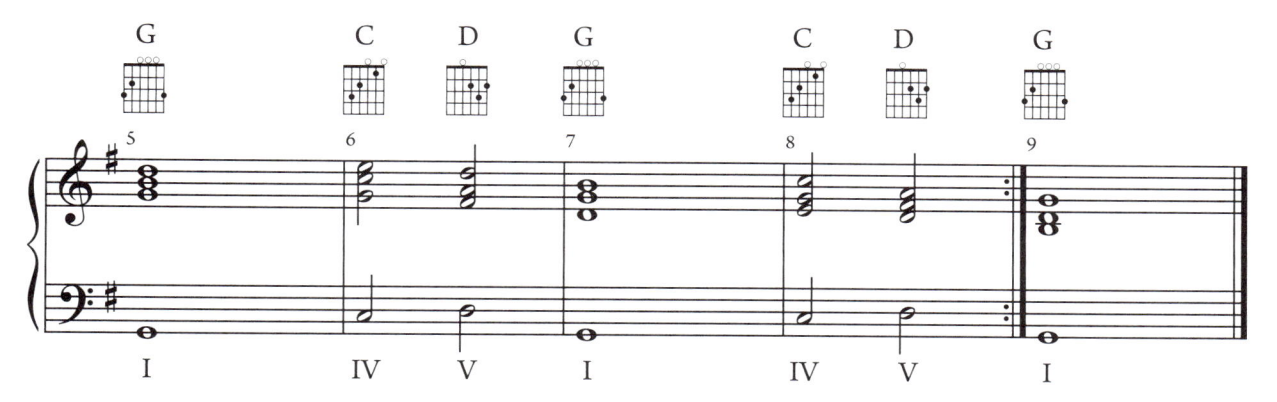

Getting oriented   Your teacher will play the tonic pitch, G, at the keyboard and then play and sing the G major scale up and down to orient you to the key. While your teacher or a class member plays the bass line, sing the bass-clef melody by itself. Then play and sing each of the treble-clef lines. Now you are ready to begin improvising your own melody.

Pitches   For the pitches of your melody, choose chord members (G, B, or D in m. 1), but also experiment with passing tones or neighbor tones between chord members (for example, you might use G–A–B in measure 1). Create an interesting contour. Let your ear guide you to create music similar to what you have already heard; some repetition of melodic and rhythmic patterns is characteristic of good improvisations.

Rhythm   For the rhythm of your melody, choose from the eight rhythmic patterns shown. You will use two patterns in each measure. Feel free to repeat patterns from measure to measure: for example, you could use four eighth notes and a half note (patterns 2 and 8) in each measure.

For a simpler exercise   Improvise only in the odd-numbered measures (over the whole-note chord), then sing the highest pitches on half notes in the even-numbered measures.

Throughout your improvisation, treat the melody given in each two-measure unit as an outline for your improvisation. Feel free to include these notes in your melody. Above all, have a good time! Don't worry if your improvisation is less than perfect. Trying is how you learn and improve.

Sample melody (improvised in odd-numbered measures)

Variation   Play the chord progression backward from the end of measure 8 until measure 1 in a rock style.

Apply It

Work space to try out your ideas

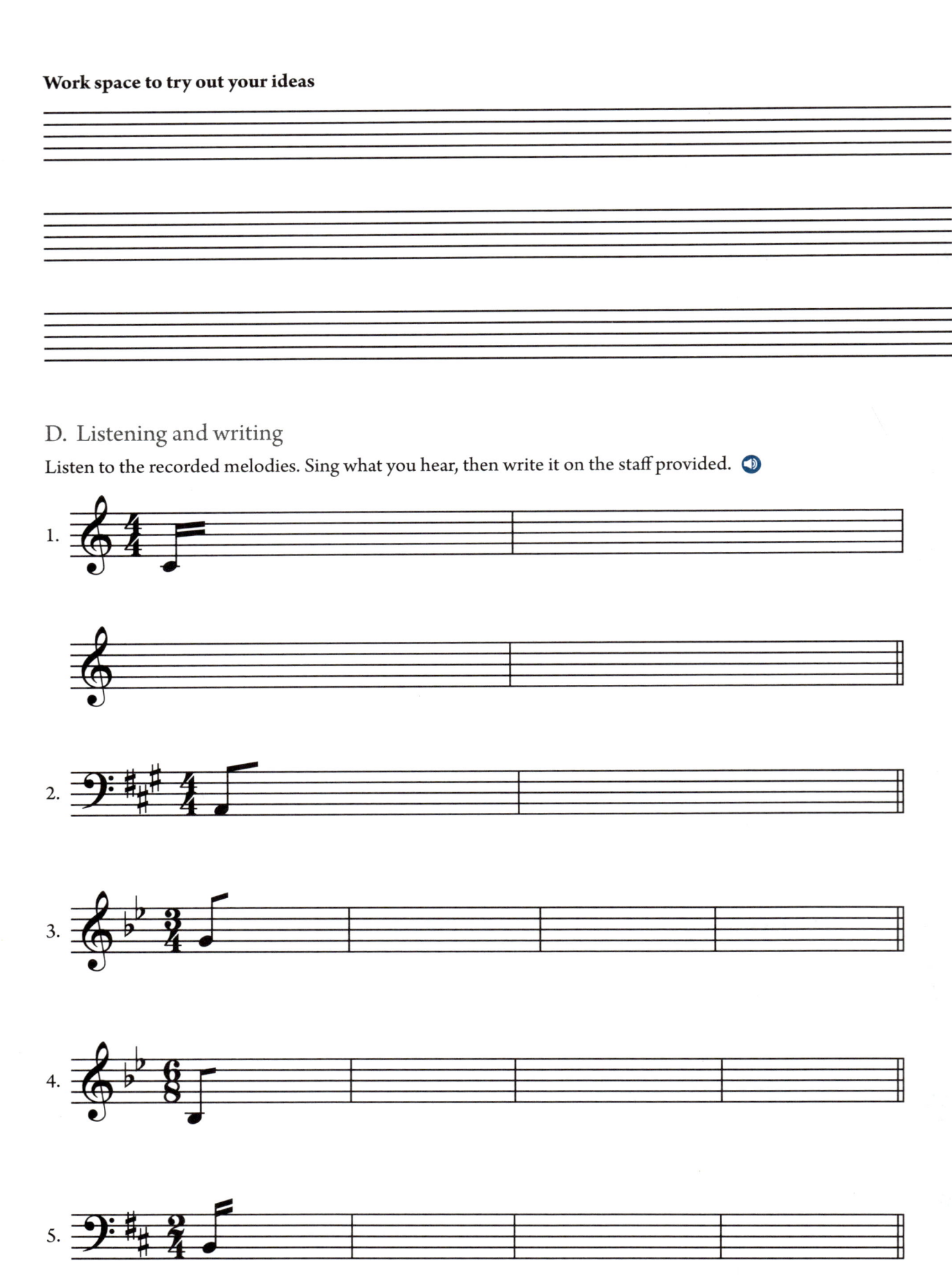

D. Listening and writing

Listen to the recorded melodies. Sing what you hear, then write it on the staff provided.

1.

2.

3.

4.

5.

CHAPTER TEN Melody Harmonization and Cadences

NAME _____

Workbook ASSIGNMENT 10.1

A. Writing triads on $\hat{1}$, $\hat{4}$, and $\hat{5}$ in major keys

Write each major scale below (using accidentals rather than key signatures), then write the specified triads in that key.

(1)

F

dominant   tonic   subdominant

(2)

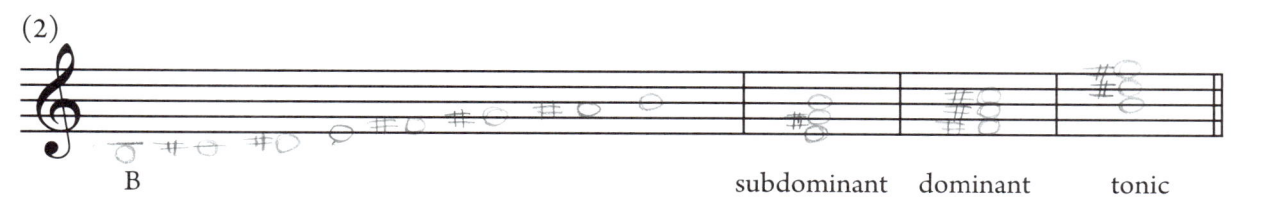

B

subdominant   dominant   tonic

(3)

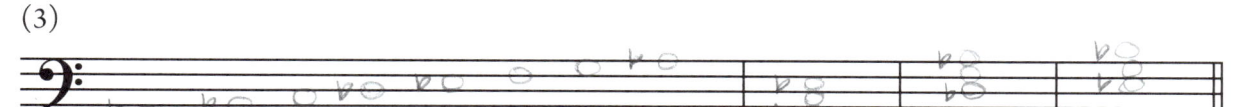

A♭

tonic   subdominant   dominant

(4)

G

tonic   dominant   subdominant

(5)

F♯

dominant   subdominant   tonic

(6)

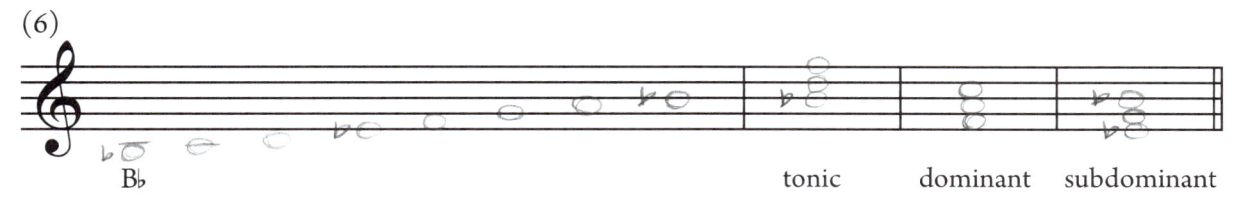

B♭

tonic   dominant   subdominant

Assignment 10.1   277

B. Writing triads on $\hat{1}$, $\hat{4}$, and $\hat{5}$ in minor keys

For each key below, write the key signature and the requested triads in that key, then label them with letter name and quality (for example, Am, D7):

	key	i tonic	iv subdominant	v minor dominant	V major dominant	V⁷ dominant seventh
(1)	c	Cm	Fm	Gm	G	G7
(2)	d	Dm	Gm	Am	A	A7
(3)	f♯	F♯m	Bm	C♯m	C♯	C♯7
(4)	b	Bm	Em	F♯m	F♯	F♯7
(5)	f	Fm	B♭m	Cm	C	C7
(6)	b♭	B♭m	E♭m	Fm	F	F7

NAME _____

Workbook ASSIGNMENT 10.2

A. Cadence types

Identify the key of each excerpt below. Then label the cadence at the end as a half cadence (HC), authentic cadence (AC), or deceptive cadence (DC). Refer to the chord symbols to identify the chords at the cadence.

(1) Robert Lowry, "How Can I Keep from Singing?," mm. 5–8

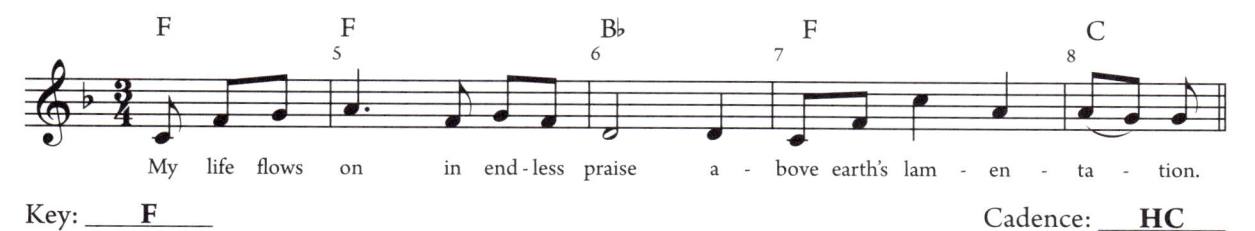

My life flows on in end-less praise a- bove earth's lam- en- ta- tion.

Key: **F**   Cadence: **HC**

(2) Ashman and Menken, "Beauty and the Beast," mm. 50–52

Tale as old as time, song as old as rhyme, Beau-ty and the Beast.

Key: **E**   Cadence: **AC**

(3) Rodgers and Hammerstein, "Edelweiss," from *The Sound of Music*, mm. 5–12

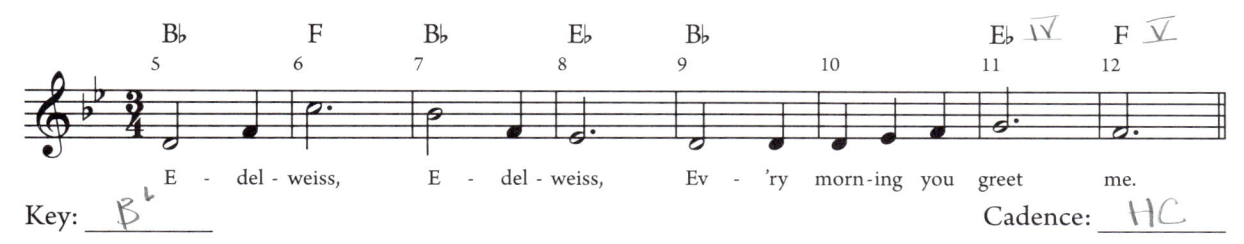

E- del- weiss, E- del- weiss, Ev- 'ry morn-ing you greet me.

Key: **B♭**   Cadence: **HC**

(4) Charnin and Strouse, "Tomorrow," mm. 26–30

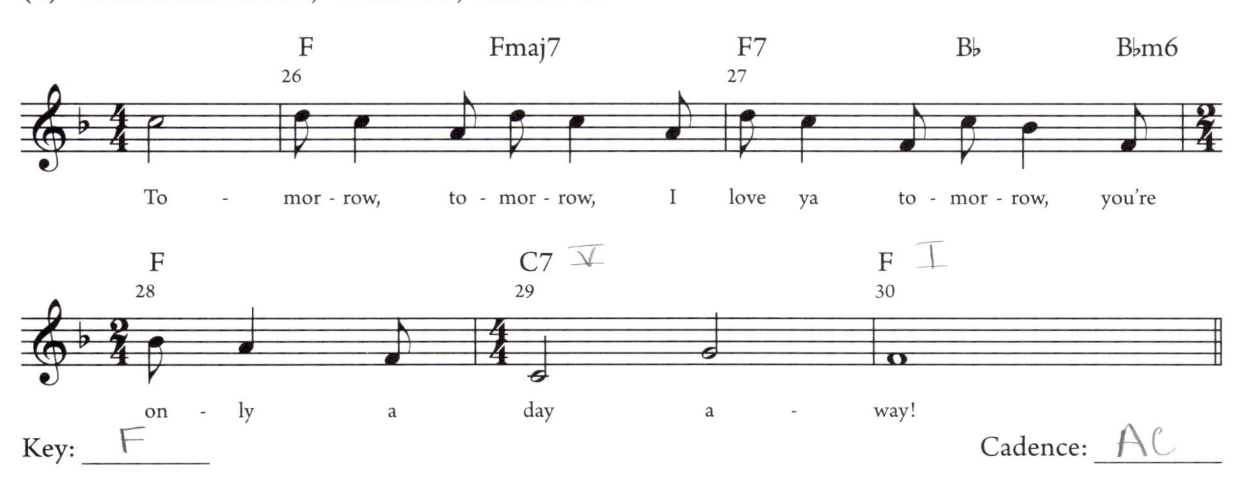

To- mor- row, to- mor- row, I love ya to- mor- row, you're on- ly a day a- way!

Key: **F**   Cadence: **AC**

(5) If the chord symbol for measure 30 of "Tomorrow" were Dm, the cadence would be a(n) **DC**

B. Interpreting chord symbols

On the staves below, write each chord specified by the symbols above the melody. Write all necessary accidentals, including those in the key signature.

(1) Bono and U2, "All Because of You," mm. 5–8

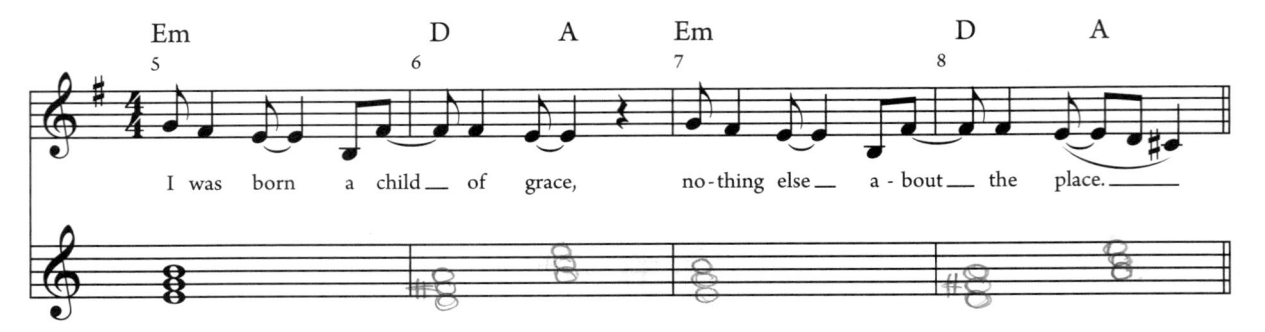

(2) Bono and U2, "One Step Closer," mm. 25–28

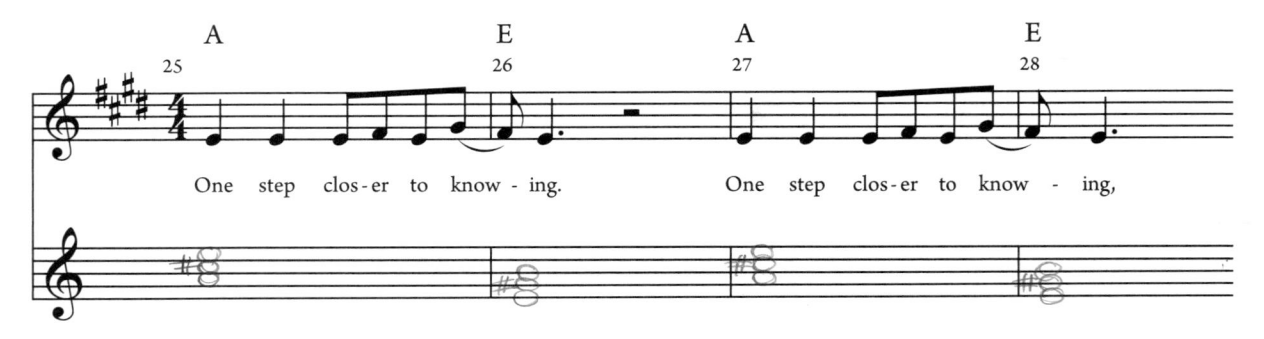

C. Matching

Match the pitches in the first column with the harmonies in the second.

_e_	(1) E–G#–B	(a)	tonic in B♭ minor
_h_	(2) B–D–F#	(b)	subdominant in C minor
_d_	(3) A–C–E	(c)	tonic in F# minor
_j_	(4) G–B♭–D	(d)	subdominant in E minor
_b_	(5) F–A♭–C	(e)	dominant in A harmonic minor
_i_	(6) C#–E–G#	(f)	dominant in B♭ harmonic minor
_a_	(7) B♭–D♭–F	(g)	subdominant in G minor
_f_	(8) F–A–C	(h)	dominant in E natural minor
_c_	(9) F#–A–C#	(i)	tonic in C# minor
_g_	(10) C–E♭–G	(j)	subdominant in D minor

CHAPTER TEN Melody Harmonization and Cadences

Workbook ASSIGNMENT 10.3

A. Harmonizing major-key melodies

For each children's song or folk tune, play or sing the melody to determine the key, write in the scale degrees, then select chords. Write the appropriate chord symbols in the blanks above the staff to represent the tonic, subdominant, and dominant seventh harmonies and the Roman numerals below, after the key indication. Circle and identify the embellishing tones as P (passing) or N (neighbor). Write one or two chords per measure. After you finish, sing the melody while playing the chords on a keyboard.

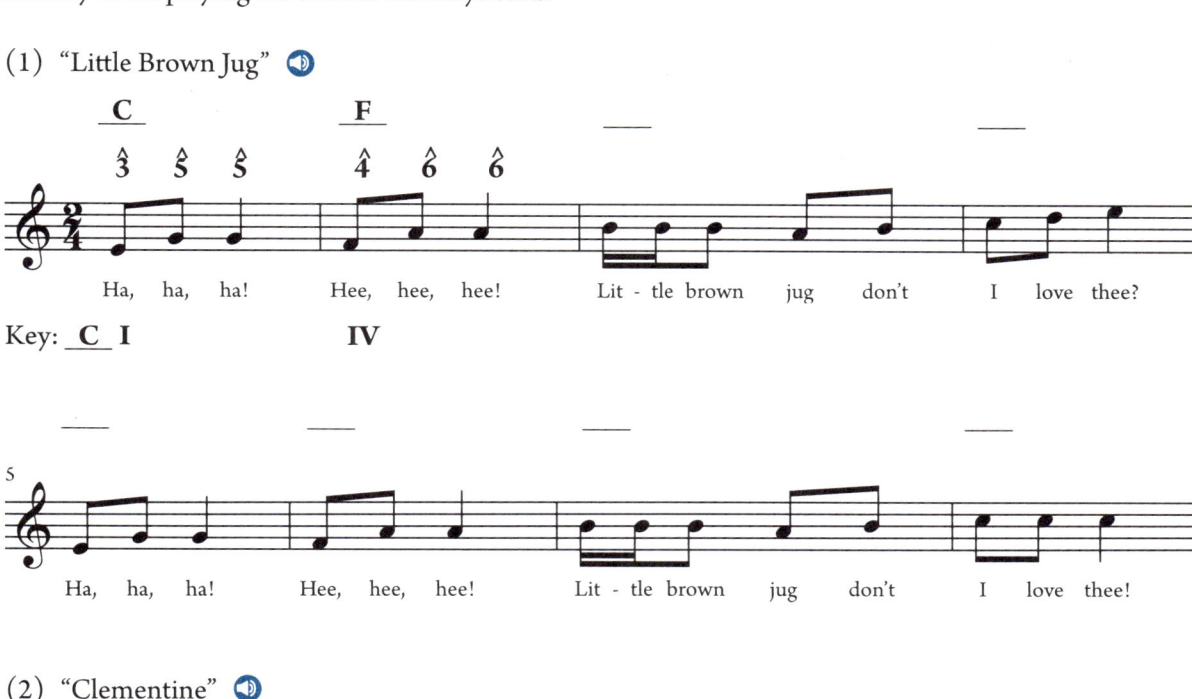

(1) "Little Brown Jug"

C   F   ___   ___

$\hat{3}$ $\hat{5}$ $\hat{5}$ $\hat{4}$ $\hat{6}$ $\hat{6}$

Ha, ha, ha!   Hee, hee, hee!   Lit-tle brown jug   don't   I love thee?

Key: __C__ I   IV

Ha, ha, ha!   Hee, hee, hee!   Lit-tle brown jug   don't   I love thee!

(2) "Clementine"

___   ___   ___   ___

In a ca-vern, in a can-yon, ex-ca-va-ting for a mine, dwelt a

Key: ___

___   ___   ___   ___

mi-ner for-ty nin-er and his daugh-ter, Cle-men-tine.

(3) "Yankee Doodle"

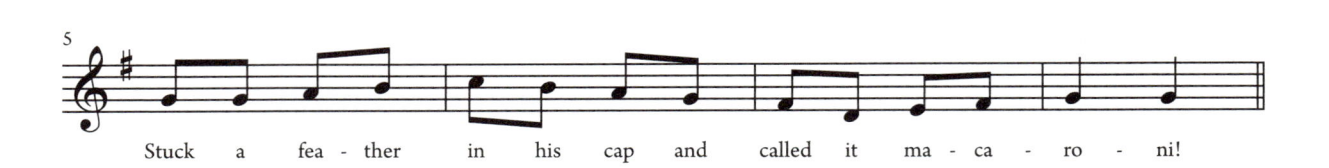

Key: ___

B. Analysis

The progression in this familiar passage is based on chords studied in this chapter. Skips between chord tones and embellishments add interest to the melody. Listen to this excerpt, then look at the bass-clef part to identify the chord for each measure. Write the chords and Roman numerals in the blanks below the staff, and circle and label any passing or neighbor tones in the treble-clef melody

Sousa, "The Stars and Stripes Forever," mm. 37–52

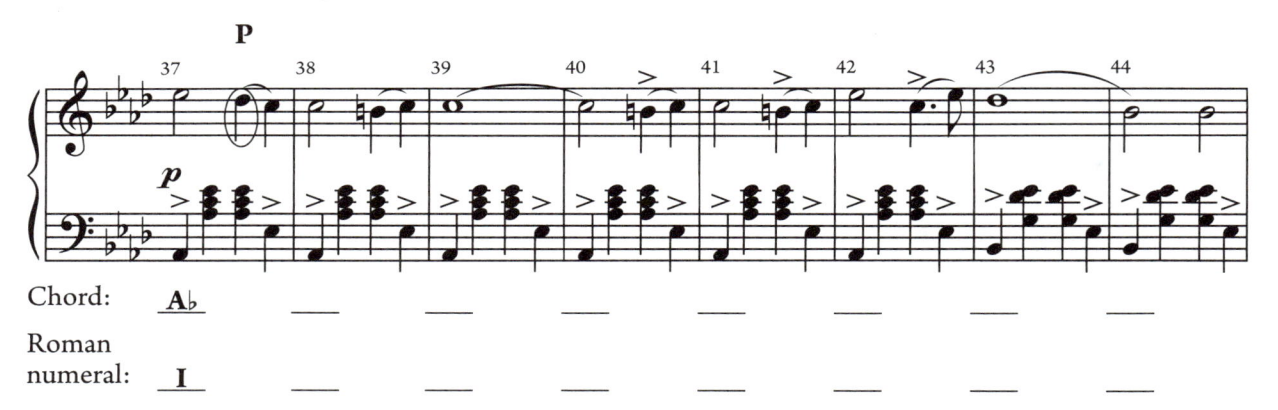

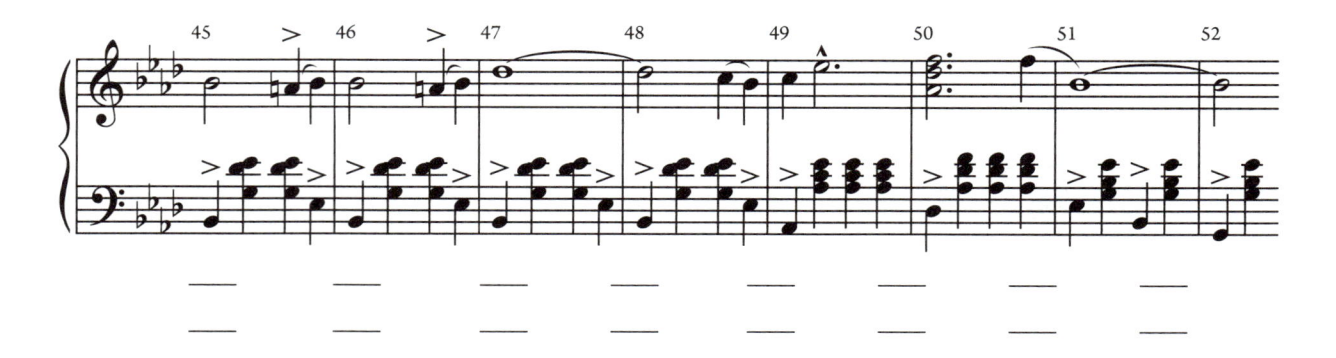

Chord: A♭
Roman numeral: I

Workbook ASSIGNMENT 10.4

A. Harmonizing minor-key melodies

Play or sing each melody to determine the key; write the scale degrees above the pitches. In the blanks above each staff, write chord symbols to harmonize the melodies, and write the Roman numerals below. Label all passing (P) and neighbor (N) tones. Sing the melody while playing the chords on a keyboard or guitar.

(1) "Wade in the Water"
(This natural minor tune is altered at the cadence with a leading tone. Choose an appropriate harmony there.)

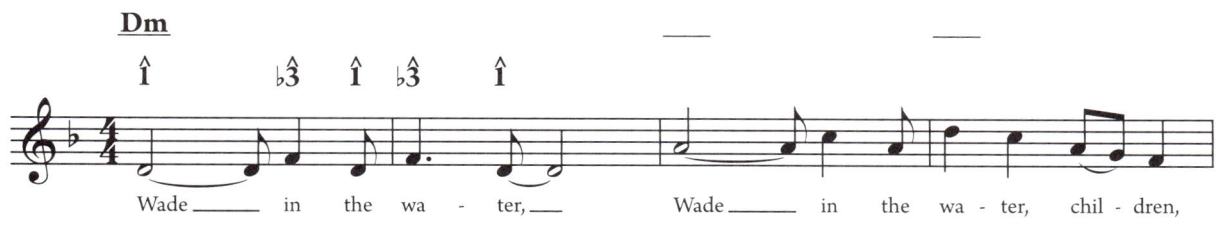

Key: d   i

(2) Gilmore, "When Johnny Comes Marching Home," mm. 9–16

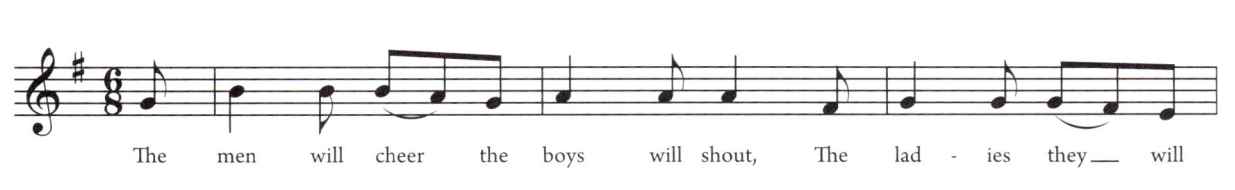

Key: ___

(3) "Hanukkah Song," mm. 1–8

Choose different harmonies for $\hat{4}$ on the rhyming words "menorah" and "horah," with an authentic cadence on "horah."

O Ha-nuk-kah, O Ha-nuk-kah, come light the me-no-rah! Let's have a par-ty, we'll all dance the

Key: ___

ho-rah. Gath-er round the ta-ble, we'll give you a treat, Se-vi-vo-nim to play with, le-vi-vot to eat.

B. Writing triads and seventh chords (review)

For each chord symbol given, write the triad or seventh chord.

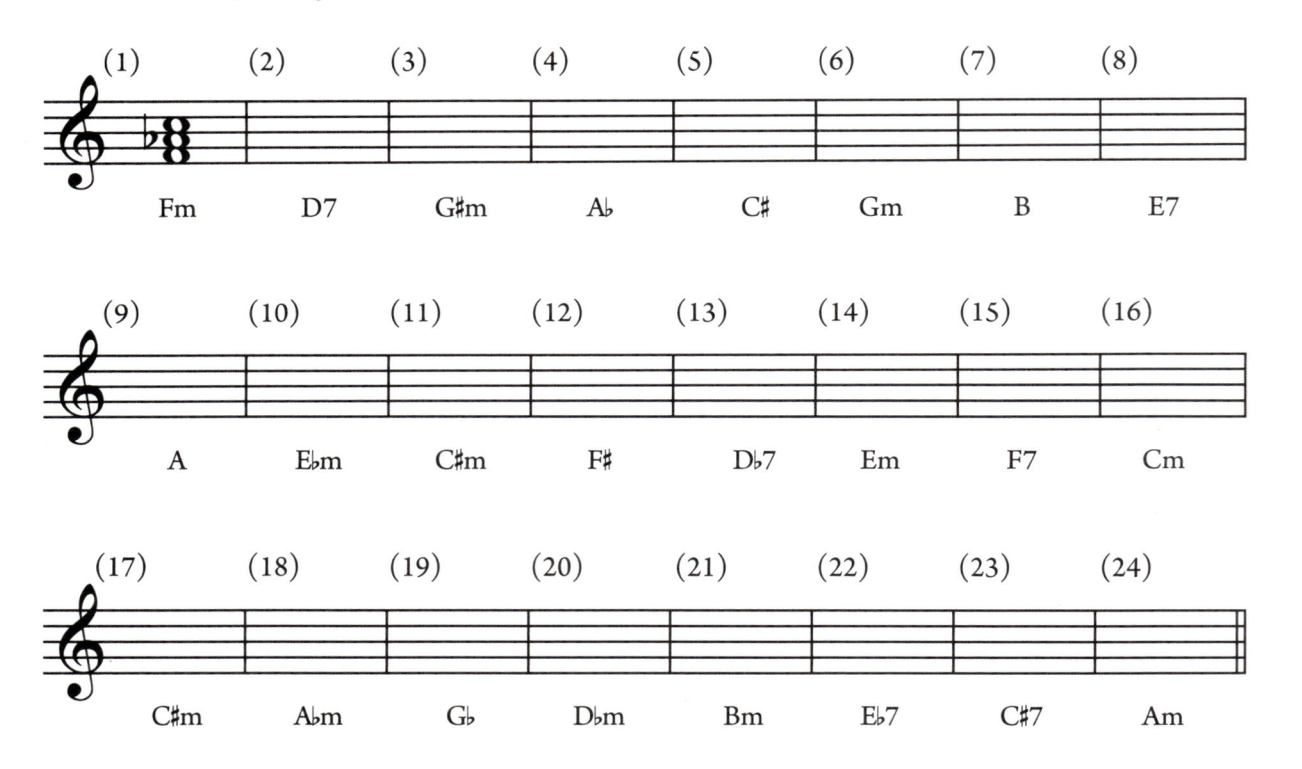

(1) Fm (2) D7 (3) G#m (4) Ab (5) C# (6) Gm (7) B (8) E7

(9) A (10) Ebm (11) C#m (12) F# (13) Db7 (14) Em (15) F7 (16) Cm

(17) C#m (18) Abm (19) Gb (20) Dbm (21) Bm (22) Eb7 (23) C#7 (24) Am

284 CHAPTER TEN Melody Harmonization and Cadences

NAME _____

Workbook — AURAL SKILLS 10.1

Listen to an excerpt from a piano work by Muzio Clementi and complete the following exercises.

(1) The rhythm may be notated in which of the following meter signatures?

a. ¢ b. 3/4 c. 6/8 d. 9/8

(2) Write the meter signature, then notate the rhythm of the melody on the staff below. Beam notes to show beat groupings.

(3) On which scale is the excerpt based?

a. major
b. natural minor (descending melodic minor)
c. ascending melodic minor
d. harmonic minor

(4) Beginning on the tonic pitch, write the melody with scale-degree numbers or solfège syllables. Your answer should begin with $\hat{1}$–$\hat{3}$–$\hat{1}$ (do–mi–do).

(5) Review your answers to questions 2–4 and notate the pitches and rhythm of the melody on the staves below. Write the appropriate meter and key signatures.

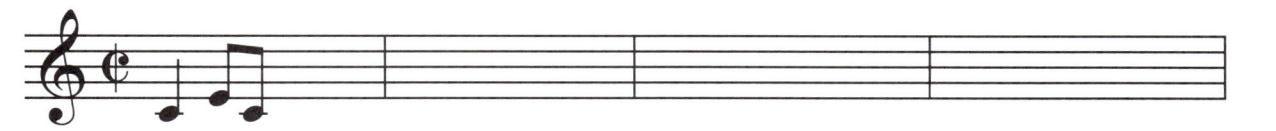

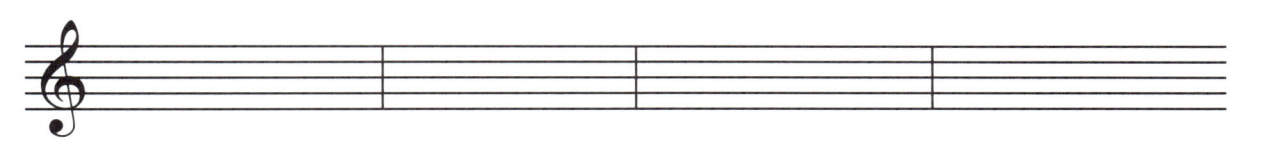

(6) The largest skip in the melody is which interval?
a. m3　　　　　　　　b. P4　　　　　　　　c. P5　　　　　　　　d. P8

(7) The cadence at measure 4, beat 1, is of which type?
a. half cadence　　　　b. authentic cadence

(8) The excerpt concludes with which type of cadence?
a. half cadence　　　　b. authentic cadence

Workbook — AURAL SKILLS 10.2

Review: Triad types

Each of the following exercises consists of recorded root-position triads. The root of each triad is notated on the staff; don't change that pitch. In the blank, write the triad's quality (M, m, A, or d). Then notate the third and fifth of the triad, including any necessary accidentals. Pay attention to the clef that is given.

For example, if you hear a minor triad whose root is B♭, write "m" in the blank, then notate the third and fifth.

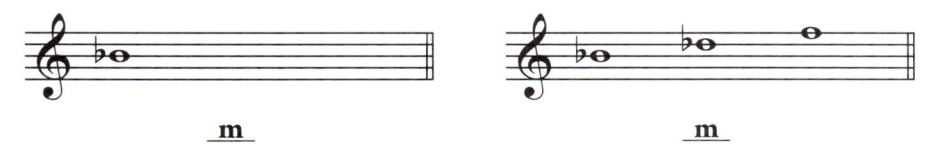

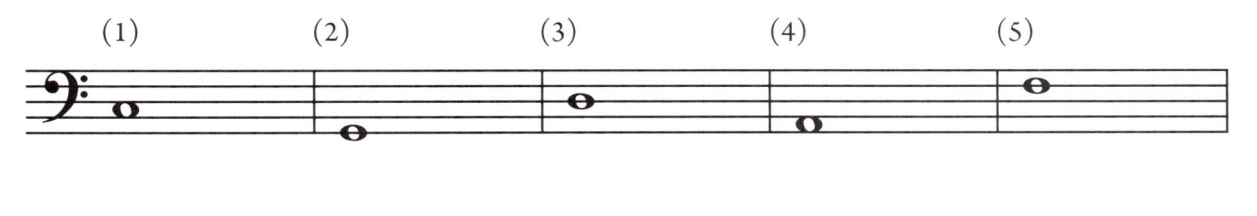

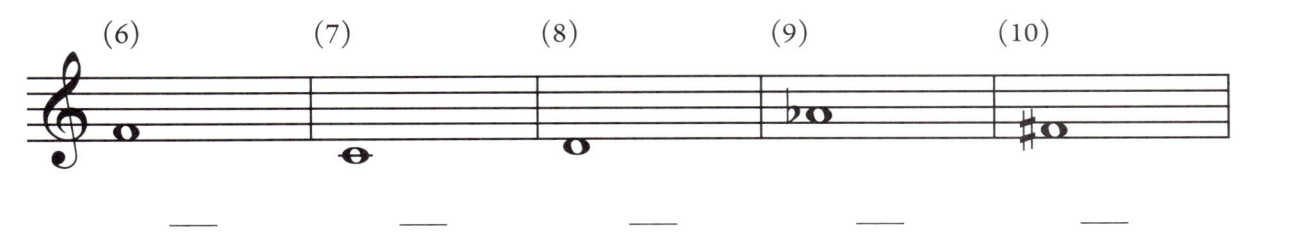

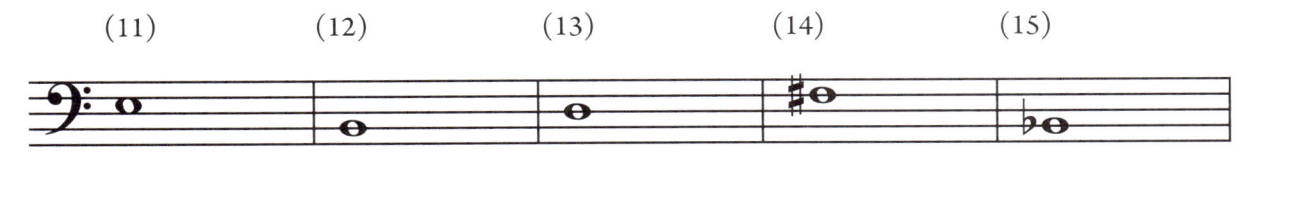

    m   m

A. Major, minor, diminished, and augmented triads (played as a melody) 🔊

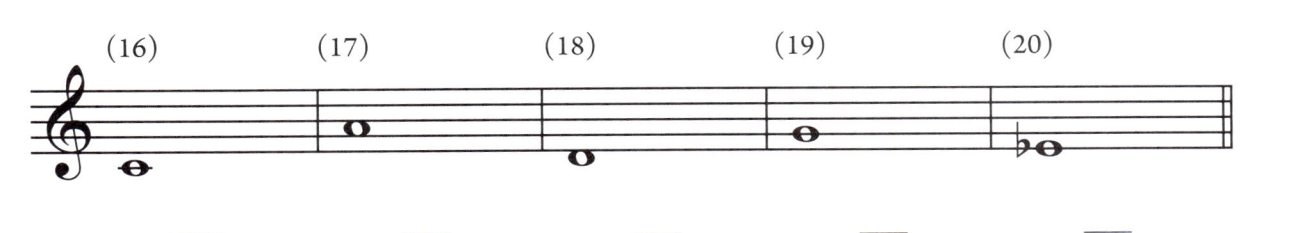

B. Major, minor, diminished, and augmented triads (played as a chord)

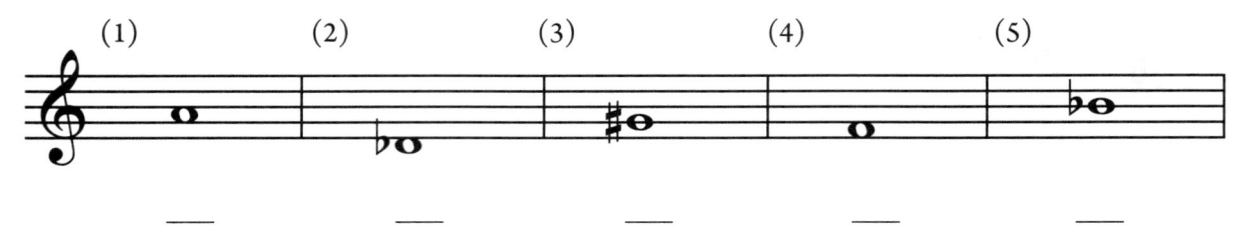

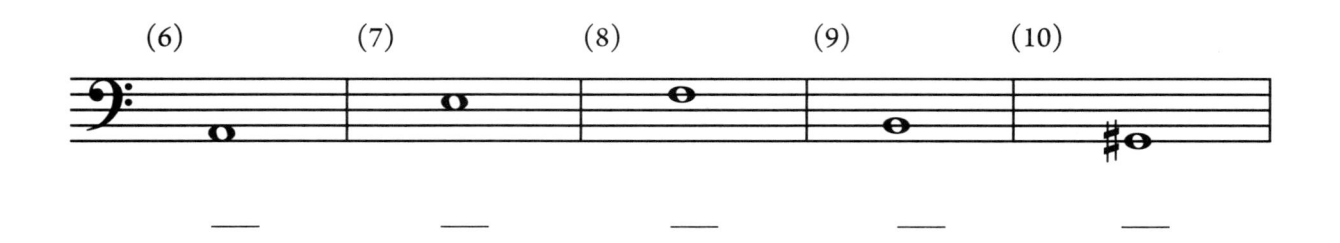

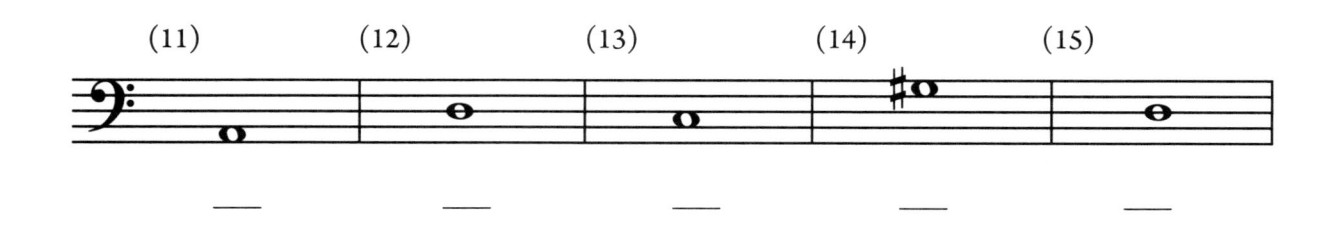

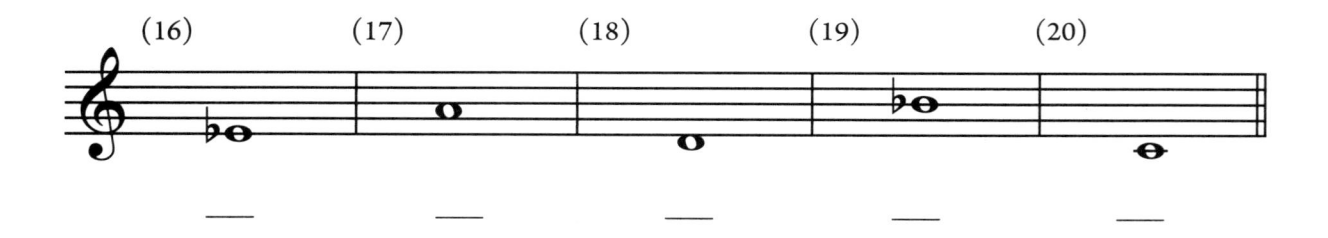

288   CHAPTER TEN Melody Harmonization and Cadences

TOPICS

- melody and paired phrases
- quaternary song form
- writing melodies
- writing keyboard accompaniments
- form in recent popular music

MUSIC

- "The Ash Grove"
- The Black Eyed Peas, "I Gotta Feeling"
- Stephen Foster, "Oh! Susanna"
- "Greensleeves"
- Jerome Kern, "Look for the Silver Lining"
- John Lennon and Paul McCartney, "Ticket to Ride"
- "Merrily We Roll Along"
- "Simple Gifts"
- Taylor Swift, "Love Story"

CHAPTER 11

Form in Folk and Popular Songs

Melody and Paired Phrases

Listen to the folk song "Greensleeves," arranged for piano, and consider the patterns of musical repetition and contrast formed by its phrases. When you consider a piece's division into sections, its patterns of repetition and contrast, and its harmonic structure (including changes of key), you are considering its **form**. Example 11.1 shows the first two phrases of the song.

EXAMPLE 11.1 "Greensleeves," mm. 1–8

The melody's first two phrases start the same but end differently: the first phrase ends with an inconclusive HC and the second with a conclusive PAC.

> **KEY CONCEPT** When two phrases are paired so that the first ends with an inconclusive cadence and the second with a conclusive cadence, they are called a **period**. The first cadence in a period is typically a HC, but may also be an IAC. The phrases themselves are called the **antecedent** (comes first and ends inconclusively) and the **consequent** (finishes the period by ending conclusively).

Musical periods are shaped not only by their cadence structure, but also by melodic repetition or contrast. When the melody of two phrases begins identically, or when the second phrase is quite similar to the first, they make a **parallel period**. Phrases are often labeled with letters to represent their design: **a a** for identical phrases and **a a'**, using the prime symbol ('), to show that the second phrase is a variant of the first. "Greensleeves" begins with a parallel period, **a a'**. When the melodic lines of phrases in a period start quite differently from each other, they form a **contrasting period** (**a b**). Figure 11.1 shows the patterns of cadences and phrase designs associated with parallel and contrasting periods.

FIGURE 11.1 Designs for parallel and contrasting periods

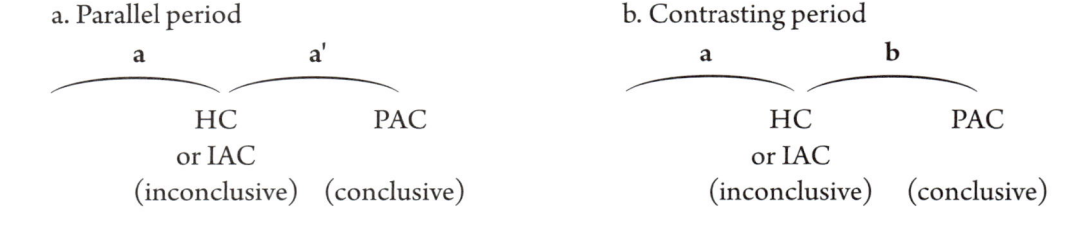

a. Parallel period

a	a'
HC or IAC	PAC
(inconclusive)	(conclusive)

b. Contrasting period

a	b
HC or IAC	PAC
(inconclusive)	(conclusive)

Quaternary Song Form

Example 11.1 shows only the first half of "Greensleeves." There are two remaining phrases, making the melody a **quaternary** (or four-phrase) **song form**. Example 11.2 shows the second half of the piece, phrases 3 and 4. Phrase 3 is a contrasting phrase, in a higher register with a dotted-quarter note high point that descends toward the cadence. Phrase 4 begins the same way as phrase 3, differing only in its last two measures and forming a parallel period. If you give each phrase a letter, the form of "Greensleeves" is **a a' b b'**.

EXAMPLE 11.2 "Greensleeves," mm. 9–16

Phrase 3: b

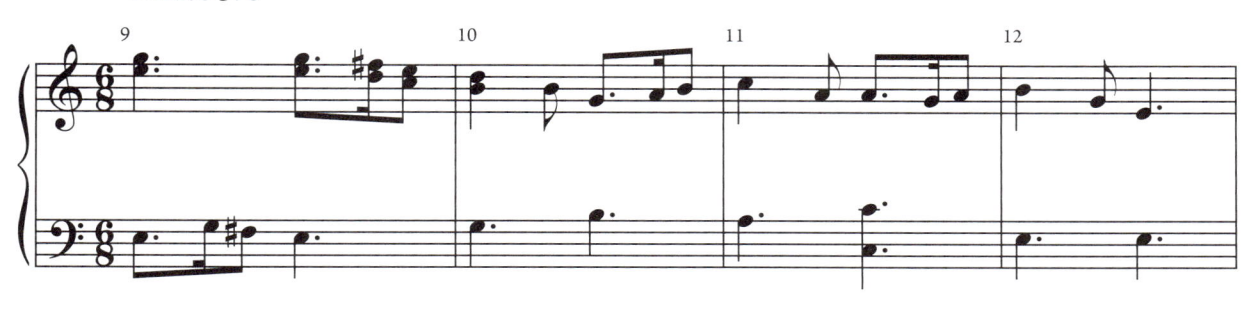

Phrase 4: b'

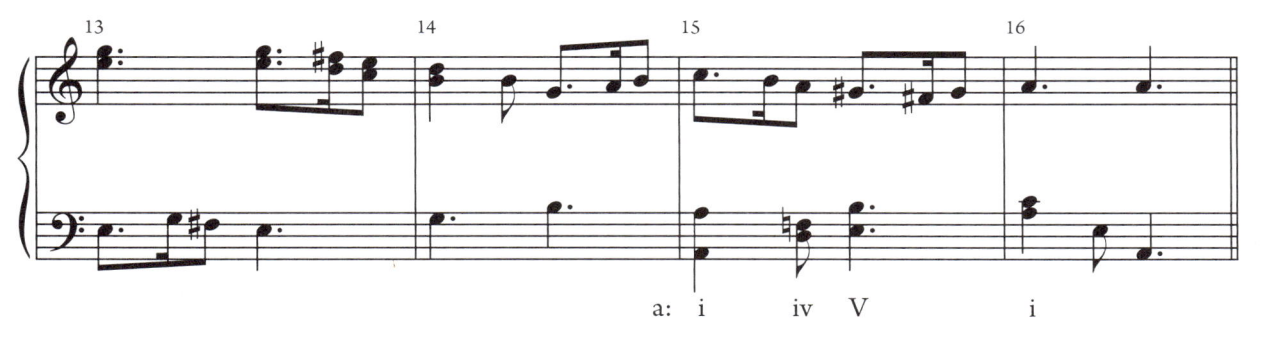

a: i   iv V   i

Not all folk songs have forms as clear-cut in their design as "Greensleeves." Listen to "Simple Gifts" (anthology, p. 394) and diagram its form. The first and second phrases begin with the same ascending fourth and have a similar rhythm and contour, so that you could label the form **a a' b a''**. On the other hand, you may feel that the differences between the first two phrases outweigh the similarities, and label it instead **a b c b'**. No matter what you decide, have musical reasons to explain why you choose each label.

Each of the folk songs considered thus far have four measures in each phrase, making a 16-bar melody. In many songs, the phrases are twice as long: the melody spans 32 measures. This length is so typical that quaternary form is often called **32-bar song form.** These song forms may be written with various phrase designs, most commonly **a a' b a'** or **a a' b a''** and **a b a c** (beginning with a contrasting period instead of a parallel one). Other typical possibilities include **a b c b** or **a b c a**.

> **TRY IT #1**
>
> Listen to "Oh! Susanna" (anthology, p. 363) while following the score. Circle the pattern that best describes its form.
>
> **a b a c**   **a a' b c**   **a a' b a'**   **a a' b b'**   **a b a' b'**

For an example of 32-bar song form, listen to the traditional folk song "The Ash Grove" while following the score in your anthology (p. 346). As you listen, think about how you would divide the song into four parts. The first part is the eight measure phrase shown in Example 11.3. The second unit of this song is the same as the first, but with a different text (note the repeat sign and additional lyrics).

EXAMPLE 11.3   "The Ash Grove," mm. 1–8

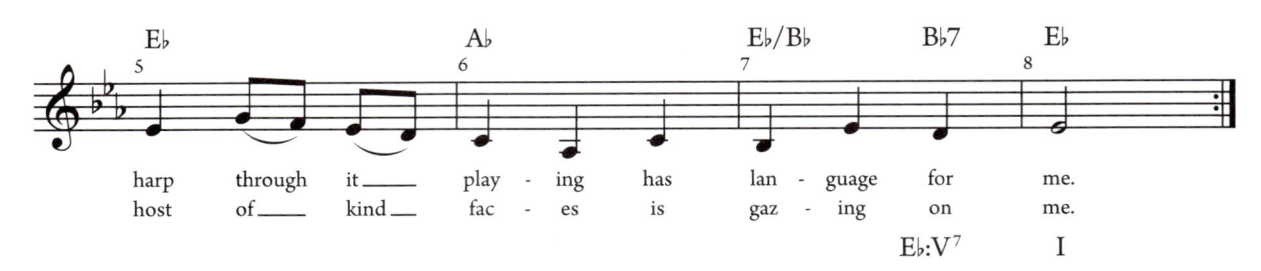

[Musical notation: mm. 1–8 of "The Ash Grove" in E♭ major, 3/4 time. Chords above staff: E♭, Fm, B♭7, E♭, A♭, E♭/B♭, B♭7, E♭. Lyrics below: "The ash grove how grace-ful, how plain-ly 'tis speak-ing. The harp through it play-ing has lan-guage for me." Second verse: "When-ev-er the light through its bran-ches is break-ing a host of kind fac-es is gaz-ing on me." Harmonic analysis at end: E♭: V⁷ I]

Now look at the second half of the song in your anthology (p. 346). These measures begin with a contrasting phrase that features a two-measure long melodic idea that is repeated twice, each time transposed down a step. This phrase ends with a half cadence. The opening melody returns after this cadence, identical to the first and second parts of the song. We can now diagram the entire form of "The Ash Grove" as **a a b a**, as shown in Figure 11.2.

FIGURE 11.2   32-bar song form in "The Ash Grove"

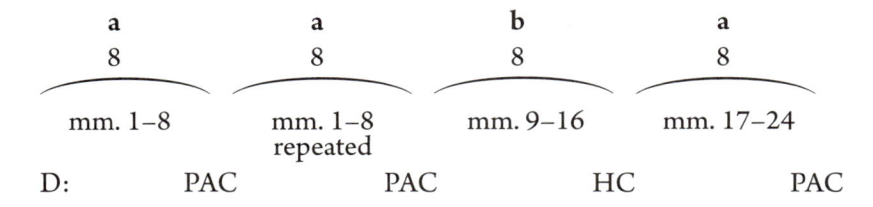

a	**a**	**b**	**a**
8	8	8	8
mm. 1–8	mm. 1–8 repeated	mm. 9–16	mm. 17–24
D: PAC	PAC	HC	PAC

> **KEY CONCEPT** In 32-bar song form, the contrasting third phrase (here **b**) is known as the **bridge** or "the middle eight." The bridge may change keys or may end inconclusively (on a HC or no cadence) to prepare for the return of the opening phrase **a**.

Listen to Jerome Kern's "Look for the Silver Lining" (anthology, p. 374); its form is shown in Figure 11.3. In this type of song, a 32-bar song form is preceded by a musical section that provides the setting and context for the song. The opening section is known as the **verse**, and the 32-bar song form is called the **refrain**. In performance, the refrain is typically repeated to make the song longer, but the verse may be heard only once at the beginning (if at all—it is sometimes omitted). **Verse–refrain** form is typical for classic Broadway show tunes and some jazz standards.

292   CHAPTER ELEVEN   Form in Folk and Popular Songs

FIGURE 11.3   Form of "Look for the Silver Lining"

Introduction	Verse	Refrain (32-bar song form)
mm. 1–2	mm. 3–11	mm. 12–43

> **TRY IT #2**
>
> Using your anthology score and recording, draw a phrase chart for the refrain of "Look for the Silver Lining," showing which measures constitute each phrase. Include phrase arcs, measure numbers, letters for phrases, and cadence types. Phrase 3 changes keys; label its cadence in A♭ major. 🔊
>
> ⌒a⌒
> mm. 12–19
>   IAC

Writing Melodies

Because there are so many types of melodies, no list of instructions can cover all the possibilities. Before beginning, you should have a style of melody in mind and should immerse yourself in examples of that style. This chapter will focus on writing periods and quaternary song forms in a folk style similar to "Greensleeves," and "The Ash Grove."

Most melodies move primarily by step (**conjunct motion**), with just a few well-placed larger intervals (**disjunct motion**). In their disjunct portions, melodies might move through the notes of a triad, with small **skips** of a third or fourth; wider jumps with larger intervals, called **leaps**, are less common. As you begin to write your own tunes, build melodic shapes that are fairly simple, with stepwise motion and small skips, and with clear harmonic goals at each cadence. As a very general principle, melodies often begin in a low or middle register, ascend to a high point, then descend to the tonic, making an arch shape. The end of each phrase is marked by one or more notes of longer duration. When phrases are paired, the first phrase will often take an arch shape but descend only to $\hat{2}$; the second phrase will then fall to the tonic to make a period.

To write a period (each phrase four measures long):

1. Map out eight blank measures on staff paper—four on the top staff and four aligned beneath them on the bottom staff—and choose a key and meter.
2. Sketch the end of each phrase first: the first ending on $\hat{3}$–$\hat{2}$ (HC) in measure 4, and the second ending on $\hat{2}$–$\hat{1}$ or $\hat{7}$–$\hat{1}$ (PAC) in measure 8.
3. Begin the melody in measure 1 on a member of the tonic triad ($\hat{1}$, $\hat{3}$, or $\hat{5}$). If you want to include an anacrusis, write one that suggests a dominant harmony (perhaps with $\hat{5}$ or $\hat{7}$), moving to $\hat{1}$ on the downbeat of measure 1. Include notes from the tonic triad in the first measure to imply a tonic chord, and embellish them with passing or neighbor tones if you wish.
4. Even though you are only writing a melody, think about a logical progression of chords that the tune implies. You started with a tonic harmony and have planned a HC in measure 4. As you plan the rest of the melody, remember the phrase model: incomplete (I–V or I–IV–V) or complete (I–V–I or I–IV–V–I). Select pitches from these harmonies to fit the model. Imply a harmonic rhythm of one or two chords per measure. (Melodies often begin with a slower harmonic rhythm that speeds up near the cadence.)

5. Sketch a melodic outline with tones from the chords you selected; continue to add passing and neighboring embellishments. If you include a leap, follow it by stepwise motion in the opposite direction. Create at least two memorable ideas, or **motives**, that you use more than once. They may be melodic or rhythmic motives.
6. Copy one or two measures of the beginning of phrase 1 into the beginning of phrase 2. Then write a continuation of phrase 2 that connects to the PAC. Where possible, use motives from the beginning of the phrase.
7. Melodies often have one high point, or **climax**. Build yours so that its highest note is stated only once or twice. (Not all songs have a single climax, but it is a good idea to keep this in mind as a goal to shape your melody.) Avoid a static melodic line: do not hover around a single pitch.

If you wish to write a 16-measure quaternary song form:

1. To write a song with **a a' b a'** structure, begin with the parallel period you have already written. It makes up the first two phrases of the form.
2. Add two more empty staves with four measures each. Write phrase 4 first by copying phrase 2. Phrase 4 can be identical to phrase 2, or you may embellish it slightly or (in a texted song) change the lyrics.
3. Now return to phrase 3, the contrasting **b** phrase, or bridge. Consider allowing this phrase to rise to the highest register of the song, making the musical climax. Create a different rhythmic pattern, such as one using longer durations, to contrast with rhythmic motives of the **a** phrases. End the bridge with a harmonically inconclusive cadence to prepare for the return of **a**.

All these principles are at work in "Oh! Susanna" (Example 11.4). The melody begins with an antecedent–consequent pair: the first phrase comes to rest on $\hat{2}$ over a half cadence (m. 4), and the second concludes with $\hat{2}-\hat{1}$ over a PAC (m. 8). Though their endings are different, the two phrases begin identically, forming a parallel period (**a a'**). The tune also illustrates several other melody-writing principles. It features a memorable ♫ ♫ rhythmic motive that recurs throughout, and it outlines the underlying harmonic progression I–V–I (shown with chord symbols) with chord tones decorated by passing and neighbor tones.

EXAMPLE 11.4   Foster, "Oh! Susanna," mm. 1–8

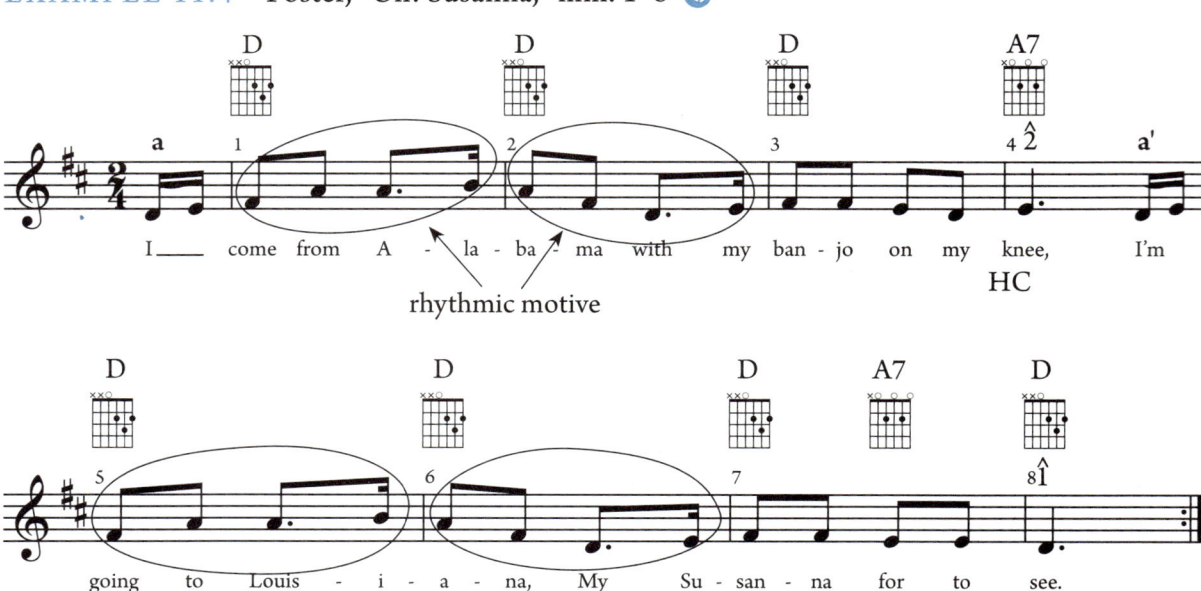

Example 11.5 shows the **b** phrase and return of the opening **a** material to complete the form. The **b** phrase contrasts with the rest of the song with its subdominant harmony and longer-duration quarter notes, and the absence of an anacrusis and the ♫♫ motive. The highest pitch in the melody, B4, heard briefly in the **a** phrases as an embellishing sixteenth-note neighbor tone, sounds for a full measure (m. 10); in its new rhythmic and harmonic context in the **b** phrase, this B4 is the climax of the song.

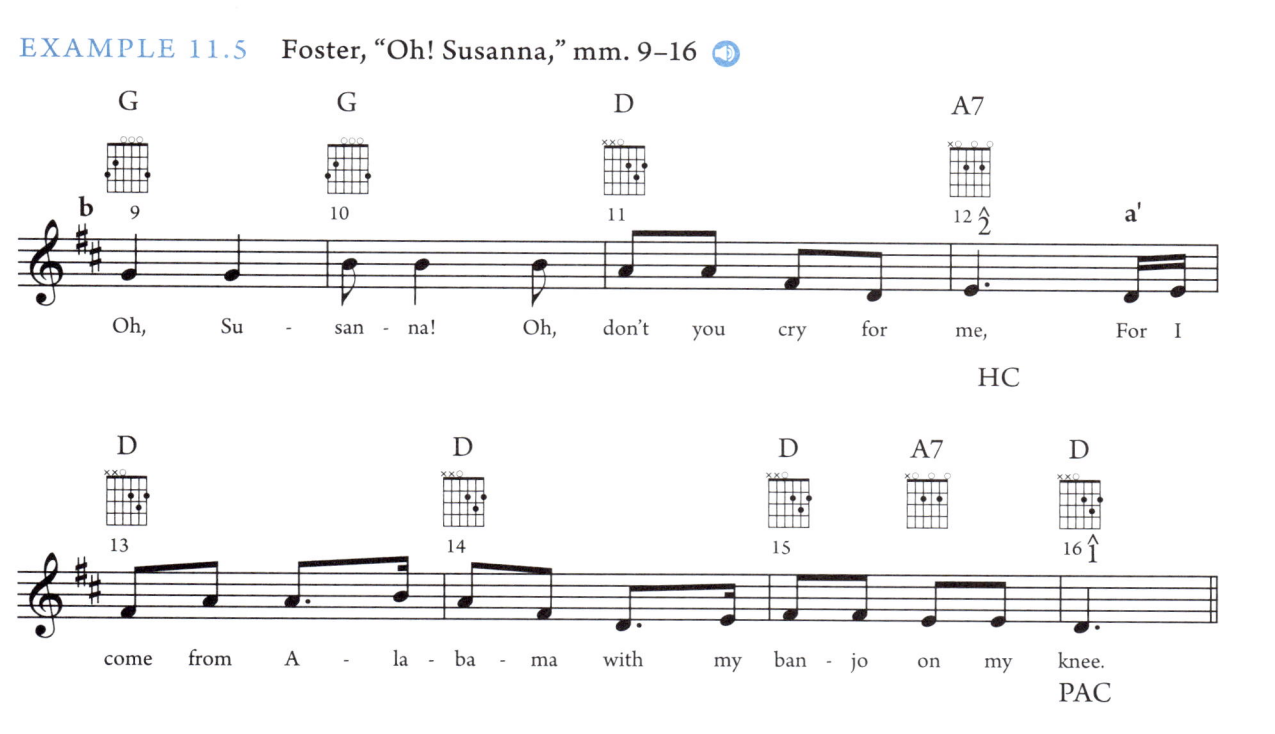

EXAMPLE 11.5   Foster, "Oh! Susanna," mm. 9–16

ASSIGNMENT 11.1, AURAL SKILLS 11.1

Writing Keyboard Accompaniments

After you have written and harmonized a melody by choosing appropriate I, IV, and V chords, you can play the chords at the keyboard by arranging the notes to fit under one hand, as shown in Example 11.6. Learn these patterns in each hand separately: they are arranged to connect one note smoothly with the next.

> **KEY CONCEPT**   When you connect chords:
> - Aim primarily for smooth motion by step or skip; avoid leaps, except in the bass.
> - If two consecutive chords share tones, keep the common tone in the same part.
> - Correctly resolve dissonant intervals and scale degrees with strong tendencies (like $\hat{7}$–$\hat{1}$).

Example 11.6 gives the basic phrase progression in parallel keys—D major and D (harmonic) minor. The fingering pattern is the same for both, but in minor keys lower $\hat{3}$

Writing Keyboard Accompaniments   295

and $\hat{6}$ by a half step in the tonic and subdominant chords. When accompanying a song, these patterns would likely be played either in the right hand with the chord roots in the left (Example 11.6b), or with the melody in the right hand and the chords in the left (Example 11.6c).

EXAMPLE 11.6   Keyboard arrangements of I, IV, and V

(a) Finger numbering

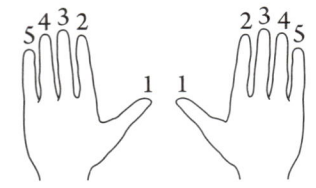

(b) Basic phrase (I–IV–V–I) with right-hand chords

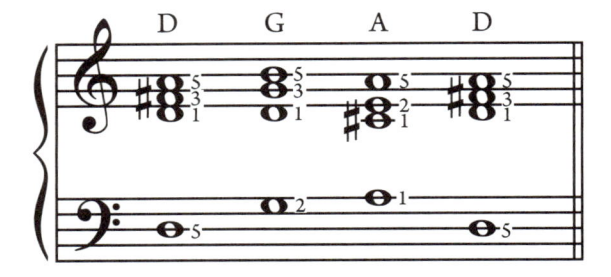

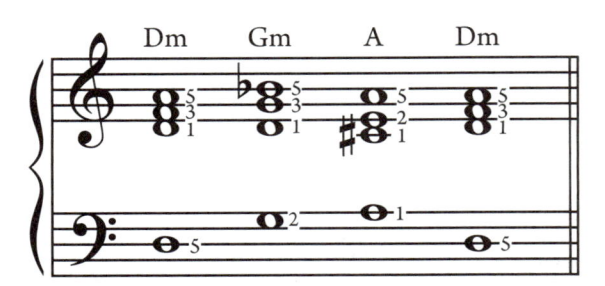

(c) Basic phrase (I–IV–V–I) with left-hand chords (melody in right hand)

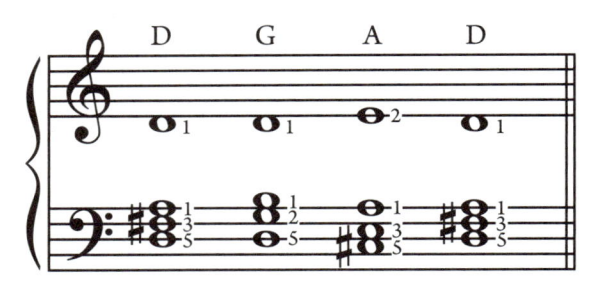

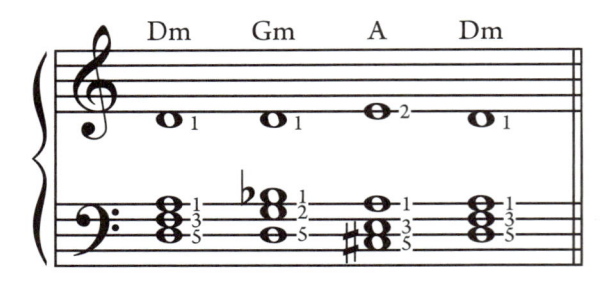

(d) In keyboard settings, avoid jumping between root-position chords (in either hand)

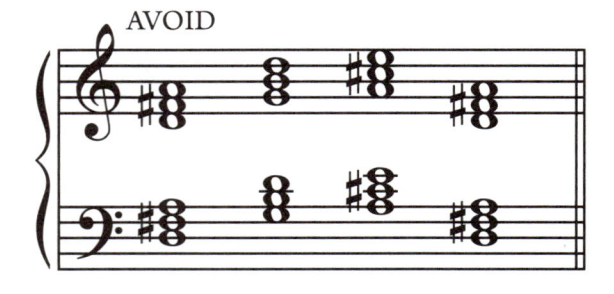

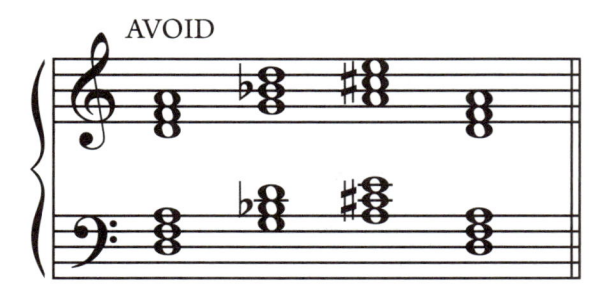

Examples 11.6b and c show the basic phrase progression (I–IV–V–I) with the chords connected correctly. Example 11.6d shows poor **chord connection**, which is avoided in keyboard settings because of its lack of smooth motion. If you wish, you may substitute a V^7 for the V chord; do this by replacing $\hat{2}$ (E, the fifth of the chord) with $\hat{4}$ (G, the seventh of the chord), as Example 11.7 shows.

EXAMPLE 11.7   Basic phrase progression with V⁷

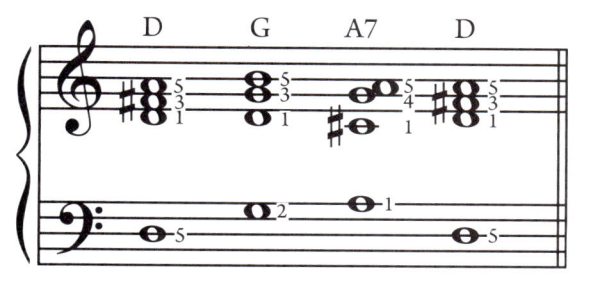

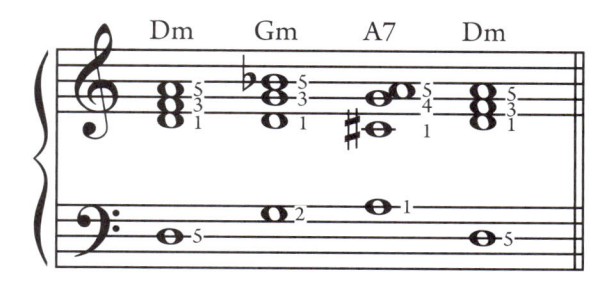

The opening portion of your melody may provide an opportunity to extend the tonic harmony with a IV chord. Example 11.8 illustrates a common way to connect I and IV.

EXAMPLE 11.8   Extending the tonic harmony with IV

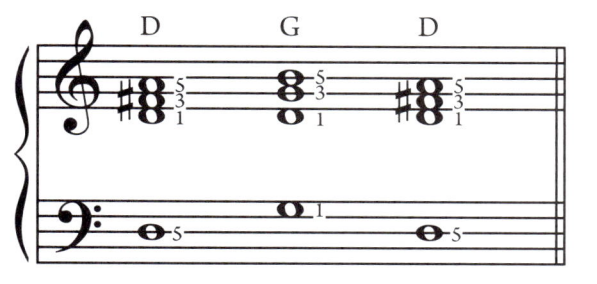

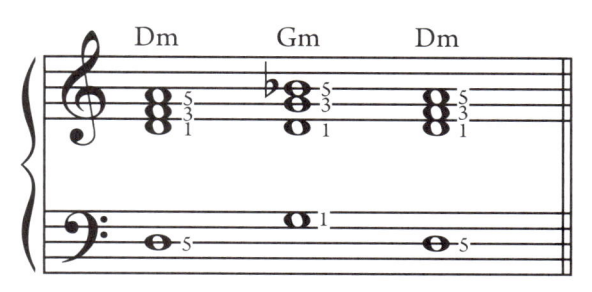

TRY IT #3

Using Example 11.6 as your model, write the chord connections specified below the staff (for one hand, as the clef indicates). Include appropriate accidentals for the key.

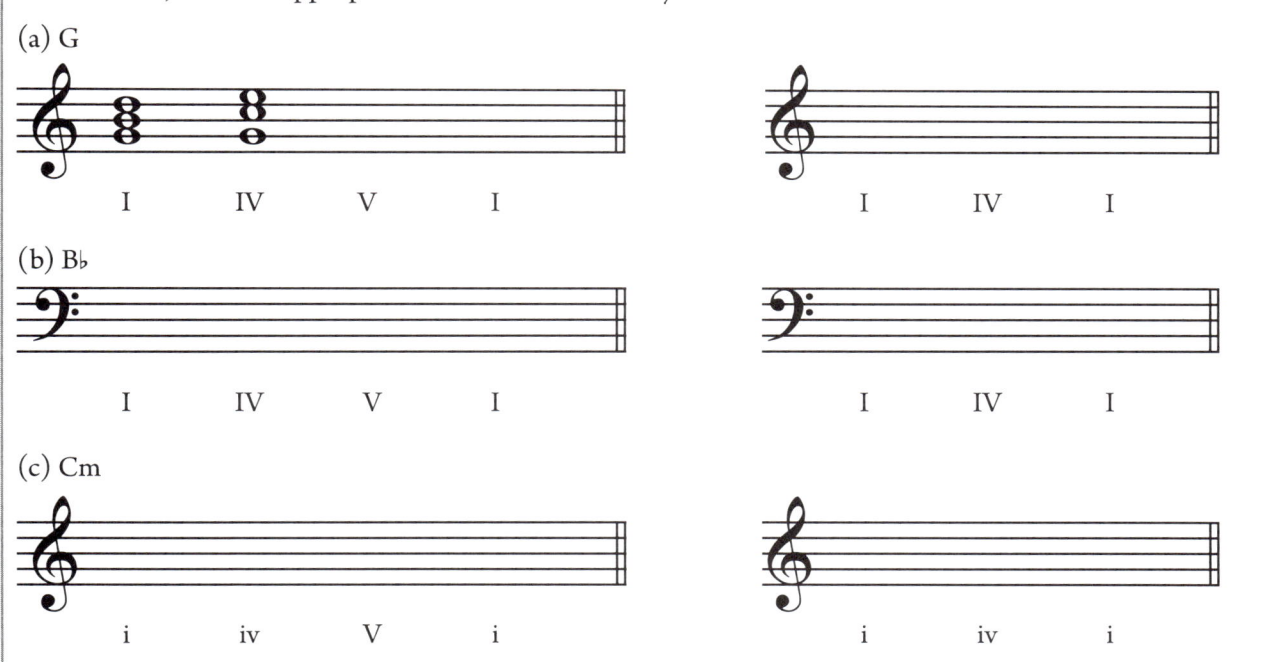

(a) G

    I   IV   V   I   I   IV   I

(b) B♭

    I   IV   V   I   I   IV   I

(c) Cm

    i   iv   V   i   i   iv   i

Another way to write keyboard accompaniments for songs is to take these basic progressions and play them in different keyboard styles. Example 11.9 shows four simple accompaniment patterns for the beginning of the familiar tune "Merrily We

Roll Along," harmonized with only I and V chords. Example 11.9a is a chordal pattern with roots in the bass on the downbeat and chords in the right hand delayed to beat 2. Example 11.9b is a more rhythmic version, where the chords come on the & of each beat (the offbeat) and $\hat{5}$ is played in the bass on beat 2, similar to a Sousa march. For a chordal accompaniment of a triple-meter melody, you might use a waltz bass—one bass note on the downbeat and chords on beats 2 and 3 (see Schubert's Waltz in B Minor, anthology, p. 392).

EXAMPLE 11.9   "Merrily We Roll Along"

(a) With chords displaced to beat 2

(b) With Sousa-style accompaniment

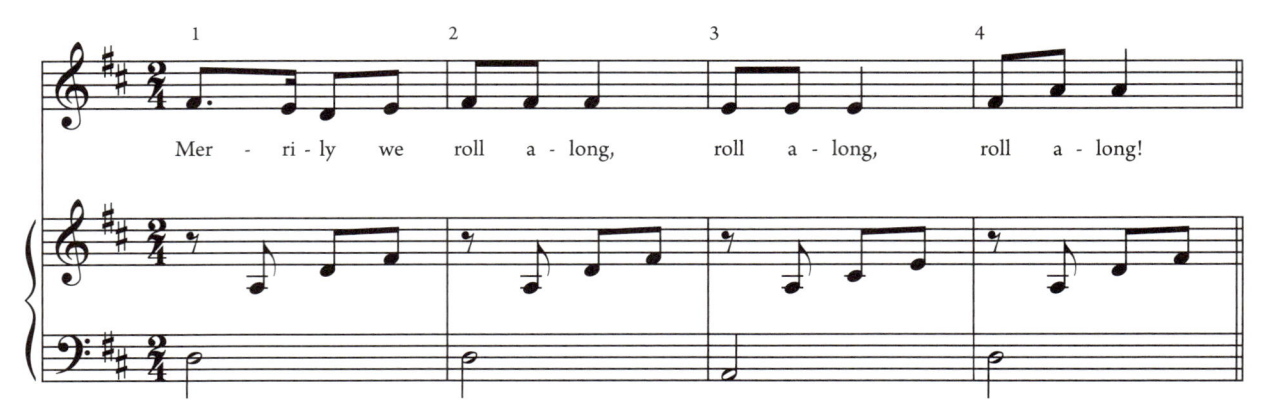

(c) With eighth-note arpeggiated accompaniment

(d) With sixteenth-note arpeggiated accompaniment

Mer - ri - ly we roll a - long, roll a - long, roll a - long!

Examples 11.9c and d show arpeggiated accompaniments, which are often used in lyrical settings. An **arpeggio** is the "spreading out" of chord tones by playing them one pitch at a time rather than together. In 11.9c the chord is arpeggiated as even eighth notes and in 11.9d as sixteenths. Try each of these to see what effects the accompaniment can have on the character of a melody.

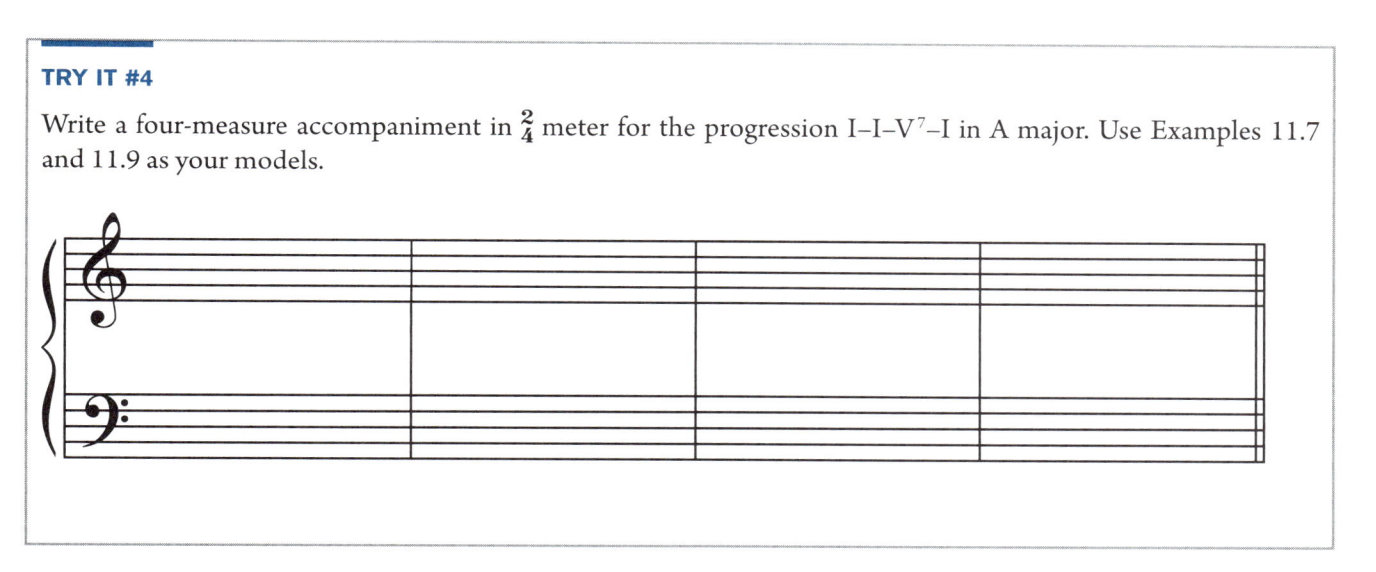

> **TRY IT #4**
>
> Write a four-measure accompaniment in $\frac{2}{4}$ meter for the progression I–I–V^7–I in A major. Use Examples 11.7 and 11.9 as your models.

ASSIGNMENT 11.2

Form in Recent Popular Music

After 1950, the terminology for labeling sections of songs began to change, as verse–refrain form became less popular.

> **KEY CONCEPT** In its new usage, the term **verse** designates a musical section that appears in a song multiple times with the same music but a different text, while **chorus** refers to a section of music that is repeated with the same (or similar) text. The verse and chorus together may act as the **a** section of a larger form.

Listen to the beginning of The Beatles' "Ticket to Ride"; the form is shown in Figure 11.4. It may help to conduct along with the song to count the measures.

FIGURE 11.4 Form in Lennon and McCartney, "Ticket to Ride"

Intro		4 measures
Verse	"I think I'm . . ."	8 measures
Chorus	"She's got a . . ."	8 measures
Verse	"She said . . ."	8 measures
Chorus	"She's got a . . ."	8 measures
Bridge	"I don't know . . ."	9 measures
Verse	"I think I'm . . ."	8 measures
Chorus	"She's got a . . ."	8 measures
Outro		2 measures

After a brief instrumental introduction (an **intro**), the song begins with the verse followed by the chorus. The music for the verse then repeats, with different text, followed by the chorus. Before the final verse and chorus, there is a **bridge**, a term that now denotes music that contrasts with the verse and chorus and appears in the second half of the song to prepare for the last statement of the verse and chorus. The verse and chorus return after the bridge. Finally, the song ends with a concluding **outro** or **coda**—instrumental music to end the song. An outro may consist of a simple "repeat and fade" or other concluding music.

This song also illustrates the use of a **hook**—a musical setting of a few words or a phrase, usually including the title, that is repeated and becomes the most "catchy" or memorable part of the song. For this song, the hook ("a ticket to ride") occurs in the chorus, as is typical, though a hook may appear elsewhere in other songs.

In recent years, song forms have expanded beyond the basic sections considered so far. Vocal sections of a song may be broken up by instrumental passages, including an **instrumental break** (a section in the middle of a song played only by instruments, often based on the verse), a **link** (a short instrumental connector between sections), and a **rap break** (like an instrumental break but with spoken rhythmic text). Intros may be extended, with new ideas entering, and sections may be repeated multiple times. For example, the song "I Gotta Feeling" by The Black Eyed Peas begins with an extended introduction, followed by four repetitions of the chorus (performed over the intro music). Prior to the first rap break, the repetition builds momentum, preparing for the entry of the spoken text, which substitutes for a sung verse. The form of the opening of this song is shown in Figure 11.5.

FIGURE 11.5 Form in the opening of The Black Eyed Peas, "I Gotta Feeling"

Instrumental intro part 1		8 measures
Instrumental intro part 2		8 measures
Chorus 1	"I gotta feeling . . ."	8 measures
Chorus 2	"A feeling . . ."	8 measures
Chorus 3	"A feeling, woohoo . . ."	8 measures
Chorus 4	"A feeling, woohoo . . ."	8 measures
Rap break (verse)	"Tonight's the night . . ."	8 measures

Songs may also include short sections before and after the chorus: a section after a verse that prepares for the entrance of the chorus is called a **prechorus**, and in very recent songs, some songwriters include a **postchorus** after a chorus to prepare for the return of the verse. A prechorus, link, and outro are all illustrated Taylor Swift's "Love Story," as shown in Figure 11.6.

FIGURE 11.6   Form in Taylor Swift, "Love Story"

Instrumental intro		8 measures
Verse 1	"We were both . . ."	8 measures
Verse 2	"I see the lights . . ."	8 measures
Prechorus	"That you were . . ."	8 measures
Chorus	"Romeo take me . . ."	8 measures
Link		2 measures
Verse 3	"So I sneak out . . ."	8 measures
Prechorus	"Cause you were . . ."	8 measures
Chorus	"Romeo take me . . ."	8 measures
Chorus	"Romeo save me . . ."	8 measures
Instrumental interlude		8 measures
Bridge	"I got tired . . ."	8 measures
Chorus	"Romeo save me . . ."	8 measures
Chorus	"Marry me Juliet . . ."	8 measures
Outro		9 measures

ASSIGNMENT 11.3

Did You Know?

Jerome Kern (1885–1945) composed many songs for Broadway shows and also wrote some of the first film scores. The song "Look for the Silver Lining" was originally composed for an unsuccessful Broadway musical, *Zip, Goes a Million*, in 1919 but reappeared in a more successful musical, *Sally*, the following year. A performance by Marion Harris, an early jazz and blues singer, was #1 on the charts in 1921. Harris's performance accompanies a romantic dance scene between Lady Mary and Matthew Crawley in the television show *Downton Abbey*. This song's optimistic text ("Always look for the silver lining, and try to find the sunny side of life") resonates with several other well-known songs in the twentieth century, including the hymn "Keep on the Sunny Side of Life," composed in 1899 but popularized by the Carter Family, and Monty Python's "Always Look on the Bright Side of Life," from the movie *The Life of Brian* (1979).

Terms You Should Know

32-bar song form	form	postchorus
arpeggio	hook	prechorus
antecedent phrase	instrumental break	quaternary song form
bridge (2 meanings)	intro	rap break
chord connection	leap	refrain
chorus	link	skip
climax	motive	verse (2 meanings)
coda	outro	verse–refrain form
conjunct motion	period	
consequent phrase	contrasting	
disjunct motion	parallel	

Questions for Review

1. How many phrases make up a period? How may they be related melodically (at the beginning) and harmonically (at the cadences)?
2. How are the phrases of quaternary song form related? What are typical formal designs, in addition to **a a' b a"**?
3. What guidelines should you follow when connecting chords?
4. What are some ways that you can turn a chordal harmonization into a piano accompaniment?
5. What are some formal sections used in recent popular songs?

Reading Review

Match the term on the left with the best answer on the right.

_____ (1) half cadence   (a) melodic presentation of a chord, one pitch at a time

_____ (2) parallel period   (b) stepwise melodic motion

_____ (3) chord connections   (c) music that is repeated with different text

_____ (4) conjunct   (d) the **b** phrase in **a a b a** form

_____ (5) disjunct   (e) consists of four phrases

_____ (6) bridge   (f) typical cadence for the first phrase of a period

_____ (7) arpeggio   (g) **a b** phrase design

_____ (8) verse   (h) **a a'** phrase design

_____ (9) contrasting period   (i) melodic motion characterized by skips and leaps

_____ (10) quaternary song form   (j) should aim for smooth motion, keeping common tones in the same part

Additional review and practice available at wwnorton.com/studyspace

Apply It

A. Reading rhythms

Rhythm review: Each of the following rhythms incorporates familiar patterns. In addition, you will encounter a march conducted in two with syncopated rhythms and two ways of indicating repetition.

Rhythm 1

Hint: Remember to conduct in two, as indicated by the "cut time" signature.

Rhythm 2

Read measures 1–4 (first ending, marked with a "1."), then repeat; this time skip from measure 3 to the second ending in measure 4 (marked with a "2.") and continue to the end.

Rhythm 3

When you reach the *D.C. al Coda* instruction, return to the beginning and perform until the ⊕ (coda sign), then skip to the ⊕ on the last line.

Rhythm 4

B. Singing at sight

Perform each of the melodies. Each includes a period; determine whether it is parallel or contrasting. Write this answer in the blank and prepare to explain your choice.

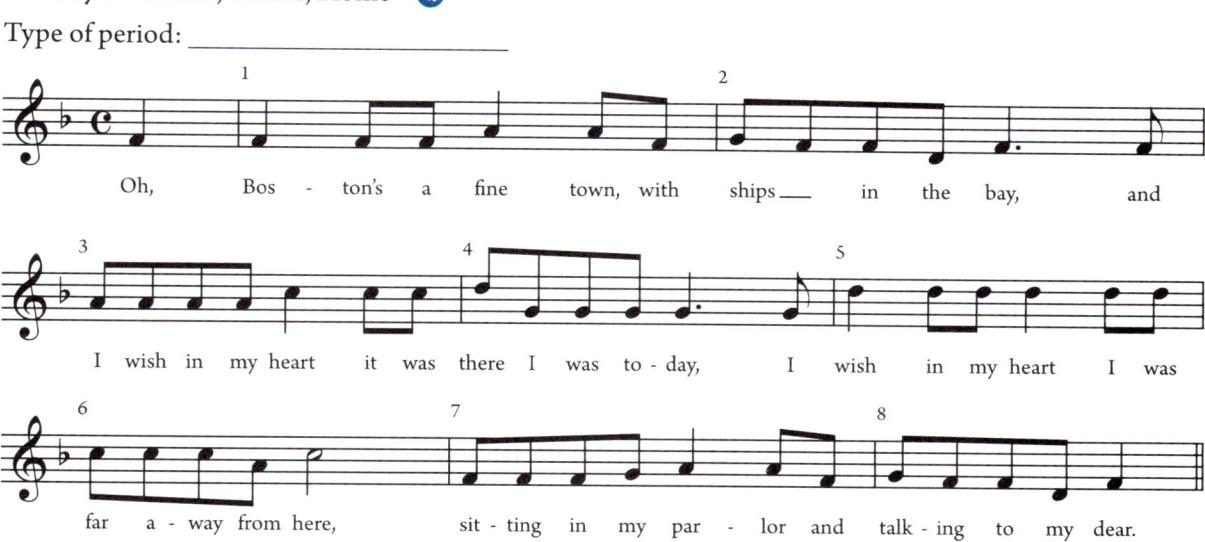

Melody 1 "Home, Dearie, Home"

Type of period: _____

Oh, Bos - ton's a fine town, with ships in the bay, and I wish in my heart it was there I was to - day, I wish in my heart I was far a - way from here, sit - ting in my par - lor and talk - ing to my dear.

Melody 2 Tony Velona and Remo Capra, "O Bambino," mm. 1–8

Type of period: _____

Melody 3 Alan Price, "The House of the Rising Sun," mm. 1–8

Type of period: _____

Very slow

There is a house in New Or - leans, they call the Ris - ing Sun, and it's been the ruin of man - y a poor boy, and God, I know I'm one.

Apply It   305

Melody 4 George Frideric Handel, "The Harmonious Blacksmith" (adapted)

Type of period in measures 5–12: _____

C. At the keyboard

1. Play the basic phrase progression below at the keyboard with your right hand, and play the root of each chord with your left hand (as shown in Example 11.7). Then play it again in the following keys: C major, F major, G major. If necessary, write it in the new key first and then play.

Basic phrase with dominant seventh

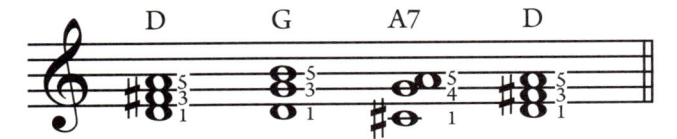

2. Play the progression again using accompanimental patterns: one note (the root) in your left hand and chords in your right hand. Be prepared to play any of the following patterns (refer to Example 11.9 for samples):

- Play the root in your left hand on beat 1 and the chord in your right on beat 2
- Play the same pattern in triple meter with the chord repeated
- Arpeggiate the chords

D. At the guitar

1. Play the basic phrase progression D–G–A7–D, using the left hand fingerings given in Appendix 8 with one of the right hand strumming patterns from Example A8.1.
2. Transpose the progression to A major, G major, and C major.
3. Perform the progression again, playing the chords as arpeggios.

NAME _____

Workbook ASSIGNMENT 11.1

A. Writing a parallel period

Write an eight-measure parallel period, following the guidelines in the chapter. After you write the first four measures, copy measures 1–2 as measures 5–6 to create a parallel structure. Use the treble-clef staff for the melody; a blank staff is provided in case you want to sketch triads or seventh chords beneath. You may write for an instrument or think in terms of a vocal phrase; if the latter, set a text to your melody. Be prepared to perform your melody in class.

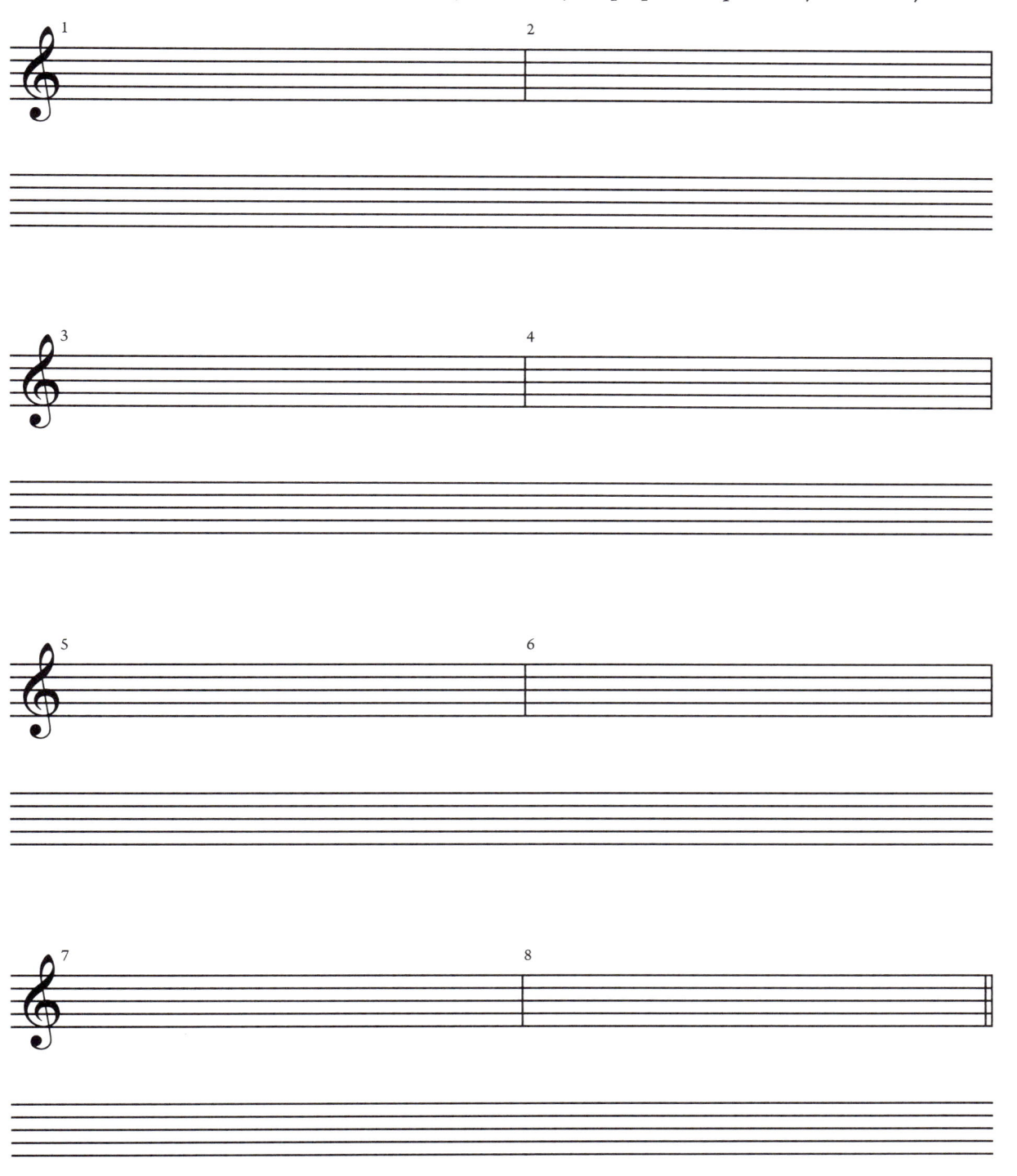

Assignment 11.1

B. Writing a contrasting period

Write an eight-measure contrasting period. After you write the first four measures, set measures 5 and following with a different melodic contour and a different rhythmic pattern. Use the treble-clef staff for the melody; as before, a blank staff is provided in case you want to sketch triads or seventh chords beneath. You may write for an instrument or think in terms of a vocal phrase; if the latter, set a text to your melody. Be prepared to perform your melody in class.

NAME _____

Workbook ASSIGNMENT 11.2

A. Writing chord progressions

Write the chord progressions below on the staff. Include the key signature, and write each chord in whole notes. Connect the chords smoothly. Commas and periods in the chord progressions indicate the end of a phrase; label the cadence at the end of each phrase (AC or HC).

(1) A♭: A♭–A♭–E♭–E♭, A♭–A♭–E♭7–A♭.

HC

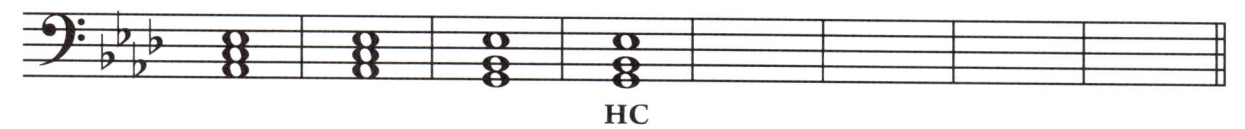

(2) F: F–C7–F–C7–C7, F–B♭–F–C7–F.

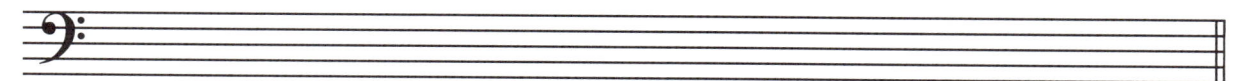

B. Writing a piano accompaniment from chord symbols

Write a piano chord in the bass clef for each chord symbol given. Circle and label any passing or neighbor tones in the melody, and identify any half or authentic cadence by writing HC or AC below the staff.

(1) "Simple Gifts," mm. 1–9

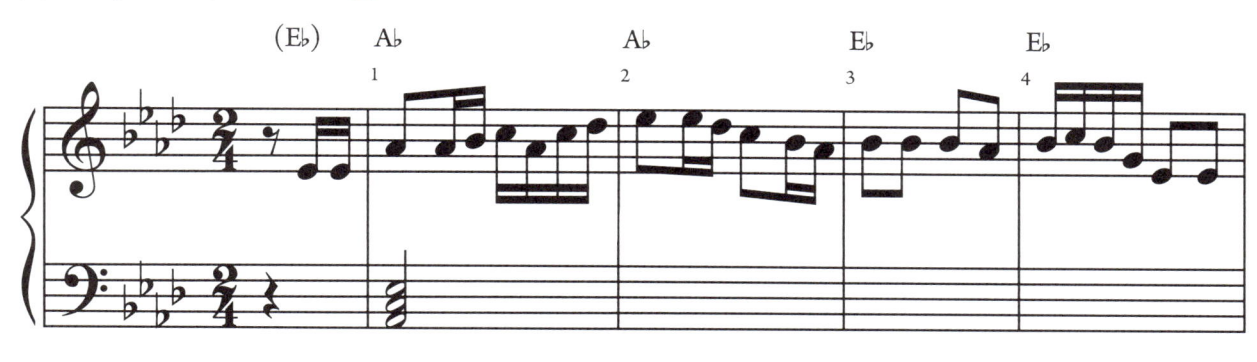

'Tis the gift to be simple, 'tis the gift to be free
'Tis the gift to come down where we ought to be
And when we find ourselves in the place just right,
'Twill be in the valley of love and delight.

Assignment 11.2 309

(2) "The Ash Grove"

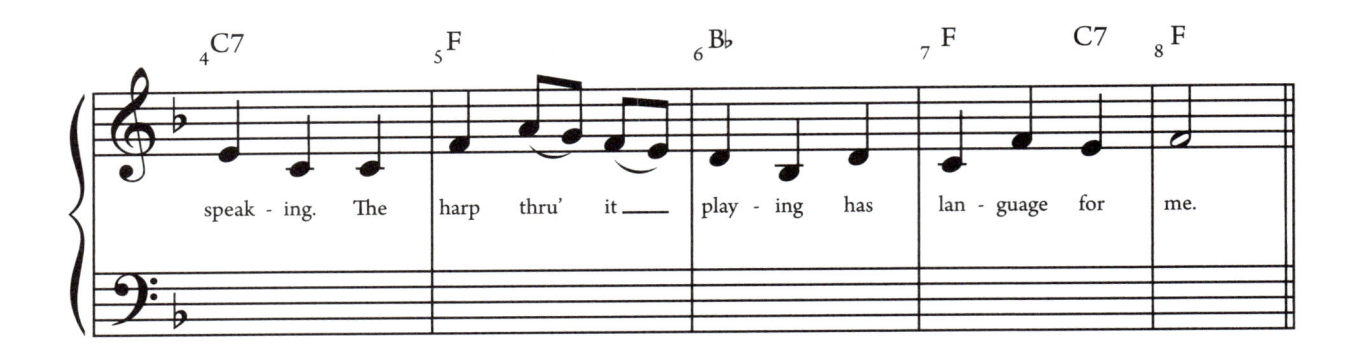

[Musical score: "The Ash Grove" in F major, 3/4 time, with chord symbols F, C7, F, C7, C7, F, B♭, F, C7, F above measures 1–8. Lyrics: "The ash grove how grace-ful, how plain-ly 'tis speak-ing. The harp thru' it play-ing has lan-guage for me."]

(3) On your own staff paper, write a full piano accompaniment for one of these melodies, 1 or 2. Take the chords you wrote and compose a piano part that could accompany a singer. Notate with right- and left-hand parts on a grand staff. Choose a chordal or arpeggiated texture, as described in the chapter. Add dynamic and tempo markings to make your accompaniment as musical as possible.

C. Analysis

Gather the notes in the left-hand part and notate them on the blank staff. Write the chord symbols for the pitches you have notated. Finally, label the circled pitches in the melody as passing (P) or neighbor (N) tones.

Mozart, Piano Sonata in C Major, K. 545, first movement, mm. 1–4

[Musical score: Allegro, mm. 1–4 of Mozart Piano Sonata K. 545, with blank staff below for notation.]

Chord symbols: C , G7 , ___ , ___ , ___ , ___

Cadence type: _____

310   CHAPTER ELEVEN   Form in Folk and Popular Songs

NAME _____

Workbook   ASSIGNMENT 11.3

A. Analysis: Lennon and McCartney, "Eight Days a Week"

Listen to this song, then fill in the form chart. Include section names (intro, verse, chorus, bridge, instrumental break, outro), the start of the first line of text in each section, and the number of measures in each section (conduct in $\frac{4}{4}$ meter and count the measures). If there is a refrain at the end of a verse, include its text and location. For any instrumental breaks, write "no text" and indicate what section the break is based on (if it is identifiable).

SECTION NAME	START OF TEXT	NUMBER OF MEASURES
Intro	(no text)	4
Verse 1	Ooh I need your . . .	16

(1) For the first verse, identify the phrases with letters and arcs, and indicate the number of measures for each.

$$\overset{\frown}{\underset{a}{4}}$$

(2) On what form is the verse based?

(3) How is the bridge similar to and different from the verses? (This question refers to the more contemporary type of "bridge," here following the first two verses.)

Assignment 11.3   311

B. Analysis: Green Day, "21 Guns"

Listen to this song (either the original Green Day version or the version from the Broadway musical *American Idiot*), then fill in the form chart. Include section names (intro, verse, chorus, bridge, instrumental break, outro), the start of the first line of text in each section, and the number of measures in each section (conduct in $\frac{4}{4}$ meter and count the measures). If there is a refrain at the end of a verse, indicate its text and location. For any instrumental breaks, write "no text" and indicate what section the break is based on (if it is identifiable).

SECTION NAME	START OF TEXT	NUMBER OF MEASURES
Intro	(no text)	4
Verse	Do you know . . .	8

CHAPTER ELEVEN Form in Folk and Popular Songs

Workbook AURAL SKILLS 11.1

Listen to an excerpt from an old popular song, and complete the following exercises.

(1) Notate the rhythm of the melody in common time.

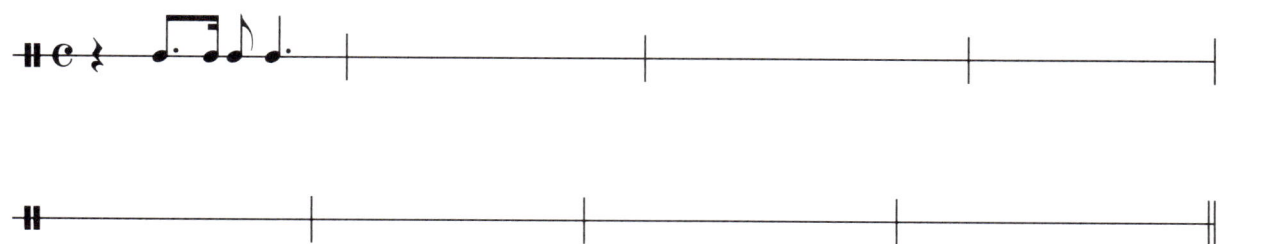

(2) Write the melody of the first phrase with scale-degree numbers or solfège syllables. The melody contains several neighbor tones that have been raised so that *re* ($\hat{2}$) becomes *ri* ($\sharp\hat{2}$), and *sol* ($\hat{5}$) becomes *si* ($\sharp\hat{5}$). Begin the melody with $\hat{3}$–$\sharp\hat{2}$–$\hat{3}$ (*mi–ri–mi*).

(3) Notate the pitches and rhythm of the first phrase on the staff below in C major.

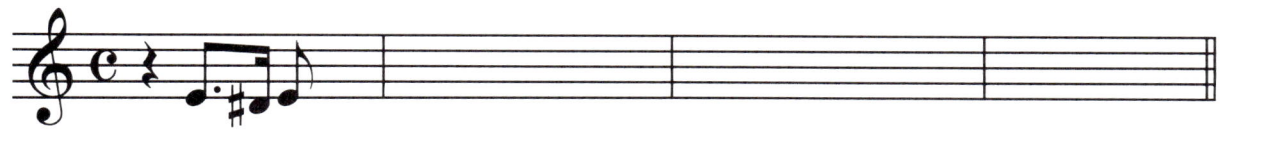

(4) The third and fourth melodic pitches create which interval?

a. M2 b. m3 c. M3 d. P4

(5) The excerpt contains two phrases based on the motive of the first measure. Which of the following statements best describes the relationship of the first phrase to the second?

a. The second phrase is an exact repetition of the first.
b. The second phrase is unrelated to the first.
c. The second phrase begins the same as the first but ends differently.
d. The second phrase begins differently from the first but ends the same.

(6) The first phrase concludes with which type of cadence?
   a. half   b. deceptive   c. imperfect authentic   d. perfect authentic

(7) Write the lowest part of the bass line of each phrase (sounding on the first and third beats) with scale-degree numbers of solfège syllables. Begin with $\hat{1}$–$\hat{5}$–$\hat{1}$ (do–sol–do).

Phrase 1:

Phrase 2:

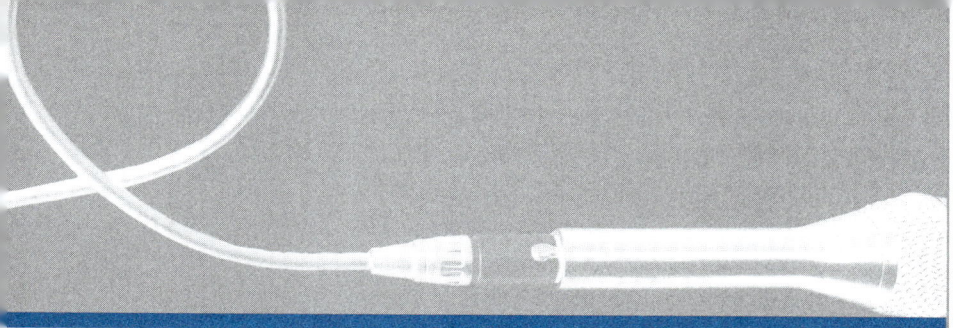

TOPICS
- pentatonic scales
- the blues scale and the 12-bar blues
- seventh chords
- chord extensions and sus chords

MUSIC
- Bobby Freeman, "Do You Want to Dance?"
- Enrique Iglesias, Paul Barry, and Mark Taylor, "Hero"
- John Newton, "Amazing Grace"
- Joel Phillips, "Blues for Norton"
- Lionel Richie, "Three Times a Lady"
- Hart A. Wand and Lloyd Garrett, "Dallas Blues"
- "Wayfaring Stranger"

CHAPTER 12

Blues and Other Popular Styles

Pentatonic Scales

In addition to major and minor scales, folk, jazz, and popular musicians typically employ pentatonic and blues scales. For an example, look at the melody for "Amazing Grace," shown in Example 12.1. In this melody, there are only five scale degrees, $\hat{1}$, $\hat{2}$, $\hat{3}$, $\hat{5}$, and $\hat{6}$ in G major. This is a **major pentatonic** scale. Since $\hat{4}$ and $\hat{7}$ are missing, there is no $\hat{7}$–$\hat{1}$ or $\hat{4}$–$\hat{3}$ half-step motion. Melodies based on the major pentatonic scale typically are harmonized with chords from the major scale.

EXAMPLE 12.1 Newton, "Amazing Grace"

(a) Score

[Musical score: "A-maz-ing grace, how sweet the sound That saved a wretch like me! I once was lost, but now am found, was blind but now I see."]

(b) G major pentatonic scale

[Musical notation showing scale degrees $\hat{1}$, $\hat{2}$, $\hat{3}$, $\hat{5}$, $\hat{6}$ — do, re, mi, sol, la]

Listen to Example 12.2, "Wayfaring Stranger," another pentatonic melody. From the key signature, the sound of the melody, and the beginning and ending notes, you might guess that the tune is in D minor, but the melody includes only five notes of the D natural minor scale: $\hat{1}$, $\flat\hat{3}$, $\hat{4}$, $\hat{5}$, and $\flat\hat{7}$. This scale is known as **minor pentatonic**. Melodies based on the minor pentatonic scale are often harmonized with chords from the natural minor scale. These are not the only possible pentatonic (five-note) scales; other pentatonic scales are heard in non-Western and popular music.

EXAMPLE 12.2   "Wayfaring Stranger"

(a) Score

I am a poor way-far-ing stran-ger a trav-'ling through this world of woe; yet there's no sick-ness, toil or dan-ger in that bright world to which I go.

(b) D minor pentatonic scale

$\hat{1}$ — do
$\flat\hat{3}$ — me
$\hat{4}$ — fa
$\hat{5}$ — sol
$\flat\hat{7}$ — te

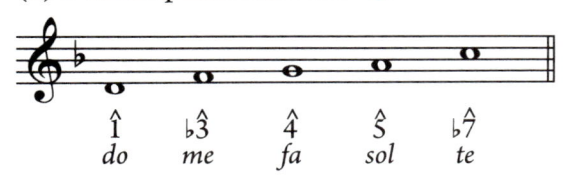

Example 12.3 compares the major and minor pentatonic scales beginning on C: both share C and G ($\hat{1}$ and $\hat{5}$), and each has the quality of the third associated with its name, major or minor.

EXAMPLE 12.3   C pentatonic scales

(a) Major pentatonic

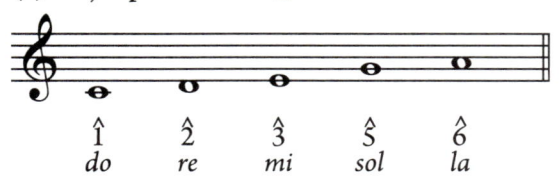

$\hat{1}$ — do
$\hat{2}$ — re
$\hat{3}$ — mi
$\hat{5}$ — sol
$\hat{6}$ — la

(b) Minor pentatonic

$\hat{1}$ — do
$\flat\hat{3}$ — me
$\hat{4}$ — fa
$\hat{5}$ — sol
$\flat\hat{7}$ — te

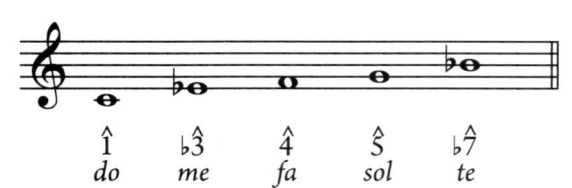

TRY IT #1

For each tonic pitch given, write the major pentatonic scale on the left and the minor pentatonic on the right. Think of the major and minor key signatures, and use the scale degrees shown in Example 12.3 to help you.

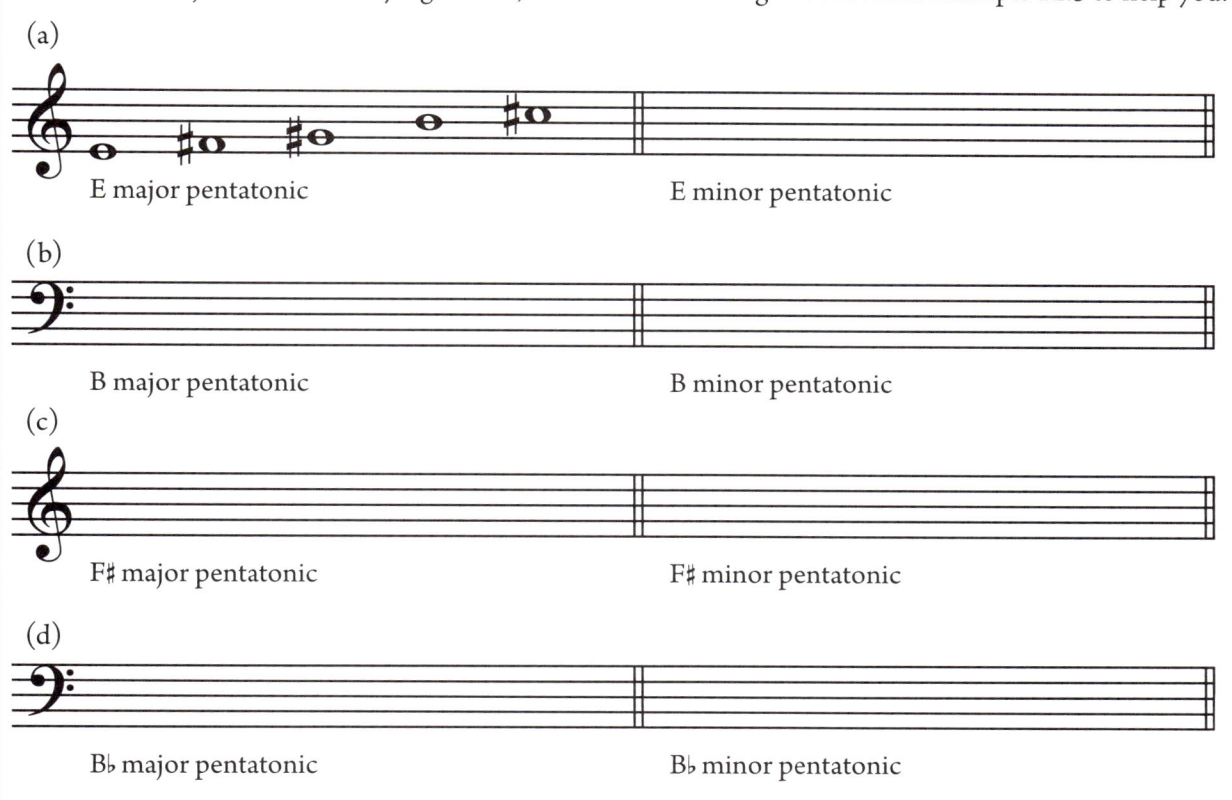

(a) E major pentatonic | E minor pentatonic

(b) B major pentatonic | B minor pentatonic

(c) F♯ major pentatonic | F♯ minor pentatonic

(d) B♭ major pentatonic | B♭ minor pentatonic

Like relative major and minor keys, there are major and minor pentatonic scales that share the same pitches, but have different tonic notes, as shown in Example 12.4.

KEY CONCEPT One easy way to remember the pattern of the pentatonic scales is to think of the black keys on a piano. Play the black keys from F♯ to F♯ (or G♭ to G♭) as shown in Example 12.4 to make a major pentatonic scale with F♯ as tonic. Then play the same collection of black keys from D♯ to D♯ (or E♭ to E♭) to make a minor pentatonic scale with D♯ as tonic.

EXAMPLE 12.4 Black-key notes as major and minor pentatonic scales

(a) Major pentatonic scale starting on F♯

$\hat{1}$ $\hat{2}$ $\hat{3}$ $\hat{5}$ $\hat{6}$
do re mi sol la

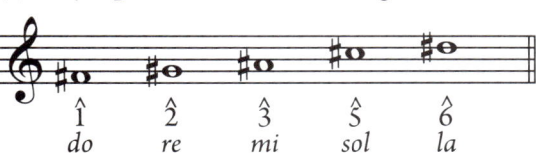

(b) Minor pentatonic scale starting on D♯

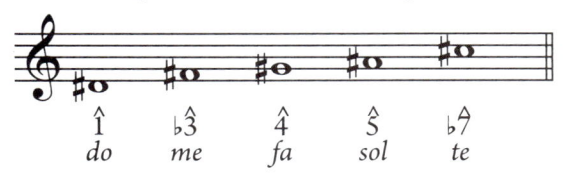

$\hat{1}$ ♭$\hat{3}$ $\hat{4}$ $\hat{5}$ ♭$\hat{7}$
do me fa sol te

The Blues Scale and the 12-Bar Blues

The blues, which grew out of African American musical practice, has become one of the most important influences on popular music in the world today. Listen to "Blues for Norton" (anthology, p. 388). It is scored for jazz **combo**, a small instrumental ensemble usually consisting of (at least) a solo instrument, keyboard, and drum set (snare drum, bass drum, and cymbals). The solo instruments in this combo are clarinet and alto saxophone. Usually, as here, the drummer's rhythms are improvised and not notated in the score.

Listen to the last few measures while following the score in Example 12.5a. The key signature suggests that the work is in F major, but the melody features a repeated and prominent ♭$\hat{3}$ (A♭). The piano part includes both A♭ and A♮, and sometimes plays $\hat{3}$ (A♮) while the solo instrument plays ♭$\hat{3}$ (A♭), as in measures 23–24. In addition, the piano has both $\hat{7}$ and ♭$\hat{7}$ (E♮ and E♭). The lowered third and seventh scale degrees are two of the possible **blue notes** in this style, which help give the blues its distinctive sound. They both come from the **blues scale**, shown in Example 12.5b.

EXAMPLE 12.5   Phillips, "Blues for Norton," mm. 20–24

(a) Score

(b) Blues scale

> **KEY CONCEPT** The blues scale shares most of its pitches with the minor pentatonic, with an added ♯$\hat{4}$/♭$\hat{5}$. A performance of a blues melody with a major-key accompaniment blurs the distinction between major and minor by including both $\hat{3}$ and ♭$\hat{3}$ and both $\hat{7}$ and ♭$\hat{7}$.

Example 12.6 shows the blues scale beginning on C; sing the scale to become familiar with its sound. The flatted fifth (here, the F♯ or G♭) changes spelling with the direction of the melody: the player's tuning on this note may be slightly higher when ascending (F♯) and slightly lower when descending (G♭). The accidentals in the scale are the blue notes. When writing blues, use the major key signature of the tonic pitch and add accidentals as needed, as in "Blues for Norton."

EXAMPLE 12.6   Blues scale on C

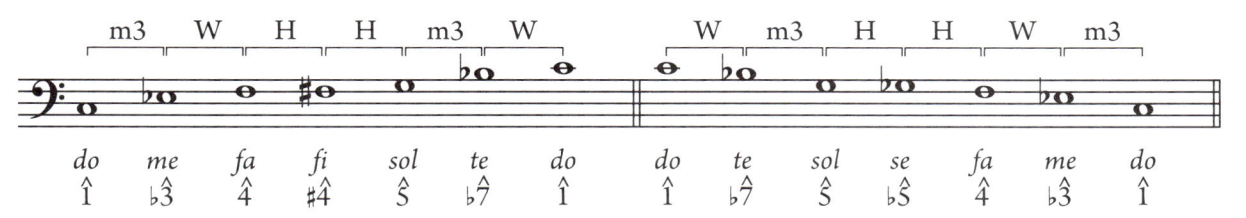

The anthology includes two scores for "Blues for Norton": one is a full score that shows what each instrumentalist plays on the recording (p. 389); more often, blues performers play from a **lead sheet** (p. 388), which gives the primary melody plus chord symbols. Instrumentalists improvise their parts from these musical cues. Follow the lead sheet as you listen to the recording. The piano part, not included in the lead sheet, is created spontaneously by the pianist, who follows the chord symbols. Likewise, the bass player not only supplies the roots of the chords, but also adds considerable melodic and rhythmic interest to the performance with improvised stepwise motion and some arpeggiations of harmonies.

Example 12.7 is the lead sheet for the first twelve bars of "Splanky." Listen while following along. (The performance also includes a long piano introduction not shown here.) Compare the pitches of Example 12.7 with the blues scale shown in Example 12.6.

EXAMPLE 12.7   Count Basie, "Splanky," mm. 1–12

> **KEY CONCEPT** Although the blues scale is based on the minor pentatonic scale, it is typically harmonized by chords from a major key. This juxtaposition of major-key harmonies with the minor pentatonic scale in the solo parts accounts for much of the distinctive character of blues compositions.

In "Splanky," the key signature provided is for C major, but the melody is based on the C minor pentatonic scale, necessitating many accidentals. Basie's melody draws on the full blues scale on C except for B♭ (which, however, is present in the C7 chord, C–E–G–B♭). The F♯ (♯$\hat{4}$) in the ascending melody in measure 3 becomes a G♭ (♭$\hat{5}$) in measure 4 when the melody descends. The notes E♮ and E♭ ($\hat{3}$ and ♭$\hat{3}$) are heard simultaneously, as is typical: the melody in measure 1 features the blue note E♭, while the C7 chord harmonizing it has E♮.

TRY IT #2

Write blues scales that begin on the pitches given below, ascending and descending. Supply the appropriate major key signature, and add accidentals. Remember to use $\sharp\hat{4}$ ascending and $\flat\hat{5}$ descending.

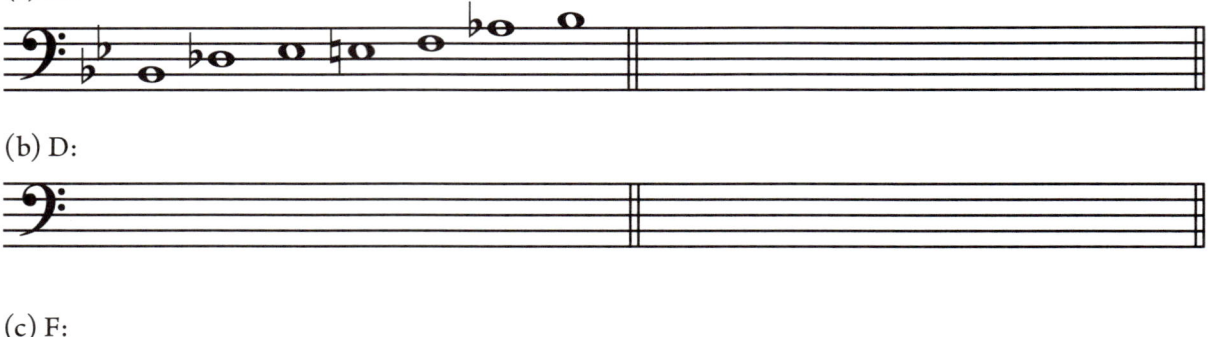

(a) B♭:

(b) D:

(c) F:

ASSIGNMENT 12.1

Another important aspect of blues style is its harmonic structure. Unlike a 32-bar song form, with four 8-measure phrases, the **12-bar blues** consists of a single harmonic progression or set of chord changes (called the **changes** by jazz musicians) that is repeated many times over the course of a performance. It is helpful to think of the progression as three 4-bar units, labeled (a), (b), and (c) in Figure 12.1.

> **KEY CONCEPT** The typical 12-bar blues progression begins with 4 measures of tonic harmony (a), followed by 2 measures of IV and 2 measures of I (b). The last 4 measures (c) feature the chords V–IV–I and end with a final tonic measure. This last measure may serve as a **turnaround**, with V or V⁷ instead of or after the tonic, leading back to the beginning (a) for another repetition of the chorus.

FIGURE 12.1   12-bar blues harmonic scheme

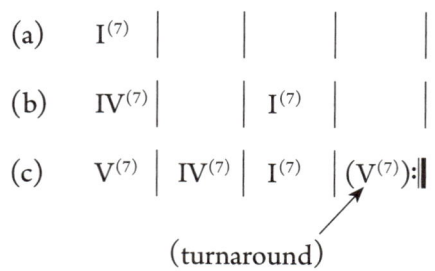

(a) | I⁽⁷⁾ | | | |
(b) | IV⁽⁷⁾ | | I⁽⁷⁾ | |
(c) | V⁽⁷⁾ | IV⁽⁷⁾ | I⁽⁷⁾ | (V⁽⁷⁾) :||

(turnaround)

Each harmony in the 12-bar blues may be played as a triad or dominant seventh chord, as shown. This basic progression may be varied by adding or omitting chords—see "Dallas Blues" (anthology, p. 395), an early blues composition, for a variant.

In popular styles such as jazz and the blues, harmonic progressions and dissonance are treated differently from their counterparts in classical styles. First, the seventh chord is considered as stable as the triad. Seventh chords may appear on any degree of the scale and on nearly every change of chord. Second, while in classical music chordal sevenths are considered a dissonance that must resolve down by stepwise motion, in popular styles sevenths may be left unresolved for their color or dramatic effect. Third, the progression V–IV (or V^7–IV^7) is an integral part of the 12-bar blues (occurring at its final cadence) and is standard practice in rock, but it is rare in classical compositions and folk songs.

Example 12.8 shows the blues chord progression for "Splanky" in lead-sheet notation, without the melody. The four slashes in each measure mean that performers should improvise on each chord for four beats—the voicing and rhythm of the chord are up to the performer, in collaboration with the other members of the combo. The chords whose symbols are given in parentheses may be omitted.

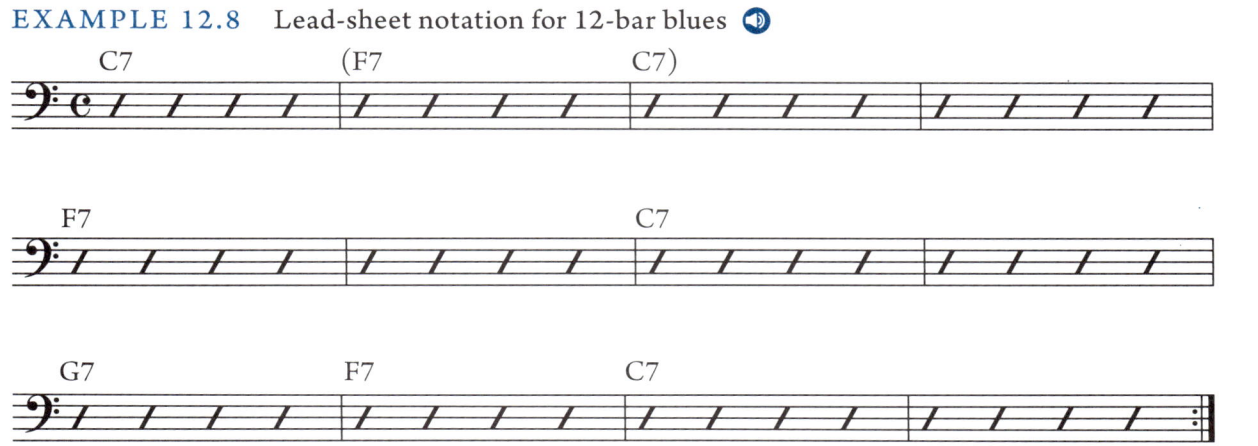

EXAMPLE 12.8   Lead-sheet notation for 12-bar blues

Listen again to "Splanky," following the chord changes; it may help to sing the chord roots along with the recording. Try out its progression at the keyboard (you can simply play the chord once per measure, or repeat it on each beat), then play through Basie's melody or create your own, drawing on the C blues scale from Example 12.6. In traditional blues practice, players first perform the initial tune and progression (together called the **head**), then with each successive chorus, various performers improvise over the chord changes. The head usually returns at the end of the performance, and sometimes in the middle as well. The 12-bar blues progression was adopted by rock musicians in the 1950s and appears in songs of many styles after that time.

Seventh Chords

Seventh chords, pervasive in popular styles, may be built on every degree of the scale, resulting in many different types of sonorities.

> **KEY CONCEPT** Seventh chords consist of four tones: a root, third, fifth, and seventh (see Chapter 9). A seventh chord is named for the quality of its triad plus the quality of its seventh.

Example 12.9 illustrates the five most common seventh-chord types, with an example of each built above middle C. A major-major seventh chord (MM7) is a major triad plus a M7; a minor-minor seventh chord (mm7) is a minor triad plus a m7. A MM7 is often called a **major seventh** for short, a mm7 is a **minor seventh**, and a major-minor seventh chord (Mm7) is a dominant seventh. A seventh chord built from a diminished triad and minor seventh (dm7) is typically called a **half-diminished seventh**, abbreviated ⌀7, and a chord built from a diminished triad and a diminished seventh (dd7) is a fully diminished seventh (or just a **diminished seventh**), abbreviated °7.

EXAMPLE 12.9   Seventh chords built above middle C

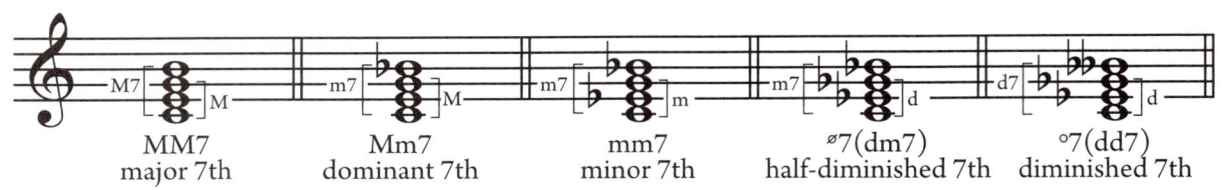

	MM7	Mm7	mm7	⌀7 (dm7)	°7 (dd7)
	major 7th	dominant 7th	minor 7th	half-diminished 7th	diminished 7th

The quality of a seventh chord in a key depends on the scale degree of its root. The seventh chords built on each degree of the G major scale are given in Example 12.10, while Example 12.11 shows seventh chords built on the G minor scale. Since $\flat\hat{7}$ is typically raised in minor, the chords on $\hat{5}$ and $\hat{7}$ are written with an F♯; the chord on the leading tone in minor is therefore a diminished seventh, while the half-diminished seventh appears on $\hat{2}$. Together, these two examples list all the seventh chords commonly found in tonal music.

EXAMPLE 12.10   Seventh chords built above the G major scale

	$\hat{1}$	$\hat{2}$	$\hat{3}$	$\hat{4}$	$\hat{5}$	$\hat{6}$	$\hat{7}$
Triad quality	M	m	m	M	M	m	d
7th quality	M	m	m	M	m	m	m
Name	major seventh	minor seventh	minor seventh	major seventh	dominant seventh	minor seventh	half-diminished seventh
Abbreviation	MM7	mm7	mm7	MM7	Mm7	mm7	⌀7
Roman numeral	I⁷	ii⁷	iii⁷	IV⁷	V⁷	vi⁷	vii⌀⁷
Chord symbol	Gmaj7	Amin7	Bmin7	Cmaj7	D7	Emin7	F♯min7(♭5) or F♯⌀7

EXAMPLE 12.11   Seventh chords built above the G minor scale

	$\hat{1}$	$\hat{2}$	$\flat\hat{3}$	$\hat{4}$	$\hat{5}$	$\flat\hat{6}$	$\hat{7}$
Triad quality	m	d	M	m	M	M	d
7th quality	m	m	M	m	m	M	d
Name	minor seventh	half-diminished seventh	major seventh	minor seventh	dominant seventh	major seventh	diminished seventh
Abbreviation	mm7	⌀7	MM7	mm7	Mm7	MM7	°7
Roman numeral	i⁷	ii⌀⁷	III⁷	iv⁷	V⁷	VI⁷	vii°⁷
Chord symbol	Gmin7	Amin7(♭5) or A⌀7	B♭maj7	Cmin7	D7	E♭maj7	F♯dim7 or F♯°7

The bottom rows of Examples 12.10 and 12.11 give the chord symbol for each seventh chord. Although seventh chords appear frequently in popular music, the labels used to designate them are not completely standardized. Alternate labels for seventh chords above C are listed in Figure 12.2.

FIGURE 12.2 Seventh-chord symbols

Seventh-chord type	Abbreviation	Chord symbol
Major	MM7	Cmaj7, CM7, Cma7, CΔ7
Dominant	Mm7	C7
Minor	mm7	Cmin7, Cmi7, Cm7, C−7
Half-diminished	ø7 or dm7	Cø7, Cmin7(♭5)
Diminished	°7 or dd7	C°7, Cdim7, Cd7

To spell a specific seventh chord above a given root, first spell the correct quality triad, then add the correct quality seventh. Example 12.12 illustrates the steps for writing a minor seventh chord above F:

(1) Spell a minor triad, F–A♭–C.
(2) Add the seventh, E (a third above the fifth of the triad).
(3) Check the seventh's quality; if it is not correct, add an accidental. Since F to E is a major seventh, lower the E to E♭.
(4) Use this shortcut to check the quality of the seventh: invert the seventh to make a second. If the second is minor, the seventh is major; if the second is major, the seventh is minor.

EXAMPLE 12.12 Steps to spell a minor seventh chord

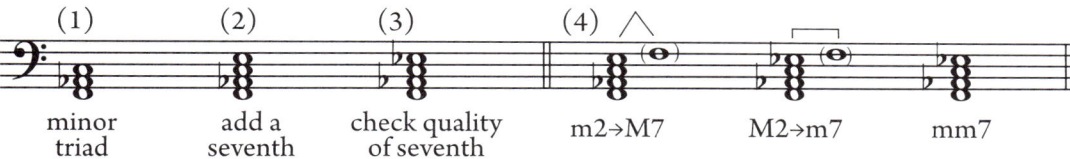

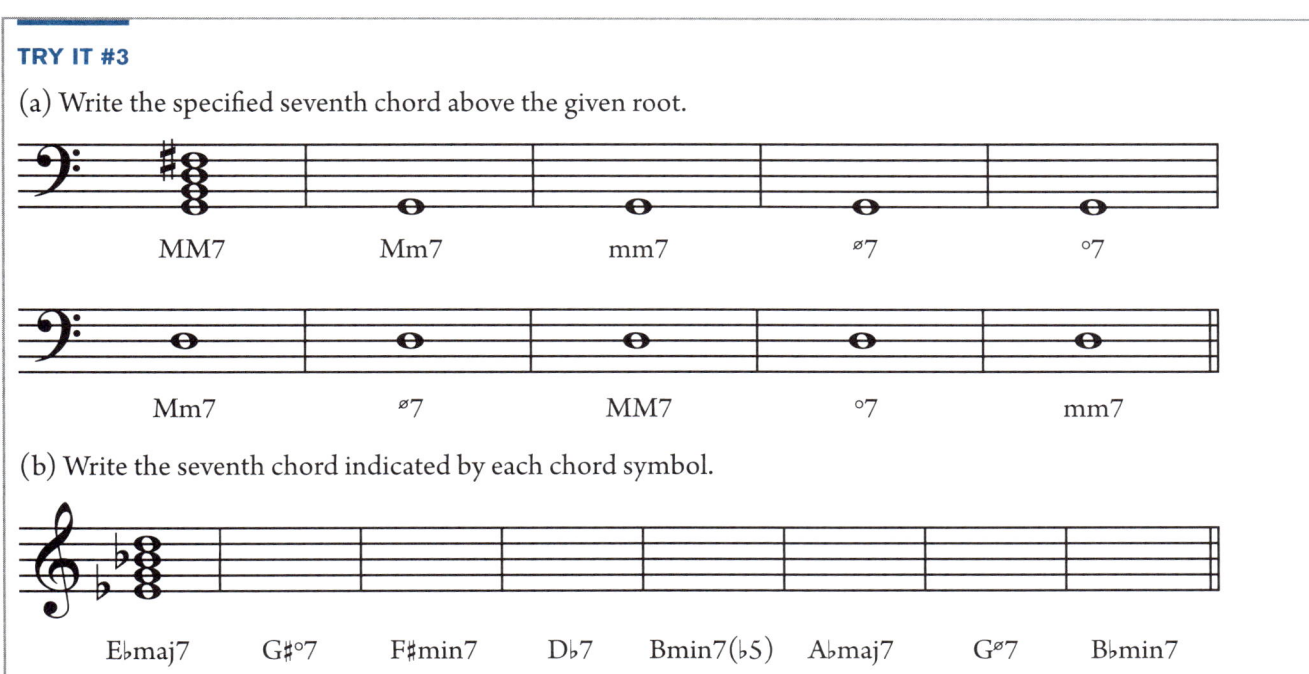

TRY IT #3

(a) Write the specified seventh chord above the given root.

MM7   Mm7   mm7   ø7   °7

Mm7   ø7   MM7   °7   mm7

(b) Write the seventh chord indicated by each chord symbol.

E♭maj7   G♯°7   F♯min7   D♭7   Bmin7(♭5)   A♭maj7   Gø7   B♭min7

ASSIGNMENT 12.2, AURAL SKILLS 12.1

Seventh Chords   323

Chord Extensions and Sus Chords

We conclude this chapter by exploring a few additional chords that you may encounter in popular music.

> **KEY CONCEPT** One way to embellish basic triads or seventh chords is to add pitches; these added pitches are sometimes called **chord extensions**.

Look at an excerpt from the Beach Boys' "Do You Want to Dance?" shown in Example 12.13. In this example, all of the chords have sevenths, and two also have a ninth added, making **ninth chords**. The basic progression is I–IV–iii–vi–ii–V–I (D–G–F♯m–Bm–Em–A–D). In measure 8, a ninth chord (Dmaj9) is created by taking a D major triad D–F♯–A, adding a seventh to make D–F♯–A–C♯ (a major-major seventh chord), then adding one more third to make the ninth: D–F♯–A–C♯–E. The same Dmaj9 chord reappears in measure 12. For MM7 or mm7 chords, the added ninth is usually a M9 (as here). In the case of the dominant seventh chord, it may be either a m9 or a M9. If you are writing in four voices and need to leave out one chord tone, omit the fifth. You may also find symbols for eleventh or thirteenth chords in some lead sheets. Simply add the eleventh (a P4) or thirteenth (a M6 or m6) above the bass in these chords.

EXAMPLE 12.13   Freeman, "Do You Want to Dance?" mm. 8–12

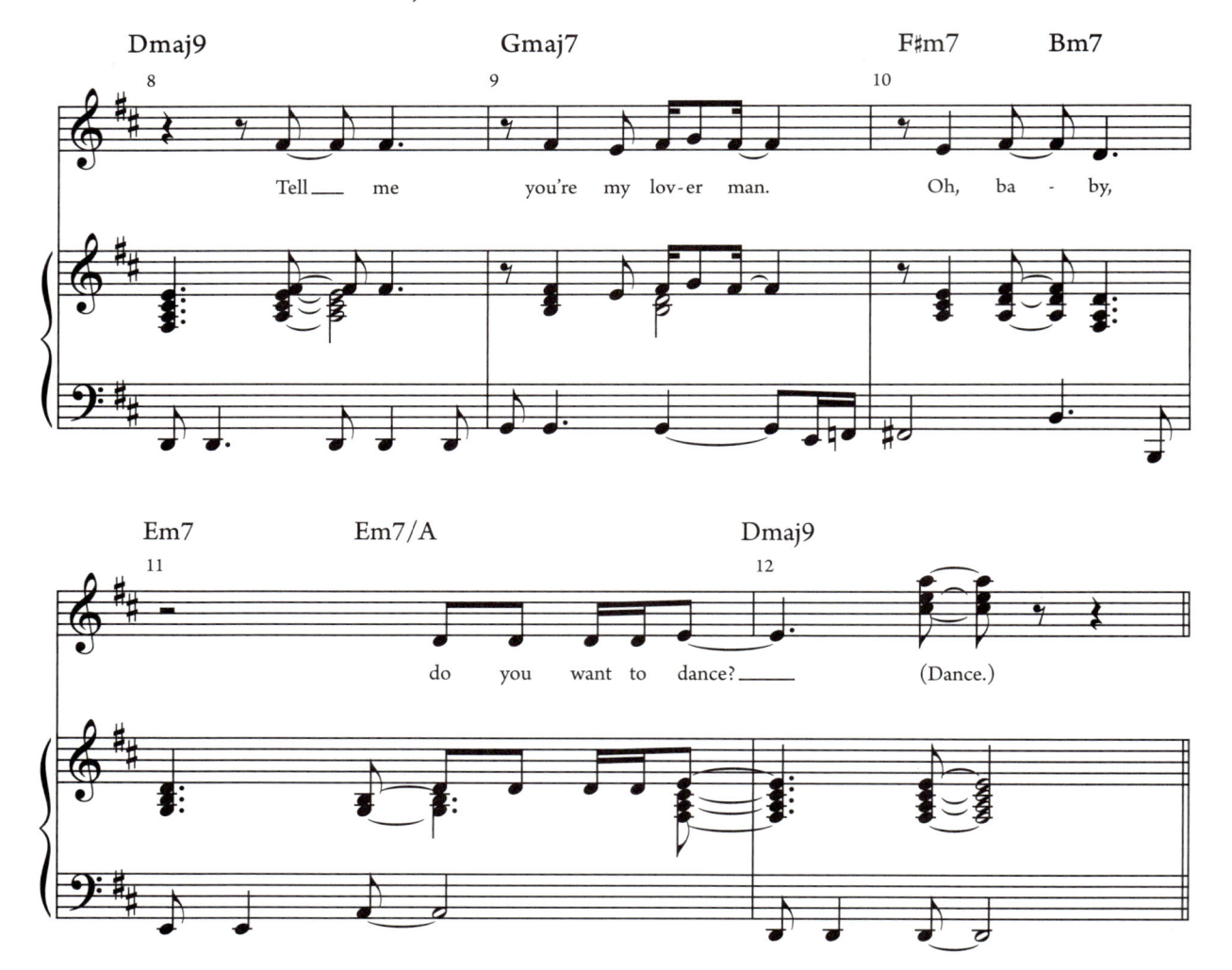

A sixth added to a triad can be indicated by "add 6" or a "6" next to the chord symbol, as in D♭6 in measure 43 of Lionel Richie's "Three Times a Lady," shown in Example 12.14. This chord is sometimes referred to as an **added-sixth chord**, and if labeled this way, the added sixth is normally a M6, whether the triad to which it is added is major or minor. In this particular example, the symbol D♭6/A♭ means to play a D♭ triad (D♭–F–A♭) with an added sixth (B♭) over an A♭ in the bass. Measures 43 and 44 also indicate the bass this way.

EXAMPLE 12.14   Richie, "Three Times a Lady," mm. 41–44

In addition to ninth chords and added-sixth chords, a third type of chord you may encounter in popular music that adds dissonance and color to a harmonic progression is a **sus** (or **sus4**) **chord**. Example 12.15, shows both the sus4 chord and another occasionally used sus chord, a sus2; the sus in these abbreviations stands for "suspended." In the typical sus (or sus4) chord, a fourth replaces the third of the chord: for example, the Dsus chord has D–G–A, with the G replacing the third (F♯) of the triad. For the sus2, the third of the triad is missing, replaced by 2. Sus chords are named for the suspension, an embellishment in classical style in which a note is held over (or suspended) from a previous chord and then resolves down by step. Unlike suspensions, dissonances in sus chords need not be held over from the previous chord and may not resolve. Example 12.15 also shows another type of chord symbol alteration; in G5, the addition of 5 means to leave out the third, resulting in a chord with only roots and fifths (G and D).

EXAMPLE 12.15   Iglesias, Barry, and Taylor, "Hero," mm. 1–4

As we near the end of this text, we challenge you to continue exploring music—by listening, playing, singing, and writing. Take some of the harmonies, forms, and styles introduced in the last two chapters and write some music of your own. Be curious, take more courses, and above all, experience music of many styles, periods, and regions. In the twenty-first century, the whole world of music is open to you. Explore and enjoy!

ASSIGNMENT 12.3, 12.4

Did You Know?

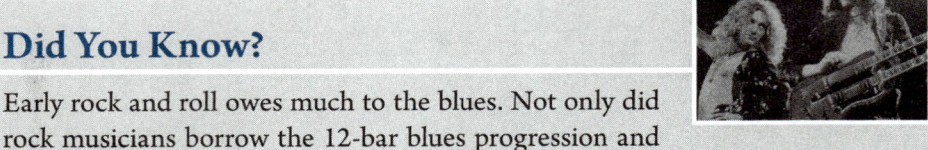

Early rock and roll owes much to the blues. Not only did rock musicians borrow the 12-bar blues progression and the blues scale, in some cases they also reworked entire blues songs—either as covers (interpretations that acknowledged the original composers) or as "new" songs of their own. Rock-music scholars (and lawyers) have debated the question of when borrowed material becomes one's own and when it is protected by copyright law. For example, some of Led Zepplin's most famous songs have blues roots, raising both scholarly and legal controversies about their authorship. These songs include "Dazed and Confused" (compare with Jake Holmes's "I'm Confused"), "Whole Lotta Love" (compare with Willie Dixon's "You Need Love"), "Bring It on Home" (compare with a song with the same title by Willie Dixon), and the "Lemon Song" (compare with Howlin' Wolf/Chester Burnett's "The Killing Floor").

Terms You Should Know

12-bar blues	diminished seventh chord	pentatonic scale
added-sixth chord	half-diminished seventh chord	major pentatonic
blue notes	head	minor pentatonic
blues scale	lead sheet	sus chord
changes	major seventh chord	turnaround
chord extensions	minor seventh chord	
combo	ninth chord	

Questions for Review

1. What distinguishes the major pentatonic from the minor pentatonic?
2. What distinguishes the minor pentatonic from the blues scale?
3. What is the standard harmonic progression for the 12-bar blues?
4. How is an extended blues piece structured (beyond the first 12 bars)?
5. Which seventh-chord types appear in jazz and popular styles?
6. How are seventh chords treated differently in popular styles and classical style?
7. Describe how seventh-chord qualities are represented in chord symbols.
8. What extensions may be added to triads and seventh chords in popular styles?
9. How are added-sixth and sus chords represented in chord symbols?
10. How are bass notes specified in chord symbols?

Reading Review

Match the term on the left with the best answer on the right.

_____ (1) sus4 chord
_____ (2) minor pentatonic
_____ (3) turnaround
_____ (4) combo
_____ (5) half-diminished seventh
_____ (6) added-sixth
_____ (7) diminished seventh
_____ (8) ninth chord
_____ (9) major pentatonic
_____ (10) lead sheet
_____ (11) blues scale
_____ (12) V–IV

(a) minor pentatonic plus $\sharp\hat{4}$ or $\flat\hat{5}$
(b) chord extension of a M6 above the root
(c) diminished triad plus diminished seventh
(d) diminished triad plus minor seventh
(e) *do–re–mi–sol–la*
(f) *do–me–fa–sol–te*
(g) progression common in blues and rock but not in classical music
(h) notation with melody and chord symbols
(i) chord extension of a third above the chordal seventh
(j) dominant chord at end of 12-bar blues to prepare for the next chorus
(k) chord with its third replaced by a fourth
(l) jazz instrumental performance group

Additional review and practice available at wwnorton.com/studyspace

Apply It

A. At the keyboard

Singing pentatonic scales

1. "Will This Circle Be Unbroken" is based on the major pentatonic scale ($\hat{1}$–$\hat{2}$–$\hat{3}$–$\hat{5}$–$\hat{6}$; *do–re–mi–sol–la*). Play C–F, the dominant and tonic pitches, and sing the song with solfège syllables or scale-degree numbers.

"Will This Circle Be Unbroken," mm. 1–4

Will	this	cir	cle	be	un	bro	ken,	by	and	by,	Lord,	by	and	by.
sol	la	do	do	mi	re	do	mi	mi	mi	re	do	re	do	la	sol
$\hat{5}$	$\hat{6}$	$\hat{1}$	$\hat{1}$	$\hat{3}$	$\hat{2}$	$\hat{1}$	$\hat{3}$	$\hat{3}$	$\hat{3}$	$\hat{2}$	$\hat{1}$	$\hat{2}$	$\hat{1}$	$\hat{6}$	$\hat{5}$

2. Bartók's "Evening in Transylvania" is based on the minor pentatonic scale ($\hat{1}$–♭$\hat{3}$–$\hat{4}$–$\hat{5}$–♭$\hat{7}$; *do–me–fa–sol–te*). Play the first pitch of the melody, E, and sing the rest with solfège syllables or scale-degree numbers.

Béla Bartók, "Evening in Transylvania," from *Ten Easy Pieces*, mm. 23–26

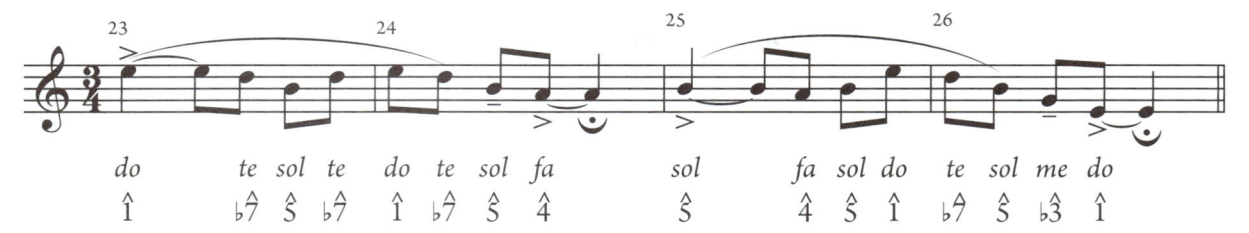

do	te	sol	te	do	te	sol	fa	sol	fa	sol	do	te	sol	me	do
$\hat{1}$	♭$\hat{7}$	$\hat{5}$	♭$\hat{7}$	$\hat{1}$	♭$\hat{7}$	$\hat{5}$	$\hat{4}$	$\hat{5}$	$\hat{4}$	$\hat{5}$	$\hat{1}$	♭$\hat{7}$	$\hat{5}$	♭$\hat{3}$	$\hat{1}$

Performing pentatonic and blues scales

As you play each of the following exercises at the keyboard, sing up and down with solfège syllables, scale-degree numbers, and letter names.

3. Major pentatonic

- Transpose "Will This Circle Be Unbroken" to G♭ major. Begin on D♭ and play only black keys.
- From each of the tonic pitches below, play a major scale. Perform the scale again, but omit $\hat{4}$ and $\hat{7}$ to create the major pentatonic scale.

(a) C   (e) E   (i) A♭
(b) D   (f) E♭   (j) G♭
(c) A   (g) F
(d) G   (h) B♭

4. Minor pentatonic

- Transpose "Evening in Transylvania" so that it begins on E♭; play only on the black keys.
- From each of the tonic pitches below, play a natural minor scale. Perform the scale again, but omit $\hat{2}$ and ♭$\hat{6}$ to create the minor pentatonic scale.

(a) C   (e) E   (i) C♯
(b) D   (f) E♭   (j) F♯
(c) A   (g) F
(d) G   (h) B♭

5. Blues

To write a blues scale, treat its letter name (A♭, for example) as the tonic of a major key, and write the blues scale using that key signature (four flats). The blue notes—♭$\hat{3}$, ♯$\hat{4}$/♭$\hat{5}$, and ♭$\hat{7}$—will always require accidentals, no matter what the key signature.

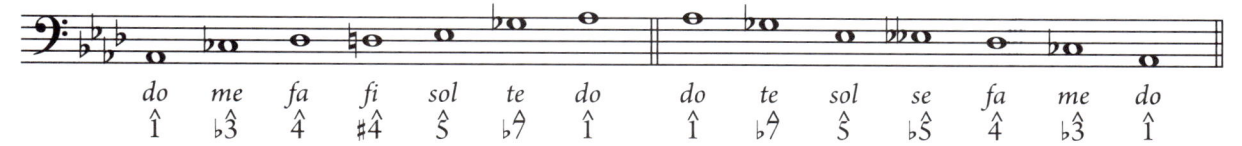

do me fa fi sol te do do te sol se fa me do
$\hat{1}$ ♭$\hat{3}$ $\hat{4}$ ♯$\hat{4}$ $\hat{5}$ ♭$\hat{7}$ $\hat{1}$ $\hat{1}$ ♭$\hat{7}$ $\hat{5}$ ♭$\hat{5}$ $\hat{4}$ ♭$\hat{3}$ $\hat{1}$

Now perform an ascending and descending blues scale starting with each note below. As you play, sing in a comfortable register with solfège syllables, scale-degree numbers, and letter names. Then notate each scale on staff paper. Write the key signature of the major tonic, and notate the accidentals for each blue note.

(a) B♭ (c) A   (e) F   (g) E
(b) E♭ (d) G   (f) D   (h) F♯

Playing and spelling seventh chords

There are two ways to think about playing the five frequently used seventh chords: (a) the triad-plus-seventh strategy and (b) the triad-plus-third strategy. Each method is summarized.

Triad-plus-seventh strategy Given a root and seventh-chord type, perform the appropriate triad, then add the correct type of seventh above its root.

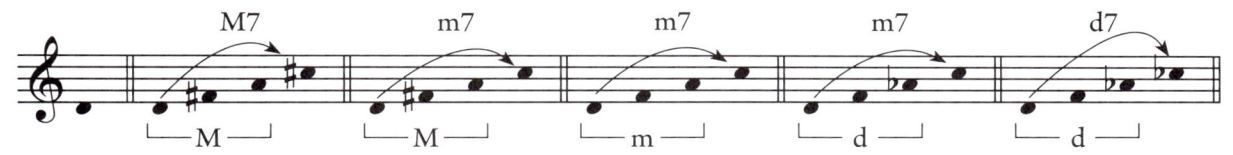

Seventh chord	Triad quality	Plus this seventh
major (MM7)	major	M7
dominant (Mm7)	major	m7
minor (mm7)	minor	m7
half-diminished (ø7)	diminished	m7
diminished (°7)	diminished	d7

Triad-plus-third strategy Given a root and seventh-chord type, perform the appropriate triad, then add the correct type of third above its fifth.

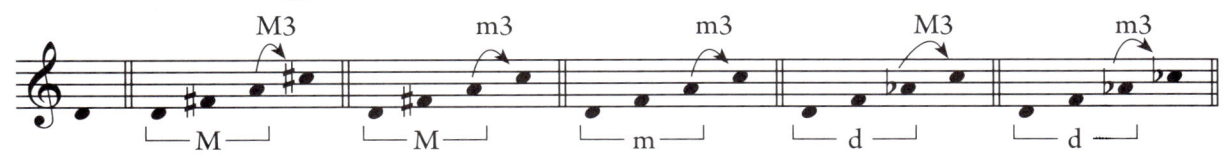

Seventh chord	Triad quality	Plus this third
major (MM7)	major	M3
dominant (Mm7)	major	m3
minor (mm7)	minor	m3
half-diminished (ø7)	diminished	M3
diminished (°7)	diminished	m3

6. Consider each pitch below to be the root of a seventh chord. Perform all five types of seventh chords from each root following either strategy. Play each at the keyboard root alone, then MM7, Mm7, mm7, ø7, and °7.

(a) D
(b) A
(c) F♯
(d) E
(e) F
(f) C♯
(g) B
(h) G
(i) E♭
(j) B♭
(k) C
(l) A♭

B. Singing at sight

Identify whether each melody uses the major or minor pentatonic scale.

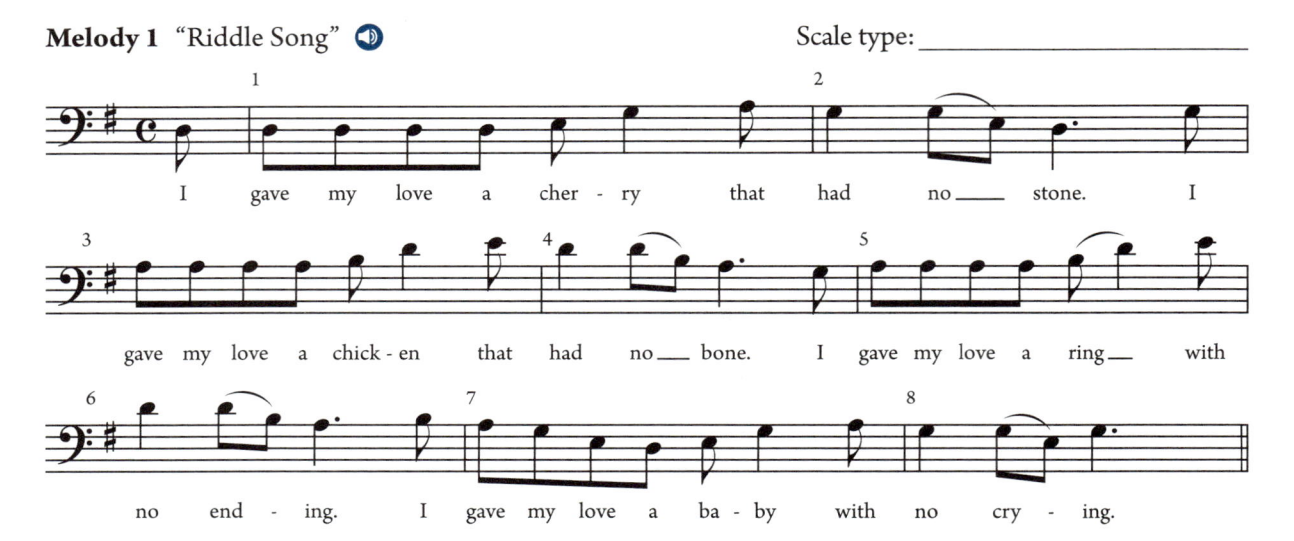

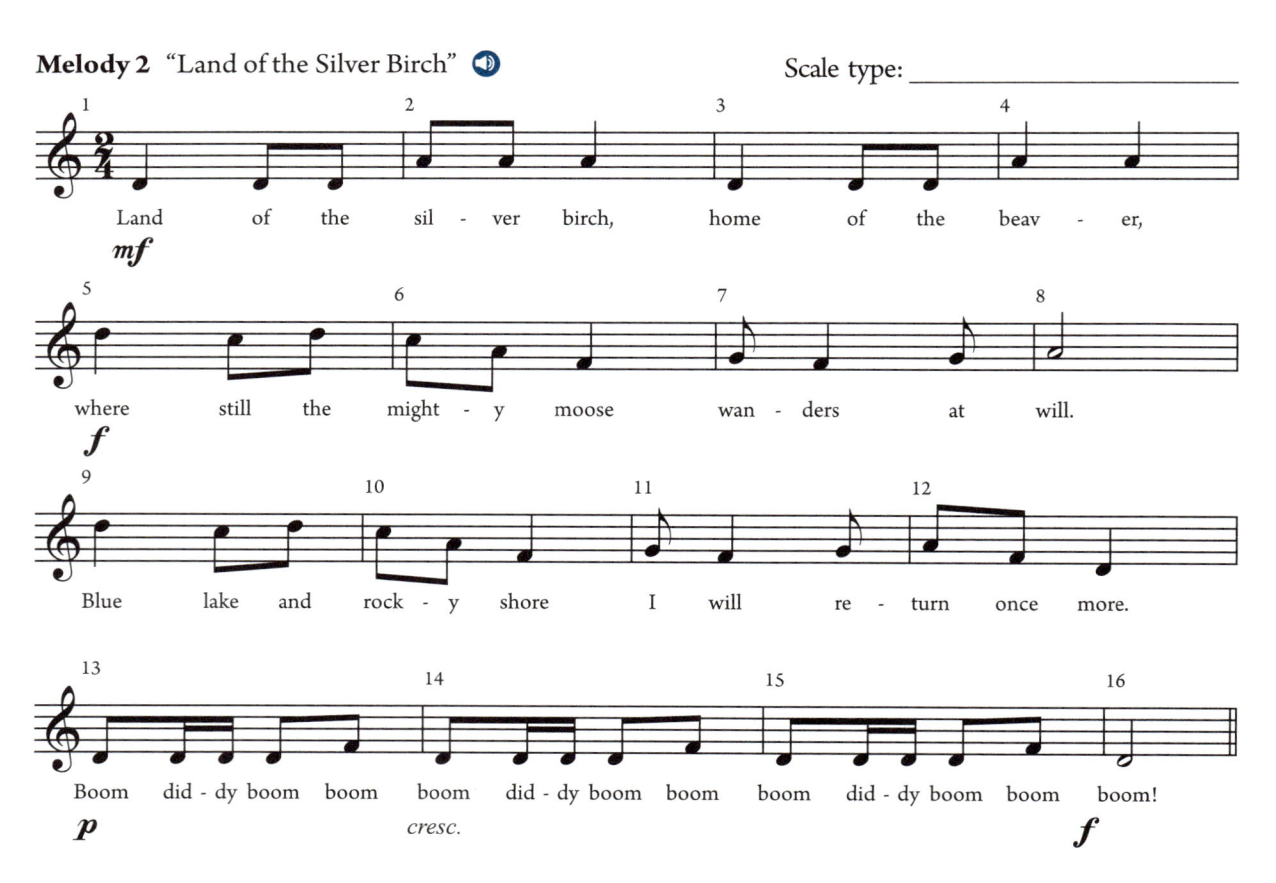

Melody 1 "Riddle Song"   Scale type: _____

I gave my love a cher-ry that had no stone. I gave my love a chick-en that had no bone. I gave my love a ring with no end-ing. I gave my love a ba-by with no cry-ing.

Melody 2 "Land of the Silver Birch"   Scale type: _____

Land of the sil-ver birch, home of the beav-er,
mf
where still the might-y moose wan-ders at will.
f
Blue lake and rock-y shore I will re-turn once more.
Boom did-dy boom boom boom did-dy boom boom boom did-dy boom boom boom!
p   *cresc.*   *f*

Melody 3 "When the Train Comes Along" 🔊 Scale type: _____

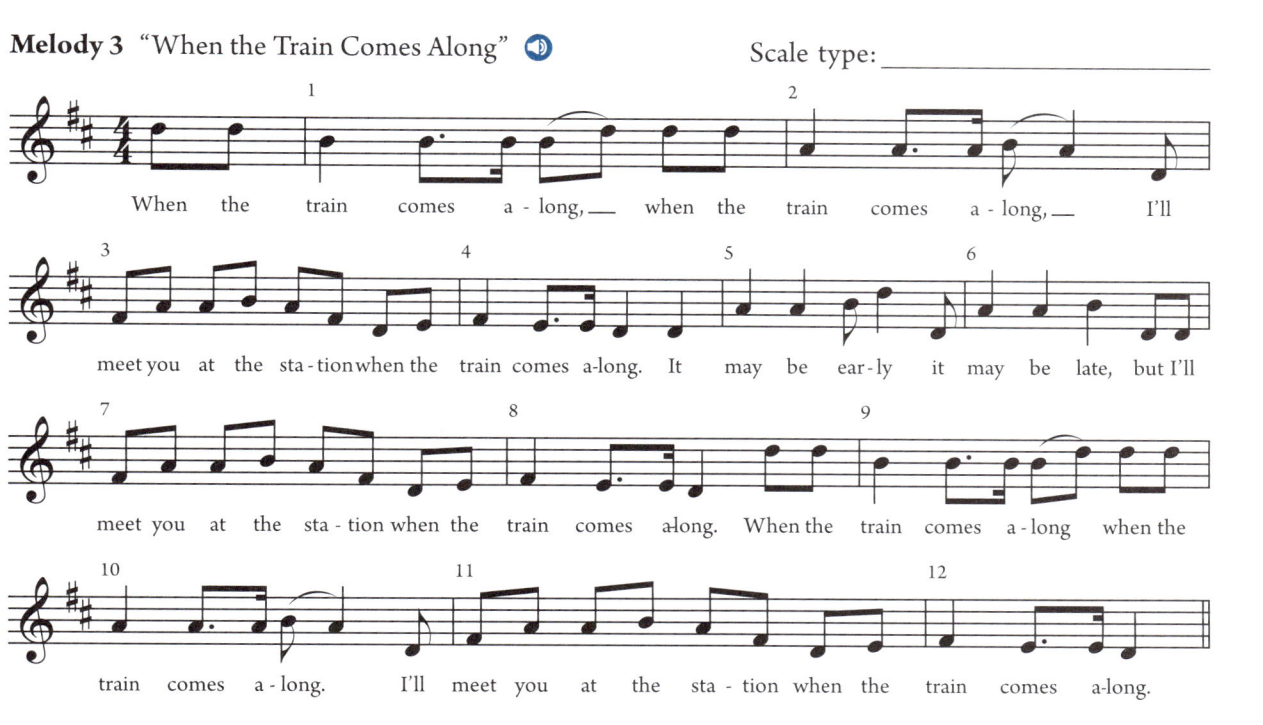

When the train comes a-long,__ when the train comes a-long,__ I'll meet you at the sta-tion when the train comes a-long. It may be ear-ly it may be late, but I'll meet you at the sta-tion when the train comes a-long. When the train comes a-long when the train comes a-long. I'll meet you at the sta-tion when the train comes a-long.

C. Swung rhythms

For swing melodies 1–3:

- When you can play the chords in rhythm, sing along as you play. If necessary (especially for notes with accidentals), use the piano to help.
- These melodies may be sung with the eighth notes swung ♩♩ = ♩♪ (triplet), and some feature syncopation.
- Swung rhythms, often used in jazz and blues, can be notated in simple quadruple meter with eighth notes beamed in groups of four: 4/4 ♪♪♪♪ ♪♪♪♪. Instead they are performed as if they were written in *compound* quadruple meter with accents on the *weak* parts of the beat: 12/8 ♩ ♪♩ ♪♩ ♪♩ ♪.
- With swung rhythms, listen for syncopations, accents, and melodic anticipations. (If it helps, rewrite in 12/8, as shown.)
- To practice swung rhythms, first, perform the example below straight (exactly as it is notated), then swing it. Compare the two recordings of the rhythm below to hear the difference between straight and swung versions of the melody.

Swing 🔊

- There are chord symbols above swing melody 3; play the chords at the keyboard. Initially, don't worry about rhythm or speed, just accuracy. When you can play the chords accurately, play them in rhythm, even if your tempo is slow.

Apply It

Swing Melody 1 Howard Washington and James White, "Lou'siana Blues," mm. 9–16
Play a G major triad to orient yourself. This excerpt begins *mi–sol* ($\hat{3}$–$\hat{5}$) and ends on *sol* ($\hat{5}$).

Down in Lou'- si - an - a where the mel - ons grow Lives the sweet-est lit - tle girl that

I love so___ My oh my heav - ens a - bove how she can love___

When she starts a lov - ing I'm in heav'n a - bove.___

Swing Melody 2 Washington and White, "Lou'siana Blues" (adapted), mm. 25–32

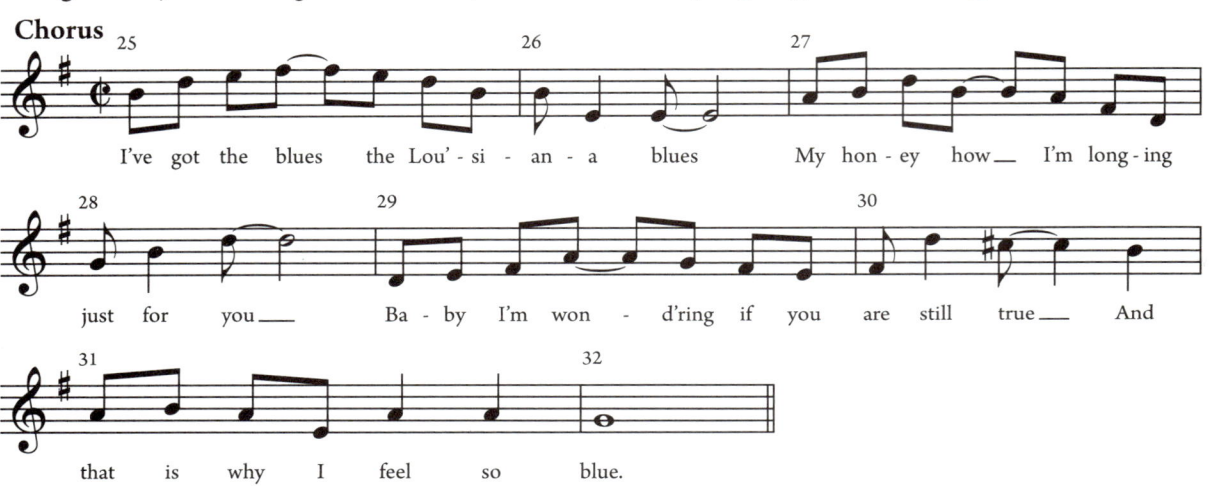

Chorus

I've got the blues the Lou'- si - an - a blues My hon - ey how___ I'm long - ing

just for you___ Ba - by I'm won - d'ring if you are still true___ And

that is why I feel so blue.

Swing Melody 3 Frank Perkins and Mitchell Parish, "Stars Fell on Alabama," mm. 1–8

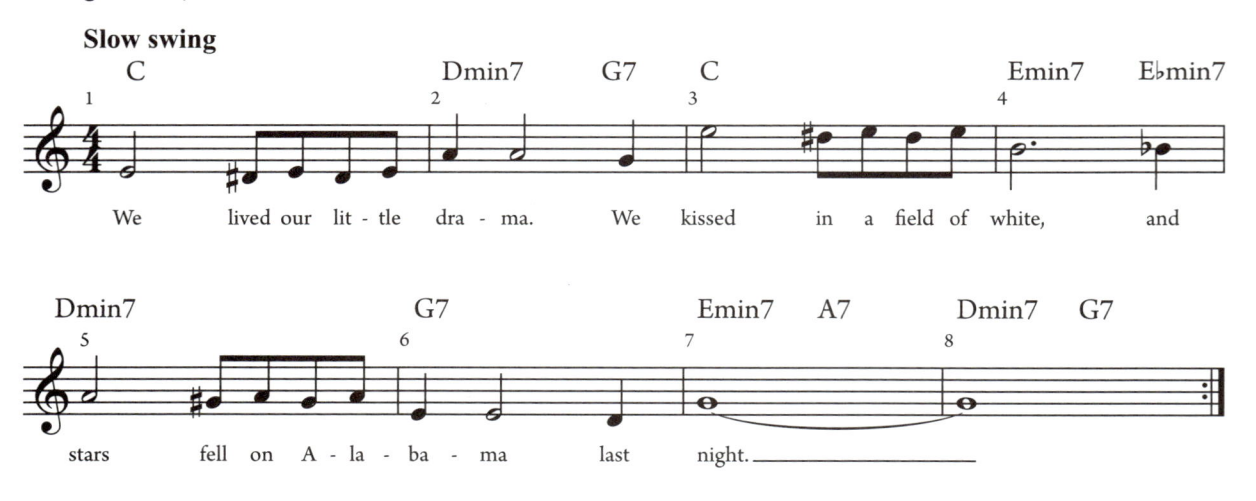

Slow swing

C | Dmin7 G7 | C | Emin7 E♭min7

We lived our lit - tle dra - ma. We kissed in a field of white, and

Dmin7 | G7 | Emin7 A7 | Dmin7 G7

stars fell on A - la - ba - ma last night.___

D. Call and response and improvisation

1. Hearing and writing blues riffs

Listen to the 12-bar blues progression with a riff (a short melodic and rhythmic idea) in the first two measures.

- Memorize the riff, then perform it in measures 5–6 and 9–10 of the progression. There will be rests in measures 3–4, 7–8, and 11–12.
- Maintain the riff's pitch, rhythm, and tempo. First, sing the riff only on "da," then use scale-degree numbers, solfège syllables, or letter names.
- Then, write the rhythm of the riff above the staff.
- Finally, notate the pitches and rhythm of the riff on the staff.

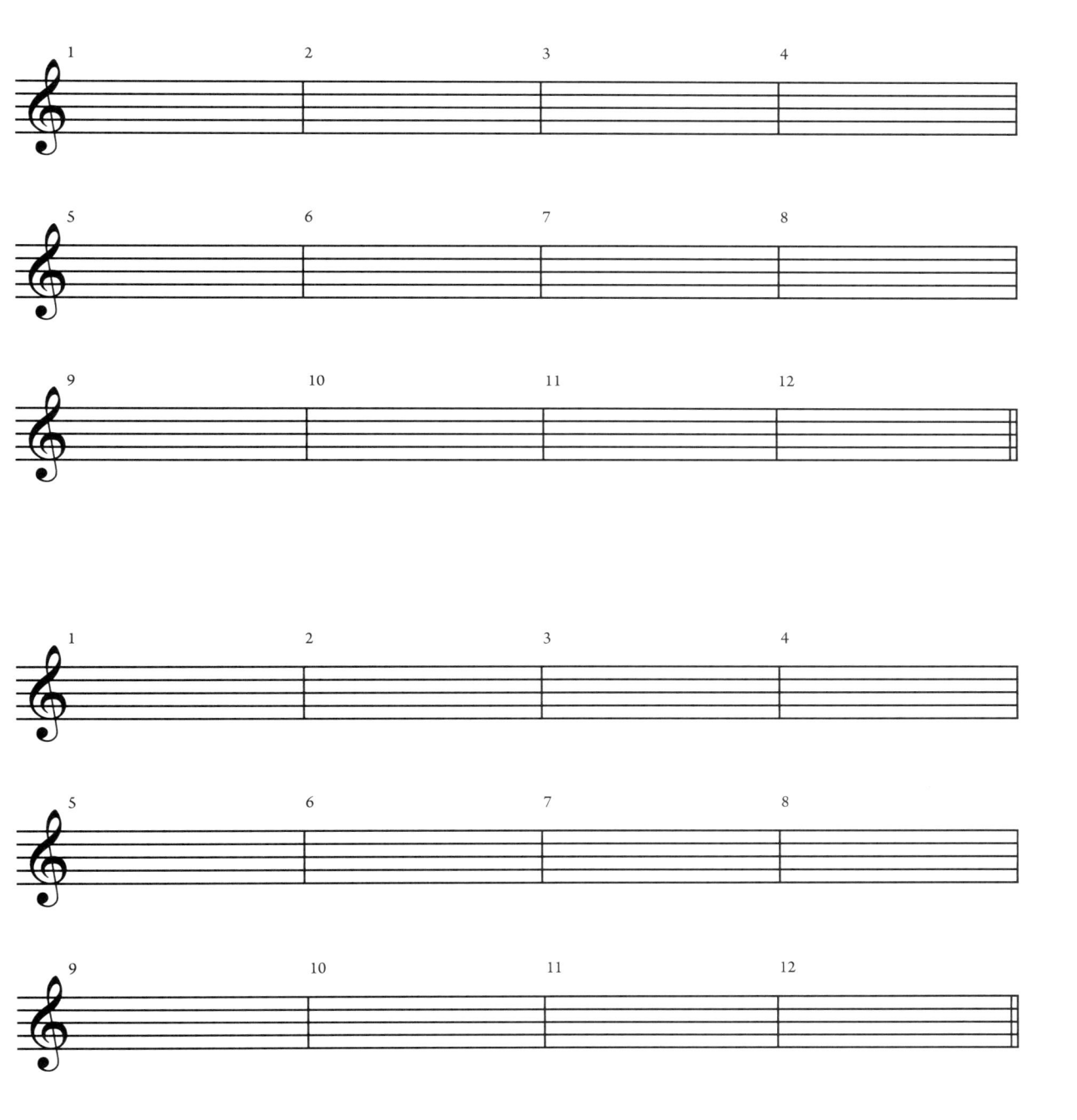

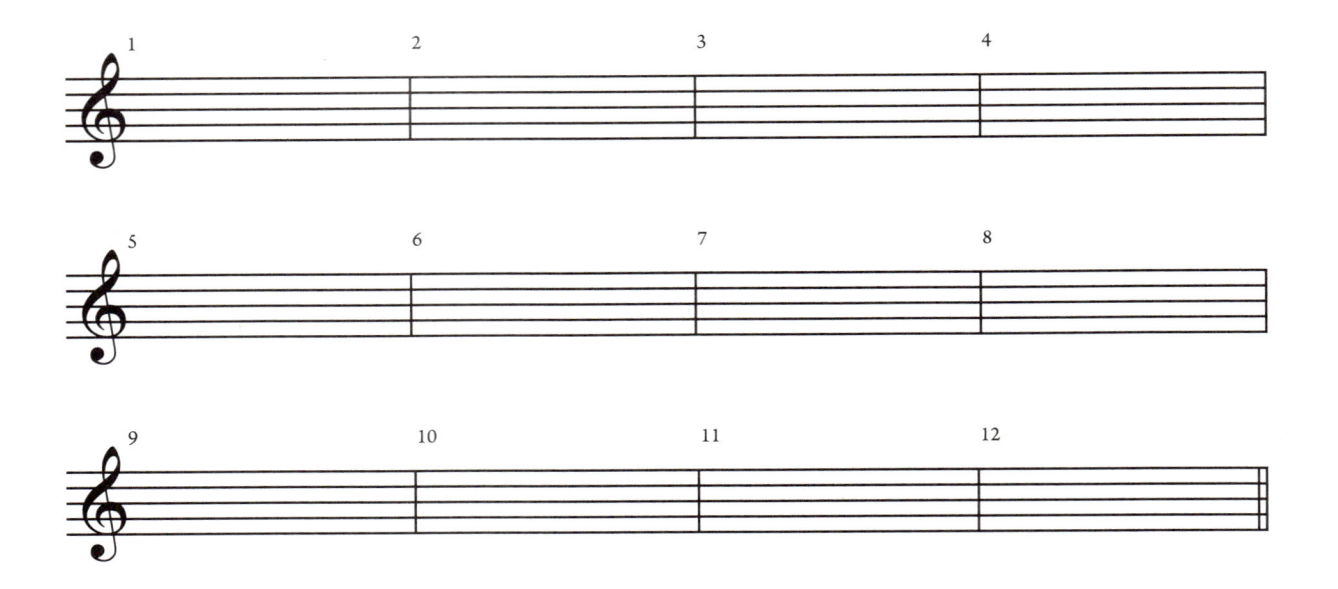

[Empty staves numbered 1–12 for student notation]

2. Improvisation

As a group, improvise based on the blues progression provided. While one or more class members play the chord progression, a soloist improvises (on voice, piano, or another instrument), choosing his or her pitches from the corresponding blues scale. Take turns swapping parts until each person has had the opportunity to improvise.

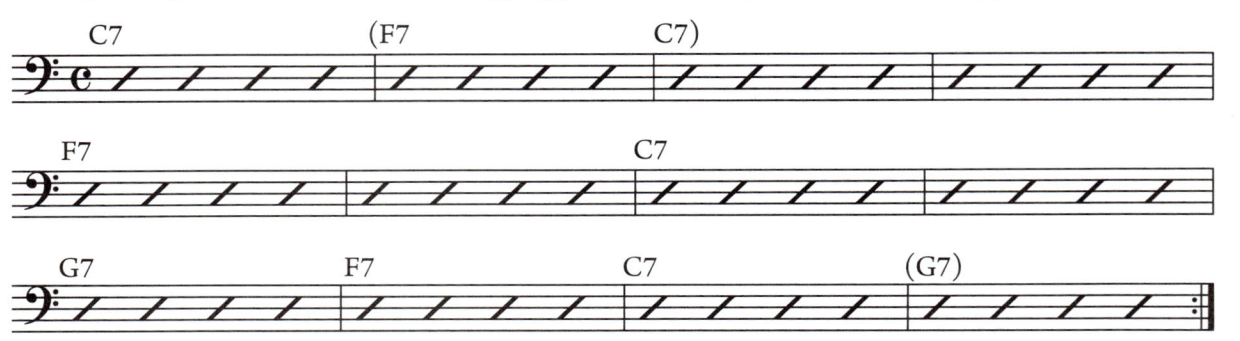

[12-bar blues progression in bass clef:
Measures 1-4: C7 | (F7) | C7) |
Measures 5-8: F7 | | C7 |
Measures 9-12: G7 | F7 | C7 | (G7) :||]

Blues scale

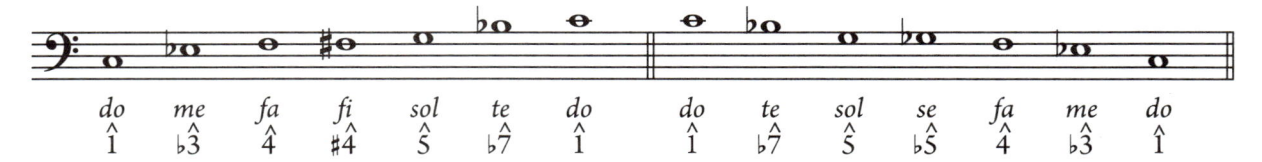

do	me	fa	fi	sol	te	do	do	te	sol	se	fa	me	do
$\hat{1}$	$\flat\hat{3}$	$\hat{4}$	$\sharp\hat{4}$	$\hat{5}$	$\flat\hat{7}$	$\hat{1}$	$\hat{1}$	$\flat\hat{7}$	$\hat{5}$	$\flat\hat{5}$	$\hat{4}$	$\flat\hat{3}$	$\hat{1}$

CHAPTER TWELVE Blues and Other Popular Styles

NAME _____

Workbook ASSIGNMENT 12.1

A. Writing pentatonic scales

(1) F minor pentatonic

(2) A♭ major pentatonic

(3) B♭ major pentatonic

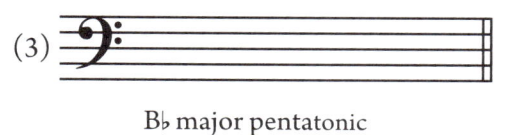

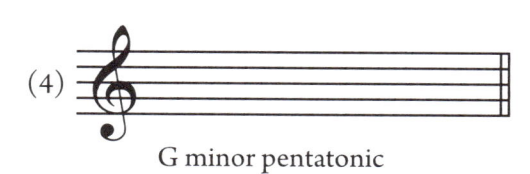

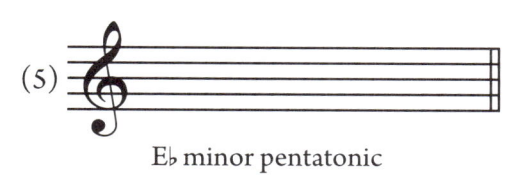

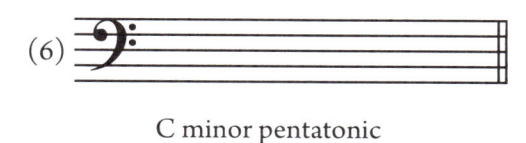

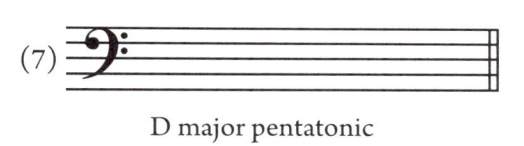

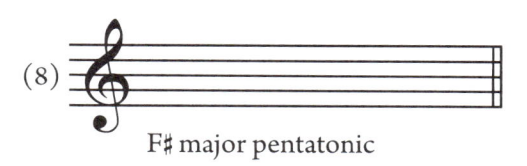

(4) G minor pentatonic

(5) E♭ minor pentatonic

(6) C minor pentatonic

(7) D major pentatonic

(8) F♯ major pentatonic

B. Identifying pentatonic scales in melodies

Identify the pentatonic scale for each melody. Write the scale beneath the melody, and write the appropriate solfège syllables or scale-degree numbers beneath the scale; write the scale type in the blank.

(1) "My Paddle's Keen and Bright" 🔊

Practice the tune on solfège syllables or scale-degree numbers for performance as a round.

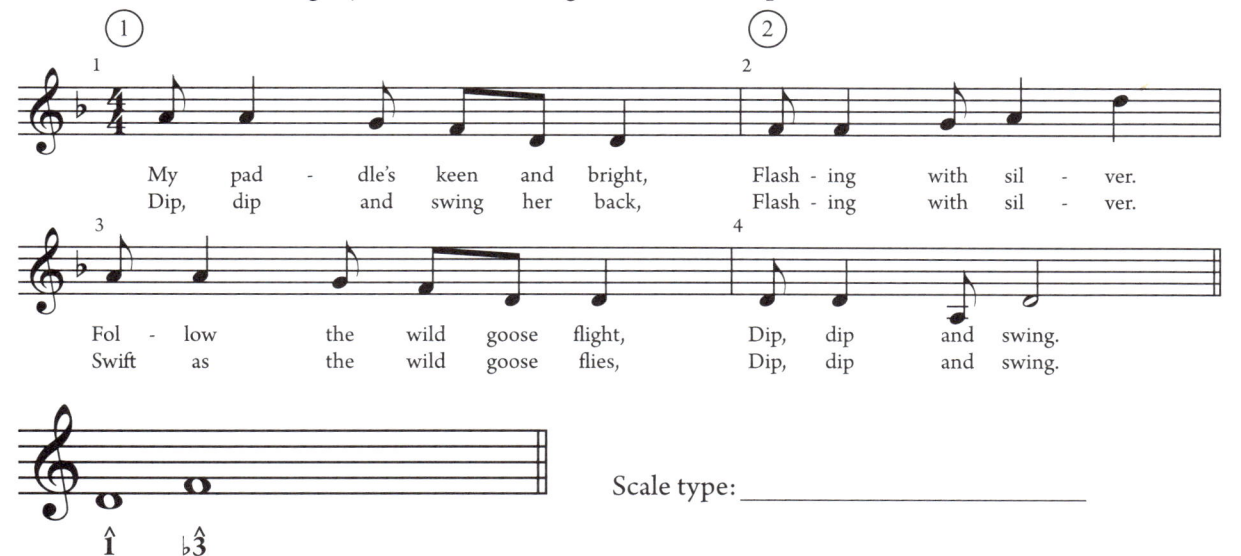

My pad-dle's keen and bright, Flash-ing with sil-ver.
Dip, dip and swing her back, Flash-ing with sil-ver.
Fol-low the wild goose flight, Dip, dip and swing.
Swift as the wild goose flies, Dip, dip and swing.

$\hat{1}$ ♭$\hat{3}$
do me

Scale type: _____

Assignment 12.1   335

(2) Robert Lowry, "How Can I Keep from Singing?" mm. 1–8

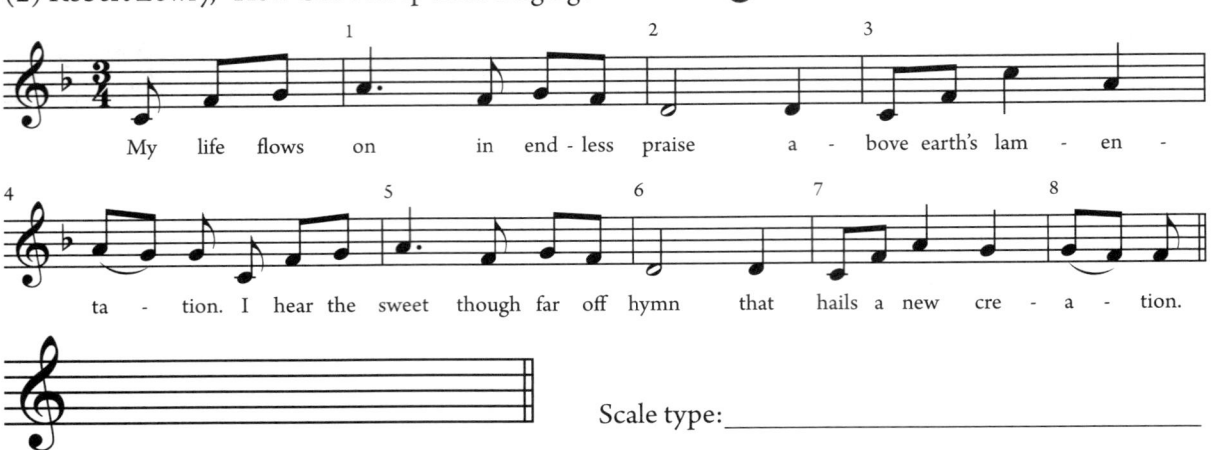

My life flows on in end-less praise a-bove earth's lam-en-ta-tion. I hear the sweet though far off hymn that hails a new cre-a-tion.

Scale type: _____

C. Blues scales

Spell the blues scales that begin on the pitches given below. Write the appropriate key signature and accidentals (both ascending and descending). Remember to use ♯4 ascending and ♭5 descending.

(1) Beginning on G:

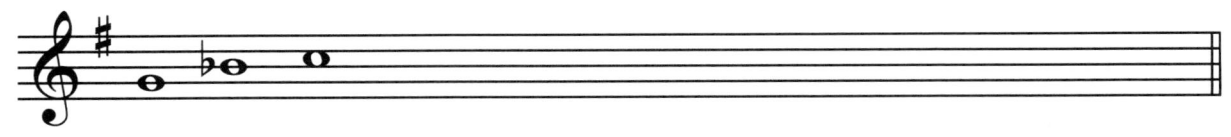

(2) Beginning on B♭:

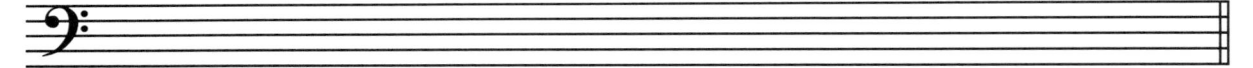

(3) Beginning on D:

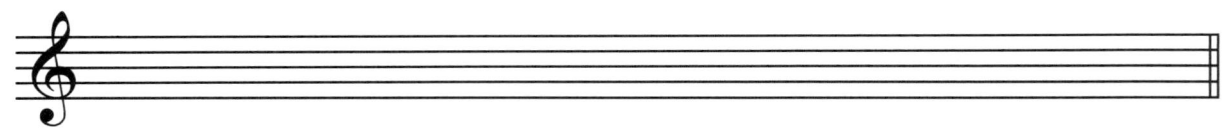

(4) Beginning on E:

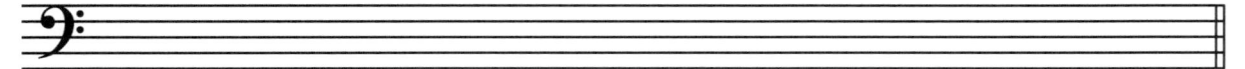

(5) Beginning on F:

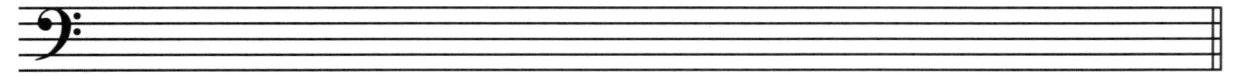

NAME _____

Workbook ASSIGNMENT 12.2

A. Spelling isolated seventh chords

Each pitch given below is the root of a seventh chord. Fill in the remaining chord members. Don't change the given pitch.

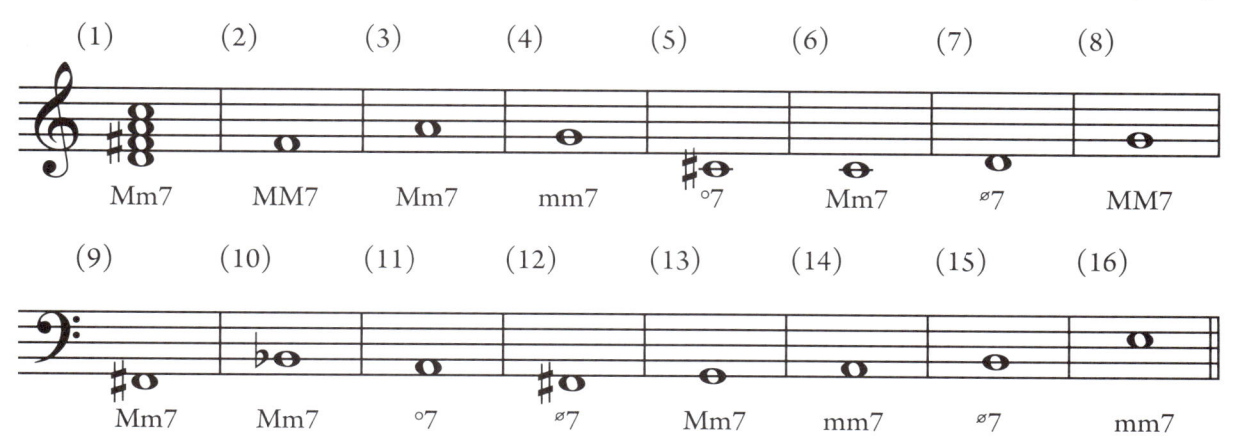

(1) Mm7 (2) MM7 (3) Mm7 (4) mm7 (5) °7 (6) Mm7 (7) ø7 (8) MM7

(9) Mm7 (10) Mm7 (11) °7 (12) ø7 (13) Mm7 (14) mm7 (15) ø7 (16) mm7

B. Writing blues progessions

Write the changes for 12-bar blues in both of the following keys. Write one chord symbol above each measure.

(1) B♭

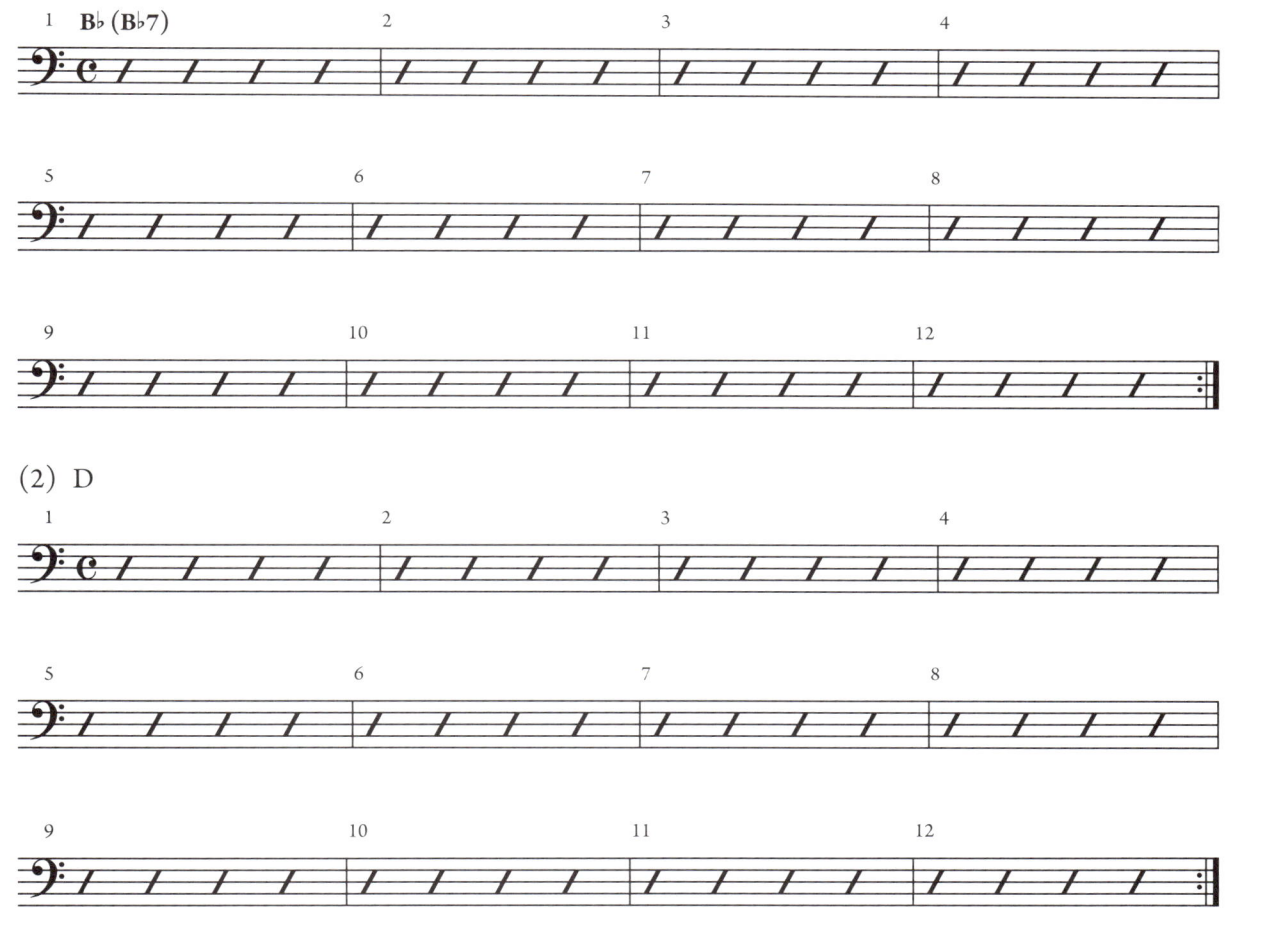

1 B♭ (B♭7) 2 3 4

5 6 7 8

9 10 11 12

(2) D

1 2 3 4

5 6 7 8

9 10 11 12

C. Analyzing a blues melody

(1) The melody of "Blues for Norton," shown below, is based on only a few short melodic ideas that are repeated and expanded. The initial melodic idea consists of two motives: a C–D–C neighbor plus a leap to A♭, and a scale segment A♭–G–F. This basic melodic idea is repeated exactly in measures 2–3, then the rhythm of the scale segment is varied in measure 4. Draw a circle around all of the C–D–C–A♭ statements and a box around all of the A♭–G–F statements. The circles and boxes may overlap. 🔊

(2) In measures 6–9, how is the melodic motive varied? In measures 10–11?

D. Writing a blues melody

Taking "Splanky" and "Blues for Norton" as your models, write three melodic ideas on the staff lines below using a blues scale in the key of your choice. Next to each melodic idea, write at least one variant (for example, change the melodic direction or add, replace, or remove a note). Then select two ideas (with their variants) and use them to make a 12-bar blues melody. Copy the melody on staff paper and be prepared to perform it in class.

Melodic idea 1:   Variants:

Melodic idea 2:   Variants:

Melodic idea 3:   Variants:

NAME _____

Workbook   ASSIGNMENT 12.3

Writing a song

Your final project is to compose either a blues song (Assignment 12.3) or a popular song (Assignment 12.4) with lyrics. Use examples in your anthology as models. On your own staff paper, notate the song on a lead sheet that shows the melody, lyrics, and chord symbols. Read the instructions in their entirety (for both types of songs)—many guidelines are applicable to both styles. Prepare to perform your song, or arrange to have it performed, in class.

General guidelines

- Write a short introduction. This might consist of the last four measures of the song or a simple chord progression that establishes a mood.
- Include a "hook"—a recurring, memorable part of the music, the lyrics of which are often the song's title.
- Recall that many song lyrics are about love—trying to find love, being in love, losing love.
- Employ text painting appropriate to your lyrics. For example, you might set the word "sun" or "moon" to the highest pitch in the phrase.
- Keep your melody and chord symbols simple; performers bring the music to life by embellishing the melodies and chords they find in lead sheets.
- Create an ending. One possibility is to play the last four measures three times, making each repetition slower and more dramatic.

Blues song

Write a song with the following form:

| Introduction | a minimum of three statements of the twelve-bar blues progression, each with different lyrics | ending or coda |

Creating the lyrics

Keep the language simple and direct or even colloquial (for example, "You ain't nothin' but a hound dog," "My mama done tol' me," etc.). Each blues progression consists of three subphrases, each four measures long: measures 1–4 state an idea; measures 5–8 restate the idea in a varied form; measures 9–12 offer an outcome or a consequence.

You could think of blues lyrics as a kind of call and response, with a refrain.

Subphrase 1 (Call)	I	I	I	I
Subphrase 2 (Response)	IV	IV	I	I
Subphrase 3 (Conclusion)	V	IV	I	I (or V^7)

The lyrics to W. C. Handy's "St. Louis Blues" are a good example:

I hate to see that evening sun go down,	call
I hate to see that evening sun go down,	response
'Cause, my baby, he's gone left this town.	conclusion
Feelin' tomorrow like I feel today,	call
If I'm feelin' tomorrow like I feel today,	response
I'll pack my truck and make my get away.	conclusion

Creating the music
- Follow the blues progression shown, or transpose it to another key of your choice.
- Choose your melodic pitches from the blues scale below, or transpose it.
- Create a two-measure motive that you can vary.
- In measure 12, write a turnaround (the V^7 chord).
- Model your song after Count Basie's "Splanky" or Phillips's "Blues for Norton" (anthology, p. 388).

Blues progression

C7 | (F7) | C7) | |
F7 | | C7 | |
G7 | F7 | C7 | (G7) |

Blues scale

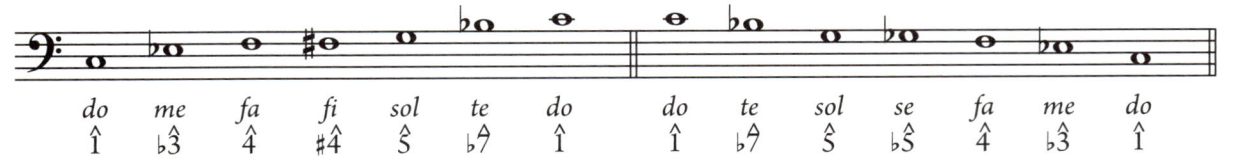

do	me	fa	fi	sol	te	do	do	te	sol	se	fa	me	do
$\hat{1}$	$\flat\hat{3}$	$\hat{4}$	$\sharp\hat{4}$	$\hat{5}$	$\flat\hat{7}$	$\hat{1}$	$\hat{1}$	$\flat\hat{7}$	$\hat{5}$	$\flat\hat{5}$	$\hat{4}$	$\flat\hat{3}$	$\hat{1}$

Work space

NAME _____

Workbook ASSIGNMENT 12.4

Writing a song

Your final project is to compose either a blues song (Assignment 12.3) or a popular song (Assignment 12.4) with lyrics. Use examples in your anthology as models. On your own staff paper, notate the song on a lead sheet that shows the melody, lyrics, and chord symbols. Read the instructions in their entirety (for both types of songs)—many guidelines are applicable to both styles. Prepare to perform your song, or arrange to have it performed, in class.

General guidelines

- Write a short introduction. This might consist of the last four measures of the song or a simple chord progression that establishes a mood.
- Include a "hook"—a recurring, memorable part of the music, the lyrics of which are often the song's title.
- Recall that many song lyrics are about love—trying to find love, being in love, losing love.
- Employ text painting appropriate to your lyrics. For example, you might set the word "sun" or "moon" to the highest pitch in the phrase.
- Keep your melody and chord symbols simple; performers bring the music to life by embellishing the melodies and chords they find in lead sheets.
- Create an ending. One possibility is to play the last four measures three times, making each repetition slower and more dramatic.

Popular song

Write a song with the following form:

| Introduction | **a a' b a'** or **a a' b a''** design, stated at least twice (with different lyrics) | ending or coda |

Creating the lyrics

1. Writing your own
- One type of four-phrase song is the ballad, which tells a story. Let the **a** phrases narrate the story, and the bridge (**b**) encapsulate its emotional impact.
- Place rhymes at the ends of phrases, and within the phrase if you like.
- Think about incorporating other poetic devices, such as alliteration and double entendre.
- Try to let the rhythm of your melody approximate that of the spoken lyrics.

2. Setting a preexisting poem
- You may choose to set a poem if you find one that inspires you and fits the formal requirements of the song form. Spend some time considering both the form and meaning of the text. Look for
    - the accents, so you can place strong and weak syllables on strong and weak beats;
    - a parallel structure in the text that might suggest parallel melodic lines;
    - rhyming line endings that might suggest "musical rhymes" (similar motives);
    - repeated words or images that might be represented as musical ideas (text painting);
    - changes in the narration or imagery that would suggest musical change; and
    - a general sentiment or mood of the text that you would like to evoke through music.

Creating the music

- Write a motive that is memorable in its rhythm, contour, and pitches. Use this motive and variations of it throughout the song.
- Each phrase should end with a cadence: **a** (HC), **a'** (PAC), **b** (HC), **a'** or **a''** (PAC).

- The bridge, **b**, should contrast with the **a** phrases: it might be in a different key, be louder or more rhythmically active, feature a different accompaniment pattern, or sound in a higher register.
- Make each phrase four or eight measures long, so that the body of your song will be sixteen or thirty-two measures. Sixteen-measure songs we have studied include "Oh! Susanna" (**a a' b a'**), "Greensleeves" (**a a' b b'**), and "When Johnny Comes Marching Home" (**a a' b c**). Thirty-two measure songs include "Look for the Silver Lining" (**a b a' c**) and "The Ash Grove" (**a a b a**).
- If you prefer, and with your teacher's permission, choose a different design, such as **a a' b b'**, **a b a b**, or **a a' b c**.
- If you want to create a simple keyboard accompaniment, use harmonic progressions and accompaniment patterns from Chapter 11 as models. Otherwise, you may simply notate melody, lyrics, and chord symbols.

Work space

NAME _____

Workbook AURAL SKILLS 12.1

Listen to a phrase from a jazz standard while you conduct, then complete the following exercises.

(1) Write the rhythm of the melody. Notate swung rhythms with straight eighth notes. Hint: Use ties to notate longer, syncopated notes across bar lines.

(2) Write the melody with scale-degree numbers or solfège syllables. Use the natural minor scale, with $\flat\hat{6}$ and $\flat\hat{7}$. Hint: The melody begins with $\hat{1}$–$\hat{1}$–$\hat{2}$–$\flat\hat{3}$–$\flat\hat{6}$ (*do–do–re–me–le*) and follows a similar pattern that is repeated two more times before changing.

(3) Notate the pitches and rhythm of the melody.

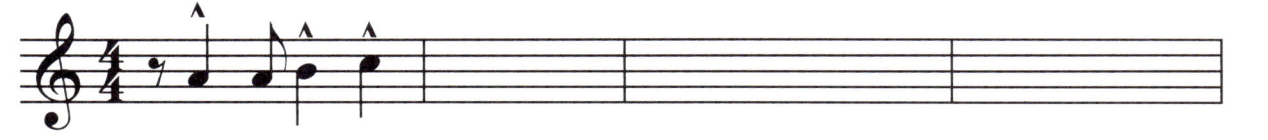

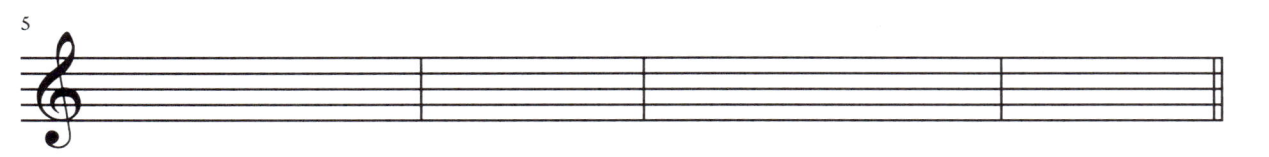

(4) Which of the following rhythmic motives is repeated in the bass line?

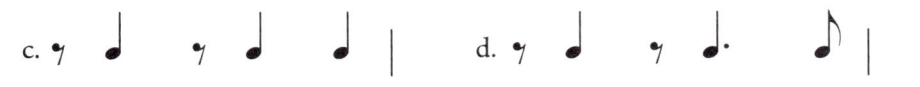

a. b.

c. d.

Aural Skills 12.1   343

(5) Which descending interval recurs three times in the bass line (separated by rests)?
a. third	b. fourth	c. fifth	d. octave

(6) The last two pitches of the bass line create which interval?
a. m3	b. P4	c. P5	d. M2

(7) The excerpt's final cadence is extended by which resolution?
a. perfect authentic	b. deceptive	c. imperfect authentic	d. plagal

Anthology

"The Ash Grove"   346

Johann Sebastian Bach, Invention in D Minor   348

Bach, Prelude in C♯ Minor, from *The Well-Tempered Clavier*, Book I   350

Ludwig van Beethoven, Piano Sonata in C Minor, Op. 13 (*Pathétique*), second movement, excerpt   354

Frédéric Chopin, Prelude in C Minor, Op. 28, No. 20   356

"Come, Ye Thankful People Come" (St. George's Windsor)   357

Stephen Foster, "Jeanie with the Light Brown Hair"   358

Foster, "Oh! Susanna"   363

Patrick S. Gilmore, "When Johnny Comes Marching Home"   364

"Greensleeves"   365

"Home on the Range"   367

Elisabeth-Claude Jacquet de la Guerre, Gigue, from Suite No. 3 in A Minor   368

Scott Joplin, "Solace"   370

Jerome Kern, "Look for the Silver Lining"   374

Wolfgang Amadeus Mozart, String Quartet in D Minor, K. 421, third movement   379

Mozart, *Variations on "Ah, vous dirai-je Maman,"* excerpts   382

"My Country, 'Tis of Thee" (America)   385

John Newton, "Amazing Grace"   386

"O God Our Help in Ages Past" (St. Anne)   387

Joel Phillips, "Blues for Norton"   388

Franz Schubert, Waltz in B Minor, Op. 18, No. 6   392

"Simple Gifts"   394

Hart A. Wand and Lloyd Garrett, "Dallas Blues"   395

"The Ash Grove"

"The Ash Grove" is a traditional Welsh folk song that has been sung to various lyrics. The words shown here are by the nineteenth-century English playwright John Oxenford. Two versions are shown: a lead sheet, in which the performer improvises an accompaniment from chord symbols, and an arrangement for piano.

a. Lead sheet

The ash grove how grace - ful, how plain - ly__ 'tis__ speak - ing. The
When - e - ver the__ light through its bran - ches is__ break - ing a

harp through it__ play - ing has lan - guage for me.
host of__ kind__ fac - es is gaz - ing on me.

The__ friends of__ my__ child - hood a - gain are__ be - fore me, each

step wakes a__ mem - ory as free - ly I roam. With

soft whis - pers__ la - den the leaves rus - tle__ o'er me. The

ash grove, the__ ash grove a - lone is my home.

b. With written-out accompaniment

Arranged by Joel Phillips

Johann Sebastian Bach (1685–1750)

Invention in D Minor

Around 1720, Bach composed fifteen two-voice contrapuntal keyboard works, called inventions, for his ten-year-old son, Wilhelm Friedemann. Bach's inventions were intended to teach students how to play two simultaneous lines on the harpsichord and how to develop a musical idea in the course of a piece.

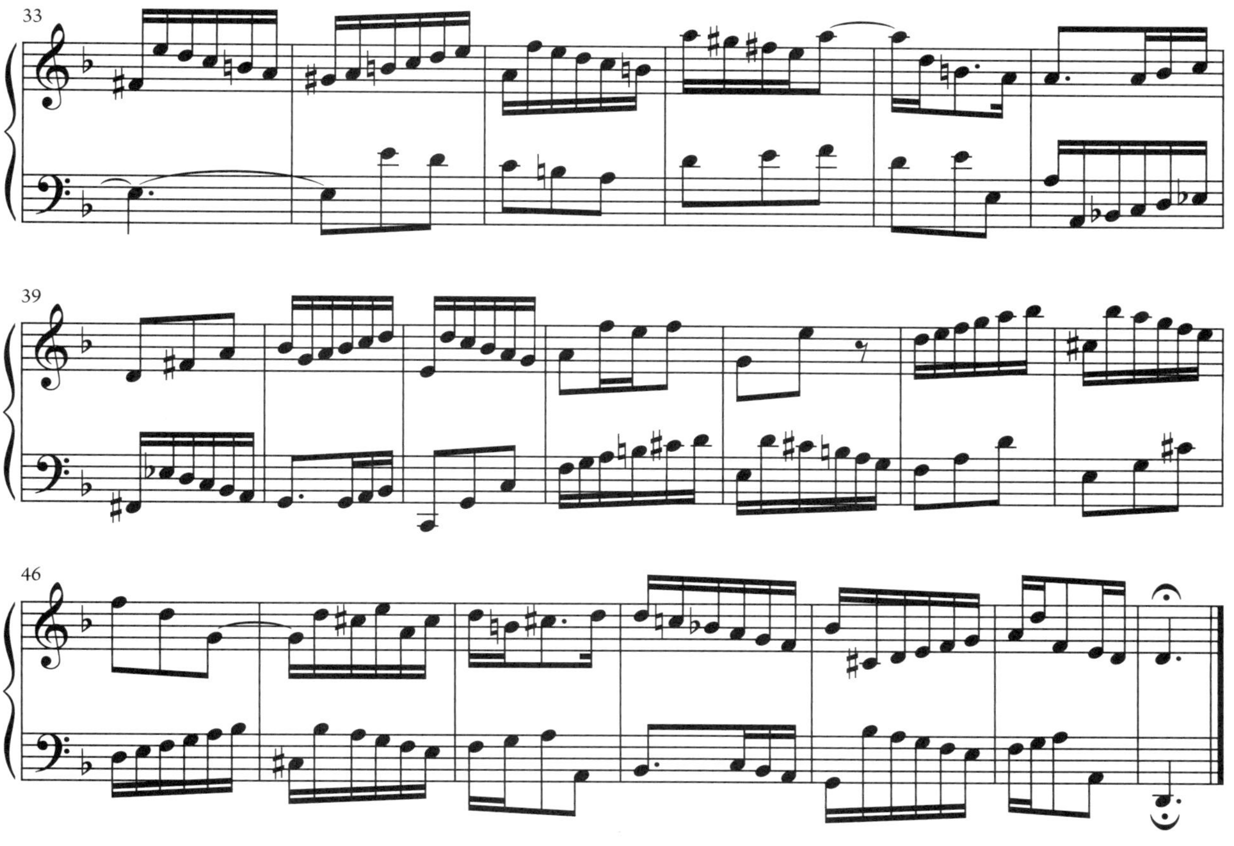
33
39
46

Johann Sebastian Bach

Prelude in C♯ Minor, from *The Well-Tempered Clavier*, Book I

The Well-Tempered Clavier consists of two books, published by Bach in 1722 and 1742, each with a prelude and fugue in all twenty-four major and minor keys. "Well-tempered" refers to tuning: a well-tempered keyboard instrument is tuned such that it can be played in any key. Previous tuning systems in use during Bach's life resulted in some keys that sounded sweet and pleasing but others that sounded less pleasing, with out-of-tune intervals. Only with this new tuning could all twenty-four keys be used equally.

Bach, Prelude in C♯ Minor, from *The Well-Tempered Clavier*, Book I

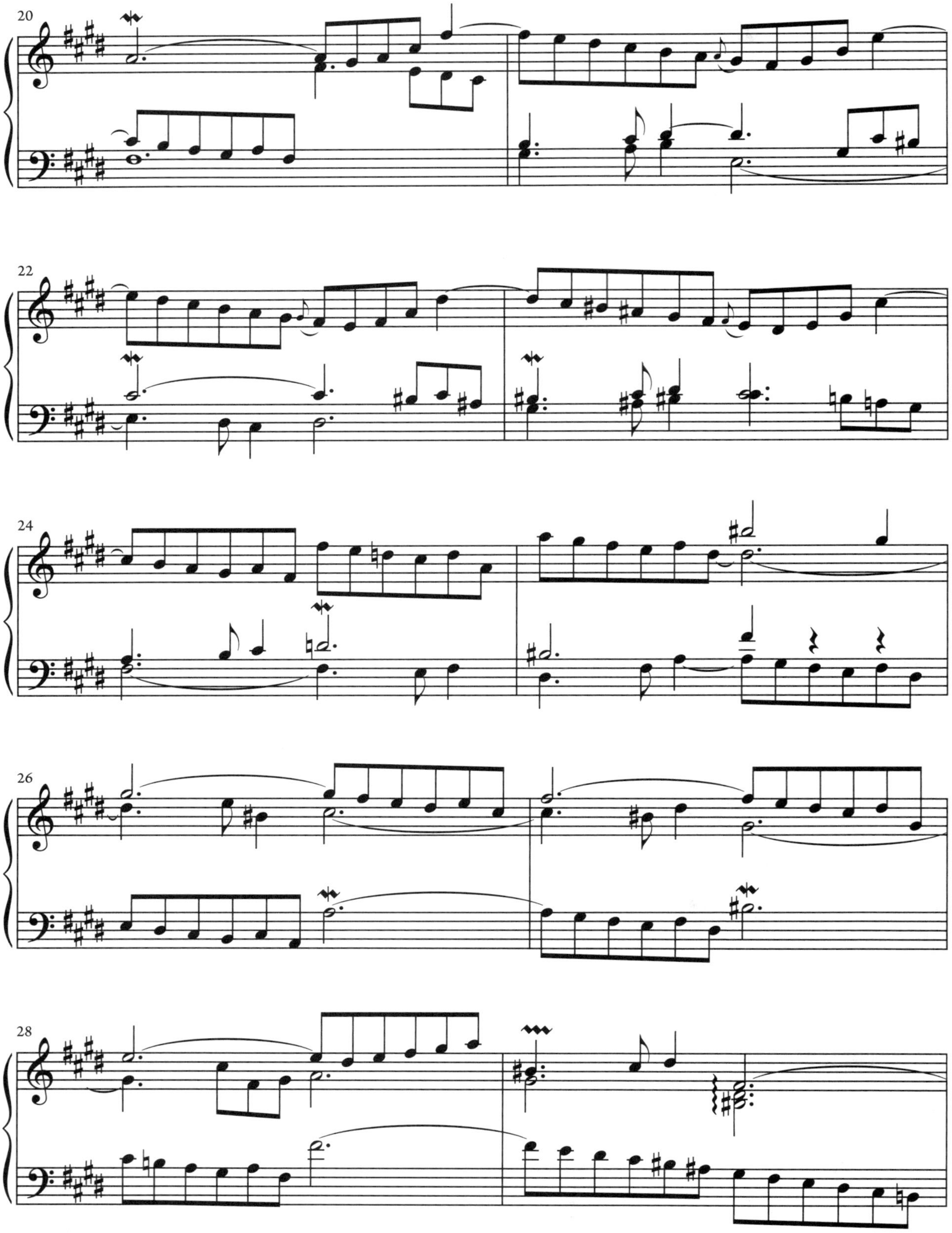

Bach, Prelude in C♯ Minor, from *The Well-Tempered Clavier*, Book I

Ludwig van Beethoven (1770–1827)
Piano Sonata in C Minor, Op. 13 (*Pathétique*), second movement, excerpt

Beethoven composed the *Pathétique* Sonata in 1799, at age twenty-seven, during his first decade composing and performing in Vienna. The subtitle, *Pathétique*, which would have appealed to nineteenth-century audiences, means "with pathos." The work was dedicated to Prince Karl von Lichnowsky, who was a supporter and patron to both Mozart and Beethoven. In the recording that accompanies this text, this excerpt is performed on fortepiano, an early keyboard from Beethoven's era.

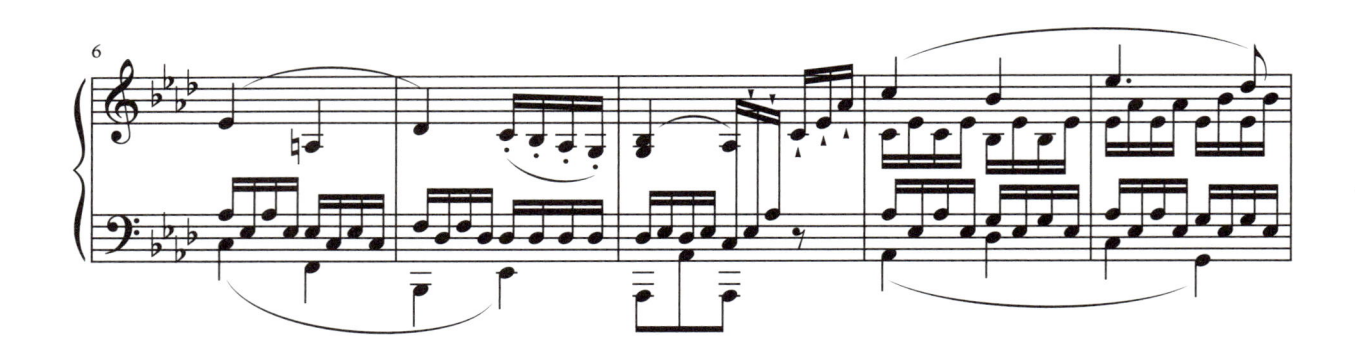

Beethoven, Piano Sonata in C Minor, Op. 13 (*Pathétique*), second movement

Frédéric Chopin (1810–1849)
Prelude in C Minor, Op. 28, No. 20

This piece is part of a collection of short preludes that Chopin composed in 1839. Like each volume of Bach's *The Well-Tempered Clavier* (p. 350), which Chopin studied, this collection consists of one prelude in each of the twenty-four major and minor keys.

"Come, Ye Thankful People Come" (St. George's Windsor)

George J. Elvey, who was organist at St. George's Church in Windsor, England, composed this tune in 1858. Though it originally had a different text, in the United States the music is most frequently sung to the text shown here, "Come, Ye Thankful People Come," and is associated with the Thanksgiving holiday.

1. Come, ye thankful people, come, Raise the song of harvest-home; All is safely gathered in, Ere the winter storms begin. God, our Maker, doth provide For our wants to be supplied; Come to God's own temple, come, Raise the song of harvest-home.

2. All the world is God's own field, Fruit unto his praise to yield; Wheat and tares together sown, Unto joy or sorrow grown. First the blade, and then the ear, Then the full corn shall appear; Grant, O harvest Lord, that we Wholesome grain and pure may be.

Stephen Foster (1826–1864)
"Jeanie with the Light Brown Hair"

Stephen Foster was a prolific songwriter of the mid-nineteenth century, whose songs, in addition to "Jeanie with the Light Brown Hair," include "Old Folks at Home," "Beautiful Dreamer," "Oh! Susanna" (p. 363), and "Camptown Races." In this song, "Jeanie" is Jane McDowell, Foster's wife.

I dream of Jeanie with the light brown hair, Borne, like a vapor, on the summer air; I see her tripping where the bright streams play,

Foster, "Jeanie with the Light Brown Hair"

I long for Jea-nie with the day-dawn smile, Ra-diant in glad-ness,
I sigh for Jea-nie, but her light form strayed Far from the fond hearts

warm with win-ning guile; I hear her mel-o-dies, like joys gone by,
round her na-tive glade; Her smiles have van-ished and her sweet songs flown,

31
Sigh - ing round my heart o'er the fond hopes that die: Sigh - ing like the night wind and
Flit - ting like the dreams that have cheered us and gone. Now the nod - ding wild flowers may
34
ad lib.
sob - bing like the rain, Wail - ing for the lost one that comes not a - gain: Oh! I
with - er on the shore While her gen - tle fin - gers will cull them no more: Oh! I
37
long for Jea - nie, and my heart bows low, Ne - ver more to find her where the bright wa - ters flow.
sigh for Jea - nie with the light brown hair, Floating, like a va - por, on the soft summer air.
ral - len - tan - do

362 ANTHOLOGY

Stephen Foster
"Oh! Susanna"

This song, published in 1848, exemplifies the style of Stephen Foster, whose parlor and minstrel songs achieved enormous popularity in his day. In fact, many of his songs continue to be so well known that they are assumed to be folk songs rather than nineteenth-century compositions. Although some of Foster's songs seem to glorify the slavery and plantations of the Old South, he was born in Pittsburgh and only visited the South once.

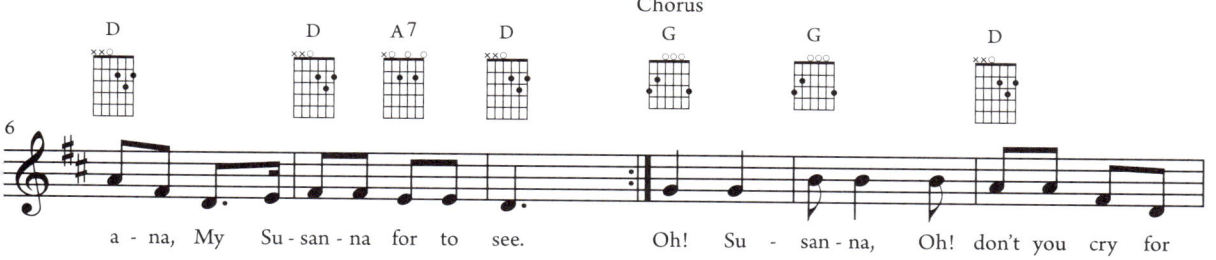

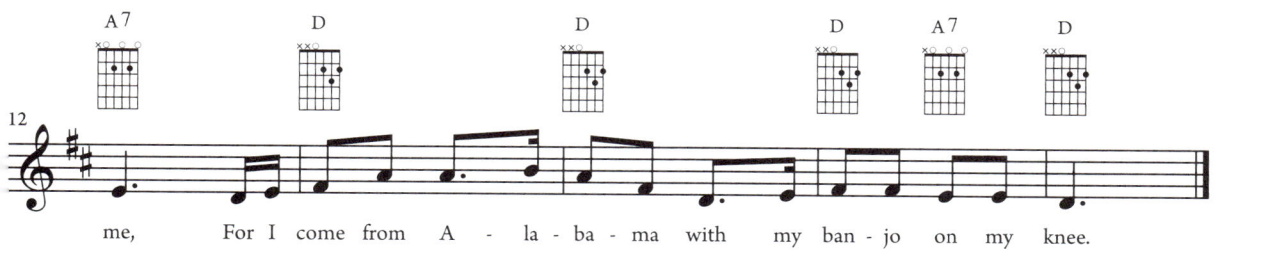

1. I come from Alabama with my banjo on my knee, I'm going to Louisiana, My Susanna for to see. Oh! Susanna, Oh! don't you cry for me, For I come from Alabama with my banjo on my knee.

2. It rained all day the night I left
   The weather was so dry;
   The sun so hot I froze myself,
   Susanna, don't you cry.
   Chorus

3. I had a dream the other night,
   When everything was still.
   I thought I saw Susanna
   A-coming down the hill.
   Chorus

4. The buckwheat cake was in her mouth,
   The tear was in her eye,
   Says I, "I'm coming from the South."
   Susanna, don't you cry.
   Chorus

Patrick S. Gilmore (1829–1892)
"When Johnny Comes Marching Home"

Patrick Gilmore was born in Ireland in 1829 and immigrated to Boston in 1849, where he was a band leader. Gilmore wrote "When Johnny Comes Marching Home" during the Civil War, when his band served the Massachusetts 24th Regiment. Two of Gilmore's lasting contributions to American culture include the founding of the first Promenade Concert in America, the forerunner of the Boston Pops concerts, and the establishment of Gilmore's Concert Garden, which became Madison Square Garden.

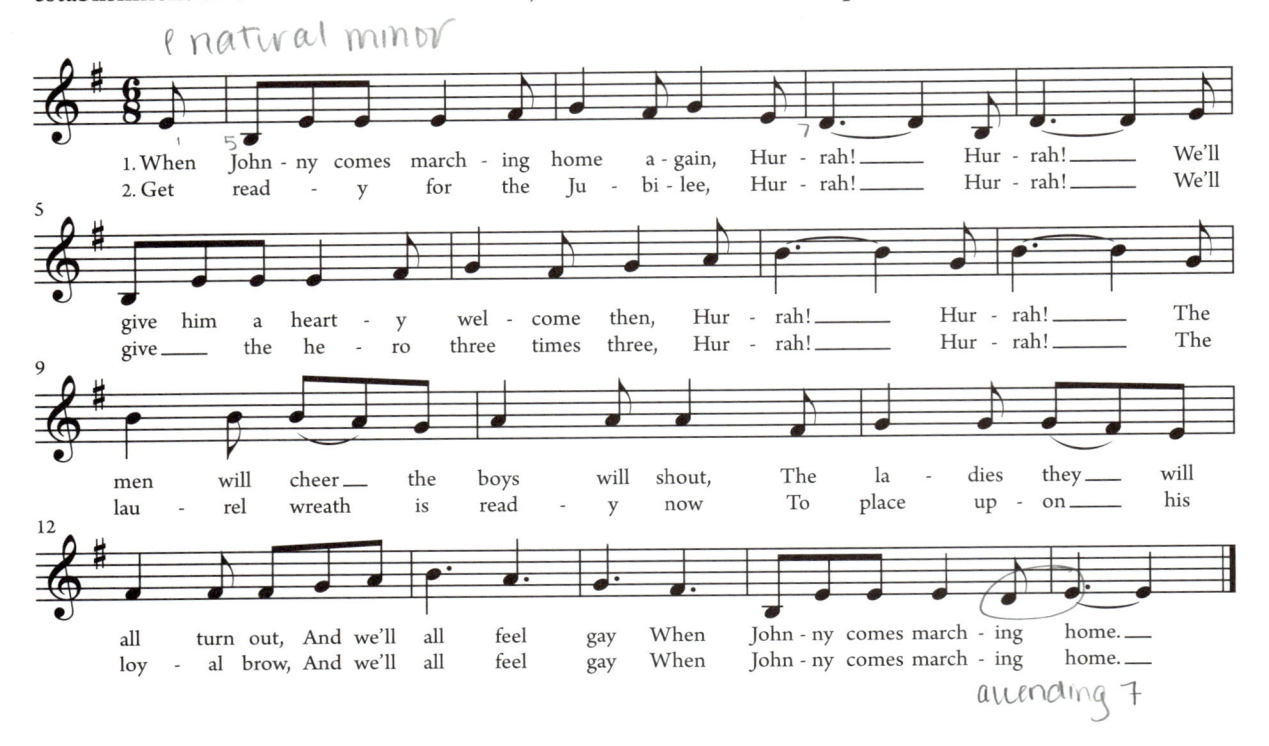

"Greensleeves"

"Greensleeves" is a traditional English folk song; though its date of composition is unknown, it is first mentioned in print in 1580. The music originally accompanied a ballad about a woman, referred to as Lady Greensleeves, who discourteously rejects a suitor. The music has also been sung with numerous other texts, including the well-known Christmas carol, "What Child Is This?" Two arrangements are shown here, the first a simple two- and three-voice setting, and the second a more highly embellished setting with some chromatic harmonies.

a. Simple arrangement

b. Embellished arrangement

Arranged by Joel Phillips

"Home on the Range"

This song, from the 1870s, is the official state song of Kansas. Its lyrics have appeared in several forms by different authors; the original, by Brewster Higley ("The Western Home"), was published in 1873, but the most familiar lyrics today are those written by John A. Lomax in 1910. The melody was composed by Daniel E. Kelly, an amateur musician who played violin with a family band. The song has become a folk anthem of the American West and has appeared in many plays and movies, including "Where the Buffalo Roam" (performed by Neil Young in 1980) and "The Messenger" (performed by Willie Nelson in 2009).

[Sheet music with lyrics:]

Oh, give me a home, where the buf-fa-lo roam, Where the deer and the an-te-lope play;— Where sel-dom is heard a dis-cour-ag-ing word, And the skies are not cloud-y all day.—

Chorus
Home, home on the range,— Where the deer and the an-te-lope play;— Where sel-dom is heard a dis-cour-a-ging word, And the skies are not cloud-y all day.—

2. How often at night when the heavens are bright
   With the lights from the glittering stars;
   Have I stood there amazed and asked as I gazed
   If their glory exceeds that of ours.
   Chorus

3. Oh, give me a land where the bright diamond sand
   Flows leisurely down the stream;
   Where the graceful, white swan goes gliding along,
   Like a maid in a heavenly dream.
   Chorus

Elisabeth-Claude Jacquet de la Guerre (1665–1729)
Gigue, from Suite No. 3 in A Minor

Elisabeth-Claude Jacquet de la Guerre was a composer and performer working primarily in Paris. She came from a family of musicians, played in the court of Louis XIV and concertized widely. She is one of the few female composers of her day whose music has survived and is still performed. She composed an opera, numerous cantatas, chamber music, and several books of compositions for harpsichord, one of which includes this gigue. This work for harpsichord is notated with ornaments—symbols above the staff that tell performers to add embellishing notes to the notated pitch. When you listen, you will hear a more florid melodic line than the one notated here.

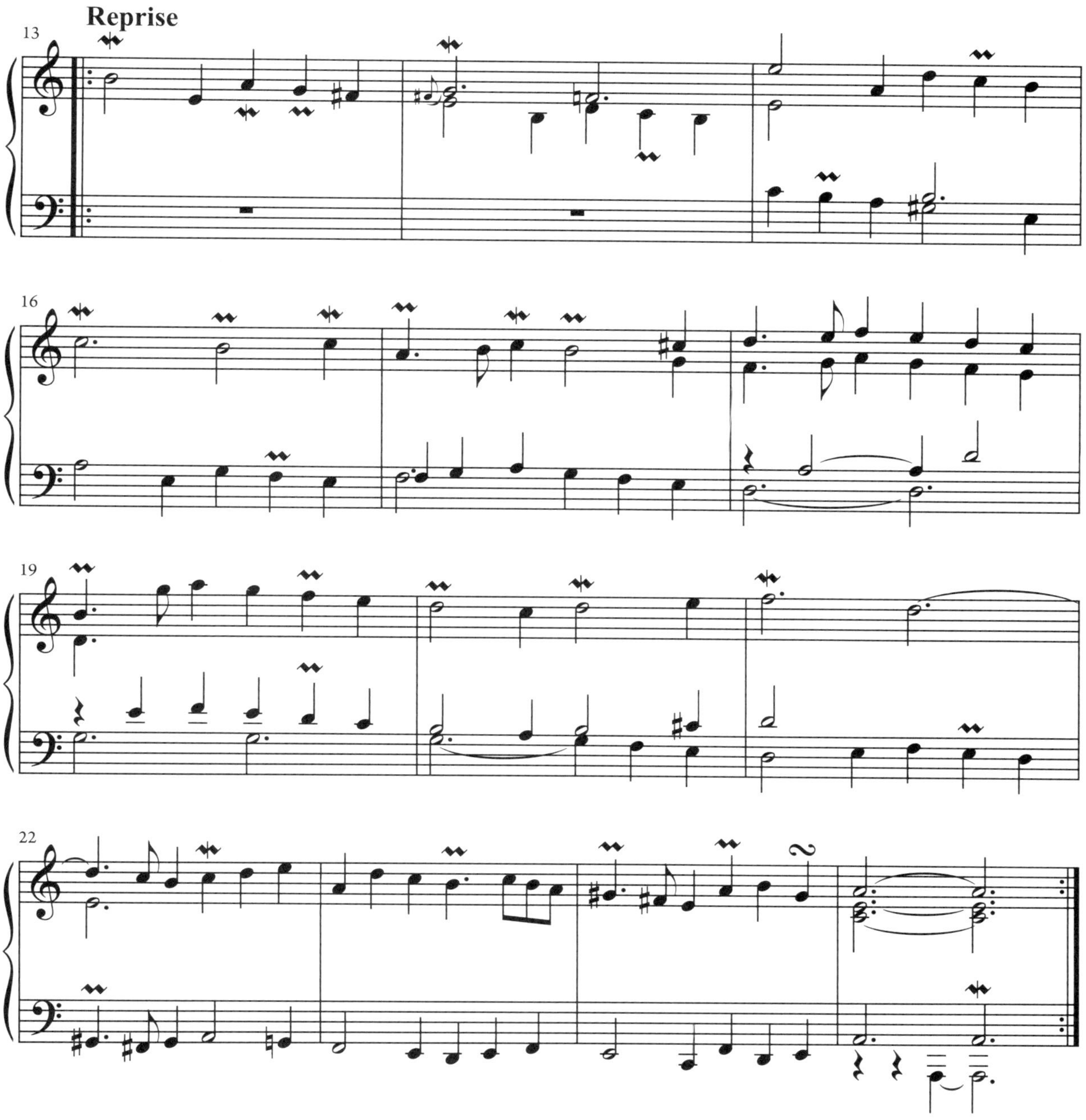
Reprise
13
16
19
22

Scott Joplin (1868–1917)
"Solace"

"Solace," published in 1909, is not a typical rag, though it does make use of the syncopation that characterizes ragtime. It is sometimes listed with the subtitle "A Mexican Serenade," and it bears some resemblance to the tango. Like other Joplin compositions, "Solace" found renewed fame as a result of its inclusion in the 1973 film *The Sting*, starring Paul Newman and Robert Redford.

Joplin, "Solace"

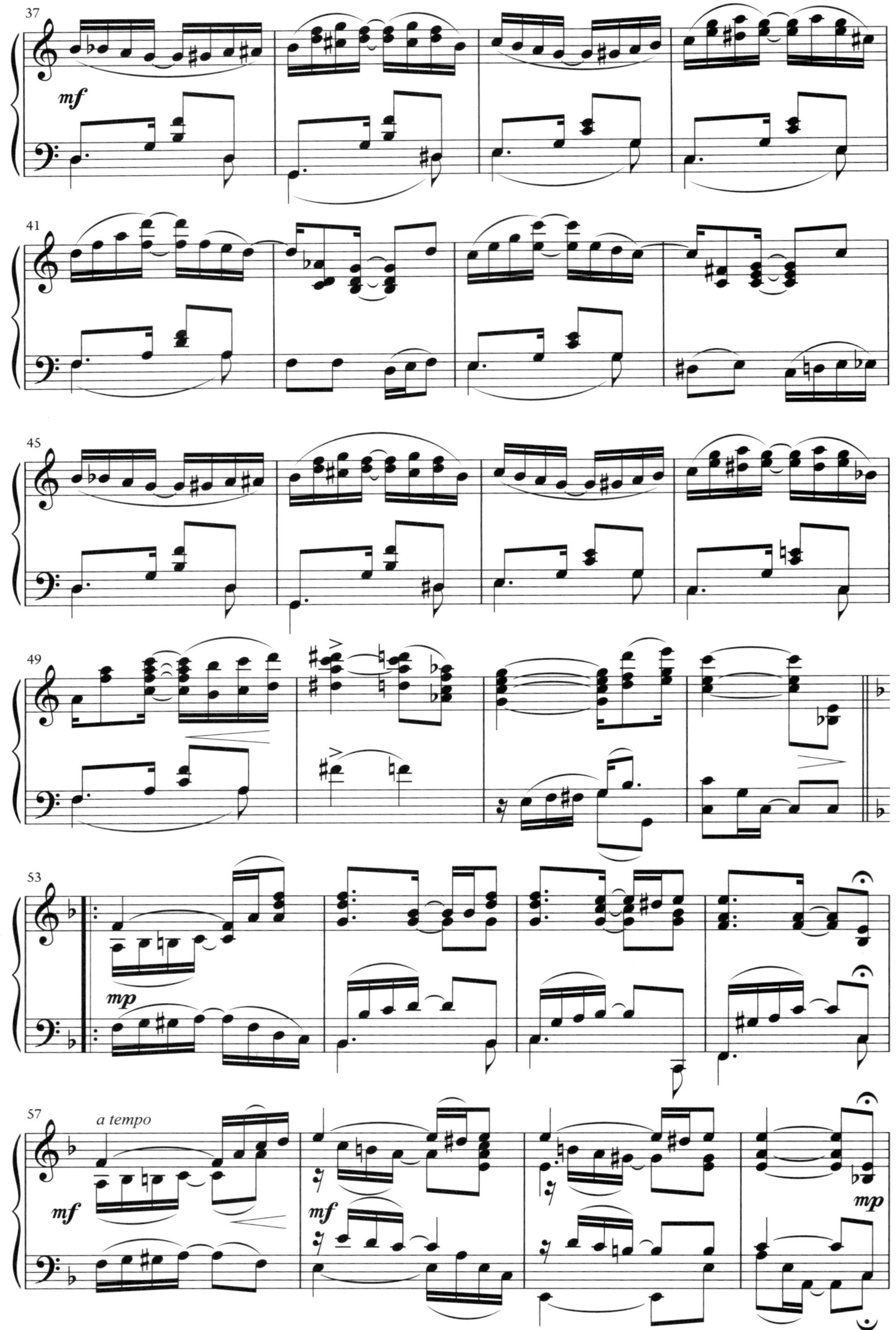
37
mf
41
45
49
53
mp
57
a tempo
mf
mf
mp

Joplin, "Solace"

Jerome Kern (1885–1945)
"Look for the Silver Lining"

Jerome Kern was a celebrated composer of songs for the musical theater and is best known for the musical *Show Boat.* Kern wrote over 700 songs; his hits include "Ol' Man River," "All the Things You Are," "A Fine Romance," and "Smoke Gets in Your Eyes." "Look for the Silver Lining" was first made popular in the musical *Sally* (1920), and was probably the inspiration for a memorable 1970s ad campaign for the International Ladies Garment Workers' Union ("Look for the union label, when you are buying a coat, dress, or blouse").

Kern, "Look for the Silver Lining"

When-e'er a cloud ap-pears in the blue Re-mem-ber some-where the sun is shin-ing And so the

24
right thing to do is make it
27
shine for you. A heart full of joy and
30
glad - ness Will al - ways ban - ish sad - ness and

34
strife So al - ways look for the sil - ver
38
lin - ing And try to find the sun - ny side of
42
1.
life.
2.
life.
fz

Wolfgang Amadeus Mozart (1756–1791)
String Quartet in D Minor, K. 421, third movement

This quartet, composed in 1783, is part of a set of six quartets that Mozart published together and dedicated to the composer Joseph Haydn. During Mozart's lifetime, Haydn's quartets were widely admired; in his "Haydn Quartets," Mozart takes inspiration from the older composer in crafting this music.

380 ANTHOLOGY

Mozart, String Quartet in D Minor, K. 421, third movement

Wolfgang Amadeus Mozart

Variations on "Ah, vous dirai-je Maman," excerpts

Mozart composed this theme and variations early in the 1780s. The theme is a French folk song, "Ah, vous dirai-je Maman," the same tune as "Twinkle, Twinkle, Little Star." Because the tune is so familiar, it makes this set an ideal vehicle for studying variation technique.

Mozart, Variations on "Ah, vous dirai-je Maman," excerpts

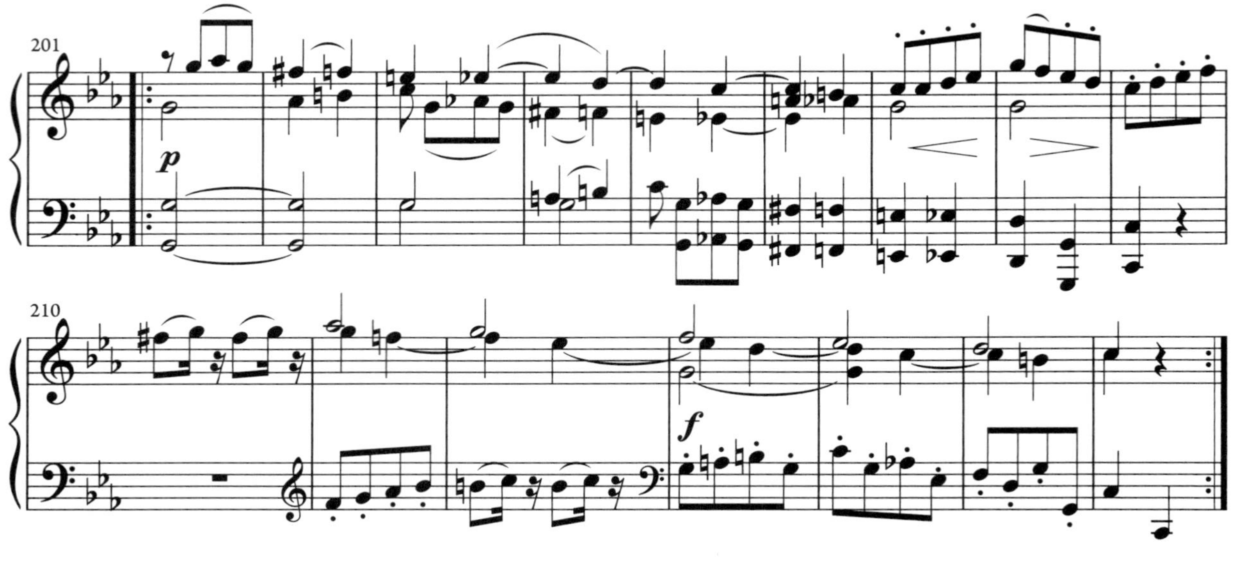
201
210

"My Country, 'Tis of Thee" (America)

This tune, sung with different texts, has been the national anthem of Britain, Germany, Denmark, and Prussia. In 1831, Samuel Francis Smith was given a score of the German version by American hymnist Lowell Mason, who asked for a translation. Instead, Smith was inspired to write new lyrics, which have become beloved as an American patriotic song.

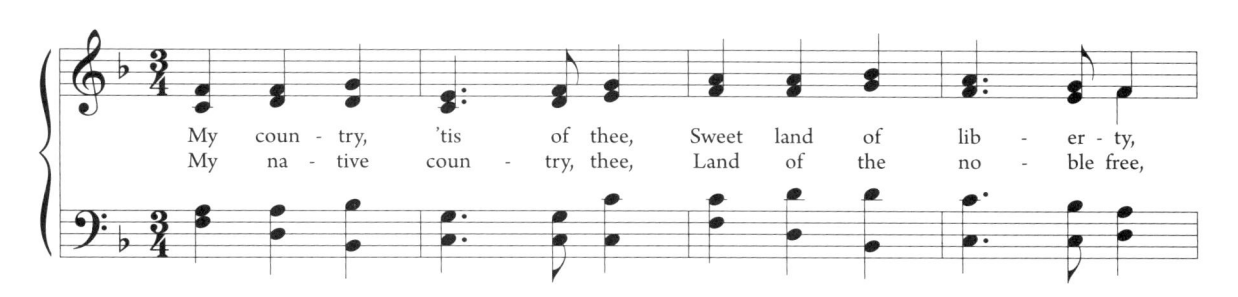

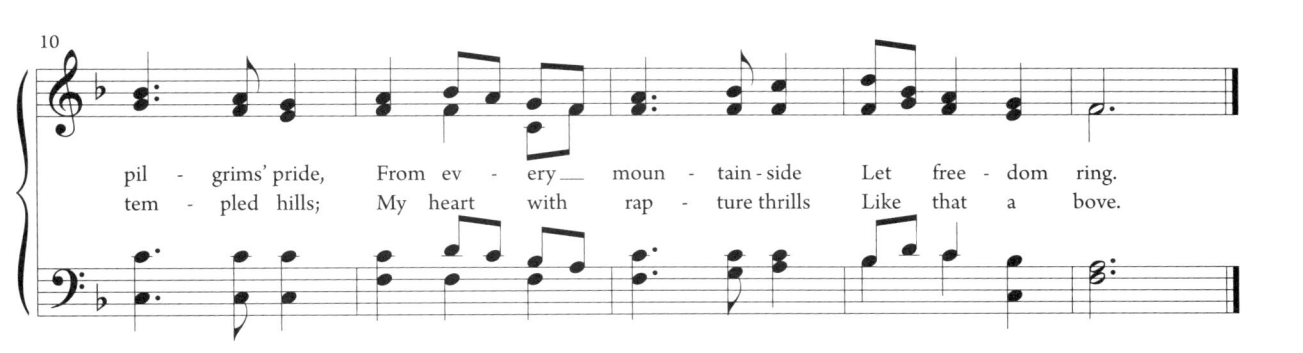

John Newton (1725–1807)

"Amazing Grace"

John Newton, composer of and collaborator on hundreds of Christian hymns, is most famous for his lyrics to "Amazing Grace." Newton's words have been sung to various melodies over the years, but in the early nineteenth century they were joined to the tune shown here. Newton was a minister of the Church of England for the last forty years of his life. He served in London and Olney, where he and collaborator William Cowper published *Olney Hymns* in 1779, which includes the text of "Amazing Grace." Newton spent his younger years as the captain of an English slave ship and converted to Christianity during a storm at sea. "Amazing Grace" is thought to be autobiographical; phrases like "a wretch like me" refer to his days as slave trader.

Amazing grace, how sweet the sound That saved a wretch like me! I once was lost, but now am found, was blind, but now I see.

Through many dangers, toils, and snares,
I have already come;
'Twas grace has brought me safe thus far,
And grace will lead me home.

The Lord has promised good to me.
His word my hope secures;
He will my shield and portion be
As long as life endures.

"O God Our Help in Ages Past" (St. Anne)

The English composer William Croft wrote and harmonized this tune in 1708. Most often, it is sung as the hymn "O God Our Help in Ages Past," to words based on Psalm 90 and written by Isaac Watts in 1719.

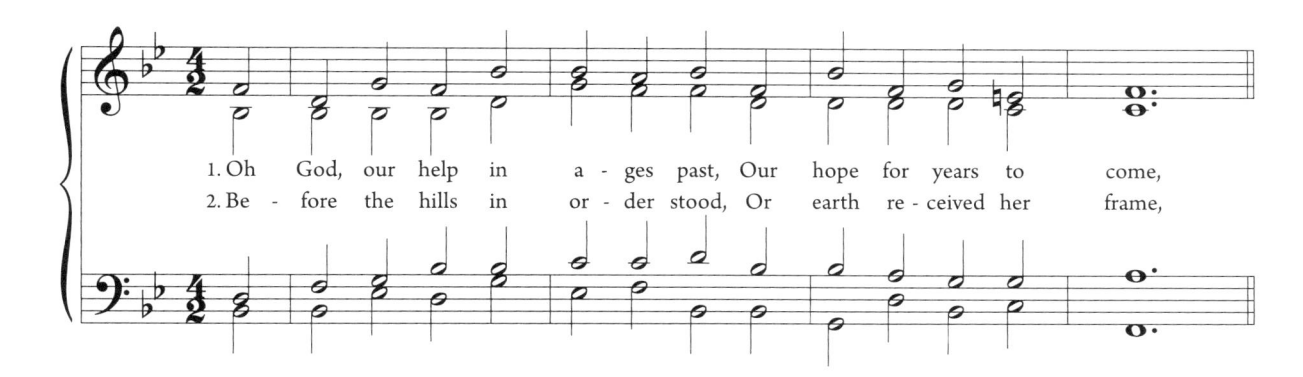

1. Oh God, our help in ages past, Our hope for years to come, Our shelter from the storm-y blast, And our e-ter-nal home.
2. Be-fore the hills in or-der stood, Or earth re-ceived her frame, From ev-er-last-ing thou art God, To end-less years the same.

Joel Phillips (b. 1958)
"Blues for Norton"

Joel Phillips, one of the authors of this text, composed "Blues for Norton" on June 6, 2006—6-6-06. Although Christians often view the number 666 negatively, Kabbalistic Jews see it as the number of creation and physical perfection of the world (according to Genesis, the world was created in six days). "Norton" has six letters, so Phillips's music is based on a six-note riff stated in each of six phrases. Ideally the work would be performed by a sextet! The smaller notes in measures 13–22 show how a second solo instrument can interact with the first in a call-and-response texture.

a. Lead sheet

b. Full score (all instruments sound as notated)

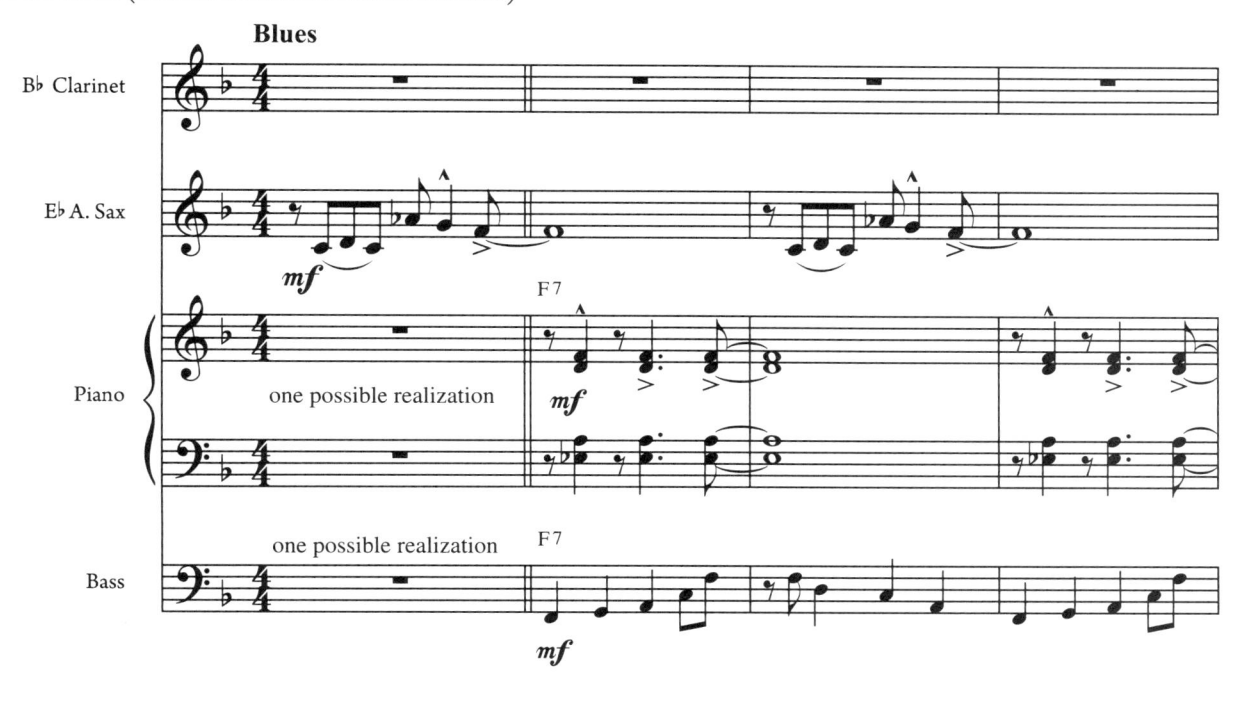

Phillips, "Blues for Norton"

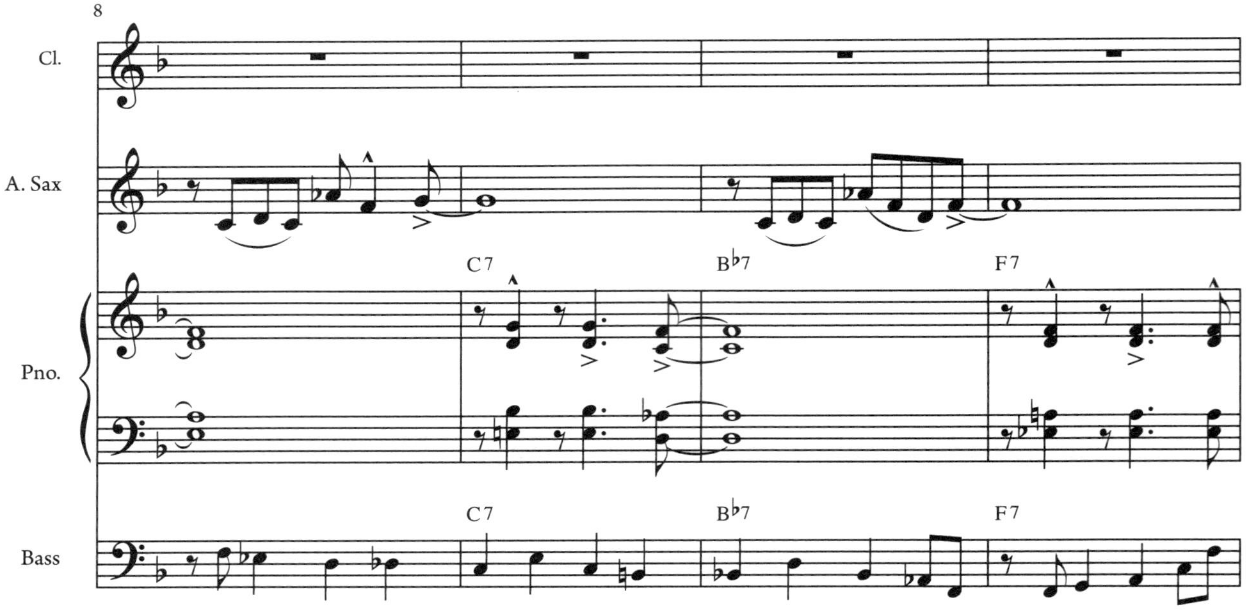
8
Cl.
A. Sax
Pno.
Bass
C7
B♭7
F7

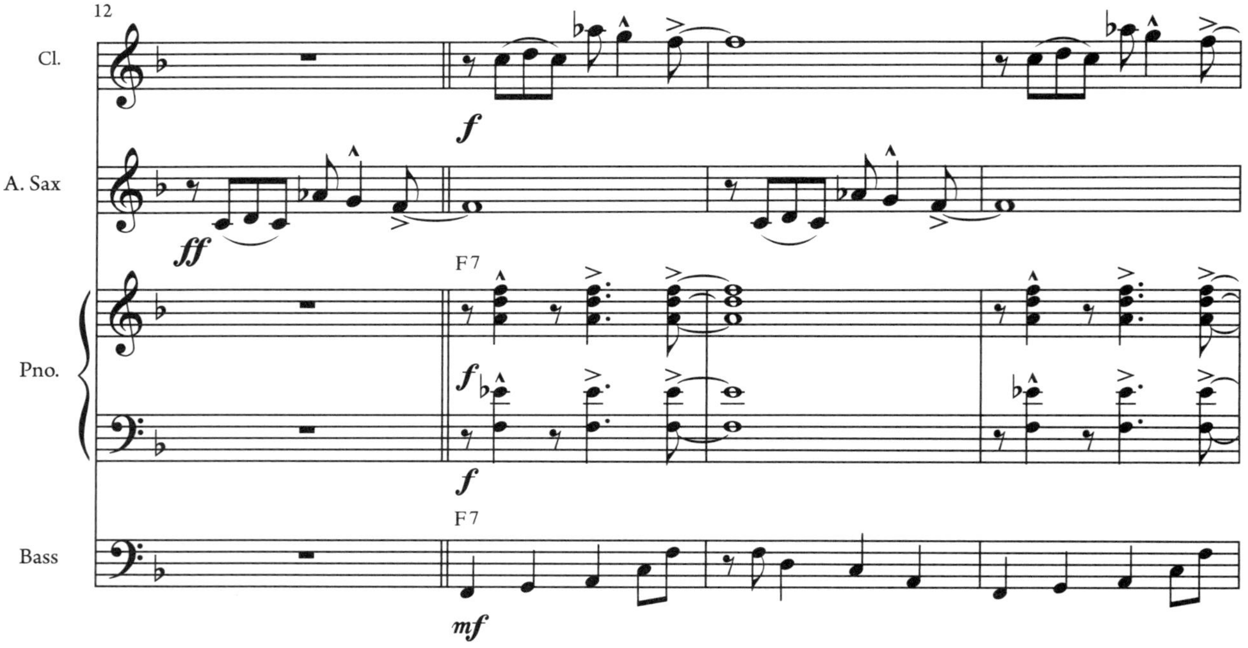
12
Cl.
A. Sax
Pno.
Bass
F7
f
ff
mf

Phillips, "Blues for Norton"

Franz Schubert (1797–1828)

Waltz in B minor, Op. 18, No. 6

The waltz is a German dance in triple meter that enjoyed great popularity in the nineteenth century. This one belongs to a set of dance pieces Schubert composed in 1815. At parties, Schubert frequently improvised short piano waltzes, like this one, for dancing.

Schubert, Waltz in B minor, Op. 18, No. 6

"Simple Gifts"

The tune "Simple Gifts" was written in 1848 by Elder Joseph Brackett Jr., a member of the American Shaker religious order. While often considered a hymn, it was originally intended for dancing, as its lyrics suggest: "to turn, turn will be our delight, 'till by turning, turning we come round right." "Simple Gifts" has been arranged by many artists, including folk singer Judy Collins and composer Aaron Copland. Even more recently, the tune was featured in a work titled "Air and Simple Gifts," composed by John Williams for the 2009 inauguration of President Barack Obama.

Hart A. Wand and Lloyd Garrett
"Dallas Blues"

Hart A. Wand was a German immigrant whose family first settled in Oklahoma after the 1889 Land Rush. He made his living primarily as a businessman, but was also a bandleader. "Dallas Blues" is one of the earliest published examples of the blues. Wand composed the tune and chord progression for piano and Garrett added the lyrics a few years later.

houn') ___ Then you stop to say, ___ "Let me go a-way from this old town ___ (this aw-ful
fare) ___ Just to come back there ___ rid-ing in a Pull-man par-lor chair ___ (a par-lor

town)." ___ There's ___ a place I know ___ folks won't pass me by, ___
chair). ___ Sent ___ a tel-e-gram, this is what I said: ___

Dal-las, Tex-as, that's the town ___ I cry! ___ (oh hear me cry!) ___ And I'm
Ba-by, bring ___ a cold towel for ___ my head ___ (my ach-ing head), ___ Got the

27
go - ing back, go - ing back to stay there till I die (un - til I die).
Dal - las Blues and your lov - in' man is al - most dead (is al - most dead).
30
I've got the Dal - las Blues and the Main Street heart dis - ease (it's buz - zin'
I'm goin' to put my - self on a San - ta Fe and go (I'm goin' to
p-f
34
'round), I've got the Dal - las Blues and the Main Street heart dis -
go), I'm goin' to put my - self on a San - ta Fe and

ease_____ (it's buz-zin' 'round),_____ Buz-zin' 'round my head_____ like a
go_____ (I'm goin' to go)_____ To that Tex-as town_____ where you

swarm of lit-tle hon-ey bees_____ (of hon-ey bees). I've got the bees)._____
nev-er see the ice and snow_____ (the ice and snow). I'm goin' to snow)._____

Appendix 1
Try It Answers

Chapter 1

TRY IT #1

(a) C (b) E (c) G (d) E (e) D (f) C (g) E (h) D (i) B (j) E (k) A
(l) E (m) F (n) B (o) D

TRY IT #2

(a) (1) B (2) C (3) F (4) G (5) D (6) A (7) D (8) F (9) G (10) E
(11) C (12) E

(b)

(1) **E** (2) **G** (3) **A** (4) **B** (5) **C** (6) **B** (7) **E**

TRY IT #3

(a) (1) F (2) G (3) D (4) B (5) F (6) A (7) C (8) G (9) B (10) E
(11) A (12) C

(b)

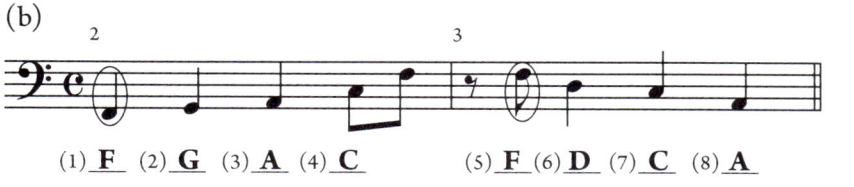

(1) **F** (2) **G** (3) **A** (4) **C** (5) **F** (6) **D** (7) **C** (8) **A**

TRY IT #4

(a) B3 (b) C6 (c) D4 (d) B5 (e) F3 (f) C4 (g) E6 (h) A5 (i) A3 (j) D6
(k) G3 (l) A2 (m) D4 (n) E2 (o) F4 (p) E3 (q) C2 (r) B3 (s) F2 (t) C3

TRY IT #5

(a) G3 (b) F3 (c) G1 (d) C2 (e) F1

Chapter 2

TRY IT #1

(a) F♯   (b) C   (c) B♭   (d) F   (e) C♯   (f) C♭   (g) G♯   (h) D♯

TRY IT #2

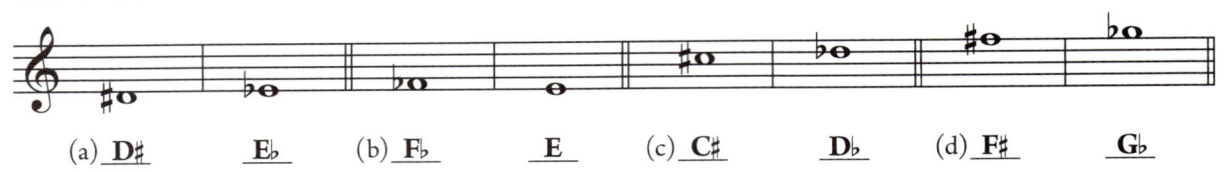

(a) D♯   E♭   (b) F♭   E   (c) C♯   D♭   (d) F♯   G♭

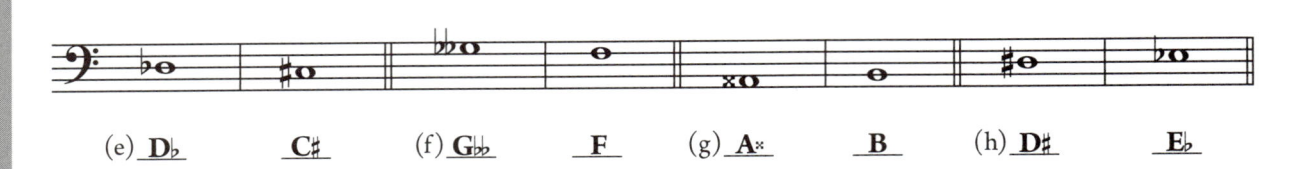

(e) D♭   C♯   (f) G𝄫   F   (g) A𝄪   B   (h) D♯   E♭

TRY IT #3

(a) (1) G♯ or A♭   (2) C♮ or B♯   (3) B♭ or A♯   (4) F or E♯   (5) D♯ or E♭   (6) G♯   (7) B♭   (8) E   (9) D♯   (10) A♭

(b) (1) H   (2) H   (3) W   (4) W   (5) H   (6) W   (7) N   (8) N   (9) W   (10) H   (11) H   (12) H   (13) W   (14) H

(c) H, W, H, W, H

Chapter 3

TRY IT #1

TRY IT #2

(a) Ma-ny were the wild notes her mer-ry voice would pour,
E   Q   S   E   H

(b) Take a sad song and make it bet-ter. Re-mem-ber to let her in-to your heart,
Q   E   E   S   H   E   Q   S   S   H

TRY IT #3

Meter signature	Beats per measure	Beat unit	Beat division
$\frac{3}{8}$	3	♪	♫
$\frac{2}{2}$	2	𝅗𝅥	♩♩
$\frac{4}{16}$	4	♬	♬♬
$\frac{3}{2}$	3	𝅗𝅥	♩♩
$\frac{3}{4}$	3	♩	♫

TRY IT #4

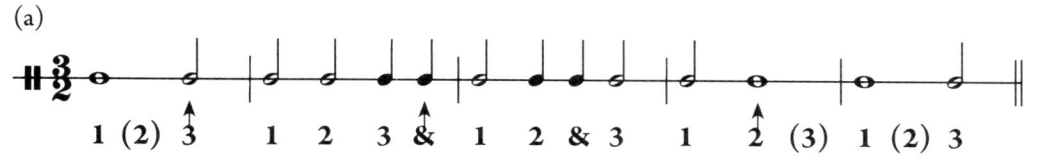

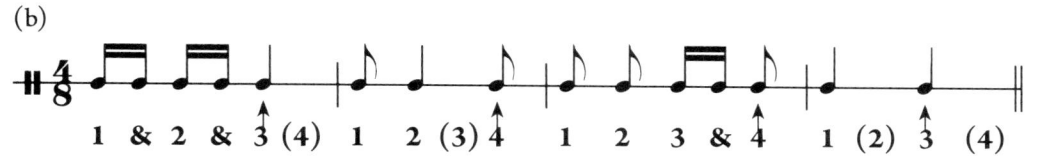

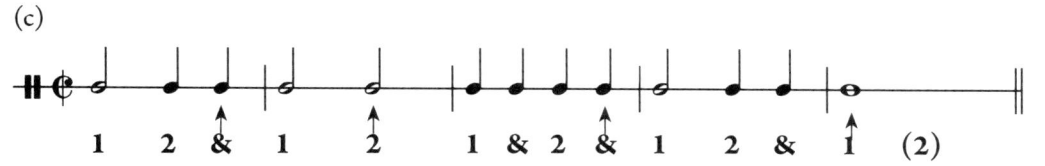

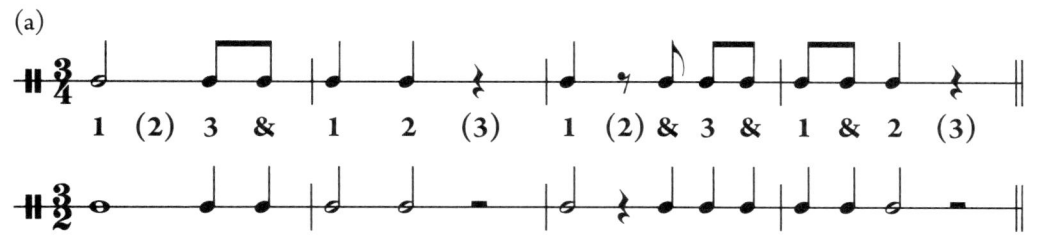

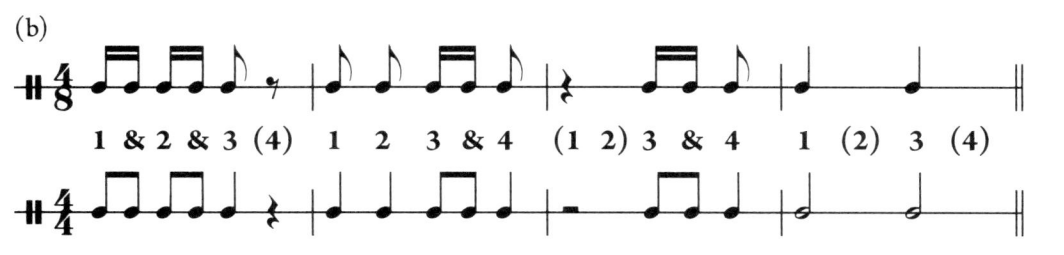

(a) $\frac{3}{2}$

1 (2) ↑3   1 2 3 &   1 2 & 3   1 ↑2 (3)   1 (2) 3

(b) $\frac{4}{8}$

1 & 2 & ↑3 (4)   1 2 (3)↑4   1 2 3 &↑4   1 (2) ↑3 (4)

(c) ¢

1 2 ↑&   1 ↑2   1 ↑& 2 ↑&   1 2 &   ↑1 (2)

TRY IT #5

(a) $\frac{3}{4}$

1 (2) 3 &   1 2 (3)   1 (2) & 3 &   1 & 2 (3)

$\frac{3}{2}$

(b) $\frac{4}{8}$

1 & 2 & 3 (4)   1 2 3 & 4   (1 2) 3 & 4   1 (2) 3 (4)

$\frac{4}{4}$

Chapter 4

TRY IT #1

(a)

1 (2) & 3 & (1) 2 3 a 1 & (2) & 3 1 (2 3)

(b)

1 e & a (2) & 1 & (2) e & a 1 a 2 & (1) & 2 a 1 (2)

(c)

1 (2) (3) & 4 & 1 a (2) & 3 (4) 1 e & a 2 a 3 & (4) & 1 (2 3 4)

TRY IT #2

1 e & a (2) e & a (1) e a (2) & 1 e & a (2) e & a (1) e a (2) &

TRY IT #3

Chapter 5

TRY IT #1

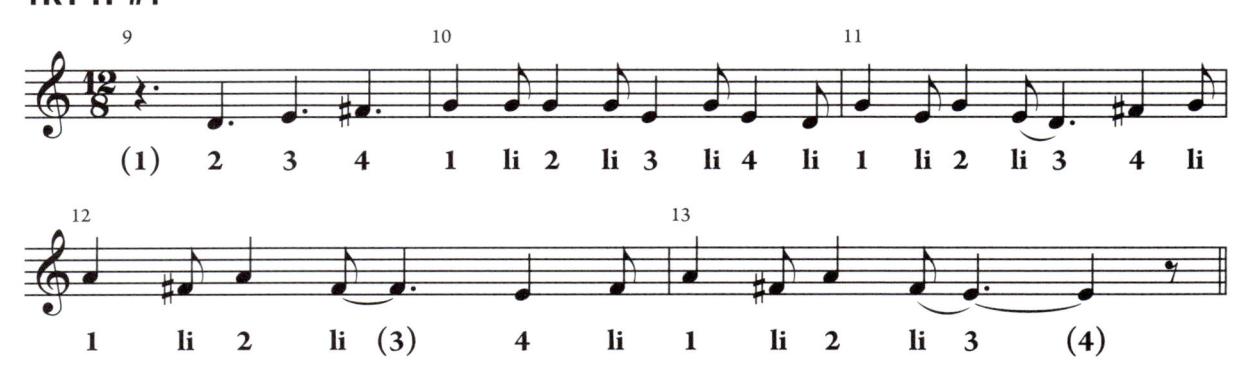

(1) 2 3 4 | 1 li 2 li 3 li 4 li | 1 li 2 li 3 4 li

1 li 2 li (3) 4 li | 1 li 2 li 3 (4)

TRY IT #2

(a)

(b)

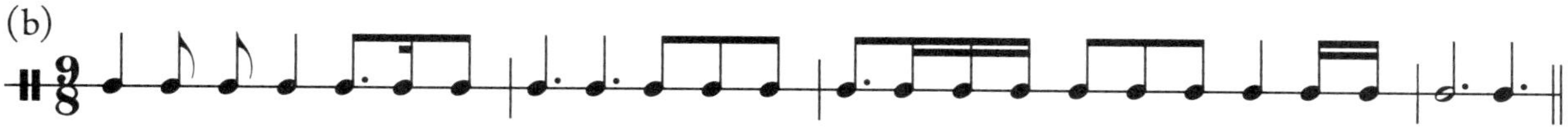

TRY IT #3

(a)

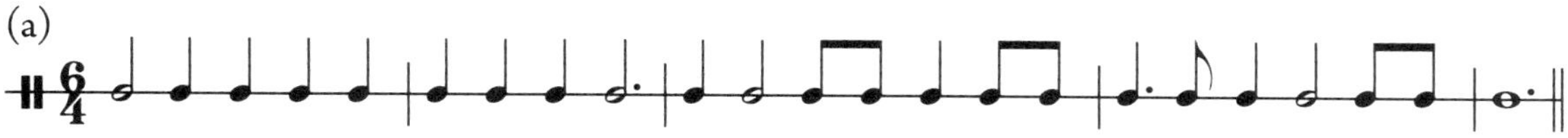

(b)

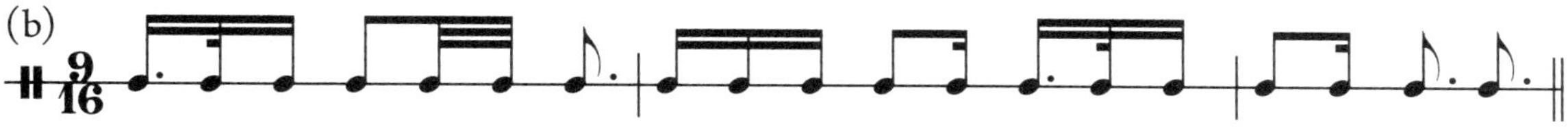

(c)

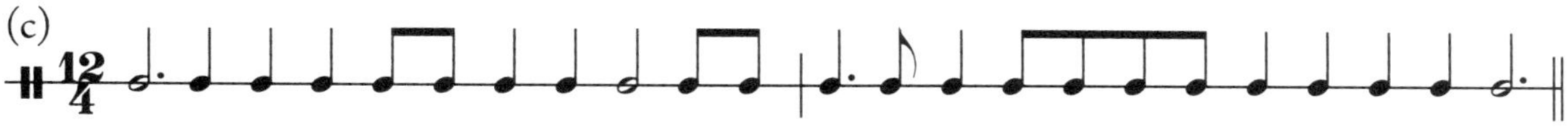

(d)

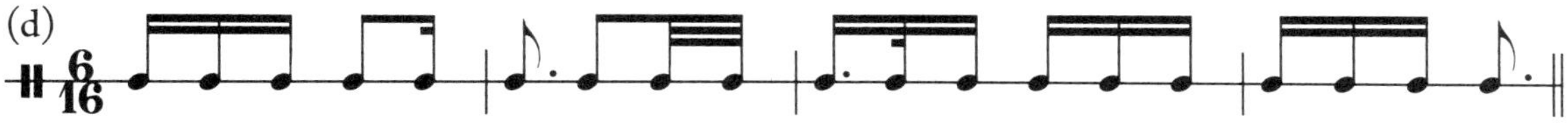

TRY IT #4

(a)

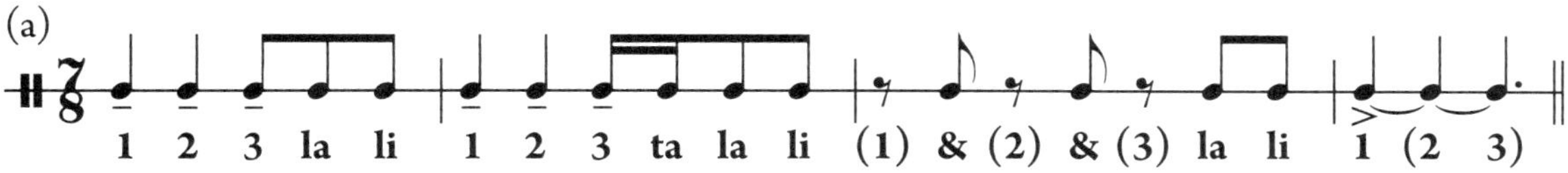
1 2 3 la li 1 2 3 ta la li (1) & (2) & (3) la li 1 (2 3)

(b)

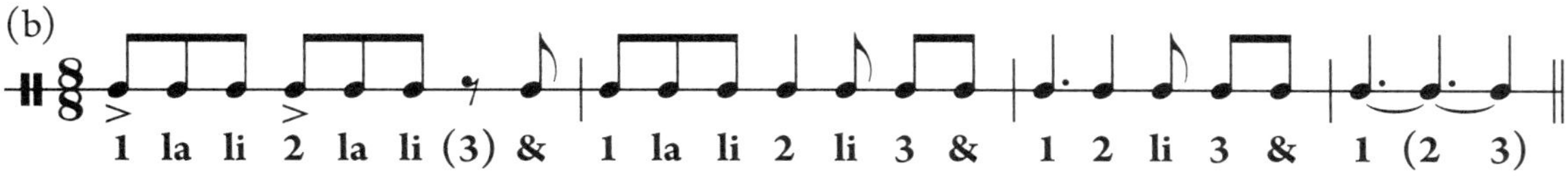
1 la li 2 la li (3) & 1 la li 2 li 3 & 1 2 li 3 & 1 (2 3)

Chapter 6

TRY IT #1

(a) (1)

(2)

(b) (1)

(2)

TRY IT #2

(a) (b)

(c) (d)

TRY IT #3

(a) (b)

(c) (d)

(e) (f)

TRY IT #4

(a) B (b) D♭ (c) A♭ (d) D (e) A (f) B♭ (g) F♯ (h) E (i) G♭ (j) F

TRY IT #5

- Key signature suggests: A♭ major
- Last six scale degrees: $\hat{1}-\hat{1}-\hat{2}-\hat{1}-\hat{7}-\hat{1}$
- First six scale degrees: $\hat{5}-\hat{5}-\hat{1}-\hat{1}-\hat{2}-\hat{3}$
- Key of piece: A♭ major

Chapter 7

TRY IT #1

(a) F major / F natural minor

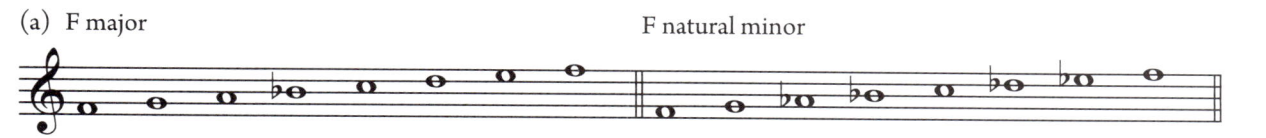

(b) B major / B natural minor

(c) A major / A natural minor

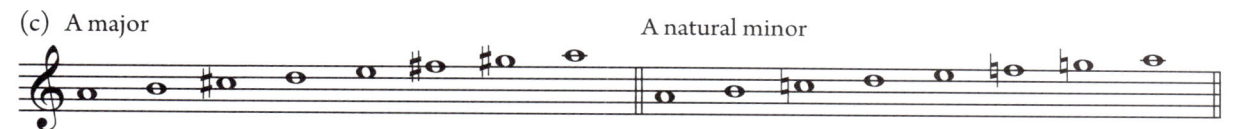

TRY IT #2

(a) C natural minor / C harmonic minor

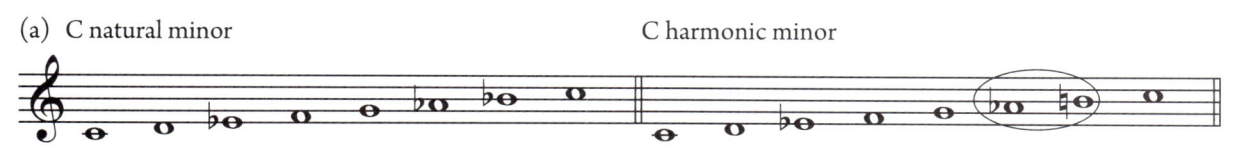

(b) F♯ natural minor / F♯ harmonic minor

(c) G natural minor / G harmonic minor

(d) C♯ natural minor / C♯ harmonic minor

TRY IT #3

(a) B melodic minor

(b) F melodic minor

TRY IT #4

(a) C♯ minor   (b) F minor   (c) B minor   (d) C minor   (e) G♯ minor   (f) D minor
(g) G minor   (h) A minor   (i) B♭ minor   (j) D♯ minor   (k) F♯ minor   (l) E minor

TRY IT #5

(a) Relative major: A 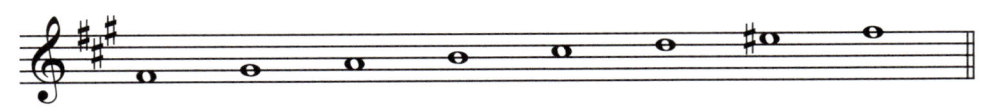 — F♯ harmonic minor scale

(b) Relative major: G 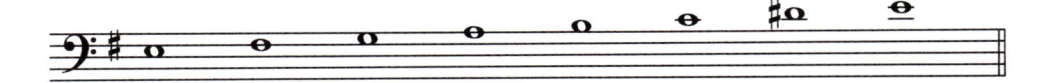 — E harmonic minor scale

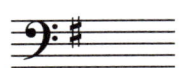

(c) Relative major: D 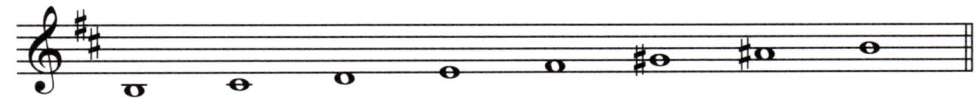 — B melodic minor scale (ascending)

(d) Relative major: D♭ 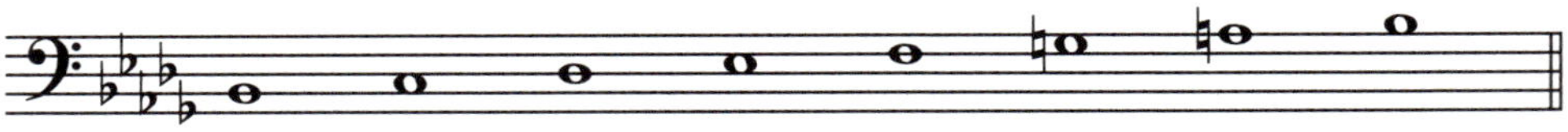 — B♭ melodic minor scale (ascending)

Chapter 8

TRY IT #1

(a) 3   (b) 7   (c) 8   (d) 2   (e) 5   (f) 3

TRY IT #2

(a) (1) P5 (2) M7 (3) M2 (4) P4 (5) M6 (6) PU (7) M3
(8) m3 (9) P4 (10) m7 (11) m6 (12) M2 (13) P5 (14) PU

(b) (1) (2) (3) (4) (5) (6) (7)

(8) (9) (10) (11) (12) (13) (14)

TRY IT #3

(a) m3 (b) m3 (c) M2 (d) P4 (e) M3 (f) P4 (g) M2 (h) P4 (i) P4 (j) m3
(k) m3 (l) m2 (m) M3 (n) P4 (o) M3 (p) m2 (q) m3 (r) P4 (s) M2 (t) P4

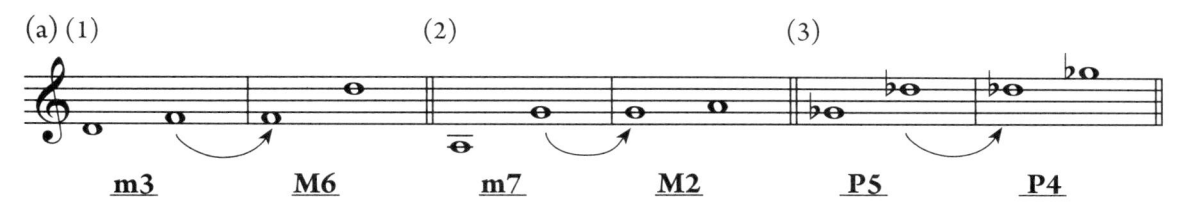

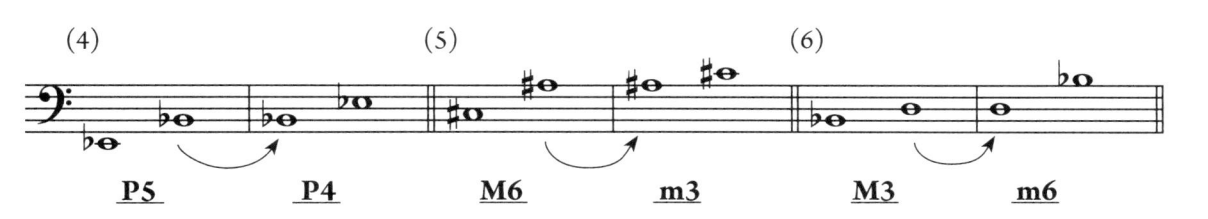

TRY IT #4

(a) (1) m3 M6 (2) m7 M2 (3) P5 P4

(4) P5 P4 (5) M6 m3 (6) M3 m6

(b) (1) (2) (3) (4) (5) (6) (7) (8) (9) (10)

(11) (12) (13) (14) (15) (16) (17) (18) (19) (20)

TRY IT #5

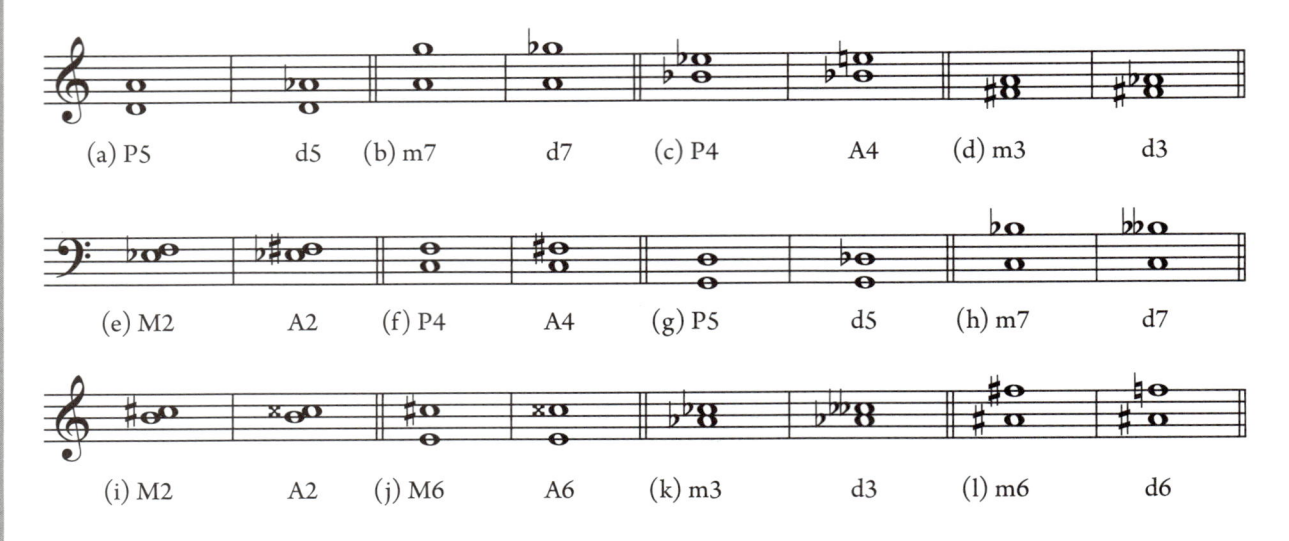

(a) P5   d5   (b) m7   d7   (c) P4   A4   (d) m3   d3

(e) M2   A2   (f) P4   A4   (g) P5   d5   (h) m7   d7

(i) M2   A2   (j) M6   A6   (k) m3   d3   (l) m6   d6

TRY IT #6

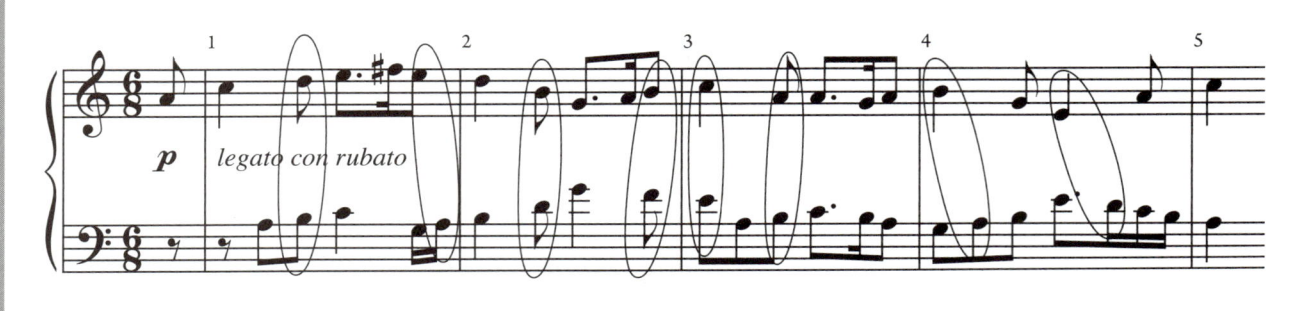

Interval:	**m10**	**P12**	**M6**	**A4**	**m6**	**m7**	**M9**	**M2**
Simple equivalent:	**m3**	**P5**					**M2**	

Chapter 9

TRY IT #1

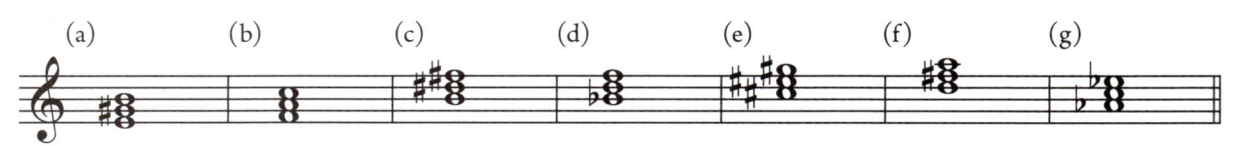

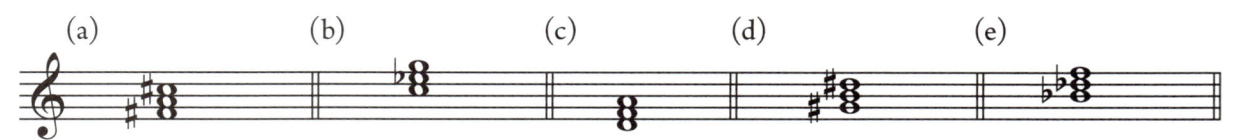

(a) (b) (c) (d) (e) (f) (g)

TRY IT #2

(a) (b) (c) (d) (e)

A-10   APPENDIX ONE   Try It Answers

TRY IT #3

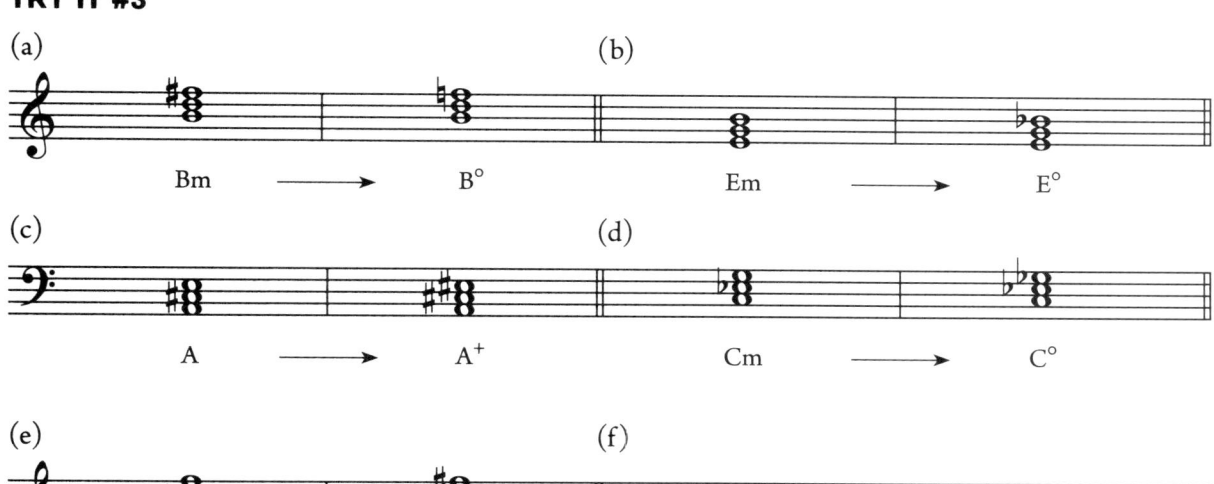

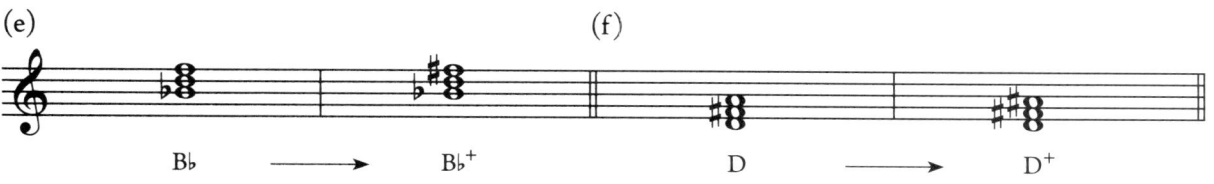

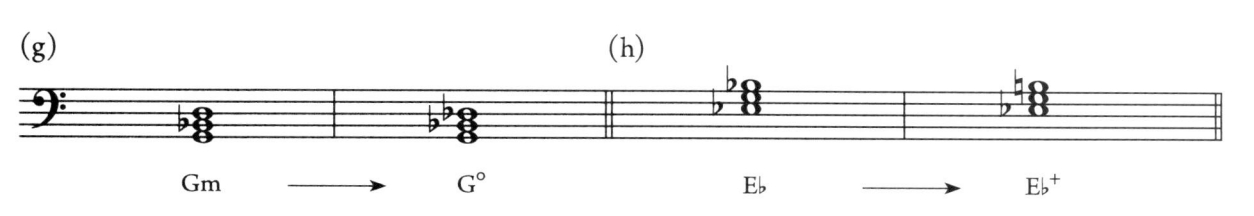

(a) Bm → B° (b) Em → E°

(c) A → A⁺ (d) Cm → C°

(e) B♭ → B♭⁺ (f) D → D⁺

(g) Gm → G° (h) E♭ → E♭⁺

TRY IT #4

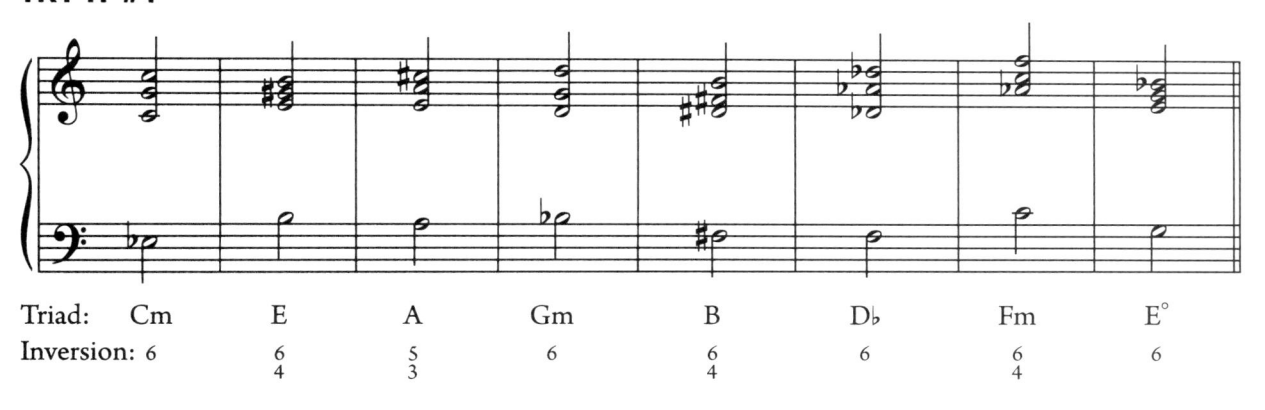

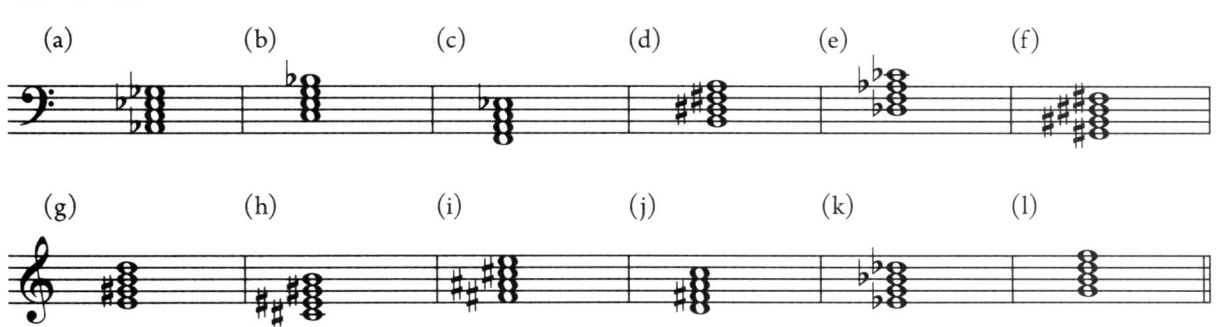

Triad:	Cm	E	A	Gm	B	D♭	Fm	E°
Inversion:	6	6/4	5/3	6	6/4	6	6/4	6

TRY IT #5

(a) (b) (c) (d) (e) (f)

(g) (h) (i) (j) (k) (l)

Chapter 10

TRY IT #1

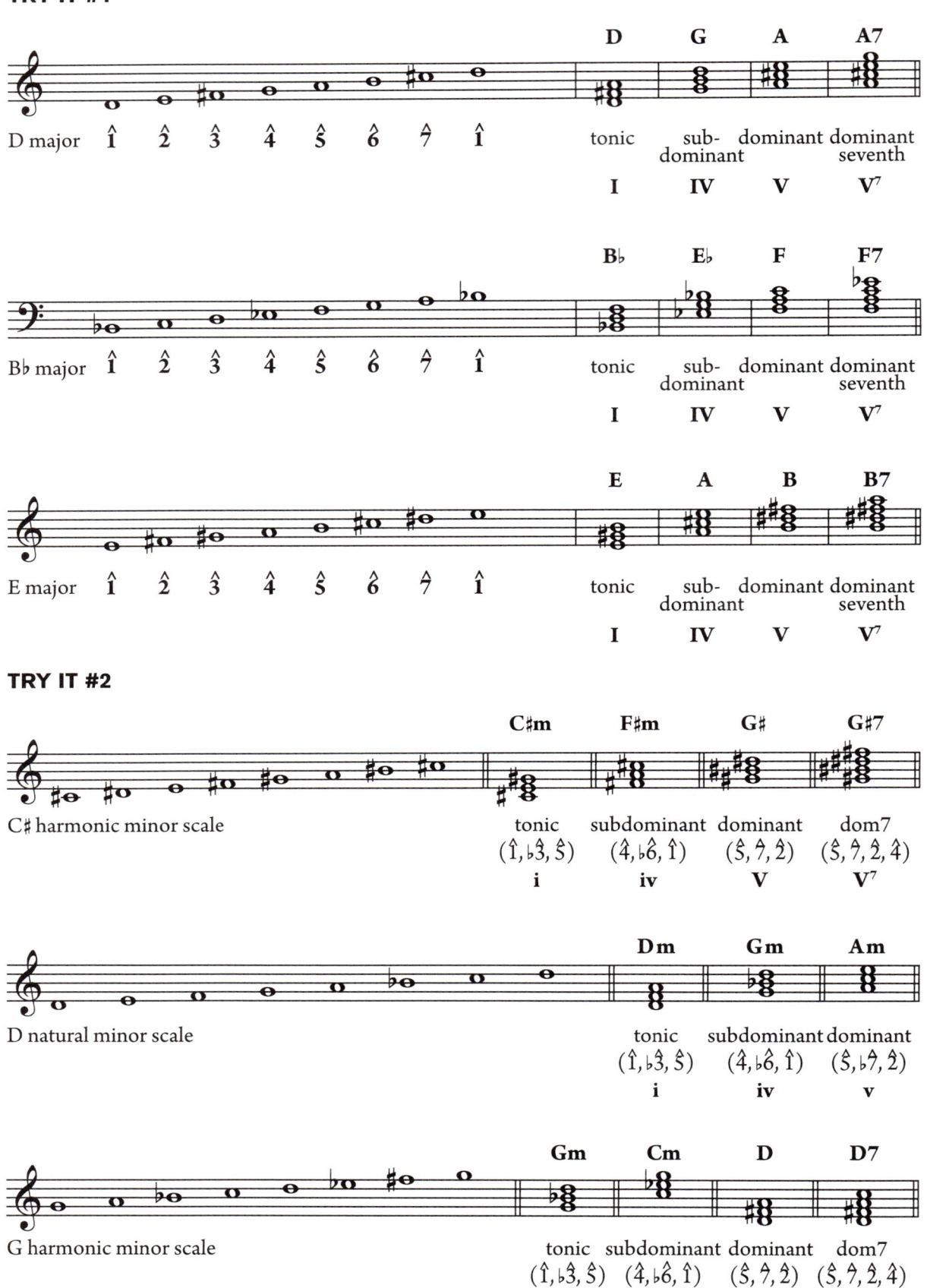

D major: $\hat{1}\ \hat{2}\ \hat{3}\ \hat{4}\ \hat{5}\ \hat{6}\ \hat{7}\ \hat{1}$

D	G	A	A7
tonic	sub-dominant	dominant	dominant seventh
I	IV	V	V⁷

B♭ major: $\hat{1}\ \hat{2}\ \hat{3}\ \hat{4}\ \hat{5}\ \hat{6}\ \hat{7}\ \hat{1}$

B♭	E♭	F	F7
tonic	sub-dominant	dominant	dominant seventh
I	IV	V	V⁷

E major: $\hat{1}\ \hat{2}\ \hat{3}\ \hat{4}\ \hat{5}\ \hat{6}\ \hat{7}\ \hat{1}$

E	A	B	B7
tonic	sub-dominant	dominant	dominant seventh
I	IV	V	V⁷

TRY IT #2

C♯ harmonic minor scale

C♯m	F♯m	G♯	G♯7
tonic	subdominant	dominant	dom7
($\hat{1}, ♭\hat{3}, \hat{5}$)	($\hat{4}, ♭\hat{6}, \hat{1}$)	($\hat{5}, \hat{7}, \hat{2}$)	($\hat{5}, \hat{7}, \hat{2}, \hat{4}$)
i	iv	V	V⁷

D natural minor scale

Dm	Gm	Am
tonic	subdominant	dominant
($\hat{1}, ♭\hat{3}, \hat{5}$)	($\hat{4}, ♭\hat{6}, \hat{1}$)	($\hat{5}, ♭\hat{7}, \hat{2}$)
i	iv	v

G harmonic minor scale

Gm	Cm	D	D7
tonic	subdominant	dominant	dom7
($\hat{1}, ♭\hat{3}, \hat{5}$)	($\hat{4}, ♭\hat{6}, \hat{1}$)	($\hat{5}, \hat{7}, \hat{2}$)	($\hat{5}, \hat{7}, \hat{2}, \hat{4}$)
i	iv	V	V⁷

A-12   APPENDIX ONE   Try It Answers

F♯ natural minor scale

tonic (1̂, ♭3̂, 5̂) — F♯m — i
subdominant (4̂, ♭6̂, 1̂) — Bm — iv
dominant (5̂, ♭7̂, 2̂) — C♯m — v

TRY IT #3
(a) Key: F, cadence: PAC (b) Key: g, cadence: HC

TRY IT #4

I am a poor way-far-ing stran-ger a trav-'ling through this world of woe;
d: i   i   i   iv   i   v

Chapter 11

TRY IT #1
a a' b a'

TRY IT #2

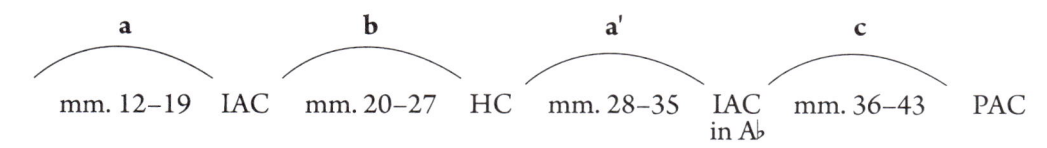

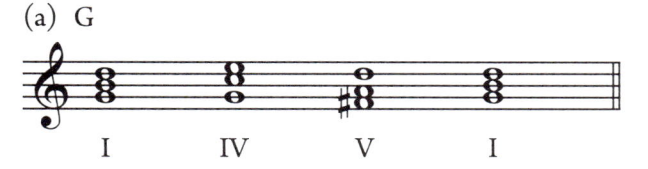

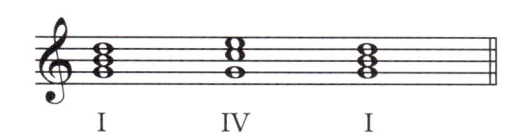

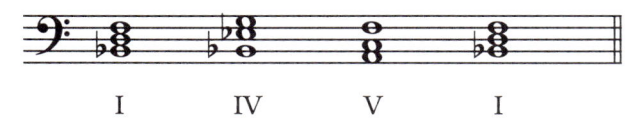

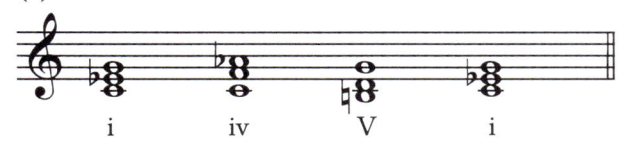

a — mm. 12–19 — IAC
b — mm. 20–27 — HC
a' — mm. 28–35 — IAC in A♭
c — mm. 36–43 — PAC

TRY IT #3

(a) G
I IV V I   I IV I

(b) B♭
I IV V I   I IV I

(c) Cm
i iv V i   i iv i

TRY IT #4

One possible answer:

Chapter 12

TRY IT #1

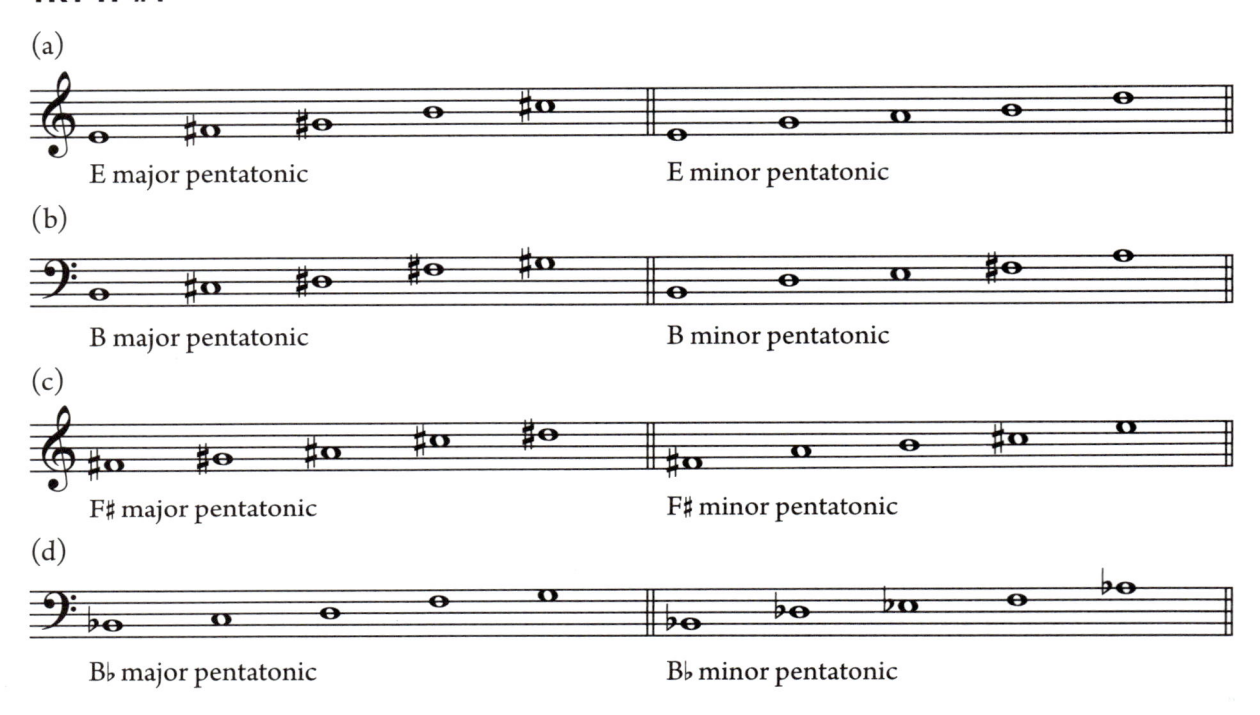

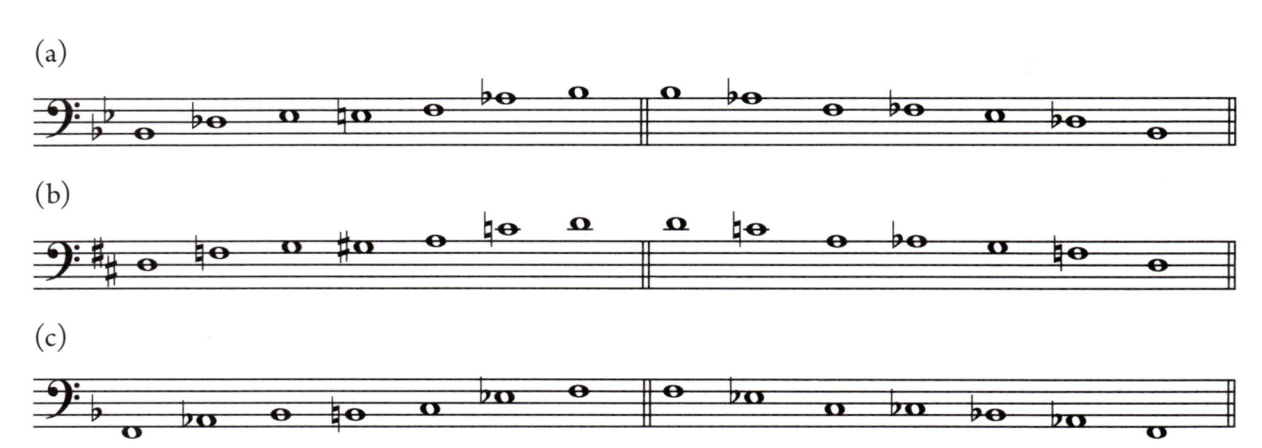

(a) E major pentatonic   E minor pentatonic

(b) B major pentatonic   B minor pentatonic

(c) F♯ major pentatonic   F♯ minor pentatonic

(d) B♭ major pentatonic   B♭ minor pentatonic

TRY IT #2

(a)

(b)

(c)

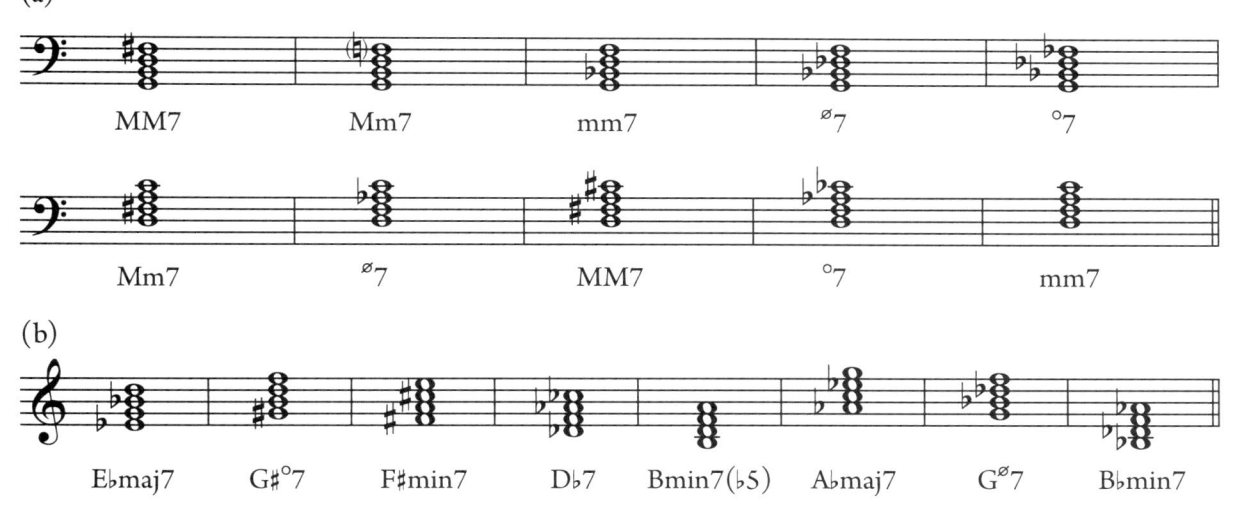

TRY IT #3

(a)

| MM7 | Mm7 | mm7 | ø7 | °7 |

| Mm7 | ø7 | MM7 | °7 | mm7 |

(b)

| E♭maj7 | G♯°7 | F♯min7 | D♭7 | Bmin7(♭5) | A♭maj7 | Gø7 | B♭min7 |

Appendix 2

Reading Review Answers

Chapter 1
(1) h (2) c (3) i (4) f (5) q (6) g (7) d (8) a
(9) o (10) p (11) r (12) j (13) l (14) n (15) e (16) m
(17) k (18) b

Chapter 2
(1) e (2) b (3) h (4) c (5) l (6) g (7) f (8) a
(9) j (10) i (11) k (12) d

Chapter 3
(1) h (2) c (3) e (4) r (5) i (6) a (7) j (8) p
(9) l (10) g (11) m (12) d (13) f (14) q (15) o (16) n
(17) b (18) k

Chapter 4
(1) c (2) a (3) b (4) f (5) h (6) e (7) i (8) d
(9) g

Chapter 5
(1) f (2) j (3) a (4) i (5) l (6) k (7) m (8) n
(9) p (10) e (11) d (12) g (13) h (14) o (15) b (16) c

Chapter 6
(1) d (2) g (3) i (4) h (5) l (6) e (7) o (8) c
(9) f (10) n (11) m (12) a (13) j (14) b (15) k

Chapter 7
(1) g (2) a (3) b (4) j (5) c (6) h (7) f (8) e
(9) d (10) i

Chapter 8
(1) e (2) i (3) a (4) j (5) o (6) u (7) f (8) v
(9) h (10) k (11) c (12) m (13) t (14) b (15) x (16) g
(17) r (18) s (19) l (20) w (21) p (22) q (23) n (24) d

Chapter 9
(1) j (2) e (3) g (4) c (5) b (6) m (7) p (8) r
(9) i (10) t (11) f (12) n (13) o (14) l (15) d (16) k
(17) a (18) h (19) q (20) s

Chapter 10
(1) e (2) d (3) k (4) c (5) i (6) n (7) m (8) f
(9) j (10) g (11) l (12) a (13) h (14) b

Chapter 11
(1) f (2) h (3) j (4) b (5) i (6) d (7) a (8) c
(9) g (10) e

Chapter 12
(1) k (2) f (3) j (4) l (5) d (6) b (7) c (8) i
(9) e (10) h (11) a (12) g

Appendix 3
Apply It Answers

Chapter 1
(B) (2) G6, C1, D6, and F6

(D)
(1) C C C D E C
(2) C B C E D C
(3) C E F G A G E D C
(4) C D F E G F E D C
(5) C B C D E D C
(6) C D E G F D E D C
(7) C E G F D E C
(8) C E G A G F D B C

Chapter 2

(A) (1) (a) D♭4   (b) G♯3   (c) D♯5   (d) A♭2   (e) G♭4   (f) E♭3   (g) A♯5
(h) G♯4   (i) B♯1   (j) F3   (k) F♯4   (l) G♭2   (m) C♯5   (n) B♭2
(o) C4   (p) B4   (q) D♯2   (r) E♭4   (s) A♯4   (t) F♯3

(A) (2)

Given Pitch	H↑	H↓	W↑	W↓
C♯4	D4	C4	D♯4	B3
A♭3	A3	G3	B♭3	G♭3
E♭5	E5	D5	F5	D♭5
G♯2	A2	G2	A♯2	F♯2
F♯4	G4	F4	G♯4	E4
D♯3	E3	D3	E♯3	C♯3
B♭5	B5	A5	C6	A♭5
A♭4	A4	G4	B♭4	G♭4
C♭2	C♯2	B1	D2	B♭1
E♯3	F♯3	E3	F𝄪3	D♯3
G♭4	G4	F4	A♭4	F♭4
F♯2	G2	F2	G♯2	E2
D♭5	D5	C5	E♭5	C♭5
A♯2	B2	A2	B♯2	G♯2
B♯3	C♯4	B3	C𝄪4	A♯3
C♭5	C5	B♭4	D♭5	B♭♭4
E♭2	E2	D2	F2	D♭2
D♯4	E4	D4	E♯4	C♯4
B♭4	B4	A4	C5	A♭4
G♭3	G3	F3	A♭3	F♭3

(3) (a) A   (b) C   (c) D   (d) F   (e) F♯ or G♭   (f) F♯ or G♭   (g) B
(h) B♭ or A♯

(B) (1) (a) ↓♮   (b) ↑♯   (c) ↑♮   (d) ↓♮   (e) ↑♯   (f) ↓♭

(2) (a) W↑   (b) H↑   (c) H↓   (d) W↑   (e) H↓   (f) H↓   (g) W↑
(h) W↓   (i) W↑   (j) H↑   (k) H↑   (l) W↓   (m) H↑   (n) H↓
(o) W↑   (p) W↓   (q) H↑   (r) W↑   (s) W↓   (t) H↑

(C)

Melody 1

Melody 2

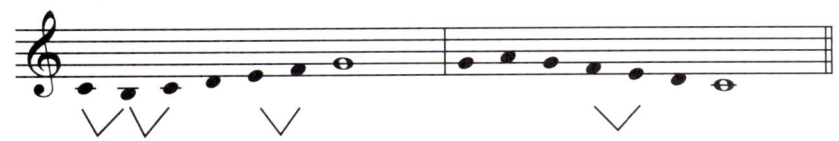

Melody 3

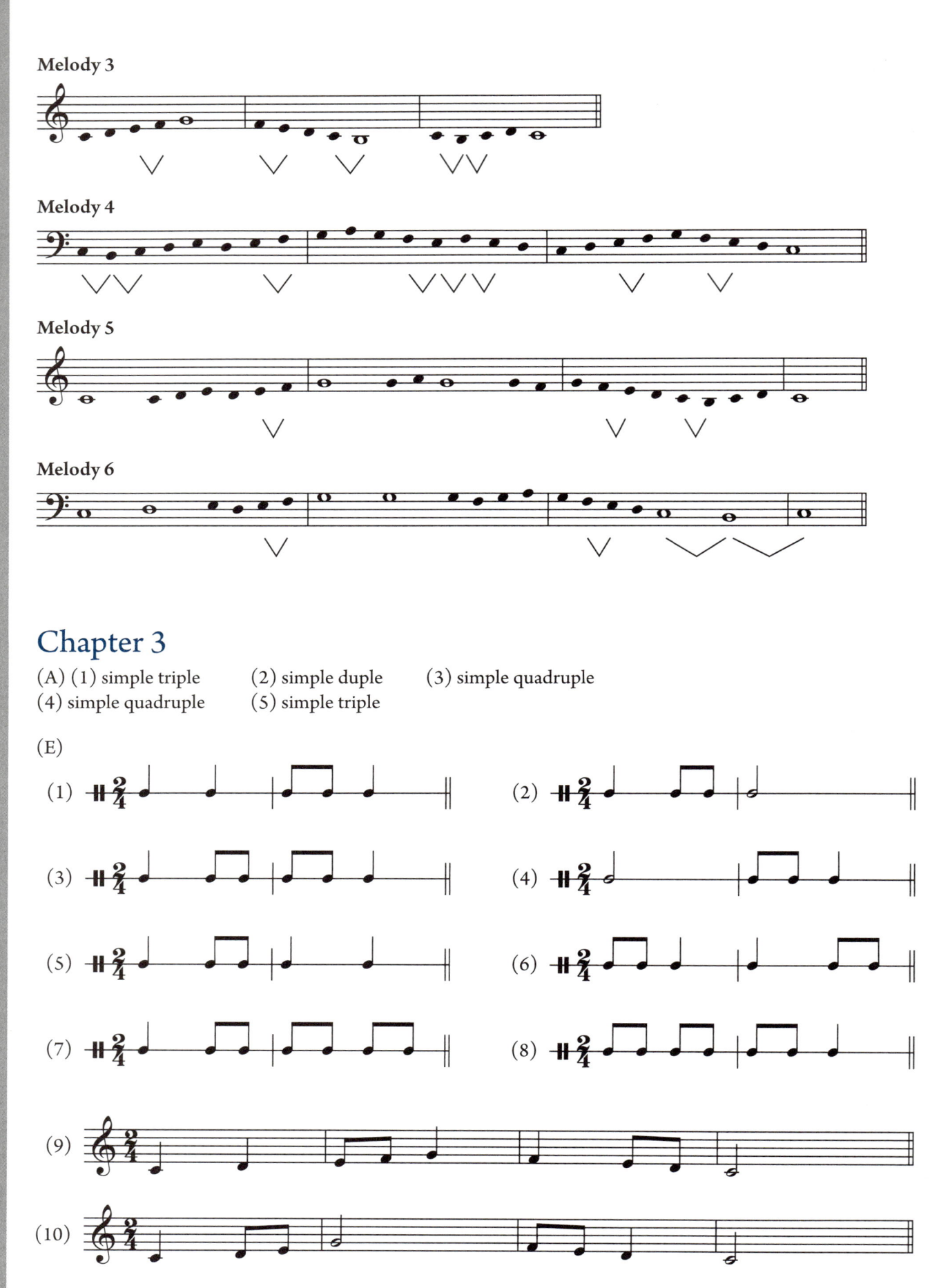

Melody 4

Melody 5

Melody 6

Chapter 3

(A) (1) simple triple (2) simple duple (3) simple quadruple
(4) simple quadruple (5) simple triple

(E)

APPENDIX THREE Apply It Answers A-21

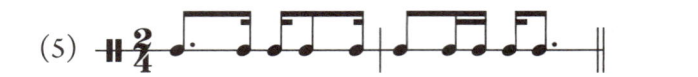

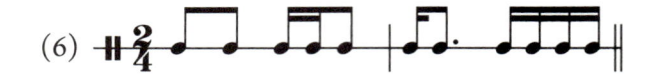

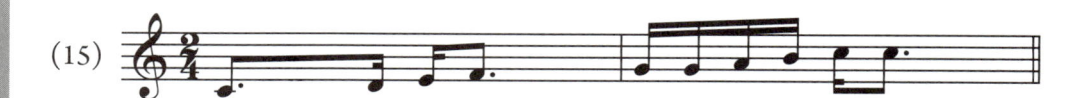

Chapter 4

(D)

Chapter 5

(A) (1) compound   (2) simple   (3) compound   (4) compound   (5) simple

(E)

(17) 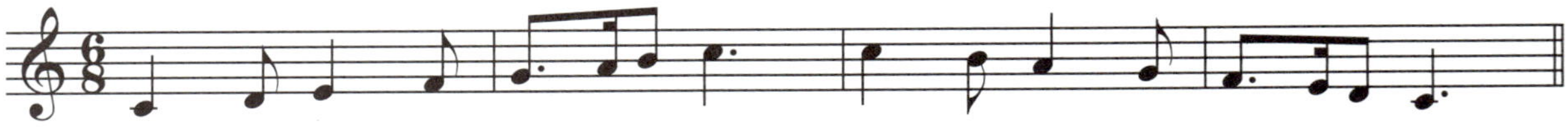

(18) 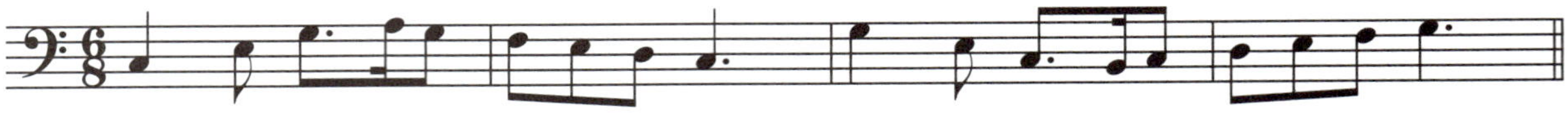

(19) 

Chapter 6

(D)

(1) 

(2) 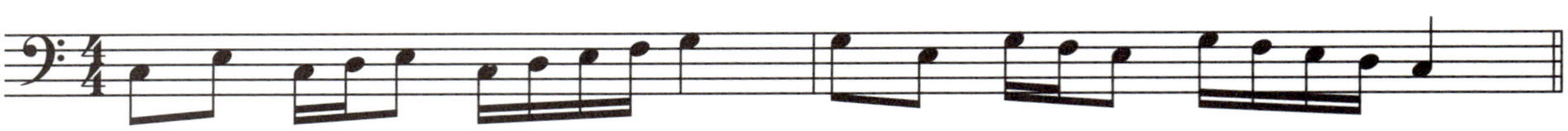

(3) 

(4) 

(5) 

Chapter 7

(C) (1) minor (2) major (3) minor (4) minor (5) major

(E)

(1) 

(2) 

(3) 

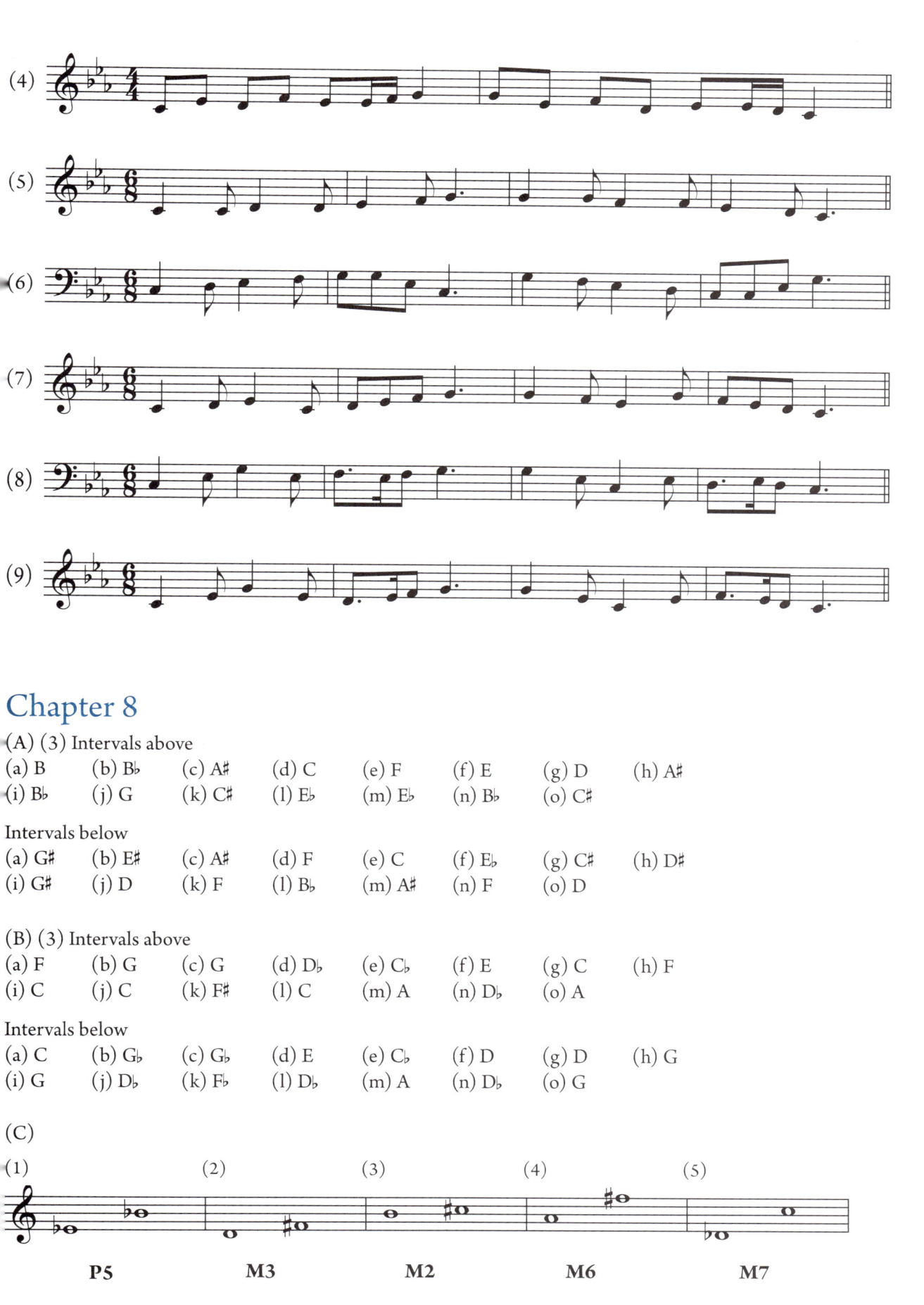

Chapter 8

(A) (3) Intervals above

| (a) B | (b) B♭ | (c) A♯ | (d) C | (e) F | (f) E | (g) D | (h) A♯ |
| (i) B♭ | (j) G | (k) C♯ | (l) E♭ | (m) E♭ | (n) B♭ | (o) C♯ |

Intervals below

| (a) G♯ | (b) E♯ | (c) A♯ | (d) F | (e) C | (f) E♭ | (g) C♯ | (h) D♯ |
| (i) G♯ | (j) D | (k) F | (l) B♭ | (m) A♯ | (n) F | (o) D |

(B) (3) Intervals above

| (a) F | (b) G | (c) G | (d) D♭ | (e) C♭ | (f) E | (g) C | (h) F |
| (i) C | (j) C | (k) F♯ | (l) C | (m) A | (n) D♭ | (o) A |

Intervals below

| (a) C | (b) G♭ | (c) G♭ | (d) E | (e) C♭ | (f) D | (g) D | (h) G |
| (i) G | (j) D♭ | (k) F♭ | (l) D♭ | (m) A | (n) D♭ | (o) G |

(C)

(1) P5 (2) M3 (3) M2 (4) M6 (5) M7

(6) (7) (8) (9) (10)

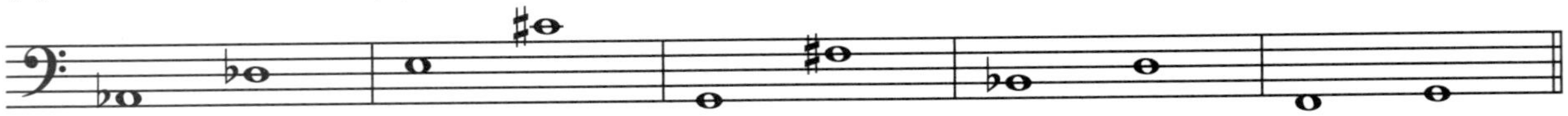

P4 M6 M7 M3 M2

(11) (12) (13) (14) (15)

m2 m3 P5 m3 m6

(16) (17) (18) (19) (20)

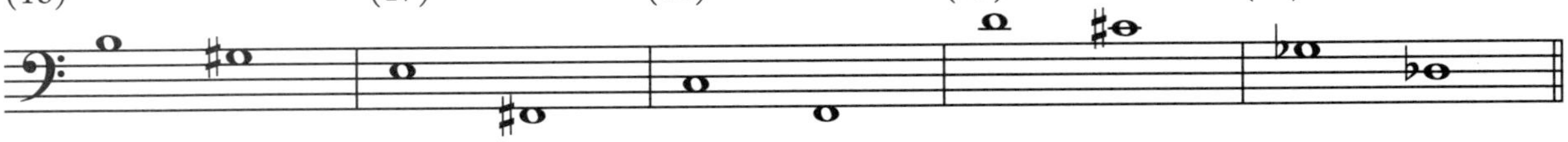

m3 m7 P5 m2 P4

(21) (22) (23) (24) (25)

m3 m2 m6 m7 P4

(26) (27) (28) (29) (30)

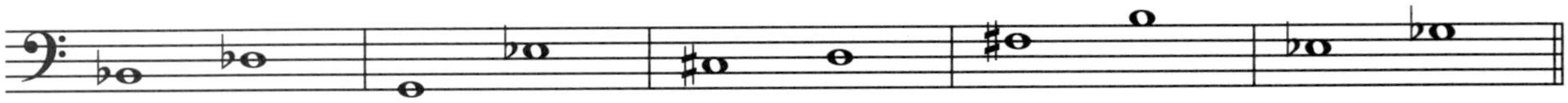

m3 m6 m2 P4 m3

(31) (32) (33) (34) (35)

M2 M6 M3 P4 M6

(36) (37) (38) (39) (40)

M6 M3 M7 M2 M7

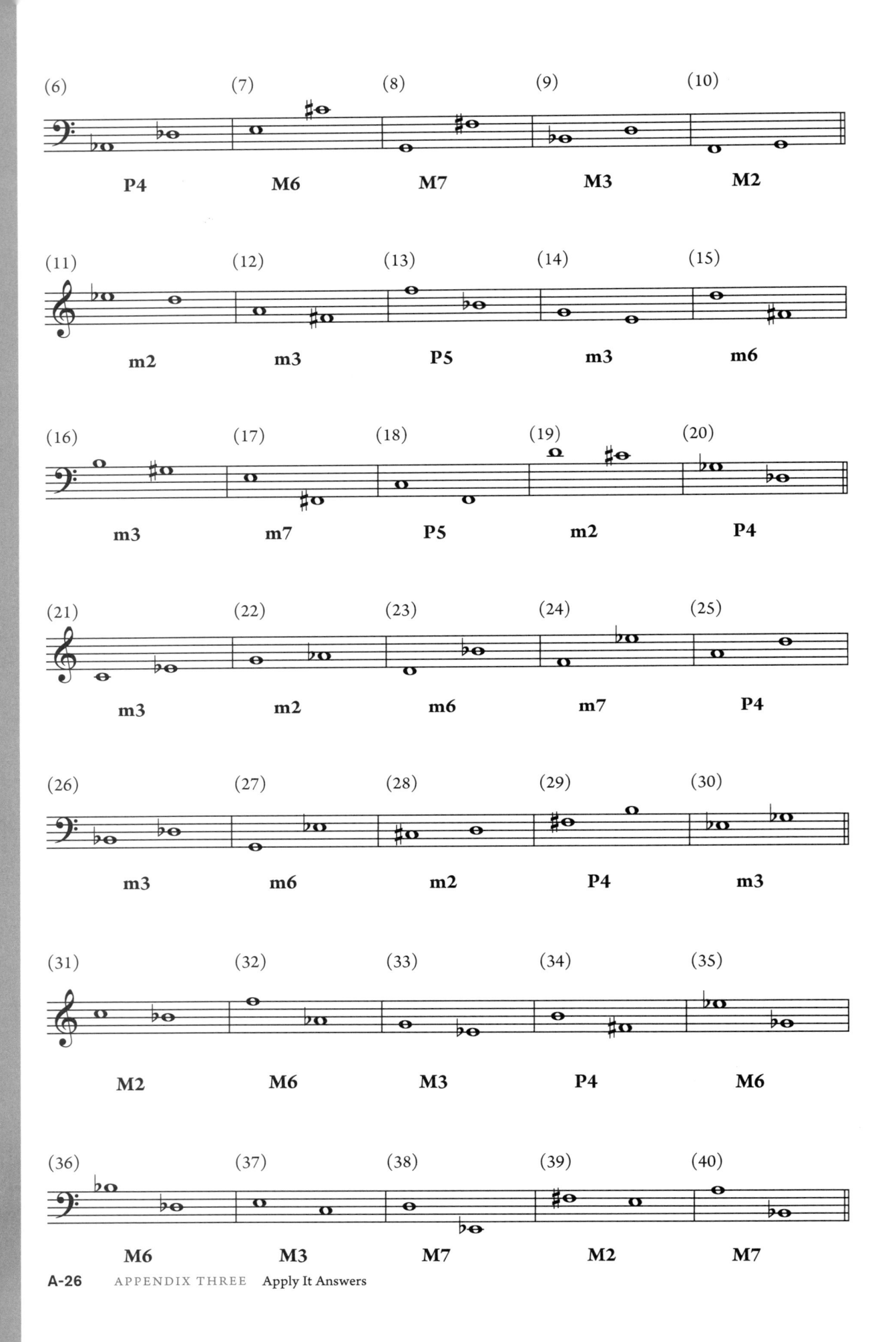

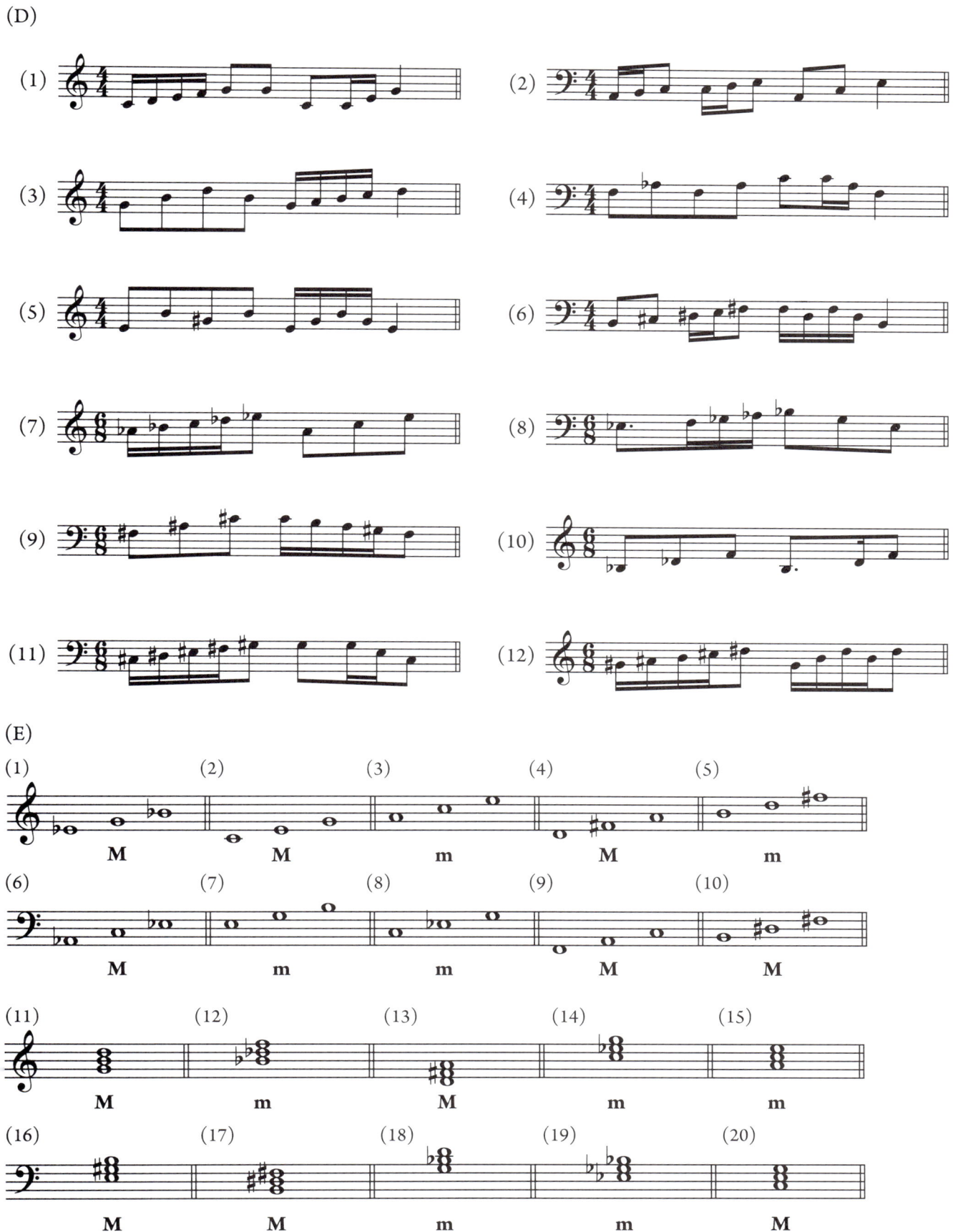

Chapter 9

(D) — sheet music exercises (1)–(12)

(E)

(1) M (2) M (3) m (4) M (5) m
(6) M (7) m (8) m (9) M (10) M
(11) M (12) m (13) M (14) m (15) m
(16) M (17) M (18) m (19) m (20) M

(21)	(22)	(23)	(24)	(25)
	d	A	A	d	A

(26)	(27)	(28)	(29)	(30)
	d	A	d	d	A

Chapter 10

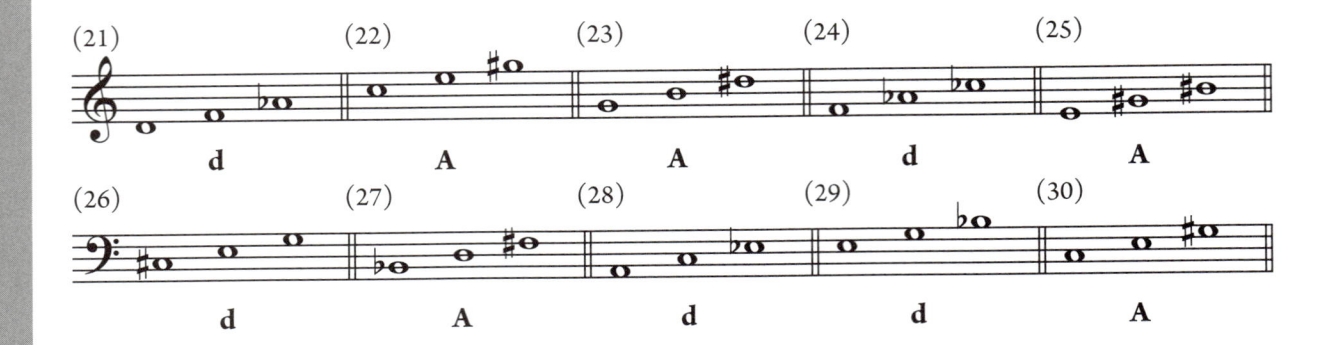

(D)

(1) – (5) [musical examples]

Chapter 11

(B) (1) contrasting period   (2) contrasting period   (3) parallel period
(4) contrasting period

Chapter 12

(B) (1) major pentatonic   (2) minor pentatonic   (3) major pentatonic

Appendix 4
Glossary

12-bar blues: See *blues progression*.

32-bar song form: See *quaternary song form*.

A

a a b a: See *quaternary song form*.

accent: Stress given to a note or some other musical element that brings it to the listener's attention. Accents can be created by playing louder or softer, using a different timbre or articulation, speeding up or slowing down, or slightly changing rhythmic durations.

accidental: A symbol that appears before a note to raise or lower its pitch chromatically, without changing its letter name. See also *sharp, flat, natural, double sharp,* and *double flat.*

accompaniment: Music played by keyboard, guitar, or other instruments providing harmonies to support a sung or played melody.

added-sixth chord: A root-position triad with an extra pitch a major sixth above the bass note.

Alberti bass: An accompaniment pattern popular in the time of Mozart, in which a three-part chord in the alto, tenor, and bass is arpeggiated with the pattern bass-alto-tenor-alto while the soprano part performs the melody.

alto: The second-highest voice in four-part (SATB) writing, notated in the treble clef, usually directly below the soprano; usually sung by women with lower voices.

alto clef: A C-clef positioned on a staff so that the middle line indicates middle C (C4).

anacrusis: A beat that precedes a downbeat, sometimes shown in an incomplete measure. Also called an upbeat or pickup.

antecedent phrase: The first phrase of a period, ending with an inconclusive cadence (usually a half cadence).

arpeggio: A chord played one pitch at a time.

articulation: How a pitch is sounded, including various ways of bowing or plucking stringed instruments and tonguing wind and brass instruments.

ascending contour: A musical line that generally goes up, from lower pitches to higher ones.

asymmetrical meter: Meter with beat units of unequal duration. These irregular beat lengths are typically (though not always) created by five or seven beat divisions grouped into unequal lengths such as 2 + 3 or 2 + 3 + 2.

augmentation: Lengthening the durations of a rhythm, often by doubling them.

augmented interval: An interval one chromatic half step larger than a major or perfect interval.

augmented second: The distance between $\flat\hat{6}$ and $\hat{7}$ in the harmonic minor scale; equivalent to three half steps.

augmented triad: A triad that has major thirds between its root and third, and between its third and fifth. The interval between its root and fifth is an augmented fifth.

authentic cadence: A conclusive cadence in which $V^{(7)}$ progresses to I.

B

bar: See *measure*.

bar line: A vertical line, extending from the top of the staff to the bottom, that indicates the end of a measure.

basic phrase: A phrase that consists of an opening tonic area (T), an optional predominant area (P), a dominant area (D), and tonic closure (T, a cadence on I).

bass: The lowest voice in four-part (SATB) writing, notated in the bass clef; usually sung by men with lower voices.

bass clef: Clef positioned on a staff to indicate F; its two dots surround the F3 line. (Also known as the F-clef.)

beam: A line that connects two or more note stems within a beat unit.

beat: The primary pulse in musical meter. Normally represents an even and regular division of musical time.

beat division: The secondary pulse in musical meter; beats may be divided into two parts (simple meter) or three parts (compound meter).

beat subdivision: A further division of the beat division into two parts; for example, a quarter note in simple meter divides into two eighths and subdivides into four sixteenths.

beat unit: The duration assigned to the basic pulse.

blue note: One of three pitches (of the blues scale) that appear in jazz and popular music for expressive effect: $\flat\hat{3}$, $\sharp\hat{4}$ (or $\flat\hat{5}$), and $\flat\hat{7}$.

blues progression: A chord progression (normally twelve bars long) typical of the blues: four measures of I, two measures each of IV and I, one measure each of V, IV, and I, finishing with I (or V for a turnaround). All harmonies may be either triads or seventh chords.

blues scale: The minor pentatonic scale plus $\sharp\hat{4}/\flat\hat{5}$. Since the blues scale includes $\flat\hat{3}$ and $\flat\hat{7}$, it blurs the distinction between major and minor when it is used over a major-key blues progression.

bridge: (1) The contrasting **b** section in an **a a b a** 32-bar song form. (2) A section in a popular song that contrasts with the verse and chorus, and enters more than halfway through the song to prepare for their return.

C

C-clef: A moveable clef that identifies which line on a staff designates middle C (C4) by the point at which its two curved lines join together in the middle. Common C-clefs include the alto and tenor clefs.

cadence: The end of a phrase, where harmonic, melodic, and rhythmic features mark the close of a complete musical thought. See also *authentic cadence, half cadence, deceptive cadence, plagal cadence.*

changing meter: Meter that changes from measure to measure.

change of mode: Transforming a melody or harmony from major to minor, or the reverse, by altering the quality of the third, sixth, and seventh scale degrees.

changes: Jazz term for harmonic progressions; short for chord changes.

chord: Pitches sounded at the same time. See also *triad, seventh chord.*

chord connection: Links between chords in a musical composition; should aim for smooth motion by step, keep common tones in the same part, and correctly resolve dissonances.

chord extensions: Pitches added to triads or seventh chords (e.g., ninths, elevenths).

chord members: The pitches that make up a chord.

chord progression: The specific order in which chords appear.

chorus: Section of music that is repeated with the same text.

chromatic: Pitches from outside a diatonic (major or natural minor) scale. The chromatic collection consists of all twelve pitches within an octave.

chromatic half step: A semitone spelling that uses the same letter name for both pitches (e.g., D and D♯).

chromatic scale: A scale consisting of all twelve pitches within the octave; the distance between each note and the next is a half step.

circle of fifths: A circular diagram representing the relationship between keys; clockwise motion around the circle shifts a key up by a P5 and removes a flat or adds a sharp; counterclockwise motion shifts a key down by a P5 and removes a sharp or adds a flat.

clef: A symbol on the far left of a staff that shows which pitch (and octave) is represented by each line and space. See also *treble clef, bass clef, C-clef, alto clef, tenor clef.*

climax: The musical high point of a melody or piece.

coda: Section at the end of a piece.

combo: A small instrumental ensemble for playing jazz or popular music, usually consisting of (at least) a solo instrument, keyboard, and drum set.

compound duple: Meter with 2 beats in a measure, each beat divided into 3 (e.g., $\frac{6}{8}$ or $\frac{6}{4}$).

compound interval: An interval larger than an octave.

compound meter: Meter where the beat divides into threes and subdivides into sixes. The top number of compound meter signatures is 6, 9, or 12 (e.g., $\frac{9}{4}$ or $\frac{6}{8}$).

compound quadruple: Meter with 4 beats in a measure, each beat divided into 3 (e.g., $\frac{12}{8}$ or $\frac{12}{4}$).

compound triple: Meter with 3 beats in a measure, each beat divided into 3 (e.g., $\frac{9}{8}$ or $\frac{9}{4}$).

conclusive cadence: A relatively strong cadence that can end a section or piece.

conducting pattern: A specific pattern, one for each meter, that conductors outline by moving their arms in the air to help keep performers playing together in time.

conjunct motion: Melodic motion that is primarily by step, making a smooth line.

consequent phrase: The second phrase of a period, ending with a strong harmonic conclusion, usually an authentic cadence.

consonance: A relative term based on acoustic properties of sound and on the norms of compositional practice. A consonant interval—unison, third, fifth, sixth, or octave—is considered pleasing to hear. A fourth is considered a consonance when written melodically but a dissonance when written harmonically.

consonance, imperfect: The intervals of major and minor thirds and sixths.

consonance, perfect: The intervals of a unison, fourth, fifth, and octave.

contour: The shape of a melody; its motion up and down. Common contours include ascending, descending, arch, V-shape, and wave.

contrary motion: Two melodic lines or voices moving in opposite directions.

contrasting period: A period in which the two phrases do not share the same initial melodic material.

crescendo: An indication to increase the dynamic level.

D

deceptive cadence (DC): The cadence $V^{(7)}$–vi in major or $V^{(7)}$–VI in minor.

deceptive resolution: Motion from $V^{(7)}$ to vi in major or $V^{(7)}$ to VI in minor that does not end a phrase.

decrescendo: See *diminuendo*.

descending contour: A melodic line that generally goes down, from higher pitches to lower ones.

diatonic half step: A semitone spelling that uses different letter names for the two pitches (e.g., D and E♭).

diatonic scale: Scales made by rotating the step pattern W–W–H–W–W–W–H; the major and natural minor scales, and the modes (Dorian, Phrygian, Lydian, Mixolydian, and Locrian) are all diatonic scales.

diminished interval: An interval one half step smaller than a minor or perfect interval.

diminished seventh chord: A seventh chord consisting of a diminished triad with a diminished seventh above its root.

diminished triad: A triad that has minor thirds between its root and third, and between its third and fifth. The interval between its root and fifth is a diminished fifth.

diminuendo: An indication to decrease the dynamic level; same as *decrescendo*.

disjunct motion: Melodic motion primarily by skip or leap that does not make a smooth line.

dissonance: A relative term based on acoustic properties of sound and on the norms of compositional practice. A dissonant interval—second, tritone, seventh, or any augmented or diminished interval—is considered unpleasant or jarring to hear. A fourth is considered a dissonance when written harmonically but a consonance when written melodically.

division: See *beat division*.

dominant: (1) Scale degree $\hat{5}$; (2) the triad built on $\hat{5}$.

dominant seventh chord: A seventh chord consisting of a major triad with a minor seventh above its root.

dot: Rhythmic notation that adds half of a note's own value to its duration (e.g., the duration of a dotted half note equals a half note plus a quarter note).

double flat: An accidental (♭♭) that lowers a pitch two half steps without changing its letter name.

double sharp: An accidental (𝄪) that raises a pitch two half steps without changing its letter name.

doubling: (1) Reinforcing a melodic line by adding voices or instruments at the unison or octave. (2) A pitch of a triad or seventh chord that appears in two parts to make four parts in SATB writing.

downbeat: The first beat of a measure, which has the strongest accent or emphasis; named for the downward motion of the conductor's hand.

duple meter: Meter with two beats in each measure.

duplet: In compound meter, a division of the beat into two, instead of three, equal parts.

duration: The length of time represented by a note or rest.

dynamic level: The degree of loudness in performance. Extends from *ppp* (very soft) to *fff* (very loud).

E

eighth note: A stemmed filled note head with one flag or beam (♪); equivalent to two sixteenth notes.

eighth rest: A silence represented by ♪; equal in duration to an eighth note.

embellishing tones: Pitches that decorate tones in a melodic line. See also *neighbor tone* and *passing tone*.

enharmonic: Different names for the same pitch (e.g., E♭ and D♯).

enharmonically equivalent intervals: Two intervals that can be respelled with enharmonically equivalent notes (e.g., A2 and m3).

enharmonic equivalence: The idea that two or more possible names for a single pitch (e.g., C♯, D♭, B𝄪) are musically the same.

extension: See *chord extension*.

F

fifth: Within a triad or seventh chord, the pitch located a fifth above the root.

figures: Arabic numerals used to represent chords as intervals above a bass note.

first inversion: A triad or seventh chord with its third in the bass.

flag: A short arc attached to the right side of a note stem, at the opposite end from the note head; each flag divides the duration of a note in half (e.g., a sixteenth note has two flags and is half of an eighth note, which has one flag).

flat: An accidental (♭) that lowers a pitch by one half step without changing its letter name.

form: A pattern of repeated, similar, and contrasting passages in a piece of music.

forte (*f*): A loud dynamic level. A louder dynamic level is *ff* (*fortissimo*); a softer dynamic level is *mf* (*mezzo forte*).

G

grand staff: Two staves, one in treble clef and one in bass clef, connected by a curly brace; typically used in piano music.

H

half cadence (HC): An inconclusive cadence ending on the dominant.

half-diminished seventh chord: A seventh chord consisting of a diminished triad with a minor seventh above its root.

half note: A stemmed hollow notehead; its duration is equivalent to two quarter notes.

half rest: A silence represented by ▬ sitting on top of the third staff line; equal in duration to a half note.

half step: The distance between a pitch and the next closest pitch on the keyboard.

harmonic interval: The span between two pitches played simultaneously.

harmonic minor scale: See *minor scale*.

harmonic rhythm: The rate at which chords change (e.g., one chord per measure or one chord per beat).

harmonize: To choose chords to accompany a melody.

head: In jazz or blues, the main musical idea played at the beginning of the piece; it recurs, alternating with sections of instrumental or vocal improvisation.

homophony: Texture in which all voices are vertically aligned to move together in the same (or nearly the same) rhythm.

hook: A musical setting of a few words or a phrase, usually including the title, that is repeated and becomes the most memorable part of a song.

I

imperfect authentic cadence (IAC): An authentic cadence weakened (1) by inverting V or (2) by the soprano ending on a scale degree other than $\hat{1}$.

inconclusive cadence: Ending that is used for the first phrase of a period or prior to the end of a section; any type of cadence other than a perfect authentic cadence.

instrumental break: Section in the middle of a song played only by instruments, often based on the verse.

interval: The distance between two pitches.

interval inversion: Transformation of an interval that results from displacing one pitch by an octave such that the interval size and quality change. When perfect intervals are inverted they remain perfect; major intervals become minor (and vice versa); augmented intervals become diminished (and vice versa). The size of an interval and its inversion sum to 9 (e.g., m2 becomes M7, P4 becomes P5, etc.).

interval quality: The difference between two intervals of the same size (e.g., third, fourth, fifth) that span a different number of semitones. Interval quality can be major, minor, perfect, diminished, or augmented.

intro: Music, usually instrumental, that introduces a popular song.

introduction: Music at the beginning of a piece that prepares for the entry of the main melody.

inverted chord: A chord with its third, fifth, or seventh (instead of the root) in the bass.

K

key: (1) Music in a major or minor key employs notes of the major or minor scale so that the first note is the primary scale degree around which all others relate hierarchically. Keys are named by the first scale degree and the type of scale used (e.g., G minor). (2) The levers on an instrument that can be depressed with a finger to make a pitch sound (e.g., piano keys).

keyboard style: Texture in which three notes of each chord are in the right hand and one in the left.

key signature: A pattern of sharps or flats (or no sharps or flats) that appears immediately following the clef on a staff, showing which notes, in any octave, are to be sharped or flatted consistently throughout the piece. The key signature helps identify the key of the piece, but each signature is used for two keys—one major and one minor.

L

leading tone: (1) Scale degree $\hat{7}$; gets its name from its tendency to lead upward toward the tonic; (2) the triad built on $\hat{7}$.

lead sheet: Performance score for jazz and popular music consisting of a melody and chord changes.

leap: A melodic interval larger than a fourth; less common in melodies than steps or skips.

ledger line: Extra lines drawn through the stems and note heads to designate a musical pitch located above or below the staff.

letter name: The name for a particular pitch, employing letters A–G, that corresponds to its place on the staff or a musical instrument.

link: A short instrumental connecter between sections of a popular song.

M

major interval: Seconds, thirds, sixths, and sevenths above $\hat{1}$ of a major scale.

major key: Music comprised of notes drawn from the major scale; the key is named by the first scale degree and type of scale (e.g., B major).

major pentachord: The first five notes of a major scale (e.g., C–D–E–F–G in C major).

major pentatonic: A five-note scale consisting of $\hat{1}$, $\hat{2}$, $\hat{3}$, $\hat{5}$, and $\hat{6}$ of a major scale.

major scale: A seven-note scale beginning $\hat{1}$ (*do*)– $\hat{2}$ (*re*)– $\hat{3}$ (*mi*) with the pattern of whole and half steps W–W–H–W–W–W–H; it shares the same key signature as its relative minor.

major seventh chord: A major triad with a major seventh above its root.

major tetrachord: A series of four notes that form an ascending W–W–H pattern; building block of a major scale.

major triad: A triad that has a major third between its root and third, and a minor third between its third and fifth. The interval between its third and fifth is a perfect fifth.

measure: A unit of grouped beats; beginning and ending with bar lines.

mediant: (1) Scale degree $\hat{3}$; (2) the triad built on $\hat{3}$.

melodic interval: The distance between two notes played one after another.

melodic minor scale: See *minor scale*.

melody: (1) A succession of pitches and rhythms in a single line; (2) the main musical idea, or "tune," in a piece of music.

melody and accompaniment: A musical texture with a melody in one part and accompanying chords in the other.

meter: The grouping and division of beats in regular, recurring patterns.

meter signature: A sign that appears at the beginning of a piece, after the clef and key signature, that indicates the meter type (duple, triple, quadruple) and beat division (simple, compound); also called a time signature.

metrical accent: An emphasis on a note resulting from its placement on a strong beat.

metronome: A mechanical device that clicks at an even rate, where the number of clicks per minute may be adjusted; used to establish a tempo for musicians to practice with a steady beat.

mezzo forte **(*mf*), *mezzo piano* (*mp*):** Medium dynamic levels between *piano* and *forte*; *mp* is louder than *p*, and *mf* is softer than *f*.

middle C: C4; the C located at the center of the piano keyboard.

minor interval: Thirds, sixths, and sevenths above $\hat{1}$ of a minor scale; seconds between $\hat{7}$ and $\hat{1}$ in a major, harmonic minor, or ascending melodic minor scale.

minor key: Music comprised of notes drawn from the minor scale; the key is named by the first scale degree and type of scale (e.g., B minor).

minor mode: Mode incorporating $\flat\hat{3}$, $\flat\hat{6}$, and $\flat\hat{7}$, with a minor tonic triad.

minor pentachord: The first five notes of a minor scale (e.g., C–D–E♭–F–G in C minor).

minor pentatonic: A five-note scale consisting of $\hat{1}$, $\flat\hat{3}$, $\hat{4}$, $\hat{5}$, and $\flat\hat{7}$ of a minor scale.

minor scale: A seven-note scale beginning $\hat{1}$ (*do*)–$\hat{2}$ (*re*)–$\flat\hat{3}$ (*me*) that occurs in three forms: natural, harmonic, and melodic. The natural minor scale is an ordered collection of pitches arranged according to the pattern of whole and half steps W–H–W–W–H–W–W; it shares the same key signature as its relative major. The harmonic minor scale has raised $\hat{7}$. The melodic minor has raised $\hat{6}$ and $\hat{7}$ ascending, but takes the natural minor form descending.

minor seventh chord: A minor triad with a minor seventh above its root.

minor triad: A triad that has a minor third between its root and third, and a major third between its third and fifth. The interval between its root and fifth is a perfect fifth.

modal scale degrees: The third, sixth, and seventh scale degrees, which are one half step lower in minor keys than in major.

modulation: A change of key, usually confirmed by a perfect authentic cadence.

monophony: A single unaccompanied line. May be performed by a single voice or instrument, or by a group playing in unison or octaves.

motive: The smallest recognizable musical idea. Motives may be characterized by their pitches, contour, and rhythm, but rarely include a cadence. Generally they are repeated (exactly or varied).

musical alphabet: The letters A, B, C, D, E, F, and G, which are used to name musical pitches.

N

natural: An accidental (♮) that cancels a sharp or flat.

natural minor scale: See *minor scale*.

neighbor tone: A melodic embellishment that decorates a pitch by moving a step above or below it, then returning to the original pitch.

ninth chord: A seventh chord with a ninth added above the bass.

note: The representation of a musical sound with a note head on the staff. The position of the note head indicates the pitch; whether the note head is filled or hollow and the presence of a stem, beam, or flag indicates the duration.

note head: A small oval used to notate a pitch on the staff. Hollow note heads normally represent a longer duration than filled note heads.

O

octave: (1) The distance of eight musical steps; the interval size 8. (2) The particular part of the musical range where a pitch sounds (e.g., C4, or middle C, is a C in a particular octave).

octave equivalence: The concept that pitches eight steps apart (sharing the same name) sound similar.

octave number: An Arabic number used with a pitch's letter name to indicate in which register that pitch sounds (e.g., C4 is the C in the fourth octave, or middle C)

offbeat: A weak beat or weak portion of a beat.

outro: In popular music, the concluding musical idea, after the last verse or chorus. May consist of a "repeat and fade" of music that has been heard before.

P

parallel keys: Major and minor keys sharing the same letter name, but with different pitches for $\hat{3}$, $\hat{6}$, and $\hat{7}$ (e.g., F major and F minor).

parallel major: The major key that has the same tonic as a given minor key (e.g., F minor's parallel major is F major). The parallel major raises the third, sixth, and seventh scale degrees of a minor key.

parallel minor: The minor key that has the tonic as a given major key (e.g., F major's parallel minor is F minor). The parallel minor lowers the third, sixth, and seventh scale degrees of a major key.

parallel motion: Two melodic lines or voices moving in the same direction by the same interval. Parallel fifths and octaves are not generally permitted in SATB writing, though parallel thirds and sixths are common.

parallel period: A period in which the two phrases begin with the same melodic material.

passing tone: A melodic embellishment that fills the space between chord members. Passing tones are approached and left by step in the same direction.

pentatonic scale: A five-note scale. See *major pentatonic* and *minor pentatonic*.

perfect authentic cadence (PAC): A strong conclusive cadence in which (1) root position V$^{(7)}$ progresses to root position I, and (2) the soprano moves from $\hat{2}$ or $\hat{7}$ to $\hat{1}$.

perfect interval: Unisons, fourths, fifths, and octaves above $\hat{1}$ in a major or minor scale.

period: A musical unit consisting of two phrases. The first phrase ends with an inconclusive cadence (usually a HC); the ending of the second answers it with a more conclusive cadence (usually a PAC).

phrase: A basic unit of musical thought, similar to a sentence in language. The typical phrase—like most sentences—has a beginning, a middle, and an end. A phrase must end with a cadence.

piano (*p*): A soft dynamic level. A softer dynamic level is *pp* (*pianissimo*); a louder dynamic level is *mp* (*mezzo piano*).

pickup: See *anacrusis*.

pitch: A musical sound in a particular octave or register.

plagal cadence (PC): The cadence IV–I (iv–i in minor), sometimes called the "Amen cadence." Because the IV–I motion often follows a conclusive authentic cadence, some musicians view plagal cadences as an extension of the tonic harmony.

postchorus: Section that follows the chorus in a popular song and prepares for the return of the verse.

prechorus: Section after the verse of a popular song that prepares for the chorus.

Q

quadruple meter: Meter with four beats in each measure.

quality: See *interval quality, triad quality*.

quarter note: A stemmed filled note head (♩); equivalent to two eighth notes.

quarter rest: A silence represented by 𝄽; equal in duration to a quarter note.

quartet: A musical texture comprised of four voices or instruments.

quaternary song form: A song form consisting of four phrases, usually with an **a a b a** or **a b c b** design. Each phrase is generally eight bars long, though some folk songs may have four-measure phrases. In **a a b a** form, the first two phrases begin the same (they may be identical or differ at the cadence). They are followed by a contrasting section (the bridge) and then a return to the opening material.

R

raised submediant: Raised $\hat{6}$ in the melodic minor scale.

rap break: Section in the middle of a popular song with spoken rhythmic text.

refrain: (1) The section of a song that recurs with the same music and text. (2) In verse–refrain form, the second section of the song, after the verse; generally in **a a b a** or quaternary song form.

register: The highness or lowness of a pitch or passage; the particular octave in which a pitch sounds.

relative keys: Major and minor keys that share the same key signature (e.g., C major and A minor).

relative major: The major key that shares the same key signature as a given minor key. The relative major has the same pitches as its relative minor but it begins on ♭$\hat{3}$ of the minor key.

relative minor: The minor key that shares the same key signature as a given major key. The relative minor has the same pitches as its relative major, but it begins on $\hat{6}$ of the major key.

resolve: To move the voices of an interval or triad from dissonance to consonance.

rest: A duration of silence.

rhythm: The durations of pitch and silence (notes and rests) used in a piece.

rhythm clef: Two short, thick, vertical lines at the beginning of a single-line staff; used to notate unpitched percussion parts.

rhythmic motive: A motive that maintains its rhythm, but changes its contour and intervals.

Roman numeral: A symbol used to represent the scale degree a chord is built on, as well as its quality.

root: The lowest pitch of a triad or seventh chord when the chord is spelled in thirds.

root position: A chord voiced with the root in the bass.

S

SATB: An abbreviation indicating the four voice ranges: soprano, alto, tenor, and bass. Also indicates a particular musical style or texture: hymn or chorale style.

scale: An ordered collection of pitches.

scale-degree names: Names for the position of a note or triad in a scale; these include tonic, supertonic, mediant, subdominant, dominant, submediant, leading tone, and subtonic.

scale-degree numbers: Numbers for the position of a note or triad in a scale, written with a caret over a number (e.g., $\hat{1}$, $\hat{5}$).

scale step: The position of a note in a scale; identified by scale degree names or scale degree numbers (e.g., tonic, $\hat{1}$).

score: Notated music.

second inversion: A triad or seventh chord voiced with its fifth in the bass.

semitone: Half step.

seventh: An interval spanning seven letter names; as a dissonance, the seventh above the root of a chord normally resolves down.

seventh chord: A four-note chord with a third, fifth, and seventh above its root; a triad with a third added above its fifth.

sharp: An accidental ($\sharp$) that raises a pitch a half step without changing its letter name.

similar motion: Two melodic lines or voices moving in the same direction, but not by the same interval. This type of motion connects two harmonic intervals that are not the same size.

simple duple: Meter with two beats in a measure, each beat divided into two (e.g., $\frac{2}{4}$).

simple interval: An interval of an octave or smaller.

simple meter: Meter where the beat divides into twos and subdivides into fours. The top number of simple meter signatures is 2, 3, or 4 (e.g., $\frac{3}{4}$ or $\frac{4}{4}$).

simple quadruple: Meter with four beats in a measure, each beat divided into two (e.g., $\frac{4}{4}$).

simple triple: Meter with three beats in a measure, each beat divided into two (e.g., $\frac{3}{4}$ or $\frac{3}{8}$).

sixteenth note: A stemmed filled notehead with two flags or beams ($\eighthnote$); two sixteenth notes equal an eighth note.

sixteenth rest: A silence represented by γ; equal in duration to a sixteenth note.

skip: A melodic interval of a third or fourth; used to move between notes of a triad.

slur: An arc that connects two (or more) different pitches. Slurs affect performance articulation but not duration. In piano music, they tell the performer to play the slurred notes smoothly; in vocal music, the slurred notes are sung on one syllable or in one breath.

solfège, fixed-do: A singing system in which a particular syllable is associated with a particular pitch (*do* is always C, *re* is always D, etc.) no matter what the key.

solfège, moveable-do: A singing system in which a particular syllable is associated with a particular scale step (*do* is always $\hat{1}$, *re* always $\hat{2}$, etc.) no matter what the key.

soprano: The highest voice in four-part (SATB) writing, notated in treble clef; usually sung by women with higher voices.

staff: The five parallel lines on which music is written. Plural form is staves.

stem: A vertical line attached to a note head; it generally extends upward if the note is written below the middle line of the staff and downward if the note is written on or above the middle line.

subdivision: See *beat subdivision*.

subdominant: (1) Scale degree $\hat{4}$; (2) the triad built on $\hat{4}$.

submediant: (1) Scale degree $\hat{6}$; (2) the triad built on $\hat{6}$.

subtonic: (1) Scale degree $\flat\hat{7}$ of the natural minor scale, located a whole step below the tonic; (2) the triad build on $\flat\hat{7}$.

supertonic: (1) Scale degree $\hat{2}$; (2) the triad built on $\hat{2}$.

sus chord: In popular music, a chord with a fourth above the bass instead of a third. The fourth does not necessarily resolve to a third.

swung eighths: A performance practice where a rhythm notated with even eighth notes is performed unevenly, with more time allotted to the first eighth and less to the second in each pair.

symmetrical meter: Meter with beat units of equal duration.

syncopation: Rhythmic displacement of accents created by dots, ties, rests, dynamic markings, or accent marks.

T

tempo: How fast or slow music is played.

tempo marking: An indication, often in Italian, printed in a score to indicate how fast the music is to be played. Typical markings, from slow to fast, include *adagio, andante, allegro, presto*.

tendency tone: A chord member or scale degree whose relation to the surrounding tones requires a particular resolution (i.e., chordal sevenths must resolve down, and leading tones must resolve up).

tenor: The second-lowest voice in four-part (SATB) writing, notated in bass clef usually directly above the bass; usually sung by men with higher voices.

tenor clef: A C-clef positioned on a staff so that the fourth line from the bottom indicates middle C (C4).

tetrachord: A four-note segment of a scale with a particular pattern of whole and half steps.

text painting: Musical depiction of the words from, or the general meaning of, a song's text or title.

texture: The number of instruments playing (solo or ensemble), the number of different melodies sounding at once, and the relationship of those melodies to each other.

third: Within a triad or seventh chord, the pitch located a third above the root.

third inversion: A seventh chord with its seventh in the bass.

tie: A small arc connecting note heads of two (or more) identical pitches to indicate the durations are to be combined together, without rearticulating the pitch. Used to notate durations extending across a bar line and for durations that cannot be represented with dotted notes.

timbre: Describes the instrumentation or quality of a musical sound.

tonic: (1) Scale degree $\hat{1}$; (2) the triad built on $\hat{1}$.

transpose: To renotate a melody or harmony at a different pitch level or in a different key while maintaining the intervals between its elements.

transcription: (1) A rhythmic pattern rewritten in a different meter, where it sounds the same if it is played at the same tempo. (2) A piece written for one instrument or ensemble arranged to be played by another (e.g., an orchestra piece transcribed for band).

treble clef: Clef positioned on a staff to indicate G by means of the end of its curving line; it circles the line that represents G4. (Also known as the G-clef.)

triad: A three-note chord with a third and fifth above its starting point, or root.

triad and seventh chord positions: See *inverted chord*.

triad names: Names for triads based on the scale degrees of their roots; these include tonic, supertonic, mediant, subdominant, dominant, submediant, leading tone, and subtonic.

triad quality: A description of a triad according to the quality of its stacked thirds and outer fifth: major, minor, diminished, or augmented.

triple meter: Meter with three beats in each measure.

triplet: In simple meter, a division of the beat into three, instead of two, equal parts.

tritone: An interval made up of three whole tones or six semitones; an augmented fourth or diminished fifth. By some definitions, only an augmented fourth is a tritone, since only this spelling of the interval spans three whole steps.

turnaround: At the end of a blues progression, a V or V^7 chord to prepare for the repeat of the progression.

two-beat triplet: In simple meter, a division of a half note into three equal quarter notes.

U

unison: The interval size 1, or the distance from a pitch to itself. Voices or instruments that are performing the same melody with the same rhythm in the same octave are said to be playing "in unison."

upbeat: The beat that precedes a downbeat; named for the upward lift of the conductor's hand. Also known as an anacrusis.

V

variation: Repetition of a passage with changes to any number of basic musical features including the melody, cadences, rhythms, key, mode, length, texture, timbre, character, and style.

verse: (1) A section of a song that returns with the same music but different text; (2) in popular song forms, the first section of verse–refrain form. In this form, the verse is usually not repeated.

verse–refrain: A song form associated with Tin Pan Alley; a verse that is not repeated sets the stage or tells the story and is followed by a refrain, which is normally in quaternary song form.

W

whole note: A stemless hollow notehead (𝐨); its duration is equivalent to two half notes.

whole rest: A silence represented by ▬ hanging below the fourth staff line; equal in duration to a whole note.

whole step: An interval that spans two adjacent half steps.

whole-tone scale: A scale with the pattern W–W–W–W–W; it has only whole steps between adjacent scale members.

Appendix 5
The Overtone Series

Every musical pitch played by an instrument, or sung by a voice, is a complex tone, consisting of a fundamental (lowest) pitch plus a series of overtones that sound faintly above it. Example A5.1 shows an overtone series above C2. Overtones (also called partials) are naturally occurring phenomena, created by the vibrations of strings, vocal chords, or columns of air. Partials are often numbered: the fundamental is the first partial, the octave above is the second partial, and so on. The partials shown with black note heads sound out of tune compared to a piano.

EXAMPLE A5.1 Overtone series with C2 Fundamental

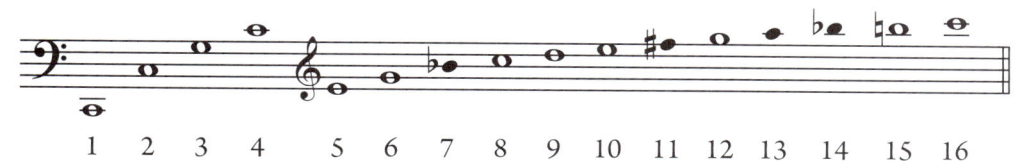

1 2 3 4 5 6 7 8 9 10 11 12 13 14 15 16

The characteristic timbre—or color—of an instrument is created by the different strengths (or amplitudes) of overtones, resulting from the shape of the instrument's resonating space. For example, a flute has a strong fundamental, a somewhat weaker second partial, and very weak higher partials. An oboe has more sound from higher overtones than from lower overtones.

The interval between the first and second partials (the octave from C to C) may be represented by the ratio 2:1 (relating the frequencies of the two pitches). Throughout the series, each ratio between partial numbers represents the interval between the pitches, such as 3:2 (C–G, perfect fifth), 4:3 (G–C, perfect fourth), 5:4 (C–E, major third), and so on. The intervals with smaller numbers tend to correspond with acoustic consonances, and higher numbers (e.g., 16:15, minor second) with dissonances. These ratios also represent the divisions of a string (e.g., on violin, guitar, or cello) where a performer would place his or her fingers to create these intervals, as Figure A5.1 shows. If you play an open string, then divide it in half and play the string again, the second pitch is an octave above the first. For brass players, changing the valve combination or slide position changes the fundamental pitch; changing the air pressure and speed move the sound between pitches in the overtone series.

FIGURE A5.1 Divisions of a string to produce P8, P5, and P4

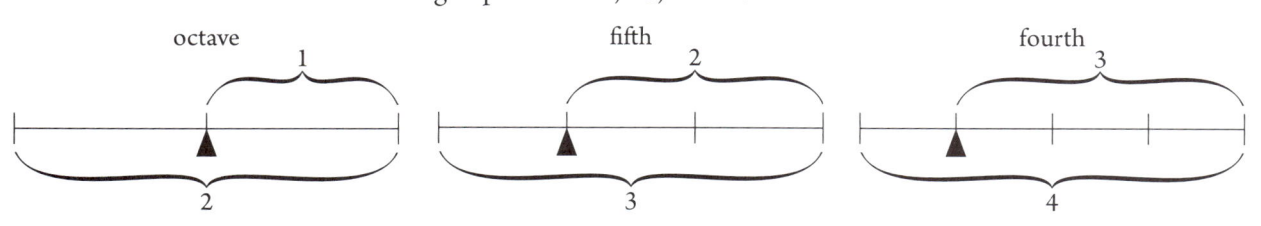

Appendix 6
The Diatonic Modes

Playing the seven white keys from C to C (with no sharps or flats) makes a C major scale, also known as the Ionian mode. Playing through the white keys starting on different notes (D to D, E to E, etc.) forms other diatonic modes, as shown in Example A6.1. There are six traditional diatonic modes (in order, from C): Ionian, Dorian, Phrygian, Lydian, Mixolydian, and Aeolian. (As a shortcut to learning the six mode names, think of a sentence that gives you the first letter of each mode, like "I don't particularly like magic acts.") A seventh mode, Locrian (Example A6.1g), was identified in the late Renaissance but deemed unusable; it was not used in composing music until the twentieth century. The traditional diatonic modes are found in twentieth- and twenty-first-century jazz, popular, and folk music, as well as in art music.

EXAMPLE A6.1 The diatonic modes as rotations of the C major scale

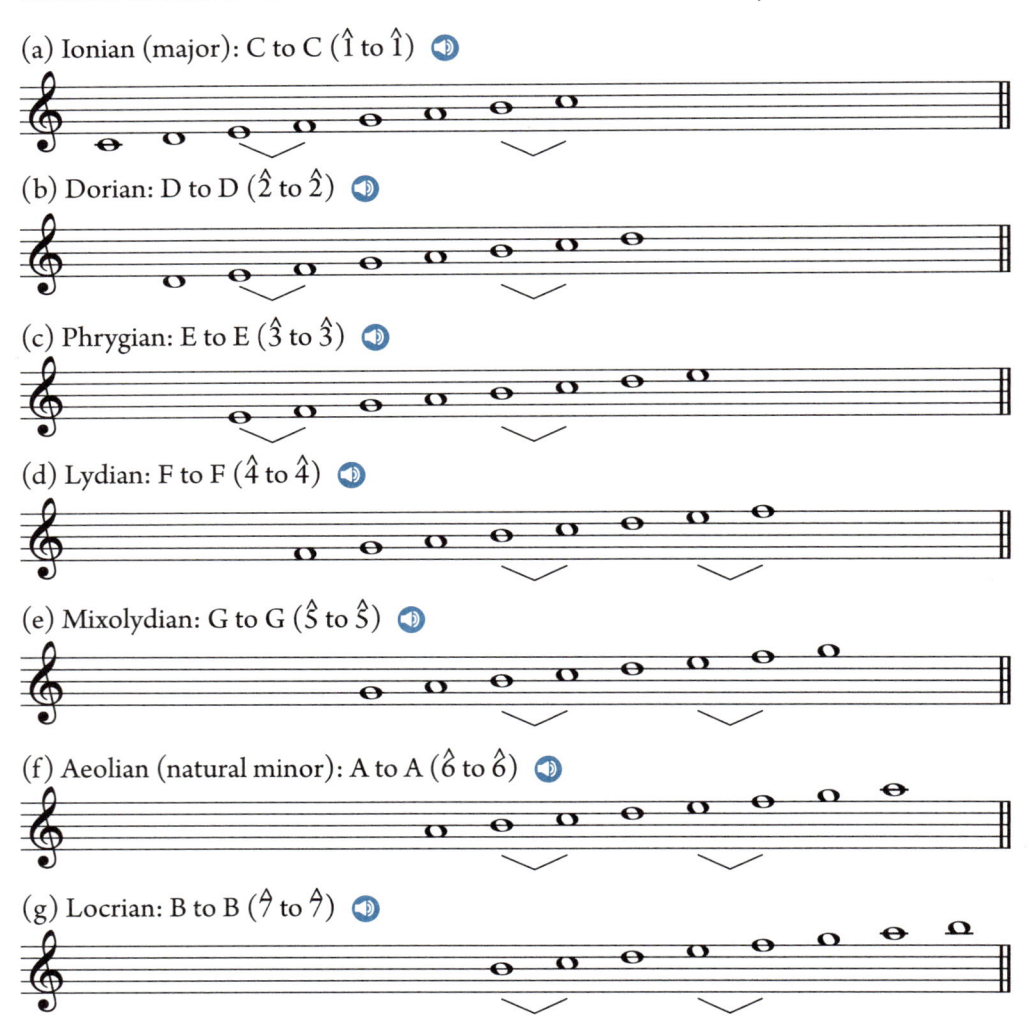

(a) Ionian (major): C to C ($\hat{1}$ to $\hat{1}$)

(b) Dorian: D to D ($\hat{2}$ to $\hat{2}$)

(c) Phrygian: E to E ($\hat{3}$ to $\hat{3}$)

(d) Lydian: F to F ($\hat{4}$ to $\hat{4}$)

(e) Mixolydian: G to G ($\hat{5}$ to $\hat{5}$)

(f) Aeolian (natural minor): A to A ($\hat{6}$ to $\hat{6}$)

(g) Locrian: B to B ($\hat{7}$ to $\hat{7}$)

One way to identify the mode of a piece is by the "relative" method: think of the major key associated with the work's key signature. Major (Ionian) melodies typically rest on $\hat{1}$ of the major key as their most stable pitch, while minor (Aeolian) melodies rest on $\hat{6}$. If $\hat{2}$ of the major key seems to function as the most stable pitch, then a melody is in Dorian mode. Look at "Greensleeves" (Example A6.2). The sharp in the key signature suggests G major, but $\hat{2}$ of that key (A) is the most stable pitch and the melody ends on A: the melody is Dorian.

EXAMPLE A6.2 "Greensleeves," mm. 1–8

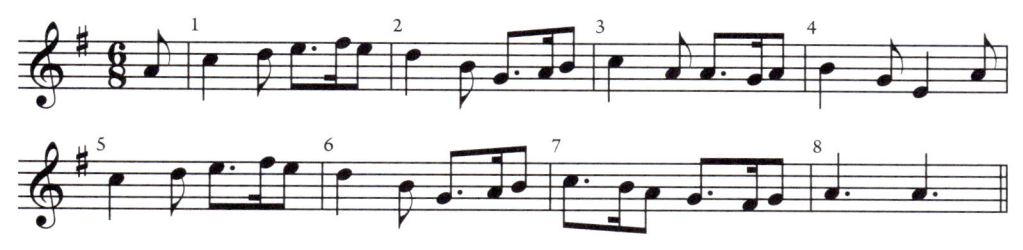

Because the major and minor scales are familiar, you may also hear the modes as alterations of these scales. The modes can be grouped into two families, according to whether the third scale degree comes from the major or minor pentachord. For each mode, one pitch is altered in comparison with the parallel major or minor scale. Example A6.3 summarizes this approach, with each mode beginning on C.

EXAMPLE A6.3 Modes (on C) grouped by families

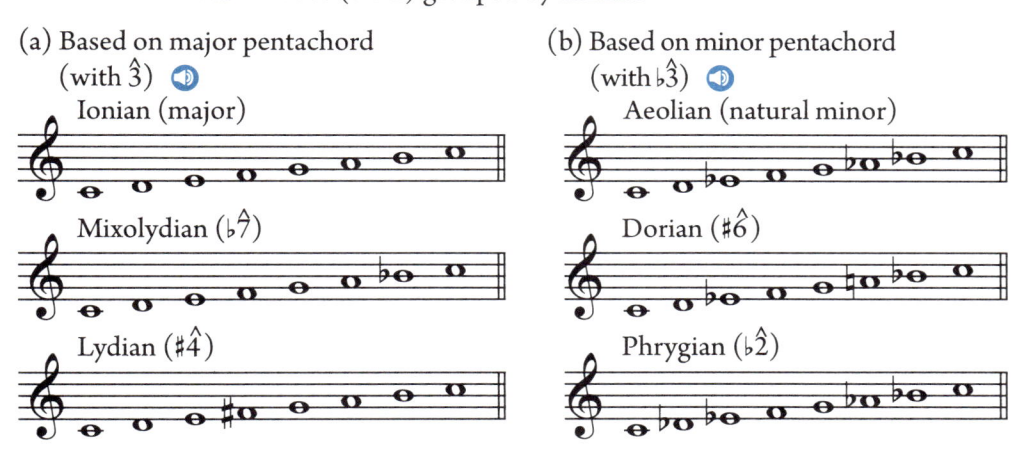

(a) Based on major pentachord
(with $\hat{3}$)
  Ionian (major)
  Mixolydian ($\flat\hat{7}$)
  Lydian ($\sharp\hat{4}$)

(b) Based on minor pentachord
(with $\flat\hat{3}$)
  Aeolian (natural minor)
  Dorian ($\sharp\hat{6}$)
  Phrygian ($\flat\hat{2}$)

To write a mode beginning on any pitch, use either the relative or parallel method, as shown in Example A6.4. Both methods yield the same result; you can write the mode using one method and check it using the other.

To write a Dorian scale beginning on G:

A. Relative method (Example A6.4a):

1. Write note heads on the staff from G to G.
2. Remember that Dorian begins on $\hat{2}$ of a major scale; G is $\hat{2}$ in F major.
3. F major has one flat, so add a flat to B.

B. Parallel method (Example A6.4b):

1. Remember that Dorian sounds like natural minor with a raised sixth scale degree.
2. Write a G natural minor scale, with two flats (B♭ and E♭).
3. Raise ♭$\hat{6}$ by changing E♭ to E♮.

EXAMPLE A6.4 Relative and parallel methods of writing modes on any pitch

(a) Relative method:

1. and 2. Write pitches G to G, and think of the scale (F major) in which G is $\hat{2}$

3. Add accidentals from key signature of F major.

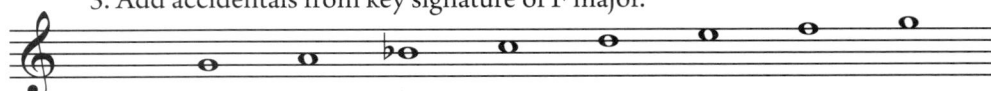

(b) Parallel method:

1. and 2. Write pitches and accidentals for G natural minor.

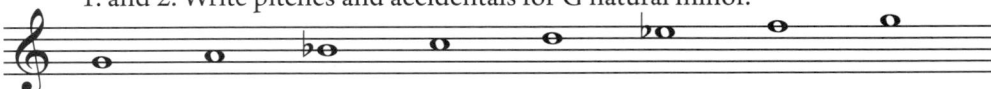

3. Raise ♭$\hat{6}$ to $\hat{6}$

Appendix 7
The C-Clefs

Music reading starts with knowledge of the treble and bass clefs, but there are other clefs as well. Instruments with a middle range, like the viola, read clefs known as C-clefs. The C-clef may appear in different positions on the staff, where its distinctive shape identifies which line is middle C by the point at which the two curved lines join together.

The two C-clefs used most often today are the alto and tenor clefs (Example A7.1). When middle C is the third line, the clef is called an alto clef (Example A7.1a, read by violists). When middle C is the fourth line, the clef is a tenor clef (Example A7.1b, read by cellists, trombonists, and bassoonists). Some players regularly read more than one clef: for example, bassoonists, trombonists, and cellists read both bass and tenor clefs.

EXAMPLE A7.1 The alto and tenor clefs

(a) Alto clef

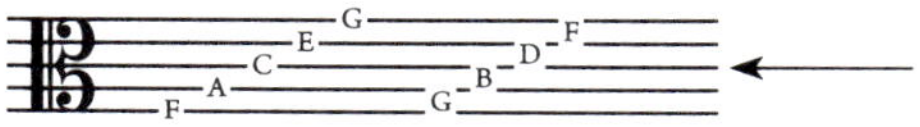

⟵ middle C (C4) (third line)

(b) Tenor clef

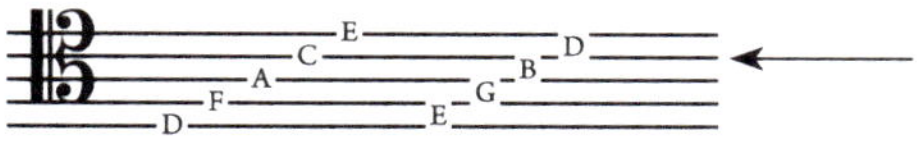

⟵ middle C (C4) (fourth line)

A C-clef may sit on any line of the staff. Depending on its position, it may be called a soprano, mezzo-soprano, alto, tenor, or baritone clef. While the only C-clefs you will probably see in modern scores are the alto and tenor clefs (shaded in Example A7.2), you may come across the others in older scores. To read these clefs, practice counting lines and spaces in thirds, as for the other clefs.

EXAMPLE A7.2 The C-clefs

Soprano clef
C E G B D D F A C

Mezzo-soprano clef
A C E G B B D F A

Alto clef
F A C E G G B D F

Tenor clef
D F A C E E G B D

Baritone clef
B D F A C C E G B

Appendix 8
Basic Guitar Chords

Guitar chords are often illustrated using fretboard diagrams—pictures showing where to place your fingers on the guitar to produce a particular chord. The six vertical lines on a diagram represent the six strings of the guitar, with the lowest-sounding string on the left and the highest-sounding on the right. The horizontal lines represent the frets (small raised bars that run perpendicular to the strings). In standard tuning, the open strings of a guitar produce E2, A2, D3, G3, B3, and E4, as shown in Figure A8.1. These pitches are customarily written an octave higher, in treble clef, as shown.

FIGURE A8.1 Open strings on the guitar

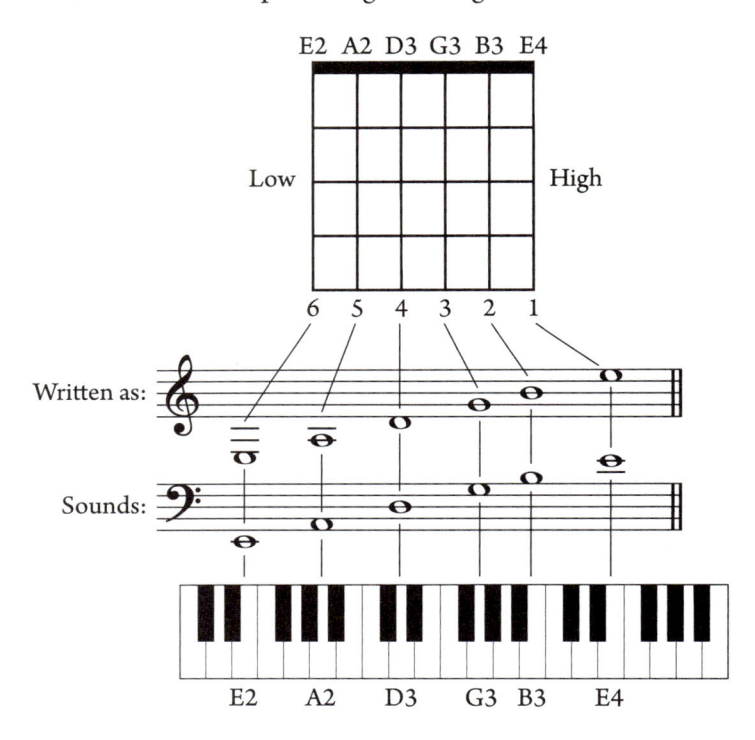

The placement of pitches on the guitar is shown in Figure A8.2. To read this diagram, look at the low string in the illustration. The open string sounds E2; if you place your finger in the space before the first fret, you produce F2, the next note is F♯2 or G♭2, the next G2, and so on. You can continue up this string to E3 on the twelfth fret (indicated by two diamonds, rather than one, as on the third, fifth, seventh, and ninth frets): fingering here sounds an octave above the open string. The diamonds shown in Figure A8.2 help performers quickly locate frets; they may vary in shape or in placement (the arrangement here is the most common). The bass guitar uses the same string arrangement as a standard guitar, but only has the four lowest strings, which are tuned to sound an octave below those on the six-string guitar (E1, A1, D2, G2).

FIGURE A8.2 Pitches on a guitar fretboard

```
              3rd      5th      7th      9th      12th     15th
High          fret     fret     fret     fret     fret     fret
E4  ┌─F───────G────────A────────B──C─────D────────E──F─────G────────A─┐ 1
B3  │─C───────D────────E──F─────G───────A─────────B──C─────D────────E─│ 2
G3  │─────A───────B────C────────D───────E──F──────G───────A─────B──C──│ 3
D3  │────E──F─────G────────A────────B──C─────────D────────E──F───────G│ 4
A2  │─────B──C────────D────────E──F─────G─────────A───────B──C────────D│ 5
E2  └─F───────G────────A────────B──C─────D────────E──F─────G────────A─┘ 6
Low
```

As an aid to performers, scores sometimes include fretboard diagrams, like the one shown in Figure A8.3b, with chord symbols. A small o at the end of a string (shown at the top of the diagram) means that the string is played but not fingered; and an x in the same position means the string should not be played (it is not part of the chord). Black dots show you where to place your fingers on the fretboard. Each chord can be played in a variety of ways, but the basic chords shown are useful for beginners. Consult other resources (online or in the library) to build your repertoire of chords.

FIGURE A8.3 How to read a fretboard diagram

(a) Finger indications

(b) Diagram

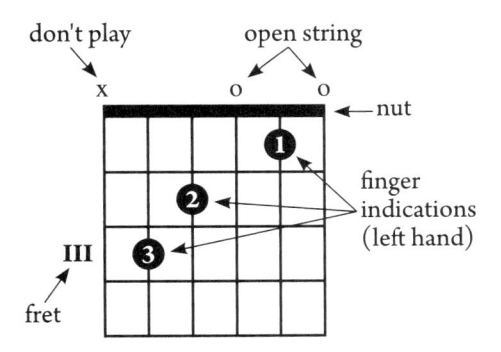

The guitar chords often taught first are E, A, D, G, and C (Figure A8.4a) and Em, Am, and Dm (Figure A8.4c). The letters below each symbol show the pitches played by each string (a dash means that a string is not played). Some basic fingerings are indicated by the finger numbers (1–4 from index finger to pinky) in this example. Guitarists often change these fingerings based on the chord progression. For example, an A major chord can be fingered 1–2–3 before a D major chord or 2–3–4 before an E major or A minor chord. The 2–1–3 fingering for A major shown in Figure A8.4a connects well to the A dominant seventh fingering shown in A8.4b. G major can be fingered 3–2–4 (as shown) to connect well to G7, or 2–1–3–4 (like the diagram for G minor in Figure A8.4d, but with the B♮ instead of B♭) to move smoothly to G minor. Three other useful, but somewhat more challenging, chords are shown in Figure A8.4d: F (index finger plays two strings), B7 (a little awkward at first), and Gm.

When placing your left hand on the fretboard, place your thumb behind the neck of the guitar and curve your fingers over to depress the strings with your fingertips. Generally place your fingers close to, but not on, the fret, as shown in the chord diagrams in Figure A8.4.

FIGURE A8.4 Basic guitar chords

(a) Major chords

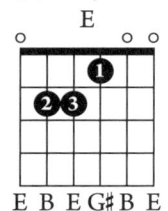

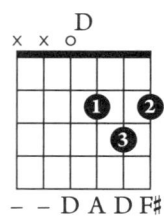

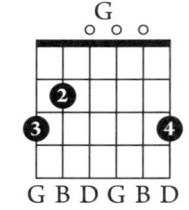

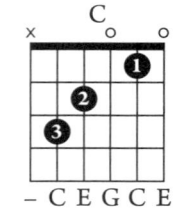

E   B E G♯ B E
A   – A E A C♯ E
D   – – D A D F♯
G   G B D G B D
C   – C E G C E

(b) Dominant seventh chords

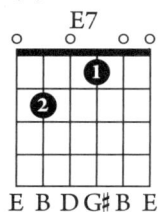

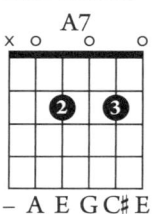

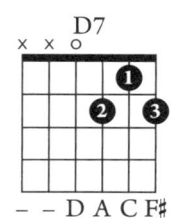

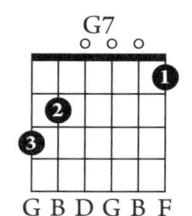

E7   E B D G♯ B E
A7   – A E G C♯ E
D7   – – D A C F♯
G7   G B D G B F

(c) Minor chords

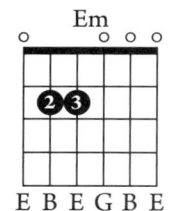

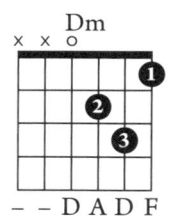

Em   E B E G B E
Am   – A E A C E
Dm   – – D A D F

(d) F major, B7, and G minor

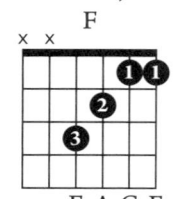

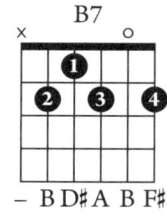

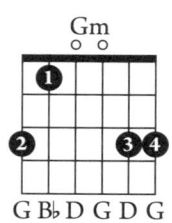

F   – – F A C F
B7   – B D♯ A B F♯
Gm   G B♭ D G D G

The chords in Figure A8.4 can be combined to play basic phrase progressions in the keys of A, D, G, or C major, and in A and D minor, as shown in Figure A8.5. You can also add ii and vi in C major (Dm and Am) and G major (Am and Em) and explore other combinations of these harmonies.

FIGURE A8.5 Progressions made from basic chords

	I	IV	V	V^7
A major	A	D	E	E7
D major	D	G	A	A7
G major	G	C	D	D7
C major	C	F	G	G7

	i	iv	v	V	V^7
A minor	Am	Dm	Em	E	E7
D minor	Dm	Gm	Am	A	A7

To strum a guitar, use your thumb or the pick to sound all of the strings that are included in the chord (leave out any marked on the chord diagram with an x). Example A8.1 shows some basic strumming patterns.

EXAMPLE A8.1 Basic guitar strumming patterns

down up down up   down down up   down down up   up down up

For an arpeggiated accompaniment, you can pluck the strings of a chord one at a time, playing the lowest-pitched note first. Explore a variety of arpeggiated patterns by plucking the strings of a chord using different rhythms in a variety of meters.

Appendix 9
Piano Fingerings for Selected Scales

In this book, class activities have used scale fingerings that are very easy for locating pitches at the keyboard. If you are interested in studying piano further (or if your teacher directs), here are standard fingerings for the major and minor scales, where the thumb is 1 and the pinky is 5. Either hand may play in any octave; scales are often learned one hand at a time, then practiced with the hands one octave apart.

EXAMPLE A9.1 Major scales

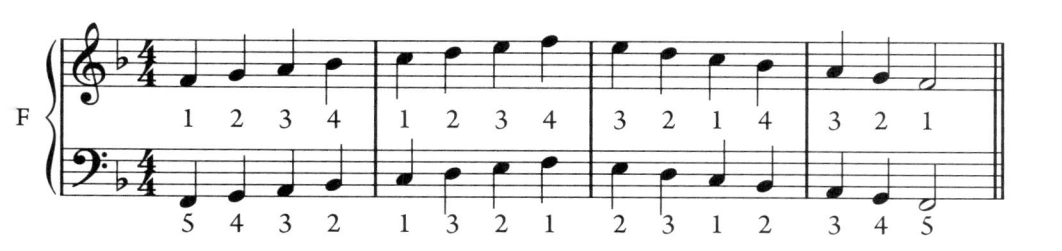

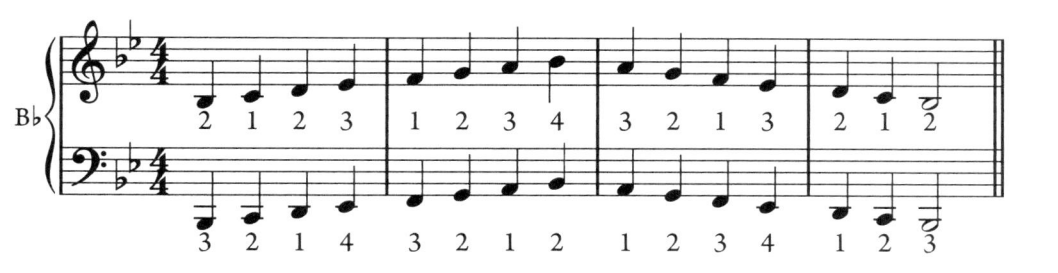

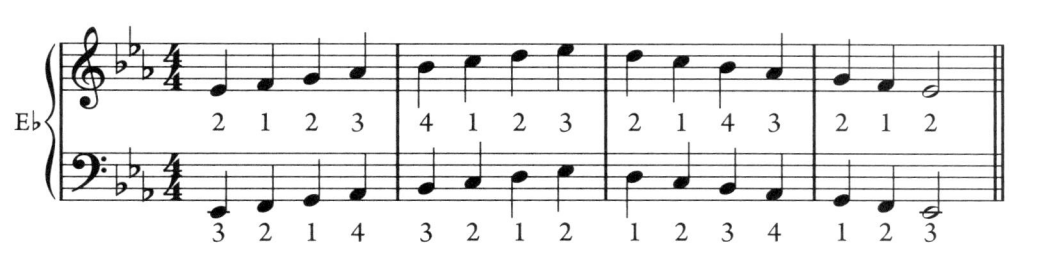

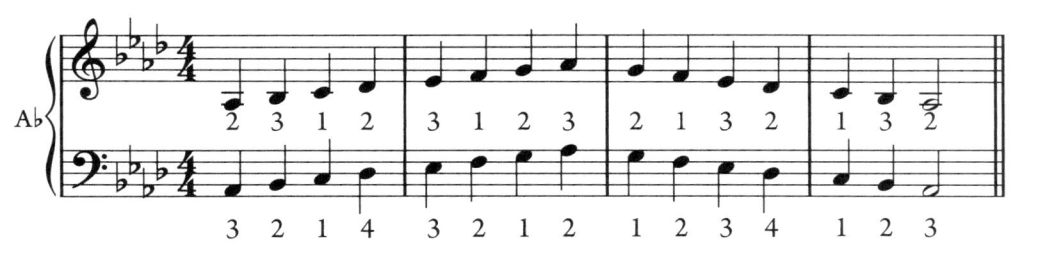

EXAMPLE A9.2 Minor scales

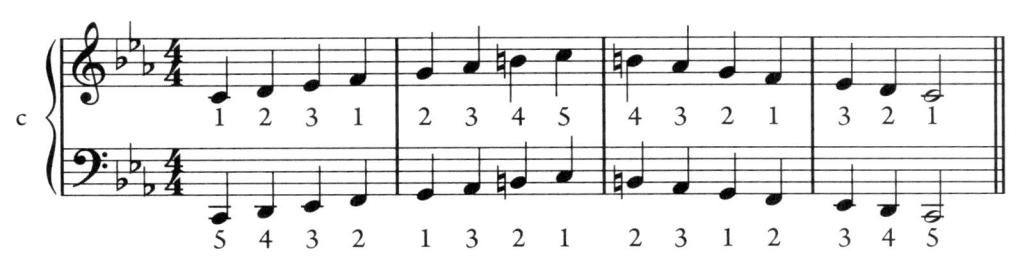

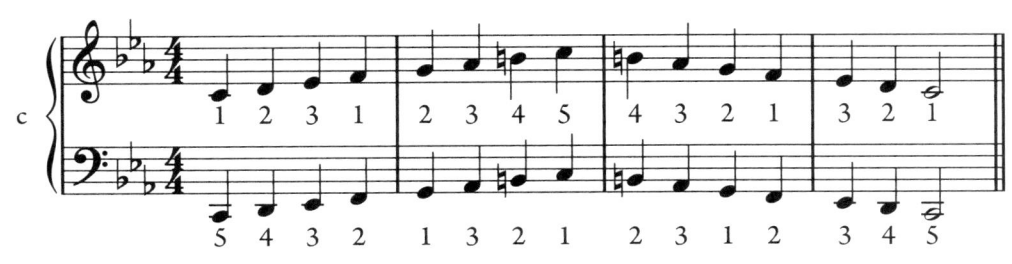

APPENDIX NINE Piano Fingerings for Selected Scales

APPENDIX NINE Piano Fingerings for Selected Scales

Appendix 10
Connecting Chords

General guidelines for connecting chords in SATB style (four-voice hymn style, with soprano, alto, tenor, and bass voices) follow. These basic principles may be adapted for keyboard and other styles. They are intended to create: (1) smooth connections between chords, by step or common tone; (2) independence of voices, minimizing motion in the same direction; and (3) the correct resolution of tendency tones, such as $\hat{7}$ and chordal sevenths.

EXAMPLE A10.1 Chord connections in authentic cadences

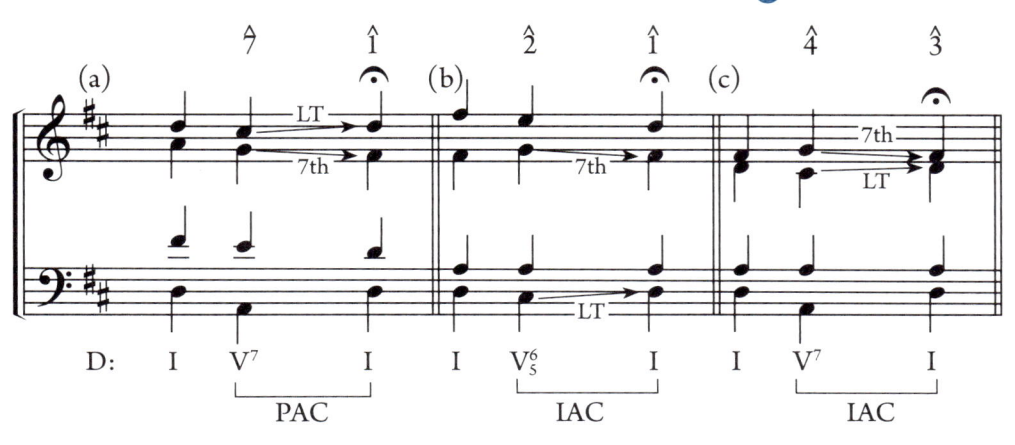

When you connect chords:

1. If the chords have a pitch or pitches in common (called **common tones**) in one of the three upper voices, try to keep these common tones in the same voice part. (In Example A10.1b and c, A3 appears in the tenor in all three chords.)
2. When there is not a common tone, move the upper voices by step if possible. (In Example A10.1, the soprano and alto move by step.) The upper parts (soprano, alto, and tenor) are more likely to move step by step or common tone than the bass, which sometimes skips between chord roots or inversions.
3. Tendency tones, such as the leading tone ($\hat{7}$) and the sevenths of chords, must move by step as marked in the example:
   - The leading tone moves up by step to $\hat{1}$.
   - Chordal sevenths move down by step.
4. Let some pairs of voices (soprano and alto, soprano and bass, tenor and alto, etc.) move in opposite directions, if possible. This is called **contrary motion**. (In Example A10.1a, the soprano and bass move up in the last two chords, while the alto and tenor move down. In c, the soprano/alto and soprano/bass pairs move in contrary motion.)

5. When pairs of voices move in the same direction, check the type of interval between them and adjust if necessary:
   - If the voices create two different intervals (called **similar motion**), the chord connection is acceptable.
   - If the voices create two intervals of the same size (called **parallel motion**), check the interval type:
     - If the intervals in parallel motion are both imperfect consonances (third to third or sixth to sixth), this is acceptable. This is shown in the soprano and alto in the last two chords of Example A10.1b, both sixths.
     - If, however, the parallel intervals are both perfect consonances (P5 to P5, P8 to P8, or PU to PU), you will need to revise the chord connection. These are called **parallel fifths**, **parallel octaves**, and **parallel unisons**, which are generally not found in SATB style, though you may see them in popular music.

Music Credits

Count Basie, Splanky. By Neal Hefti. © 1958 (renewed) WB Music Corp. All rights reserved. Used with permission of Alfred Publishing Co., Inc. **John Cage, 4′33″.** Copyright © 1960 by Henmar Press, Inc. Used by permission. All rights reserved.

Photo Credits

1 iStockphoto; **13** Klein Stephane/Corbis Sygma; **35** Bettmann/Corbis; **47** iStockphoto; **58** Lebrecht Music & Arts/Edition Peters 1800–2010; **73** iStockphoto; **81** Roger Ressmeyer/Corbis; **110** Michael Ochs Archives/Corbis; **138** © Lebrecht Music & Arts/Lebrecht Music & Arts; **155** Jon Helgason/Dreamstime.com; **168** National Gallery Collection; by the kind permission of the Trustees of the National Gallery, London/Corbis; **185** Timur Arbaev/Dreamstime.com; **203** Culver Pictures/The Art Archive at Art Resource, NY; **223:** Peter Borg/Westminster Choir College of Rider University; **236** Wikimedia Commons; **269** Bettmann/Corbis; **301** © Lebrecht Music & Arts.

Index of Musical Examples

"21 Guns" (Green Day), 312

"Ah, Belinda, I am prest," from *Dido and Aeneas* (Purcell), 180
"All Because of You" (Bono and U2), 280
"All Time High" (Barry and Rice), 30
"Alleluia" (Boyce), 274
"Alleluia" (Mozart), 209
"Am Flusse" (Schubert), 210
"Amazing Grace" (Newton), 1, 24, 45–46, 49, 52, 54–55, 315, 386
"American Pie" (McLean), 78
Anonymous, Minuet in D Minor, from the Anna Magdalena Bach Notebook, 218
Arlen, Harold, "We're Off to See the Wizard," from *The Wizard of Oz*, 114
"Ash Grove, The," 127–28, 129, 187, 291–92, 293, 310, 346–47
Ashman, Howard, "Beauty and the Beast," 279
"Aus meines Herzens Grunde" (Bach), 211

Bach, Johann Sebastian
    "Aus meines Herzens Grunde," 211
    Invention in D Minor, 158, 198, 348–49
    "Jesu, Priceless Treasure," 273
    Musette, BWV Anh. 126, 143
    "O Haupt voll blut und Wunden," 71
    Passacaglia in C Minor, 60
    Prelude, from Cello Suite No. 2, 5
    Prelude in C Major, from *The Well-Tempered Clavier*, Book I, 50
    Prelude in C♯ Minor, from *The Well-Tempered Clavier*, Book I, 350–53
    "Wachet auf," 180, 261–62
"Banana Boat Song," 209
Barry, John, "All Time High," 30
Barry, Paul, "Hero," 325
Bartók, Béla
    "Bulgarian Rhythm," 107
    "Change of Time," 124
    "Evening in Transylvania," 328
    "Fifth Chords," 124
    "From the Diary of a Fly," 124
    "In the Style of a Folk Song," 124
    "Syncopation," 109
    "Unison," 124
Basie, Count, "Splanky," 319, 321
Beatles, "Ticket to Ride," 300
"Beautiful Dreamer" (Foster), 99
"Beauty and the Beast" (Ashman and Menken), 279

Beethoven, Ludwig van
    Pathétique Sonata, 71, 354–55
    Sonata for Violin and Piano, Op. 30, no. 2, first movement, 172
    Sonatina in G, Romanze, 143
    String Quartet in F Major, Op. 18, No. 1, second movement, 119
"Before the Parade Passes By," from *Hello Dolly!* (Herman), 117
"Better Times Are Coming" (Foster), 272
Black Eyed Peas, "I Gotta Feeling," 300–301
Bliss, Philip B., "Wonderful Words of Life," 115
"Blue Rondo à la Turk" (Brubeck), 108
"Blues for Norton" (Phillips), 6, 44, 56, 57, 218, 263, 318–19, 338, 388–91
Bono
    "All Because of You," 280
    "Miracle Drug," 69
    "One Step Closer," 280
Boyce, William, "Alleluia," 274
Brubeck, Dave, "Blue Rondo à la Turk," 108
"Bulgarian Rhythm," from *Mikrokosmos* (Bartók), 107
Burleske (L. Mozart), 240
"Butterfly, The," 119

Canon for Three Violins and Keyboard in D Major (Pachelbel), 250
"Can't Help Falling in Love," from *Blue Hawaii* (Weiss, Peretti, and Creatore), 87
Capra, Remo, "O Bambino," 305
Cerf, Christopher, "Dance Myself to Sleep," from *Sesame Street*, 100
"Change of Time" (Bartók), 124
Charnin, Martin, "Tomorrow," 279
"Chartres," 264
Chopin, Fryderyk, Prelude in C Minor, Op. 28, No. 20, 60, 356
"Circle of Life," from *The Lion King* (John and Rice), 8
Clarke, Jeremiah, *Trumpet Voluntary*, 180
"Clementine," 281
"Come, Follow Me," 144
"Come, Ye Thankful People Come" (St. George's Windsor), 48, 52, 60, 225, 255, 357
Corelli, Arcangelo, Allemanda, from Trio Sonata, Op. 4, No. 5, 162
Creatore, Luigi, "Can't Help Falling in Love," from *Blue Hawaii*, 87
Croce, Jim, "Time in a Bottle," 160
"Cruella de Vil" (Leven), 31

"Dallas Blues" (Wand and Garrett), 320, 395–98
"Dance Myself to Sleep," from *Sesame Street* (Cerf and Stiles), 100
"Do You Want to Dance?" (Freeman), 324
"Dona nobis pacem," 273
"Down in the Valley," 241
"Drink to Me Only," 150

"Edelweiss" (Rodgers and Hammerstein), 279
Edwards, Clara, "Into the Night," 87
"Eight Days a Week" (Lennon and McCartney), 311
"Evening in Transylvania" (Bartók), 328

"Fifth Chords" (Bartók), 124
"For He's a Jolly Good Fellow," 264–65
Foster, Stephen
    "Beautiful Dreamer," 99
    "Better Times Are Coming," 272
    "Jeanie with the Light Brown Hair," 24, 51, 216, 358–62
    "Oh! Susanna!", 47, 48, 134, 136, 260, 291, 294–95, 363
Frasier, theme from (Miller), 44
Freeman, Bobby, "Do You Want to Dance?", 324
"Frog in the Bog, The" (Loomis), 143
"From the Diary of a Fly" (Bartók), 124

Garrett, Lloyd, "Dallas Blues," 320, 395–98
Gilmore, Patrick, "When Johnny Comes Marching Home," 97, 98, 157, 283, 364
"Girl from Ipanema, The" (Jobim and Moraes), 92
"Girls on the Beach" (Wilson and Love), 79
"Go Down, Moses," 266–68
Green Day, "21 Guns," 312
"Greensleeves," 186, 202, 289–91, 365–66

Hammerstein, Oscar, II
    "Edelweiss," 279
    "If I Loved You," 69
Handel, George Frideric
    "The Harmonious Blacksmith," 306
    "How Beautiful Are the Feet of Them," from *Messiah*, 122
    "Rejoice Greatly," from *Messiah*, 120
"Hanukkah Song," 284
Harburg, E. Y., "We're Off to See the Wizard," from *The Wizard of Oz*, 114
Harline, Leigh, "Hi-Diddle-Dee-Dee," from *Pinocchio*, 117

A-55

"Harmonious Blacksmith, The" (Handel), 306
Haydn, Joseph
    Piano Sonata No. 9, Scherzo, 172
    Seven German Dances, No. 6, 240
"Hello Goodbye" (Lennon and McCartney), 20
Hensel, Fanny Mendelssohn
    "Schwanenlied," 119
    "Waldeinsam," 172
Herman, Jerry, "Before the Parade Passes By," from *Hello Dolly!*, 117
"Hero" (Iglesias, Barry, and Taylor), 325
"Hey Jude" (Lennon and McCartney), 51
"Hi-Diddle-Dee-Dee," from *Pinocchio* (Harline and Washington), 117
Holst, Gustav, Second Suite in F for Military Band, "Song of the Blacksmith," 109
"Home, Dearie, Home," 305
"Home on the Range," 45–46, 101, 103, 264, 266, 367
Horner, James, "My Heart Will Go On," 65
"House of the Rising Sun, The" (Price), 305
"How Beautiful Are the Feet of Them," from *Messiah* (Handel), 122
"How Can I Keep from Singing" (Lowry), 210, 279, 336

"I Gotta Feeling" (Black Eyed Peas), 300–301
"I Guess That's Why They Call It the Blues" (John, Taupin, and Johnstone), 106, 123
"I Had a Little Nut Tree," 240
"I Will Always Love You" (Parton), 81
"If I Loved You" (Rodgers and Hammerstein), 69
Iglesias, Enrique, "Hero," 325
"Imagine" (Lennon), 4
"Imperial March," from *The Empire Strikes Back* (Williams), 44
"In the Style of a Folk Song" (Bartók), 124
"Into the Night" (Edwards), 87
"It Takes Two," from *Hairspray* (Shaiman and Wittman), 123

Jacquet de la Guerre, Elisabeth, Gigue, from Suite No. 3 in A Minor, 104, 121, 368–69
"Jeanie with the Light Brown Hair" (Foster), 24, 51, 216, 358–62
"Jesu, Priceless Treasure" (Bach), 273
Jobim, Antônio Carlos, "The Girl from Ipanema," 92
Joel, Billy, "Piano Man," 24
John, Sir Elton
    "Circle of Life," from *The Lion King*, 8
    "I Guess That's Why They Call It the Blues," 106, 123
    "Your Song," 65
Johnstone, Davey, "I Guess That's Why They Call It the Blues," 106, 123
Joplin, Scott
    "Pine Apple Rag," 44, 78
    "Solace," 10–11, 27, 28–29, 32, 71, 75, 76, 92, 370–73

Kander, John, Theme from *New York, New York*, 80
Kern, Jerome, "Look for the Silver Lining," 80, 292, 374–78
King, Carole, "You've Got a Friend," 92

"Land of the Silver Birch," 330
Larson, Jonathan, "Seasons of Love," from *Rent*, 65
Lennon, John
    "Eight Days a Week," 311
    "Hello Goodbye," 20
    "Hey Jude," 51
    "Imagine," 4
    "Norwegian Wood," 99
Lerner, Alan Jay, "Wand'rin' Star," from *Paint Your Wagon*, 87
Leven, Mel, "Cruella de Vil," 31
"Lil' Liza Jane," 142
"Lindenbaum, Der," from *Winterreise* (Schubert), 150
"Little Brown Jug," 281
Lloyd Webber, Andrew, "Memory," from *Cats*, 123
Loesser, Frank, "Luck Be a Lady," from *Guys and Dolls*, 93
Loewe, Frederick, "Wand'rin' Star," from *Paint Your Wagon*, 87
"Look for the Silver Lining" (Kern), 80, 292, 374–78
Loomis, Harvey Worthington, "The Frog in the Bog," 143
"Lou'siana Blues" (Washington and White), 332
Love, Mike, "Girls on the Beach," 79
"Love Me Tender" (Presley), 150
"Love Story" (Swift), 301
Lowry, Reverend R., "How Can I Keep from Singing," 210, 279, 336
"Luck Be a Lady," from *Guys and Dolls* (Loesser), 93

"Masters in This Hall," 150
McCartney, Paul
    "Eight Days a Week," 311
    "Hello Goodbye," 20
    "Hey Jude," 51
    "Norwegian Wood," 99
McLean, Don, "American Pie," 78
"Memory," from *Cats* (Lloyd Webber), 123
Menken, Alan, "Beauty and the Beast," 279
"Merrily We Roll Along," 297–99
"Michael Finnigin," 60, 266
"Midnight Train to Georgia" (Weatherly), 93
Miller, Bruce, *Frasier*, theme from, 44
"Miracle Drug" (Bono and U2), 69
Mission Impossible, Theme from (Schifrin), 11, 108
Moraes, Vinius de, "The Girl from Ipanema," 92
Mozart, Leopold, *Burleske*, 240

Mozart, Wolfgang Amadeus
    "Alleluia," 209
    Piano Sonata in C Major, K. 545, 53, 211, 310
    String Quartet in D Minor, K. 421, third movement, 60, 167, 379–81
    "Sull' aria," from *The Marriage of Figaro*, 120
    Variations on "Ah, vous dirai-je Maman," 22, 52, 73, 155–56, 160, 218, 382–84
    Variations on "Lison dormait," 62
"Music Alone Shall Live," 210
"My Country, 'Tis of Thee," 47, 48, 223–24, 230–31, 232, 233, 234, 236, 262, 385
"My Heart Will Go On" (Horner), 65
"My Paddle's Keen and Bright," 335

Nelson, Willie, "On the Road Again," 30
New York, New York, Theme from (Kander), 80
Newton, John, "Amazing Grace," 1, 24, 45–46, 49, 52, 54–55, 316, 386
"Norwegian Wood" (Lennon and McCartney), 99
"Nun danket," 246

"O Bambino" (Velona and Capra), 305
"O God Our Help in Ages Past" (St. Anne), 387
"O Haupt voll blut und Wunden" (Bach), 71
"O magnum mysterium" (Victoria), 180
"Oh! Susanna!" (Foster), 47, 48, 134, 136, 260, 291, 294–95, 363
"Old Hundredth," 244
"On the Road Again" (Nelson), 30
"Once More My Soul," 173
"One Step Closer" (Bono and U2), 280

Pachelbel, Johann, Canon for Three Violins and Keyboard in D Major, 250
Parish, Mitchell, "Stars Fell on Alabama," 332
Parton, Dolly, "I Will Always Love You," 81
Pathétique Sonata (Beethoven), 71, 354–55
Peretti, Hugo, "Can't Help Falling in Love," from *Blue Hawaii*, 87
Perkins, Frank, "Stars Fell on Alabama," 332
Phillips, Joel, "Blues for Norton," 6, 44, 56, 57, 218, 263, 318–19, 338, 388–91
"Piano Man" (Joel), 24
"Pine Apple Rag" (Joplin), 44, 78
Presley, Elvis, "Love Me Tender," 150
Price, Alan, "The House of the Rising Sun," 305
Purcell, Henry, "Ah, Belinda, I am prest," from *Dido and Aeneas*, 180

"Rejoice Greatly," from *Messiah* (Handel), 120
Rice, Tim
    "All Time High," 30
    "Circle of Life," from *The Lion King*, 8
Richie, Lionel, "Three Times a Lady," 69, 325

"Riddle Song," 330
Robinson, Smokey, "You've Really Got a Hold on Me," 101, 106
Rodgers, Richard
    "Edelweiss," 279
    "If I Loved You," 69
Root, George F., "There's Music in the Air," 210
"Rosa Mystica," 263

St. George's Windsor, 48, 52, 60, 225, 255, 357
"St. James Infirmary," 240
Schifrin, Lalo, Theme from *Mission Impossible,* 11, 108
Schubert, Franz
    Allegretto, D. 915, 172
    "Am Flusse," 210
    "Der Lindenbaum," from *Winterreise,* 150
    Waltz in B Minor, 71, 157–58, 257–59, 298, 392–93
    Wanderer Fantasy, Op. 15, Adagio, 172
"Schwanenlied" (Hensel), 119
"Seasons of Love," from *Rent* (Larson), 65
Seven German Dances, No. 6 (Haydn), 240
Shaiman, Marc, "It Takes Two," from *Hairspray,* 123
"Shalom, Chaverim," 150
"Shenandoah," 209
"Silent Night," 98
"Simple Gifts," 137, 185, 203, 291, 309, 394
"Solace" (Joplin), 10–11, 27, 28–29, 32, 71, 75, 76, 92, 370–73
Sousa, John Philip, "The Stars and Stripes Forever," 44, 53, 127, 282
"Splanky" (Basie), 319, 321
"Stars and Stripes Forever, The" (Sousa), 44, 53, 127, 282
"Stars Fell on Alabama" (Perkins and Parish), 332

Stiles, Norman, "Dance Myself to Sleep," from *Sesame Street,* 100
Strouse, Charles, "Tomorrow," 279
"Sull' aria," from *The Marriage of Figaro* (Mozart), 120
Swift, Taylor, "Love Story," 301
"Syncopation" (Bartók), 109

Taupin, Bernie
    "I Guess That's Why They Call It the Blues," 106, 123
    "Your Song," 65
Taylor, Mark, "Hero," 325
"There's Music in the Air" (Root), 210
"Three Times a Lady" (Richie), 69, 325
"Ticket to Ride" (The Beatles), 300
"Time in a Bottle" (Croce), 160
"Tomorrow" (Charnin and Strouse), 279
Trumpet Voluntary (Clarke), 180
Twain, Shania, "You're Still the One," 92
"Twinkle, Twinkle, Little Star," 130

U2
    "All Because of You," 280
    "Miracle Drug," 69
    "One Step Closer," 280
"Unison" (Bartók), 124

Variations on "Ah, vous dirai-je Maman" (Mozart), 22, 52, 73, 155–56, 160, 218, 382–84
Variations on "Lison dormait" (Mozart), 62
Velona, Tony, "O Bambino," 305
Victoria, Tomás Luis de, "O magnum mysterium," 180

"Wachet auf" (Bach), 180, 261–62
"Wade in the Water," 283

"Waldeinsam" (Hensel), 172
Wand, Hart A., "Dallas Blues," 320, 395–98
Wanderer Fantasy, Op. 15, Adagio (Schubert), 172
"Wand'rin' Star," from *Paint Your Wagon* (Lerner and Loewe), 87
Washington, Howard, "Lou'siana Blues," 332
Washington, Ned, "Hi-Diddle-Dee-Dee," from *Pinocchio,* 117
"Wayfaring Stranger," 266–67, 268–69, 316
Weatherly, Jim, "Midnight Train to Georgia," 93
Weiss, George David, "Can't Help Falling in Love," from *Blue Hawaii,* 87
"We're Off to See the Wizard," from *The Wizard of Oz* (Arlen and Harburg), 114
"When Johnny Comes Marching Home" (Gilmore), 97, 98, 157, 283, 364
"When the Train Comes Along," 331
White, James, "Lou'siana Blues," 332
"Will This Circle Be Unbroken," 328
Williams, John, "Imperial March," from *The Empire Strikes Back,* 44
Wilson, Brian, "Girls on the Beach," 79
Wittman, Scott, "It Takes Two," from *Hairspray,* 123
Wonder, Stevie, "You Are the Sunshine of My Life," 20
"Wonderful Words of Life" (Bliss), 115

"Yankee Doodle," 282
"You Are the Sunshine of My Life" (Wonder), 20
"Your Song" (John and Taupin), 65
"You're Still the One" (Twain), 92
"You've Got a Friend" (King), 92
"You've Really Got a Hold on Me" (Robinson), 101, 106

Index of Terms and Concepts

12-bar blues, 318–21, 326
32-bar song form, 291–93

accelerando, 48
accents
    displaced, 77–78
    metrical, 49
accidentals, 27–32
    double flats, 30–31
    double sharps, 30–31
    flats, 27–29
    naturals, 27–29
    sharps, 27–29
adagio, 48
added-sixth chord, 325
alla breve, 53
allegretto, 48
allegro, 48
alto, 223
anacrusis, 52, 55
andante, 48
andantino, 48
antecedent phrase, 290
arpeggio, 299
arrangements, keyboard, 295–98
articulation, 76
ascending contour, 1
asymmetrical meters, 107–9
augmentation, 78
augmented intervals, 197–200, 202
augmented second, 158
augmented triads, 226
authentic cadence, 260–61, 265

bar, 49
bar lines, 1, 49
basic phrase, 260
    subdominant in, 264–65
bass, 223
bass clef, 5–6
    drawing a, 11
    ledger lines and, 7, 9
beams, 50
    in compound meters, 101
    notating, 50
    for rhythmic patterns, 75
beat
    strong, 49
    weak, 49
beat division, 54–55, 99
beat subdivisions, 73–75
    in compound meters, 100–102

beat unit, 52, 53
    in compound meters, 97, 102, 104
blue notes, 318
blues scale, 318–21
bridge (in 32-bar song form), 292–93
bridge (in later popular music), 300

cadences, 259
    authentic, 260–61, 265
    deceptive, 261–62
    half, 260–61
    imperfect authentic, 261
    perfect authentic, 261
    plagal, 262
    types of, 260–64
change in mode, 156
changes, 320
changing meter, 108–9
chords, 223. *See also* chord extensions; dominant
        seventh chord; seventh chords; triads
chord connection, 296
chord extensions, 324–26
chord members, 224, 230
chord progressions, 260
    keyboard arrangements of, 295–98
chorus, 300
chromatic half steps, 33, 128
chromatic scale, 128
circle of fifths, 137
    minor key signatures and, 165–66
clave rhythm pattern, 77
clefs, 3–6
    bass, 5–6
    rhythm, 55
    treble, 3–4
climax, 294
combo, 318
common time, 53
compound intervals, 201–2
compound meter, 97–105
    compound duple, 97–98, 102
    compound quadruple, 99, 102
    compound triple, 99, 102
    meter signatures for, 98–100, 102
    other, 102–5
    subdivisions, 100–102
    syncopation in, 105–7
conducting patterns, 48
conjunct motion, 293
consequent phrase, 290
consonant intervals, 202–3
contour, musical, 1

contrasting period, 290
cut time, 53, 77

deceptive cadence, 261–62
deceptive resolution, 262
descending contour, 1
diatonic half steps, 33, 130
diatonic scales, 130
diminished intervals, 197–200, 202
diminished seventh chord, 322–23
diminished triads, 224, 226
disjunct motion, 293
dissonant intervals, 202–3
dominant, 131
dominant seventh chord, 233–35
    inversion, 234–35
    in major keys, 256–57
    melody harmonization with, 255–59,
        266–68
    in minor keys, 257–59, 266–68
    spelling, 234
dominant triad, 225
    in major keys, 256, 257
    melody harmonization with, 255–59, 265,
        266–68
    in minor keys, 257–59
dot, 52–53, 56
dotted notes, 53
dotted rests, 56
dotted-half note beat unit, 104
dotted-quarter beat unit, 97
double flats, 30–31
double sharps, 30–31
doubling (in chords), 224
doubly augmented intervals, 200
doubly diminished intervals, 200
downbeat, 49
duple meter, 47–48, 52
    compound, 97–98
duplets, 105–7
dynamic levels, 49

eighth note, 50
eighth rest, 56
embellishing tones, 265–66
    neighbor tones, 265–66
    passing tones, 265–66
enharmonic spellings, 28–29, 30–31
    for augmented and diminished intervals, 200

F-clef. *See* bass clef
fifth (of chord), 224, 230

A-58

figures, 231
first-inversion chords, 231, 234–35
fixed *do* solfège, 131
flags, 50
flats, 27–29
flatted fifth, 318–19
form, 289–314
    32-bar song form, 291–93
    in later popular music, 299–301
    period, 290, 293–94
    quaternary song form, 290–93, 294–95
    verse-refrain form, 292–93
forte, 49
fortissimo, 49
four-phrase song form, 290–93

G-clef. *See* treble clef
grand staff, 10–11
grave, 48
Guidonian hand, 138
guitar tabs, 260

half cadence, 260–61
half note, 50
half rest, 56
half step, 28, 32–35
    chromatic, 33, 128
    diatonic, 33, 130
    hearing, 34–35
half-diminished seventh chord, 322–23
harmonic intervals, 186
harmonic minor, 157–59, 161
harmonic rhythm, 259
harmonization, 259–60
head, 321
hexachord, 138
homophonic texture, 223
hook, 300
hymn style, 223

imperfect authentic cadence, 261
improvisation, 80
instrumental break, 300
intervals, 31, 185–222
    compound, 201–2
    consonant, 202–3
    dissonant, 202–3
    enharmonically equivalent, 200
    half step, 28, 32–35
    harmonic, 186
    melodic, 185
    simple, 201
    sizes, 185
    spelling methods for, 191–97
    spelling triads by, 227, 229–30
    unisons, 186–87
    whole step, 30, 32–35
interval inversion, 190, 195–96
interval quality, 187–90
    augmented, 197–200, 202
    diminished, 197–200, 202

doubly augmented, 200
doubly diminished, 200
major, 188–97, 202
minor, 188–97, 202
perfect, 188–91, 202
intro, 300
inverted chords, 230–31, 234–35
inverting intervals, 190

key signatures, 133
    determining, 135–36
    identifying key from score, 165–66
    for major keys, 133–37
    for minor keys, 164–66
    spelling triads by, 227–28
keyboard, piano
    half and whole steps on, 32–33
    ledger lines and, 6–9
    naming white keys on, 2–3, 28
    with octave numbers, 6
keyboard arrangements, 295–98
    styles of, 297–99
keyboard style, 232, 235

larghetto, 48
largo, 48
lead sheet, 319, 321
leading tone, 131, 226, 227
leading-tone triad, 225
leaps, melodic, 293
ledger lines, 6–9
    drawing, 12
    landmarks for, 8
letter names, pitch, 1–2, 28–29
link, 300

major intervals, 188–97, 202
major keys, 130
    melody harmonization in, 256–57, 266
    seventh chords in, 322
    signatures for, 133–37
major pentatonic scale, 315, 316–17
major scales, 129–30, 161
    spelling triads by, 227, 228–29
    writing, 131–33
major seventh chord, 321–23
major tetrachord, 132
major triad, 224–25, 226
measure, 1, 49
mediant, 131
mediant triad, 225
melodic intervals, 185
melodic minor, 160–61
melodies, writing, 293–95
melody and accompaniment texture, 258
melody harmonization
    with basic phrase model, 259–60, 264–65, 266–69
    embellishments, 265–66
    with triads and dominant seventh chord, 255–59

meter
    asymmetrical, 107–9
    changing, 108–9
    compound, 97–105
    duple, 47–48, 52
    quadruple, 47–48, 52
    simple, 47–72
    symmetrical, 107
    triple, 47–48
meter signatures, 51–53
    for compound meters, 98–100, 102
    for simple meters, 51–53
metrical accents, 49
mezzo forte, 49
mezzo piano, 49
middle C, 3
minor dominant seventh chord, 266–68
minor intervals, 188–97, 202
minor mode, 156
minor pentatonic scale, 316–17, 318, 319
minor scales and keys, 155–85
    harmonic minor, 157–59, 161
    identifying from score, 167–68
    melodic minor, 160–61
    melody harmonization in, 257–59, 266–68
    natural minor, 156–57, 161
    parallel keys, 155–56
    seventh chords in, 322
    signatures for, 164–66
minor seventh chord, 321–23
minor triad, 224–25, 226
modal scale degrees, 156
moderato, 48
modulation, 163
motives, 294
movable *do* solfège, 131
musical alphabet, 3
musical contour, 1

natural minor, 156–57, 161
    relative, 163
naturals, 27–29
neighbor tones, 265–66
ninth chord, 324, 325
notation guidelines
    beaming of rhythmic patterns, 75
    beams and flags, 50
    beams in compound meters, 101
    clefs, 11
    for duplets, 107
    ledger lines, 12
    note heads, 3
    notes and stems, 12
    unisons and seconds with stems, 186–87
notes, 1
    eighth, 50
    half, 50
    quarter, 50
    sixteenth, 50
    whole, 50
note heads, drawing, 3, 12

octave, 2, 188, 202
octave equivalence, 2
octave numbers, naming pitches with, 6, 7
outro, 300

parallel keys, 155–56
    parallel major, 156
    parallel minor, 156
parallel period, 290
passing tones, 265–66
pentatonic scales, 315–17
    major pentatonic, 315, 316–17
    minor pentatonic, 316–17, 318, 319
perfect authentic cadence, 261
perfect intervals, 188–91, 202
periods, 290
    contrasting, 290
    parallel, 290
    writing, 293–94
phrases, 259
    antecedent, 290
    consequent, 290
    keyboard arrangements of, 295–98
    paired, 289–90
pianissimo, 49
piano (dynamic), 49
piano keyboard
    half and whole steps on, 32–33
    ledger lines and, 6–9
    naming white keys on, 2–3, 28
pickup, 52, 55
pitch, 1
pitch notation, 1–9
    ledger lines for, 6–9
    letter names, 1–2, 28–29
    naming with octave numbers, 6
    staff, 3
    treble and bass clefs, 3–6
    writing pitches in score, 11–13
    writing pitches with accidentals, 31–32
plagal cadence, 262
postchorus, 301
prechorus, 301
prestissimo, 48
presto, 48

quadruple meter, 47–48, 52
quality (of triad), 224
quarter note, 49
quarter rest, 56
quarter-note beat, rhythmic subdivisions of, 74
quaternary song form, 290–93
    writing, 294–95

raised submediant, 161
rap break, 300
refrain, 292–93
register, 7
relative keys, 162–65
    relative major, 163–64
    relative minor, 163–64

resolution, 202–3
rests, 56–57
    in compound meters, 101
    eighth, 56
    half, 56
    quarter, 56
    sixteenth, 56
    whole, 56
rhythm, 49
    counting in simple meters, 54–55
rhythm clef, 55
rhythmic notation, 49–51
    dots in, 52–53
rhythmic variations in performance, 80–81
riff, 333
ritardando, 48
rock and roll, 326
Roman numerals, 225, 227
root (of chord), 224, 230
root-position chords, 230, 231, 234–35

SATB, 223
scales, 127–30
    blues, 318–21
    chromatic, 128
    comparing, 161–62
    diatonic, 130
    major, 129–30, 161
    pentatonic, 315–17
    whole-tone, 129
scale degrees, 130–31
    dominant, 131
    leading tone, 131
    mediant, 131
    in minor, 161
    modal, 156
    raised submediant, 161
    subdominant, 131
    submediant, 131
    subtonic, 161
    supertonic, 131
    tonic, 130, 131
scale steps. *See* scale degrees
score, 1
    writing music in a, 11–13
second-inversion chords, 231, 234–35
semitone. *See* half step
seventh (of chord), 224, 230
seventh chords, 321–23
    diminished, 322–23
    dominant, 233–35
    half-diminished, 322–23
    major, 321–23
    minor, 321–23
    spelling, 323
    symbols for, 323
seventh chord positions and inversions, 234–35
    first inversion, 234–35
    root position, 234–35
    second inversion, 234–35
    third inversion, 234–35

sharps, 27–29
simple intervals, 201
simple meters, 47–72
    counting rhythms in, 54–55
    duple, 47–48, 52
    meter signatures for, 51–53
    quadruple, 47–48, 52
    triple, 47–48
sixteenth note, 50
sixteenth rest, 56
skips, melodic, 293
slurs, 76
solfège, 131, 138
    fixed *do*, 131
    movable *do*, 131
soprano, 223
staff (staves), 1
    grand staff, 10–11
    ledger lines and, 6–9
staff notation, 3
stems, 1
    drawing, 12
strong beat, 49
subdominant, 131
subdominant triad, 225
    in basic phrase model, 264–65
    in major keys, 256, 257
    melody harmonization with, 255–59, 266–68
    in minor keys, 257–59
submediant, 131
submediant triad, 225
subtonic, 161
supertonic, 131
supertonic triad, 225
sus chords, 325
swung eighths, 80
symmetrical meter, 107
syncopation, 77–78, 81
    in asymmetrical meters, 108
    in compound meters, 105–7

tacet, 58
tempo, 48
tempo markings, 48
tendency tone, 131
tenor, 223
tetrachord, 132
    major, 132
texture, 223
    homophonic, 223
    melody and accompaniment, 258
third (of chord), 224, 230
third-inversion chords, 234–35
ties, 76
tonic, 130, 131
tonic triad, 225
    in major keys, 255–56, 257
    melody harmonization with, 255–59, 266–68
    in minor keys, 257–59

transpose, 130
treble clef, 3–4
    drawing a, 11
    ledger lines and, 6–7, 8–9
triads, 223–33
    melody harmonization with, 255–59
    names of, 225
    spelling, 227–30
triad positions and inversions, 230–31
    first inversion, 231
    root position, 230, 231
    second inversion, 231
triad qualities, 224
    augmented, 226
    diminished, 224, 226
    major, 224–25, 226
    in major keys, 224–25
    minor, 224–25, 226
    in minor keys, 226–27
triple meter, 47–48
triplets, 79
tritone, 198
turnaround, 320
two-beat triplets, 79–80

unison, 186
upbeat, 49, 52, 55

verse (in 32-bar song form), 292–93

verse (in later popular music), 299–300
verse-refrain form, 292–93
vivace, 48

weak beat, 49
whole note, 50
whole rest, 56
whole steps, 30, 32–35
    hearing, 34–35
whole tone. *See* whole steps
whole-tone scale, 129
writing music in a score, 11–13
writing pitches with accidentals, 31–32